Regional Economic Effects of Alternative Highway Systems

Regional Economic Effects of Alternative Highway Systems

Curtis C. Harris, Jr.
University of Maryland

With the assistance of:
Jay O. Casey
Stanley J. Hille
Charles E. Olson

Ballinger Publishing Company ● Cambridge, Mass.
A Subsidiary of J.B. Lippincott Company

International Standard Book Number: 0-88410-412-5

Library of Congress Catalog Card Number: 74-11357

Printed in the United States of America

Library of Congress Cataloging in Publication Data

Harris, Curtis C
      Regional economic effects of alternative highway systems.
      Includes bibliographical references.
      1. Roads—Economic aspects—United States—Mathematical models. I. Title.
HE336.E3H34   388.1'1'0973   74-11357
ISBN 0-88410-412-5

To My Parents

Contents

List of Tables

List of Figures and Maps

FIGURES

MAPS

Preface

Billions of dollars are spent on highways in the United States each year, but knowledge about the regional economic impacts of these highways is limited. Some highways are built in response to changes in the location of economic activity, but others may cause changes in the location of economic activity. A number of attempts have been made to measure economic impacts of highways, but the results are often inconclusive and incomplete. Research studies that have been successful are limited in scope, usually evaluating effects of one highway in one small geographic area. None of the studies developed so far has been successful in evaluating complete national highway systems. It is the purpose of this study to fill this gap.

The model used in this book is designed to measure regional economic impacts of highway systems for all regions in the United States. Moreover, it is designed to evaluate planned hypothetical alternative highway systems. The model is the Multiregional, Multi-Industry Forecasting Model presented elsewhere.[a] However, some modifications were necessary for this highway evaluation application. Because of the modifications, and in order to allow the reader to have a complete picture of the model, the basic model description is repeated here. If the reader requires more detail on the methodology or data estimation procedures he will find it in the previous volumes.

In Chapter One of this book the forecasting model is described, and a review of other work is presented for the purpose of pointing out the need for a study that evaluates complete national highway systems. Chapter Two describes the forecasting model in detail and gives the statistical parameters obtained from fitting the equations to the data. Chapter Three describes the

[a]See Curtis C. Harris, Jr., *The Urban Economies, 1985: A Multiregional Multi-Industry Forecasting Model*, Lexington, Mass.: Lexington Books (D.C. Heath) 1973; and Curtis C. Harris, Jr. and Frank E. Hopkins, *Locational Analysis: An Interregional Econometric Model of Agriculture, Mining, Manufacturing and Services*, Lexington, Mass.: Lexington Books (D.C. Heath), 1972.

alternative highway systems that are evaluated with the forecasting model. Chapter Four presents the procedures used to derive the transportation variables that are used to help explain the location of industry. It also describes how these transportation variables as national highway systems are added. Chapter Five summarizes the economic and demographic results of the study. Energy requirements and pollution emissions are tied to the economic results in Chapter Six. Concluding remarks are made in the final chapter. Summary information for each economic area is given in the Appendix.

The study was financed by the Federal Highway Administration under Contract FH-11-7766. The main body of the research was finished in January 1973. It was concerned with the regional economic and demographic effects of alternative highway systems. Supplemental work, including the attachment of resource requirements and pollution emissions, was completed in February 1974. The book consists of the January 1973 report to the Federal Highway Administration, with minor revisions, plus parts of supplemental reports.

Research of this nature cannot be undertaken without the help of many people. I have acknowledged the assistance of three individuals on the title page—Jay O. Casey, Stanley J. Hille, and Charles E. Olson. Mr. Casey, now with American University, was responsible for the substantial computer work that was necessary for this application of the Multiregional, Multi-Industry Forecasting Model. Professor Hille of the University of Alabama (formerly with the University of Maryland), and Professor Olson of the University of Maryland served as my experts in transportation economies. They planned the geographical placement of the hypothetical highway systems as given in Chapter Three and related this study to other studies in Chapters One and Four. Professor Hille also helped in incorporating energy requirements in the model, as reported in Chapter Six.

Professors Everett Carter, Jerome Hall, and Richard McCuen, all of the University of Maryland, helped augment the model with engineering cost data for highway construction and maintenance that was necessary to find the energy requirements associated with building and maintaining highways. Mr. Richard Davis of the University of Maryland programmed some of the final display tables. Mr. Martin Stein of the Maryland Department of Transportation (formerly with the Federal Highway Administration) reviewed and commented on most of the reports. Comments were also received by David Goettee and Walter Bottiny of the Federal Highway Administration and Ali Parhizgari of the University of Maryland.

I am indebted to Professor Clopper Almon of the University of Maryland for use of his national interindustry forecasting model. His data and projections are used as control totals for the regional data and projections. Also I would like to thank Professor John H. Cumberland of the University of Maryland for use of some of the pollution emissions data estimated by his environmental research project.

Regional Economic Effects of Alternative Highway Systems

Chapter One

Introduction—The Need to Evaluate Highway Systems

Should national highway systems be built for the purpose of stimulating the economies of certain regions or should they just be built to serve the people wherever they happen to be located? Regardless of the objective, highway construction does have an impact on regional development and growth. A major highway system serving a particular area can have an effect on the area's economy in three ways.

1. The construction expenditures are large; and as they are spent in a region, they generate employment and income in other sectors of the economy with multiplying effects.
2. New or improved highways reduce the interregional transportation costs, and thus have an effect on the location of industries.
3. New highway systems reduce the amount of traffic congestion within a region, making it more attractive as a location for industry and people.

Since new highway systems cannot serve all the people and all the industries, the economic impacts will vary by region. A new highway system will improve the competitive advantage of some regions relative to others. Although the highway system could improve the efficiency of the national economy, it is unlikely that all regions will have positive gains as a result of a new highway system. If full employment economy is assumed, the gains in some regions will be offset by losses in others.

If a new highway system is planned, the planners should know what the economic impacts will be on the various regions. Only then can they fully evaluate the benefits and costs of the highway system. This book presents a Multiregional, Multi-industry Forecasting Model[a] that can be used to project the

[a]See Curtis C. Harris, Jr., *The Urban Economies, 1985: A Multiregional Multi-Industry Forecasting Model*, Lexington, Mass.: Lexington Books (D.C. Heath), 1973;

changes in regional economies that would result from the construction of new national highway systems. Projections are made to 1990 under five assumptions as to the existence of highway systems. They are as follows.

1. The *Base Year* system, which assumes that construction on the National System of Interstate and Defense Highways (Interstate system) stopped in 1970.
2. The *Completed Interstate* system, which assumes that the Interstate system as now planned will be completed by 1976 and that no new national highway systems are added after 1976.
3. The *Extended Primary* system, which is a hypothetical system that extends the Interstate system to smaller cities during the 1977-1968 period.
4. The *Economic Development* system, which is a hypothetical system that is designed to serve the low income areas of the United States and to complement the interstate system after 1977.
5. The *Urban system*, which is a hypothetical system in which additional urban highways would be added between 1977 and 1986 for the purpose of reducing congestion in the major cities that now have the most congestion.

Comparison of the 1990 economic and demographic projections under these five alternatives reveals the several impacts of the assumed highway systems. The results of the study show that both low income and small areas benefit by the Extended Primary and Economic Development systems, with relatively more areas benefiting from the Economic Development system. The Urban system stimulates growth in the major urban areas, but the percent gains are not very large. The benefits of the Completed Interstate system by size classification of the areas are mixed, but the low income areas do not benefit.

Although the projections are made by economic areas, the results are summarized in Table 1-1 by census region. The New England and Mountain regions have the greatest percent population increase from the Completed Interstate system. The Extended Primary system favors the East-South Central and Mountain regions. The Economic Development system favors the East-South Central and the West-South Central regions, and the Urban system favors the Middle Atlantic and East-North Central regions. Overall, the construction of new highways reduces the truck costs per dollar of output shipped and stimulates interregional shipments. New highways reduce average transport costs, therefore reducing the incentive of industries to relocate.

The remainder of this introduction briefly describes the forecasting

---

and Curtis C. Harris, Jr. and Frank E. Hopkins, *Locational Analysis: An Interregional Econometric Model of Agriculture, Mining, Manufacturing and Services* Lexington, Mass.: Lexington Books (D.C. Heath), 1972. Even though this book reports on a major application of a model that was published previously, the basic model description is repeated here in order to give the reader a complete view of the study.

model and reviews other work for the purpose of pointing out the need for a study that evaluates a complete nationwide highway system.

THE MULTIREGIONAL, MULTI-INDUSTRY FORECASTING MODEL

The Multiregional, Multi-Industry Forecasting Model is designed both to make long run regional forecasts under reasonable assumptions and to evaluate impacts of alternative government decisions. Essentially, forecasts are made assuming no exogenous changes in governmental spending; then forecasts are made with a set of predetermined changes. Comparison between the sets of forecasts shows the economic impacts of the governmental decisions. This application of the model to evaluate regional impacts of alternative highway systems is only one of many possible applications.

The forecasting model starts by forecasting output by industry in each area for the first year after the base year. The output or change in output of each industry sector is explained by the marginal costs or prices that firms face in each location. In addition, agglomeration effects also help to explain output location. After output has been determined, then payrolls, employment, population, and personal income are derived. Also, the final demand sectors are forecast—consumption and governmental expenditures are related to income, investment is related to output, and foreign exports are determined exogenously.

The model is recursive. The supply and demand data in the year t are used to forecast variables in the year $t + 1$; then the forecasts are used as data to make forecasts for the year $t + 2$. A simplified flow chart of the forecasting model is presented in Figure 1-1. The left-hand side of the chart itemizes the data and computations for the year t. The connecting lines show how the data are used to make forecasts in year $t + 1$. After $t + 1$ forecasts are made, they are realigned as data, as given in the left-hand side of the chart, in order to forecast for year $t + 2$. In any given year, predetermined changes may be made in the data, such as changes in governmental expenditures or in the highway system.

An important set of variables used to determine the location of output is the set referred to as transport shadow prices in Figure 1-1. These variables are the cost of transporting a marginal unit of a commodity either into or out of a region. They were derived by determining both rail and truck costs by weight class of shipping a unit of good between each pair of regions. The least-cost method of shipping a unit good in each weight class for each commodity is determined and these unit costs are used in the linear programming transportation algorithm in order to produce the marginal costs.

Changes in the highway system will directly affect the cost of shipping a commodity between regions, thus they will have an effect on the transport shadow prices. If highway improvements lead to a decrease in truck travel time between two points, while the rail costs remain the same, then more

TABLE 1.1 POPULATION PROJECTIONS FOR 1990 BY CENSUS REGION
UNDER FIVE ALTERNATIVE HIGHWAY SYSTEMS POPULATION IN
THOUSANDS

AREA	BASE YEAR	COMPLETED INTERSTATE	EXTENDED PRIMARY
1 NEW ENGLAND	14096.7	14466.2	14536.1
2 MIDDLE ATLANTIC	48284.5	47938.4	48013.0
3 EAST NORTH CENTRAL	53542.4	53348.1	53281.2
4 WEST NORTH CENTRAL	20588.7	20432.7	20608.2
5 SOUTH ATLANTIC	40069.2	39841.6	39765.2
6 EAST SOUTH CENTRAL	17860.1	17849.6	18098.6
7 WEST SOUTH CENTRAL	26914.2	26761.0	26746.6
8 MOUNTAIN	10345.1	10862.1	11038.4
9 PACIFIC	37955.9	38157.1	37569.4

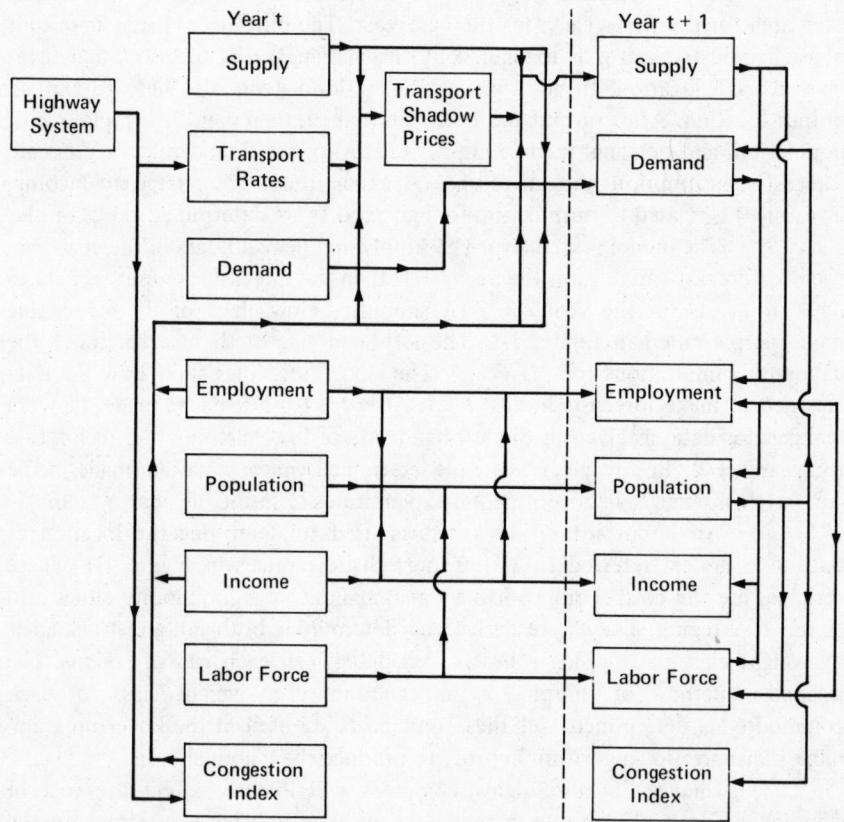

Figure 1-1. Simplified Flow Chart of Multiregional, Multi-Industry Forecasting Model.

ECONOMIC DEVELOPMENT	URBAN	PERCENT			
		CI/BY	EP/CI	ED/CI	U/CI
14442.0	14487.5	102.6	100.5	99.8	100.1
47678.9	48416.3	99.3	100.2	99.5	101.0
53231.8	53582.7	99.6	99.9	99.8	100.4
20494.7	20337.5	99.2	100.9	100.3	99.5
40126.1	39829.9	99.4	99.8	100.7	100.0
18318.7	17797.8	99.9	101.4	102.6	99.7
27112.9	26559.6	99.4	99.9	101.3	99.2
10963.9	10777.3	105.0	101.6	100.9	99.2
37287.7	37868.1	100.5	98.5	97.7	99.2

shipments would go by truck, thus reducing the total transportation costs of shipping a unit of good. The model will incorporate the effects of highway changes on the transport costs, and determine the effect on industry location.

The quality of the highway system within each region may also affect the attractiveness of that region for the location of certain industries. In the equations that explain the location of output, highway quality is incorporated in a regional congestion index; the index will be used as an explanatory variable.

In addition to cost savings and highway quality, the construction of the highway itself may have an influence on the regional economies. Highway construction is part of the final demand for goods in a region, and the income of the construction workers contributes to the income of the region; thus industries that supply construction materials and consumer expenditures will be affected by the location of the highway construction. While construction will have some impact on the expansion of the economy of a region during the construction phase, it should be noted that when the construction stops, decreases in the economy may occur.

One of the major advantages that this model has over the typical impact model is that regional demand and supply are interrelated, whereas in other models they are not. For example, in an input-output model, it is necessary to predetermine levels of final demand for each region and then use interdependence coefficients to produce the changes in output. While this approach may have merit at the national level, it seems inappropriate at the regional level. Since the national economy is essentially a closed economy, final demand forecasts can be predetermined; but, for a region, the final demand levels influence the output levels—which in turn determine income levels, which in turn determine major components of final demand sectors. Since the location of demand and supply need not be in the same region, it is necessary for a model to specify these interrelationships and allow changes in the location of output and resources to take place.

In tracing out impacts with an input-output model, all trade and technical coefficients are assumed to remain constant, and the effect of changes in final demand, such as government expenditures, are fed through the model to determine the effects on output, income, and employment. This procedure may be satisfactory for short run analysis or for small incremental changes in final demand, but obviously it is deficient for measuring long run impacts. The Multiregional, Multi-Industry Forecasting Model presented here is designed for tracing out long run impacts, and it produces a time stream of the economic changes. Since all variables are interrelated in the model, everything is allowed to change over time and, as a result, many indirect effects of government decisions can be brought to light that would not show up in other models. Many government decisions have an effect on industry location, making it more profitable for an industry to relocate from one region to another. The regional forecasting model is designed to handle these relocations.

The Multiregional, Multi-Industry Forecasting Model was originally applied using counties as regions.[b] However, since there are 3,112 county-type areas, the model is very costly to operate; therefore, counties have been aggregated into 173 economic areas as determined by the Office of Business Economics (OBE).[c] These areas not only will make it less expensive to operate the model, but they also seem to be a more appropriate regional delineation than counties for evaluating highway impacts.

Most of the major highways in recent years have been built either to improve the travel time between major cities or to improve the travel time within a metropolitan area. Each of the OBE economic areas has a major city as its center; therefore, estimating travel time and vehicle costs between OBE economic areas is almost identical to estimating the time and cost between cities. We use the population centers as geographic points from which to compute the distances between areas.

Since the economies of regions change as the highway system changes, the energy requirements and environmental quality of the regions also change. Therefore energy and pollution coefficients are developed and applied to the economic projections in order to measure energy requirements and pollution emissions. This work, which is reported in Chapter Six, is very preliminary in nature.

[b]Curtis C. Harris, Jr., *The Urban Economies 1985.*
[c]The Office of Business Economics has since changed its name to Bureau of Economic Analysis.

THE NEED FOR A SYSTEMS STUDY

Many studies have been conducted over the years concerning the impact of highways on economic development. For example, McCarthy[d] found that plant location was greatly influenced by good highways along with the more traditional market and labor locational factors. Similarly, Barloon[e] indicated that the Interstate system of highways was allowing for an "interregional liberation" of a large and growing portion of industry. Freight can now move greater distances at higher speeds thereby reducing the need to locate near particular markets.

The total impact of the Interstate system is undoubtedly enormous. Assuming that time savings are of consequence to motorists, one can visualize this impact in that a transcontinental driving trip will be reduced from 96 to 48 hours upon completion of the Interstate system. In trucking, the impact is even more spectacular. A St. Louis over-the-road truck driver's productivity has doubled in the last twelve years due to improved roads, and distance between engine overhauls has increased from 170,000 to 300,000 miles. Moreover, accident rates in the area have been halved and the running times of bus transportation has been reduced by one-third nationwide.[f]

Utilizing currently accepted benefit measures, Francis Turner estimates that Interstate system benefits (without counting time savings) have already exceeded the $43 billion spent on its construction.[g] While the overall benefits of past highway programs cannot be questioned, it is necessary to determine what the potential economic impacts of highways will be on economic development in *specific regions*. Perhaps, justification for transportation facilities will be determined with different criteria after the 1976 Interstate system completion date. As one region becomes more like the other from a transportation viewpoint (a natural consequence of ubiquitous highways), alternative locational possibilities will occur for industry. Industrial location could therefore be more heavily influenced by factors other than those necessitated by the confinements of the earlier transportation system.[h]

[d]James F. McCarthy, *Highways, Trucks, and New Industry: A Study of Changing Patterns in Plant Location*, Washington, D.C.: ATA Foundation, 1963, p. 12.

[e]Marvin J. Barloon, "The Interrelationship of the Changing Structure of American Transportation and Changes in Industrial Location," *Land Economics* XLI (2): 174.

[f]Juan Cameron, "How the Interstate Changed the Face of the Nation, and Why the Remaining Links in the Superhighway System Are Meeting with Such Fierce Opposition," *Fortune*, July 1971, p. 78.

[g]Quoted in ibid.

[h]Marvin J. Barloon, op. cit., p. 179.

Most research efforts have done much to uncover benefits of highway improvements,[i] but they have not provided the tools for predicting impacts of future highways on regional economic development. Certain researchers have measured impacts of highways on specific areas, but they fail to account for interregional effects.

Two studies were conducted in the state of Ohio. One examines the economic impact of Interstate Route 71 in Northeastern Ohio (containing the towns of Mansfield and Ashland). It stated that there were no apparent population changes attributed to the interstate highway, except location shifts to the access zones at the SR13 and US30 interchanges.[j]

A somewhat contradicting conclusion was given in a study conducted by Ohio University. It found a positive relationship between the level of highway capacity in a county and its income, and that poorer areas were more responsive to highway improvements than were prosperous areas.[k]

Interstate 29's economic impact in South Dakota was found to be significant for highway oriented business: these businesses expanded faster than those in the control area for the study period. However, other retail business showed had no visible impact from the appearance of the highway.[l]

These studies are not definitive because they generally employ a methodology that compares an impact area to a control area, therefore they cannot be utilized for forecasting.

Another group of studies attempted to evaluate the effects of highway development upon a whole region, namely that of Appalachia. The findings of these studies conclude that there has been growth in employment greater than the national average; however, it is open to question whether this growth has resulted from highways or from renewed demand for natural resources found in the area. In fact, a study of West Virginia highways concludes that while travel times were reduced in major markets, relative disadvantages between cities remained about the same.[m]

[i]Herbert Mohring and Mitchell Harwitz, *Highway Benefits: An Analytical Framework*, Evanston, Ill.: Northwestern University Press, p. 62, p. 52; Martin M. Stein and Barbara Faigin, *Regional Economic Effects of Highway Investment*, Office of Programs and Policy Planning, Socio-Economic Studies Division, U.S. Department of Transportation, Federal Highway Administration, Washington, D.C.

[j]Ohio Department of Highways, Division of Planning and Programming, Bureau of Planning Survey, Interim Report, *Economic Impact Study, Interstate Route 71*, 1971, p. 28.

[k]Robert L. Williams and Rajinder K. Koohal, *Highways and Economics Development in Ohio*, Volume 1, Athens, Ohio: Ohio University Research Institute, 1970.

[l]C.P. Jorgenson, William T. Voss, Russel L. DeLancey, Lloyd DeLancey, *Economic Impact Study, South Dakota Interstate 29*, Research and Planning Division, South Dakota Department of Highways, 1967, pp. j-1.

[m]Isaac Shafron and Frederick J. Wegmann, "The Influence of the Highway Network Structure on the Economic Development of West Virginia," *Highway Research Record Number 285*, Highway Research Board, National Research Council, National Academy of Science, Washington, D.C., 1969.

Wheat[n] studied the effects of freeways on city growth by examining value added by industry and utilizing experimental and control group methodology. He found that intercity freeways stimulate manufacturing growth in regions where travel is impeded by congestion or topographic irregularities.

A study conducted in the city of Evanston, Wyoming measured highway impact with an input-output model.[o] This study provided interesting information, but it did not attempt to account for interregional shifts. A related input-output study on the impact of Interstate Highway 80 on Southwestern Wyoming suffered from the same shortcomings.[p]

Stein and Mosbaek[q] present a case that interregional input-output analysis is needed to fill in some of the gaps left by other studies. One major advantage of an interregional model is that it can measure impacts in areas other than the area in which the highway is constructed. Gains in one area may be offset by losses in adjacent area. Another advantage of the interregional input-output models is that hypothetical investments can be simulated during the planning process.

Current interregional input-output studies have not filled in all of the research gaps. They are useful in measuring the impacts of the construction phase of highway construction, but they fail to account for changes in the location of industry and people due to the highway improvements, and they are not very well suited for long run forecasting. In order to predict locational changes between regions, an understanding of the relationship of location decisions to selective regional changes in transport cost and regional congestion must be made. It is these remaining gaps that the Multiregional, Multi-Industry Forecasting Model is designed to fill.

Measuring Benefits

The above literature review indicated that benefits accrue directly to users and indirectly to the economy through increased productive capacity and industrial development benefits. These benefits occur as a consequence of lowered line-haul transportation costs and, often, the substitution of one newly cheaper mode of transportation for another. One of the key problems, then, is

[n]Leonard A. Wheat, "The Effects of Modern Highways on Urban Manufacturing Growth," *Highway Research Record, Number 277*, Highway Research Board, National Research Council, National Academy of Science, Washington, D.C., 1969, p. 10.

[o]Raymond W. Hooker and Kenneth R. Potter, *An Input-Output Analysis of the Economic Impact of I-80 on Evanston, Wyoming*, Division of Economic Research College of Commerce and Industry, University of Wyoming, Laramie, Wyoming, 1970.

[p]Karen Lou Madsen, *An Estimated 1967 Input-Output Model for Southwestern Wyoming*, Division of Economic Research, College of Commerce and Industry, University of Wyoming, Laramie, Wyoming, 1968.

[q]Martin M. Stein, Ernest J. Mosbaek, "Evaluation of Alternative Transportation Investment Decisions: Modification and Use of a Multiregional Input-Output Model," *High Research Record, Number 348*, Highway Research Board, National Research Council, National Academy of Science, Washington, D.C., 1971.

to discover how line-haul truck costs are related to reduced grades, improved curves, wider pavement, and smoother road surfaces. Additionally, better constructed roads can result in utilization of larger trucks, thereby reducing labor costs per ton-mile as well as operating costs relating to engine wear, maintenance, and so forth.

Since the roads being compared in this study all have improved surfaces, the savings will show up in increased average speed for the vehicles. Thus, truck costs can best be quantified in terms of speed relationships. These costs are fuel consumption, tire wear, depreciation, interest, maintenance costs, and time savings (improving vehicle turnaround and having driver costs lowered).

In order to determine the effects of improved highways on costs, one must examine the engineering literature. Perhaps the most comprehensive treatment of this subject is by Winfrey,[r] who gives a detailed analysis of the effects of grades, curves, etc. on the above costs. Unfortunately, however, no generalizations are made concerning the overall effects when one upgrades from one type of highway to the next, nor is there any discussion of the effect of topography on operating costs.

Other literature indicates that some line-haul costs go up as others go down when the roads are improved, thus only improvements related to time saving are of value. In fact, one study stated that the impact of speed changes on road use savings are fairly modest (more so for trucks than for passenger cars).[s] Similar conclusions were given by Paul S. Claffy.[t]

Many studies are available on the savings of time as related to user benefits. Most of them have related the willingness of truckers to pay tolls to the value of time saved. This method was used by the Chicago Area Transportation Studies as well as for studies of turnpike users.[u]

A group of studies based on research conducted by the Texas Transportation Institute attempted a different approach to this problem.[v] Their

[r]Robley Winfrey, *Economic Analysis for Highways*, Scranton, Pa.: International Textbook Company, 1969, pp. 331-359.

[s]Jan De Weille, *Quantification of Road User Savings*, World Bank Staff Occasional Paper Number Two, International Bank for Reconstruction and Development, Washington, D.C., 1966, p. 40.

[t]Paul S. Claffy, *Running Costs of Motor Vehicles as Affected by Highway Design—Interim Report*, National Cooperative Highway Research Program; Report 13, Highway Research Board, National Research Council, National Academy of Sciences, Washington, D.C., 1965.

[u]Roger L. Creighton, *Urban Transportation Planning* Urbana, Ill.: University of Illinois Press, 1970.

[v]Allen William Ward, *An Analysis of Variations in the Value of Time Savings to Trucks* (thesis), Texas A&M University, College Station, Texas, 1965; Charles R. Haning and William F. McFarland, *Value of Time Saved to Commercial Motor Vehicles Through Use of Improved Highways*, Texas Transport Institute, Texas A&M, College Station, Texas, 1963; William G. Adkins, Allen W. Ward, and William F. McFarland, *Values of Time Saving of Commercial Vehicles*, National Cooperative Highway Research Program, Report 33, Highway Research Board, National Research Council, National Academy of Sciences, Washington, D.C., 1967; Charles R. Haning and C.V. Wootan, "Value of Commerical Motor

sole purpose was to evaluate the benefit per hour saved with improved highways. Utilizing carrier ICC records a net operating revenue approach was used, which assumes that the value of time savings will be reflected in the net operating profits of commercial highway users.[w]

Other studies have reviewed value of time to passenger cars. These again use route selection models and attempt to relate the value of time saved to various trip purposes (work, social-recreational, personal business, vacation, school).[x] User benefits include lower operating costs, reduced travel time, better driving conditions, and greater safety. The approach in this book is to focus on the reduced travel time, assuming that it will result in lower truck operating costs. Better driving and safety conditions are unfortunately unmeasurable in terms of relocation of industry.

Use of the Multiregional, Multi-Industry Forecasting Model is made in an attempt to fill in the gaps left in previous research by measuring regional effects of highway systems. The model could be applied to highway systems of any size, but in this study only national networks are evaluated.

Vehicle Time Saved," *Highway Research Record Number 82*, Highway Research Board, National Research Council, National Academy of Sciences, Washington, D.C., 1965.

[w]Ward, *op. cit.,* p. 11.

[x]Thomas C. Thomas and Gordon I. Thompson, *The Value of Time Saved by Trip Purpose*, Menlo Park, Calif.: Stanford Research Institute, 1970.

Chapter Two

The Model

The Multiregional, Multi-Industry Forecasting Model (referred to hereafter as the regional forecasting model) is presented in this chapter along with the parameters that were estimated for each equation.[a] The chapter is divided into five parts. The first part describes the sectoring scheme used to classify the variables. The second part gives the notation used in the equations, and the third part presents the equations. The equations and their parameters are explained in the fourth part. The last part describes the economic areas that are used as geographic units.

THE SECTORS

Table 2.1 shows the number and names of the sectors used in the model. Subscripts used in the equations refer to the numbers given in the table. The Industry sectors correspond closely to the input-output sectors used by the Office of Business Economics (OBE). After the publication of the 1958 national input-output table, OBE published additional industry detail in the food and kindred products, the primary nonferrous metals, and the utility sectors. These additional sectors are included in our set of industries; and in addition, OBE's wholesale and retail trade sector is divided into separate sectors, with retail trade further broken down into eleven types of retail outlets. OBE's industry set contains two government enterprises and three dummy industries. Because of lack of regional data the government enterprises are made part of final demand along with the general government, and two dummy industries—business travel and office supplies—are added to the business service sector. The third dummy sector, scrap, is dropped.

[a]Except for minor differences the model is the same as presented in Harris, *The Urban Economics, 1986,* op. cit., pp. 9-31. The same notation and equation format are preserved.

Table 2-1.   Sectors Used in the Forecasting Model

Industry Sectors		SIC Numbers
1	Livestock	Part01, Part02
2	Crops	Part01, Part02
3	Forestry & fishery products	08, 09
4	Agricultural services	071, 072, 073, 074
5	Iron ore mining	101, 106
6	Nonferrous ore mining	102, 103, 104, 105, 108, 109
7	Coal mining	11, 12
8	Petroleum mining	131, 132
9	Minerals mining	141, 142, 144, 145, 148, 149
10	Chemical mining	147
11	New construction	138, Part15, Part16, Part17
12	Maintenance construction	Part15, Part16, Part17
13	Ordnance	19
14	Meat packing	201
15	Dairy products	202
16	Canned and frozen foods	203
17	Grain mill products	204
18	Bakery products	205
19	Sugar	206
20	Candy	207
21	Beverages	208
22	Misc. food products	209
23	Tobacco	21
24	Fabrics & yarn	221, 222, 223, 224, 226, 228
25	Rugs, tire cord, misc. textiles	227, 229
26	Apparel	225, 23, 3992, −239
27	Household textiles & upholst.	239
28	Lumber & prod., exc. containers	24, −244
29	Wooden containers	244
30	Household funiture	251
31	Office furniture	25, −251
32	Paper & prod., exc. containers	26, −265
33	Paper containers	265
34	Printing & publishing	27
35	Basic chemicals	281, 286, 287, 289
36	Plastics & synthetics	282
37	Drugs, cleaning & toilet items	283, 284
38	Paint & allied products	285
39	Petroleum refining	29
40	Rubber & plastic products	30
41	Leather tanning	311, 312
42	Shoes & other leather products	31, −311, −312
43	Glass & glass products	321, 322, 323
44	Stone & clay products	324, 325, 326, 327, 328, 329
45	Iron & steel	331, 332, 3391, 3399
46	Copper	3331, 3351, 3362
47	Aluminum	3334, 3352, 3361
48	Other non-ferrous metals	3332, 3333, 3339, 334, 3356, 3357, 3369, 3392
49	Metal containers	341, 3491
50	Heating, plumbing, struc. metal	343, 344
51	Stampings, screw mach. prod.	345, 346
52	Hardware, plating, wire prod.	342, 347, 348, 349, −3491
53	Engines & turbines	351

Table 2-1 continued

Industry Sectors		SIC Numbers
54	Farm machinery & equipment	352
55	Construction & mining mach.	3531, 3532, 3533
56	Material handling equipment	3534, 3535, 3536
57	Metalworking mach. & equip.	354
58	Special industrial machinery	355
59	General industrial machinery	356
60	Machine shops & misc. mach.	359
61	Office & computing machines	357
62	Service industry machines	358
63	Electric apparatus & motors	361, 362
64	Household appliances	363
65	Electric light & wiring equipment	364
66	Communication equipment	365, 366
67	Electronic components	367
68	Batteries & engine elec. equipment	369
69	Motor vehicles	371
70	Aircraft & parts	372
71	Ships, trains, trailers, cycles	373, 374, 375, 379
72	Instruments & clocks	381, 382, 384, 387
73	Optical & photographic equip.	383, 385, 386
74	Misc. manufactured products	39, -3992
75	Transportation	40, 41, 42, 44, 45, 46, 47
76	Communication	481, 482, 489
77	Radio, TV broadcasting	483
78	Electric utility	491, 4931
79	Gas utility	492, 4932
80	Water utility	494, 495, 496, 497
81	Wholesale trade	50
82	Finance & insurance	60, 61, 62, 63, 64, 66, 67
83	Real estate & rental	65, -654
84	Hotels, personal & repair svc.	70, 72, 76, -7694, -7699
85	Business services	654, 73, 7694, 7699, 81, 89, -736, -892
86	Automobile repair services	75
87	Amusements & recreation	78, 79
88	Medical & educational instit.	736, 80, 82, 84, 86, 892
89	Lumber, houseware, farm equip. stores	52
90	General merchandise stores	53, -532
91	Food stores	54
92	Automotive dealers	55, 2554
93	Gasoline service stations	554
94	Apparel, accessory stores	56
95	Furniture stores	57
96	Eating, drinking places	58
97	Drug and proprietary stores	591
98	Other retail stores	59, -591
99	Nonstore retailers	532

Extra Labor Sectors

100	Federal civilian government	
101	State and local government	
102	Domestic services	
103	Armed forces	

(Continued)

Table 2-1 continued

Industry Sectors	*SIC Numbers*

Extra Import Sectors

100   Noncompetitive industry imports
101   Noncompetitive consumer imports

Equipment Purchasing Sectors

1   Farm
2   Mining
3   Oil & gas wells
4   Construction
5   Ordnance
6   Meat products
7   Tobacco
8   Fabrics & yarn
9   Rugs, Tire Cord
10   Apparel
11   Household textiles and upholst.
12   Lumber & prod. exc. containers
13   Wooden containers
14   Household furniture
15   Office furniture
16   Paper, exc. containers
17   Paper containers
18   Printing & publishing
19   Basic chemicals
20   Plastics and synthetics
21   Drugs, cleaning, & toilet items
22   Paint
23   Petroleum refining
24   Rubber & plastic
25   Leather tanning
26   Shoes & other leather products
27   Glass & products
28   Stone & clay products
29   Iron & steel
30   Non-ferrous metals
31   Metal containers
32   Heating, plumbing, struc. metal
33   Stampings, screw mach. products
34   Hardware, plating, wire prod. & valves
35   Engines & turbines
36   Farm machinery & equipment
37   Construction & material handling equipment
38   Metal working machinery
39   Special industrial machinery
40   General industrial machinery
41   Machine shops & misc.
42   Office & computing machines
43   Service industry machinery
44   Electric apparatus & motors
45   Household appliances
46   Electric lighting & wirings

Table 2-1 continued

Industry Sectors	*SIC Numbers*

Equipment Purchasing Sectors

47 Communication equipment
48 Electronic components
49 Batteries, X-ray, & engine elec. equipment
50 Motor vehicles
51 Aircraft & parts
52 Ships, trains, & cycles
53 Instruments & clocks
54 Optical & photographic equip.
55 Misc. manufacturing
56 Transportation
57 Communication
58 Utility
59 Trade
60 Finance & insurance
61 Service
62 Dairy products
63 Canned & frozen foods
64 Grain mill products
65 Bakery products
66 Sugar
67 Confectionery
68 Beverages
69 Miscellaneous foods

Construction Sectors

1 Residential
2 Additions & alterations to residences
3 Non-housekeeping residential construction
4 Industrial
5 Offices
6 Stores, restaurants & garages
7 Religious
8 Educational
9 Hospital & institutional
10 Misc. non-residential buildings
11 Farm construction
12 Oil & gas well drilling & exploration
13 Railroad
14 Telephone
15 Electric utility
16 Gas & petroleum pipelines
17 All other private construction
18 Highway
19 Military
20 Conservation
21 Sewer systems
22 Water systems
23 Public residential construction
24 Public industrial construction
25 Public educational

(Continued)

Table 2–1 continued

Industry Sectors	*SIC Numbers*

26	Public hospital
27	Other public structures
28	Miscellaneous public

General Government Sectors

1	National aeronautics & space administration
2	Federal government not listed elsewhere
3	Federal government enterprises
4	Expenditres from or sales to the livestock sector
5	Expenditures from or sales to the crop sector
6	Expenditures from or sales to the forestry & fisheries sector
7	Expenditures from or sales to the lumber sector
8	State & local government

Population Age Sectors

1	Ages 14 and under
2	Ages 15–34
3	Ages 35–64
4	Ages 65 and over

Population Race Sectors

| 1 | White |
| 2 | Nonwhite |

Output, employment, earnings, personal consumer expenditures, defense expenditures, exports, and imports are reported by 99 industry sectors. There are four extra labor sectors used to report employment and earnings, and two extra import sectors for imported goods that do not compete directly with domestic goods. Equipment is reported by 69 equipment purchasing sectors which either correspond directly to individual industry sectors or some combination of industry sectors. Construction is reported by 28 types—seventeen private and eleven public. Data on general government expenditures, excluding expenditures for construction and employee compensation, are classified into eight functional categories. There are four population age groups used to report population and death data; and two population race sectors used for reporting population, births, and deaths.

NOTATION

BIR_{rj}^{t} Births by race r of residents in region j in year t.

CGS_{j}^{t} Highway congestion index in region j in year t.

CLF_j^t — Civilian labor force by place of residence in region j in year t.

CMS_j^t — Capacity miles of service of highways in region j in year t.

CN_{ij}^t — Construction, both private and public, by construction type i located in region j in year t.

COM_j^t — Net number of commuters in region j in year t (a positive sign indicates commuters coming into region j and a negative sign indicates commuters going out of region j).

CPE_j^t — Civilian persons employed, residing in region j in year t.

CUE_j^t — Civilian unemployment of persons residing in region j in year t.

D_{ij}^t — Total demand for goods classified by industry i located in region j in year t.

DEF_{ij}^l — Defense expenditures, excluding construction and employee compensation, for goods produced in industry i located in region j in year t.

DEH_{arj}^t — Deaths by age group a and race r of residents in region j in year t.

DEN_j^t — Population per square mile in region j in year t.

EMP_{ij}^t — Employment by labor sector i working in region j in year t.

EQ_{ij}^t — Equipment purchases by equipment purchasing sector i located in region j in year t.

ERN_j^t — Earnings of civilian residents in region j in year t.

EX_{ij}^t — Foreign exports of goods produced by industry i exiting the country through ports in region j in year t.

GOV_{ij}^t — General (nondefense) government expenditures, excluding construction and employee compensation, by function type i located in region j in year t.

HCN_j^t — Exogenous highway construction expenditures of a national highway system in region j in year t.

IM_{ij}^t — Foreign imports of goods classified by sector i entering the country through ports in region j in year t.

MB_{ikj}^t — Major buying sector k located in region j that bought goods from industry i in year t.

MJH_j^t — Number of multijob holders working in region j in year t.

MS_{ikj}^t — Major supplying sector k located in region j that sold goods to industry i in year t.

NPM^t_{arj} — Net civilian population migration by age group a and race r of persons out of (or into) region j in year t.

NR — Number of regions.

NY — Number of forecast years.

PAY^t_{ij} — Earnings by labor sector i located in region j in year t.

PCE^t_{ij} — Personal consumption expenditures of goods classified by industry i in region j in year t.

PEC^t_j — Population associated with change in persons employed residing in region j in year t.

PI^t_j — Personal income of residents in region j in year t.

PLS^t_j — Population associated with labor force surplus (or deficit) residing in region j in year t.

POP^t_{arj} — Population by age group a and race r residing in region j in year t.

PR^t_j — Property income of residents in region j in year t.

Q^t_{ij} — Output of industry i located in region j in year t.

QD^t_{ij} — Output less defense expenditures of industry i located in region j in year t.

S^t_{ij} — Total supply of goods classified by industry i located in region j in year t.

SQM_j — Square miles of region j.

SS^t_j — Personal contributions for social insurance of residents in region j in year t.

T^t_{ikj} — Transport cost of shipping a unit of commodity i from region k to region j in year t.

TI^t_{ij} — Transport cost of obtaining a marginal unit of input from industry i into region j in year t.

TQ^t_{ij} — Transport cost of shipping a marginal unit of output from industry i out of region j in year t.

TR^t_j — Transfer payments of residents in region j in year t.

VL^t_j — Value of land per acre in region j in year t.

VMT^t_j — Vehicle miles traveled in region j in year t.

WR^t_{ij} Annual earnings per worker in labor sector i working in region j in year t.

c^t_{ik} Construction coefficient (national sales from industry i to construction type k per unit of total construction by type k) in year t.

e^t_{ik} Equipment coefficient (national sales from industry i to equipment purchasing sector k per unit of total equipment purchased by sector k) in year t.

g^t_{ik} Government coefficient (national sales from industry i to government function k per unit total government purchases by function k) n year t.

q^t_{ik} Input-output technical coefficient (national sales from industry i to industry k per unit of output for industry k) in year t.

f_{ik} Denotes the functional relationship in sector i in equation k.

Δ Denotes change between year t and $t-1$ (e.g. $\Delta Q^t_{ij} = Q^t_{ij} - Q^{t-1}_{ij}$).

$i \rightarrow k$ A matching of elements i to elements k.

$\in$ Denotes "is an element of."

THE EQUATIONS

The subscript j is used to denote the region, where $j = 1, \ldots, NR$. In this application of the model, number of regions (NR) is 173, the number of OBE economic areas. If a variable does not have a subscript j, it is a national value. The number of sectors in each sector group (see Table 2-1) is unique to the model and some equations give particular sectors special treatment; therefore, the sector numbers are used as subscripts in the equations.

In the equations, superscript t ($t = 1, \ldots, NY$) denotes the forecast year, and $t-1$ denotes the prior year for which either data are available or forecasts have already been made. The parameters in the functional relationships are estimated using economic areas as observations and with superscript t representing the year 1966 and $t-1$ representing 1965. These are the years for which complete data are available. The model is recursive—data for year $t-1$ are used to make forecasts for year t, then the year t forecasts become data and are used to make forecasts for $t + 1$ and so on. In this application of the model forecasts are made to the year 1990, and the takeoff year is 1970. The regional estimates for 1970 are a mixture of actual data and forecasts.

The following equations are given in the logical order needed for making the forecasts.

Government Expenditures, Excluding Construction and Employee Compensation

$$DEF_{ij}^{t} = DEF_{ij}^{t-1} \cdot DEF_{i}^{t}/DEF_{i}^{t-1} \qquad (i = 1, \ldots, 99) \qquad (2.1)$$

$$GOV_{ij}^{t} = f_{i2}(PI_{j}^{t-1}) \qquad (i = 2, 3, 8) \qquad (2.2)$$

$$GOV_{ij}^{t} = GOV_{ij}^{t-1} \cdot GOV_{i}^{t}/GOV_{i}^{t-1} \qquad (i = 1, 4, 5, 6, 7) \qquad (2.3)$$

Output, Excluding Construction

$$\Delta QD_{ij}^{t} = f_{i4}(TQ_{ij}^{t-1}, TI_{s_k j}^{t-1}, WR_{ij}^{t-1}, \qquad \begin{array}{l} (i = 1, \ldots, 88) \\ (i \neq 11, 12, 75, 81) \end{array} \qquad (2.4)$$

$$VL_{j}^{t-1}, Q_{ij}^{t-1}, EQ_{hj}^{t-1}, MB_{ikj}^{t-1}, \qquad \begin{array}{l} (k \leqslant 1, \ldots, 4) \\ (s_k \in \max\limits_{s} q_{si}) \end{array}$$

$$MS_{ikj}^{t-1}, CGS_{j}^{t-1}, \qquad (h \to i)$$

$$DEN_{j}^{t-1})$$

$$QD_{ij}^{t} = \Delta QD_{ij}^{t} + QD_{ij}^{t-1} \qquad \begin{array}{l} (i = 1, \ldots, 88) \\ (i \neq 11, 12, 75, 81) \end{array} \qquad (2.5)$$

$$Q_{ij}^{t} = QD_{ij}^{t} + DEF_{ij}^{t} \qquad \begin{array}{l} (i = 1, \ldots, 88) \\ (i \neq 11, 12, 75, 81) \end{array} \qquad (2.6)$$

$$Q_{ij}^{t} = Q_{ij}^{t-1} \cdot \sum_{k=1}^{88} Q_{kj}^{t} / \sum_{k=1}^{88} Q_{kj}^{t-1} \qquad \begin{array}{l} (i = 75, 81, 89, \ldots, 99) \\ (k \neq 11, 12, 75, 81) \end{array} \qquad (2.7)$$

Gross Investment

$$EQ_{ij}^{t} = f_{i8}(Q_{kj}^{t}, EQ_{ij}^{t-1}) \qquad \begin{array}{l} (i = 1, \ldots, 69) \\ (k \to i) \end{array} \qquad (2.8)$$

$$CN_{ij}^{t} = f_{i9}(PI_{j}^{t-1}) \qquad (i = 1, 2, 17) \qquad (2.9)$$

$$CN_{ij}^{t} = f_{i10}(Q_{kj}^{t-1}, CN_{ij}^{t-1}) \qquad \begin{array}{l} (i = 3, \ldots, 16) \\ (k \to i) \end{array} \qquad (2.10)$$

$$CN_{ij}^{t} = f_{i11}(PI_{j}^{t-1}, CN_{ij}^{t-1}) \qquad (i = 18, \ldots, 28) \qquad (2.11)$$

Construction Output

$$Q^t_{11j} = \sum_{k=1}^{28} c^t_{11k} \cdot CN^t_{kj} \tag{2.12}$$

$$Q^t_{12j} = \sum_{k=1}^{99} q^t_{12k} \cdot Q^t_{kj} + \sum_{h=1}^{8} g^t_{12h} \cdot \quad (k \neq 12) \tag{2.13}$$

$$GOV^t_{hj} + DEF^t_{12j}$$

Employment

$$\Delta EMP^t_{ij} = f_{i14}(\Delta Q^t_{ij}, EQ^t_{kj}, Q^t_{ij}) \qquad (i = 1, \ldots, 99) \tag{2.14}$$

$$EMP^t_{100j} = f_{15}(\sum_{k=2}^{7} GOV^t_{kj}) \tag{2.15}$$

$$EMP^t_{101j} = f_{16}(GOV^t_{8j}) \tag{2.16}$$

$$EMP^t_{102j} = f_{17}(PI^{t-1}_j) \tag{2.17}$$

$$EMP^t_{103j} = EMP^{t-1}_{103j} \cdot EMP^t_{103} / EMP^{t-1}_{103} \tag{2.18}$$

$$MJH^t_j = \sum_{k=3}^{102} EMP^t_{kj} \cdot MJH^{t-1}_j / \qquad (k \neq 100, 101) \tag{2.19}$$

$$\sum_{k=3}^{102} EMP^{t-1}_{kj}$$

$$COM^t_j = \sum_{k=3}^{102} EMP^t_{kj} \cdot COM^{t-1}_j / \tag{2.20}$$

$$\sum_{k=3}^{102} EMP^{t-1}_{kj}$$

$$CPE^t_j = \sum_{k=1}^{102} EMP^t_{kj} - MJH^t_j - COM^t_j \tag{2.21}$$

Population

$$BIR_{rj}^t = f_{r22}(POP_{2rj}^{t-1}) \qquad\qquad (r = 1, 2) \qquad\qquad (2.22)$$

$$DEH_{arj}^t = f_{ar23}(POP_{arj}^{t-1}) \qquad\qquad \begin{array}{l}(a = 1, 2, 3, 4)\\(r = 1, 2)\end{array} \qquad (2.23)$$

$$PLS_j^{t-1} = (CLF_j^{t-1} - CPE_j^{t-1} \cdot CLF^{t-1} / \qquad\qquad (2.24)$$

$$CPE^{t-1}) \cdot \sum_{a=1}^{4} \sum_{r=1}^{2} POP_{arj}^{t-1} / CLF_j^{t-1}$$

$$PEC_j^t = \Delta CPE_j^t \cdot \sum_{a=1}^{4} \sum_{r=1}^{2} POP_{arj}^{t-1} / CLF_j^{t-1} \qquad\qquad (2.25)$$

$$NPM_{arj}^t = f_{ar26}(PLS_j^{t-1}, PEC_j^t, \Delta EMP_{103j}^t, \begin{array}{l}(a = 2, 3)\\(r = 1, 2)\end{array} \qquad (2.26)$$

$$\sum_{i=1}^{102} PAY_{ij}^{t-1} / \sum_{i=1}^{102} EMP_{ij}^{t-1})$$

$$NPM_{1rj}^t = f_{r27}(\sum_{i=2}^{3} NPM_{irj}^t) \qquad\qquad (r = 1, 2) \qquad\qquad (2.27)$$

$$NPM_{4rj}^t = f_{r28}(POP_{4rj}^t) \qquad\qquad (r = 1, 2) \qquad\qquad (2.28)$$

$$POP_{arj}^t = POP_{arj}^{t-1} + (BIR_{arj}^t - DEH_{arj}^t \qquad \begin{array}{l}(a = 1, 2, 3, 4)\\(r = 1, 2)\end{array} \qquad (2.29)$$

$$+ BIR_{arj}^{t-1} - DEH_{arj}^{t-1}) \cdot 0.5$$

$$+ NPM_{arj}^t + (EMP_{103j}^t - EMP_{103j}^{t-1})b_{ar}$$

$$(\sum_{a=1}^{4} \sum_{r=1}^{2} b_{ar} = 1)$$

Labor Force and Unemployment

$$CLF_j^t = f_{30}(\sum_{a=2}^{3} \sum_{r=1}^{2} POP_{arj}^t, PLS_j^{t-1}) \qquad\qquad (2.30)$$

$$CUE_j^t = CLF_j^t - CPE_j^t \tag{2.31}$$

Income

$$PAY_{ij}^t = f_{i32}\left(EMP_{ij}^t, EQ_{kj}^{t-1}, \sum_{h=13}^{74} PAY_{hj}^{t-1}\Big/ \quad (i=1,\ldots,99) \atop (k{\to}i)\right. \tag{2.32}$$

$$\sum_{h=13}^{74} EMP_{hj}^{t-1}$$

$$PAY_{ij}^t = EMP_{ij}^{t-1} \cdot PAY_{ij}^{t-1}/EMP_{ij}^{t-1} \quad (i=100,\ldots,103) \tag{2.33}$$

$$WR_{ij}^t = PAY_{ij}^t/EMP_{ij}^t \quad (i=1,\ldots,103) \tag{2.34}$$

$$ERN_j^t = CPE_j^t \cdot \sum_{i=3}^{102} PAY_{ij}^t\Big/\sum_{i=3}^{102} EMP_{ij}^t \tag{2.35}$$

$$TR_j^t = f_{36}\left(\sum_{a=1}^{4}\sum_{r=1}^{2} POP_{arj}^t, CUE_j^t\right) \tag{2.36}$$

$$PR_j^t = f_{37}(ERN_j^t) \tag{2.37}$$

$$SS_j^t = CPE_j^t \cdot SS_j^{t-1}/CPE_j^{t-1} \tag{2.38}$$

$$PI_j^t = ERN_j^t + TR_j^t + PR_j^t - SS_j^t + PAY_{103j}^t \tag{2.39}$$

Personal Consumption Expenditures

$$PCE_{ij}^t = f_{i40}(PI_j^t, PCE_j^{t-1}) \quad (i=1,\ldots,99) \tag{2.40}$$

International Trade

$$EX_{ij}^t = EX_{ij}^{t-1} \cdot EX_i^t/EX_i^{t-1} \quad (i=1,\ldots,99) \tag{2.41}$$

$$IM_{ij}^t = IM_{ij}^{t-1} \cdot IM_i^t/IM_i^{t-1} \quad (i=1,\ldots,99) \tag{2.42}$$

$$IM_{ij}^t = IM_{ij}^{t-1} \cdot IM_i^t / IM_i^{t-1} \qquad (i = 100, 101) \qquad (2.43)$$

Total Supply

$$S_{ij}^t = Q_{ij}^t + IM_{ij}^t \qquad (i = 1, \ldots, 99) \qquad (2.44)$$

Total Demand

$$D_{ij}^t = \sum_{k=1}^{99} q_{ik}^t \cdot Q_{kj}^t + \sum_{k=1}^{69} e_{ik}^t \cdot EQ_{kj} \quad (i = 1, \ldots, 99) \quad (2.45)$$

$$+ \sum_{k=1}^{28} c_{ik}^t \cdot CN_{kj}^t + \sum_{k=1}^{8} g_{ik}^t \cdot GOV_{kj}^t$$

$$+ PCE_{ij}^t + DEF_{ij}^t + EX_{ij}^t$$

Marginal Transport Costs
(Shadow Prices)

$$TQ_{ij}^t, TI_{ij}^t = f_{i46}(S_{ik}^t, D_{ik}^t, T_{ikh}^t) \qquad \begin{matrix} (i = 1, \ldots, 74) \\ (i \neq 4, 11, 12) \\ (h, k = 1, \ldots, NR) \end{matrix} \qquad (2.46)$$

Other Variables

$$VL_j^t = f_{47}(PR_j^t) \qquad (2.47)$$

$$MS_{ikj}^t \in Q_{hj}^t \qquad \begin{matrix} (i, h = 1, \ldots, 99) \\ (k \leqslant 4) \end{matrix} \qquad (2.48)$$

$$MB_{ikj}^t \in Q_{hj}^t, PCE_{hj}^t, DEF_{hj}^t, EX_{hj}^t, \qquad \begin{matrix} (i, h = 1, \ldots, 99) \\ (m = 1, \ldots, 69) \end{matrix} \qquad (2.49)$$
$$EQ_{mj}^t, CN_{nj}^t, GOV_{vj}^t \qquad \begin{matrix} (n = 1, \ldots, 28) \\ (v = 1, \ldots, 8) \\ (k \leqslant 4) \end{matrix}$$

$$DEN_j^t = \sum_{a=1}^{4} \sum_{r=1}^{2} POP_{arj}^t / SQM_j \qquad (2.50)$$

$$CMS_j^t = f_{51} \left(\sum_{a=1}^{4} \sum_{r=1}^{2} POP_{arj}^t, HCN_j^t \right) \qquad (2.51)$$

$$VMT_j^t = f_{52} \left(\sum_{a=1}^{4} \sum_{r=1}^{2} POP_{arj}^t \right) \qquad (2.52)$$

$$CGS_j^t = VMT_j^t / CMS_j^t \qquad (2.53)$$

EXPLANATION AND RESULTS OF THE EQUATIONS

When the economic area forecasts are made, they are controlled to sum to a predetermined set of national forecasts. This procedure assures that the sum of the regional forecasts are reasonable, and since the national model is an input-output model, the industry forecasts are consistent with each other.

In order to convert the regional model so that it allocates national totals, it is necessary to enter the variables as regional shares in the equations. If a variable is a level variable (for one point in time), it is expressed as a relative regional share. Thus:

becomes
$$X_j^t \quad \rightarrow \quad X_j^t / X^t$$

Where X_j^t is any level variable in region j period t and X without the subscript is the national value of the variable. If the variable in question is a change variable (between two points in time), it is expressed as an absolute regional share. Thus:

becomes
$$X_j^t - X_j^{t-1} = \Delta X_j^t \quad \rightarrow \quad X_j^t - X_j^{t-1} \cdot X^t / X^{t-1}$$

The absolute regional share is the difference between the regional level of X in period t and what it would have been if it had grown at the national rate from period $t-1$.

The sum of the relative regional shares over all areas is always equal to one, and the sum of the absolute regional shares is always equal to zero. Since the sums remain the same in the forecast years as in the base year, the equations will allocate the national values to regions. In other words, the regional model forecasts regional shares, then the national values are applied to obtain the regional values.

The national model used here was developed by Professor Clopper

Almon of the University of Maryland,[b] and all the data in the regional model have been adjusted so as to be consistent with the data in the national model. The national model is a dynamic input-output model that forecasts the national economy under various assumptions as to final demand spending. The model is recursive, forecasting final demand spending for one year and generating a set of outputs consistent with that final demand spending and with the labor force. The income generated by the output is used to help forecast the final demand spending in the next year, and then the model keeps recycling from year to year until the last forecast year is reached.

Government Expenditures

Government expenditures (excluding construction and employee compensation) are, for the most part, treated exogenously, although expenditures on some functions are allowed to change with income. Equation 2.1 holds the regional distribution of defense expenditures by industry constant over time. Regional defense expenditures by industry only change by the same percentage as the national defense expenditures in that industry. The location of the government's defense expenditures is assumed to be the same as the location of the industry that produces the goods or services.

General federal government expenditures, the federal government enterprises (mostly post offices), and the state and local government expenditures are hypothesized to depend directly on the prior level of personal income as given in Equation 2.2. The parameters for these three questions are given in Table 2-2.

The regional distributions of other nondefense government expenditures are held constant, with the regional levels changing only as the national levels change, as given in Equation 2.3. These functions include NASA and government purchases of livestock, crops, forestry and fisheries, and lumber. These latter four expenditures categories were given special treatment because the federal government sells as well as buys goods and services to these sectors. The data show for 1966 that the net effect of these transactions was negative for crops and forestry and fisheries. That is, on balance, the federal government sold crops from the Commodity Credit Corporation's inventories and furnished services to the forestry and fisheries industry, mostly in the form of forest management.

Output, Excluding Construction

Equation 2.4, which is the principal equation driving the forecasting model, forecasts the change in regional output by industry. The dependent variable is the change in output after defense expenditures have been subtracted

---

[b]Clopper Almon Jr., Margaret R. Buckler, Lawrence M. Horowitz, and Thomas C. Reimbold, *1985 Interindustry Forecasts of the American Economy*, Lexington, Mass.: Lexington Books (D.C. Heath), 1974.

Table 2-2.   Equation (2.2) Explaining the Level of 1966
Government Expenditures

Sector	No. Observations	R^2	Constant	1965 Personal Income
2 General Federal Income	173	.8619	.00046 (.00039)	.92078 (.02819)
3 Federal enterprises	173	.9835	-.00009 (.00014)	1.01541 (.01005)
8 State and local government	173	9799	-.00000 (.00015)	1.00017 (.01095)

from output. Defense expenditures are subtracted out because the location of defense expenditures is defined as the location of the production, and because of the practice of using cost-plus contracts. The location of goods produced for defense is often not influenced by regional variations of input prices.

The regional change in output is hypothesized to be a function of selected input prices and agglomeration variables.[c] The results of these equations are given in Table 2-3. This table shows the overall fit of the equations (R^2) for explaining both the change in output and the level of output. The equations were fitted using the change in output as the dependent variable; however, since our objective is to forecast output, the R^2 associated with the level of output (measuring how well the regional variation in output is explained by the equations) is the appropriate number to examine.

Transportation costs have considerable regional variation; therefore, the independent variables in Equation 2.4 include the marginal transport cost of shipping a unit of output out of each region and the marginal transport cost of obtaining a unit of major inputs into each region. The location of commodity-producing industries is often influenced by the transportation cost of shipping the commodities to markets. Similarly, the location of industries is often influenced by the transportation cost of obtaining its most important inputs. In Equation 2.4 up to four input transportation cost variables were used for each industry, depending on the importance of the commodity inputs. The transportation variables are computed using a linear programming transportation algorithm. The marginal cost of shipping output (TQ) was significant in twelve of the equations, and 28 equations had at least one input shadow price (TI) as a significant variable. (The significant criterion is that the coefficient must be greater than its standard error.) The industry having the greatest influence on

[c]The theoretical background of Equation 2.4 and other equations were presented in Harris, *The Urban Economics, 1985, op. cit.,* pp. 33–45.

TABLE 2.3

EQUATIONS (2.4) EXPLAINING CHANGE IN OUTPUT BY INDUSTRY SECTOR   1965-1966

1 LIVESTOCK

$$\Delta QD(1,T) = 1201 - 94431\ Q(1,T-1) - 8647R\ TI(17,T-1) - 44690\ FQ(1,T-1) + 139215\ CGS(T-1) + 35961\ Q(14,T-1)$$
$$(632)\quad (30110) \qquad (80910) \qquad (39967) \qquad (8087R) \qquad (26432)$$
$$+ 31293\ Q(4,T-1)$$
$$(23462)$$

NO. OBSV. = 171   R-SQUARE = .0764   R-SQUARE (LEVEL OF OUTPUT) = .9898

2 CROPS

$$\Delta QD(2,T) = 751 - 59557\ Q(2,T-1) + 54134\ FQ(1,T-1) + 54418\ Q(35,T-1)$$
$$(417)\quad (28622) \qquad (40056) \qquad (16225)$$

NO. OBSV. = 169   R-SQUARE = .1017   R-SQUARE (LEVEL OF OUTPUT) = .9902

3 FORESTRY & FISHERY PRODUCTS

$$\Delta QD(3,T) = 6974 - 715432\ VL(T-1) - 1263611\ CGS(T-1) + 120812\ PCF(3,T-1) + 185174\ Q(4,T-1) + 266257\ Q(25,T-1)$$
$$(4312)\quad (265794) \qquad (723160) \qquad (94807) \qquad (152540) \qquad (72806)$$

NO. OBSV. = 73   R-SQUARE = .2669   R-SQUARE (LEVEL OF OUTPUT) = .9957

4 AGRICULTURAL SERVICES

$$\Delta QD(4,T) = 6703 + 224423\ Q(4,T-1) - 1380870\ CGS(T-1)$$
$$(3766)\quad (156506) \qquad (681370)$$

NO. OBSV. = 170   R-SQUARE = .0248   R-SQUARE (LEVEL OF OUTPUT) = .9696

5 IRON ORE MINING

$$\Delta QD(5,T) = 6294 - 22278\ Q(5,T-1) - 736104\ TI(55,T-1) + 133635\ CN(18,T-1) + 56362\ FX(5,T-1)$$
$$(2828)\quad (16918) \qquad (313652) \qquad (97168) \qquad (30759)$$

NO. OBSV. = 24   R-SQUARE = .3746   R-SQUARE (LEVEL OF OUTPUT) = .9915

6 NON-FERROUS ORE MINING

$$\Delta QD(6,T) = 57781 - 215297\ Q(6,T-1) - 2154073\ TQ(6,T-1) - 2165405\ TI(35,T-1) - 5220808\ CGS(T-1) + 685774\ Q(46,T-1)$$
$$(23620)\quad (177210) \qquad (1184371) \qquad (2044381) \qquad (1953490) \qquad (261315)$$

NO. OBSV. = 56   R-SQUARE = .1840   R-SQUARE (LEVEL OF OUTPUT) = .9971

7 COAL MINING

$$\Delta QD(7,T) = 7584 - 180468\ Q(7,T-1) + 1236227\ TQ(7,T-1) + 649379\ CN(18,T-1)$$
$$(7563)\quad (91720) \qquad (1103472) \qquad (590463)$$

NO. OBSV. = 57   R-SQUARE = .088R   R-SQUARE (LEVEL OF OUTPUT) = .9917

8 PETROLEUM MINING

$$\Delta QD(8,T) = 587 + 440483\ Q(8,T-1) - 1554994\ CGS(T-1) + 214054\ Q(85,T-1)$$
$$(8931)\quad (156884) \qquad (1504989) \qquad (130418)$$

NO. OBSV. = 68   R-SQUARE = .1453   R-SQUARE (LEVEL OF OUTPUT) = .9893

9 MINERALS MINING

$\Delta QD(9,T) = 427 + 217439 \, Q(9,T-1) - 313765 \, TI(40,T-1)$
(1955) (97990) (302286)
NO. OBSV. = 162   R-SQUARE = .0348   R-SQUARE (LEVEL OF OUTPUT) = .9565

10 CHEMICAL MINING

$\Delta QD(10,T) = 36919 - 2306089 \, TI(55,T-1) - 254744 \, VL(T-1) - 3723521 \, CGS(T-1) + 291753 \, Q(45,T-1)$
(9938) (794986) (229162) (1260031) (146689)
NO. OBSV. = 27   R-SQUARE = .5333   R-SQUARE (LEVEL OF OUTPUT) = .9964

14 MEAT PACKING

$\Delta QD(14,T) = 1545 + 293304 \, Q(14,T-1) - 688988 \, DEN(T-1) + 166740 \, FX(14,T-1)$
(2067) (178868) (241265) (71413)
NO. OBSV. = 150   R-SQUARE = .0617   R-SQUARE (LEVEL OF OUTPUT) = .9911

15 DAIRY PRODUCTS

$\Delta QD(15,T) = 2061 + 420299 \, Q(15,T-1) - 775543 \, VL(T-1)$
(1236) (126808) (179212)
NO. OBSV. = 171   R-SQUARE = .1050   R-SQUARE (LEVEL OF OUTPUT) = .9694

16 CANNED & FROZEN FOODS

$\Delta QD(16,T) = 3157 + 57738 \, Q(16,T-1) - 596162 \, TI(3,T-1)$
(1639) (29836) (275302)
NO. OBSV. = 123   R-SQUARE = .0697   R-SQUARE (LEVEL OF OUTPUT) = .9928

17 GRAIN MILL PRODUCTS

$\Delta QD(17,T) = 6315 + 274979 \, Q(17,T-1) - 451483 \, WR(17,T-1) - 1130404 \, CGS(T-1) + 152867 \, DEN(T-1)$
(3125) (68420) (402183) (374040) (80310)
NO. OBSV. = 153   R-SQUARE = .1198   R-SQUARE (LEVEL OF OUTPUT) = .9969

18 BAKERY PRODUCTS

$\Delta QD(18,T) = 7898 + 114637 \, Q(18,T-1) - 509428 \, TI(19,T-1) - 1145740 \, CGS(T-1) + 202184 \, Q(17,T-1)$
(3464) (70737) (474123) (357681) (70490)
NO. OBSV. = 165   R-SQUARE = .1054   R-SQUARE (LEVEL OF OUTPUT) = .9969

19 SUGAR

$\Delta QD(19,T) = - 2174 + 84236 \, Q(19,T-1) + 204768 \, DEN(T-1)$
(2718) (72495) (135493)
NO. OBSV. = 42   R-SQUARE = .1327   R-SQUARE (LEVEL OF OUTPUT) = .9914

20 CANDY

$\Delta QD(20,T) = 32097 + 544880 \, Q(20,T-1) - 5461734 \, TQ(20,T-1) - 2516700 \, VL(T-1)$
(19331) (320941) (2957061) (1425497)
NO. OBSV. = 80   R-SQUARE = .0967   R-SQUARE (LEVEL OF OUTPUT) = .6826

(CONTINUED)

TABLE 2.3   (CONTINUED)

21 REVERAGES

NO. OBSV. = 162   R-SQUARE = .0935   R-SQUARE (LEVEL OF OUTPUT) = .7723

$$\Delta QD(21,T) = \underset{(57294)}{135611} + \underset{(738663)}{1490819}\, Q(21,T-1) - \underset{(2599602)}{4192528}\, TQ(21,T-1) - \underset{(6427589)}{11011429}\, TI(49,T-1) - \underset{(1439482)}{3655959}\, VI(T-1) - \underset{(3320440)}{6848254}\, CGS(T-1)$$
$$+ \underset{(459164)}{734386}\, Q(43,T-1)$$

22 MISC. FOOD PRODUCTS

NO. OBSV. = 151   R-SQUARE = .1574   R-SQUARE (LEVEL OF OUTPUT) = .9908

$$\Delta QD(22,T) = \underset{(4265)}{8316} - \underset{(48707)}{112774}\, Q(22,T-1) - \underset{(4470019)}{976392}\, TI(49,T-1) - \underset{(158105)}{175655}\, TI(43,T-1) - \underset{(257163)}{408940}\, TI(17,T-1) + \underset{(35659)}{112018}\, EQ(69,T-1)$$
$$+ \underset{(63410)}{109540}\, DEN(T-1)$$

23 TOBACCO

NO. OBSV. = 38   R-SQUARE = .1466   R-SQUARE (LEVEL OF OUTPUT) = .9999

$$\Delta QD(23,T) = \underset{(1657)}{2703} - \underset{(204475)}{318965}\, VL(T-1) + \underset{(83796)}{197980}\, Q(33,T-1)$$

24 FABRICS & YARN

NO. OBSV. = 65   R-SQUARE = .1218   R-SQUARE (LEVEL OF OUTPUT) = .9901

$$\Delta QD(24,T) = \underset{(204432)}{42919} - \underset{(1054540)}{2003229}\, TQ(24,T-1) - \underset{(1987526)}{4381454}\, TI(2,T-1) - \underset{(1696074)}{1734195}\, CGS(T-1) + \underset{(316776)}{782717}\, DEN(T-1)$$

25 RUGS, TIRE CORD, MISC. TEXTILES

NO. OBSV. = 26   R-SQUARE = .3759   R-SQUARE (LEVEL OF OUTPUT) = .5561

$$\Delta QD(25,T) = \underset{(102273)}{199377} - \underset{(316653)}{973768}\, Q(25,T-1) - \underset{(9586662)}{13574611}\, TI(36,T-1) - \underset{(12348786)}{16686885}\, TI(1,T-1) + \underset{(284599)}{449984}\, Q(27,T-1)$$

26 APPAREL

NO. OBSV. = 120   R-SQUARE = .1875   R-SQUARE (LEVEL OF OUTPUT) = .9945

$$\Delta QD(26,T) = \underset{(1085)}{2365} - \underset{(39617)}{71523}\, Q(26,T-1) - \underset{(159036)}{261946}\, VL(T-1)$$

27 HOUSEHOLD TEXTILES & UPHOLST.

NO. OBSV. = 95   R-SQUARE = .0454   R-SQUARE (LEVEL OF OUTPUT) = .9639

$$\Delta QD(27,T) = \underset{(2769)}{2768} - \underset{(359302)}{603493}\, VL(T-1) + \underset{(79279)}{165343}\, EQ(11,T-1)$$

28 LUMBER & PROD, EXC. CONTAINERS

NO. OBSV. = 153   R-SQUARE = .0286   R-SQUARE (LEVEL OF OUTPUT) = .9937

$$\Delta QD(28,T) = \underset{(520H)}{7656} - \underset{(362335)}{675503}\, TQ(28,T-1) - \underset{(646949)}{708964}\, WR(28,T-1) + \underset{(53326)}{78075}\, Q(12,T-1)$$

29 WOODEN CONTAINERS

$\Delta QD(29,T) = - 6680 + 478236\ FQ(13,T-1)$
            (6576)   (328049)

NO. OBSV. = 82   R-SQUARE = .0259   R-SQUARE (LEVEL OF OUTPUT) = .9943

30 HOUSEHOLD FURNITURE

$\Delta QD(30,T) = 36073 + 1320165\ Q(30,T-1) - 7010286\ WR(30,T-1)$
            (38743)   (427049)   (5613646)

NO. OBSV. = 117   R-SQUARE = .0807   R-SQUARE (LEVEL OF OUTPUT) = .9789

31 OFFICE FURNITURE

$\Delta QD(31,T) = 3862 + 70955\ EQ(15,T-1) - 665722\ TI(28,T-1)$
            (3228)   (59823)   (480298)

NO. OBSV. = 118   R-SQUARE = .0248   R-SQUARE (LEVEL OF OUTPUT) = .9937

32 PAPER & PROD. EXC. CONTAINERS

$\Delta QD(32,T) = - 1384 - 547804\ Q(32,T-1) + 385603\ DEN(T-1) + 396795\ Q(35,T-1)$
            (2893)   (306231)   (311069)   (263867)

NO. OBSV. = 124   R-SQUARE = .0460   R-SQUARE (LEVEL OF OUTPUT) = .9869

33 PAPER CONTAINERS

$\Delta QD(33,T) = 7600 - 1828718\ TI(35,T-1) + 323075\ DEN(T-1)$
            (7021)   (1227826U)   (223005)

NO. OBSV. = 110   R-SQUARE = .0332   R-SQUARE (LEVEL OF OUTPUT) = .9871

34 PRINTING & PUBLISHING

$\Delta QD(34,T) = - 527 - 65193\ W(34,T-1) + 155000\ CN(18,T-1)$
            (645)   (27811)   (92452)

NO. OBSV. = 168   R-SQUARE = .0329   R-SQUARE (LEVEL OF OUTPUT) = .9975

35 BASIC CHEMICALS

$\Delta QD(35,T) = - 3943 - 732648\ Q(35,T-1) + 552257\ EQ(19,T-1) + 445137\ DEN(T-1) + 362495\ Q(2,T-1)$
            (3391)   (369450)   (244697)   (288429)   (338504)

NO. OBSV. = 141   R-SQUARE = .0519   R-SQUARE (LEVEL OF OUTPUT) = .9800

36 PLASTICS & SYNTHETICS

$\Delta QD(36,T) = - 28896 + 1691380\ Q(36,T-1) + 917876\ Q(24,T-1)$
            (23961)   (1417581)   (615609)

NO. OBSV. = 84   R-SQUARE = .0526   R-SQUARE (LEVEL OF OUTPUT) = .9933

(CONTINUED)

TABLE 2.3 (CONTINUED)

37 DRUGS, CLEANING & TOILET ITEMS   NO. OBSV. = 98   R-SQUARE = .1868   R-SQUARE (LEVEL OF OUTPUT) = .9860

$\Delta QD(37,T) = 7729 - 151121\ Q(37,T-1) - 807750\ WR(37,T-1) - 960335\ CGS(T-1) + 215739\ DEN(T-1) + 427698\ Q(35,T-1)$
(6883)   (93490)   (713911)   (697855)   (200773)   (148962)
$+ 113384\ Q(40,T-1)$
(88381)

38 PAINT & ALLIED PRODUCTS   NO. OBSV. = 81   R-SQUARE = .1122   R-SQUARE (LEVEL OF OUTPUT) = .9946

$\Delta QD(38,T) = 17550 - 532772\ Q(38,T-1) + 2885117\ TI(35,T-1) + 895536\ CN(18,T-1)$
(9327)   (222369)   (1728434)   (785801)

39 PETROLEUM REFINING   NO. OBSV. = 82   R-SQUARE = .0508   R-SQUARE (LEVEL OF OUTPUT) = .9881

$\Delta QD(39,T) = 7600 - 1408011\ TI(35,T-1) + 214561\ EQ(23,T-1)$
(7677)   (1294662)   (114614)

40 RUBBER & PLASTIC PRODUCTS   NO. OBSV. = 117   R-SQUARE = .0302   R-SQUARE (LEVEL OF OUTPUT) = .9658

$\Delta QD(40,T) = -1228 - 172276\ Q(40,T-1) + 348968\ CN(18,T-1)$
(1963)   (92917)   (250549)

41 LEATHER TANNING   NO. OBSV. = 43   R-SQUARE = .1953   R-SQUARE (LEVEL OF OUTPUT) = .9827

$\Delta QD(41,T) = 34583 - 4612304\ TQ(41,T-1) - 1382396\ DEN(T-1)$
(14656)   (3011460)   (482108)

42 SHOES & OTHER LEATHER PRODUCTS   NO. OBSV. = 89   R-SQUARE = .1239   R-SQUARE (LEVEL OF OUTPUT) = .9722

$\Delta QD(42,T) = 969 - 419399\ Q(42,T-1) - 222238\ VL(T-1) + 324961\ EQ(26,T-1) + 387484\ Q(24,T-1)$
(2320)   (131511)   (266127)   (117936)   (174624)

43 GLASS & GLASS PRODUCTS   NO. OBSV. = 83   R-SQUARE = .0577   R-SQUARE (LEVEL OF OUTPUT) = .9940

$\Delta QD(43,T) = 9014 - 266872\ Q(43,T-1) - 1347732\ TI(35,T-1) + 122962\ EQ(27,T-1)$
(6989)   (134604)   (1249286)   (81114)

44 STONE & CLAY PRODUCTS   NO. OBSV. = 168   R-SQUARE = .0299   R-SQUARE (LEVEL OF OUTPUT) = .9966

$\Delta QD(44,T) = 3697 + 164920\ Q(44,T-1) - 790641\ CGS(T-1)$
(1983)   (88290)   (367063)

45 IRON & STEEL

$\Delta QD(45,T) = 2090 + 139652\ Q(45,T-1) - 506455\ TI(5,T-1) - 91658\ DEN(T-1) + 59368\ Q(35,T-1)$
(1919)   (23155)   (296344)   (56723)   (53739)

NO. OBSV. = 97   R-SQUARE = .3534   R-SQUARE (LEVEL OF OUTPUT) = .9962

46 COPPER

$\Delta QD(46,T) = -1815 + 97856\ Q(46,T-1)$
(3012)   (92327)

NO. OBSV. = 59   R-SQUARE = .0174   R-SQUARE (LEVEL OF OUTPUT) = .8350

47 ALUMINUM

$\Delta QD(47,T) = 77893 - 6897113\ TQ(47,T-1) - 5635706\ TI(60,T-1) - 1872973\ CGS(T-1) + 604517\ DEN(T-1)$
(32939)   (3274412)   (2738851)   (1722330)   (364988)

NO. OBSV. = 92   R-SQUARE = .0921   R-SQUARE (LEVEL OF OUTPUT) = .9567

48 OTHER NON-FERROUS METALS

$\Delta QD(48,T) = 12141 - 220481\ Q(48,T-1) + 2200162\ TI(47,T-1) + 345048\ FQ(30,T-1)$
(9713)   (120590)   (1623929)   (152239)

NO. OBSV. = 79   R-SQUARE = .1041   R-SQUARE (LEVEL OF OUTPUT) = .9645

49 METAL CONTAINERS

$\Delta QD(49,T) = 9747 + 131165\ Q(49,T-1) - 296128\ VL(T-1) - 1297899\ CGS(T-1) + 44768\ Q(45,T-1)$
(5715)   (73228)   (235301)   (804924)   (44703)

NO. OBSV. = 48   R-SQUARE = .1132   R-SQUARE (LEVEL OF OUTPUT) = .9882

50 HEATING, PLUMBING, STRUC METAL

$\Delta QD(50,T) = 16327 - 6612848\ Q(50,T-1) - 7961326\ TI(47,T-1) + 2756747\ FQ(32,T-1) + 7271752\ DEN(T-1) + 1288021\ CN(4,T-1)$
(460961) (1724304)   (7864724)   (1048424)   (1460220)   (1259689)

NO. OBSV. = 151   R-SQUARE = .1860   R-SQUARE (LEVEL OF OUTPUT) = .9945

51 STAMPINGS, SCREW MACHINE PROD.

$\Delta QD(51,T) = 24870 + 292574\ Q(51,T-1) - 2079328\ TI(47,T-1) - 2053606\ VL(T-1) + 197654\ Q(46,T-1)$
(12366) (103257)   (2023336)   (339507)   (117258)

NO. OBSV. = 76   R-SQUARE = .3501   R-SQUARE (LEVEL OF OUTPUT) = .9874

52 HARDWARE, PLATING, WIRE PROD.

$\Delta QD(52,T) = -4563 - 747395\ Q(52,T-1) + 513648\ DEN(T-1) + 206506\ Q(46,T-1) - 652613\ Q(35,T-1)$
(3115)   (253039)   (3745381)   (1580371)   (289548)

NO. OBSV. = 108   R-SQUARE = .1055   R-SQUARE (LEVEL OF OUTPUT) = .9880

53 ENGINES & TURBINES

$\Delta QD(53,T) = 3235 + 124129\ Q(53,T-1) - 1158352\ TI(60,T-1)$
(4812)   (60054)   (945604)

NO. OBSV. = 52   R-SQUARE = .1161   R-SQUARE (LEVEL OF OUTPUT) = .9935

(CONTINUED)

TABLE 2.3 (CONTINUED)

54 FARM MACHINERY & EQUIPMENT
$$\Delta QD(54,T) = 3196 - 842214\ CGS(T-1) + 54715\ DEN(T-1) + 256522\ CN(18,T-1)$$
$$(1042)\quad (200291)\quad\quad (38991)\quad\quad (74843)$$
NO. OBSV. = 110   R-SQUARE = .1771   R-SQUARE (LEVEL OF OUTPUT) = .9943

55 CONSTRUCTION & MINING MACHINES
$$\Delta QD(55,T) = -1916 + 73660\ EQ(37,T-1) + 47892\ FX(55,T-1)$$
$$(1225)\quad (57186)\quad\quad (24929)$$
NO. OBSV. = 88   R-SQUARE = .1035   R-SQUARE (LEVEL OF OUTPUT) = .9762

56 MATERIAL HANDLING EQUIPMENT
$$\Delta QD(56,T) = 3942 + 28936\ Q(56,T-1) - 886923\ CGS(T-1) + 210511\ CN(18,T-1)$$
$$(1475)\quad (25490)\quad\quad (253871)\quad\quad (87611)$$
NO. OBSV. = 85   R-SQUARE = .1502   R-SQUARE (LEVEL OF OUTPUT) = .9935

57 METALWORKING MACHINERY & EQUIP
$$\Delta QD(57,T) = -3762 - 182050\ Q(57,T-1) + 447988\ CN(18,T-1) + 185657\ EQ(29,T-1)$$
$$(3442)\quad (117137)\quad\quad (352605)\quad\quad (86602)$$
NO. OBSV. = 80   R-SQUARE = .0757   R-SQUARE (LEVEL OF OUTPUT) = .9738

58 SPECIAL INDUSTRIAL MACHINERY
$$\Delta QD(58,T) = 213 + 142704\ Q(58,T-1) - 379075\ DEN(T-1) + 152984\ CN(18,T-1) + 27393\ FX(58,T-1)$$
$$(1043)\quad (61222)\quad\quad (145790)\quad\quad (108582)\quad\quad (26417)$$
NO. OBSV. = 98   R-SQUARE = .0890   R-SQUARE (LEVEL OF OUTPUT) = .9986

59 GENERAL INDUSTRIAL MACHINERY
$$\Delta QD(59,T) = 3645 - 788831\ DEN(T-1) + 154612\ EX(59,T-1) + 200644\ Q(63,T-1)$$
$$(1888)\quad (241906)\quad\quad (54972)\quad\quad (121101)$$
NO. OBSV. = 88   R-SQUARE = .1155   R-SQUARE (LEVEL OF OUTPUT) = .9941

60 MACHINE SHOPS & MISC MACHINERY
$$\Delta QD(60,T) = 813 + 134826\ Q(60,T-1) - 278054\ DEN(T-1)$$
$$(1127)\quad (91351)\quad\quad (128678)$$
NO. OBSV. = 136   R-SQUARE = .0340   R-SQUARE (LEVEL OF OUTPUT) = .9937

61 OFFICE & COMPUTING MACHINES
$$\Delta QD(61,T) = 72999 - 1570556\ Q(61,T-1) - 70883427\ CGS(T-1) + 2925220\ DEN(T-1) + 4288222\ Q(67,T-1)$$
$$(59881)\quad (1057498)\quad\quad (9685855)\quad\quad (2172741)\quad\quad (1238122)$$
NO. OBSV. = 67   R-SQUARE = .2897   R-SQUARE (LEVEL OF OUTPUT) = .9950

62 SERVICE INDUSTRY MACHINES
$$\Delta QD(62,T) = 5329 - 745222\ Q(62,T-1) - 1327341\ TQ(62,T-1) + 398599\ EQ(43,T-1) + 570486\ CN(18,T-1)$$
$$(3741)\quad (214828)\quad\quad (653450)\quad\quad (153362)\quad\quad (359284)$$
NO. OBSV. = 86   R-SQUARE = .1406   R-SQUARE (LEVEL OF OUTPUT) = .9877

63 ELECTRIC APPARATUS & MOTORS

ΔQD(63,T) = 4297 - 481268 Q(63,T-1)
            (3897) (200051)

NO. OBSV. = 88   R-SQUARF = .0631   R-SQUARE (LEVEL OF OUTPUT) = .9655

64 HOUSEHOLD APPLIANCES

ΔQD(64,T) = 6411 - 2436535 TQ(64,T-1) - 463935 DFN(T-1) + 816113 CN(1R,T-1)
            (440A) (1089997)   (244396)   (495011)

NO. OBSV. = 67   R-SQUARE = .0932   R-SQUARE (LEVEL OF OUTPUT) = .9760

65 ELECTRIC LIGHT & WIRING EQUIP.

ΔQD(65,T) = 1758 - 417908 Q(65,T-1) + 882408 TQ(65,T-1) + 768075 CN(1R,T-1) + 113166 Q(45,1-1)
            (4319) (127617)   (815021)   (439068)   (92681)

NO. OBSV. = 70   R-SQUARE = .1574   R-SQUARE (LEVEL OF OUTPUT) = .9875

66 COMMUNICATION EQUIPMENT

ΔQD(66,T) = -762 - 206997 Q(66,T-1) + 299068 DEN(T-1)
            (2362) (102275)   (207336)

NO. OBSV. = 91   R-SQUARF = .0446   R-SQUARE (LEVEL OF OUTPUT) = .9864

67 ELECTRONIC COMPONENTS

ΔQD(67,T) = 29313 + 3788509 Q(67,T-1) - 10831387 CGS(T-1)
            (45399) (765843)   (6849995)

NO. OBSV. = 89   R-SQUARE = .2235   R-SQUARE (LEVEL OF OUTPUT) = .9946

68 BATTERIES & ENGINE ELEC EQUIP.

ΔQD(68,T) = -1750 + 241206 Q(68,T-1)
            (4312)   (178187)

NO. OBSV. = 71   R-SQUARF = .0259   R-SQUARE (LEVEL OF OUTPUT) = .9868

69 MOTOR VEHICLES

ΔQD(69,T) = 5744 - 205425 Q(69,T-1) - 1170947 DFN(T-1) + 636477 PCF(69,T-1) + 243214 FX(69,T-1)
            (3250) (91568)   (391667)   (321952)   (98091)

NO. OBSV. = 86   R-SQUARF = .1094   R-SQUARE (LEVEL OF OUTPUT) = .9929

70 AIRCRAFT & PARTS

ΔQD(70,T) = 12058 - 2268752 T(160,T-1)
            (10910) (1896561)

NO. OBSV. = 77   R-SQUARE = .0187   R-SQUARE (LEVEL OF OUTPUT) = .9535

71 SHIPS, TRAINS, TRAILRS, CYCLFS

ΔQD(71,T) = 11843 - 67700 Q(71,T-1) - 885674 TQ(71,T-1) - 527985 WK(71,T-1) - 565672 CGS(T-1)
            (3655) (61351)   (208655)   (465852)   (381851)

NO. OBSV. = 115   R-SQUARE = .7123   R-SQUARE (LEVEL OF OUTPUT) = .9947

(CONTINUED)

TABLE 2.3   (CONTINUED)

72   INSTRUMENTS & CLOCKS

$\Delta QD(72,T) = 4387 - 354507 \; Q(72,T-1) - 893341 \; VL(T-1) + 132114 \; Fx(72,T-1) + 463473 \; Q(51,T-1)$
                (3189)   (147775)   (423076)   (67113)   (125794)

NO. OBSV. = 83   R-SQUARF = .1721   R-SQUARE (LEVEL OF OUTPUT) = .9980

73   OPTICAL & PHOTOGRAPHIC EQUIP.

$\Delta QD(73,T) = 8243 - 1405554 \; TI(35,T-1)$
                (7866)   (1255233)

NO. OBSV. = 65   R-SQUARF = .0195   R-SQUARE (LEVEL OF OUTPUT) = .9935

74   MISC. MANUFACTURED PRODUCTS

$\Delta QD(74,T) = 9140 + 297655 \; Q(74,T-1) - 1703370 \; CGS(T-1)$
                (7535)   (100943)   (1158792)

NO. OBSV. = 129   R-SQUARF = .0655   R-SQUARE (LEVEL OF OUTPUT) = .9577

76   COMMUNICATION

$\Delta QD(76,T) = 34208 + 4404002 \; PI(T-1) - 10322943 \; CGS(T-1)$
                (22476)   (743312)   (4011481)

NO. OBSV. = 173   R-SQUARE = .1742   R-SQUARE (LEVEL OF OUTPUT) = .9944

77   RADIO, TV BROADCASTING

$\Delta QD(77,T) = - 106 - 212181 \; TI(66,T-1) + 223755 \; CN(18,T-1)$
                (1359)   (193049)   (91096)

NO. OBSV. = 164   R-SQUARF = .0426   R-SQUARE (LEVEL OF OUTPUT) = .9989

78   ELECTRIC UTILITY

$\Delta QD(78,T) = 34208 + 4404902 \; PI(T-1) - 10322943 \; CGS(T-1)$
                (22476)   (743312)   (4011481)

NO. OBSV. = 173   R-SQUARE = .1742   R-SQUARE (LEVEL OF OUTPUT) = .9944

79   GAS UTILITY

$\Delta QD(79,T) = 36717 + 4479355 \; PI(T-1) - 10924504 \; CGS(T-1)$
                (25295)   (792293)   (4399882)

NO. OBSV. = 158   R-SQUARF = .1790   R-SQUARE (LEVEL OF OUTPUT) = .9944

80   WATER UTILITY

$\Delta QD(80,T) = 20109 - 2088966 \; TI(35,T-1) - 961813 \; VL(T-1) + 193546 \; Q(80,T-1)$
                (7887)   (1178093)   (510693)   (162596)

NO. OBSV. = 102   R-SQUARF = .0602   R-SQUARE (LEVEL OF OUTPUT) = .9947

82   FINANCE & INSURANCE

$\Delta QD(82,T) = - 605 + 104644 \; PI(T-1)$
                (583)   (42339)

NO. OBSV. = 173   R-SQUARF = .0345   R-SQUARE (LEVEL OF OUTPUT) = .9988

83 REAL ESTATE & RENTAL

$$\Delta QD(83,T) = 9584 + 783984\ PI(T-1) - 1008427\ WR(83,T-1) - 1426377\ CGS(T-1)$$
$$(4567)\quad (1113168)\qquad\qquad (712358)\qquad\qquad (654074)$$

NO. OBSV. = 169   R-SQUARE = .2340   R-SQUARE (LEVEL OF OUTPUT) = .9995

84 HOTELS, PERSONAL & REPAIR SVC.

$$\Delta QD(84,T) = 20986 - 2031229\ TI(67,T-1) - 1599401\ VL(T-1)$$
$$(7871)\quad (1192767)\qquad\qquad (347258)$$

NO. OBSV. = 173   R-SQUARE = .1131   R-SQUARE (LEVEL OF OUTPUT) = .9831

85 BUSINESS SERVICES

$$\Delta QD(85,T) = 409 - 198804\ VL(T-1) + 131488\ CN(18,T-1)$$
$$(681)\quad (89155)\qquad\qquad (89518)$$

NO. OBSV. = 165   R-SQUARE = .0303   R-SQUARE (LEVEL OF OUTPUT) = .9975

86 AUTOMOBILE REPAIR SERVICES

$$\Delta QD(86,T) = 1495 - 433715\ Q(86,T-1) + 175011\ Q(39,T-1)$$
$$(2349)\quad (222182)\qquad\qquad (165161)$$

NO. OBSV. = 173   R-SQUARE = .0220   R-SQUARE (LEVEL OF OUTPUT) = .9926

87 AMUSEMENTS & RECREATION

$$\Delta QD(87,T) = -1206 + 207898\ PI(T-1)$$
$$(1897)\quad (137381)$$

NO. OBSV. = 172   R-SQUARE = .0133   R-SQUARE (LEVEL OF OUTPUT) = .9865

88 MEDICAL & EDUCATIONAL INSTIT.

$$\Delta QD(88,T) = 1930 - 333961\ TI(37,T-1)$$
$$(1197)\quad (182230)$$

NO. OBSV. = 173   R-SQUARE = .0193   R-SQUARE (LEVEL OF OUTPUT) = .9996

other industries was the chemical industry, since the marginal transportation cost of obtaining chemicals was significant in seven equations.

Other variables representing input prices in Equation 2.4 are the wage rate and the value of land. The wage rate is the annual earnings per worker in each industry, and the value of land is the value of agricultural land per acre. Agricultural land is used as a variable since new plants are often built on land that was previously free of structures. The wage rate variable was significant in six equations, and the value of land helped explain changes in output in fifteen equations.

Capital expenditures also may influence industry location. It is possible for interest rates and the construction costs per square foot to vary by region, thus influencing management's decision to locate new plants. Interest rates, however, do not show much regional variation since the money market is essentially a nationwide market and is not divided into regional markets.[d] There may be some regional variation in construction costs per square foot, but unfortunately we do not have the data on the square footage of construction, therefore we cannot use this as a variable in the equation.

Existing capital stock may be more important in influencing future location decisions than the cost of building new plants. Once a plant has been located, it is unlikely that it will be abandoned in the short run. A firm's markets may change location, but yet the firm may not change location because of the sunk costs of the existing plant. In order for it to be profitable to abandon the existing plant and build a new one elsewhere, the returns from the new location would have to be greater than the returns from the old location plus the fixed cost associated with the plant. If the plant were abandoned, the firm would still have to incur the fixed costs.

In order to capture the influence of capital stock on location, the level of output and the prior equipment investment are entered into Equation 2.4. The level of output was significant in 55 equations, explaining the change in output. Since output serves as an agglomeration variable as well as a proxy for capital stock, it was allowed to enter the equation with either sign on its coefficient. There may be external economies of firms in the same industry locating together because they share in a skilled labor market or because they specialize and buy and sell to each other. Output entered 26 times with a positive sign and 29 times with a negative sign. The equipment variable entered into fifteen equations.

Other explanatory variables in Equation 2.4 represent agglomeration variables. Firms may locate near principal buyers and suppliers even though the transport costs of shipping output or obtaining the inputs is unimportant. Proximity to other related firms improves the communication between the firms

[d]Paul A. Meyer, "Price Discrimination, Regional Loan Rates, and the Structure of the Banking System," *Journal of Finance*, Vol. XXII, No. 1, March 1967.

and partially overcomes the uncertainty associated with distance. Moreover, these other firms may share the same labor market. For each industry the important buyers and important suppliers of both commodities and services were identified and variables representing up to four buyers and up to four suppliers were used in the equation. These variables are given in Equations 2.48 and 2.49.

The variables representing major suppliers are the outputs of the other industries. The variables representing major buyers are the outputs of other industries when the other industries are the buyers or purchasers by final demand sectors when sales are to final demand. For example, if an industry sells to individual consumers, then the value of personal consumption expenditures is used as a variable to represent the major buyers. The output of at least one major supplying industry was significant in explaining the location of eighteen industries, and at least one variable representing a major buyer was significant in 34 industry equations. The highway construction activity (CN_{18}) was significant in fourteen equations.

There are two other agglomeration variables in Equation 2.4—the highway congestion index and the population density. The greater the congestion in a region, the more likely it will adversely affect the industry growth; however growth may be either directly or indirectly related to population density. The highway congestion variable entered into 25 equations, and the population density was significant in 21 equations, thirteen with a positive sign and eight with a negative sign.

Once the change in output less defense expenditures is estimated with Equation 2.4, then forecasts of total output are derived as explained in Equations 2.5 and 2.6.

The transportation and trade industries as well as the construction industries are given special treatment. The output in transportation and trade industries is measured by the markup margins of these industries. It is the difference between the value of goods when received by the industries and the value of the goods when sold by these industries. Both the trade and transportation sectors handle all types of goods and both have to be located near the sectors that they serve, although not necessarily in the same region. Therefore, as given in Equation 2.7, the output in the transportation and trade sectors was allowed to change at the same rate at which output in the regular industry sectors changed. The derivation of output in the construction industries will be discussed later.

Gross Investment

The data on gross investment include equipment purchases by 69 equipment purchasing sectors and construction by 28 types of construction. The equipment purchasing sectors are almost identical to the industry sectors, except that some of the industry sectors had to be combined in order to form one equipment purchasing sector. There is, however, a direct matching of the industry sectors into the equipment purchasing sectors. The construction sectors include seventeen private types of construction and eleven public types of construction.

Equipment expenditures by sector are forecast using the level of output of the corresponding industry or industries and the prior level of equipment expenditures as given in Equation 2.8. The results are given in Table 2-4. The prior level of equipment expenditures was significant in 24 of the equations.

Equation 2.9 shows that residential construction is forecast by relating it to personal income. The higher the personal income, the higher the expected level of construction. The personal income variable is lagged, since the

TABLE 2.4
EQUATIONS EXPLAINING THE 1966 LEVEL OF EQUIPMENT
BY EQUIPMENT PURCHASING SECTOR

EQUATION (2.8)

EQUIPMENT SECTOR	NO. OBSV.	R-SQ	CONSTANT	1965 OUTPUT	NO.	1965 EQUIP.
1 FARM	169	.3603	.00320 (.00041)	.46262 (.04770)	1-4	
2 MINING	173	.9788	.00016 (.00012)	.96972 (.01091)	9,10, 5-7	
3 OIL & GAS WELLS	155	.9710	-.00007 (.00024)	1.01152 (.01414)	8	
4 CONSTRUCTION	173	.9514	.00148 (.00017)	.74372 (.01285)	11,12	
5 ORDNANCE	135	.8033	.00110 (.00089)	.91336 (.03919)	13	
6 MEAT PRODUCTS	147	.5052	.00197 (.00068)	.36111 (.08495)	14	.37720 (.07682)
7 TOBACCO	42	.8287	.00126 (.00461)	1.05126 (.07558)	23	
8 FABRICS & YARN	75	.7641	.00059 (.00207)	.98645 (.06415)	24	
9 RUGS, TIRE CORD	80	.7451	.00415 (.00145)	.74658 (.04944)	25	
10 APPAREL	125	.2030	.00538 (.00171)	.34291 (.06127)	26	
11 HOUSEHOLD TEXTILES & UPHOLST.	93	.2692	.00689 (.00224)	.44333 (.07657)	27	
12 LUMBER & PROD. EXC. CONTAINERS	119	.4847	.00314 (.00113)	.77111 (.07351)	28	
13 WOODEN CONTAINERS	98	.2661	.00467 (.00171)	.42494 (.14119)	29	.30810 (.10161)
14 HOUSEHOLD FURNITURE	102	.7158	.00047 (.00129)	1.05116 (.06624)	30	
15 OFFICE FURNITURE	88	.5706	.00293 (.00171)	.36570 (.11525)	31	.55014 (.11007)

TABLE 2.4 (CONT'D)

EQUIPMENT SECTOR	NO. OBSV.	R-SQ	CONSTANT	1965 OUTPUT	NO.	1965 EQUIP.
16 PAPER, EXC. CONTAINERS	96	.3683	.00402 (.00143)	.53798 (.11877)	32	.16721 (.09838)
17 PAPER CONTAINERS	86	.7450	.00286 (.00113)	.82545 (.05269)	33	
18 PRINTING & PUBLISHING	125	.8090	.00178 (.00078)	.59946 (.03679)	34	.21309 (.05135)
19 BASIC CHEMICALS	115	.3798	.00288 (.00128)	.51574 (.12990)	35	.20333 (.10592)
20 PLASTICS & SYNTHETICS	104	.7869	.00141 (.00120)	.24812 (.09475)	36	.68723 (.04649)
21 DRUGS, CLEANING & TOILET ITEMS	98	.7934	.00223 (.00120)	.82368 (.04290)	37	
22 PAINT	89	.5271	.00474 (.00162)	.59142 (.06066)	38	
23 PETROLEUM REFINING	79	.7995	-.00099 (.00220)	.20261 (.15463)	39	1.14702 (.12500)
24 RUBBER & PLASTIC	104	.6940	.00256 (.00104)	.35238 (.07780)	40	.44642 (.08762)
25 LEATHER TANNING	53	.3308	.00875 (.00562)	.61640 (.12276)	41	
26 SHOES & OTHER LEATHER PRODUCTS	67	.5443	.00357 (.00335)	.94224 (.10695)	42	
27 GLASS & PRODUCTS	96	.4073	.00355 (.00204)	.40378 (.11762)	43	.30147 (.06769)
28 STONE & CLAY PRODUCTS	125	.4484	.00322 (.00087)	.34395 (.09737)	44	.33153 (.08497)
29 IRON & STEEL	85	.7628	.00223 (.00138)	.33815 (.05531)	45	.49791 (.05317)
30 NON-FERROUS METALS	77	.3564	.00509 (.00228)	.54382 (.15133)	46-48	.22548 (.17699)
31 METAL CONTAINERS	75	.8509	.00147 (.00146)	.95206 (.04665)	49	
32 HEATING, PLUMBING, STRUC. METAL	114	.8830	-.00029 (.00062)	.58324 (.06165)	50	.53657 (.05335)
33 STAMPINGS, SCREW MACH. PRODUCTS	106	.9593	-.00001 (.00050)	1.02205 (.02065)	51	
34 HARD., PLAT., WIRE PROD. & VALVES	108	.9214	-.00062 (.00064)	.57250 (.05595)	52	.53840 (.05268)
35 ENGINES & TURBINES	76	.6303	.00308 (.00198)	.55013 (.11891)	53	.28119 (.12634)
36 FARM MACHINERY & EQUIPMENT	124	.4197	.00282 (.00153)	.68667 (.07310)	54	
37 CONST. & MATERIAL HANDLING EQP.	106	.5735	.00112 (.00158)	.56723 (.12417)	55,56	.37594 (.10894)
38 METAL WORKING MACHINERY	111	.8977	-.00012 (.00077)	1.02017 (.03298)	57	
39 SPECIAL INDUSTRIAL MACHINERY	88	.9379	-.00012 (.00072)	1.06953 (.02967)	58	

(CONT'D)

TABLE 2.4 (CONT'D)

EQUIPMENT SECTOR	NO. OBSV.	R-SQ	CONSTANT	1965 OUTPUT	NO.	1965 EQUIP.
40 GENERAL INDUSTRIAL MACHINERY	114	.8900	-.00009 (.00067)	1.02311 (.03399)	59	
41 MACHINE SHOPS & MISC.	124	.9098	-.00037 (.00054)	1.07866 (.03075)	60	
42 OFFICE & COMPUTING MACHINES	109	.7157	.00068 (.00131)	.79876 (.09117)	61	.17707 (.08220)
43 SERVICE INDUSTRY MACHINERY	69	.3092	.00723 (.00249)	.67703 (.12363)	62	
44 ELECTRIC APPARATUS & MOTORS	92	.8077	.00174 (.00102)	.31782 (.09082)	63	.57238 (.06766)
45 HOUSEHOLD APPLIANCES	78	.5816	.00297 (.00201)	.81951 (.07973)	64	
46 ELECTRIC LIGHTING & WIRINGS	77	.4442	.00475 (.00254)	.67331 (.08697)	65	
47 COMMUNICATION EQUIPMENT	105	.7777	.00235 (.00108)	.80616 (.04247)	66	
48 ELECTRONIC COMPONENTS	99	.6935	.00222 (.00143)	.14927 (.11266)	67	.67215 (.09507)
49 BATTERY, X-RAY, ENG. ELEC. EQP.	83	.8177	.00186 (.00122)	.40185 (.07868)	68	.46973 (.05225)
50 MOTOR VEHICLES	90	.8990	.00077 (.00139)	.97411 (.03481)	69	
51 AIRCRAFT & PARTS	97	.9187	.00050 (.00093)	1.11892 (.03414)	70	
52 SHIPS, TRAINS & CYCLES	97	.7334	.00072 (.00135)	.65248 (.09608)	71	.51695 (.07961)
53 INSTRUMENTS & CLOCKS	78	.5685	.00449 (.00201)	.76434 (.07639)	72	
54 OPTICAL & PHOTOGRAPHIC EQP.	69	.9429	.00151 (.00152)	.96326 (.02895)	73	
55 MISC. MANUFACTURING	145	.9071	.00182 (.00053)	.74433 (.02051)	74	
56 TRANSPORTATION	173	.9992	.00001 (.00004)	.99806 (.00217)	75	
57 COMMUNICATION	173	.9992	-.00004 (.00003)	1.00763 (.00222)	76,77	
58 UTILITY	173	.9923	-.00003 (.00008)	1.00505 (.00675)	78-80	
59 TRADE	173	.9213	-.00231 (.00040)	2.33667 (.05222)	81., 89-99	
60 FINANCE & INSURANCE	173	.9771	-.00091 (.00023)	1.15780 (.01356)	82	
61 SERVICE	173	.9899	.00057 (.00013)	.90077 (.00696)	83-88	
62 DAIRY PRODUCTS	151	.7791	.00038 (.00049)	.50202 (.06694)	15	.48034 (.05552)
63 CANNED & FROZEN FOODS	141	.7719	.00121 (.00062)	.87398 (.04029)	16	
64 GRAIN MILL PRODUCTS	138	.5315	.00081 (.00100)	.91645 (.07378)	17	

TABLE 2.4 (CONT'D)

EQUIPMENT SECTOR	NO. OBSV.	R-SQ	CONSTANT	1965 OUTPUT	NO.	1965 EQUIP.
65 BAKERY PRODUCTS	148	.8701	.00041 (.00045)	.96993 (.03102)	18	
66 SUGAR	67	.8731	-.00196 (.00182)	1.23909 (.05860)	19	
67 CONFECTIONERY	97	.9503	-.00071 (.00083)	1.08323 (.02541)	20	
68 BEVERAGES	153	.8274	.00049 (.00050)	.94534 (.03514)	21	
69 MISCELLANEOUS FOODS	147	.7955	.00021 (.00065)	.82213 (.05660)	22	.17064 (.04951)

personal income of the current year would not be known to individuals when construction decisions are made. The parameters of these equations are given in the first section of Table 2-5.

Equation 2.10 shows that forecasting other private construction is made by relating it to the prior level of output of appropriate industry sectors and to the prior level of construction. One or more of the industry secrtors can be associated with each of these types of private construction. For example, the equation for explaining industrial construction would use the output of all manufacturing industries. The numbers of the industries associated with each type of construction is given in the second section of Table 2-5, along with the parameters of the equations.

Public construction is forecast using Equation 2.11. It is explained by the prior level of personal income and the prior level of construction expenditures. As personal income increases, tax revenues increase, and it is more likely that public construction will increase. The parameters of these equations are given in the third section of Table 2-5.

Construction Output

By definition, new construction output is the value added in the construction industry. For each dollar of construction, a certain proportion is used for buying materials and a certain proportion is in the form of income payments, such as wages to laborers. Using national coefficients for each type of construction that express the value added portion of construction, the region construction output was forecast as given in Equation 2.12. These outputs were summed over all construction types to obtain the regional output level for construction. By definition, the location of output in the construction industry is identical to the location of the demand for the construction services.

The output for maintenance construction is forecast in a similar fashion, as given in Equation 2.13. Maintenance construction sells its services to the industry sectors and to the government sectors; therefore, national coefficients were applied to industry output and the level of government expenditures to forecast output in the maintenance construction industry.

TABLE 2.5
EQUATIONS EXPLAINING THE 1966 LEVEL OF CONSTRUCTION BY SECTOR

EQUATION (2.9)

PRIVATE SECTORS RELATED TO INCOME	NO. OBSV.	R-SQ	CONSTANT	1965 PERSONAL INCOME
1 RESIDENTIAL	173	.8493	.00172 (.00031)	.70227 (.02262)
2 ADD. & ALT. TO RESIDENCES	173	.8493	.00172 (.00031)	.70227 (.02262)
17 ALL OTHER PRIVATE CONSTRUCTION	171	.7523	.00157 (.00045)	.73269 (.03234)

EQUATION (2.10)

PRIVATE SECTORS RELATED TO OUTPUT	NO. OBSV.	R-SQ	CONSTANT	1965 OUTPUT	NO.	1965 CONSTR.
3 NON-HOUSEKEEPING RES. CONST.	171	.5971	.00295 (.00046)	.49713 (.03141)	84	
4 INDUSTRIAL	169	.8059	.00099 (.00040)	.70774 (.04816)	13-74	.12750 (.05372)
5 OFFICES	173	.9031	.00160 (.00035)	.72404 (.01814)	81-83	
6 STORES, RESTAURANTS & GARAGES	172	.8708	.00191 (.00032)	.67201 (.01985)	85,86 89-99	
7 RELIGIOUS	171	.8314	.00249 (.00031)	.57416 (.01989)	88	
8 EDUCATIONAL	158	.8856	.00094 (.00040)	.86343 (.02485)	68	
9 HOSPITAL AND INSTITUTIONAL	168	.7994	.00240 (.00037)	.59863 (.02327)	88	
10 MISC. NON-RESIDENTIAL BUILDINGS	152	.4665	.00200 (.00112)	.70603 (.06165)	75,77 87	
11 FARM CONSTRUCTION	125	.0224	.00503 (.00255)	.45617 (.27145)	1,2	
12 OIL, GAS WELL DRILLING & EXPLOR.	110	.9690	-.00020 (.00035)	1.02245 (.01758)	8	
13 RAILROAD	173	.9992	.00001 (.00004)	.99760 (.00218)	75	
14 TELEPHONE	173	.9989	-.00003 (.00004)	1.00443 (.00258)	76	
15 ELECTRIC UTILITY	173	.9802	-.00008 (.00012)	1.01336 (.01102)	78	
16 GAS & PETROLEUM PIPELINES	82	.0252	.01069 (.00213)			.18701 (.12992)

EQUATION (2.11)

PUBLIC SECTORS	NO. OBSV.	R-SQ	CONSTANT	1965 PERSONAL INCOME	1965 CONSTR.
18 HIGHWAY	165	.8411	.00168 (.00040)	.55129 (.03483)	.19817 (.07405)
19 MILITARY	137	.5008	.00139 (.00084)	.21475 (.04992)	.62529 (.06755)

TABLE 2.5 (CONT'D)

PRIVATE SECTORS RELATED TO OUTPUT	NO. OBSV.	R-SQ	CONSTANT	1965 OUTPUT	NO.	1965 CONSTR.
20 CONSERVATION	163	.4309	.00043 (.00114)	.09556 (.07761)		.84102 (.08079)
21 SEWER SYSTEMS	169	.6286	.00227 (.00051)	.61943 (.03684)		
22 WATER SYSTEMS	173	.7269	-.00262 (.00084)	-.09934 (.07578)		1.55288 (.09032)
23 PUBLIC RESIDENTIAL	164	.6565	.00269 (.00046)	.56695 (.03222)		
24 PUBLIC INDUSTRIAL	173	.5155	.00127 (.00067)	.24262 (.06875)		.53851 (.08739)
25 PUBLIC EDUCATIONAL	173	.9237	.00155 (.00022)	.73260 (.01610)		
26 PUBLIC HOSPITAL	153	.8584	-.00216 (.00066)	1.12920 (.06503)		.25450 (.07883)
27 OTHER PUBLIC STRUCTURES	172	.6799	.00033 (.00060)	.49709 (.05240)		.44745 (.05900)
28 MISCELLANEOUS PUBLIC	173	.5155	.00127 (.00067)	.24262 (.06875)		.53851 (.08739)

Employment

The change in employment by industry shown in Equation 2.14 is a function of the change in output, equipment purchases, and the level of output. The results of fitting the equations for the 99 industry sectors are given in Table 2-6.

The employment in federal government given in Equation 2.15 is a function of the general federal government expenditures in the same period. As government expenditures increase, employment is expected to increase. The same type of functional relationship is used to explain the employment in state and local government as given in Equation 2.16. The parameters in these two equations are as follows:.

$$EMP^t_{100} = \underset{(.0008)}{.0021} + \underset{(.0563)}{.6418} \sum_{k=2}^{7} GOV^t_k \quad (R^2 = .4317)$$

$$EMP^t_{101} = \underset{(.0001)}{.0014} + \underset{(.0082)}{.7563}\ GOV^t_8 \quad (R^2 = .9804)$$

Employment of domestic servants in households, as given in Equation 2.17, is assumed to be a function of the personal income of the prior period. The greater the personal income, the greater the demand for domestic servants. The equation is as follows.

TABLE 2.6
EQUATIONS EXPLAINING THE 1965-1966 CHANGE IN EMPLOYMENT

EQUATION (2.14)

INDUSTRY	NO. OBSV.	R-SQ	CONSTANT	1965-'66 CHANGE IN OUTPUT	1965 EQUIP. NO.		1966 OUTPU'
1 LIVESTOCK	173	.0631	1958 (921)	.0067 (.0043)	-338699 (124024)	1	
2 CROPS	173	.0515	-226 (521)	.0124 (.0048)	-124635 (88582)	1	16398 (6966
3 FORESTRY AND FISHERY PRODUCTS	128	.7341	8 (5)	.0189 (.0010)			-71 (20
4 AGRICULTURAL SERVICES	172	.4431	0 (12)	.0702 (.0060)			
5 IRON ORE MINING	53	.9419	-36 (16)	.0289 (.0013)	3154 (1420)	2	37 (30
6 NON-FERROUS ORE MINING	100	.8903	0 (10)	.0234 (.0008)			
7 COAL MINING	89	.5608	1 (15)	.0244 (.0023)			
8 PETROLEUM MINING	117	.0969	-28 (20)		3590 (1022)	3	
9 MINERALS MINING	168	.5101	2 (10)	.0100 (.0008)			
10 CHEMICAL MINING	40	.4434	-5 (29)	.0108 (.0022)	3317 (1983)	2	-87 (51
11 NEW CONSTRUCTION	173	.0847	473 (212)	.0072 (.0022)	-81816 (22166)	4	
12 MAINTENANCE CONSTRUCTION	173	.4206	146 (55)	.0185 (.0040)	-25248 (6228)	4	
13 ORDNANCE	141	.7684	38 (34)	.0210 (.0010)	-5274 (1560)	5	
14 MEAT PACKING	171	.3922	51 (22)	.0042 (.0006)	3516 (2735)	6	-1223 (312
15 DAIRY PRODUCTS	173	.7612	0 (7)	.0179 (.0008)			
16 CANNED AND FROZEN FOODS	165	.5462	16 (23)	.0145 (.0011)	-2290 (1563)	63	
17 GRAIN MILL PRODUCTS	166	.8813	-8 (6)	.0109 (.0003)	1461 (410)	64	
18 BAKERY PRODUCTS	173	.6566	-4 (9)	.0251 (.0015)	924 (720)	65	
19 SUGAR	61	.4132	-5 (18)	.0060 (.0011)	645 (476)	66	
20 CANDY	126	.3460	0 (11)	.0296 (.0037)			
21 BEVERAGES	171	.7900	0 (8)	.0146 (.0006)			
22 MISC. FOOD PRODUCTS	169	.4999	14 (9)	.0097 (.0008)	-2393 (528)	69	
23 TOBACCO	52	.9000	-20 (43)	.0148 (.0007)	1360 (688)	7	

TABLE 2.6 (CONT'D)

INDUSTRY	NO. OBSV.	R-SQ	CONSTANT	1965-'66 CHANGE IN OUTPUT	1965 EQUIP. NO.		1966 OUTPUT
24 FABRICS AND YARN	120	.2562	59 (85)	.0070 (.0011)	-6624 (3368)	8	
25 RUGS, TIRE CORD, MISC. TEXTILES	120	.5390	46 (33)	.0204 (.0021)			-5418 (1384)
26 APPAREL	163	.5896	-11 (43)	.0459 (.0032)	2005 (1770)	10	
27 HOUSEHOLD TEXTILES AND UPHOLST.	132	.6153	44 (23)	.0237 (.0032)	-5640 (921)	11	
28 LUMBER AND PROD. EXC. CONTAINERS	173	.5346	0 (19)	.0344 (.0025)			
29 WOODEN CONTAINERS	134	.7392	3 (6)	.0589 (.0032)	1265 (343)	13	-1545 (524)
30 HOUSEHOLD FURNITURE	151	.5281	-7 (27)	.0461 (.0036)	1490 (1325)	14	
31 OFFICE FURNITURE	136	.4277	-28 (15)	.0249 (.0028)	-5831 (1175)	15	9590 (1322)
32 PAPER AND PROD. EXC. CONTAINERS	145	.3512	22 (27)	.0200 (.0024)	6162 (2198)	16	-9450 (2704)
33 PAPER CONTAINERS	130	.4430	-36 (23)	.0163 (.0017)	5069 (1268)	17	
34 PRINTING AND PUBLISHING	173	.7434	21 (21)	.0523 (.0026)	4817 (1644)	19	-8475 (1185)
35 BASIC CHEMICALS	166	.6606	42 (26)	.0169 (.0010)	2951 (2611)	19	-9865 (3216)
36 PLASTICS AND SYNTHETICS	122	.8443	7 (18)	.0231 (.0009)	-1438 (743)	20	
37 DRUGS, CLEANING AND TOILET ITEMS	127	.0622	-32 (35)	.0018 (.0010)	4425 (1630)	21	
38 PAINT AND ALLIED PRODUCTS	105	.9069	6 (6)	.0238 (.0008)	-613 (271)	22	
39 PETROLEUM REFINING	125	.2239	12 (15)	.0023 (.0004)	-838 (622)	23	
40 RUBBER AND PLASTIC PRODUCTS	146	.6721	26 (38)	.0292 (.0018)	-3799 (2274)	24	
41 LEATHER TANNING	76	.7993	14 (10)	.0441 (.0028)	-727 (477)	25	-383 (373)
42 SHOES AND OTHER LEATHER PRODUCTS	123	.7417	-31 (35)	.0654 (.0039)	3936 (1462)	26	
43 GLASS AND GLASS PRODUCTS	127	.3485	33 (17)	.0190 (.0027)	-811 (679)	27	-3240 (1167)
44 STONE AND CLAY PRODUCTS	173	.7336	0 (14)	.0337 (.0016)			
45 IRON AND STEEL	146	.6458	142 (49)	.0101 (.0012)	2835 (2521)	29	-23215 (2808)
46 COPPER	92	.6543	15 (20)	.0075 (.0007)	1968 (1154)	30	-2993 (775)
47 ALUMINUM	114	.5443	37 (34)	.0145 (.0013)			-3628 (2159)

(CONT'D)

TABLE 2.6 (CONT'D)

INDUSTRY	NO. OBSV.	R-SQ	CONSTANT	1965-'66 CHANGE IN OUTPUT	1965 EQUIP.	NO.	1966 OUTPUT
48 OTHER NON-FERROUS METALS	110	.4289	43 (30)	.0070 (.0008)	-4789 (1728)	30	
49 METAL CONTAINERS	84	.1059	2. (33)	.0044 (.0018)	-1280 (1078)	31	
50 HEATING. PLUMBING. STRUC. METAL	170	.6904	29 (18)	.0337 (.0019)	5223 (1899)	32	-1012 (218
51 STAMPINGS. SCREW MACHINE PROD.	136	.8107	16 (16)	.0238 (.0010)	-1869 (789)	33	
52 HARDWARE. PLATING. WIRE PROD.	162	.8523	0 (14)	.0410 (.0013)			
53 ENGINES AND TURBINES	77	.8774	-6 (30)	.0348 (.0016)	-2179 (1905)	35	3076 (1772
54 FARM MACHINERY AND EQUIPMENT	155	.8777	30 (12)	.0313 (.0010)	-1714 (1089)	36	-2895 (997
55 CONSTRUCTION AND MINING MACHINES	138	.7491	37 (17)	.0269 (.0018)	-1159 (1020)	37	-3889 (114
56 MATERIAL HANDLING EQUIPMENT	120	.9138	12 (9)	.0259 (.0008)	-1262 (424)	37	
57 METALWORKING MACHINERY AND EQUIP.	138	.7140	35 (15)	.0399 (.0026)	-4804 (691)	38	
58 SPECIAL INDUSTRIAL MACHINERY	135	.8027	25 (13)	.330 (.0016)	-3349 (689)	39	
59 GENERAL INDUSTRIAL MACHINERY	142	.5460	1 (18)	.0287 (.0022)			
60 MACHINE SHOPS AND MISC. MACHINERY	165	.7487	-6 (9)	.0550 (.0025)	1246 (603)	41	
61 OFFICE AND COMPUTING MACHINES	127	.9268	-1 (23)	.0213 (.0006)	7096 (1667)	42	-679 (1715
62 SERVICE INDUSTRY MACHINES	112	.5984	27 (27)	.0164 (.0015)	7750 (2014)	43	-1041 (246
63 ELECTRIC APPARATUS AND MOTORS	115	.8271	101 (41)	.0420 (.0019)	-5703 (3147)	44	-574 (416
64 HOUSEHOLD APPLIANCES	99	.7335	29 (41)	.0310 (.0020)	-2311 (1651)	45	
65 ELECTRIC LIGHT AND WIRING EQUIP.	97	.8968	2 (16)	.0424 (.0015)			
66 COMMUNICATION EQUIPMENT	133	.9177	93 (47)	.0396 (.0011)	-21275 (2271)	47	
67 ELECTRONIC COMPONENTS	129	.8790	17 (36)	.0356 (.0014)	-6508 (2809)	48	437 (318
68 BATTERIES AND ENGINE ELEC. EQUIP.	100	.8647	19 (20)	.0405 (.0020)	-1744 (826)	49	
69 MOTOR VEHICLES	139	.5709	2 (83)	.0149 (.0011)			
70 AIRCRAFT AND PARTS	146	.1673	-56 (139)	.0063 (.0014)	9424 (5583)	51	
71 SHIPS. TRAINS. TRAILERS. CYCLES	149	.8491	-18 (48)	.0469 (.0016)	2897 (2516)	52	

TABLE 2.6 (CONT'D)

INDUSTRY	NO. OBSV.	R-SQ	CONSTANT	1965-'66 CHANGE IN OUTPUT	1965 EQUIP. NO.		1966 OUTPUT
72 INSTRUMENTS AND CLOCKS	117	.5925	27 (24)	.0262 (.0021)	-2702 (952)	53	
73 OPTICAL AND PHOTOGRAPHIC EQUIP.	103	.2472	-41 (35)	.0090 (.0042)	4661 (829)	54	
74 MISC. MANUFACTURED PRODUCTS	165	.8945	25 (18)	.0670 (.0025)	-4116 (1124)	55	
75 TRANSPORTATION	173	.5450	137 (56)	.0230 (.0020)	-23682 (3272)	56	
76 COMMUNICATION	173	.2090	30 (34)	.0297 (.0045)	-5138 (2389)	57	
77 RADIO, TV BROADCASTING	171	.0130	-13 (25)		2557 (1712)	57	
78 ELECTRIC UTILITY	173	.1666	0 (32)	.0077 (.0013)			
79 GAS UTILITY	170	.2236	36 (30)	.0173 (.0028)	-6131 (2435)	58	
80 WATER UTILITY	123	.7477	1 (3)	.0110 (.0006)			
81 WHOLESALE TRADE	173	.5498	-132 (50)	.0339 (.0029)	22992 (2802)	59	
82 FINANCE AND INSURANCE	173	.6355	134 (34)	.0366 (.0021)	-23152 (2281)	60	
83 REAL ESTATE AND RENTAL	173	.8174	29 (21)	.0052 (.0003)	-4941 (1638)	61	
84 HOTELS, PERSONAL AND REPAIR SVC.	173	.2688	-65 (61)	.0496 (.0063)	11490 (3695)	61	
85 BUSINESS SERVICES	173	.4828	-197 (60)	.0017 (.0006)	34176 (3434)	61	
86 AUTOMOBILE REPAIR SERVICES	173	.3974	0 (11)	.0155 (.0015)			
87 AMUSEMENTS AND RECREATION	173	.8568	22 (16)	.0531 (.0017)	-3776 (859)	61	
88 MEDICAL AND EDUCATIONAL INSTIT.	173	.0237	46 (74)		-8013 (3932)	61	
89 LUMBER, HSEWARE, FARM EQP. STORES	173	.2732	0 (12)	.0316 (.0039)			
90 GENERAL MERCHANDISE STORES	173	.8984	-58 (28)	.1263 (.0036)	10184 (1808)	59	
91 FOOD STORES	173	.8105	-74 (18)	.0957 (.0037)	12955 (1250)	59	
92 AUTOMOTIVE DEALERS	173	.5962	-2 (20)	.0674 (.0049)	11700 (1674)	59	-11168 (3279)
93 GASOLINE SERVICE STATIONS	173	.8251	-13 (8)	.1349 (.0048)	2435 (465)	59	
94 APPAREL, ACCESSORY STORES	173	.9057	-51 (9)	.1101 (.0030)	8959 (534)	59	
95 FURNITURE STORES	173	.8885	-19 (6)	.0749 (.0020)	3394 (360)	59	

(CONT'D)

TABLE 2.6 (CONT'D)

INDUSTRY	NO. OBSV.	R-SQ	CONSTANT	1965-'66 CHANGE IN OUTPUT	1965 EQUIP.	NO.	1966 OUTPUT
96 EATING, DRINKING PLACES	173	.8735	-36 (31)	.1134 (.0053)	6357 (2802)	59	
97 DRUG AND PROPRIETARY STORES	173	.8108	-18 (7)	.0952 (.0036)	3351 (460)	59	
96 OTHER RETAIL STORES	173	.6274	-22 (13)	.0809 (.0055)	4002 (970)	59	
99 NON-STORE RETAILERS	173	.8721	0 (6)	.0936 (.0027)			

$$EMP^t_{102} = .0023 + .6052\ PI^{t-1} \qquad (R^2 = .7950)$$
$$\phantom{EMP^t_{102} = }(.0003) \quad (.0235)$$

The number of armed forces in each region is allowed to grow at the same rate as the level of armed forces in the nation, as shown in Equation 2.18. This formula holds the regional distribution of armed forces constant, although the levels of the armed forces can be predetermined for each region, as can defense expenditures.

In order to forecast population, income, and unemployment by place of residence, it is necessary to convert the employment from the number of jobs by place of work to the number of persons employed by place of residence. Equation 2.19 derives the number of multijob holders. The ratio of multijob holders to employment in the non-agriculture, nongovernment sectors in the prior period is held constant for the forecast year. The commuters are forecast as given in Equation 2.20 by allowing the commuting rate to be held constant. The commuting rate is the net number of commuters expressed as a percent of the employment in nonagriculture and nonmilitary sectors. The number of civilian persons employed by place of residence is given in Equation 2.21. It is the sum of the jobs in a region minus the multijob holders minus the net commuters. A negative sign on net commuters indicates that residents are commuting out of a region to work in other regions.

Population

Population is forecast by age and race group. As shown in Equation 2.29, the population forecast consists of adding estimates of births, net migration, and the change in the number of armed forces to the previous year's population and subtracting estimates of deaths. The births and deaths are forecast by relating them to the previous year's population, as given in Equations 2.22 and 2.23. The parameters of these equations are given in the first two sections of Table 2-7.

Table 2-7. Equations Explaining 1966 Births, 1966 Deaths, and 1965–1966 Population Migration

Equation (2.22)

Sector	No. Obsv.	R^2	Constant	1965 Pop.
White births	173	.9952	-.00001 (.00006)	1.00086 (.00531)
Nonwhite births	173	.9883	.00009 (.00010)	.9842 (.0082)

Equation (2.23)

Sector	No. Obsv.	R^2	Constant	1965 Pop.
White deaths 0–14	173	.9942	.0004 (.00006)	.924 (.005)
White deaths 15–34	173	.9800	.001 (.0002)	.875 (.009)
White deaths 35–64	173	.9956	-.0002 (.0001)	1.027 (.005)
White deaths 65 & over	173	.9954	-.00001 (.0001)	1.001 (.005)
Nonwhite deaths 0–14	170	.9786	-.0002 (.0001)	1.041 (.012)
Nonwhite deaths 15–34	169	.9635	.0001 (.0002)	1.011 (.015)
Nonwhite deaths 35–64	173	.9650	.0003 (.0002)	.952 (.014)
Nonwhite deaths 65 & over	172	.9886	.0001 (.0001)	.999 (.008)

(Continued)

Table 2-7 continued

Equation (2.26)

Sector	No. Obsv.	R^2	Constant	1965 Pop. Surplus	1965-66 Expected Pop. Change	1965-66 Change in Military	1965 Avg. Wage Rate
White migration 15–34	173	.0620	-9163 (4301)	-	-	-	764768 (227556)
White migration 35–64	173	.1027	-3966 (3892)	-	.043 (.017)	.995 (.345)	476897 (205931)
Nonwhite migration 15–34	173	.1601	-5833 (1511)	.042 (.012)	-	-	372684 (80019)
Nonwhite migration 35–64	173	.1233	-4350 (1131)	-.018 (.009)	-	-	274310 (59883)

Equation (2.27)

Sector	No. Obsv.	R^2	Constant	1965-66 Migration 15–64
White migration 0–14	173	.1701	-10377 (2366)	-.722 (.122)
Nonwhite migration 0–14	173	.2651	-2030 (378)	-.456 (.058)

Equation (2.28)

Sector	No. Obsv.	R^2	Constant	1965 Population 65 & Over
White migration 65 & over	173	.9670	674 (186)	1151325 (16260)
Nonwhite migration 65 & over	173	.9313	-43 (29)	128967 (2680)

The age breakdown of population is important in explaining population migration. There are four age groups used—namely, 0-14, 15-34, 35-64, and 65 and over. The migration in the middle two groups, which is the working age population, is explained with variables representing labor conditions of the region. Net migration in these two groups, as given in Equation 2.26, is assumed to be a function of (1) the change in civilian persons employed, modified by the labor force participation rate as given in Equation 2.25; (2) the labor force surplus or deficit, modified by the labor force participation rate as given in Equation 2.24; (3) the change in the number of armed forces stationed in the region; and (4) the average wage rate in the region. The results of these equations are given in the third section of Table 2-7. Note that the average wage rate was a significant variable in each of the equations.

Both the change in employment and labor surplus variables were modified by the labor force participation rate, since labor force participation varies by region. It is assumed that the population migrating into a region has the same employment opportunities as the population already there. For example, one of the reasons for the large regional variation in labor force participation rates is the availability of job opportunities for women. If the labor force participation rate is low, it is likely that there is not a high percentage of women in the labor force and the incoming female migrants are assumed to have the same opportunities as the existing female population.

Net migration for the first age group, those 14 or younger, is related directly to the migration in the working age groups as shown in Equation 2.27. The results as given in the fourth section of Table 2-7 show that the coefficient on the independent variable had the wrong sign; therefore a substitute relationship was used in the model that allows the population in the 14 and under age groups to have the same regional distribution as the population in the 15-34 age groups.

Population migration in the older age group, those 65 or older, is explained largely by noneconomic conditions. In Equation 2.28 migration of these older people is assumed to be a function of the number of people in the age group.

The results of migration equations, particularly in the 14 and under age groups, were poor since the net migration as defined is not purely a migration figure but also accounts for the aging of population from the lower age groups to the next highest group. In any one region, for example, the components of the difference between the population in the 14 and under group between two years is made up of births, deaths, net migrants, and the 14-year-olds who move into the 15-34 age group. Since the birth rate in 1966 was lower than it was in 1952, the migration as we compute it can easily be negative in the 14 and under group at the same time that the migration in the 15-34 group is positive. The migration in the 15-34 age group, as we define it, includes the 14-year-olds turning 15 and excludes the 34-year-olds turning 35.

Labor Force and Unemployment

Labor force is assumed to be a function of the population in the working age groups and the population associated with labor force surplus or deficit. This type of equation, as given in Equation 2.30, will allow the labor force participation rates to change with economic conditions. The labor force surplus is defined in relationship to the national unemployment rate. If a region's unemployment rate is greater than the nation's, then the region would have surplus labor. If it is lower than the nation's, then it would have a labor deficit. Studies have shown that participation in the labor force is directly related to the employment opportunities.[e] The higher the employment rate, the higher the labor force participation rate. As the national economy or regional economy slows down and the unemployment rate goes up, then the labor force participation rate goes down. The labor force equation is:

$$CLF^t = -\;\;\underset{(.0001)}{.0009} + \underset{(.0102)}{1.1637} \sum_{a=2}^{3} \sum_{r=1}^{2} POP^t_{ar}$$

$$-\;\;\underset{(.0000000042)}{.0000000187}\;\;PLS^{t-1} \qquad (R^2 = .9870)$$

The civilian unemployment is defined as the difference between the civilian labor force and the number of civilian persons employed.

Income

The earnings by industry sector are hypothesized to be a function of the employment, equipment investment, and the prior average manufacturing wage, as shown in Equation 2.32. The greater the employment, the greater the earnings. The equipment investment is used in the employment equations, since as equipment is added there may be a tendency to reduce or slow down the rate of increase in the amount of employment in some industries. Equipment is often added to replace labor, but at the same time it increases the efficiency or productivity of labor; therefore in other industries there would be a tendency for wage rates in highly productive industries to rise, and a direct relationship between the amount of earnings and the amount of equipment would be expected. The prior average manufacturing wage is expected to be a significant explanatory variable in those industries where increases in the wage rate lags behind increases in the average manufacturing wage rate. The parameters of the earnings equations for the 99 industry sectors are given in Table 2-8.

Earnings in the extra labor sectors are estimated by applying the prior wage rates in the sectors, as given in Equation 2.33. By definition,

---

[e]Sophia Cooper, and Denis F. Johnston, "The Outlook for the Labor Force at Mid-Decade." Paper presented before American Statistical Association, Chicago, December 1964.

TABLE 2.8

EQUATIONS EXPLAINING 1966 EARNINGS BY INDUSTRY SECTOR

EQUATION (2.32)

INDUSTRY	NO. OBSV.	R-SQ	CONSTANT	1966 EMPLOY.	1965 EQUIP.	NO.	1965 MFG. WAGE RATE
1 LIVESTOCK	172	.5214	-.002 (.001)	.348 (.055)	.517 (.061)	1	7.534 (4.352)
2 CROPS	173	.5950	-.000 (.000)	.576 (.067)	.504 (.072)	1	
3 FORESTRY AND FISHERY PRODUCTS	126	.9308	-.009 (.003)	1.159 (.029)			24.527 (7.878)
4 AGRICULTURAL SERVICES	172	.9638	-.003 (.001)	1.128 (.019)	-.057 (.030)	1	8.022 (2.152)
5 IRON ORE MINING	51	.9962	-.000 (.001)	1.084 (.011)	-.141 (.057)	2	
6 NON-FERROUS ORE MINING	95	.9773	-.003 (.002)	1.104 (.021)	-.095 (.046)	2	6.572 (6.305)
7 COAL MINING	86	.9624	-.010 (.004)	.973 (.029)	.146 (.088)	2	26.670 (12.473)
8 PETROLEUM MINING	114	.9243	-.001 (.001)	1.158 (.031)			
9 MINERALS MINING	168	.8584	-.004 (.001)	1.035 (.040)	.064 (.028)	2	9.083 (3.879)
10 CHEMICAL MINING	38	.9176	-.019 (.013)	.977 (.055)	-.216 (.213)	2	66.507 (38.756)
11 NEW CONSTRUCTION	173	.9548	-.005 (.001)	1.145 (.020)			12.047 (2.733)
12 MAINTENANCE CONSTRUCTION	173	.9825	-.004 (.001)	1.103 (.012)			8.903 (2.254)
13 ORDNANCE	141	.9936	-.003 (.001)	1.146 (.013)	-.024 (.018)	5	5.862 (3.744)
14 MEAT PACKING	171	.9605	-.005 (.001)	1.004 (.026)	.071 (.020)	6	14.554 (2.161)
15 DAIRY PRODUCTS	173	.9793	-.002 (.001)	1.133 (.018)	-.024 (.014)	62	5.128 (1.658)

(Continued)

TARIF 2.8 (CONT'D)

INDUSTRY	NO. OBSV.	R-SQ	CONSTANT	1966 EMPLOY.	1965 EQUIP. NO.	1965 MFG. WAGE RATE
16 CANNED AND FROZEN FOODS	165	.9454	-.006 (.001)	1.040 (.021)		16.089 (3.601)
17 GRAIN MILL PRODUCTS	166	.9817	-.003 (.001)	1.129 (.013)		7.701 (1.862)
18 BAKERY PRODUCTS	173	.9882	-.003 (.001)	1.101 (.009)		5.794 (1.890)
19 SUGAR	60	.9638	.002 (.001)	.902 (.023)		
20 CANDY	109	.9796	-.001 (.000)	1.127 (.016)		
21 BEVERAGES	171	.9883	-.003 (.001)	1.168 (.010)		5.134 (1.917)
22 MISC. FOOD PRODUCTS	169	.9902	-.002 (.001)	1.189 (.013)	-.023 (.010) 69	3.549 (1.926)
23 TOBACCO	49	.9709	-.011 (.006)	1.151 (.030)		24.955 (17.718)
24 FABRICS AND YARN	105	.9881	-.003 (.002)	1.025 (.012)		7.664 (4.660)
25 RUGS, TIRE CORD, MISC. TEXTILES	106	.9704	-.006 (.002)	1.125 (.031)	-.084 (.025) 9	16.399 (6.009)
26 APPAREL	163	.9897	-.005 (.001)	1.199 (.010)		10.526 (3.396)
27 HOUSEHOLD TEXTILES AND UPHOLST.	132	.9864	-.004 (.002)	1.057 (.011)		11.484 (4.899)
28 LUMBER AND PROD. EXC. CONTAINERS	173	.9622	-.008 (.001)	1.183 (.032)	.084 (.021) 12	19.488 (2.778)
29 WOODEN CONTAINERS	134	.9567	-.006 (.001)	1.042 (.021)	.029 (.013) 13	16.742 (3.068)
30 HOUSEHOLD FURNITURE	151	.9787	-.004 (.001)	1.014 (.012)		11.222 (2.600)
31 OFFICE FURNITURE	136	.9873	-.002 (.001)	1.127 (.013)	-.052 (.011) 15	5.169 (2.914)

32	PAPER AND PROD. EXCL. CONTAINERS	145 .9906	.000 (.000)	.981 (.010)	.017 16 (.009)	5.578 (2.335)
33	PAPER CONTAINERS	126 .9913	-.002 (.001)	1.006 (.009)		
34	PRINTING AND PUBLISHING	173 .9943	-.001 (.000)	1.181 (.008)	-.042 18 (.010)	
35	BASIC CHEMICALS	166 .9889	-.000 (.000)	1.092 (.011)	-.015 19 (.010)	
36	PLASTICS AND SYNTHETICS	122 .9758	-.003 (.001)	1.028 (.015)		7.128 (2.781)
37	DRUGS, CLEANING AND TOILET ITEMS	127 .9805	-.003 (.002)	.918 (.012)		11.531 (5.707)
38	PAINT AND ALLIED PRODUCTS	105 .9974	-.001 (.001)	1.027 (.005)		3.029 (2.126)
39	PETROLEUM REFINING	119 .9936	-.000 (.000)	1.059 (.010)	-.008 23 (.007)	
40	RUBBER AND PLASTIC PRODUCTS	136 .9807	-.002 (.001)	1.009 (.021)	.026 24 (.024)	5.078 (3.768)
41	LEATHER TANNING	67 .9877	-.005 (.003)	.968 (.024)	.071 25 (.025)	12.362 (9.450)
42	SHOES AND OTHER LEATHER PRODUCTS	109 .9963	-.003 (.001)	1.039 (.006)		8.853 (2.661)
43	GLASS AND GLASS PRODUCTS	118 .9831	-.002 (.001)	1.024 (.013)		6.004 (3.296)
44	STONE AND CLAY PRODUCTS	173 .9846	-.002 (.001)	1.063 (.013)	.011 28 (.011)	5.950 (1.607)
45	IRON AND STEEL	132 .9957	-.002 (.001)	1.040 (.006)		4.521 (2.076)
46	COPPER	87 .9867	-.003 (.002)	1.070 (.014)		7.104 (5.703)
47	ALUMINUM	106 .9887	-.000 (.000)	1.074 (.011)		

(CONT'D)

TABLE 2.8 (CONT'D)

INDUSTRY	NO. OBSV.	R-SQ	CONSTANT	1966 EMPLOY.	1965 EQUIP.	NO.	1965 MFG. WAGE RATE
48 OTHER NON-FERROUS METALS	102	.9941	-.000 (.000)	1.071 (.008)			
49 METAL CONTAINERS	79	.9664	-.001 (.001)	1.014 (.039)	.079 (.034)	31	
50 HEATING, PLUMBING, STRUC. MFTAI	169	.9917	-.002 (.000)	1.060 (.013)	.014 (.010)	32	3.660 (1.434)
51 STAMPINGS, SCRFW MACHINE PROD.	136	.9896	-.000 (.000)	1.055 (.009)			
52 HARDWARE, PLATING, WIRE PROD.	161	.9941	-.002 (.001)	1.014 (.007)			5.965 (1.731)
53 ENGINES AND TURBINES	77	.9871	-.003 (.002)	.904 (.019)	.074 (.020)	35	8.061 (6.189)
54 FARM MACHINERY AND EQUIPMENT	153	.9802	-.001 (.000)	1.137 (.021)	.025 (.020)	36	
55 CONSTRUCTION AND MINING MACHINES	136	.9895	-.000 (.000)	1.032 (.011)	.020 (.009)	37	
56 MATERIAL HANDLING EQUIPMENT	120	.9932	-.001 (.000)	1.109 (.008)			
57 METALWORKING MACHINERY AND EQUIP.	138	.9801	-.001 (.000)	1.115 (.014)			
58 SPECIAL INDUSTRIAL MACHINERY	122	.9933	-.003 (.001)	1.043 (.008)			9.487 (2.374)
59 GENERAL INDUSTRIAL MACHINERY	142	.9941	-.002 (.001)	1.025 (.007)			4.275 (1.915)
60 MACHINE SHOPS AND MISC. MACHINERY	165	.9917	-.001 (.001)	1.073 (.008)			2.111 (1.922)
61 OFFICE AND COMPUTING MACHINES	127	.9881	-.002 (.001)	1.057 (.014)	-.032 (.011)	42	4.005 (3.067)
62 SERVICE INDUSTRY MACHINES	104	.9876	-.003 (.001)	1.071 (.013)			6.947 (3.099)
63 ELECTRIC APPARATUS AND MOTORS	114	.9861	-.004 (.001)	.993 (.021)	.030 (.016)	44	10.134 (3.288)

		N	R²					
64	HOUSEHOLD APPLIANCES	99	.9844	-.007 (.001)	1.053 (.014)			17.683 (4.277)
65	ELECTRIC LIGHT AND WIRING EQUIP.	97	.9962	-.003 (.001)	.951 (.009)	.032 41 (.010)		9.437 (2.753)
66	COMMUNICATION EQUIPMENT	133	.9814	-.000 (.000)	1.050 (.013)			
67	ELECTRONIC COMPONENTS	129	.9895	-.003 (.001)	.998 (.016)	.028 48 (.014)		8.247 (3.179)
68	BATTERIES AND ENGINE ELEC. EQUIP.	100	.9745	-.003 (.002)	.977 (.023)	.033 49 (.014)		7.410 (4.942)
69	MOTOR VEHICLES	139	.9993	.000 (.000)	1.057 (.003)			-2.430 (1.243)
70	AIRCRAFT AND PARTS	142	.9759	-.000 (.000)	1.078 (.014)			
71	SHIPS, TRAINS, TRAILERS, CYCLES	149	.9850	-.001 (.000)	1.140 (.014)	.012 52 (.010)		9.507 (2.900)
72	INSTRUMENTS AND CLOCKS	112	.9928	-.003 (.001)	1.019 (.009)			
73	OPTICAL AND PHOTOGRAPHIC EQUIP.	96	.9783	-.001 (.001)	1.151 (.018)			
74	MISC. MANUFACTURED PRODUCTS	165	.9971	-.002 (.001)	1.009 (.004)			6.869 (1.662)
75	TRANSPORTATION	173	.9903	-.001 (.000)	1.180 (.009)			
76	COMMUNICATION	173	.9921	-.000 (.000)	.972 (.007)			1.629 (1.369)
77	RADIO, TV BROADCASTING	171	.9472	-.000 (.000)	1.084 (.020)			
78	ELECTRIC UTILITY	173	.9918	-.002 (.000)	1.004 (.007)			4.577 (1.247)
79	GAS UTILITY	170	.9786	-.001 (.00)	1.070 (.020)	-.060 58 (.019)		3.360 (1.937)

(CONT'D)

TABLE 2.8 (CONT'D)

INDUSTRY	NO. OBSV.	R-SQ	CONSTANT	1966 EMPLO.	1965 EQUIP. NO.	1965 MFG. WAGE RATE
80 WATER UTILITY	123	.9804	-.002 (.002)	1.056 (.014)		4.970 (4.681)
81 WHOLESALE TRADE	173	.9976	-.002 (.000)	1.105 (.004)		3.085 (.880)
82 FINANCE AND INSURANCE	173	.9961	-.001 (.000)	1.135 (.005)		
83 REAL ESTATE AND RENTAL	173	.9931	-.003 (.001)	1.072 (.007)		6.278 (2.033)
84 HOTELS, PERSONAL AND REPAIR SVC.	173	.9693	-.001 (.000)	1.167 (.016)		
85 BUSINESS SERVICES	173	.9884	-.001 (.000)	1.136 (.009)		
86 AUTOMOBILE REPAIR SERVICES	173	.9513	-.001 (.000)	1.130 (.020)		
87 AMUSEMENTS AND RECREATION	173	.9383	.000 (.002)	1.526 (.031)		-10.350 (6.866)
88 MEDICAL AND EDUCATIONAL INSTIT.	173	.9668	-.002 (.001)	1.037 (.015)		6.814 (2.869)
89 LUMBER, HSEWARE, FARM EQP. STORES	173	.9755	-.003 (.000)	1.087 (.014)		6.041 (1.273)
90 GENERAL MERCHANDISE STORES	173	.9938	-.001 (.000)	1.074 (.007)		1.582 (1.148)
91 FOOD STORES	173	.9668	-.003 (.001)	1.113 (.016)		6.069 (2.717)
92 AUTOMOTIVE DEALERS	173	.9835	-.003 (.000)	1.161 (.012)		5.307 (1.411)
93 GASOLINE SERVICE STATIONS	173	.9909	-.001 (.000)	1.015 (.015)	.065 59 (.006)	1.557 (1.064)
94 APPAREL, ACCESSORY STORES	173	.9949	-.001 (.000)	1.144 (.006)		
95 FURNITURE STORES	173	.9936	-.002 (.000)	1.139 (.007)		4.595 (1.162)

96 EATING, DRINKING PLACES	173	.9821	-.001 (.000)	1.247 (.013)	2.946 (2.863)
97 DRUG AND PROPRIETARY STORES	173	.9473	-.002 (.001)	1.123 (.021)	
98 OTHER RETAIL STORES	173	.9850	-.001 (.000)	1.190 (.011)	
99 NON-STORE RETAILERS	173	.9940	-.001 (.000)	1.107 (.007)	

government household real wage rates do not change over time, and all income figures are expressed in constant 1969 dollars in this study.

The earnings by place of work as given in Equation 2.35 are adjusted to earnings by place of residence by applying the nonagriculture average earnings rate to the number of civilian persons employed. This adjustment procedure assumes that the commuters have the same average wage rate as the noncommuters.

In order to derive the personal income of the region, transfer payments, property income, and military pay are added to the civilian earnings and, in order to be consistent with OBE's definition of personal income, social security payments by the workers are subtracted out. This is shown in Equation 2.39. Transfer payments as given in Equation 2.36 are assumed to be a function of the population and the level of unemployment. Transfer payments consist of pensions, social security payments, unemployment insurance payments, and welfare payments, all of which are related to the amount of population and unemployment in the region.

Property income as given in Equation 2.37 is assumed to be a function of earnings. A large proportion of the property income is rental income, and as earnings increase in a region, rents also have a tendency to increase. The social security payments are estimated by applying the prior year's ratio of social security payments to civilian persons employed to the current year's civilian persons employed, as shown in Equation 2.38. The parameters of Equations 2.36 and 2.37 are as follows.

$$TR^t = -\ \underset{(.0001)}{.0007} + \underset{(.0105)}{1.1262} \sum_{a=1}^{4} \sum_{r=1}^{2} POP_{ar}^t \quad (R^2 = .9853)$$

$$PR^t = -\ \underset{(.0001)}{.0004} + \underset{(.0082)}{1.0657}\ ERN^{t-1} \quad\quad (R^2 = .9899)$$

Unemployment was not significant in explaining transfer payments because of its high collinearity with population.

Personal Consumption Expenditures

Personal consumption expenditures, as given in Equation 2.40, are forecast by industry sector and they are assumed to be a function of the level of personal income and the prior level of consumption expenditures. As incomes go up, consumption is expected to go up. The results of these equations are given in Table 2-9.

International Trade

Regional exports to foreign countries by industry are measured at the ports of embarkation; imports are measured at the ports of disembarkation.

TABLE 2.9
EQUATIONS EXPLAINING THE 1966
PERSONAL CONSUMPTION EXPENDITURE BY INDUSTRY SECTOR

EQUATION (2.40)

INDUSTRY	NO. OBSV.	R-SQ	CONSTANT	1966 PERSONAL INCOME	1965 PERSONAL CONSUMPTION
1 LIVESTOCK	173	9868	.00020 (.00012)	.96497 (.00855)	
2 CROPS	173	.9873	.00017 (.00011)	.97112 (.00842)	
3 FORESTRY AND FISHERY PRODUCTS	173	.3790	.00201 (.00087)	.65304 (.06392)	
7 COAL MINING	173	.7314	-.00082 (.00072)	1.14184 (.05292)	
9 MINERALS MINING	173	.8996	.00161 (.00025)	.72220 (.01845)	
13 ORDNANCE	173	.8901	.00174 (.00025)	.69844 (.01877)	
14 MEAT PACKING	173	.9889	.00009 (.00011)	.98416 (.00799)	
15 DAIRY PRODUCTS	173	.9888	.00011 (.00011)	.98178 (.00799)	
16 CANNED AND FROZEN FOODS	173	.9889	.00009 (.00011)	.98418 (.00799)	
17 GRAIN MILL PRODUCTS	173	.9884	.00015 (.00011)	.97387 (.00806)	
18 BAKERY PRODUCTS	173	.9889	.00009 (.00011)	.98448 (.00799)	
19 SUGAR	173	.9889	.00011 (.00011)	.98061 (.00795)	
20 CANDY	173	.9889	.00009 (.00011)	.98437 (.00799)	
21 BEVERAGES	173	.9889	.00009 (.00011)	.98393 (.00798)	
22 MISC. FOOD PRODUCTS	173	.9889	.00011 (.00011)	.98043 (.00795)	
23 TOBACCO	173	.9651	.00076 (.00017)	.86901 (.01263)	
24 FABRICS AND YARN	173	.9829	.00016 (.00013)	.97220 (.00980)	
25 RUGS, TIRE CORD, MISC. TEXTILES	173	.9454	.00144 (.00019)	.75008 (.01378)	
26 APPAREL	173	.9905	-.00043 (.00011)	1.07415 (.00806)	
27 HOUSEHOLD TEXTILES AND UPHOLST.	173	.9622	.00087 (.00018)	.85031 (.01290)	
28 LUMBER AND PROD. EXC. CONTAINERS	173	.5680	.00278 (.00047)	.51987 (.03467)	
30 HOUSEHOLD FURNITURE	173	.9889	-.00047 (.00012)	1.08198 (.00877)	

(CONT'D)

TABLE 2.9 (CONT'D)

INDUSTRY	NO. OBSV.	R-SQ	CONSTANT	1966 PERSONAL INCOME	1965 PERSONAL CONSUMPTION
31 OFFICE FURNITURE	173	.9777	-.00006 (.00016)	1.01004 (.01167)	
32 PAPER AND PROD. EXC. CONTAINERS	173	.8562	.00201 (.00028)	.65245 (.02045)	
33 PAPER CONTAINERS	158	.8343	-.00049 (.00056)	1.10207 (.03933)	
34 PRINTING AND PUBLISHING	173	.9632	-.00183 (.00027)	1.31691 (.01967)	
35 BASIC CHEMICALS	173	.8844	.00197 (.00025)	.65999 (.01825)	
36 PLASTICS AND SYNTHETICS	173	.9678	.00037 (.00018)	.93661 (.01307)	
37 DRUGS. CLEANING AND TOILET ITEMS	173	.9372	.00116 (.00021)	.79995 (.01584)	
38 PAINT AND ALLIED PRODUCTS	173	.6604	.00176 (.00052)	.69582 (.03816)	
39 PETROLEUM REFINING	173	.9483	.00149 (.00018)	.74245 (.01325)	
40 RUBBER AND PLASTIC PRODUCTS	173	.8477	.00217 (.00027)	.62503 (.02026)	
42 SHOES AND OTHER LEATHER PRODUCTS	173	.9918	.00003 (.00009)	.99562 (.00694)	
43 GLASS AND GLASS PRODUCTS	173	.6774	.00278 (.00037)	.51895 (.02738)	
44 STONE AND CLAY PRODUCTS	173	.7115	.00245 (.00038)	.57586 (.02804)	
45 IRON AND STEEL	173	.9362	-.00010 (.00028)	1.01799 (.02033)	
47 ALUMINUM	173	.9807	.00025 (.00014)	.95640 (.01026)	
48 OTHER NON-FERROUS METALS	173	.9809	.00024 (.00014)	.95781 (.01023)	
50 HEATING. PLUMBING. STRUC. METAL	173	.9241	.00152 (.00022)	.73695 (.01615)	
51 STAMPINGS. SCREW MACHINE PROD.	173	.9854	-.00043 (.00014)	1.07492 (.00999)	
52 HARDWARE, PLATING. WIRE PROD.	173	.9790	.00102 (.00013)	.82421 (.00924)	
53 ENGINES AND TURBINES	173	.8452	.00176 (.00031)	.69495 (.02274)	
54 FARM MACHINERY AND EQUIPMENT	173	.9467	.00004 (.00024)	.99350 (.01802)	
57 METALWORKING MACHINERY AND EQUIP.	173	.9577	-.00020 (.00023)	1.03463 (.01663)	
58 SPECIAL INDUSTRIAL MACHINERY	173	.9678	.00037 (.00018)	.93662 (.01307)	
61 OFFICE AND COMPUTING MACHINES	173	.8839	.00133 (.00029)	.77052 (.02136)	

TABLE 2.9 (CONT'D)

INDUSTRY	NO. OBSV.	R-SQ	CONSTANT	1966 PERSONAL INCOME	1965 PERSONAL CONSUMPTION
62 SERVICE INDUSTRY MACHINES	173	.9552	.00102 (.00018)	.82284 (.01363)	
63 ELECTRIC APPARATUS AND MOTORS	173	.9700	.00096 (.00015)	.83475 (.01123)	
64 HOUSEHOLD APPLIANCES	173	.9591	.00063 (.00019)	.89083 (.01406)	
65 ELECTRIC LIGHT AND WIRING EQUIP.	173	.9458	.00144 (.00019)	.75141 (.01375)	
66 COMMUNICATION EQUIPMENT	173	.9620	.00051 (.00019)	.91140 (.01384)	
67 ELECTRONIC COMPONENTS	172	.9622	.00024 (.00020)	.95926 (.01458)	
68 BATTERIES AND ENGINE ELEC. EQUIP.	173	.8216	.00231 (.00029)	.60081 (.02141)	
69 MOTOR VEHICLES	173	.8862	.00156 (.00027)	.73062 (.02002)	
70 AIRCRAFT AND PARTS	173	.8451	.00177 (.00031)	.69432 (.02273)	
71 SHIPS, TRAINS, TRAILERS, CYCLES	173	.9043	.00161 (.00024)	.72108 (.01794)	
72 INSTRUMENTS AND CLOCKS	173	.9712	.00046 (.00016)	.92122 (.01213)	
73 OPTICAL AND PHOTOGRAPHIC EQUIP.	173	.8891	.00165 (.00026)	.71403 (.01929)	
74 MISC. MANUFACTURED PRODUCTS	173	.9521	.00107 (.00019)	.81509 (.01399)	
75 TRANSPORTATION	173	.9785	.00078 (.00013)	.86587 (.00981)	
76 COMMUNICATION	173	.9724	-.00012 (.00018)	1.02036 (.01314)	
78 ELECTRIC UTILITY	173	.9478	.00126 (.00019)	.78235 (.01403)	
79 GAS UTILITY	173	.8623	.00049 (.00038)	.91589 (.02799)	
80 WATER UTILITY	169	.9920	.00003 (.00014)	.04974 (.01734)	.94584 (.01181)
81 WHOLESALE TRADE	173	.9899	.00003 (.00010)	.99552 (.00769)	
82 FINANCE AND INSURANCE	173	.9628	-.00175 (.00027)	1.30331 (.01959)	
83 REAL ESTATE AND RENTAL	173	.9205	-.00325 (.00048)	1.56160 (.03509)	
84 HOTELS, PERSONAL AND REPAIR SVC.	173	.8546	.00117 (.00034)	.79756 (.02516)	
85 BUSINESS SERVICES	173	.9440	-.00359 (.00041)	1.62149 (.03020)	
86 AUTOMOBILE REPAIR SERVICES	173	.9723	.00035 (.00016)	.93864 (.01211)	

(CONT'D)

TABLE 2.9 (CONT'D)

INDUSTRY	NO. OBSV.	R-SQ	CONSTANT	1966 PERSONAL INCOME	1965 PERSONAL CONSUMPTION
87 AMUSEMENTS AND RECREATION	173	.8826	-.00193 (.00050)	1.33404 (.03720)	
88 MEDICAL AND EDUCATIONAL INSTIT.	173	.9586	-.00058 (.00024)	1.10053 (.01750)	
89 LUMBER, HSEWARE, FARM EQP. STORES	173	.8847	.00299 (.00018)	.48355 (.01335)	
90 GENERAL MERCHANDISE STORES	173	.9507	.00068 (.00021)	.88158 (.01535)	
91 FOOD STORES	173	.9828	.00067 (.00012)	.88376 (.00895)	
92 AUTOMOTIVE DEALERS	173	.8386	.00229 (.00028)	.60404 (.02027)	
93 GASOLINE SERVICE STATIONS	173	.8119	.00228 (.00030)	.60519 (.02228)	
94 APPAREL, ACCESSORY STORES	173	.9869	.00006 (.00012)	.98985 (.00872)	
95 FURNITURE STORES	173	.9684	.00094 (.00016)	.83733 (.01156)	
96 EATING, DRINKING PLACES	173	.9489	.00076 (.00021)	.86857 (.01541)	
97 DRUG AND PROPRIETARY STORES	173	.8642	.00189 (.00028)	.67294 (.02040)	
98 OTHER RETAIL STORES	173	.9488	.00132 (.00019)	.77104 (.01370)	
99 NON-STORE RETAILERS	173	.9744	.00151 (.00026)	.02945 (.02408)	.71013 (.01108)

As shown by Equations 2.41, 2.42, and 2.43, the regional distribution of foreign exports and imports is held constant from year to year.

Imports that are competitive with goods produced in the United States are classified by industry sector. Goods that are not competitive, such as natural rubber and mahogany lumber, are grouped into two extra import sectors. The first extra import sector contains those noncompetitive imports that are used as material inputs for further processing. The noncompetitive goods that are used directly by individual consumers are classified in the second extra import sector.

Total Supply and Demand

The supply of the commodities produced classified by industry is the sum of the domestic output in that industry and the competitive imports of that commodity as given in Equation 2.44.

The demand for the commodities classified by industry sectors as given in Equation 2.45 is the sum of the demand by sectors using the commodities as intermediate goods and the demand by sectors using them as final goods. Final demand by industry sector is available for personal consumption expenditures, defense expenditures and exports. The industry demand in other sectors is estimated using coefficients from a national input-output model. National technical coefficients are applied to regional outputs to obtain the intermediate demand, and national equipment coefficients by equipment purchasing sector are applied to equipment expenditures totals to obtain equipment demand by industry sector. Similarly, national construction coefficients by type of construction are applied to the construction totals to obtain construction demand by industry sector, and national government coefficients are applied to government regional totals in order to obtain regional demand for government expenditures.

Marginal Transport Costs

The marginal transportation costs (shadow prices) are expressed in Equation 2.46 as a function of supply, demand, and transport rates; however, they are computed using a linear programming transportation algorithm. In order to obtain these estimates it is necessary to have total supply and total demand by industry sector for each region and the transport cost of shipping a unit of good between each pair of regions.

Other Variables

The value of land is forecast by relating it to the property income of the region, as given in Equation 2.47. A proportion of the property income is a return from investment in land; therefore there should be a direct relationship between the level of property income and the land value. The parameters of the equation are:

$$VL^t = \underset{(.0003)}{.0035} + \underset{(.0190)}{.3860} \ PR^t \qquad\qquad (R^2 = .7062)$$

The industry location equations include agglomeration variables representing major suppliers and buyers. These major suppliers and buyers were identified with a national input-output model. The major suppliers were selected by examining the columns of the input-output table. The entries in the columns show the amount of goods being supplied by other industries. The major suppliers are represented by their output levels as shown in Equation 2.48.

The major buyers were selected by examining the rows of the national input-output table, which show the sales of domestic output to the various industry and final demand sectors. A major buyer could be represented by the output of another industry or by an equipment purchasing sector or by a government sector or by other final demand sectors, as shown in Equation 2.49.

The population density (Equation 2.50) and the highway congestion index are other agglomeration variables in the equation to explain industry location. This congestion index is computed (using data on urbanized areas furnished by FHWA) by dividing capacity miles of service (CMS) into vehicle miles traveled (VMT), as given in Equation 2.53. Equations 2.51 and 2.52 show that CMS is a function of population and exogenous highway construction expenditures (HCN) of a national highway system, and that VMT is a function of population. Before 1977 the exogenous expenditures are for the Interstate highway system and for years after 1976 they will be for an alternative hypothetical system. The parameters of these equations are:

$$CMS^t = -291.88 + .00133 \sum_{a=1}^{4} \sum_{r=1}^{2} POP_{ar}^t + .00704\ HCN^t$$
$$(83.24)\quad (.00038)$$

$$VMT^t = -331.85 + .00078 \sum_{a=1}^{4} \sum_{r=1}^{2} POP_{ar}^t$$
$$(32.97)\quad (.00001)$$

The R^2's are .9316 and .9558 respectively. CMS and VMT are entered in the equation as actual values, and POP and HCN are entered as relative regional shares.

ECONOMIC AREAS

The model is designed to apply to any set of regions that encompass the entire nation. Although most of the basic data were available by counties, it was decided to use economic areas as the regions in this study for two principal reasons: (1) the concept of an economic area is probably more meaningful for evaluating alternative highway systems than using political subdivisions, such as counties, as the areas of study; (2) the forecasting model is less costly to operate with few regions and this fact is important for being able to evaluate alternative highway systems. If the model were run at the county level, the cost of solving the linear programming algorithms would be too high. The changes in highway systems directly affect transportation costs; therefore, it is essential that the linear programming algorithms be run more frequently in this study than they would be in an application that did not allow highway systems to change.

In selecting the economic areas, alternative sets of areas were evaluated with four criteria: (1) the areas should be based on the nodal concept; (2) the areas should contain entire metropolitan areas; (3) the areas should be useful for measuring intercity travel; and (4) the areas should encompass the entire nation.

The alternative regional classifications examined for possible use in this study include the county, the state, the Standard Metropolitan Statistical

Area (SMSA), the Office of Business Economics Economic Area of the United States (OBE Area), the Census of Transportation Production Area, the Bureau of the Census Economic Area, the Bureau of the Census Functional Area, and the Census Region. The OBE Area classification is the only one that satisfies all four criteria. The OBE economic areas[f] are shown in Map 2-1.

OBE describes the economic areas as follows:

> The economic areas which have been delineated are based on the nodal-functional area concept. That is, to each urban center are attached the surrounding county units where the economic activity is focused directly or indirectly on that of the center. Each economic area combines the place of residence and place of work of employees as nearly as possible. Therefore, there is a minimum of commuting across the economic area boundaries.
>
> Each economic area approaches self-sufficiency in its residentiary industry sector; that is, while each economic area specializes in producing goods and/or services for "export" to other economic areas (and abroad) most of the services (and some goods) required by the residents and businesses of the area are provided within the area.

The mechanical procedures used in delineating the OBE Economic Areas are as follows

> First, economic centers were identified. Standard metropolitan statistical areas were chosen where possible. Each SMSA has a large city at its center which serves both as a wholesale and retail trade center and as a labor market center. However, not all SMSA's were made centers of economic areas because some are integral parts of larger metropolitan complexes. The New York City area, for instance, encompasses not only the New York City SMSA but also Jersey City, Newark, Patterson-Clifton-Passaic, Stamford, Norwalk and Bridgeport SMSA's. The Seattle economic area includes Seattle-Everett and the Tacoma SMSA's. In rural parts of the country, where there were no SMSA's, cities of from 25,000 to 50,000 population were utilized as economic centers provided that two other criteria were met. These other criteria were: (1) that the city form a wholesale trade center for the area; and (2) that the area as a whole have a population minimum of about 200,000 people. (There are some exceptions to the size criteria in sparsely populated areas.) After identifying economic centers, intervening counties were allocated to the centers. This assignment was made on the basis of comparative time and distance of travel to the economic centers, the

---

[f]"OBE Economic Areas of the United States," Regional Economics Division, Office of Business Economics, U.S. Department of Commerce (mimeo), September 1967.

journey to work pattern around the economic centers, the interconnection between counties because of journey to work, the road network, the linkage of counties by such other economic ties as could be found, and certain geographic features.

In places where the commuting pattern of adjacent economic centers overlap, counties were included in the economic area containing the center with which there was the greatest commuting connection. In the case of cities where the commuting pattern overlapped to a great degree, no attempt was made to separate the two cities; instead, both were included in the same economic area.

In the more rural parts of the country, the journey to work information was insufficient to establish boundaries of the economic areas. In these areas, distance of travel to the economic centers was the major determinant.

The Interstate highway system has been designed to serve both intercity and intrametropolitan travel, and future alternative systems are likely to be designed either for the same purposes or to aid a region in its economic development. Intercity highway systems can be evaluated with OBE areas since each contains a central city and travel between areas is measured by the travel between the central cities. Metropolitan highway systems can be evaluated since each SMSA is contained within an OBE area. An economic development highway system can be evaluated since most economic development takes place around a city that is a growth center and the OBE areas also are likely to be economic development areas.

Chapter Three

The Alternative Highway Systems

Included in this section is a complete description of the three future hypothetical alternative national highway systems that are evaluated with the forecasting model. In order to estimate the construction costs of the alternative systems, it was necessary to estimate the per mile cost of each route in the Interstate system. The construction cost estimating procedures are included in the second part of this chapter. The final part of the chapter discusses the congestion index that is used to help explain the location of industry and to determine the allocation of funds under the Urban system.

DESCRIPTION OF FUTURE ALTERNATIVE
HIGHWAY SYSTEMS

After the completion of the Interstate highway system in 1976, it is assumed that there will be funds available for additional national highway systems to be constructed between 1977 and 1986. The proposed systems are set forth as hypothetical alternatives whose economic impact can be studied using the Multiregional, Multi-Industry Forecasting Model. The three systems described herein are: (1) the Extended Primary system, (2) the Economic Development system, and (3) the Urban system.

The Extended Primary System

Objective. This highway system is designed to meet the needs of smaller cities that are not being served by the Interstate system. Most of these cities have less than 50,000 population and many of them are located in regions with low population densities. The likely benefit of such a system would be the decentralization of industry, shifting economic activity from larger to smaller cities. Because the principal purpose of this alternative highway system will be to improve transportation to the smaller and more remote cities, it is likely that less than half the expenditures on it will be for urban highways. In those states that would receive little funding for this system because of their population densities or existing Interstate highway links, some funds will be appropriated for improved highways, e.g., beltways, in their larger urban areas. This would make the distribution of federal funds more equitable to the states.

Expenditures. Federal expenditures on this system, measured in 1969 prices, are assumed to be $40 billion for the period 1977 to 1986. For each $7 of federal funds, the states will be required to appropriate $3, resulting in a total expenditure of some $57 billion. The relative expenditures in this system for rural and urban highways will depend on the priority of the network segments and will not be predetermined. Predetermined percentages for the states would not be desirable as some states need more improved rural highways while others require relatively more for urban highways. A state specializing in agriculture, for example, should have most of its highway funds spent for rural improvements, while a more urbanized state should be spending its funds more for urban highways.

Allocation of Federal Funds. The federal funds are divided into three equal portions as a first approximation. One portion is allocated to states according to the 1970 population. The second portion is allocated according to the square root of the land area of the state. And the third portion is allocated according to the miles of federal aid highways located in the state. This procedure is the one currently used by the Federal Highway Administration (FHWA). Because the Extended Primary system is intended to provide better nationwide highways to the smaller cities, there may be deviation from this formula if some states have more small cities than others. However, every state will receive at least 50 percent of what it would receive under the above formula and no state will receive more than 150 percent of its formula allocation.

Quality of Roads. All segments in the Extended Primary system will be constructed according to Interstate highway system standards. Rural and urban cost per mile, in constant prices, is assumed to be the same as the expected completion costs of the Interstate highway system. In estimating the cost per mile of a new highway segment, the cost of the closest Interstate segment will be used.

Nodal Points in the System. Nodal counties were found by ranking counties within each state by the size of their 1970 urban population. The nodal point in each county is the center of the largest city in the county. Those cities that already have nodal points in the Interstate system are eliminated from consideration for the Extended Primary system, but highway segments may link these cities with smaller cities.

Placement of Road Segments. After the nodal points had been selected, road segments are placed to serve these nodes. The segments are designed to form an integrated network with the existing and planned Interstate system. The segments in the Extended Primary system incorporate smaller cities into the Interstate's intercity network. A node is considered to be served by the new system if it has at least one road of Interstate quality which meets or crosses another road of at least primary highway quality. The other road could either be another segment in the new system or an existing highway of at least primary quality.

Priority of Segments. After the segments in the Extended Primary system had been placed, they were ranked according to the population that they serve. Expenditures were allocated to the new highway segments according to their priority rating within each state until the total funds were exhausted. The network attribute of the system was preserved, and the effect of the limited amount of funds is to prevent the extension of the network to the smallest cities.

Urban Mileage. The urban mileage of road segments was determined by the population size of the cities and towns that the roads go through, and by the miles of beltways to be constructed.

Major Links in the System. The major links in the Extended Primary system, as determined by the criteria listed above, are shown on Map 3-1. The rural and urban mileages, and the rural and urban construction costs by state, are presented in Table 3-1. The difference between the total construction costs and the $57 billion available for the Extended Primary system would be the expenditures for preliminary engineering and the purchase of rights-of-way. The numbers on the map correspond to the highway segments listed in the table.

The Economic Development System

Objective. This highway system has the purpose of reducing transportation cost to the economically depressed areas of the nation. It should result in a shift of industry from the highly developed areas to the underdeveloped areas.

Expenditures. The total amount of federal funds will be $40 billion during the ten-year period 1977 to 1986. Since the Economic Development system is designed to help the poorer areas in the nation, state matching funds are not required. Not all the states will be served with this system.

Allocation of Federal Funds. The economic areas were ranked according to their per capita income and nodal points within each economic area

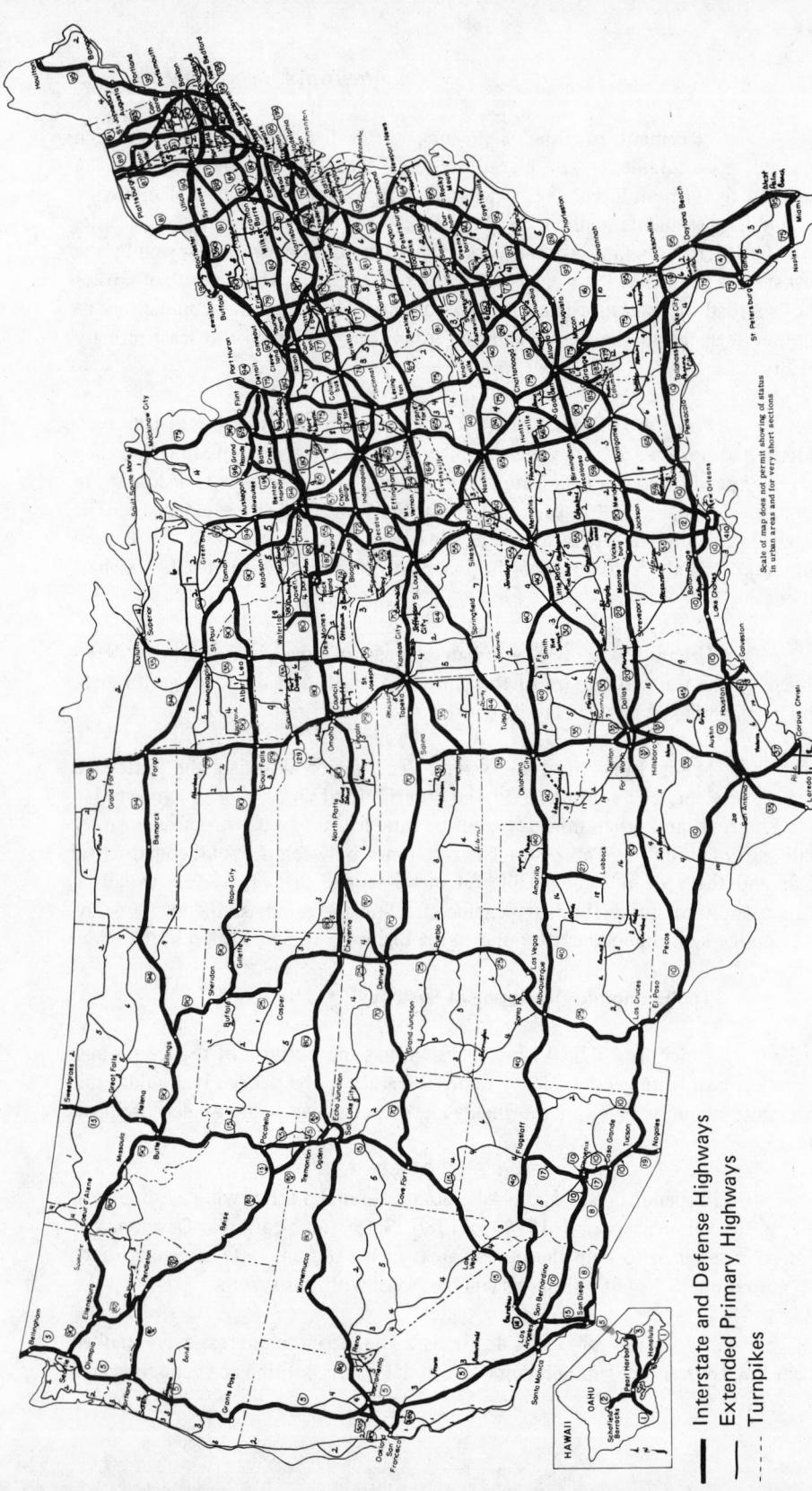

Map 3–1   The National System of Interstate and Defense Highways and Extended Primary Highways

Interstate and Defense Highways

Extended Primary Highways

Turnpikes

Scale of map does not permit showing of status in urban areas and for very short sections

TABLE 3.1
ESTIMATED MILEAGE AND COST BY HIGHWAY SEGMENT UNDER THE EXTENDED PRIMARY SYSTEM
(COST IN MILLIONS OF 1969 DOLLARS)

STATE	NUMBER ON MAP 3.1	RURAL		URBAN		TOTAL	
		MILES	COST	MILES	COST	MILES	COST
	1	73	87.7	20	34.1	93	121.8
	2	63	75.7	14	23.8	77	99.6
	3	98	104.0	19	46.4	117	150.3
	4	45	45.1	14	51.9	59	96.9
	5	16	12.8	7	8.4	23	21.2
	6	127	169.3	27	241.8	154	411.0
	7	85	95.1	15	31.0	100	126.2
	8	122	136.8	18	32.9	140	169.7
ALABAMA	TOTAL	629	726.5	134	470.2	763	1196.7
	1	197	118.4	23	103.7	220	222.0
	2	237	168.3	12	33.1	249	201.3
	3	69	55.3	1	1.5	70	56.8
	4	131	105.0	5	7.5	136	112.5
	5	144	106.0	12	51.1	156	157.0
	6	148	118.6	0	.0	148	118.6
	7	0	.0	20	90.1	20	90.1
	BELTWAYS	0	.0	30	45.1	30	45.1
ARIZONA	TOTAL	926	671.4	103	332.0	1029	1003.5
	1	85	68.1	25	55.1	110	123.2
	2	79	63.3	9	19.8	88	83.1
	3	7	6.3	1	2.9	8	9.2
	4	30	27.0	10	18.0	40	45.1
	5	139	135.3	29	111.3	168	246.6
	6	49	39.3	3	6.6	52	45.9
	7	84	75.7	16	46.5	100	122.2
	8	54	54.1	8	35.3	62	89.3
	9	118	94.5	22	48.5	140	143.0
ARKANSAS	TOTAL	645	563.7	123	343.9	768	907.6
	1	349	419.4	90	378.6	439	798.0
	2	380	456.7	72	302.9	452	759.6
	3	201	241.6	39	164.1	240	405.6
	4	125	150.2	11	46.3	136	196.5
	5	135	243.4	3	12.9	138	256.3
CALIFORNIA	TOTAL	1190	1511.3	215	904.7	1405	2416.0
	1	227	218.8	22	33.5	249	252.3
	2	132	104.0	24	36.6	156	140.5
	3	398	260.8	25	36.4	423	297.2
	4	294	281.5	29	50.6	323	332.1
COLORADO	TOTAL	1051	865.1	100	156.9	1151	1022.1
	1	56	185.1	15	84.1	71	269.2
	2	30	84.7	18	110.6	48	195.3
CONNECTICUT	TOTAL	86	269.8	33	194.7	119	464.5
	1	79	94.9	31	177.0	110	271.9
DELAWARE	TOTAL	79	94.9	31	177.0	110	271.9
	1	193	154.6	37	18.5	230	173.2
	2	78	62.5	7	18.2	85	80.7
	3	137	109.8	13	33.9	150	143.6
	4	153	133.6	15	24.3	168	157.9
	5	134	93.9	17	47.7	151	141.6
	6	46	37.3	14	19.6	60	56.9
	BELTWAYS	0	.0	105	273.4	105	273.4
FLORIDA	TOTAL	741	591.7	208	435.7	949	1027.4
	1	52	46.9	8	22.4	60	69.3
	2	132	106.9	30	60.1	162	167.0
	3	24	21.6	12	33.7	36	55.3
	4	26	23.4	9	25.2	35	48.7
	5	10	9.0	12	33.7	22	42.7
	6	114	117.8	18	49.1	132	166.9
	7	82	73.9	13	36.5	95	110.4
	8	81	73.0	11	30.8	92	103.9
	9	47	42.4	5	14.0	52	56.4
	10	15	10.5	0	.0	15	10.5
	11	26	23.4	9	13.5	35	37.0
	12	74	66.7	9	25.2	83	91.9
	BELTWAYS	0	.0	100	274.4	100	274.4
GEORGIA	TOTAL	683	615.6	236	618.7	919	1234.2

77

(Continued)

TABLE 3.1
ESTIMATED MILEAGE AND COST BY HIGHWAY SEGMENT UNDER THE EXTENDED PRIMARY SYSTEM
(COST IN MILLIONS OF 1969 DOLLARS)

STATE	NUMBER ON MAP 3.1	RURAL		URBAN		TOTAL	
		MILES	COST	MILES	COST	MILES	COST
	1	148	222.3	2	3.2	150	225.5
	2	81	121.7	9	14.4	90	136.1
	3	77	46.3	8	5.6	85	51.9
	4	99	148.7	7	11.2	106	159.9
	6	50	30.0	5	3.5	55	33.6
IDAHO	TOTAL	455	569.1	31	38.0	486	607.0
	1	176	211.5	66	587.7	242	799.2
	2	127	248.6	19	120.3	146	368.9
	3	68	81.7	19	205.5	87	287.2
	4	63	138.8	12	98.6	75	237.4
ILLINOIS	TOTAL	434	680.7	116	1012.1	550	1692.7
	1	85	90.1	10	35.3	95	125.4
	2	102	112.4	24	93.7	126	206.1
	3	105	141.2	12	36.5	117	177.7
	4	71	75.4	26	59.5	97	134.9
	5	77	71.6	11	27.9	88	99.6
	6	62	65.3	12	40.1	74	105.4
	7	65	89.2	16	54.5	81	143.7
	8	71	71.1	18	30.3	89	101.5
	9	85	90.5	25	60.8	110	151.3
INDIANA	TOTAL	723	806.9	154	438.6	877	1245.5
	1	299	239.6	47	107.9	346	347.4
	2	233	198.5	50	56.8	283	255.3
	3	29	26.1	1	1.0	30	27.1
	4	53	47.8	10	10.0	63	57.8
	5	67	60.4	16	16.0	83	76.4
	6	9	7.2	9	9.9	18	17.1
	7	15	12.0	5	9.5	20	21.5
	8	14	11.2	2	8.4	16	19.6
	9	88	70.5	6	11.0	94	81.5
	BELTWAYS	0	.0	90	92.1	90	92.1
IOWA	TOTAL	807	673.3	236	322.7	1043	996.0
	1	105	72.5	27	53.8	132	126.3
	2	342	274.0	22	45.1	364	319.1
	3	251	172.1	22	50.3	273	222.3
	4	62	37.3	5	15.5	67	52.8
	5	22	24.2	13	23.4	35	47.7
	BELTWAYS	0	.0	60	156.2	60	156.2
KANSAS	TOTAL	782	580.1	149	344.3	931	924.4
	1	18	23.4	12	62.5	30	85.9
	2	173	225.2	19	74.9	192	300.2
	3	259	332.8	23	70.9	282	403.7
	4	89	115.9	10	28.0	99	143.9
KENTUCKY	TOTAL	539	697.4	64	236.4	603	933.7
	1	246	246.4	44	193.9	290	440.3
	2	7	14.7	12	66.1	19	80.8
	3	113	237.7	26	143.2	139	380.9
LOUISIANA	TOTAL	366	498.8	82	403.2	448	902.0
	1	72	86.5	22	55.1	94	141.6
	2	160	192.3	10	25.0	170	217.3
	4	82	98.6	9	22.5	91	121.1
MAINE	TOTAL	314	377.4	41	102.7	355	480.0
	1	54	146.0	5	40.6	59	186.6
	2	191	516.5	29	235.3	220	751.8
MARYLAND	TOTAL	245	662.5	34	275.8	279	938.4
	1	192	346.1	27	321.8	219	667.9
	2	72	101.0	42	159.8	114	260.8
	3	26	36.5	18	68.5	44	105.0
	4	12	16.8	3	11.4	15	28.2
	5	31	43.5	7	26.6	38	70.1
	BELTWAYS	0	.0	40	476.7	40	476.7
MASSACHUSETTS	TOTAL	333	543.8	137	1064.9	470	1608.8

TABLE 3.1
ESTIMATED MILEAGE AND COST BY HIGHWAY SEGMENT UNDER THE EXTENDED PRIMARY SYSTEM
(COST IN MILLIONS OF 1969 DOLLARS)

STATE	NUMBER ON MAP 3.1	RURAL		URBAN		TOTAL	
		MILES	COST	MILES	COST	MILES	COST
	1	276	304.1	17	71.5	293	375.6
	2	68	357.4	18	26.8	86	384.2
	3	320	448.7	25	105.2	345	553.9
	4	217	249.3	19	94.3	236	343.6
MICHIGAN	TOTAL	881	1359.4	79	297.9	960	1657.3
	1	153	122.6	35	63.1	188	185.7
	2	226	168.0	24	145.5	250	313.5
	3	144	115.4	25	152.7	169	268.1
	4	148	118.6	8	14.4	156	133.0
	5	126	101.0	6	36.7	132	137.6
	6	136	103.5	10	18.0	146	121.5
MINNESOTA	TOTAL	933	728.9	108	430.5	1041	1159.4
	1	50	40.1	24	64.9	74	105.0
	2	58	46.5	12	32.5	70	78.9
	3	26	20.8	19	51.4	45	72.2
	4	125	100.2	15	40.6	140	140.7
	5	48	38.5	8	21.6	56	60.1
	6	85	68.1	2	5.4	87	73.5
	7	32	25.6	2	3.0	34	28.6
	BELTWAYS	0	.0	40	84.1	40	84.1
MISSISSIPPI	TOTAL	424	339.7	122	303.5	546	643.2
	1	56	52.1	19	71.6	75	123.7
	2	106	98.0	22	76.7	128	174.7
	3	199	171.9	28	99.4	227	271.2
	4	65	52.1	9	34.3	74	86.3
	5	135	118.2	10	34.6	145	152.7
	6	150	150.2	12	32.3	162	182.6
	7	244	244.4	15	41.0	259	285.3
	BELTWAYS	0	.0	30	93.1	30	93.1
MISSOURI	TOTAL	955	886.8	145	482.9	1100	1369.7
	1	255	191.9	23	29.0	278	220.9
	2	348	226.0	36	43.3	384	269.3
	3	240	152.6	16	14.0	256	166.7
	4	80	48.1	10	2.0	90	50.1
	5	144	86.5	3	.6	147	87.1
	6	231	138.8	14	2.8	245	141.6
MONTANA	TOTAL	1298	844.0	102	91.7	1400	935.7
	1	9	4.5	6	11.4	15	15.9
	2	123	61.6	29	55.2	152	116.8
	3	178	89.1	15	28.5	193	117.7
	4	44	22.0	4	7.6	48	29.6
	5	35	17.5	7	13.3	42	30.8
	6	314	157.2	28	53.3	342	210.5
	BELTWAYS	0	.0	60	114.2	60	114.2
NEBRASKA	TOTAL	703	352.0	149	283.5	852	635.6
	1	68	40.9	22	72.7	90	113.6
	2	265	159.2	10	33.1	275	192.3
	3	141	84.7	13	43.0	154	127.7
	4	282	141.2	23	64.5	305	205.7
	5	156	93.7	4	13.2	160	107.0
NEVADA	TOTAL	912	519.8	72	226.4	984	746.3
	1	95	158.9	35	43.0	130	201.9
	BELTWAYS	0	.0	25	62.6	25	62.6
NEW HAMPSHIRE	TOTAL	95	158.9	60	105.6	155	264.5
	1	107	321.5	12	75.7	119	397.2
	2	49	147.2	7	44.2	56	191.4
	BELTWAYS	0	.0	20	126.2	20	126.2
NEW JERSEY	TOTAL	156	468.7	39	246.1	195	714.8
	1	184	126.2	29	53.4	213	179.6
	2	214	150.0	30	49.6	244	199.6
	3	145	87.2	34	55.6	179	143.0
	4	208	145.8	25	42.6	233	188.4

(Continued)

TABLE 3.1
ESTIMATED MILEAGE AND COST BY HIGHWAY SEGMENT UNDER THE EXTENDED PRIMARY SYSTEM
(COST IN MILLIONS OF 1969 DOLLARS)

STATE	NUMBER ON MAP 3.1	RURAL MILES	RURAL COST	URBAN MILES	URBAN COST	TOTAL MILES	TOTAL COST
	5	16	11.2	8	11.2	24	22.4
	6	106	74.3	7	9.8	113	84.1
NEW MEXICO	TOTAL	873	594.8	133	222.3	1006	817.2
	1	78	132.8	40	288.4	118	421.3
	2	78	125.0	18	76.3	96	201.3
	3	127	198.1	56	202.5	183	400.6
	4	138	210.1	11	43.0	149	253.1
	5	89	142.6	4	17.6	93	160.2
	6	80	128.2	5	19.5	85	147.7
	7	83	133.0	24	93.7	107	226.8
	BELTWAYS	0	.0	100	390.6	100	390.6
NEW YORK	TOTAL	673	1069.9	258	1131.7	931	2201.6
	1	249	174.6	28	5.6	277	180.2
	2	34	23.8	24	4.8	58	28.6
	3	82	57.5	20	4.0	102	61.5
	4	73	85.1	18	18.7	91	103.9
	5	66	79.3	7	11.9	73	91.2
	6	57	65.0	2	2.0	59	67.0
	7	105	87.4	17	33.2	122	120.6
	8	84	70.4	13	11.6	97	82.0
	9	45	49.6	5	5.0	50	54.6
	BELTWAYS	0	.0	60	135.2	60	135.2
NORTH CAROLINA	TOTAL	795	692.8	194	232.1	989	924.8
	1	294	173.5	45	40.5	339	213.9
	2	217	108.7	12	13.2	229	121.9
	3	80	40.1	9	9.9	89	50.0
	BELTWAYS	0	.0	40	44.1	40	44.1
NORTH DAKOTA	TOTAL	591	322.2	106	107.7	697	429.9
	1	102	138.8	25	93.7	127	232.6
	2	93	118.5	44	178.7	137	297.2
	3	46	59.9	28	145.8	74	205.7
	4	76	119.5	15	51.1	91	170.6
	5	110	148.2	44	208.3	154	356.6
OHIO	TOTAL	427	584.9	156	677.6	583	1262.6
	1	57	45.7	10	23.0	67	68.7
	2	63	50.5	18	27.0	81	77.5
	3	72	57.7	28	30.8	100	88.5
	4	122	97.8	9	11.5	131	109.3
	5	81	64.9	8	12.0	89	76.9
	6	173	138.6	12	12.4	185	151.0
	BELTWAYS	0	.0	30	45.1	30	45.1
OKLAHOMA	TOTAL	568	455.1	115	162.0	683	617.1
	1	43	51.7	6	21.0	49	72.7
	3	380	456.7	46	161.2	426	618.0
	4	38	45.7	8	28.0	46	73.7
	6	95	114.2	5	17.5	100	131.7
OREGON	TOTAL	556	668.2	65	227.9	621	896.1
	1	143	214.8	24	60.1	167	274.9
	2	44	66.1	12	30.0	56	96.1
	3	87	130.7	3	7.5	90	138.2
	4	30	51.1	12	239.2	42	290.2
	5	45	67.6	6	15.0	51	82.6
	6	88	132.2	20	50.1	108	182.3
	7	51	76.6	15	37.7	66	114.3
	8	141	225.4	12	99.8	153	325.2
PENNSYLVANIA	TOTAL	629	964.6	104	539.3	733	1503.9
	1	46	96.7	19	74.2	65	171.0
RHODE ISLAND	TOTAL	46	96.7	19	74.2	65	171.0
	1	23	20.7	4	.4	27	21.1
	2	87	68.6	19	8.4	106	77.0
	3	138	96.7	15	3.0	153	99.8

TABLE 3.1

ESTIMATED MILEAGE AND COST BY HIGHWAY SEGMENT UNDER THE EXTENDED PRIMARY SYSTEM
(COST IN MILLIONS OF 1969 DOLLARS)

STATE	NUMBER ON MAP 3.1	RURAL MILES	RURAL COST	URBAN MILES	URBAN COST	TOTAL MILES	TOTAL COST
	4	65	62.5	4	10.0	69	72.5
	5	86	60.3	6	1.2	92	61.5
	6	51	40.0	10	6.2	61	46.2
	BELTWAYS	0	.0	90	163.3	90	163.3
SOUTH CAROLINA	TOTAL	450	348.8	148	192.5	598	541.3
	1	221	122.5	32	26.8	253	149.3
	2	184	148.2	21	11.4	205	159.6
	3	134	119.2	8	6.2	142	125.4
	BELTWAYS	0	.0	50	95.1	50	95.1
SOUTH DAKOTA	TOTAL	539	389.9	111	139.6	650	529.5
	1	34	40.9	8	13.6	42	54.5
	2	180	162.3	34	91.7	214	254.0
	3	61	67.2	22	22.0	83	89.2
	4	54	54.1	6	12.6	60	66.7
	5	37	40.8	14	14.0	51	54.8
	6	114	106.3	23	62.7	137	169.0
	7	12	10.8	8	27.2	20	38.1
	BELTWAYS	0	.0	40	136.2	40	136.2
TENNESSEE	TOTAL	492	482.2	155	380.2	647	862.4
	1	162	97.4	44	101.4	206	198.7
	2	108	64.9	20	34.1	128	99.0
	3	39	39.1	18	32.5	57	71.5
	4	119	76.6	21	39.4	140	116.0
	5	119	71.5	19	32.3	138	103.9
	6	136	88.8	51	109.3	187	198.1
	7	11	6.6	13	22.1	24	28.7
	8	111	66.7	36	82.9	147	149.6
	9	218	167.1	35	61.8	253	228.9
	10	86	60.3	2	4.2	88	64.5
	11	182	109.4	24	40.9	206	150.2
	12	123	98.6	18	12.6	141	111.2
	13	26	15.6	19	41.9	45	57.5
	14	90	63.1	15	31.5	105	94.6
	15	128	106.2	18	31.5	146	137.7
	16	240	165.0	17	24.1	257	189.1
	17	41	24.6	13	22.1	54	46.8
	18	40	36.1	7	6.3	47	42.4
	19	31	18.6	1	1.7	32	20.3
	20	126	75.7	21	35.8	147	111.5
TEXAS	TOTAL	2136	1451.7	412	768.4	2548	2220.1
	1	72	57.7	11	27.5	83	85.2
	2	119	89.8	8	21.2	127	111.1
	3	151	107.7	14	39.9	165	147.5
	4	129	103.4	5	12.5	134	115.9
	5	138	110.6	7	17.5	145	128.1
	6	96	67.3	6	17.4	102	84.7
UTAH	TOTAL	705	536.4	51	136.1	756	672.5
	1	148	216.4	17	48.8	165	265.2
VERMONT	TOTAL	148	216.4	17	48.8	165	265.2
	1	97	106.9	36	23.4	133	130.3
	2	107	117.9	21	21.0	128	138.9
	3	113	135.8	20	196.3	133	332.1
	4	40	44.1	11	1.1	51	45.2
	5	21	23.1	3	.3	24	23.4
	6	71	103.8	12	90.5	83	194.3
	BELTWAYS	0	.0	20	196.3	20	196.3
VIRGINIA	TOTAL	449	531.5	123	529.0	572	1060.5
	1	115	253.4	17	61.3	132	314.7
	2	219	482.5	21	75.7	240	558.3
	3	84	101.0	17	22.1	101	123.1
WASHINGTON	TOTAL	418	836.9	55	159.1	473	996.0
	1	15	40.6	26	210.9	41	251.5

(Continued)

TABLE 3.1
ESTIMATED MILEAGE AND COST BY HIGHWAY SEGMENT UNDER THE EXTENDED PRIMARY SYSTEM
(COST IN MILLIONS OF 1969 DOLLARS)

STATE	NUMBER ON MAP 3.1	RURAL		URBAN		TOTAL	
		MILES	COST	MILES	COST	MILES	COST
	2	49	132.5	16	129.8	65	262.3
	3	108	286.4	6	42.9	114	329.3
WEST VIRGINIA	TOTAL	172	459.5	48	383.6	220	843.1
	1	106	79.6	68	96.2	174	175.9
	2	174	129.1	25	36.1	199	165.2
	3	114	82.3	11	21.7	125	104.1
	4	89	62.4	11	66.1	100	128.5
	5	125	87.6	16	24.0	141	111.7
	6	267	213.9	17	37.4	284	251.3
	7	35	28.0	10	14.0	45	42.1
	BELTWAYS	0	.0	50	153.2	50	153.2
WISCONSIN	TOTAL	910	683.1	208	448.8	1118	1131.8
	1	286	171.9	19	22.8	305	194.7
	2	207	124.4	13	26.0	220	150.4
	3	42	25.2	8	16.0	50	41.3
	4	216	148.8	10	14.0	226	162.9
	5	145	87.1	6	7.2	151	94.3
WYOMING	TOTAL	896	557.5	56	86.1	952	643.6
U.S. TOTAL		29858	29601.7	5637	16987.7	35495	46589.4

were selected. Links in the highway system were planned to serve these nodes, starting with the lowest income areas until the total funds were allocated. The allocation to any state or economic area was not predetermined, but depended on their highway needs.

Quality of Roads. All segments in the new highway system were constructed according to Interstate system standards. Rural and urban costs per mile, in constant prices, were assumed to be the same as the expected completion costs of the Interstate system. In determining the cost of a new highway segment, the cost from the closest Interstate segment was used.

Nodal Points in the System. Each economic area has one or more central cities and these central cities are designated as nodal points in the Economic Development system. The economic areas are delineated to form what may be called "little economies," with economic activity centered in the designated cities.

Placement of Road Segments. Road segments in the Economic Development system tie into the Interstate system. A network of segments was planned, and each nodal point is served by at least one new road segment. This new road segment meets or crosses either with another new road segment in the nodal county or with an existing road of at least primary quality.

Priority of Segments. The new segments in the system were given a priority rating according to the per capita income of the economic area that it serves. Expenditures were allocated to road segments according to the priority ratings (beginning with the lowest average income) until the total amount of money was exhausted.

Rural-Urban Mileage. Separate rural and urban mileage was coded in order to estimate the cost of each segment, but there were no restrictions on the proportion of mileage or money that could be spent on either rural or urban highways.

Major Links in the System. The major links in the Economic Development system are shown in Map 3-2. Table 3-2 presents, by segment, the rural and urban mileage, and the rural and urban construction costs of the system. The difference between the total construction costs and the $40 billion available for the Economic Development system would be the expenditures for preliminary engineering and the purchase of rights-of-way. The numbers on the map correspond to the segment numbers in the table. They indicate the priority rating of the segment.

The Urban System

Objective. This system is designed to reduce urban congestion where it is the greatest. It favors large metropolitan areas, and thus will influence industry to centralize and concentrate in large cities.

Expenditures. The total amount of federal funds is $40 billion during the ten-year period 1977 to 1986. Since not all states and cities are served by this system, no matching state funds are required.

Allocation of Funds. Allocation of funds was determined by the value of FHWA's arterial highway congestion index for urbanized areas. Urbanized areas were ranked according to the congestion index and funds were allocated to the most congested urbanized area until its congestion index fell to the value of the congestion index in the second most congested city. Then funds were allocated to the first and second urbanized areas until their congestion indexes were reduced to the value of the third most congested area. Then funds were allocated to the first, second, and third city until their congestion indexes were reduced to the congestion index of the fourth most congested area. This procedure was continued until the total amount of funds was exhausted.

Quality of Roads. All segments in the Urban system are to be constructed according to Interstate system standards. The urban cost per mile, in constant prices, is assumed to be the same as the expected completion costs of the Interstate system. In determining the cost of a new highway segment, the cost from the closest Interstate segment was used.

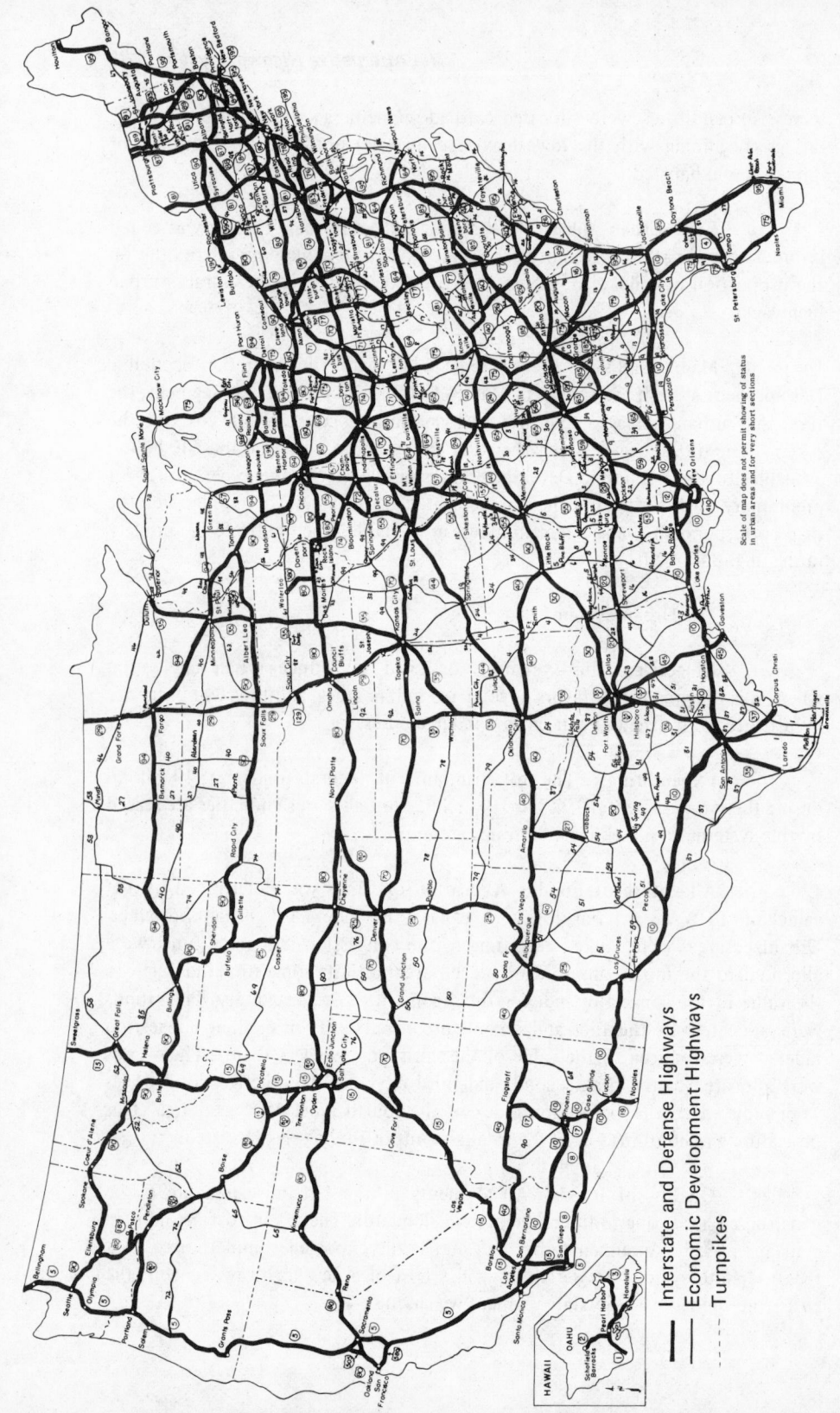

Map 3-2. The National System of Interstate and Defense Highways and Economic Development Highways

Interstate and Defense Highways

Economic Development Highways

Turnpikes

Scale of map does not permit showing of status in urban areas and for very short sections

TABLE 3.2
ESTIMATED MILEAGE AND COST BY HIGHWAY SEGMENT UNDER THE ECONOMIC DEVELOPMENT SYSTEM
(COST IN MILLIONS OF 1969 DOLLARS)

NUMBER ON MAP 3.2	RURAL MILES	COST	URBAN MILES	COST	TOTAL MILES	COST
1	422	252.7	90	195.8	512	448.4
2	190	137.7	26	5.2	216	137.9
3	401	380.3	80	150.5	481	530.8
4	360	316.4	40	92.7	400	409.1
5	448	394.1	114	297.1	562	691.1
6	362	492.7	66	306.1	428	798.9
7	48	43.1	12	34.7	60	77.8
8	308	369.8	32	58.7	340	428.5
9	431	468.8	86	428.9	517	897.7
10	419	362.2	80	209.9	499	572.2
11	391	415.6	50	122.7	441	538.3
12	351	435.3	33	154.5	384	589.7
13	593	604.4	85	137.6	678	742.0
14	407	329.4	74	86.6	481	416.0
15	79	62.2	14	5.6	93	67.8
16	332	559.6	48	240.4	380	800.0
17	310	494.7	82	453.4	392	948.2
18	588	657.4	57	162.0	645	819.3
19	470	407.2	62	236.6	532	643.8
20	95	83.0	12	19.6	107	102.6
21	350	830.4	61	491.8	411	322.2
22	406	371.6	45	90.9	451	462.5
23	448	358.5	48	79.0	496	437.6
24	494	438.0	58	152.6	552	590.5
25	115	131.1	26	23.7	141	154.9
26	263	236.6	29	6.3	292	242.9
27	307	174.1	38	47.7	345	221.8
28	125	103.8	7	17.9	132	121.6
29	155	165.4	31	68.5	186	233.9
30	169	166.4	9	28.8	178	195.3
31	549	342.1	51	86.9	600	429.0
32	203	134.8	51	108.9	254	243.7
33	368	332.6	64	161.4	432	493.9
34	105	83.8	8	17.6	113	101.4
35	67	56.8	14	32.1	81	88.9
36	147	102.7	23	4.6	170	107.3
37	773	495.9	53	103.5	826	599.4
38	242	298.7	44	93.0	286	391.7
39	183	219.1	6	10.2	189	229.3
40	725	430.5	75	128.3	800	558.8
41	103	147.7	7	14.2	110	161.9
42	201	155.1	21	127.7	222	282.8
43	89	79.9	12	36.3	101	116.2
44	103	65.3	13	38.2	116	103.5
45	180	143.9	27	29.2	207	173.1
46	410	232.0	46	104.5	456	336.5
47	119	71.2	19	32.2	138	103.5
48	349	269.1	67	227.4	416	496.5
49	470	313.2	44	83.0	514	396.2
50	162	140.7	5	8.7	167	149.4
51	516	338.1	60	94.3	576	432.4
52	386	326.0	31	39.5	417	365.5
53	609	358.4	72	74.7	681	433.2
54	502	352.8	96	144.8	598	497.6
55	121	132.8	27	19.8	148	152.6
56	229	177.7	60	75.8	289	253.6
57	228	347.2	60	182.4	288	529.6
58	86	61.9	11	37.2	97	99.1
59	244	170.4	38	79.6	282	250.1
60	219	356.5	22	124.3	241	480.9
61	277	250.3	61	378.4	338	628.6
62	45	35.2	6	.6	51	35.8
63	196	144.8	14	67.1	210	211.8
64	36	32.3	6	5.1	42	37.4
65	222	174.9	6	28.6	228	203.6
66	91	72.6	4	11.6	95	84.2
67	218	319.3	23	73.8	241	393.2
68	194	129.1	20	71.8	214	201.0
69	298	192.4	37	41.2	335	233.6

(Continued)

TABLE 3.2
ESTIMATED MILEAGE AND COST BY HIGHWAY SEGMENT UNDER THE ECONOMIC DEVELOPMENT SYSTEM
(COST IN MILLIONS OF 1969 DOLLARS)

NUMBER ON MAP 3.2	RURAL MILES	RURAL COST	URBAN MILES	URBAN COST	TOTAL MILES	TOTAL COST
70	76	75.8	16	55.9	92	131.7
71	99	133.7	18	58.5	117	192.2
72	317	333.9	25	141.6	342	475.5
73	351	329.7	16	67.7	367	397.3
74	354	247.5	23	9.6	377	257.0
75	118	219.4	17	28.9	135	248.4
76	415	384.8	28	60.5	443	445.2
77	97	75.5	11	30.3	108	105.9
78	382	328.9	47	98.7	429	427.6
79	323	250.1	16	21.6	339	271.6
80	59	82.4	13	33.7	72	116.1
81	77	62.9	18	48.3	95	111.2
82	141	118.9	16	45.0	157	163.9
83	80	58.3	31	44.5	111	102.8
85	174	111.8	24	25.1	198	136.9
86	274	1407.0	52	665.0	326	2071.9
87	285	170.6	28	52.0	313	222.6
88	119	95.0	22	30.5	141	125.5
89	75	71.9	16	55.9	91	127.8
90	144	119.6	12	16.9	156	136.5
91	102	126.5	10	46.7	112	173.2
92	121	67.2	16	44.7	137	111.9
94	38	56.9	2	5.0	40	61.9
95	182	100.6	42	104.2	224	204.8
96	45	71.8	7	27.2	52	99.1
98	87	172.5	12	55.1	99	227.6
99	290	296.2	51	275.9	341	522.1
U.S. TOTAL	24927	23894.8	3388	9503.2	28315	33398.0

Placement of Road Segments. Individual road segments in the Urban system are not identified. Additional freeway mileage as determined by the above procedure will consist of either new highways in the urbanized areas or additional lanes on existing Interstate quality roads. Table 3-3 presents information on the expenditures for the Urban system by DOT urbanized areas. It shows the value of the congestion index for each of these urbanized areas before construction of the additional links, the additional miles of freeways to be built, and the construction costs by area. The additional links will bring down the congestion index to .4291 for each area listed. The difference between the total construction costs and the $40 billion available for the Urban system would be the expenditures for preliminary engineering and the purchase of rights-of-way.

ESTIMATING EXOGENOUS HIGHWAY CONSTRUCTION COSTS

The construction costs of the alternative future highway systems must be estimated as accurately as possible in order to provide realistic figures on the amounts to be spent in each of the regions under the different alternatives. The highway construction costs, it will be recalled, play a significant role in

Table 3-3. Estimated Mileage and Cost by Urban Areas Under the Urban System

DOT Urbanized Area	1968 Congestion Index	Additional Freeway Miles	Cost (1969 Prices (000.000)
Chicago, Ill.	.7624	720.5	6052.0
New Orleans, La.	.6418	47.4	260.9
Philadelphia, Pa.	.6304	286.8	2323.1
San Francisco, Calif.	.6231	325.8	1075.1
Miami, Fla.	.6103	96.3	443.0
Detroit, Mich.	.6053	340.7	3066.4
New York, NY	.5860	958.8	13902.2
Baltimore, Md.	.5816	92.9	297.2
Cincinnati, Ohio	.5759	75.2	391.2
Los Angeles, Calif.	.5750	591.3	2483.6
Washington, D.C.	.5484	129.4	2187.2
St. Louis, Mo.	.5425	100.3	381.3
Huntsville, Ala.	.5318	6.7	11.4
Cleveland, Ohio	.5248	111.9	895.0
Madison, Wisc.	.5203	6.3	25.8
Boston, Mass.	.5098	114.4	1361.0
Honolulu, Hawaii	.4987	9.7	160.5
Erie, Pa.	.4963	3.5	69.5
Louisville, Ky.	.4954	24.9	129.5
Birmingham, Ala.	.4945	14.2	52.6
Atlanta, Ga.	.4730	36.9	103.2
Ft. Lauderdale, Fla.	.4715	11.1	28.8
Norfolk, Va.	.4699	12.4	121.8
Dayton, Ohio	.4695	14.2	48.4
Akron, Ohio	.4666	8.8	34.3
Florence, Ala.	.4655	1.2	2.0
Memphis, Tenn.	.4588	8.5	28.8
Providence, RI	.4533	10.0	84.3
Columbus, Ohio	.4529	9.9	51.7
Oklahoma City, Okla.	.4455	6.6	29.7
Salt Lake City, Utah	.4435	2.5	7.2
Houston, Tex.	.4401	10.9	54.5
Montgomery, Ala.	.4391	.6	1.0
Sacramento, Calif.	.4291[a]	.0	.0
Totals		4190.6	36164.2

[a]Congestion Index is reduced to this level for all the urban areas listed.

determining the overall economic activity in each of the regions. The greater the construction activity in a given region, the more jobs there will be, the higher the level of income, the more will be spent, and so forth.

The forecasting model requires that the highway construction data for each region be separated into endogenous and exogenous components. The endogenous highway construction is assumed to be a function of the personal income of the region, as given in Equation 2.9; the exogenous component is predetermined as a planned highway system. Past, present, and future construction on the Interstate system is assumed to be exogenous, and other highway construction is considered endogenous. Construction on the future highway systems to be evaluated in this study is assumed to be exogenous.

Estimates of annual Interstate highway construction in constant dollars were made from three computer data files acquired from FHWA. These data allowed the estimation of annual rural and urban Interstate highway construction expenditures by route number within each state. The data files used were as follows.

1. Total obligations on Interstate highway construction to October 31, 1969.
2. Mileage and construction cost, in 1968 prices, to complete the Interstate system from November 1, 1969 (The 1970 Estimate of the Cost of Completing the Interstate System).
3. Mileage and period of construction of each Interstate highway segment (PR-511, Report of the Status of the Interstate System).

In addition, price indices on highway construction were acquired.[a]

The first step was to determine the cost per mile of the uncompleted portion of the Interstate highway system. In the second step the data on mileage and periods of construction were used to determine the number of miles completed in each calendar year. When the construction period covered more than one year the mileage of the road segment was proportioned to the years according to the number of months the segment was under construction. This procedure has the effect of spreading the construction costs of a segment evenly over the period. In the third step the cost per mile in 1968 prices was applied to miles in each year to obtain a first approximation of annual Interstate highway construction costs in 1968 prices. In the fourth step the highway construction price index was applied to the first approximations of the real highway cost in each year, and the total for all years was obtained.

By applying a price index the real highway cost was converted into an estimate of current dollar cost. The current dollar cost estimates for each year were adjusted proportionally to make them sum to the actual current dollar cost as given in data file number 1. In the last step the construction price index was reapplied to obtain a time series in constant 1969 prices.

In order to estimate the cost of construction of future highway systems, the cost per mile of the Interstate highway system is used. It is being assumed that the highway quality of new systems will be the same as the Interstate system. These data are shown in Table 3-4 for urban and rural highways by route within each state. When links in hypothetical future highway systems were coded, the cost per mile of the closest appropriate Interstate

[a]*Price Trends for Federal-Aid Highway Construction*, Federal Highway Administration, U.S. Department of Transportation, First Quarter 1971.

TABLE 3.4
ESTIMATED RURAL AND URBAN COST PER MILE BY STATE AND ROUTE UNDER THE INTERSTATE SYSTEM
(COST IN 1969 DOLLARS)

STATE	ROUTE	URBAN			RURAL		
		MILES	COST	COST/MILE	MILES	COST	COST/MILE
ALABAMA	010	11.06	113652841.	10272710.	56.75	77641023.	1368099.
ALABAMA	020	9.44	26443043.	2800993.	77.54	77834322.	1003772.
ALABAMA	059	36.60	134344768.	3670168.	212.46	211667370.	996264.
ALABAMA	065	50.50	86384643.	1710703.	324.96	405605280.	1248165.
ALABAMA	085	15.73	18788412.	1194687.	66.86	52544653.	785933.
ALABAMA	359	2.30	7661319.	3331008.	.00	0.	0.
ALABAMA	459	11.90	0.	0.	20.93	85563425.	4087967.
ALABAMA	565	12.98	23214000.	1788367.	6.85	25708383.	3753049.
ALABAMA	759	3.00	10443255.	3481085.	1.50	2894702.	1929801.
ARIZONA	008	3.19	10164794.	3187844.	180.17	85132330.	472503.
ARIZONA	010	38.35	171922346.	4483054.	364.26	224808216.	617161.
ARIZONA	015	.00	0.	0.	30.15	53013447.	1758485.
ARIZONA	017	19.14	27549962.	1439601.	117.54	117139861.	996594.
ARIZONA	019	6.05	7038062.	1163967.	58.06	45480229.	783363.
ARIZONA	040	2.11	3270213.	1549660.	363.47	282315656.	776715.
ARIZONA	710	3.20	11420936.	3564710.	.00	0.	0.
ARKANSAS	030	16.37	47377387.	2893325.	130.23	118646920.	911082.
ARKANSAS	040	24.83	55289188.	2227026.	268.82	276255208.	841652.
ARKANSAS	055	5.81	10303004.	1774171.	66.12	58969275.	891894.
ARKANSAS	430	6.32	19383340.	3065637.	6.78	31908236.	4708738.
ARKANSAS	540	8.40	14196939.	1690819.	.00	0.	0.
ARKANSAS	630	6.37	0.	0.	.00	0.	0.
CALIFORNIA	005	143.16	603738576.	4217324.	666.29	822418208.	1234330.
CALIFORNIA	008	20.66	71823593.	3476018.	156.90	173454156.	1105481.
CALIFORNIA	010	80.49	301949340.	3751430.	163.53	157033268.	960275.
CALIFORNIA	015	23.92	160117692.	6692485.	223.39	344569648.	1542473.
CALIFORNIA	040	1.44	975710.	678100.	158.38	103451725.	653169.
CALIFORNIA	080	46.87	203072190.	4332874.	143.77	251711168.	1750792.
CALIFORNIA	105	10.20	208398256.	20431201.	.00	0.	0.
CALIFORNIA	205	.00	0.	0.	13.31	17426050.	1309459.
CALIFORNIA	210	47.10	222360874.	4721293.	2.77	23981736.	8642067.
CALIFORNIA	280	44.83	242489644.	5409533.	16.04	53028649.	3306646.
CALIFORNIA	380	3.34	34756723.	10418335.	.00	0.	0.
CALIFORNIA	405	65.31	277418292.	4247777.	8.93	22563633.	2525848.
CALIFORNIA	505	.00	0.	0.	30.75	19205506.	624553.
CALIFORNIA	580	18.33	56828930.	3100297.	44.03	75428780.	1713284.
CALIFORNIA	605	28.44	107017506.	3763180.	.00	0.	0.
CALIFORNIA	680	28.61	95331746.	3331828.	34.83	77225378.	2217453.
CALIFORNIA	805	28.56	160494838.	5619161.	.00	0.	0.
CALIFORNIA	880	11.17	30549526.	2734274.	.00	0.	0.
COLORADO	025	53.22	62683518.	1177919.	254.58	131189961.	515322.
COLORADO	070	26.06	48331614.	1854412.	434.15	536613848.	1236006.
COLORADO	080S	13.96	31853539.	2281539.	175.47	69673000.	397072.
COLORADO	225	12.53	17458581.	1392899.	.00	0.	0.
COLORADO	270	5.40	8913002.	1649717.	.00	0.	0.
COLORADO	470	26.33	68124170.	2587321.	.00	0.	0.
CONNECTICUT	084	47.57	264914094.	5568566.	60.02	196496328.	3273575.
CONNECTICUT	086	16.18	123469702.	7631008.	20.43	49735425.	2434431.
CONNECTICUT	091	40.35	186272824.	4616978.	16.93	76681278.	4529570.
CONNECTICUT	095	13.19	94394848.	7154889.	39.91	67117305.	1681635.
CONNECTICUT	291	23.89	120786030.	5056336.	2.55	19261553.	7553550.
CONNECTICUT	484	1.31	18100064.	13768009.	.00	0.	0.
CONNECTICUT	684	1.43	0.	0.	.00	0.	0.
DELAWARE	095	12.48	70674031.	5661452.	.00	0.	0.
DELAWARE	295	2.65	1422095.	537259.	.00	0.	0.
DELAWARE	495	11.68	93010499.	7960199.	.00	0.	0.
FLORIDA	004	17.99	49632617.	2759497.	117.79	82181434.	697683.
FLORIDA	010	14.61	7303560.	499753.	353.62	269263480.	761451.
FLORIDA	075	30.62	78421809.	2561040.	444.02	380585512.	857138.
FLORIDA	095	90.32	233692342.	2587302.	252.95	195121538.	771393.
FLORIDA	110	6.45	13797493.	2138225.	.00	0.	0.
FLORIDA	195	4.42	20298565.	4593013.	.00	0.	0.
FLORIDA	295	18.71	34631996.	1851262.	17.04	22714309.	1332961.
FLORIDA	395	1.20	10008322.	8322929.	.00	0.	0.
GEORGIA	016	7.22	16085662.	2229186.	161.77	117309157.	725154.
GEORGIA	020	29.82	45637347.	1530506.	176.95	159682274.	902413.
GEORGIA	024	.00	0.	0.	4.21	9088906.	2160086.
GEORGIA	059	.00	0.	0.	20.55	17771711.	864635.
GEORGIA	075	44.26	125537486.	2836526.	312.48	284817496.	911464.

(Continued)

TABLE 3.4
ESTIMATED RURAL AND URBAN COST PER MILE BY STATE AND ROUTE UNDER THE INTERSTATE SYSTEM
(COST IN 1969 DOLLARS)

STATE	ROUTE	URBAN			RURAL		
		MILES	COST	COST/MILE	MILES	COST	COST/MILE
GEORGIA	085	20.67	47798508.	2312116.	152.79	128512566.	841127.
GEORGIA	095	.00	0.	0.	113.55	160472450.	1413172.
GEORGIA	185	3.57	2258702.	632788.	37.70	44167042.	1171540.
GEORGIA	285	63.36	122206212.	1928771.	.00	0.	0.
GEORGIA	475	.00	0.	0.	16.06	10789155.	671706.
GEORGIA	485	5.62	44766957.	7959749.	.00	0.	0.
IDAHO	015	9.40	6832499.	726752.	190.22	106379287.	559251.
IDAHO	015W	1.96	1949071.	993068.	61.27	30752263.	501936.
IDAHO	080N	8.82	11915387.	1351539.	275.11	128542556.	467242.
IDAHO	090	5.21	8380816.	1609679.	68.26	104275780.	1527649.
IDAHO	180	1.74	311234.	178614.	1.94	0.	0.
ILLINOIS	024	.00	0.	0.	38.65	78822234.	2039341.
ILLINOIS	055	27.04	221607408.	8194337.	182.38	404384636.	2217261.
ILLINOIS	057	22.45	103952826.	4629466.	342.20	381938768.	1116142.
ILLINOIS	064	11.10	38959957.	3510785.	113.13	144460704.	1276927.
ILLINOIS	070	11.23	101730839.	9056365.	153.76	205258212.	1334947.
ILLINOIS	072	.00	121787.	0.	74.34	126735908.	1704925.
ILLINOIS	074	29.89	92968130.	3110630.	190.95	197309796.	1033290.
ILLINOIS	080	12.01	28285579.	2354598.	151.86	178618686.	1176185.
ILLINOIS	090	12.81	139013362.	10848413.	14.88	17487604.	1175067.
ILLINOIS	094	45.94	387705864.	8439447.	1.14	2072868.	1816977.
ILLINOIS	180	.00	0.	0.	14.00	46252658.	3304790.
ILLINOIS	255	8.49	36779744.	4332125.	10.86	43205148.	3978375.
ILLINOIS	270	3.80	340553.	89523.	11.64	43137177.	3706297.
ILLINOIS	280	7.94	12288932.	1548463.	.51	9552404.	18588462.
ILLINOIS	474	6.16	41934276.	6809355.	8.32	9909872.	1191289.
ILLINOIS	494	20.87	900327912.	43139814.	.00	0.	0.
INDIANA	064	2.69	7685527.	2860086.	123.80	179827202.	1452550.
INDIANA	065	37.42	145280516.	3882427.	232.26	256659624.	1104607.
INDIANA	069	15.54	6004591.	386284.	146.97	150160848.	1021732.
INDIANA	070	25.72	96451594.	3749891.	133.18	127438740.	956880.
INDIANA	074	6.47	3215586.	496616.	150.27	137803374.	917066.
INDIANA	080	14.58	62206256.	4266303.	.00	0.	0.
INDIANA	094	4.46	9135801.	2048195.	26.08	49214402.	1886694.
INDIANA	164	.00	0.	0.	14.30	20481681.	1432285.
INDIANA	265	1.84	4293000.	2333152.	4.89	10993553.	2248170.
INDIANA	275	.00	0.	0.	3.31	22535149.	6811632.
INDIANA	465	44.50	97738364.	2196357.	10.26	23580433.	2297490.
IOWA	029	19.23	36674611.	1907127.	134.92	103484863.	767026.
IOWA	035	15.14	16781286.	1108468.	210.12	176786474.	841362.
IOWA	074	5.19	17519765.	3373056.	.00	0.	0.
IOWA	080	25.39	24909521.	980901.	276.58	259704078.	938984.
IOWA	080N	.00	0.	0.	17.45	18486441.	1059326.
IOWA	129	.50	13882617.	27765234.	.00	0.	0.
IOWA	235	14.44	49940619.	3459552.	.00	0.	0.
IOWA	280	5.16	17360112.	3364725.	4.69	3840808.	819518.
IOWA	380	13.14	55497766.	4223574.	59.05	47403425.	802794.
IOWA	480	.77	10477892.	13563614.	.00	0.	0.
IOWA	680	.00	0.	0.	.00	4303149.	0.
KANSAS	035	20.80	34008790.	1635322.	89.17	74264016.	832790.
KANSAS	035W	19.07	72763781.	3816143.	79.11	57157278.	722545.
KANSAS	070	13.71	42603767.	3107244.	366.45	212490914.	579864.
KANSAS	235	16.96	22105900.	1303542.	.00	0.	0.
KANSAS	435	13.63	25933817.	1903351.	15.10	59202127.	3920671.
KANSAS	470	6.89	8447242.	1226707.	.00	0.	0.
KANSAS	635	9.06	58169622.	6418225.	.00	0.	0.
KANSAS	670	.80	23614319.	29517899.	.00	0.	0.
KENTUCKY	024	4.81	9510681.	1977273.	88.58	136911592.	1545646.
KENTUCKY	064	15.96	83076030.	5204883.	182.12	239259690.	1313736.
KENTUCKY	065	8.59	44417082.	5173441.	84.06	84318027.	1003106.
KENTUCKY	071	6.82	15479870.	2268957.	74.36	89553650.	1204346.
KENTUCKY	075	13.88	39544453.	2849298.	177.72	227691776.	1281163.
KENTUCKY	264	24.68	81531028.	3303144.	.00	0.	0.
KENTUCKY	275	12.79	81508362.	6374758.	11.72	17811986.	1520226.
KENTUCKY	471	4.80	39837957.	8299575.	.00	0.	0.
LOUISIANA	010	57.72	314878984.	5455719.	223.76	467364672.	2088662.
LOUISIANA	012	6.58	9170775.	1392876.	80.17	86760894.	1082157.
LOUISIANA	020	70.03	88948071.	4439860.	174.42	166535162.	954816.
LOUISIANA	055	.00	0.	0.	67.32	106372855.	1580045.
LOUISIANA	059	.30	2255.	7567.	11.50	14583302.	1268021.
LOUISIANA	110	8.87	53792545.	6066986.	.00	0.	0

TABLE 3.4

ESTIMATED RURAL AND URBAN COST PER MILE bY STATE AND ROUTE UNDER THE INTERSTATE SYSTEM
(COST IN 1969 DOLLARS)

ATE	ROUTE	U R B A N			R U R A L		
		MILES	COST	COST/MILE	MILES	COST	COST/MILE
UISIANA	210	7.73	10094416.	1305266.	4.86	39934714.	8211388.
UISIANA	220	5.14	20306893.	3950757.	12.47	50730021.	4068165.
UISIANA	410	16.89	229853106.	13608828.	27.19	139626808.	5135226.
UISIANA	610	4.03	30719457.	7615870.	.00	0.	0.
INE	095	5.35	13152303.	2456206.	246.40	306162784.	1242555.
INE	195	.35	1585489.	4529970.	1.71	3615277.	2114197.
INE	295	8.64	61387344.	7101364.	2.31	7387744.	3191250.
INE	395	1.51	2649133.	1753425.	.00	0.	0.
RYLAND	070	.00	0.	0.	54.54	95625248.	1753426.
RYLAND	070N	14.51	108858902.	7501709.	31.66	39392909.	1244066.
RYLAND	070S	14.12	79732104.	5645750.	18.50	16545458.	894228.
RYLAND	081	.00	0.	0.	12.53	22429650.	1789832.
RYLAND	083	17.59	182847418.	10393651.	17.33	18242640.	1052882.
RYLAND	095	39.79	612993560.	15407062.	6.57	45030689.	6855000.
RYLAND	170	3.00	42564638.	14188213.	.00	0.	0.
RYLAND	270	1.85	2772403.	1498596.	.00	0.	0.
RYLAND	295	.82	819913.	997192.	.00	0.	0.
RYLAND	395	.70	11987021.	17124316.	.00	0.	0.
RYLAND	495	43.25	129214368.	2987692.	.00	0.	0.
RYLAND	695	28.35	90995944.	3209262.	.00	0.	0.
RYLAND	895	.68	0.	0.	.00	0.	0.
SSACHUSETTS	086	.00	0.	0.	6.73	11522425.	1712099.
SSACHUSETTS	090	.20	0.	0.	.00	0.	0.
SSACHUSETTS	091	32.45	123583361.	3807986.	24.39	34590279.	1418032.
SSACHUSETTS	093	14.44	116451792.	8063598.	12.87	22940331.	1782773.
SSACHUSETTS	095	46.36	552265072.	11911535.	31.56	57710318.	1828414.
SSACHUSETTS	195	9.04	48626802.	5376658.	17.50	53774861.	3073522.
SSACHUSETTS	290	13.54	69635210.	5143145.	7.06	13047980.	1848516.
SSACHUSETTS	291	4.03	18578301.	4609683.	.00	0.	0.
SSACHUSETTS	295	.72	2853451.	3938510.	3.54	7446461.	2103363.
SSACHUSETTS	391	4.88	37509958.	7683468.	.00	0.	0.
SSACHUSETTS	495	34.24	88680632.	2589772.	55.39	125794517.	2271074.
SSACHUSETTS	695	5.35	299825884.	56065511.	.00	0.	0.
SSACHUSETTS	895	4.19	14321277.	3417966.	14.07	36401978.	2587205.
CHIGAN	069	7.36	30912452.	4198401.	104.38	142539344.	1365633.
CHIGAN	075	96.91	409677920.	4227396.	292.55	328080492.	1121463.
CHIGAN	094	80.91	174749882.	2159889.	186.80	205648318.	1100875.
CHIGAN	U96	57.69	333605484.	5782838.	137.13	174324920.	1271208.
CHIGAN	194	3.56	5942958.	1669110.	.00	0.	0.
CHIGAN	196	14.86	42133896.	2835125.	64.82	64583683.	996290.
CHIGAN	275	2.40	22557702.	9399042.	27.60	78184021.	2832754.
CHIGAN	296	3.58	9475333.	2649208.	.00	0.	0.
CHIGAN	375	1.09	9929744.	9114503.	.00	0.	0.
CHIGAN	475	15.38	87506383.	5688389.	1.64	3663766.	2227966.
CHIGAN	496	9.10	40034158.	4400191.	3.05	2814521.	923771.
CHIGAN	675	4.83	25442263.	5266944.	3.10	13737504.	4425901.
CHIGAN	696	28.53	256720992.	8997231.	.00	0.	0.
NNESOTA	035	13.47	81054789.	6019294.	211.57	150548370.	711589.
NNESOTA	035E	38.74	105697325.	2728376.	.83	1960007.	2347569.
NNESOTA	035W	42.17	131832511.	3126384.	1.06	7843443.	7370368.
NNESOTA	090	5.18	9411134.	1816821.	276.02	212614324.	770281.
NNESOTA	094	34.47	210168492.	6096866.	204.81	163659938.	799075.
NNESOTA	335	2.72	29544681.	10862015.	.00	0.	0.
NNESOTA	394	10.16	39072276.	3846959.	.00	0.	0.
NNESOTA	494	41.47	100070007.	2412802.	2.33	5578397.	2389766.
NNESOTA	535	1.80	35781197.	19893793.	.00	0.	0.
NNESOTA	694	22.40	38220830.	1706288.	.00	0.	0.
SSISSIPPI	010	2.13	7802236.	3666847.	76.76	124783184.	1625604.
SSISSIPPI	020	24.04	68064229.	2831329.	108.09	93203005.	862238.
SSISSIPPI	055	27.89	75266512.	2698783.	270.03	218589122.	809509.
SSISSIPPI	059	23.20	35364284.	1524598.	152.64	120598343.	790084.
SSISSIPPI	110	3.50	31122276.	8892079.	.40	612319.	1530798.
SSISSIPPI	220	10.80	26858595.	2486907.	.00	0.	0.
SSOURI	029	23.98	44098626.	1838698.	103.39	117037298.	1132011.
SSOURI	035	14.99	43407933.	2895472.	98.07	90814152.	926050.
SSOURI	044	34.41	106305128.	3089214.	211.80	204579856.	969209.
SSOURI	U55	21.17	50865234.	2402426.	193.01	189406204.	981333.
SSOURI	057	.00	0.	0.	22.34	24319427.	1088523.
SSOURI	070	43.81	167433470.	3821881.	214.41	170133914.	793499.

(Continued)

TABLE 3.4
ESTIMATED RURAL AND URBAN COST PER MILE BY STATE AND ROUTE UNDER THE INTERSTATE SYSTEM
(COST IN 1969 DOLLARS)

STATE	ROUTE	URBAN			RURAL		
		MILES	COST	COST/MILE	MILES	COST	COST/MILE
MISSOURI	155	.00	0.	0.	10.61	23583479.	2222527.
MISSOURI	229	6.03	31900362.	5290010.	8.65	9344915.	1080905.
MISSOURI	244	21.05	30623276.	1454907.	.00	0.	0.
MISSOURI	255	3.83	7105383.	1855595.	.00	0.	0.
MISSOURI	270	15.98	13450922.	841764.	.00	0.	0.
MISSOURI	435	40.65	94581843.	2326555.	10.50	30217894.	2877895.
MISSOURI	470	9.55	25175465.	2635539.	7.07	11521274.	1628751.
MISSOURI	635	3.71	13128432.	3542905.	.00	0.	0.
MISSOURI	670	.60	10570681.	17617801.	.00	0.	0.
MONTANA	015	9.22	18548034.	2010848.	394.99	275559368.	697638.
MONTANA	U90	16.12	15980611.	991352.	531.92	416830164.	783634.
MONTANA	094	3.53	698840.	197772.	251.50	146092668.	580877.
MONTANA	115	.00	0.	0.	1.43	56033.	39222.
MONTANA	315	.85	299355.	354005.	.00	0.	0.
NEBRASKA	080	14.22	26566098.	1867637.	451.34	241481622.	535035.
NEBRASKA	080S	.00	0.	0.	2.14	846010.	394889.
NEBRASKA	129	.70	2790957.	3987082.	2.37	7734617.	3263551.
NEBRASKA	180	2.96	4231619.	1429601.	.72	5993157.	8330257.
NEBRASKA	480	3.91	44116138.	11278373.	.00	0.	0.
NEBRASKA	680	6.67	5341932.	801027.	6.28	21915584.	3490277.
NEVADA	015	11.33	31999812.	2823454.	117.21	56459779.	481701.
NEVADA	080	8.59	28261371.	3290393.	412.75	240261494.	562103.
NEW HAMPSHIRE	089	5.08	6870588.	1352584.	58.85	80702168.	1371295.
NEW HAMPSHIRE	093	18.13	18604946.	1026323.	106.56	225182012.	2113138.
NEW HAMPSHIRE	095	3.02	33777853.	11178551.	1.48	5708509.	3849154.
NEW HAMPSHIRE	193	5.55	2732212.	492290.	.00	305596.	0.
NEW JERSEY	U76	5.07	39381029.	7764058.	.00	0.	0.
NEW JERSEY	078	19.51	199336732.	10219485.	36.25	101720818.	2806417.
NEW JERSEY	080	35.93	225461024.	6275202.	31.38	120366761.	3835183.
NEW JERSEY	095	20.33	129094339.	6350290.	22.90	68927063.	3009915.
NEW JERSEY	195	5.70	25014872.	4388574.	1.30	46245318.	35573322.
NEW JERSEY	278	1.15	8268760.	7192373.	.00	0.	0.
NEW JERSEY	280	16.63	166085670.	9988447.	.00	0.	0.
NEW JERSEY	287	44.37	201276910.	4536132.	18.95	62062536.	3274442.
NEW JERSEY	295	34.79	156951068.	4511169.	32.76	87968169.	2684877.
NEW JERSEY	495	.65	21887872.	33673650.	.00	0.	0.
NEW JERSEY	895	2.40	30706170.	12794238.	1.70	7114404.	4184944.
NEW MEXICO	010	9.37	16091160.	1718027.	160.55	81600587.	508248.
NEW MEXICO	025	29.45	42020979.	1426657.	436.90	298618800.	683496.
NEW MEXICO	040	28.25	53500356.	1894078.	352.53	258262458.	732599.
NEW YORK	078	2.40	258595600.	107748167.	.00	0.	0.
NEW YORK	081	43.26	143709396.	3322341.	144.36	196316694.	1359941.
NEW YORK	084	10.38	27133707.	2615150.	61.42	181441056.	2954103.
NEW YORK	087	38.16	167423344.	4387756.	150.33	240744190.	1601405.
NEW YORK	088	14.63	70404298.	4811810.	106.16	372902360.	3512717.
NEW YORK	090	23.32	90044546.	3860500.	6.42	9952544.	1550241.
NEW YORK	095	19.68	284831544.	14471339.	.00	0.	0.
NEW YORK	190	22.36	101761871.	4551916.	.00	0.	0.
NEW YORK	278	28.60	305500208.	10681146.	.00	0.	0.
NEW YORK	287	11.36	63852941.	5622370.	.00	0.	0.
NEW YORK	290	10.09	37811331.	3746375.	.00	0.	0.
NEW YORK	295	12.78	176677192.	13826911.	.00	0.	0.
NEW YORK	478	1.10	17755834.	16141668.	.00	0.	0.
NEW YORK	481	9.71	43902042.	4523134.	.00	0.	0.
NEW YORK	490	17.10	95531049.	5585795.	17.39	25798566.	1483553.
NEW YORK	495	6.52	141287934.	21667160.	.00	0.	0.
NEW YORK	587	1.44	3478496.	2417488.	.00	0.	0.
NEW YORK	678	2.45	56542010.	23104567.	.00	0.	0.
NEW YORK	684	17.12	3111213.	181702.	10.26	17565553.	1712042.
NEW YORK	687	3.60	11313808.	3142725.	.00	0.	0.
NEW YORK	690	13.02	69303537.	5321305.	.00	0.	0.
NEW YORK	695	7.70	232863958.	30242072.	.00	0.	0.
NEW YORK	787	10.34	182360958.	17629654.	.00	0.	0.
NEW YORK	790	1.08	9021.	8359.	.00	0.	0.
NEW YORK	878	15.66	415847868.	26551873.	.00	0.	0.
NEW YORK	890	8.28	47216483.	5699134.	.00	0.	0.
NEW YORK	895	1.18	209745.	177457.	.00	0.	0.
NORTH CAROLINA	026	.00	0.	0.	41.33	42860938.	1037131.
NORTH CAROLINA	040	36.77	62558598.	1701309.	247.41	297622716.	1202961.
NORTH CAROLINA	077	10.28	36482066.	3549607.	90.94	92829167.	1020745.
NORTH CAROLINA	085	42.89	42618917.	993586.	189.86	208812566.	1099811.

TABLE 3.4
ESTIMATED RURAL AND URBAN COST PER MILE BY STATE AND ROUTE UNDER THE INTERSTATE SYSTEM
(COST IN 1969 DOLLARS)

TATE	ROUTE	URBAN			RURAL		
		MILES	COST	COST/MILE	MILES	COST	COST/MILE
ORTH CAROLINA	095	4.11	929792.	226166.	180.68	133875182.	740937.
ORTH DAKOTA	029	.00	0.	0.	221.42	155007672.	700070.
ORTH DAKOTA	094	9.17	9971797.	1087701.	354.63	187001444.	527320.
ORTH DAKOTA	194	.00	0.	0.	1.22	2922165.	2389233.
HIO	070	44.43	160858956.	3620211.	194.63	242910000.	1248088.
HIO	071	56.01	291366688.	5201903.	195.68	236599840.	1209125.
HIO	074	6.23	26801202.	4304825.	13.73	21511692.	1566213.
HIO	075	70.94	240797944.	3394204.	142.60	191884276.	1345626.
HIO	077	40.44	156204546.	3862178.	124.20	170920630.	1376207.
HIO	080	14.26	19530045.	1369974.	4.29	30661672.	7144938.
HIO	080S	13.96	23848387.	1707760.	43.31	42617502.	983907.
HIO	090	59.37	204142254.	3438691.	44.42	93048282.	2094712.
HIO	270	33.48	87009618.	2598687.	23.17	66716959.	2879201.
HIO	271	20.39	24986502.	1225252.	16.56	42856718.	2588372.
HIO	275	23.10	41718949.	1805988.	29.88	73319772.	2454099.
HIO	277	3.72	12026567.	3231812.	.00	0.	0.
HIO	280	5.05	11422064.	2262542.	.87	7467967.	8597596.
HIO	290	10.94	87018453.	7955165.	.00	0.	0.
HIO	470	.16	3261191.	20382447.	6.24	16744617.	2683432.
HIO	471	.54	18887170.	34832895.	.00	0.	0.
HIO	475	13.57	39757597.	2928846.	7.05	17831244.	2530052.
HIO	480	40.07	153859000.	3639410.	3.35	206362.	61590.
HIO	675	13.64	51227319.	3755669.	12.31	24287532.	1972992.
HIO	680	14.55	44159967.	3034632.	2.29	2489872.	1087280.
KLAHOMA	035	38.50	59355392.	1541771.	199.99	154686347.	773464.
KLAHOMA	040	57.30	60947957.	1063626.	281.13	213276632.	758634.
KLAHOMA	044	14.69	34344620.	2337959.	3.92	3172513.	810061.
KLAHOMA	240	17.20	32876449.	1911483.	.00	0.	0.
KLAHOMA	244	16.09	69264199.	4304951.	.00	0.	0.
KLAHOMA	440	8.71	39487691.	4531292.	.00	0.	0.
KLAHOMA	444	2.54	20248504.	7970109.	.00	0.	0.
REGON	005	42.02	146553226.	3487814.	268.04	310874412.	1159792.
REGON	080N	24.31	167837972.	6904939.	326.99	338254836.	1034438.
REGON	082	.00	0.	0.	14.80	40662276.	2747451.
REGON	105	3.61	11520483.	3192400.	.00	0.	0.
REGON	205	19.45	155742478.	8006068.	2.99	299957.	100292.
REGON	305	3.30	20234723.	6131734.	.00	0.	0.
REGON	405	3.47	121918110.	35138994.	.00	0.	0.
REGON	505	1.44	11446822.	7949217.	.00	0.	0.
ENNSYLVANIA	070	6.54	11301542.	1728946.	77.85	104090708.	1337116.
ENNSYLVANIA	076	35.56	89016604.	2503279.	.00	0.	0.
ENNSYLVANIA	078	4.49	41683288.	9281860.	51.80	158577046.	3061187.
ENNSYLVANIA	079	9.38	186184398.	19854884.	174.42	289991976.	1662570.
ENNSYLVANIA	080	4.89	11991607.	2453399.	316.36	464205784.	1467357.
ENNSYLVANIA	081	33.28	84722285.	2546087.	208.05	315271080.	1515374.
ENNSYLVANIA	081E	2.53	12628380.	4984887.	26.29	30921680.	1176110.
ENNSYLVANIA	083	18.45	48029201.	2602786.	33.01	48492860.	1468901.
ENNSYLVANIA	084	.00	0.	0.	50.89	87991266.	1729133.
ENNSYLVANIA	090	.00	0.	0.	47.62	67868805.	1425308.
ENNSYLVANIA	095	48.53	494473244.	10189370.	4.93	10221300.	2074535.
ENNSYLVANIA	176	.00	0.	0.	11.58	14252568.	1230467.
ENNSYLVANIA	279	7.81	0.	0.	5.10	45237191.	8870037.
ENNSYLVANIA	283	2.38	4493809.	1888702.	.79	0.	0.
ENNSYLVANIA	476	21.38	159717168.	7470886.	.00	0.	0.
ENNSYLVANIA	479	.00	65006191.	0.	.00	0.	0.
ENNSYLVANIA	676	3.96	32214047.	8141142.	.00	0.	0.
ENNSYLVANIA	695	7.80	99360340.	12738505.	.00	0.	0.
ENNSYLVANIA	876	.91	0.	0.	.00	0.	0.
ENNSYLVANIA	895	2.10	34147787.	16260851.	.00	0.	0.
HODE ISLAND	084	3.77	14198362.	3766144.	13.52	16245064.	1201558.
HODE ISLAND	095	24.35	94013109.	3860204.	15.89	34135944.	2148185.
HODE ISLAND	195	4.25	32313958.	7609750.	.00	0.	0.
HODE ISLAND	295	23.90	72886935.	3049207.	.00	0.	0.
HODE ISLAND	895	12.28	103456000.	8424375.	.00	0.	0.
OUTH CAROLINA	020	19.76	0.	0.	126.40	104736902.	828605.
OUTH CAROLINA	026	28.55	38655354.	1354054.	198.44	138376558.	697310.
OUTH CAROLINA	077	3.88	0.	0.	70.89	74776234.	1054771.
OUTH CAROLINA	085	15.67	2072638.	132237.	93.53	80645095.	862258.
OUTH CAROLINA	095	.00	0.	0.	203.42	175532530.	862897.

(Continued)

TABLE 3.4
ESTIMATED RURAL AND URBAN COST PER MILE BY STATE AND ROUTE UNDER THE INTERSTATE SYSTEM
(COST IN 1969 DOLLARS)

STATE	ROUTE	URBAN			RURAL		
		MILES	COST	COST/MILE	MILES	COST	COST/MILE
SOUTH CAROLINA	126	3.86	1481989.	383494.	.00	363106.	0.
SOUTH CAROLINA	185	3.08	2628091.	852354.	.00	0.	0.
SOUTH CAROLINA	385	6.38	4409599.	690889.	.00	0.	0.
SOUTH CAROLINA	585	2.31	0.	0.	.00	868298.	0.
SOUTH DAKOTA	029	4.23	178475.	42148.	252.05	175150874.	694903.
SOUTH DAKOTA	090	.00	0.	0.	417.05	309386472.	741852.
SOUTH DAKOTA	190	.89	1703301.	1904903.	.76	858586.	1128893.
SOUTH DAKOTA	229	8.04	11242548.	1398810.	3.92	1989572.	508084.
TENNESSEE	024	16.95	36250483.	2139233.	162.08	159919450.	986649.
TENNESSEE	040	45.32	153001154.	3375591.	428.37	373404400.	871689.
TENNESSEE	055	12.53	30578436.	2440504.	.00	0.	0.
TENNESSEE	065	23.15	46622517.	2014055.	101.61	80536592.	792609.
TENNESSEE	075	13.66	23382876.	1711557.	130.82	162433908.	1241661.
TENNESSEE	081	.00	0.	0.	76.63	73490393.	959053.
TENNESSEE	124	1.95	8307680.	4254288.	.00	0.	0.
TENNESSEE	155	.00	0.	0.	15.37	29723123.	1933211.
TENNESSEE	240	26.07	62864868.	2411439.	.00	0.	0.
TENNESSEE	255	5.54	19713215.	3557583.	.00	0.	0.
TENNESSEE	265	2.92	10633916.	3644037.	.00	0.	0.
TENNESSEE	440	7.50	17703127.	2360417.	.00	0.	0.
TENNESSEE	640	10.82	12012648.	1110346.	.00	0.	0.
TEXAS	010	101.82	218432270.	2145330.	784.98	516191464.	657584.
TEXAS	020	104.55	177877980.	1701447.	511.15	331465348.	648473.
TEXAS	027	13.61	11616021.	853492.	98.49	91983192.	933934.
TEXAS	030	26.97	19559128.	725251.	143.93	110293508.	766309.
TEXAS	035	90.51	149827408.	1655350.	314.90	194398258.	617342.
TEXAS	035E	43.20	85529595.	1979737.	57.10	57213781.	1002027.
TEXAS	035W	15.10	51909383.	3438381.	62.76	40822185.	650413.
TEXAS	037	26.70	62584101.	2343999.	118.52	75157186.	634155.
TEXAS	040	9.67	21752817.	2249501.	164.10	97842648.	596238.
TEXAS	045	99.04	175526116.	1772305.	193.13	196742906.	1018714.
TEXAS	110	.96	21781067.	22749051.	.00	0.	0.
TEXAS	345	1.29	30827219.	23804803.	.00	0.	0.
TEXAS	410	40.35	38095061.	944088.	.00	0.	0.
TEXAS	610	39.04	196232824.	5026827.	.00	0.	0.
TEXAS	635	41.34	102280609.	2474329.	.00	0.	0.
TEXAS	820	48.73	101597613.	2084940.	.00	0.	0.
UTAH	015	51.98	128820758.	2478235.	354.93	271868352.	765974.
UTAH	070	.00	0.	0.	230.61	163121860.	707338.
UTAH	080	11.81	33969740.	2877279.	189.47	140665106.	742410.
UTAH	080N	3.07	3404789.	1108149.	84.28	61330204.	727710.
UTAH	215	22.44	59546478.	2653432.	6.97	14408045.	2066051.
VERMONT	089	5.94	15313729.	2577828.	128.85	176015006.	1366074.
VERMONT	091	7.23	25184535.	3484824.	174.74	258998238.	1482173.
VERMONT	093	.00	0.	0.	11.00	16631851.	1511986.
VERMONT	189	1.41	223277.	158571.	.00	0.	0.
VIRGINIA	064	55.72	235230246.	4221652.	212.88	329239616.	1546600.
VIRGINIA	066	6.97	57179965.	8202745.	69.40	94736435.	1365078.
VIRGINIA	077	.00	0.	0.	58.51	175093644.	2992485.
VIRGINIA	081	1.03	73298.	71317.	334.10	381162136.	1140866.
VIRGINIA	085	.00	0.	0.	65.58	63491013.	968196.
VIRGINIA	095	8.95	87639959.	9795214.	144.96	174825842.	1206019.
VIRGINIA	195	3.34	36517000.	10919611.	.00	0.	0.
VIRGINIA	264	11.75	47776795.	4064806.	.00	0.	0.
VIRGINIA	266	.60	9610745.	15958802.	.00	0.	0.
VIRGINIA	295	.00	0.	0.	36.90	115357319.	3126215.
VIRGINIA	381	.10	207023.	2014273.	1.23	1205252.	977231.
VIRGINIA	464	5.73	30839111.	5384607.	.00	0.	0.
VIRGINIA	495	1.34	12438050.	9309144.	21.27	57027967.	2680516.
VIRGINIA	564	2.92	9972600.	3414606.	.00	0.	0.
VIRGINIA	581	4.02	10176640.	2531758.	2.57	3749664.	1459329.
VIRGINIA	595	1.10	0.	0.	.00	0.	0.
VIRGINIA	664	9.20	0.	0.	.00	0.	0.
WASHINGTON	005	124.88	446147460.	3572651.	118.32	254672762.	2152390.
WASHINGTON	082	8.60	11152223.	1296252.	105.71	123945014.	1172520.
WASHINGTON	090	42.11	316499820.	7515908.	261.83	262619078.	1003021.
WASHINGTON	182	11.44	43435191.	3796783.	23.76	25427596.	1070185.
WASHINGTON	205	5.06	15132064.	2990526.	5.89	43102532.	7317917.
WASHINGTON	405	28.62	72895984.	2546770.	.00	0.	0.
WEST VIRGINIA	064	28.46	148037230.	5201951.	94.61	242012752.	2557936.
WEST VIRGINIA	070	6.92	69295358.	10006879.	7.68	16168101.	2104287.

TABLE 3.4
ESTIMATED RURAL AND URBAN COST PER MILE BY STATE AND ROUTE UNDER THE INTERSTATE SYSTEM
(COST IN 1969 DOLLARS)

ATE	ROUTE	U R B A N			R U R A L		
		MILES	COST	COST/MILE	MILES	COST	COST/MILE
EST VIRGINIA	077	9.36	139058860.	14852749.	92.63	324989428.	3508513.
EST VIRGINIA	079	4.41	35625021.	8078236.	159.26	428117952.	2688147.
EST VIRGINIA	081	.00	0.	0.	26.91	34670360.	1288339.
EST VIRGINIA	470	3.92	65760595.	16775662.	.00	0.	0.
ISCONSIN	057	26.80	37150744.	1386222.	83.70	70753872.	845327.
ISCONSIN	090	2.96	4382926.	1480696.	190.36	137892286.	724373.
ISCONSIN	094	31.83	129863542.	4080412.	234.11	195158996.	833624.
ISCONSIN	535	1.25	10910684.	8701476.	.00	0.	0.
ISCONSIN	794	3.82	75618169.	19789087.	.00	0.	0.
ISCONSIN	894	10.52	25948791.	2467636.	.00	0.	0.
YOMING	025	8.21	16202880.	1974523.	300.55	192925950.	641914.
YOMING	080	7.67	9047947.	1180262.	408.61	243133906.	595024.
YOMING	090	.00	0.	0.	211.77	166569408.	786548.
YOMING	180	1.11	13005298.	11716484.	.00	0.	0.
AWAII	001	19.50	321058276.	16466991.	8.76	20520032.	2341883.
AWAII	002	1.03	0.	0.	7.57	31786468.	4196233.
AWAII	003	4.00	31407574.	7851894.	12.40	148910620.	12008383.
ISTRICT OF COLUMBIA	066	3.51	209409878.	59660935.	.00	0.	0.
ISTRICT OF COLUMBIA	070S	2.30	35852808.	15588177.	.00	0.	0.
ISTRICT OF COLUMBIA	095	8.46	372899324.	44098207.	.00	0.	0.
ISTRICT OF COLUMBIA	266	1.65	95096102.	57479176.	.00	0.	0.
ISTRICT OF COLUMBIA	295	10.72	180818370.	16865837.	.00	0.	0.
ISTRICT OF COLUMBIA	495	.12	0.	0.	.00	0.	0.
ISTRICT OF COLUMBIA	695	3.12	81390561.	26076259.	.00	0.	0.

highway link was applied. Since these costs were in constant prices, they are assumed to be applicable to future highway systems.

By coding highway links into OBE economic areas, estimates of highway construction expenditures were made under the Interstate system and each of the three future alternative systems. These data are shown in Table 3-5. When they were entered into the forecasting model, it was necessary to specify the timing of these expenditures; that is, the total expenditures under each alternative had to be allocated to each of the years in which the system is to be constructed. In order to allocate the construction expenditures under the Interstate system between 1971 and 1976, it was assumed that the total expenditures would be spent evenly through the period.

The objective of the Extended Primary system is to serve cities that are not being served by the Interstate system. The highway links in this system are planned to extend the Interstate system to other cities in order of size. Since most of the larger cities in the United States will be served by the Interstate system, the links in the Extended Primary system would serve the middle-sized cities. In order to determine the timing of these expenditures between 1976 and 1986, it was assumed that some expenditures would take place in each of the years, but the timing of the bulk of the expenditures would vary according to the population density of the area.

The economic areas were classified into five groups according to their population density. The bulk of the construction expenditures in Group 1 (highest density) were assumed to occur near the beginning of the ten-year period, whereas the bulk of the expenditures in Group 5 were assumed to take

TABLE 3.5
EXOGENOUS HIGHWAY CONSTRUCTION COSTS BY OBE ECONOMIC AREA
UNDER ALTERNATIVE HIGHWAY SYSTEMS
(THOUSANDS OF DOLLARS)

AREA	COMPLETED INTERSTATE (1971-'76)	EXTENDED PRIMARY (1977-'86)	ECONOMIC DEVELOPMENT (1977-'86)	URBAN (1977-'86)
1 BANGOR. MAINE	60129.6	251400.0	.0	.0
2 PORTLAND. MAINE	102798.0	227900.0	139200.0	.0
3 BURLINGTON. VT.	274722.7	189200.0	496500.0	.0
4 BOSTON. MASS.	1313195.1	1740200.0	75600.0	1445300.0
5 HARTFORD. CONN.	661636.0	673900.0	.0	.0
6 ALB.-SCHEN.-TROY. N. Y.	295048.6	454600.0	48000.0	.0
7 SYRACUSE. N. Y.	95934.8	319900.0	.0	.0
8 ROCHESTER. N. Y.	27235.0	117000.0	147300.0	.0
9 BUFFALO. N. Y.	13416.0	907500.0	153600.0	.0
10 ERIE. PA.	63722.4	.0	.0	69500.0
11 WILLIAMSPORT. PA.	9008.3	413760.0	36000.0	.0
12 BINGHAMTON. N. Y. - PA.	274698.9	331400.0	374800.0	.0
13 WIL-BARRE-HAZLE. PA.	74623.0	195500.0	138500.0	.0
14 NEW YORK. N. Y.	1639649.4	546600.0	118800.0	13902199.5
15 PHILA.. PA. - N. J.	1330118.6	619500.0	.0	2323099.9
16 HARRISBURG. PA.	132336.	536200.0	159000.0	.0
17 BALTIMORE. MD.	673419.7	887700.0	1892800.0	297200.0
18 WASH.. D. C. - MD. - VA.	965485.6	102600.0	124400.0	2187199.9
19 STAUNTON. VA.	65555.0	.0	269100.0	.0
20 ROANOKE. VA.	46201.7	270300.0	537400.0	.0
21 RICHMOND. VA.	277145.0	419000.0	161400.0	.0
22 NOR.-PORTS.. VA.	128456.4	429200.0	213100.0	121800.0
23 RALEIGH. N. C.	105004.7	197500.0	496700.0	.0
24 WILMINGTON. N. C.	.0	162200.0	172800.0	.0
25 GR-WINS SALEM-H PT. N.C.	208745.3	87100.0	41600.0	.0
26 CHARLOTTE. N. C.	154801.7	499100.0	181300.0	.0
27 ASHEVILLE. N. C.	90065.3	30500.0	194400.0	.0
28 GREENVILE. S. C.	33485.2	115000.0	53400.0	.0
29 COLUMBIA. S. C.	66019.0	148900.0	39900.0	.0
30 FLORENCE. S. C.	24629.9	161000.0	368900.0	.0
31 CHARLESTON. S. C.	36100.9	56000.0	73300.0	.0
32 AUGUSTA. GA.	23801.1	50500.0	231400.0	.0
33 SAVANNAH. GA.	99893.6	.0	409500.0	.0
34 JACKSONVILLE. FLA.	129910.7	377700.0	301700.0	.0
35 ORLANDO. FLA.	38761.8	158600.0	90000.0	.0
36 MIAMI. FLA.	110672.1	226400.0	33800.0	471800.0
37 TAMPA-ST. PETE. FLA.	336648.7	253400.0	214600.0	.0
38 TALLAHASSEE. FLA.	133035.0	161200.0	224100.0	.0
39 PENSACOLA. FLA.	60359.3	49600.0	105500.0	.0
40 MONTGOMERY. ALA.	48311.1	601100.0	594100.0	1000.0
41 ALBANY. GA.	.0	412400.0	554200.0	.0
42 MACON. GA.	19750.2	49200.0	249600.0	.0
43 COLUMBUS. GA.-ALA.	96395.2	102000.0	201900.0	.0
44 ATLANTA. GA.	265055.8	467300.0	202900.0	103200.0
45 BIRMINGHAM. ALA.	188179.4	218300.0	610400.0	52600.0
46 MEMPHIS. TENN.-ARK.	126008.6	507400.0	425600.0	28800.0
47 HUNTSVILLE. ALA	48922.4	219700.0	286300.0	13400.0
48 CHATTANOOGA. TENN.-GA.	231673.0	25800.0	106300.0	.0
49 NASHVILLE. TENN.	190780.0	325400.0	231700.0	.0
50 KNOXVILLE. TENN.	85747.2	310100.0	478900.0	.0
51 BRISTOL. VA.-TENN.	101466.0	131800.0	135500.0	.0
52 HUNT-ASH. W.VA.-KY.-OHIO	592196.3	421800.0	356200.0	.0
53 LEXINGTON. KY.	40061.2	262700.0	558300.0	.0
54 LOUISVILLE. KY.-IND.	138691.0	.0	33400.0	129500.0
55 EVANSVILLE. IND.-KY.	122509.5	262900.0	281700.0	.0
56 TERRE HAUTE. IND.	16895.3	40400.0	76800.0	.0
57 SPRINGFIELD. ILL.	168785.8	225000.0	143200.0	.0
58 CHAMPAIGN-URBANA. ILL.	63899.1	.0	.0	.0
59 LAFAY-W. LAFAY. IND.	21220.7	101900.0	26600.0	.0
60 INDIANAPOLIS. IND.	167194.2	374900.0	58600.0	.0
61 MUNCIE. IND.	14364.8	71100.0	.0	.0
62 CIN.. OHIO-KY.-IND.	370564.9	167500.0	331200.0	391200.0
63 DAYTON. OHIO	98283.3	.0	.0	48400.0
64 COLUMBUS. OHIO	152915.1	419200.0	518400.0	51700.0
65 CLARKSBURG. W. VA.	202191.8	328800.0	593900.0	.0
66 PITTSBURGH. PA.	418295.2	1222500.0	27000.0	.0
67 YOUNGSTOWN-WARREN. OHIO	42689.1	.0	.0	.0
68 CLEVELAND. OHIO	392091.2	158900.0	.0	929300.0
69 LIMA. OHIO	4770.8	94400.0	128400.0	.0
70 TOLEDO. OHIO	194187.4	317000.0	.0	.0

TABLE 3.5
EXOGENOUS HIGHWAY CONSTRUCTION COSTS BY OBE ECONOMIC AREA
UNDER ALTERNATIVE HIGHWAY SYSTEMS
(THOUSANDS OF DOLLARS)

AREA	COMPLETED INTERSTATE (1971-'76)	EXTENDED PRIMARY (1977-'86)	ECONOMIC DEVELOPMENT (1977-'86)	URBAN (1977-'86)
71 DETROIT, MICH.	717771.0	.0	.0	3066399.9
72 SAGINAW, MICH.	63699.1	227100.0	157900.0	.0
73 GRAND RAPIDS, MICH.	55549.4	332100.0	112300.0	.0
74 LANSING, MICH.	163320.8	251700.0	.0	.0
75 FORT WAYNE, IND.	3548.3	117800.0	12700.0	.0
76 SOUTH BEND, IND.	14009.6	93200.0	3900.0	.0
77 CHICAGO, ILL.	1043659.7	602500.0	60200.0	6051999.8
78 PEORIA, ILL.	140242.8	47700.0	.0	.0
79 DAV-R IS-MOL, IOWA-ILL.	47619.3	154700.0	15000.0	.0
80 CEDAR RAPIDS, IOWA	65993.5	60700.0	.0	.0
81 DUBUQUE, IOWA	.0	517000.0	453000.0	.0
82 ROCKFORD, ILL.	5671.1	439800.0	159600.0	.0
83 MADISON, WIS.	20355.3	152600.0	139400.0	25800.0
84 MILWAUKEE, WIS.	186295.5	212200.0	20800.0	.0
85 GREEN BAY, WIS.	.0	467000.0	232500.0	.0
86 WAUSAU, WIS.	.0	192600.0	128500.0	.0
87 DULUTH-SUP, MINN.-WIS.	15142.2	427800.0	370000.0	.0
88 EAU CLAIRE, WIS.	8879.9	140500.0	235800.0	.0
89 LA CROSSE, WIS.	32242.1	30000.0	101300.0	.0
90 ROCHESTER, MINN.	23742.9	.0	51400.0	.0
91 MINN.-ST. PAUL, MINN.	417374.0	882600.0	555300.0	.0
92 GRAND FORKS, N. D.	26427.5	276000.0	141600.0	.0
93 MINOT, N. D.	.0	257600.0	275000.0	.0
94 GREAT FALLS, MONT.	109277.0	502500.0	403400.0	.0
95 BILLINGS, MONT.	173291.9	437200.0	255200.0	.0
96 BISMARCK, N. D.	3657.0	71900.0	117800.0	.0
97 FAR-MOOR, N. D.-MINN.	89926.9	22000.0	174300.0	.0
98 ABERDEEN, S. D.	69981.6	113300.0	187800.0	.0
99 SIOUX FALLS, S. D.	49715.4	208800.0	101600.0	.0
100 RAPID CITY, S. D.	105042.3	180400.0	185200.0	.0
101 SCOTTSBLUFF, NEBR.	33540.5	188500.0	.0	.0
102 GRAND ISLAND, NEBR.	4935.5	187500.0	.0	.0
103 SIOUX CITY, IOWA-NEBR.	29758.5	247800.0	99400.0	.0
104 FORT DODGE, IOWA	7432.2	71200.0	26400.0	.0
105 WATERLOO, IOWA	101427.3	120000.0	72700.0	.0
106 DES MOINES, IOWA	21200.1	259500.0	188700.0	.0
107 OMAHA, NEBR.-IOWA	66230.0	267100.0	.0	.0
108 LINCOLN, NEBR.	4848.0	145000.0	34190.0	.0
109 SALINA, KANS.	50751.3	29200.0	78000.0	.0
110 WICHITA, KANS.	41122.7	472400.0	224500.0	.0
111 KANSAS CITY, MO.-KANS.	502227.7	540800.0	323400.0	.0
112 COLUMBIA, MO.	9300.9	197200.0	349500.0	.0
113 QUINCY, ILL.	.0	412500.0	171900.0	.0
114 ST. LOUIS, MO.-ILL.	471816.6	272200.0	.0	381300.0
115 PADUCAH, KY.	212476.5	375800.0	432400.0	.0
116 SPRINGFIELD, MO.	37686.7	424500.0	592100.0	.0
117 L ROCK-N I ROCK, ARK.	65388.9	362200.0	250200.0	.0
118 FORT SMITH, ARK.-OKLA.	24797.0	94600.0	121800.0	.0
119 TULSA, OKLA.	62302.3	201400.0	209900.0	.0
120 OKLAHOMA CITY, OKLA.	147293.4	218800.0	55400.0	29700.0
121 WICHITA FALLS, TEX.	967.5	226600.0	226000.0	.0
122 AMARILLO, TEX.	170096.8	252500.0	279900.0	.0
123 LUBBOCK, TEX.	34564.6	42300.0	173600.0	.0
124 ODESSA, TEX.	134619.8	117900.0	170900.0	.0
125 ABILENE, TEX.	20471.4	87800.0	139700.0	.0
126 SAN ANGELO, TEX.	51493.4	133800.0	432100.0	.0
127 DALLAS, TEX.	300997.5	217600.0	120500.0	.0
128 WACO, TEX.	79570.7	30500.0	207300.0	.0
129 AUSTIN, TEX.	7264.2	73200.0	251300.0	.0
130 TYLER, TEX.	10144.7	175800.0	372800.0	.0
131 TEXARKANA, TEX.-ARK.	55648.1	173200.0	138600.0	.0
132 SHREVEPORT, LA.	98094.4	159400.0	295300.0	.0
133 MONROE, LA.	40586.3	191400.0	533400.0	.0
134 GREENVILLE, MISS.	4716.1	567000.0	545800.0	.0
135 JACKSON, MISS.	51312.7	28600.0	236800.0	.0
136 MERIDIAN, MISS.	75625.6	222500.0	388000.0	.0
137 MOBILE, ALA.	200033.4	131400.0	344100.0	.0
138 NEW ORLEANS, LA.	741740.1	414800.0	305300.0	260900.0

(Continued)

TABLE 3.5
EXOGENOUS HIGHWAY CONSTRUCTION COSTS BY OBE ECONOMIC AREA
UNDER ALTERNATIVE HIGHWAY SYSTEMS
(THOUSANDS OF DOLLARS)

AREA	COMPLETED INTERSTATE (1971-'76)	EXTENDED PRIMARY (1977-'86)	ECONOMIC DEVELOPMENT (1977-'86)	URBAN (1977-'86)
139 LAKE CHARLES, LA.	57517.2	296600.0	473600.0	.0
140 BEAU-P ART-ORANGE, TEX.	.0	.0	25200.0	.0
141 HOUSTON, TEX.	94665.4	201000.0	40800.0	54500.0
142 SAN ANTONIO, TEX.	149990.5	468000.0	742900.0	.0
143 CORPUS CHRISTI, TEX.	68516.8	198200.0	119500.0	.0
144 BROWN-HARL-S BENITO, TEX	.0	149600.0	329900.0	.0
145 EL PASO, TEX.	92157.1	393800.0	490200.0	.0
146 ALBUQUERQUE, N. M.	176160.3	225400.0	231700.0	.0
147 PUEBLO, COL.	38729.1	271300.0	204000.0	.0
148 DENVER, COL.	258125.6	96500.0	37800.0	.0
149 GRAND JUNCTION, COL.	177737.1	830000.0	377000.0	.0
150 CHEYENNE, WYO.	180483.8	330400.0	266800.0	.0
151 SALT LAKE CITY, UTAH	382112.8	446700.0	151100.0	7200.0
152 IDAHO FALLS, IDAHO	49753.6	118800.0	69900.0	.0
153 BUTTE, MONT.	138122.5	101800.0	127500.0	.0
154 SPOKANE, WASH.	265726.9	478100.0	30100.0	.0
155 SEATTLE-EVERETT, WASH.	274504.6	871600.0	.0	.0
156 YAKIMA, WASH.	371326.0	30600.0	150400.0	.0
157 PORTLAND, ORE.-WASH.	449319.6	453600.0	189000.0	.0
158 EUGENE, ORE.	56909.0	441100.0	137100.0	.0
159 BOISE CITY, IDAHO	35304.0	.0	245200.0	.0
160 RENO, NEV.	124038.0	492600.0	47400.0	.0
161 LAS VEGAS, NEV.	65664.1	368200.0	.0	.0
162 PHOENIX, ARIZ.	444589.9	689000.0	274000.0	.0
163 TUCSON, ARIZONA	25384.7	312900.0	64200.0	.0
164 SAN DIEGO, CALIF.	326710.7	.0	.0	.0
165 L. A.-LONG BEACH, CALIF.	853745.3	411600.0	.0	2483599.9
166 FRESNO, CALIF.	109449.1	304200.0	.0	.0
167 STOCKTON, CALIF.	93145.2	100800.0	.0	.0
168 SACRAMENTO, CALIF.	107415.3	341100.0	.0	.0
169 REDDING, CALIF.	31733.3	111000.0	.0	.0
170 EUREKA, CALIF.	.0	270000.0	.0	.0
171 S FRAN-OAKLAND, CALIF.	282049.4	873600.0	.0	1075100.0
172 ANCHORAGE, ALASKA	.0	.0	.0	.0
173 HONOLULU, HAWAII	414619.0	.0	.0	160500.0
U.S. TOTAL	28621177.5	46589366.5	33398000.0	36164193.0

place near the end of the ten-year period. The table below shows what fraction of the total expenditures were assigned to the years within each of the five groups of areas.

Year			Groups		
	1	2	3	4	5
1977	4/33	1/33	1/32	1/31	1/33
1978	7/33	3/33	1/32	1/31	1/33
1979	8/33	7/33	2/32	1/31	1/33
1980	5/33	8/33	5/32	1/31	1/33
1981	3/33	6/33	7/32	3/31	2/33
1982	2/33	3/33	7/32	6/31	3/33
1983	1/33	2/33	5/32	8/31	5/33
1984	1/33	1/33	2/32	6/31	8/33
1985	1/33	1/33	1/32	3/31	7/33
1986	1/33	1/33	1/32	1/31	4/33

The Economic Development highway system is designed to serve areas with low income; therefore, the timing of the construction expenditures between the years 1977 and 1986 depends on the ranking of the areas according to their per capita income. The economic areas were classified into six groups, and it was assumed that the construction period within any area would last for a five-year period. Each of the six groups was assigned a different starting date for their highway system. Group 1, which has the lowest per capita income, was assigned a construction period from 1977 to 1981; Group 2 was given the construction period 1978 to 1982; and so on. The annual distribution of the expenditures over the five-year period within each area as assumed to be the same. The first and fifth construction year received 1/16 of the expenditures, the second and fourth construction years received 4/16 of the expenditures, and the third construction year received 6/16 of the construction expenditures.

The construction expenditures under the Urban highway system were allocated to the economic areas according to the amount of congestion as measured by FHWA's congestion index. The areas receiving money under this alternative were classified into eight groups. Since most of the money goes to Group 1, which has the greatest amount of congestion, some of the money was assumed to be spent in each of the ten years of the 1977-1986 period. The construction period in each of the other seven groups was assumed to be shorter, with the construction period of the eighth group reduced to three years. The following table shows the annual distribution of the highway expenditures for each of the eight groups.

Year	Groups 1	2	3	4	5	6	7	8
1977	1/44	–	–	–	–	–	–	–
1978	3/44	1/47	1/36	–	–	–	–	–
1979	5/44	4/47	4/36	1/29	1/26	–	–	–
1980	6/44	6/47	6/36	4/29	5/26	1/19	1/8	–
1981	7/44	8/47	7/36	6/29	7/26	5/19	3/8	1/4
1982	7/44	9/47	7/36	7/29	7/26	7/19	3/8	2/4
1983	6/44	8/47	6/36	6/29	5/26	5/19	1/8	1/4
1984	5/44	6/47	4/36	4/29	1/26	1/19	–	–
1985	3/44	4/47	1/36	1/29	–	–	–	–
1986	1/44	1/47	–	–	–	–	–	–

CONGESTION WITHIN A REGION

Transportation networks are made up of nodes and connectors. The connectors are the highways, railways, waterways, and airways that link activity centers together, while nodes are the centers of economic activity and intersections of the connectors. Improvement in the network may change not only the relative

attractiveness of various economic centers to industry, it may also affect the mobility (or congestion) within an activity center. The level of congestion within a center can affect the efficiency of trade among industries as well as pickup and delivery of less-than-vehicle-load shipments within the center. Thus an index of congestion within a region is needed to help explain industry location.

A 1968 congestion index (CGS) for 250 urbanized areas was computed with data furnished by FHWA. The index is vehicle miles traveled (VMT) divided by capacity miles of service (CMS). Vehicle miles traveled is the daily vehicle miles traveled on arterial highways (DAVMT) adjusted by a peak-hour factor (PHF). The capacity miles of service is the freeway miles (FM) times the hourly freeway capacity (HFC) plus the surface arterial miles (SM) times the hourly surface arterial highway capacity (HSC). The formula is:

$$CGS = \frac{VMT}{CMS} = \frac{DAVMT \cdot PHF}{FM \cdot HFC + SM \cdot HSC}$$

With the data furnished by FHWA it was possible to compute this index for most urbanized areas. The urbanized area index was used to allocate construction expenditures under the Urban system alternative, as previously shown in Table 3-3. But in order to use the congestion index to help explain industry location, it is necessary to recompute it for OBE economic areas.

Each of the urbanized areas was assigned to an OBE economic area. In the economic areas that contain more than one urbanized area, the vehicle miles traveled and the capacity miles of service were aggregated to obtain an average congestion index for the economic area.

There were some economic areas that did not contain an urbanized area as reported by FHWA. In these cases, the vehicle miles traveled and the capacity miles of service were estimated by using a regression equation, which expressed them as a function of the population. Since the areas without data were small populated areas, the observations in the regression were limited to areas with less than 750,000 population. The formulas are as follows.

VMT $= -21.5 + .00027\,POP$ $(R^2 = .39)$

CMS $= 35.0 + .00076\,POP$ $(R^2 = .23)$

Table 3-6 shows the congestion index computed for each of the OBE economic areas.

TABLE 3.6
CONGESTION INDEX, VEHICLE MILES TRAVELED AND CAPACITY
MILES IN SERVICE IN URBANIZED AREAS BY OBE ECONOMIC AREA

OBE NO.	OBE NAME	POPULATION (000)	VMT	CMS	CONGESTION INDEX VMT/CMS
1	BANGOR, MAINE	323	37	177	.21
2	PORTLAND, MAINE	719	99	388	.26
3	BURLINGTON, VT.	467	30	111	.27
4	BOSTON, MASS.	5993	3892	8870	.44
5	HARTFORD, CONN.	2812	978	2969	.33
6	ALB.-SCHEN.-TROY, N. Y.	1316	224	901	.25
7	SYRACUSE, N. Y.	1431	213	752	.28
8	ROCHESTER, N. Y.	948	390	1112	.35
9	BUFFALO, N. Y.	1767	477	1208	.39
10	ERIE, PA.	451	96	194	.50
11	WILLIAMSPORT, PA.	414	88•	431•	.20
12	BINGHAMTON, N. Y. - PA.	766	122	426	.29
13	WIL-BARRE-HAZLE, PA.	680	253	1102	.23
14	NEW YORK, N. Y.	17921	13432	23040	.58
15	PHILA., PA. - N. J.	7075	3968	7276	.55
16	HARRISBURG, PA.	1650	439	1342	.33
17	BALTIMORE, MD.	2558	1325	2279	.58
18	WASH., D. C. - MD. - VA.	2822	2225	4057	.55
19	STAUNTON, VA.	392	85•	420•	.20
20	ROANOKE, VA.	827	171	581	.29
21	RICHMOND, VA.	986	345	871	.40
22	NOR.-PORTS., VA.	1174	729	1723	.42
23	RALEIGH, N. C.	1606	229	881	.26
24	WILMINGTON, N. C.	479	30	109	.28
25	GR-WINS SALEM-H PT, N.C.	1114	280	1286	.22
26	CHARLOTTE, N. C.	1434	346	1204	.29
27	ASHEVILLE, N. C.	389	54	175	.31
28	GREENVILLE, S. C.	795	200	740	.27
29	COLUMBIA, S. C.	603	198	917	.22
30	FLORENCE, S. C.	425	93•	452•	.21
31	CHARLESTON, S. C.	435	140	355	.39
32	AUGUSTA, GA.	473	81	314	.26
33	SAVANNAH, GA.	418	72	269	.27
34	JACKSONVILLE, FLA.	986	298	977	.30
35	ORLANDO, FLA.	853	270	910	.30
36	MIAMI, FLA.	2014	1860	3653	.51
37	TAMPA-ST. PETE, FLA.	1525	728	2088	.35
38	TALLAHASSEE, FLA.	324	33	132	.25
39	PENSACOLA, FLA.	352	101	353	.29
40	MONTGOMERY, ALA.	707	96	218	.44
41	ALBANY, GA.	468	31	158	.20
42	MACON, GA.	505	60	297	.20
43	COLUMBUS, GA.-ALA.	515	88	266	.33
44	ATLANTA, GA.	2113	1485	3139	.47
45	BIRMINGHAM, ALA.	1749	510	1212	.42
46	MEMPHIS, TENN.-ARK.	1741	489	1065	.46
47	HUNTSVILLE, ALA	682	186	365	.51
48	CHATTANOOGA, TENN.-GA.	694	204	740	.28
49	NASHVILLE, TENN.	1397	285	815	.35
50	KNOXVILLE, TENN.	916	144	454	.32
51	BRISTOL, VA.-TENN.	783	42	115	.36
52	HUNT-ASH, W.VA.-KY.-OHIO	1384	232	1258	.18
53	LEXINGTON, KY.	760	91	274	.33
54	LOUISVILLE, KY.-IND.	1168	696	1405	.50
55	EVANSVILLE, IND.-KY.	755	75	242	.31
56	TERRE HAUTE, IND.	246	37	178	.21
57	SPRINGFIELD, ILL.	492	117	394	.30
58	CHAMPAIGN-URBANA, ILL.	377	79	248	.32
59	LAFAY-W. LAFAY, IND.	240	28	127	.22
60	INDIANAPOLIS, IND.	1515	812	1933	.42
61	MUNCIE, IND.	536	85	301	.28
62	CIN., OHIO-KY.-IND.	1839	1138	2009	.57
63	DAYTON, OHIO	1107	668	1521	.44
64	COLUMBUS, OHIO	1695	752	1749	.43
65	CLARKSBURG, W. VA.	334	69•	359•	.19
66	PITTSBURGH, PA.	3699	1684	4209	.40
67	YOUNGSTOWN-WARREN, OHIO	757	311	1210	.26
68	CLEVELAND, OHIO	4160	2905	5990	.48

(Continued)

TABLE 3.6
CONGESTION INDEX, VEHICLE MILES TRAVELED AND CAPACITY
MILES IN SERVICE IN URBANIZED AREAS BY OBE ECONOMIC AREA

OBE NO.	OBE NAME	POPULATION (000)	VMT	CMS	CONGESTION INDEX VMT/CMS
69	LIMA, OHIO	271	31	147	.21
70	TOLEDO, OHIO	1016	329	1108	.30
71	DETROIT, MICH.	4988	4779	8413	.57
72	SAGINAW, MICH.	752	165	529	.31
73	GRAND RAPIDS, MICH.	1053	353	1447	.24
74	LANSING, MICH.	977	387	1412	.27
75	FORT WAYNE, IND.	566	137	914	.33
76	SOUTH BEND, IND.	725	208	716	.29
77	CHICAGO, ILL.	7878	6166	8088	.76
78	PEORIA, ILL.	602	162	506	.32
79	DAV-R IS-MOL, IOWA-ILL.	594	132*	600*	.22
80	CEDAR RAPIDS, IOWA	308	89	417	.21
81	DUBUQUE, IOWA	296	25	129	.19
82	ROCKFORD, ILL.	545	114	452	.25
83	MADISON, WIS.	421	134	258	.52
84	MILWAUKEE, WIS.	1954	1172	3022	.39
85	GREEN BAY, WIS.	881	156	621	.25
86	WAUSAU, WIS.	334	70*	365*	.19
87	DULUTH-SUP, MINN.-WIS.	434	85	412	.21
88	EAU CLAIRE, WIS.	202	33*	221*	.15
89	LA CROSSE, WIS.	261	36	124	.29
90	ROCHESTER, MINN.	235	27	191	.14
91	MINN.-ST. PAUL, MINN.	2704	1671	5074	.33
92	GRAND FORKS, N. D.	238	40*	249*	.16
93	MINOT, N. D.	194	30*	209*	.14
94	GREAT FALLS, MONT.	236	31	137	.23
95	BILLINGS, MONT.	240	35	160	.22
96	BISMARCK, N. D.	145	20*	171*	.12
97	FAR-MOOR, N. D.-MINN.	338	34	177	.19
98	ABERDEEN, S. D.	136	15*	153*	.10
99	SIOUX FALLS, S. D.	365	41	231	.18
100	RAPID CITY, S. D.	239	44*	263*	.17
101	SCOTTSBLUFF, NEBR.	107	9*	132*	.07
102	GRAND ISLAND, NEBR.	320	67*	353*	.19
103	SIOUX CITY, IOWA-NEBR.	461	58	335	.17
104	FORT DODGE, IOWA	269	51*	292*	.18
105	WATERLOO, IOWA	425	67	315	.21
106	DES MOINES, IOWA	753	193	918	.21
107	OMAHA, NEBR.-IOWA	761	267	936	.29
108	LINCOLN, NEBR.	312	73	325	.23
109	SALINA, KANS.	372	80*	401*	.20
110	WICHITA, KANS.	750	214	1061	.20
111	KANSAS CITY, MO.-KANS.	2200	1216	3379	.36
112	COLUMBIA, MO.	386	31	156	.20
113	QUINCY, ILL.	296	60*	324*	.18
114	ST. LOUIS, MO.-ILL.	3159	1857	3457	.54
115	PADUCAH, KY.	575	138*	624*	.22
116	SPRINGFIELD, MO.	822	93	376	.25
117	L ROCK-N L ROCK, ARK.	862	198	723	.27
118	FORT SMITH, ARK.-OKLA.	283	53	277	.19
119	TULSA, OKLA.	953	367	1034	.35
120	OKLAHOMA CITY, OKLA.	1120	669	1501	.45
121	WICHITA FALLS, TEX.	470	103	450	.23
122	AMARILLO, TEX.	485	109*	512*	.21
123	LUBBOCK, TEX.	375	110	458	.24
124	ODESSA, TEX.	337	61	268	.23
125	ABILENE, TEX.	290	64	431	.15
126	SAN ANGELO, TEX.	138	32	133	.24
127	DALLAS, TEX.	2399	2170	7175	.30
128	WACO, TEX.	408	94	382	.25
129	AUSTIN, TEX.	505	159	800	.20
130	TYLER, TEX.	548	82	332	.25
131	TEXARKANA, TEX.-ARK.	334	42	186	.23
132	SHREVEPORT, LA.	454	141	364	.39
133	MONROE, LA.	553	53	226	.23
134	GREENVILLE, MISS.	569	133*	604*	.22
135	JACKSON, MISS.	527	137	518	.26

TABLE 3.6
CONGESTION INDEX, VEHICLE MILES TRAVELED AND CAPACITY
MILES IN SERVICE IN URBANIZED AREAS BY OBE ECONOMIC AREA

OBE NO.	OBE NAME	POPULATION (000)	VMT	CMS	CONGESTION INDEX VMT/CMS
136	MERIDIAN, MISS.	419	89•	437•	.20
137	MOBILE, ALA.	729	341	1011	.34
138	NEW ORLEANS, LA.	2128	744	1637	.45
139	LAKE CHARLES, LA.	737	40	206	.19
140	BEAU-P ART-ORANGE, TEX.	393	224	1010	.22
141	HOUSTON, TEX.	2118	1729	4156	.42
142	SAN ANTONIO, TEX.	1215	614	2080	.30
143	CORPUS CHRISTI, TEX.	530	160	833	.19
144	BROWN-HARL-S BENITO, TEX	395	82	550	.15
145	EL PASO, TEX.	687	186	502	.37
146	ALBUQUERQUE, N. M.	545	197	632	.31
147	PUEBLO, COL.	458	155	903	.17
148	DENVER, COL.	1334	855	2884	.30
149	GRAND JUNCTION, COL.	235	46•	271•	.17
150	CHEYENNE, WYO.	219	39•	247•	.16
151	SALT LAKE CITY, UTAH	1013	380	925	.41
152	IDAHO FALLS, IDAHO	303	61•	328•	.19
153	BUTTE, MONT.	231	39•	244•	.16
154	SPOKANE, WASH.	644	179	687	.26
155	SEATTLE-EVERETT, WASH.	2059	1747	4337	.40
156	YAKIMA, WASH.	405	35	142	.25
157	PORTLAND, ORE.-WASH.	1507	749	2399	.31
158	EUGENE, ORE.	524	76	301	.25
159	BOISE CITY, IDAHO	254	49	136	.36
160	RENO, NEV.	189	50	174	.29
161	LAS VEGAS, NEV.	275	124	449	.28
162	PHOENIX, ARIZ.	1190	629	1638	.38
163	TUCSON, ARIZONA	413	211	1005	.21
164	SAN DIEGO, CALIF.	1188	997	2344	.43
165	L. A.-LONG BEACH, CALIF.	9816	9147	16734	.55
166	FRESNO, CALIF.	1042	212	901	.24
167	STOCKTON, CALIF.	628	84	233	.36
168	SACRAMENTO, CALIF.	1056	616	1435	.43
169	REDDING, CALIF.	181	26•	196•	.13
170	EUREKA, CALIF.	126	14•	148•	.09
171	S FRAN-OAKLAND, CALIF.	4766	3989	6496	.61
172	ANCHORAGE, ALASKA	265	52	167	.31
173	HONOLULU, HAWAII	727	261	522	.50

• ESTIMATED WITH REGRESSION EQUATION.

Chapter Four

Transport Costs

The equation for explaining industry location uses marginal transportation costs as independent variables. These costs are a composite of truck and rail costs; and as new highway systems are constructed, the truck costs change. The changes improve the competitive position of some areas relative to other areas.

The first part of this chapter discusses the theory behind the transport variables that are used in the forecasting model. The second part describes the procedure for estimating the data that are used to compute the transport variables.[a] The third part describes how the National Highway Network Model (TRANSNET) is used to compute the savings in truck costs associated with the new highway systems.

MARGINAL TRANSPORT COSTS

The theory supporting Equation 2.4 is related to the Ricardian theory of rents. This theory assumes that firms produce and supply markets at different levels of constant cost. The supply curve of a market is a stepped function, as illustrated in Figure 4-1, with the firms ranked by their costs from the least to the highest.

Given the market demand curve, both the price and the identity of the producing firms are determined. The price is such that the costs of the marginal firm are just covered. Since costs of other firms in the industry are lower, they receive rents. The vertical distance between the price line and the supply curve is the per unit rent received by each firm. If the demand curve were to shift outward, then additional firms would start up production and the existing firms would receive higher rents. If the demand curve were to shift downward, the marginal firms would shut down and the remaining firms would receive lower rents.

[a]Material in these first two parts is equivalent to material in *The Urban Economies, op. cit.,* pp. 33–37, and 64–67.

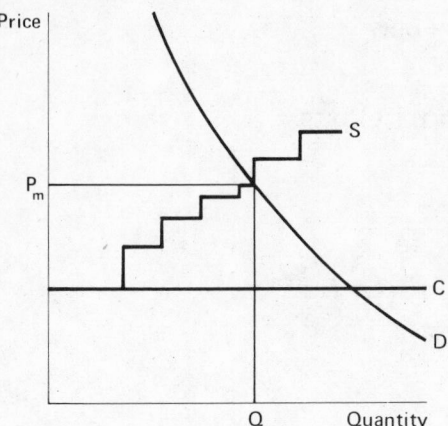

Figure 4-1.   Market Equilibrium with One Market.

It is assumed that the difference in the production costs of these firms is due to the location of the firms and that production has a tendency to decrease in poor locations and increase in good locations. The firms at the poor locations see that other firms are receiving higher rents; therefore, they always have an incentive to move to better locations. Or, firms in good locations expand their production, forcing firms in poorer locations out of business.

Any cost item could vary by location. Suppose all costs were the same at each location except for the wage rate. In this case, the vertical distance between the supply curve and the line C would be the wage premium per unit of output that some firms have to pay above the firm paying the lowest wage rate. Firms paying the higher wage rates would have incentive to move to locations where the wage rate was lower. Thus, the regional wage rate is used as a variable in Equation 2.4 to help explain the change in regional output. The same reasoning can be applied to other cost items.

Other things being equal, firms paying higher prices for inputs will have a tendency to move to locations where the prices are lower. The handling of transport costs requires further explanation.

If all costs were equal at all locations except for the cost of transporting the product to the market, then Figure 4-1 could be used to illustrate the transportation cost of each supplier shipping to the market. There is an additional complication, however, since most firms sell their products in more than one market at different locations. In the case of many markets, which transportation cost should be used in explaining the output change of the industry? Fortunately, transportation variables can be derived that are equivalent in concept to the one market situation by using linear programming. Using the transportation algorithm, it is necessary to know the supply and demand at each location and the transport rates of shipping a commodity between the locations. Table 4-1 illustrates this problem, assuming three markets and three supplying firms located in different regions. It is assumed that the firms act as competitors.

The solution to the linear programming transportation algorithm produces marginal transport costs (shadow prices). The three markets of the example are illustrated in Figure 4-2. Market 4 is supplied by firms S_2 and S_3. Supplier S_3 is the marginal supplier, therefore establishes the market price at $3. In this illustration the $3 is the marginal transportation cost. Since it is being assumed that all other costs are constant, the x axis has been moved upwards to this constant cost line. Supplier S_2 receives a rent of $2 supplying market 4, while the marginal supplier S_3 receives zero rent. Supplier S_3 also supplies market 5 and the rent received there is also zero. Supplier S_1, on the other hand, supplies two markets, 5 and 6, and receives a rent of $1 in each market.

As illustrated in Table 4-1, there are two sets of shadow prices. One set is the transport costs of shipping marginal units of the commodity out of each of the supplying firms (TQ_i) and the other set is the transportation costs of obtaining marginal units of the commodity into each of the markets (TI_j). The shadow prices in the illustration have been set so that the most poorly located supplying firm has a shadow price TQ of zero and the other supplying

Table 4-1. Equilibrium Commodity Flows, Rents, and Shadow Prices

		Markets			Supply S_i	Rent RT_i	Shadow Price TQ_i
		D_4	D_5	D_6			
S u p p l i e r s	S_1	0 $3	2 $4	1 $3	3	$1	$-1
	S_2	4 $1	0 $5	0 $6	4	$2	$-2
	S_3	3 $3	2 $5	0 $8	5	$0	$0
Demand D_j		7	4	1			
Shadow Price TI_j		$3	$5	$4			

X_{ij} ← Commodity flow from supplier i to market j

T_{ij} Unit transport cost from supplier i to market j

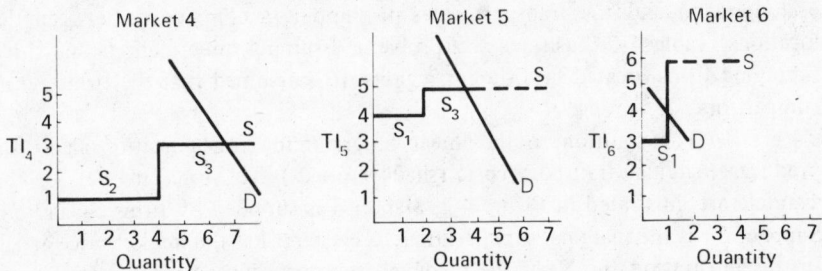

Figure 4-2. Market Equilibrium in Three Markets.

firms have negative shadow prices. The market shadow prices are then computed using:

$$TI_j = T_{ij} - TQ_i \qquad (4.1)$$

which holds for all ij with positive shipments from supplier i to market j.

The rents received by each supplying firm as given by the RT_i column in Table 4-1 are identical to the supply shadow prices TQ_i except for the change in sign. The equation for the market price (above the constant cost of production) is:

$$TI_j = T_{ij} + RT_i \qquad (4.2)$$

Therefore, combining Equations 4.1 and 4.2, rent is:

$$RT_i = -TQ_i \qquad (4.3)$$

In explaining the location of the firms in an industry, the rents (or supply shadow prices as computed from the linear programming problem) are used to represent the transportation variable of shipping the final product. Firms that receive low rents will have a tendency to relocate closer to the market in order to receive higher rents. In addition, firms are also concerned about the transportation cost of obtaining the material supplies that are used as inputs. The locations of each of the firms in the above illustration are also markets for material supplies. Therefore, in order to obtain a transportation variable representing the cost of obtaining material supplies, the linear programming algorithm is solved for these material supplying industries.

For example, when trying to explain the change in output in the household furniture industry, the market shadow price of obtaining an additional unit of lumber at the furniture industry location would be one of the costs that would influence the location of the furniture industry. In Equation 2.4 the marginal transport cost of shipping an additional unit of the product out of each region, TQ, is used as an explanatory variable and up to four market transport variables of the material supplying industries, TI, are used.

Data Requirements

A linear 'programming algorithm was solved for each of the 71 commodity industries in this study in order to produce the marginal transportation costs (shadow prices). For each commodity an area-to-area matrix was set up that contained the transport costs of shipping a unit of the commodity between each pair of OBE economic areas. In addition to the unit transport costs, other data required to solve the linear programming algorithm are the total supply and total demand in each area. As the forecasts are made, the supply and demand change in each area; and as new highway systems are constructed, the unit transport costs also change.

As given in Equation 2.44, the total supply for each commodity in a particular area is the sum of the area's output and the amount that is imported from other nations through ports in the area. The total demand for each commodity in each area is estimated with the combination of actual data and the use of national technical coefficients as given in Equation 2.45. Table 4-2 illustrates the availability of area data and the use of national coefficients. The intermediate demand by industry is estimated with national input-output coefficients. The equipment and construction components of final demands by industry are estimated by applying national capital coefficients to area totals of equipment and construction by sector. The government demand by industry sector is also estimated by assuming that each area industry's distribution of government expenditures by sector is the same as the national distribution. Actual estimates were available by industry sector for personal consumer expenditures, federal defense expenditures and exports to foreign nations going through ports in the area.[b]

UNIT TRANSPORT COST

As is well known, the price level of transportation services is not determined by the competitive market, but is regulated by the Interstate Commerce Commission (ICC). The ICC approves or disapproves rates proposed by the carriers under criteria outlined by Congress.[c] The rate setting procedure for each carrier is a function of intermode competition, national aims outlined in the National Transportation Acts, and provision for an adequate rate of return for the carrier.

[b]Procedures for estimating total supply and total demand by area were described in *Locational Analysis, op. cit.*, Appendixes A and B. Procedures for estimating unit transport cost are summarized here, but were given in detail in *Locational Analysis*, Appendix C.

[c]Charles F. Phillips, Jr., *The Economics of Regulation*, Homewood, Ill.: Richard D. Irwin, 1966, pp. 441-482, reviews the historical development of transportation rate regulation in the United States.

Table 4-2.   Components of Total Demand by Industry[a]

Intermediate Demand by Industry Sector *1 2 3 4 5 6 7 8 9 10 11 12 ... 99*	*Final Demand*							*Total Demand*
	PCE *1*	*Equipment* *1 2 3 4 5 ... 69*	*Construction* *1 2 3 ... 28*	*DEF* *1*	*FG* *1 ... 7*	*SL* *1*	*Ex* *1*	
1								
2								
3								
4								
5								
6								
.								
.								
99								
Totals								

[a]Direct economic area data estimates are available for sections filled in with cross lines. Other estimates are made using national coefficients.

Explanation of final demand sectors:

PCE	Personal consumption expenditures
EQUIPMENT	Gross private equipment by 69 purchasing sectors
CONSTRUCTION	Private and public construction by 28 types
DEF	Federal defense expenditures
FG	Federal government purchases by seven functional groupings, excluding construction
SL	State and local government purchases, excluding construction
EX	Gross foreign exports

For our purposes we can ignore the political aspects of the nation's transportation policy and concentrate upon the cost incurred by the carrier in transporting a commodity between areas and the markup that the carrier can apply to this cost. This procedure will determine the rates carriers can charge their customers. Fortunately, both the costs and the markup ratios can be obtained through publications of the Bureau of Accounts of the ICC.

The rate estimating procedure for the two modes of transportation considered in the forecasting model—rail and truck—is expressed in:

$$_kC_{ij}^w = {_k}TER_i^w + {_k}LH_{ij}^w + TER_j^w \qquad (4.4)$$

where k = mode of transport, 1 for rail, 2 for truck

i = region originating shipment

j = region of destination

w = weight class of shipment

TER = terminal cost

LH = line-haul cost

$_kC_{ij}^w$ = total cost to carriers of shipping a unit bundle in weight class w between areas i and j by mode of transport k,

and

$$T_{ij} = \sum_{w=1}^{n} a^w \left[\frac{Min}{k} \left({_k}C_{ij}^w \cdot MUP_k \right) \right] \qquad (4.5)$$

where MUP_k = markup ratio of the kth mode

a^w = number of shipments in the unit shipment bundle of the wth weight class

n = number of weight classifications

T_{ij} = transportation rate of shipping a unit bundle between the ith and jth areas

Equation 4.4 is the general form for calculating the cost incurred by the kth mode for shipping a commodity between the ith and jth areas. Equation 4.5 specifies the formulation used to calculate the unit transport costs that are used as coefficients in the linear programming algorithm. Aggregation over all weight classes of the minimum value of the cost by mode for each weight class multiplied by the markup ratio times the number of shipments in each weight class yields the coefficient. Terminal costs include the expenses of pickup or delivery, platform handling, and billing and collecting, while line-haul costs consist of the expenses of the carrier while the shipment is in transit. The unit shipment bundle reflects the national distribution of shipments by weight for each commodity.

Since trucking has lower terminal cost and higher line-haul cost than rail, small shipments will normally be shipped by truck and large shipments by rail. The coefficients reflect not only the influence of distance between areas, but also the weight of shipment and competition between modes for the shipment of commodities.

Distance measurements between counties were obtained from the Bureau of Public Roads.[d] These measurements are particularly useful for the location model, since they approximate actual land transportation routes, rather than the unsophisticated straight airline distances. Distances between economic areas were measured as the distance between the central city counties of each area.

The weight class information by mode of transportation for each commodity was obtained from the 1963 *Census of Transportation.* The industrial classification scheme used in the *Census of Transportation* differs from the SIC codes, therefore a relationship between both systems was established.

Other Modes of Transport

There are five principal modes of transportation—rail, highway (common carrier and private truck), water, air, and pipeline; but transportation rates are calculated only for rail and highway traffic. Pipelines were eliminated from consideration since they are highly specialized carriers, transporting mostly petroleum products. Air transport is normally utilized when time, rather than cost, is the major constraint affecting the shipper. The time constraint usually occurs because of spoilage possibilities (flowers and fresh food) or emergency shipments (spare parts).[e]

It is not expected that industry location would be influenced by air transport rates, since only in abnormal circumstances would inputs or outputs be shipped by air. Water transportation achieves cost advantages over rail and highway only at very long distances or for large bulk items;[f] but except for petroleum products, the percentage of shipments by water is small, therefore water transport was not included in the model. Although it would have been possible to include transportation costs for these other three modes in the model, the time and effort involved would have been too great considering the

[d]Glenn E. Brokke, *Nationwide Highway Travel*, Bureau of Public Roads, (mimeo) U.S. Department of Commerce, June 9, 1966.

[e]John B. Lansing, *Transportation and Economic Policy*, New York: The Free Press, 1966, pp. 333-336.

[f]Edgar M. Hoover, *The Location of Economic Activity*, New York: McGraw-Hill, 1948.

relative unimportance of these modes compared with the rail and highway modes.

Rail Rate Calculation

The method used to calculate rail transportation rates was derived from a paper by Merrill J. Roberts,[g] who applies a markup ratio classified by commodity type to out-of-pocket costs. Out-of-pocket costs are the expenses incurred by the carrier, both terminal and line-haul, to transport a commodity from origin to destination, averaged over an extended time period, excluding allocation of capital equipment depreciation rates and overhead expenses. They are similar to total variable cost where the variation refers to many, not just one shipment. The markup ratios used by Roberts are ratios of revenue to out-of-pocket costs by commodity found in the ICC Bureau of Accounts *Distribution of Rail Revenue Contribution by Commodity Group—1960.*

The latest publication of this series is for the year 1961; however, a substitute publication, *Procedures for Developing Rail Revenue Contribution by Commodity and Territory,* is issued yearly. While not providing the ratios, it does provide the necessary statistics and outlines and method used to calculate these ratios for 1965. The data were listed by shipments within and between three major regions: Official (New England, Middle Atlantic, Eastern, and Midwest), South (east of the Mississippi River), and West.

Out-of-pocket costs, rather than fully distributed costs, were used as the base to obtain estimates of the transportation rates, because of the de facto policy of the ICC in settling rate controversies. Roberts[h] reports that in a survey of 350 ICC decisions on rate reduction controversies between March 14, 1960, and May 25, 1962, only eight of 252 that presented cost data used fully distributed cost information; the remainder used out-of-pocket cost information. Thus by not requiring fully distributed cost in its hearings, the ICC has allowed out-of-pocket costs to be the base upon which rates are formulated. Additional support for using out-of-pocket cost as a basis for approximating rail rates has been supplied in a statement by the Bureau of Accounts of the ICC:[i]

> . . . Rates based solely on the fully distributed costs . . . would not have the benefit of being guided by that prominent principle of ratemaking which involves the recognition of derived demand . . . also. . . known as differential charging, product discrimination. . . . Regardless of terminology, rates made without adherence to this principle will result in reductions on high-grade traffic and concomi-

[g]Merrill J. Roberts, "Transport Costs, Pricing, and Regulation," in *Transportation Economics*, compiled papers of a conference of the Universities-National Bureau Committee for Economic Research, New York: Columbia University Press, 1965, pp. 3-42.
[h]*Ibid.*
[i]Interstate Commerce Commission, Bureau of Accounts, *Distribution of Rail Revenue Contribution by Commodity Group*, 1960, p. 2.

tant increases on low-grade volume traffic. Historically, rates reflect continuous interplay of economic forces. . . . Therefore, the ratios of revenue to out-of-pocket costs . . . have a ratemaking significance which is not possessed by the ratios of revenue to fully distributed costs. . . .

Highway Cost Calculation

The procedure used for calculating common carrier trucking costs was derived from *Cost of Transporting Freight by Class I and Class II Motor Carriers of General Commodities for 1965*, compiled by the Interstate Commerce Commission. The out-of-pocket costs of the motor carriers plus a markup adequate to insure sufficient revenue, including a reasonable return on invested capital, are used as the rate the common carrier would charge its customers. It is assumed in this study that these charges apply to all trucking, including intrastate common carriers, and private trucking not under ICC jurisdiction.

The motor carrier cost information is divided into thirteen regions. The regional delineation is not a simple disaggregation of the country into thirteen contiguous regions, but is a hierarchy of regions, beginning with the nation (Transcontinental) and ending on an elementary level (within New England). The markup ratios that the ICC recommends be applied to out-of-pocket cost differ regionally because of regional differentials in interest rates.

The unit transport rates derived apply to all commodities, assuming average operating conditions. Actual variations in operating conditions that affect rates include circuitry of routes, density of shipment, partial pickup and delivery service, jointness of round trips, and running speed.

INTERAREA TRANSPORT COST SAVINGS

Highway construction and improvements that result in substantially lower transport costs may, over a period of time, induce change in the regional location of industry. Better highway networks reduce the line-haul costs of moving freight between regions, lower pickup and delivery costs, and reduce intraregional production costs by increasing freight and passenger mobility within a defined region.[j] While it is not common to distinguish transport cost reductions between regions from those within regions, it is useful to analyze highway improvements in this context so as to provide for assessment of the regional impact of such improvements.

Other Studies

Past attempts at evaluating benefits of improved highways are not suitable for measuring interarea transport cost savings. These studies fall into three distinct categories.

[j]Department of Research and Transport Economics, American Trucking Associations, *Highways, Trucks, and New Industry*, Washington, D.C., 1963, pp. 15-22.

1. Those treating speed advances as being measurable from the tolls being paid by toll road users.
2. Engineering studies of particular types of highway improvements.
3. Efforts to measure time savings per hour from carrier reports to the ICC.

The now famous *Highway Cost Allocation Study* exemplifies the type of study that treats speed improvements as being reflected in the willingness of individuals to pay tolls. Benefits of toll roads are a composite of driving strain.[k] This type of analysis does not provide an adequate basis for estimating savings to shippers related to improvement of segments of the highway system. Thus methodology more sensitive to specific highway betterment was needed for the study presented in this book.

Engineering studies treat micro improvements in highways in great detail, but do not make broad analyses that are useful for evaluating new highway systems. For example, the elimination of curves, improvement of road surfaces, and the reduction of grades are examined in terms of reduction in fuel costs, tire wear, engine oil consumption, maintenance, etc. But there are no generalizations made about reductions in operating costs that are associated with changing a roadway from one-lane to two-lane, or unlimited access to limited access under various topographical, weather, or traffic conditions.[l] Neither is it recognized that operating costs increase with speed. These efforts provide an excellent background for studying the enigma, but they do not provide the data for analysis of problems linking improved roads to reductions in shipping costs.

Several excellent studies conducted through the Texas Transportation Institute made giant strides toward solving the problem of transport savings.[m] Utilizing carrier data from the ICC records, benefits for major regions were measured in terms of value of time saved. Unfortunately these figures are not useful for measuring interarea transport savings when the interarea routes consist of road segments of different qualities. Moreover, the procedure would estimate the benefits from an improvement in speed from 20 to 30 miles per hour to be the same as it would for an improvement from 50 to 60 miles per hour. ICC data (presented later) clearly show that marginal cost reductions of a given increment in speed decline as speeds increase.

The data generated by most other studies do not yield straightforward estimates of the likely reduction in trucking rates associated with a given highway improvement, since there is a lack of an adequate data base on which improvements can be measured—that is, little information is available that shows vehicle costs by highway type. While the engineering indicate the reductions in fuel, rubber, and driver time associated with a given highway advancement, no data are available on trucking costs by highway type under

[k]U.S. Department of Commerce, Bureau of Public Roads, *Supplementary Report of the Highway Cost Allocation Study*, 1965.
[l]Winfrey, *Economic Analysis for Highways, op. cit.,* pp. 298-359.
[m]See footnote *v*, Chapter 1.

varying terrain and traffic conditions to use as a basis for which to subtract the appropriate cost reduction.

Estimating Truck Transport Savings

The ICC data and rate making procedures used in the study provide a clear and straightforward basis for linking motor carrier costs with speed. The rate formulas reflect realistic economic costs in major regions of the United States.

The ICC data does have limitations. Operations on high quality roads are mixed with operations on low quality roads, and no attempt is made to determine trucking costs on a highway segment-by-segment basis. In addition, actual motor carrier rates once they have been determined by ICC may not change as costs change. In this study it is assumed that reductions in highway transportation costs will be passed on to the consumer in the form of lower rates because of the high level of competition between private and for-hire motor carriers. If for-hire motor transportation costs become too high, business firms will purchase their own trucks. This can be done even by very small firms, since entry costs are at a minimum.[n]

The cost of transporting a unit bundle from the ith to the jth area as computed with Equations 4.4 and 4.5 is based on average operating conditions in the ith area, plus terminal costs at both ends. The ICC data used in these formulas reflect average conditions and do not relate operating costs to particular road types. However, the ICC data does include information on the average speed for each region and tables that show the relationship between operating costs per vehicle mile and assumed that range from 15 mph to 45 mph. These data, along with DOT's National Highway Network Model of the United States (TRANSNET), developed from a traffic assignment model, are used to adjust the line-haul costs in Equation 4.4 for changes in speed due to highway improvements.

TRANSNET uses a road network system whereby all the principal highways in the United States have been coded into links. Data are available on the type of highway, the number of miles, the speed, and the terrain characteristics of the area for each link. The model assigns a given trip between two points in the most efficient manner and computes the time of the trip in terms of minutes.

The nodes in TRANSNET were matched with the central city nodes of the OBE economic areas. Each of the highway links were classified into the

[n]See Walter Y. Oi and Arthur P. Hurter, Jr. *Economics of Private Truck Transportation*, Dubuque, Iowa: Wm. C. Brown, 1965, for a complete discussion of private motor competition with for-hire motor transport as well as with rail transportation. Empirical evidence gathered in this study indicates all size firms conduct private transportation. Competition is especially intense on the short haul. For-hire motor transportation forces competition from rail on the long haul. Thus it is believed that the above assumption is realistic.

economic areas, making it possible to compute the number of miles and the average speed for each major type of highway within each area.

Using the ICC relationship between speed and line-haul cost, the truck vehicle cost per mile was substituted for the speed data in TRANSNET. The network model was then run in order to compute the minimum truck vehicle cost path between each of the economic areas. The following paragraphs explain how the changes in average truck costs are computed.

The first step is a computation of the average cost of operating trucks from each economic area to each other economic area. The operating costs are determined by adjusting the ICC data for speed conditions and urban area penalties on a link-by-link basis. TRANSNET requires data on average speed by type of road and on the time (penalty) lost incurred by a vehicle going through or around major urban areas.

The highway links between area centers have been classified into five types of highways: (1) Limited Access—Divided Toll, (2) Limited Access—Divided Free, (3) Other Divided, (4) Principal Through Highways, and (5) Local Connectors. These highway types have been further classified into four speed categories, depending on terrain. Thus, for practical purposes, the basic highway network of the United States has been divided into twenty speed categories (sixteen if the distinction between "toll" and "free" limited access highways is dropped).

The estimates of speeds in TRANSNET are a composite of automobile and truck speeds; therefore, in order to obtain reasonably correct truck speeds the TRANSNET speeds were adjusted. First, the relative rolling speeds of motor trucks to automobiles had to be determined. A 1966 World Bank paper[o] indicates that trucks average 90 percent of auto speeds on paved roads; speeds utilized in this study were assumed to be 19.4 percent trucks and 80.6 percent autos. The following computation was made to determine the truck rolling speed:

given $\quad S \quad = .806AS + .194TS$

and $\qquad TS = .887AS$

therefore $\quad TS = .907S$

where $\quad S \quad$ = weighted speed of all vehicles

$\qquad AS$ = average auto speed

$\qquad TS$ = average truck speed

The final adjustment that was necessary to derive the average truck

[o]Jan de Weille, *Quantification of Road User Savings*, International Bank for Reconstruction and Development, Washington, D.C., 1966.

speeds was to reduce the "rolling speeds" for stops. For this purpose it was assumed that trucks are rolling 85 percent of the time they are on the road. The 85 percent figure was determined on the assumption that truck drivers make, on the average, two food and fuel stops totaling 90 minutes during a ten-hour shift. The estimates of truck speeds by speed category are given in Table 4-3.

The per mile vehicle operating costs for eight ICC regions for 1965 at operating speeds between 15 and 45 miles per hour are presented in Table 4-4. (There are thirteen ICC "Regions," but five of them are overlapping.) These data make clear the inverse relationship between speed and unit cost for the range of speeds shown.

The per mile vehicle operating costs at the assumed speeds for the various highway types of state are shown in Table 4-5. The cost figures for the assumed speeds were obtained through the use of linear interpolation of the ICC data given in Table 4-4. The figures in Table 4-5 are used in TRANSNET to compute the minimum truck vehicle cost path between each pair of areas.

In addition to improving the links in the system, highway improvements can make it easier to go from one link to another. High speed access interchange can be substituted for regular intersections; other improvements can also reduce the "friction" at intersections. TRANSNET contains a set of time penalties for intersections in urban areas in the basic highway network. The time penalties, measured in minutes, reflect the added cost of getting through or around urban areas. They are given in Table 4-6.

The time penalties used in TRANSNET were adjusted upward by

Table 4-3. Truck Speeds by Speed Category

Speed Category	Vehicle Category	Limited Access Divided Toll & Free	Other Divided	Principal Through Highways	Local Connectors
A	DOT Network	54.0	48.0	42.0	25.0
(Lowest)	Truck-Rolling	49.0	43.5	38.1	22.7
	Truck-Average	41.6	37.0	32.4	19.3
B	DOT Network	58.0	50.0	44.0	30.0
(Low)	Truck-Rolling	52.6	45.3	39.9	27.2
	Truck-Average	44.7	38.5	33.9	23.1
C	DOT Network	60.0	52.0	46.0	30.0
(Mid)	Truck-Rolling	54.4	47.2	41.7	27.2
	Truck-Average	46.2	40.1	35.4	23.1
D	DOT Network	62.0	58.0	49.0	35.0
(High)	Truck-Rolling	56.2	52.6	44.4	31.7
	Truck-Average	47.8	44.7	37.8	27.0

Computations:
   Truck-Rolling = (DOT Network Speed) × .907
   Truck-Average = (Truck Rolling) × .85

Table 4–4. Total Line Haul Cost per Vehicle Mile (1965) at Various Speeds for Eight ICC Regions

Region	Average Speed	Average Cost (¢)	Cost per Vehicle Mile at Various Speeds						
			15 mph	20 mph	25 mph	30 mph	35 mph	40 mph	45 mph
1 Central	35.4	39.992	66.145	54.799	47.992	43.453	40.212	37.781	35.890
2 Middle Atlantic	32.3	40.353	65.612	53.822	46.747	42.031	38.662	36.136	34.170
3 Middle West	39.6	37.495	67.794	55.601	48.285	43.407	39.923	37.310	35.278
4 New England Group I	25.3	43.343	58.414	49.158	43.605	39.903	37.259	35.275	33.733
5 Pacific	38.7	40.880	75.062	61.108	52.735	47.154	43.167	40.177	37.851
6 Rocky Mountain	39.1	39.107	72.248	58.806	50.741	45.364	41.523	38.643	36.403
7 Southern	37.3	33.335	57.182	47.210	41.227	37.238	34.389	32.253	30.590
8 South West	41.3	34.525	64.981	53.024	45.850	41.067	37.651	35.089	33.096

Source: *Cost of Transporting Freight by Class I and Class II Motor Common Carriers of General Commodities 1965*, ICC, Table 11 for each region.

Table 4-5.   Average Truck Speeds and Cost per Vehicle Mile by Speed Category

State	Speed Category[a]	Limited Access		Other Divided		Principal Through Highways		Local Connectors	
		ATS	CVM	ATS	CVM	ATS	CVM	ATS	CVM
Ala	C	46.2	30.19	40.1	32.22	35.4	34.21	23.1	43.50
Ariz	D	47.8	36.55	44.7	37.99	37.7	41.49	27.0	50.50
Ark	B	44.7	33.22	38.5	35.86	33.9	38.40	23.1	48.58
Cal	C	46.2	37.29	40.1	40.13	35.4	42.91	23.1	55.92
Colo	C	46.2	35.87	40.1	38.60	35.4	41.29	23.1	53.81
Colo	D	47.8	35.15	44.7	36.54	37.7	39.91	27.0	48.59
Conn	B	44.7	33.83	38.5	35.87	33.9	37.84	23.1	45.72
Del	C	46.2	33.70	40.1	36.10	35.4	38.46	23.1	49.34
Fla	B	44.7	30.69	38.5	32.89	33.9	35.02	23.1	43.50
Ga	B	44.7	30.69	38.5	32.89	33.9	35.02	23.1	43.50
Idaho	C	46.2	35.86	40.1	38.60	35.4	41.29	23.1	53.81
Ill	C	46.2	35.44	40.1	37.74	35.4	40.02	23.1	50.58
Ind	C	46.2	35.44	40.1	37.74	35.4	40.02	23.1	50.58
Iowa	C	46.2	34.79	40.1	37.27	35.4	39.71	23.1	51.07
Kan	D	47.8	34.14	44.7	35.40	37.7	38.46	27.0	46.33
Ky	A	42.5	31.72	37.1	33.54	32.4	35.87	19.3	48.61
La	B	44.7	33.22	38.5	35.86	33.9	38.40	23.1	48.57
Maine	C	46.2	33.70	40.1	35.24	35.4	37.10	23.1	45.72
Md	C	46.2	33.36	40.1	36.10	35.4	38.46	23.1	49.43
Mass	C	46.2	33.36	40.1	35.24	35.4	37.10	23.1	45.72
Mich	C	46.2	35.44	40.1	37.74	35.4	40.02	23.1	50.58
Minn	C	46.2	34.79	40.1	37.27	35.4	39.71	23.1	51.06
Miss	C	46.2	30.19	40.1	32.22	35.4	34.22	23.1	43.50
Mo	C	46.2	34.79	40.1	37.27	35.4	39.71	23.1	51.06
Mont	C	46.2	35.86	40.1	38.60	35.4	41.29	23.1	53.81
Mont	D	47.8	35.15	44.7	36.54	37.7	39.91	27.0	48.59
Neb	D	47.8	34.14	44.7	35.40	37.7	38.46	27.0	46.33
Nev	D	47.8	36.55	44.7	37.99	37.7	41.49	27.0	50.50

NH	C	46.2	33.36	40.1	35.24	35.4	37.10	23.1	45.72
NJ	C	46.2	33.70	40.1	36.10	35.4	38.46	23.1	49.44
NM	D	47.8	35.15	44.7	36.54	37.7	39.91	27.0	48.60
NY	B	44.7	34.29	38.5	36.89	33.9	39.40	23.1	49.44
NC	B	44.7	30.69	38.5	32.89	33.9	35.02	23.1	43.50
ND	D	47.8	34.14	44.7	35.40	37.7	38.46	27.0	46.33
Ohio	C	46.2	35.44	40.1	37.74	35.4	40.02	23.1	50.58
Okla	B	44.7	33.22	38.5	35.86	33.9	38.40	23.1	48.58
Ore	B	44.7	37.99	38.5	41.07	33.9	43.62	23.1	55.92
Pa	B	44.7	34.29	38.5	36.89	33.9	39.40	23.1	49.44
RI	B	44.7	33.82	38.5	35.87	33.9	37.84	23.1	45.72
SC	B	44.7	30.69	38.5	32.89	33.9	35.02	23.1	43.50
SD	D	47.8	34.14	44.7	35.40	37.7	38.46	27.0	46.33
Tenn	A	42.5	31.72	37.1	33.54	32.4	35.87	19.3	48.61
Texas	D	47.8	31.98	44.7	33.22	37.7	36.22	27.0	43.94
Utah	C	46.2	35.86	40.1	38.60	35.4	41.29	23.1	53.81
Vt	C	46.2	33.36	40.1	35.24	35.4	37.10	23.1	45.72
Va	C	46.2	30.19	40.1	32.22	35.4	34.22	23.1	43.50
Wash	B	44.7	37.99	38.5	41.07	33.9	43.62	23.1	55.92
W Va	B	44.7	34.29	38.5	36.89	33.9	39.40	23.1	49.44
Wisc	C	46.2	34.79	40.1	37.27	35.4	39.71	23.1	51.06
Wyo	D	47.8	35.15	44.7	36.54	37.7	39.91	27.0	48.59

[a]See Table 4-3.

Table 4-6.   Time and Cost Urban Area Penalties for Use in TRANSNET

Urban Area	TRANSNET Penalty	Assumed Truck Penalty	Truck Cost per Minute[a]	Truck Penalty Cost
300,000-800,000 pop.	5 min	7 min.	22.6¢	$1.58
800,000-1,500,000 pop.	7 min.	9 min.	22.6¢	2.03
Over 1,500,000 pop.	11 min.	13 min.	22.6¢	2.94
Chicago, Detroit, Los Angeles, Philadelphia	18 min.	20 min.	22.6¢	4.52
New York	22 min.	24 min.	22.6¢	5.42

[a]Computed using the 1965 median hourly truck operating cost of $13.58, obtained from ICC data.

two minutes to reflect the greater difficulty trucks have in traveling through urban areas. The time penalties were converted to dollar costs applying the cost per minute to the time penalty. The cost per minute estimate is based on 1965 ICC vehicle cost data for the Eastern Central Region of the United States. The hourly cost of $13.58 of operating the average truck in the Eastern Central Region was the median for the thirteen ICC regions. The adjusted time and cost penalty figures are also shown in Table 4-6. The numbers in the last columns are used in TRANSNET.

Using the vehicle cost data in place of the speed and time penalty data, TRANSNET was run to estimate minimum cost paths between the economic areas under four assumptions concerning the national highway system. The links in the national network were furnished by DOT for the Base Year and the Completed Interstate systems. The network was then upgraded twice to include the links of the Extended Primary and Economic Development systems, as given in Maps 3-1 and 3-2 in Chapter Three. The Urban system does not involve changes in the national network.

Reductions in the cost of operating the average truck from the ith area to the jth area over lowest cost routes for each of the three future alternative highway systems were placed on a percentage basis relative to the Base Year system. For example, if the line-haul cost of operating a truck from the ith to the jth area dropped from $1,000 under the Base Year system to $900 under the Completed Interstate system, the drop would be 10 percent. These percentage reductions were applied to the line-haul of moving a unit of each commodity, as given in Equation 4.4, in order to find the cost of moving the unit under each of the assumed future alternative highway systems. In this way, the transport rates used in the linear programming algorithm and eventually the shadow prices in the forecasting model are adjusted to reflect changes in speed due to improvements in the highway network.

Table 4-7 presents sample results from running TRANSNET. The numbers show line-haul costs between pairs of economic areas of each of the three future alternatives relative to the Base Year system.

TABLE 4.7

LINE HAUL COSTS BY THREE ALTERNATIVE HIGHWAY SYSTEMS BETWEEN SELECTED OBE ECONOMIC AREAS
RELATIVE TO THE BASE YEAR ALTERNATIVE

BASE YEAR = 1000

	NEW YORK N.Y.			WASHINGTON D.C.			COLUMBIA S.C.			GREEN BAY WIS.			ST. LOUIS MO.			FRESNO CALIF.		
	CI	FP	ED	CI	EP	ED	CI	FP	ED	CI	EP	ED	CI	EP	ED	CI	EP	ED
HOUSTON, MASS.	995	980	995	991	991	991	981	981	981	973	973	973	993	993	993	988	986	988
HARTFORD, CONN.	997	968	997	990	990	990	979	979	979	965	965	965	992	992	992	985	983	985
ALB.-SCHEN.-TROY, N.Y.	995	975	995	994	994	994	981	981	981	980	980	980	991	991	991	991	989	991
SYRACUSE, N.Y.	977	983	977	983	983	983	966	966	966	978	978	978	997	997	997	991	989	991
BUFFALO, N.Y.	1000	959	1000	1000	984	1000	962	955	962	975	973	975	995	995	995	990	988	990
NEW YORK, N.Y.	1000	1000	1000	992	992	992	976	976	976	966	963	966	992	988	992	985	981	985
PHILA.-PA.-N.J.	974	950	974	1000	1000	1000	976	976	976	978	971	978	995	995	995	977	974	977
HARRISBURG, PA.	985	963	985	1000	1000	1000	974	974	974	976	968	976	996	996	996	984	981	984
BALTIMORE, MD.	985	969	985	1001	1000	1000	974	974	974	967	966	967	997	993	997	981	974	981
WASH., D.C. - MD. - VA.	987	974	987	1000	1000	1000	971	971	971	977	978	977	997	990	997	977	974	977
RALEIGH, N.C.	984	977	984	983	983	983	953	953	953	961	958	961	970	970	970	976	973	976
CHARLOTTE, N.C.	989	979	989	984	984	984	914	914	900	976	966	976	964	960	964	975	972	975
MIAMI, FLA.	975	972	975	991	987	991	900	900	900	969	966	969	972	972	972	976	973	976
TAMPA-ST. PETE, FLA.	974	984	975	973	973	973	983	983	983	976	976	976	962	971	962	967	967	967
ATLANTA, GA.	991	984	991	994	990	994	982	974	982	978	964	978	967	967	967	963	961	963
BIRMINGHAM, ALA.	987	983	987	986	986	986	938	938	938	962	958	962	953	953	953	961	966	967
MEMPHIS, TENN.-ARK.	992	988	992	992	992	992	927	927	927	966	961	964	959	959	959	971	966	969
NASHVILLE, TENN.	990	986	990	989	989	989	957	957	941	950	938	960	954	947	947	973	969	973
HUNT.-ASH.-W.VA.-KY.-OHIO	965	946	965	957	957	957	1000	1000	1000	962	956	960	972	947	972	973	969	973
LOUISVILLE, KY.-IND.	992	983	992	974	974	974	933	933	933	971	957	952	972	972	953	976	969	973
INDIANAPOLIS, IND.	988	983	988	994	989	994	996	988	996	952	941	941	997	997	997	982	978	982
CIN.-OHIO-KY.-IND.	991	985	991	999	993	993	996	990	997	952	952	952	998	998	998	983	976	982
COLUMBUS, OHIO	989	983	989	999	992	999	956	951	951	963	950	943	995	995	995	985	982	985
PITTSBURGH, PA.	987	958	987	999	999	999	953	946	953	971	970	965	996	996	996	990	988	990
CLEVELAND, OHIO	977	963	970	999	999	999	980	971	962	965	965	953	986	986	984	990	987	990
DETROIT, MICH.	977	977	977	999	999	999	980	971	977	953	953	911	984	984	964	987	985	987
CHICAGO, ILL.	983	979	983	986	986	984	992	987	992	911	911	911	964	964	964	988	986	988
MILWAUKEE, WIS.	983	980	983	999	999	985	990	987	987	855	854	854	970	941	963	987	984	986
MINN.-ST. PAUL, MINN.	984	981	984	995	986	986	990	987	990	1000	923	918	964	941	936	997	991	997
KANSAS CITY, MO.-KANS.	979	976	979	960	960	945	961	961	961	1011	990	1002	936	936	1000	976	972	976
ST. LOUIS, MO.-ILL.	992	988	992	970	970	950	973	973	973	937	937	937	1000	1000	1000	987	982	987
DALLAS, TEX.	990	986	990	988	988	989	942	942	950	974	967	959	991	991	992	973	982	973
NEW ORLEANS, LA.	986	983	986	989	984	984	939	939	931	985	971	980	989	987	986	961	940	959
HOUSTON, TEX.	971	965	971	967	967	967	979	979	979	973	951	954	984	984	984	949	938	950
DENVER, COL.	988	986	988	977	977	977	982	982	982	994	982	989	976	976	976	952	940	952
SAN ANTONIO, TEX.	975	967	975	979	977	979	967	967	973	973	951	954	1000	1000	1000	969	962	969
SEATTLE-EVERETT, WASH.	988	971	979	979	968	979	961	961	973	973	954	970	1000	1000	976	977	969	977
PORTLAND, ORE.-WASH.	987	987	987	986	982	986	960	960	982	987	964	971	986	986	986	960	946	960
PHOENIX, ARIZ.	981	981	981	982	982	982	964	964	967	973	972	971	1000	1002	1000	999	974	999
SAN DIEGO, CALIF.	975	967	975	975	975	975	959	959	962	980	973	977	990	981	988	974	960	974
L.A.-LONG BEACH, CALIF.	988	987	988	977	975	975	959	959	956	987	967	970	988	988	980	999	960	999
S FRAN-OAKLAND, CALIF.	986	985	986	991	985	987	959	959	956	987	981	985	983	980	980	987	974	987

Chapter Five

Economic and Demographic Projections

In this chapter the major results of the study are summarized, with tables that show the highlights of the 1990 economic and demographic projections associated with the alternative highway systems. The Appendix Tables include additional detail for all the OBE economic areas.

Each OBE economic area is designed as a functional unit with an urban center serving adjacent rural counties. Growth of the overall area is likely to be neither extremely fast nor extremely slow, since it is possible to have migration from rural to urban counties within a given economic area. Some of the faster growing areas are Honolulu; Houston; Jackson, Mississippi; and Hartford. There are eight economic areas that are projected to have a decline in population by 1990; these are mostly concentrated in the midwestern area of South Dakota and Nebraska.

COMPARISON OF ALTERNATIVES

The national control totals used for these projections were the same for all of the alternative highway systems considered. When two alternatives are compared, any gains that regions show with respect to jobs, population, or income would have to be offset by losses in other regions.

The 1990 results show that 54 of 173 OBE areas will gain in population with the Completed Interstate system over and above what they would have received if work on the Interstate had been stopped in 1970. Compared with the Completed Interstate system, the Extended Primary system shows that 1990 population would be higher in 97 areas. Under the Economic Development system, 90 areas are expected to have population higher than it would be with just the Completed Interstate system, while under the Urban system, only 39 areas are expected to have higher population.

The comparison of population and economic variables among the

TABLE 5.1 POPULATION PROJECTIONS FOR 1990 BY POPULATION
SIZE GROUP UNDER FIVE ALTERNATIVE HIGHWAY SYSTEMS
POPULATION IN THOUSANDS

1970 POPULATION GROUP	BASE YEAR	COMPLETED INTERSTATE	EXTENDED PRIMARY
1 GREATER THAN 5 MILLION	81045.7	81206.4	80680.0
2 2 MILLION TO 5 MILLION	58391.9	58303.1	57842.4
3 1 MILLION TO 2 MILLION	62586.6	62694.2	62686.2
4 700,000 TO 1 MILLION	22015.3	21879.1	22097.3
5 500,000 TO 700,000	17397.7	17480.6	17784.4
6 300,000 TO 500,000	21590.2	21432.9	21669.7
7 LESS THAN 300,000	6629.4	6660.5	6896.7

TABLE 5.2 PER CAPITA INCOME PROJECTIONS FOR 1990 BY PER
CAPITA INCOME SIZE GROUP UNDER FIVE ALTERNATIVE HIGHWAY
SYSTEMS

1970 INCOME GROUP	BASE YEAR	COMPLETED INTERSTATE	EXTENDED PRIMARY
1 GREATER THAN $4,500	7885.	7849.	7819.
2 $4,000 TO $4,500	6720.	6752.	6733.
3 $3,500 TO $4,000	6147.	6139.	6123.
4 $3,000 TO $3,500	5278.	5273.	5319.
5 $2,500 TO $3,000	4502.	4501.	4599.
6 LESS THAN $2,500	3614.	3557.	3692.

various alternatives can be meaningful even though the 1990 projections themselves differ from expectations. The 1990 numbers are estimated with a given set of assumptions, but the only assumptions that change between the alternative computer runs are those pertaining to highway systems. Thus, since everything is held constant except the highway system, comparison of the results should give reasonable measures of the impacts of the alternative systems.

Table 5-1 through 5-5 show the highlights of the results. In Table 5-1 the areas were grouped by 1970 population size. Comparison of the 1990 numbers of any two alternative highway systems indicate which population size groups gain or lose population. It can be seen that the smallest areas would gain population with both the Extended Primary and Economic Development systems, relative to what they would have if these new systems are not built.

Table 5-2 gives the 1990 per capita income projections, with the areas grouped into income groups according to their 1970 per capita income. The numbers show that low income areas would benefit in terms of per capita income both by the Extended Primary and Economic Development systems over and above what they would have if these systems were not built.

Table 5-3 shows the major 1990 shifts in jobs and population that would take place as a result of a particular highway system. For example, compared to the location of the 1990 population in the Base Year system, 2.3 million people would have to locate somewhere else in 1990 if the Interstate

ECONOMIC DEVELOPMENT	URBAN	PERCENT CI/BY	EP/CI	ED/CI	U/CI
80570.5	82001.6	100.2	99.4	99.2	101.0
57667.7	58403.4	99.8	99.2	98.9	100.2
62294.9	62307.3	100.2	100.0	99.4	99.4
22184.3	21732.4	99.4	101.0	101.4	99.3
17859.9	17341.0	100.5	101.7	102.2	99.2
22089.6	21273.0	99.3	101.1	103.1	99.3
6989.7	6597.9	100.5	103.5	104.9	99.1

ECONOMIC DEVELOPMENT	URBAN	PERCENT CI/BY	EP/CI	ED/CI	U/CI
7811.	8001.	99.5	99.6	99.5	101.9
6744.	6787.	100.5	99.7	99.9	100.5
6109.	6059.	99.9	99.7	99.5	98.7
5318.	5210.	99.9	100.9	100.8	98.8
4658.	4449.	100.0	102.2	103.5	98.9
3789.	3529.	98.4	103.8	106.5	99.2

system were completed. These figures are the total of all positive shifts between an alternative and the Base Year system summed over all economic areas.[a] A greater number of people would have to reside and work in different locations under the Economic Development system than under any of the other systems. Their percentages at the right of the table express these shifts as a percent of the United States total. For example, 4.8 percent of the total 1990 construction jobs would locate in different areas under the Economic Development system than they would under the Base Year system.

Table 5-4 shows the 1990 population projections for each of the economic areas under the five alternative highway systems, with the areas ranked by their 1970 population. Comparison of these numbers show the impact of each of the alternative highway systems. For example, the 1990 population in the New York area would be the highest under the Urban system and lowest under the Extended Primary system. Compared to the Completed Interstate system, New York's 1990 population under the Urban system would be 2 percent higher.

Table 5-5 shows the 1990 per capita income projections for each economic area under the five alternative systems, with the areas ranked by their 1970 per capita income. It can be seen that the lowest income areas would have

[a]Since the U.S. totals are the same under all alternatives, the sum of the positive shifts is equal to the sum of the negative shifts.

TABLE 5.3 SUM OF 1990 INTERAREA SHIFTS FROM BASE YEAR
SYSTEM BY FOUR ALTERNATIVE HIGHWAY SYSTEMS

U.S.A.

		U.S. TOTAL	COMPLETED INTERSTATE
JOBS BY INDUSTRY		1	2
1	NATURAL RESOURCES (1-10)	2323.2	24.2
2	CONSTRUCTION (11,12)	3904.7	24.2
3	MANUFACTURING (13-74)	26829.4	570.9
4	PUBLIC UTILITIES (75-80)	5287.2	96.5
5	WHOLESALE TRADE (81)	6003.5	80.2
6	RETAIL TRADE (86,89-99)	18435.1	308.7
7	F.I.RE. (82,83)	8242.5	4.4
8	SERVICES (84,85,87,88,102)	22816.3	32.7
9	STATE & LOCAL GOVT. (101)	12525.1	121.5
10	FEDERAL GOVERNMENT (100)	3085.6	26.8
11	MILITARY (103)	1700.1	.0
TOTAL JOBS (000)		111152.7	1248.9
CIVILIAN PERSONS EMPLOYED		104925.3	1170.3
CIVILIAN LABOR FORCE		109166.3	1182.3
POPULATION (000)		269656.6	2369.3
PERSONAL INCOME (000,000)		1658774.7	21654.6

higher per capita incomes under the Extended Primary and Economic Development systems over and above what they would have under the Completed Interstate system. Completing the Interstate, however, would reduce the per capita income below what it would be under the Base Year system in these low income areas.

Completed Interstate vs. Base Year

The Interstate system was designed to facilitate intercity travel between the larger cities in the United States. However, since the highways go through or near other cities, cities of any size can benefit from the Interstate system. Each of the OBE economic areas contains a central city, and many of these cities qualify to receive links under the Interstate system. In general, the larger cities are projected to benefit by the Interstate system; however, New York and Los Angeles are notable exceptions.

Comparing 1990 projections by percent population change, the areas that gain the most population under the Completed Interstate system are Phoenix, Arizona; Burlington, Vermont; and Billings, Montana. The areas that show the greatest losses under the Completed Interstate system are Buffalo, New York; Bismark, North Dakota; and Raleigh, North Carolina. Burlington, Vermont was also a large gainer when measured by the per capita income.

Other areas having large gains in per capita income are Cheyenne, Wyoming, and Clarksburg, West Virginia. The areas that would lose the most per

EXTENDED PRIMARY 3	ECONOMIC DEVELOPMENT 4	URBAN 5	PERCENT OF U.S. TOTAL			
			2/1	3/1	4/1	5/1
41.5	48.5	35.0	1.0	1.8	2.1	1.5
68.1	188.8	42.1	.6	2.3	4.8	1.1
743.7	762.0	861.0	2.1	2.8	2.8	3.2
188.7	208.4	137.6	1.8	3.6	3.9	2.6
114.6	120.8	119.3	1.3	1.9	2.0	2.0
444.0	474.3	459.7	1.7	2.4	2.6	2.5
7.4	8.1	5.5	.1	.1	.1	.1
36.0	38.8	37.1	.1	.2	.2	.2
164.0	176.7	173.2	1.0	1.3	1.4	1.4
36.2	39.0	38.3	.9	1.2	1.3	1.2
.0	.0	.0	.0	.0	.0	.0
1786.0	1946.9	1864.9	1.1	1.6	1.8	1.7
1666.2	1815.6	1751.0	1.1	1.6	1.7	1.7
1696.0	1815.5	1717.0	1.1	1.6	1.7	1.6
3001.2	3330.5	2868.6	.9	1.1	1.2	1.1
30379.1	33176.2	31769.2	1.3	1.8	2.0	1.9

capita income because of the Completed Interstate system are Brownsville, Texas; Omaha, Nebraska; and Eureka, California. The areas with the lowest 1970 per capita income would benefit the least in terms of income gains with the Completed Interstate system. The benefits by population size group are mixed. New England and the Pacific regions would have the largest percent gain in population as a result of the Completed Interstate system.

Extended Primary vs. Completed Interstate

Many of the areas that benefit by the Completed Interstate system in 1990 are made relatively worse off by the Extended Primary system. The Extended Primary system would improve the competitive position of additional areas, thus relatively lowering the 1990 population and income in areas that already have highway systems. The Extended Primary system benefits the smaller economic areas relative to the larger areas. In terms of per capita income, the poorest areas are made better off with the Extended Primary system, and the higher income areas are made worse off. The East-South Central and the Mountain census regions are the largest gainers from the Extended Primary system. The Pacific region would have lower population with this system.

Comparing 1990 projections by percent population change, the areas that show the largest gains due to the Extended Primary system are Grand Junction, Colorado; Minot, North Dakota; and Scottsbuff, Nebraska. The areas that would lose the highest percent of the population under the Extended

TABLE 5.4

POPULATION PROJECTIONS FOR 1990 BY ORF ECONOMIC AREA
UNDER FIVE ALTERNATIVE HIGHWAY SYSTEMS
WITH AREAS RANKED BY 1970 POPULATION. *

AREA	1970	BASE YEAR	COMPLETED INTERSTATE	EXTENDED PRIMARY	ECONOMIC DEVELOPMENT	URBAN	PERCENT CI/BY	EP/CI	ED/CI	U/CI
14 NEW YORK, N. Y.	18228.3	22848.1	22673.4	22505.2	22538.9	23125.4	99.2	99.3	99.4	102.0
165 L. A.-LONG BEACH, CALIF.	10436.1	15656.1	15516.2	15358.1	15314.1	15540.2	99.1	99.0	98.7	100.2
77 CHICAGO, ILL.	8194.0	11176.1	11259.7	11190.7	11192.5	11473.9	100.7	99.4	99.4	101.9
15 PHILA., PA.- N. J.	7281.8	9459.7	9671.5	9639.1	9617.6	9774.1	102.2	99.7	99.4	101.1
4 BOSTON, MASS.	6339.0	7771.1	7883.1	7933.8	7847.1	7919.5	101.4	100.6	99.5	100.5
71 DETROIT, MICH.	5207.8	7260.4	7277.8	7260.8	7259.7	7327.7	100.2	99.8	99.8	100.8
171 S FRAN-OAKLAND, CALIF.	5090.9	6874.1	6929.7	6790.5	6802.3	6840.9	100.8	99.0	98.2	98.7
68 CLEVELAND, OHIO	4255.6	6231.6	6146.4	5960.1	6005.6	6168.4	98.6	97.0	97.7	99.0
66 PITTSBURGH, PA.	3716.2	3783.3	3778.3	3843.9	3767.1	3783.1	98.7	101.7	100.1	100.1
114 ST. LOUIS, MO.-ILL.	3248.2	3997.1	4012.1	3959.0	3941.1	4033.6	100.4	98.7	98.2	100.5
18 WASH., D. C. - MD. - VA.	3090.2	4776.6	4810.2	4734.4	4719.8	4962.6	100.7	98.4	98.4	103.2
5 HARTFORD, CONN.	2964.6	4647.6	4777.5	4747.9	4703.0	4767.7	102.8	99.4	98.4	99.8
91 MINN.-ST. PAUL, MINN.	2935.4	3819.0	3782.2	3779.0	3777.1	3762.7	99.0	99.9	99.9	99.5
127 DALLAS, TEX.	2736.5	3813.7	3777.9	3754.4	3742.1	3745.8	99.1	99.4	99.4	99.2
17 BALTIMORE, MD.	2670.2	3413.6	3469.1	3492.5	3587.3	3475.0	101.6	100.7	103.4	100.2
36 MIAMI, FLA.	2430.9	3902.2	3735.1	3671.2	3640.7	3780.2	95.7	98.3	97.5	101.2
155 SEATTLE-EVERETT, WASH.	2363.9	3633.0	3595.4	3584.8	3486.4	3570.6	99.0	99.7	97.0	99.3
141 HOUSTON, TEX.	2362.8	3974.4	3927.5	3885.5	3894.2	3909.2	99.8	98.9	98.9	99.5
44 ATLANTA, GA.	2296.7	3199.8	3194.7	3199.9	3181.7	3194.0	99.8	100.2	99.6	100.0
111 KANSAS CITY, MO.-KANS.	2249.2	3184.0	3215.4	3192.0	3180.5	3187.6	101.1	99.3	99.4	99.1
138 NEW ORLEANS, LA.	2148.6	3237.8	3337.3	3305.0	3318.1	3328.7	103.1	99.0	99.4	99.7
84 MILWAUKEE, WIS.	2066.2	2778.2	2743.5	2732.9	2732.0	2734.1	98.8	99.6	99.3	99.7
62 CIN. OHIO-KY-IND.	1889.0	2655.8	2697.2	2668.3	2701.1	2718.4	100.6	98.9	99.3	100.8
37 TAMPA-ST. PETE. FLA.	1797.8	2695.0	2710.7	2697.2	2659.2	2667.7	100.6	98.1	98.3	98.4
9 BUFFALO, N. Y.	1749.4	2319.1	2088.9	2302.0	2172.6	2070.7	96.1	110.2	101.6	99.1
64 COLUMBUS, OHIO	1765.3	2268.7	2184.7	2205.8	2205.6	2184.6	96.7	100.5	100.5	99.5
45 BIRMINGHAM, ALA.	1723.5	2310.8	2306.7	2287.5	2366.6	2305.0	99.8	99.2	102.6	99.9
16 HARRISBURG, PA.	1700.5	2399.2	2384.9	2394.6	2362.7	2365.7	99.4	100.4	99.1	99.2
46 MEMPHIS, TENN.-ARK.	1637.3	2200.6	2179.8	2260.2	2234.7	2175.5	99.1	101.0	100.2	99.8
157 PORTLAND, ORE.-WASH.	1621.2	2292.6	2342.4	2304.2	2268.8	2311.5	101.4	99.1	97.6	99.4
23 RALEIGH, N. C.	1613.2	2066.4	1943.2	1934.0	2017.1	1915.3	94.0	99.5	103.8	98.6
60 INDIANAPOLIS, IND.	1523.4	2200.9	2176.3	2184.5	2160.9	2172.3	100.4	100.4	100.0	99.8
148 DENVER, COL.	1496.4	2288.4	2225.6	2254.1	2272.5	2275.2	99.9	99.9	98.6	99.5
26 CHARLOTTE, N. C.	1444.7	2224.2	2225.1	2245.9	2225.6	2229.1	100.0	100.9	100.0	100.2
7 SYRACUSE, N. Y.	1426.8	1873.7	1831.9	1837.8	1803.8	1811.8	97.2	100.3	98.5	98.9
49 NASHVILLE, TENN.	1357.9	1754.7	1761.2	1766.5	1762.5	1762.1	100.4	100.3	100.1	100.1
164 SAN DIEGO, CALIF.	1331.8	2081.2	2142.2	2018.4	2034.8	2103.5	102.9	94.2	95.0	98.2
6 ALB.-SCHEN.-TROY, N. Y.	1316.4	1677.0	1695.4	1704.3	1677.3	1685.0	101.1	100.5	98.9	99.4
162 PHOENIX, ARIZ.	1314.4	1684.3	2058.7	2080.7	2038.2	2039.6	122.2	101.1	99.0	99.1
52 HUNT-ASH. W.VA.-KY.-OHIO	1310.0	1408.4	1461.4	1469.0	1459.2	1461.1	103.8	100.5	99.8	100.0
142 SAN ANTONIO, TEX.	1229.3	1845.6	1853.9	1847.7	1875.7	1827.4	100.5	101.2	101.2	98.6

Rank	City										
22	NOR.-PORTS., VA.	1225.9	1539.0	1518.3	1550.9	1513.2	1536.0	98.6	102.1	99.7	101.2
54	LOUISVILLE, KY.-IND.	1220.9	1597.8	1584.5	1540.2	1566.9	1593.9	99.2	97.2	98.9	100.6
63	DAYTON, OHIO	1159.7	1780.0	1769.7	1745.3	1750.9	1768.0	99.4	98.6	99.9	99.9
120	OKLAHOMA CITY, OKLA.	1156.8	1674.3	1661.0	1637.2	1616.3	1653.0	99.2	98.6	97.3	99.5
25	GR-WINS SALEM-H PT, N.C.	1142.7	1747.3	1759.4	1746.6	1744.2	1746.6	100.7	99.3	99.1	99.3
73	GRAND RAPIDS, MICH.	1124.1	1690.8	1684.1	1690.6	1679.2	1676.2	99.6	100.4	99.5	99.5
168	SACRAMENTO, CALIF.	1089.4	1265.0	1252.0	1243.0	1214.2	1225.5	99.0	99.3	97.0	97.9
151	SALT LAKE CITY, UTAH	1061.7	1097.6	1160.6	1161.7	1127.6	1146.6	105.7	100.1	97.2	98.8
70	TOLEDO, OHIO	1051.3	1324.0	1385.2	1393.9	1323.0	1350.9	104.6	100.6	95.5	97.5
34	JACKSONVILLE, FLA.	1036.7	1654.3	1629.9	1624.4	1621.8	1614.0	99.5	99.7	99.5	99.0
166	FRESNO, CALIF.	1034.6	1339.3	1334.0	1328.8	1316.2	1294.6	99.6	99.6	98.7	97.0
74	LANSING, MICH.	1014.4	1637.9	1637.9	1636.6	1629.0	1637.8	100.2	99.9	99.5	100.0
8	ROCHESTER, N.Y.	1009.3	1349.2	1311.7	1307.6	1331.5	1312.3	97.2	99.7	100.5	100.5
119	TULSA, OKLA.	941.4	1387.4	1360.2	1356.2	1366.7	1353.1	98.0	99.7	100.5	100.5
21	RICHMOND, VA.	926.1	1258.8	1323.2	1358.4	1308.9	1317.4	105.1	102.7	98.9	99.6
35	ORLANDO, FLA.	904.8	1163.3	1135.6	1118.2	1128.7	1117.0	97.6	99.4	98.5	100.4
85	GREEN BAY, WIS.	864.5	1147.2	1113.6	1136.6	1177.8	1122.0	97.4	101.7	99.0	99.6
50	KNOXVILLE, TENN.	831.3	1026.9	1007.4	1067.5	1094.8	1003.6	98.1	106.0	99.1	99.6
117	L ROCK-N L ROCK, ARK.	817.7	1262.2	1254.7	1277.5	1273.4	1240.0	99.4	100.7	101.5	99.0
20	ROANOKE, VA.	798.4	1260.4	1253.1	1262.1	1277.3	1277.0	99.4	101.9	101.9	99.3
116	SPRINGFIELD, MO.	794.2	1035.5	1023.8	1052.3	1065.3	1016.7	98.9	102.8	104.0	99.8
28	GREENVILLE, S.C.	782.8	1125.9	1111.0	1107.1	1107.2	1109.1	98.7	99.7	99.7	99.9
72	SAGINAW, MICH.	771.0	1019.0	1014.1	1027.1	1031.2	1013.1	99.5	101.3	101.7	98.8
107	OMAHA, NEBR.-IOWA	770.6	990.7	940.2	955.7	881.0	928.5	94.9	101.6	93.7	98.8
106	DES MOINES, IOWA	768.6	861.9	845.7	852.7	848.0	843.8	98.1	100.6	100.3	99.8
55	EVANSVILLE, IND.-KY.	765.4	875.4	927.7	951.5	951.5	850.2	97.5	108.8	111.4	99.5
67	YOUNGSTOWN-WARREN, OHIO	762.2	918.6	907.8	905.3	904.7	909.6	98.8	99.7	99.7	100.2
173	HONOLULU, HAWAII	753.4	1319.2	1452.4	1332.0	1332.3	1439.3	110.1	91.2	91.7	99.1
12	BINGHAMTON, N.Y. - PA.	749.2	749.2	742.8	734.6	737.6	727.1	99.1	98.9	98.9	97.9
51	BRISTOL, VA.-TENN.	748.4	762.2	816.0	862.7	843.7	804.3	97.9	105.7	103.4	98.6
53	LEXINGTON, KY.	747.1	833.7	833.7	832.2	819.0	826.2	98.2	100.4	110.8	99.6
139	LAKE CHARLES, LA.	740.6	849.7	849.7	944.6	993.6	920.2	98.6	100.1	105.3	97.5
76	SOUTH BEND, IND.	728.3	960.8	955.3	956.6	950.7	955.7	98.8	99.5	100.5	100.0
2	PORTLAND, MAINE	724.1	966.6	755.6	765.8	765.8	756.9	98.9	102.2	101.4	100.2
110	WICHITA, KANS.	718.2	759.3	880.9	908.4	890.7	872.7	98.9	103.1	101.1	99.1
137	MOBILE, ALA.	692.0	890.5	1086.4	1069.3	1115.0	1075.0	101.0	98.4	102.6	98.9
48	CHATTANOOGA, TENN.-GA.	687.2	1075.7	951.6	950.0	945.2	741.4	103.1	99.8	99.9	99.9
13	WIL-BARRE-HAZLE, PA.	686.9	922.9	760.8	756.1	751.5	741.4	97.3	99.4	98.8	97.5
154	SPOKANE, WASH.	681.5	782.0	830.7	861.1	786.4	813.5	108.7	103.7	94.7	97.9
40	MONTGOMERY, ALA.	671.3	764.2	950.9	1000.4	985.1	947.3	98.8	105.2	103.6	99.6
145	EL PASO, TEX.	643.4	962.3	724.1	761.7	773.7	720.8	98.2	105.2	106.8	99.6
47	HUNTSVILLE, ALA	628.6	737.2	934.1	951.6	965.0	933.6	97.8	101.9	103.3	100.0
167	STOCKTON, CALIF.	610.8	955.4	705.8	702.1	694.5	698.4	99.5	99.7	98.9	99.5
78	PEORIA, ILL.	605.2	705.8	702.1	710.0	705.2	714.8	101.1	99.5	99.0	100.4
79	COLUMBIA, S. C.		700.0	712.0	709.0	971.1	956.7	100.4	98.8	99.3	97.8
79	DAV-R IS-MOL, IOWA-Ill.		738.6	720.5	723.8	702.3	712.0	97.5	100.5	99.5	98.8

* POPULATION IN THOUSANDS.

(Continued)

POPULATION PROJECTIONS FOR 1990 BY ORE ECONOMIC AREA
UNDER FIVE ALTERNATIVE HIGHWAY SYSTEMS
WITH AREAS RANKED BY 1970 POPULATION. *

TABLE 5.4

AREA	1970	BASE YEAR	COMPLETED INTERSTATE	EXTENDED PRIMARY	ECONOMIC DEVELOPMENT	URBAN	PERCENT CI/BY	EP/CI	ED/CI	U/CI
75 FORT WAYNE, IND.	597.4	867.4	856.2	865.2	852.2	859.3	98.7	101.1	99.5	100.4
146 ALBUQUERQUE, N. M.	572.7	685.4	715.9	714.8	734.7	708.6	104.5	99.8	102.6	99.0
87 ROCKFORD, ILL.	560.4	757.0	740.8	776.7	757.6	737.3	97.9	104.8	102.3	99.5
129 AUSTIN, TEX.	559.6	840.7	836.0	831.6	834.7	833.6	98.8	100.2	100.5	99.5
115 PADUCAH, KY.	558.5	676.3	705.1	747.5	769.0	694.7	104.3	106.0	109.1	98.5
130 TYLER, TEX.	553.4	745.5	731.7	740.8	750.0	728.5	98.1	101.2	102.5	98.5
61 MUNCIE, IND.	551.7	681.5	678.4	679.3	676.8	686.6	99.5	100.1	99.8	100.3
158 EUGENE, ORE.	541.3	802.4	797.3	811.4	788.2	783.0	99.4	101.8	98.9	98.2
133 MONROE, LA.	537.8	764.9	765.8	764.4	829.4	753.9	100.1	100.6	108.3	98.5
143 CORPUS CHRISTI, TEX.	516.3	701.2	694.9	704.2	705.9	697.6	99.8	100.0	100.7	99.7
135 JACKSON, MISS.	510.4	824.7	824.1	811.1	837.1	816.2	99.9	98.4	101.6	99.0
147 PUEBLO, COL.	509.6	518.7	509.6	514.9	522.9	506.8	98.2	101.0	102.6	99.5
134 GREENVILLE, MISS.	506.6	627.7	598.6	605.7	663.2	593.1	95.4	111.2	110.8	99.1
3 BURLINGTON, VT.	502.1	580.5	713.5	721.6	803.4	709.4	122.9	101.1	112.6	99.4
42 MACON, GA.	496.2	653.1	636.8	631.8	653.3	635.2	97.5	99.2	102.6	99.4
57 SPRINGFIELD, ILL.	491.0	519.6	536.6	554.7	546.2	537.7	103.3	103.4	101.8	100.2
43 COLUMBUS, GA.--ALA.	488.1	638.7	644.2	659.6	660.6	644.8	100.9	102.4	102.6	100.1
24 WILMINGTON, N. C.	487.1	608.2	601.2	627.9	635.7	589.6	98.8	104.4	105.7	98.1
32 AUGUSTA, GA.	461.5	583.2	574.5	571.5	606.0	570.6	98.5	99.5	105.5	99.3
41 ALBANY, GA.	460.8	580.7	566.3	611.1	628.3	560.9	97.5	107.9	111.0	99.1
10 ERIE, PA.	460.0	553.1	527.7	495.8	500.1	545.5	95.4	94.0	94.8	103.4
121 WICHITA FALLS, TEX.	455.8	589.8	579.1	589.4	599.5	570.3	98.2	101.8	103.5	98.5
83 MADISON, WIS.	454.6	607.7	593.3	606.8	606.7	591.8	97.6	102.3	102.3	99.7
163 TUCSON, ARIZONA	454.2	623.8	615.3	618.1	607.1	609.9	98.6	100.5	98.7	99.3
103 SIOUX CITY, IOWA-NEBR.	453.5	485.6	481.2	504.5	485.7	478.0	99.1	104.8	100.9	99.3
132 SHREVEPORT, LA.	437.8	552.6	546.6	567.4	598.9	541.6	99.0	103.8	109.5	99.0
127 AMARILLO, TEX.	430.8	432.8	436.0	438.7	444.7	437.4	100.8	100.8	102.0	100.3
31 CHARLESTON, S. C.	429.0	611.9	605.7	596.0	602.0	597.6	98.5	98.4	99.4	98.7
87 DULUTH-SUP, MINN.-WIS.	426.3	435.7	429.7	457.8	462.7	427.5	98.6	106.5	107.7	99.5
105 WATERLOO, IOWA	419.4	455.1	454.9	454.1	453.4	451.4	100.0	99.8	99.7	99.2
11 WILLIAMSPORT, PA.	417.8	490.7	471.2	491.8	468.2	474.0	96.0	104.4	99.4	100.6
33 SAVANNAH, GA.	407.8	586.3	589.8	582.9	617.3	585.9	100.6	98.8	104.7	99.3
156 YAKIMA, WASH.	404.7	539.6	603.8	580.1	597.3	590.2	111.9	96.1	98.9	97.8
128 WACO, TEX.	403.9	527.4	528.8	522.2	546.7	527.0	100.3	98.7	103.4	99.7
30 FLORENCE, S. C.	400.7	537.8	524.5	530.2	564.5	520.4	97.5	101.1	107.6	99.7
112 COLUMBIA, MO.	397.1	462.1	439.4	484.3	516.0	435.5	95.1	110.2	117.4	99.1
19 STAUNTON, VA.	395.1	541.4	540.7	529.3	556.0	531.0	99.9	97.9	102.8	98.2
140 BEAU-P ART-ORANGE, TEX.	394.7	548.9	539.2	532.6	535.6	534.5	98.2	99.3	98.8	99.1
136 MERIDIAN, MISS.	393.4	460.3	451.2	492.4	504.5	448.8	98.0	109.1	111.8	99.5
27 ASHEVILLE, N. C.	391.6	527.3	523.5	512.1	534.7	512.9	99.3	97.8	102.1	98.0
58 CHAMPAIGN-URBANA, ILL.	390.4	431.6	427.9	423.7	424.1	428.2	99.1	99.0	99.1	100.1

#	City										
39	PENSACOLA, FLA.	382.3	426.6	417.2	381.4	431.6	409.9	97.8	91.4	103.4	98.3
99	SIOUX FALLS, S. D.	365.0	349.4	347.7	357.4	351.9	347.8	99.5	102.8	101.2	100.0
144	BROWN-HARL'S RENITO. TEX	355.6	527.3	512.4	520.4	551.1	507.6	97.2	101.6	107.5	99.1
86	WAUSAU, WIS.	350.3	461.6	456.5	473.9	470.1	453.1	98.9	103.8	103.0	99.3
109	SALINA, KANS.	349.0	367.0	362.6	347.4	361.1	357.1	98.8	95.8	99.6	98.5
38	TALLAHASSEE, FLA.	344.5	344.5	437.7	454.6	447.9	434.1	104.6	102.3	103.9	99.2
97	FAR-MOOR, N. D-MINN.	335.4	335.1	333.5	339.1	332.5	332.1	99.5	96.5	101.7	99.6
80	CEDAR RAPIDS, IOWA	330.1	344.9	335.3	323.6	319.6	334.2	97.2	96.5	95.3	99.7
131	TEXARKANA, TEX-ARK.	329.8	360.7	354.4	356.0	356.0	351.3	98.4	102.0	100.3	99.0
123	LUBBOCK, TEX.	328.7	377.5	361.9	325.7	361.9	354.2	96.1	90.0	107.2	97.9
65	CLARKSBURG, W. VA.	326.8	351.3	382.4	471.7	287.7	376.2	108.9	107.9	123.3	98.4
108	LINCOLN, NEBR.	324.0	374.0	296.3	292.8	471.7	296.1	99.2	101.4	98.8	99.9
102	GRAND ISLAND, NEBR.	323.8	321.3	316.6	305.2	305.2	315.9	98.5	103.6	96.4	99.8
1	BANGOR, MAINE	321.8	338.2	336.5	322.7	350.2	334.1	99.5	107.1	95.9	99.3
124	ODESSA, TEX.	319.2	333.1	342.4	350.2	349.1	333.1	102.8	98.5	102.3	97.3
161	LAS VEGAS, NEV.	317.3	317.3	363.5	369.6	384.4	357.4	97.3	101.7	96.1	98.3
81	DUBUQUE, IOWA	301.9	362.1	361.1	384.4	358.3	358.3	99.7	107.4	106.5	99.2
172	ANCHORAGE, ALASKA	300.4	318.6	314.9	300.8	301.3	313.5	98.8	95.7	95.5	99.5
152	IDAHO FALLS, IDAHO	300.2	335.3	330.7	333.9	333.9	328.5	98.6	101.0	101.0	99.3
113	QUINCY, ILL.	299.1	317.1	309.4	318.6	327.8	311.0	97.6	106.0	103.0	100.5
118	FORT SMITH, ARK.-OKLA.	289.3	405.9	403.8	407.9	407.9	401.9	99.5	100.0	101.0	100.6
69	LIMA, OHIO		303.2	298.3	327.2	327.2	296.6	98.4	103.1	109.7	99.4
89	LA CROSSE, WIS.	276.2	312.6	309.1	278.1	313.3	305.2	98.9	96.3	106.1	98.7
104	FORT DODGE, IOWA	269.5	276.0	267.9	266.9	261.0	265.8	97.1	99.6	97.4	99.2
159	BOISE CITY, IDAHO	266.1	265.5	315.6	311.2	333.6	316.3	98.1	98.6	106.6	100.2
125	ABILENE, TEX.	265.5	280.1	271.4	267.5	285.7	265.2	97.0	98.5	105.2	97.7
56	TERRE HAUTE, IND.	264.8	257.7	305.2	300.3	360.3	305.9	97.8	98.4	101.2	100.2
149	GRAND JUNCTION, COL.	252.7	284.7	308.1	343.1	325.1	315.2	108.2	116.9	111.4	98.9
59	LAFAY-W. LAFAY. IND.	251.9	250.8	315.1	310.4	324.9	310.4	99.3	103.2	96.6	100.1
95	BILLINGS, MONT.	250.8	263.5	293.0	324.9	250.6	290.0	112.2	110.9	106.9	99.3
90	ROCHESTER, MINN.	246.9	261.1	261.1	250.6	287.7	257.2	99.1	96.0	99.1	98.5
153	BUTTE, MONT.	246.1	305.2	309.5	306.6	312.9	310.3	101.4	101.1	101.0	100.3
100	RAPID CITY, S. D.	234.9	213.6	215.4	220.3	219.5	214.9	100.8	102.3	101.9	99.8
150	CHEYENNE, WYO.	231.9	248.7	270.5	285.6	229.3	269.8	108.7	105.6	106.6	99.8
94	GREAT FALLS, MONT.	229.3	277.6	291.1	293.7	319.5	268.4	104.9	109.8	109.8	99.1
92	GRAND FORKS, N. D.	222.6	238.3	235.8	250.9	251.2	232.4	99.0	106.4	106.5	98.6
88	EAU CLAIRE, WIS.	219.9	281.6	272.0	283.0	302.3	271.1	96.6	104.1	111.1	99.7
160	RENO, NEV.	206.7	302.0	310.3	321.4	305.5	304.0	102.8	98.3	98.0	98.0
93	MINOT, N. D.	182.2	209.6	208.3	239.2	247.5	204.0	99.4	114.8	118.8	97.9
169	REDDING, CALIF.	176.9	224.2	218.3	213.7	211.4	208.8	97.3	97.9	96.8	95.6
96	BISMARCK, N. D.	144.9	159.5	150.0	152.0	159.5	147.9	94.0	101.3	106.8	98.6
98	ABERDEEN, S. D.	132.9	120.5	127.7	131.4	137.6	127.9	105.9	102.9	107.8	100.2
126	SAN ANGELO, TEX.	125.0	143.2	141.7	157.8	185.4	140.6	99.0	111.3	130.8	99.2
170	EUREKA, CALIF.	121.9	140.7	143.6	151.6	140.1	134.6	102.1	105.5	97.6	93.7
101	SCOTTSBLUFF, NEBR.	105.7	109.3	108.0	120.6	104.1	107.8	98.8	111.6	96.3	99.7

• POPULATION IN THOUSANDS.

TABLE 5.5

PER CAPITA INCOME PROJECTIONS FOR 1990 BY ORE ECONOMIC AREA
UNDER FIVE ALTERNATIVE HIGHWAY SYSTEMS
WITH AREAS RANKED BY 1970 PER CAPITA INCOME.

| AREA | 1970 | BASE YEAR | COMPLETED INTERSTATE | EXTENDED PRIMARY | ECONOMIC DEVELOPMENT | URBAN | PERCENT | | | |
							I/BY	EP/CI	ED/CI	U/CI
160 RENO, NEV.	5160.	9419.	9327.	9609.	9387.	9442.	99.0	103.0	100.6	101.2
172 ANCHORAGE, ALASKA	4699.	7731.	7774.	7769.	7759.	7749.	100.6	99.9	99.8	99.7
171 S FRAN-OAKLAND, CALIF.	4689.	7083.	6861.	6945.	6862.	6950.	96.9	101.2	100.0	101.3
77 CHICAGO, ILL.	4600.	7584.	7635.	7616.	7623.	7943.	100.7	99.8	99.8	104.0
14 NEW YORK, N.Y.	4589.	8366.	8355.	8268.	8281.	8446.	99.9	99.0	99.1	101.1
173 HONOLULU, HAWAII	4556.	5969.	6010.	5961.	5920.	6048.	100.7	99.2	98.5	100.6
5 HARTFORD, CONN.	4468.	6655.	6727.	6732.	6667.	6654.	101.1	100.1	99.1	98.9
17 BALTIMORE, MD.	4400.	7176.	7368.	7452.	7656.	7297.	102.7	101.1	103.9	99.0
165 L. A.-LONG BEACH, CALIF.	4392.	6393.	6345.	6324.	6348.	6375.	99.3	99.7	100.0	100.5
71 DETROIT, MICH.	4373.	8212.	8221.	8121.	8153.	8448.	100.1	98.8	99.2	102.8
12 BINGHAMTON, N.Y. - PA.	4292.	6607.	6604.	6675.	6723.	6525.	100.0	101.1	101.8	98.8
80 CEDAR RAPIDS, IOWA	4260.	7009.	7004.	6921.	6951.	6918.	99.9	98.8	99.2	98.8
18 WASH., D.C. - MD. - VA.	4235.	6733.	6739.	6713.	6736.	6737.	100.1	99.6	100.0	100.0
168 SACRAMENTO, CALIF.	4133.	4815.	4732.	4793.	4658.	4730.	98.3	101.3	98.4	100.0
4 BOSTON, MASS.	4086.	6485.	6570.	6611.	6538.	6577.	101.3	100.6	99.5	100.1
36 MIAMI, FLA.	4065.	7411.	7317.	7248.	7276.	7287.	98.7	99.1	99.5	99.6
155 SEATTLE-EVERETT, WASH.	4049.	6354.	6346.	6358.	6344.	6308.	99.9	100.2	100.0	99.4
15 PHILA. - N.J.	4015.	6370.	6543.	6472.	6483.	6624.	102.7	98.9	99.1	101.2
167 STOCKTON, CALIF.	4004.	5697.	5675.	5701.	5652.	5676.	99.6	100.5	99.6	100.0
170 EUREKA, CALIF.	4001.	5610.	5328.	5589.	5381.	5534.	95.0	104.9	101.0	103.9
21 RICHMOND, VA.	3995.	5866.	5882.	5908.	5893.	5845.	100.3	100.2	100.0	99.4
78 PEORIA, ILL.	3984.	6585.	6702.	6485.	6508.	6581.	101.8	96.8	97.1	98.2
82 ROCKFORD, ILL.	3982.	6650.	6600.	7199.	6895.	6477.	99.3	109.1	104.5	98.2
60 INDIANAPOLIS, IND.	3981.	7178.	7089.	6949.	6850.	6832.	98.8	98.0	96.6	96.4
148 DENVER, COL.	3951.	6137.	6139.	6029.	6031.	6063.	100.0	98.2	98.2	98.8
84 ROCHESTER, N.Y.	3935.	6953.	6848.	6742.	6809.	6715.	98.5	98.5	99.4	98.1
44 MILWAUKEE, WIS.	3923.	6571.	6489.	6404.	6406.	6336.	98.8	98.7	98.7	97.6
58 CHAMPAIGN-URBANA, ILL.	3908.	5769.	5773.	5702.	5714.	5686.	100.1	98.8	99.0	98.5
127 DALLAS, TEX.	3903.	5846.	5831.	5746.	5778.	5744.	99.7	98.5	99.1	98.5
62 CIN. - OHIO-KY.-IND.	3902.	6662.	6780.	6551.	6822.	6792.	101.8	96.6	100.6	100.2
68 CLEVELAND, OHIO	3883.	6231.	6213.	6120.	6122.	6143.	99.7	98.5	98.5	98.9
57 SPRINGFIELD, ILL.	3879.	6422.	6683.	6921.	6895.	6570.	104.0	103.6	103.2	98.3
111 KANSAS CITY, MO.-KANS.	3878.	5701.	5740.	5750.	5771.	5697.	100.7	100.2	100.5	99.3
161 LAS VEGAS, NEV.	3858.	5522.	5523.	5526.	5517.	5559.	100.0	100.0	99.9	100.7
108 LINCOLN, NEBR.	3854.	7741.	7720.	7735.	7730.	7673.	99.7	100.2	100.1	99.4
110 WICHITA, KANS.	3850.	5746.	5704.	5874.	5758.	5660.	99.3	103.0	100.9	99.2
83 MADISON, WIS.	3845.	5873.	5817.	6113.	6222.	5763.	99.0	105.1	107.0	99.1
91 MINN-ST. PAUL, MINN.	3836.	7042.	6996.	7044.	7047.	6780.	99.3	100.7	100.7	96.9
141 HOUSTON, TEX.	3834.	5924.	5829.	778.	5751.	5778.	98.4	99.1	98.7	99.1
63 DAYTON, OHIO	3805.	6578.	6485.	395.	6429.	6318.	98.6	98.6	99.1	97.4
75 FORT WAYNE, IND.	3763.	6534.	6448.	5474.	6472.	6373.	98.7	100.4	99.1	98.8

#	City											
124	ODESSA, TEX.	3741.	4607.	4681.	4687.	4928.	4740.	101.6	100.1	100.3	105.3	101.3
61	MUNCIE, IND.	3739.	6653.	6647.	6668.	6651.	6543.	99.9	100.1	100.1	100.1	98.4
157	PORTLAND, ORE.--WASH.	3732.	5817.	5924.	5932.	5916.	5867.	101.8	100.1	99.9	99.3	99.0
54	LOUISVILLE, KY.--IND.	3700.	4936.	4983.	4985.	4949.	4942.	100.9	100.0	100.0	99.3	99.2
79	DAV-R IS-MOL, IOWA-ILL.	3693.	5421.	5461.	5460.	5460.	5414.	100.7	99.8	99.8	100.0	99.1
59	LAFAY-W LAFAY, IND.	3684.	5832.	5780.	5728.	5728.	5743.	99.1	100.6	99.1	100.6	99.4
44	ATLANTA, GA.	3683.	6074.	6040.	6001.	5982.	5995.	99.0	98.9	98.9	98.6	98.8
67	YOUNGSTOWN-WARREN, OHIO	3667.	6300.	6240.	6122.	6122.	6092.	99.0	97.8	97.8	98.1	97.6
66	PITTSBURGH, PA.	3657.	6457.	6490.	6542.	6405.	6377.	100.5	100.8	100.8	98.7	98.3
70	TOLEDO, OHIO	3648.	6516.	6554.	6090.	6419.	6459.	100.6	99.7	99.7	97.9	98.6
74	LANSING, MICH.	3648.	6050.	6072.	6090.	6041.	5991.	100.4	100.3	100.3	99.5	98.7
169	REDDING, CALIF.	3648.	4764.	4738.	4846.	4666.	4768.	99.5	102.3	102.3	98.5	100.6
114	ST. LOUIS, MO--ILL.	3647.	6078.	6101.	6018.	6014.	6061.	100.4	98.6	98.6	98.6	99.3
164	SAN DIEGO, CALIF.	3647.	5174.	5167.	5132.	5135.	5128.	99.9	99.3	99.3	99.4	99.3
90	ROCHESTER, MINN.	3642.	6358.	6350.	6342.	6427.	6243.	99.9	100.9	100.9	101.2	99.1
9	BUFFALO, N.Y.	3633.	6688.	6671.	6730.	6723.	6612.	99.7	100.9	100.8	100.8	99.1
22	NOR-PORTS.. VA.	3631.	5145.	5158.	5141.	5141.	5138.	100.2	99.7	99.4	101.0	100.8
6	ALB--SCHEN--TROY, N.Y.	3628.	5560.	5618.	5663.	5589.	5598.	101.0	99.4	99.7	99.6	99.6
106	DES MOINES, IOWA	3617.	5719.	5621.	5702.	5702.	5552.	98.3	100.8	100.8	101.4	98.8
162	PHOENIX, ARIZ.	3599.	6538.	6646.	6739.	6731.	6570.	101.6	101.4	101.3	101.3	98.9
109	SALINA, KANS.	3582.	5860.	5853.	5757.	5864.	5776.	99.9	98.4	98.4	100.2	98.7
154	SPOKANE, WASH.	3551.	5419.	5508.	5490.	5498.	5490.	101.6	101.6	101.6	101.8	99.7
10	ERIE, PA.	3550.	5041.	4893.	4858.	4854.	5074.	97.1	99.3	99.2	103.7	103.7
101	SCOTTSBLUFF, NEBR.	3539.	6021.	5997.	6039.	6039.	5928.	99.2	100.1	99.3	97.8	98.9
76	SOUTH BEND, IND.	3525.	6440.	6376.	6383.	6332.	6224.	93.8	102.5	95.5	97.8	97.8
107	OMAHA, NEBR-IOWA	3517.	5256.	4929.	5051.	4705.	4822.	98.6	100.8	100.8	97.1	97.1
16	HARRISBURG, PA.	3499.	5636.	5558.	5472.	5472.	5394.	99.7	100.3	100.4	97.6	97.6
105	WATERLOO, IOWA	3476.	6212.	6194.	6211.	6220.	6045.	100.8	105.0	105.0	110.6	97.6
122	AMARILLO, TEX.	3470.	5035.	4958.	5145.	5428.	5000.	100.0	111.8	111.8	110.6	98.5
94	GREAT FALLS, MONT.	3454.	4925.	5915.	5484.	5484.	4933.	97.6	101.7	99.7	99.5	99.1
102	GRAND ISLAND, NEBR.	3443.	6063.	5708.	6019.	5895.	5864.	96.6	98.5	99.7	101.5	99.5
64	COLUMBUS, OHIO	3429.	5911.	5468.	5621.	5791.	5489.	100.2	99.4	100.0	101.5	96.2
69	LIMA, OHIO	3409.	5456.	4614.	5448.	5448.	5441.	99.0	100.7	99.7	99.5	100.4
35	ORLANDO, FLA.	3393.	4661.	5048.	4647.	4602.	4631.	98.9	99.1	99.6	99.7	98.7
34	JACKSONVILLE, FLA.	3380.	5106.	5329.	5244.	5278.	4982.	100.5	98.4	99.1	99.6	99.1
37	TAMPA-ST. PETF, FLA.	3359.	5303.	4828.	5329.	5276.	5283.	101.5	103.8	100.2	103.9	100.2
38	TALLAHASSEE, FLA.	3339.	4759.	5266.	5013.	5017.	4840.	100.9	99.2	103.9	99.4	98.6
25	GR-WINS SALFM-H PT, N.C.	3335.	5500.	5247.	5204.	5515.	5472.	100.2	99.6	99.4	99.3	99.4
28	GREENVILLE, S.C.	3331.	5257.	5266.	5247.	5229.	5236.	100.0	99.6	99.3	100.7	100.4
140	REAU-P ART-ORANGE, TFX.	3331.	4910.	4910.	4891.	4875.	4932.	99.5	100.8	100.7	101.3	98.4
104	FORT DODGE, IOWA	3327.	7030.	6998.	7057.	7047.	6887.	100.4	101.3	100.7	103.5	97.9
73	GRAND RAPIDS, MICH.	3327.	5949.	5917.	5940.	5940.	5794.	99.7	100.7	103.5	100.5	99.8
20	ROANOKE, VA.	3322.	4531.	4519.	4549.	4677.	4508.	98.0	102.6	100.5	102.0	99.8
163	TUCSON, ARIZONA	3311.	4293.	4209.	4319.	4229.	4186.	96.9	107.4	102.0	107.4	99.1
2	PORTLAND, MAINE	3311.	5754.	5731.	5848.	5842.	5678.	97.6	101.3	99.3	99.3	98.6
11	WILLIAMSPORT, PA.	3304.	5521.	5353.	5746.	5315.	5279.	99.7	101.4	101.4	99.7	96.3
7	SYRACUSE, N.Y.	3292.	5346.	5219.	5287.	5135.	5028.	99.7	101.3	101.5	98.4	101.5
166	FRESNO, CALIF.	3277.	4311.	4298.	4358.	4284.	4364.	99.7	101.4	101.5	96.3	101.5

(Continued)

PER CAPITA INCOME PROJECTIONS FOR 1990 BY ORF ECONOMIC AREA
UNDER FIVE ALTERNATIVE HIGHWAY SYSTEMS
WITH AREAS RANKED BY 1970 PER CAPITA INCOME.

TABLE 5.5

AREA	1970	BASE YEAR	COMPLETED INTERSTATE	EXTENDED PRIMARY	ECONOMIC DEVELOPMENT	URBAN	PERCENT CI/BY	EP/CI	ED/CI	U/CI
156 YAKIMA, WASH.	3276.	4647.	4773.	4795.	4746.	4833.	102.7	100.5	99.4	101.3
3 BURLINGTON, VT.	3263.	4790.	5787.	5982.	6204.	5697.	120.8	103.4	107.2	98.4
120 OKLAHOMA CITY, OKLA.	3260.	4883.	4849.	4792.	4770.	4815.	99.3	98.8	98.4	99.3
113 QUINCY, ILL.	3250.	6349.	6256.	6807.	6593.	6150.	98.5	108.8	105.4	98.3
119 TULSA, OKLA.	3250.	5347.	5327.	5265.	5334.	5222.	99.6	98.8	100.1	98.0
72 SAGINAW, MICH.	3207.	5170.	5164.	5160.	5148.	5151.	99.9	99.9	99.7	99.8
45 BILLINGS, MONT.	3205.	4942.	5079.	5396.	5240.	5055.	102.8	106.2	103.2	99.5
103 SIOUX CITY, IOWA-NEBR.	3190.	6021.	5988.	6122.	6035.	5914.	99.4	100.2	100.3	98.8
123 LUBBOCK, TEX.	3184.	4964.	4966.	5119.	4984.	4975.	100.0	103.1	100.4	100.2
151 SALT LAKE CITY, UTAH	3180.	5527.	5630.	5697.	5606.	5574.	101.9	101.2	99.6	99.0
146 ALBUQUERQUE, N.M.	3172.	4486.	4581.	4598.	4810.	4531.	102.1	100.8	105.0	99.0
26 CHARLOTTE, N.C.	3165.	5797.	5791.	5838.	5748.	5735.	99.9	100.8	99.3	99.0
152 IDAHO FALLS, IDAHO	3157.	6216.	6224.	6276.	6229.	6176.	100.2	100.0	100.0	99.2
150 CHEYENNE, WYO.	3154.	5338.	5666.	6106.	6188.	5517.	106.1	107.8	109.2	97.4
147 PUEBLO, COL.	3148.	5946.	5952.	5969.	5991.	5907.	100.1	100.3	100.7	99.3
67 DULUTH-SUP, MINN-WIS.	3139.	6197.	6193.	6278.	6333.	6133.	99.9	101.3	103.8	98.8
100 RAPID CITY, S.D.	3135.	4873.	4869.	5054.	5033.	4812.	99.9	101.1	103.4	98.8
99 SIOUX FALLS, S.D.	3132.	6854.	6849.	6923.	6914.	6791.	99.9	101.6	100.9	99.2
159 BOISE CITY, IDAHO	3130.	5685.	5712.	5586.	6280.	5625.	100.5	97.6	109.9	99.2
138 NEW ORLEANS, LA.	3114.	5103.	5201.	5137.	5149.	5162.	101.9	98.8	99.0	99.2
58 EUGENE, ORE.	3101.	4296.	4238.	4331.	4275.	4228.	98.6	102.2	100.9	99.8
55 EVANSVILLE, IND-KY.	3097.	5948.	5950.	6077.	6157.	5860.	99.7	102.5	103.8	98.6
125 ABILENE, TEX.	3091.	4092.	4078.	4086.	4104.	4075.	99.7	100.2	100.8	99.9
39 PENSACOLA, FLA.	3089.	4493.	4538.	4564.	4522.	4550.	101.0	100.6	99.6	100.3
56 TERRE HAUTE, IND.	3082.	5497.	5480.	5359.	5599.	5376.	99.7	97.8	102.2	98.1
121 WICHITA FALLS, TEX.	3076.	4415.	4402.	4480.	4581.	4377.	99.7	101.6	102.2	101.0
19 STAUNTON, VA.	3065.	3773.	3761.	3823.	3843.	3798.	99.7	99.4	104.1	99.4
153 BUTTE, MONT.	3064.	4507.	4505.	4459.	4577.	4471.	100.0	99.0	101.6	99.2
149 GRAND JUNCTION, COL.	3063.	6349.	6450.	6779.	6751.	6365.	101.6	105.1	104.7	98.7
85 GREEN BAY, WIS.	3051.	5603.	5419.	5790.	5708.	5364.	96.7	106.8	105.3	99.0
13 WIL-BARRE-HAZLE, PA.	3044.	5287.	5256.	5281.	5293.	5177.	99.4	100.7	100.5	98.5
126 AUSTIN, TEX.	3038.	4912.	4889.	4885.	5012.	4858.	99.5	99.9	102.5	99.4
129 SAN ANGELO, TEX.	3037.	4447.	4432.	4477.	4518.	4433.	99.7	101.0	101.9	100.0
89 LA CROSSE, WIS.	3007.	4434.	4519.	4560.	4859.	4397.	101.9	101.0	107.5	100.0
17 COLUMBIA, MO.	2980.	5314.	5265.	5408.	5471.	5235.	99.1	102.7	103.9	99.4
81 DUBUQUE, IOWA	2963.	5063.	5063.	5506.	5535.	5019.	100.0	108.7	109.3	99.1
32 AUGUSTA, GA.	2936.	4540.	4560.	4513.	4632.	4523.	100.4	99.0	101.6	99.1
47 HUNTSVILLE, ALA.	2930.	5145.	5067.	5255.	5208.	4982.	98.5	103.7	102.8	98.3

No.	City							Index			
49	NASHVILLE, TENN.	2920.	5336.	5411.	5412.	5444.	5250.	101.4	100.0	100.6	97.0
130	TYLER, TEX.	2911.	4193.	4230.	4218.	4327.	4174.	99.4	100.9	103.2	99.6
48	CHATTANOOGA, TENN.-GA.	2911.	4727.	4887.	4902.	4954.	4822.	103.7	99.7	101.1	98.4
86	WAUSAU, WIS.	2910.	5331.	5442.	5442.	4812.	5259.	99.8	101.8	101.5	100.4
1	BANGOR, MAINE	2906.	5331.	5442.	5319.	5218.	5259.	99.1	102.3	98.1	98.9
M8	EAU CLAIRE, WIS.	2870.	4617.	4660.	4577.	4901.	4540.	99.1	100.8	107.1	99.2
145	EL PASO, TEX.	2869.	4719.	4753.	4677.	4791.	4626.	98.4	101.6	102.4	98.4
42	MACON, GA.	2866.	4261.	4544.	4329.	4193.	4179.	97.0	98.4	106.6	98.1
98	ABERDEEN, S. D.	2862.	5462.	5646.	5631.	5969.	5407.	102.8	103.4	108.2	99.0
137	MOBILE, ALA.	2838.	3982.	3928.	3874.	4102.	3941.	99.2	98.6	103.0	99.0
135	JACKSON, MISS.	2824.	4779.	4684.	4740.	4928.	4670.	98.2	98.8	104.0	98.5
46	MEMPHIS, TENN.-ARK.	2870.	5081.	5115.	4989.	5114.	4866.	99.8	102.5	102.5	97.5
45	BIRMINGHAM, ALA.	2816.	4999.	4990.	4999.	5129.	4894.	99.2	98.7	102.8	98.9
117	L ROCK-N L ROCK, ARK.	2811.	4474.	4523.	4437.	4485.	4390.	98.8	101.9	101.1	98.9
29	COLUMBIA, S. C.	2808.	3897.	3867.	3849.	3814.	3867.	98.8	100.5	98.9	100.5
128	WACO, TEX.	2806.	3790.	3805.	3798.	3885.	3782.	100.0	100.2	102.3	99.6
24	WILMINGTON, N. C.	2780.	3523.	3574.	3504.	3587.	3552.	99.5	102.0	103.4	101.4
142	SAN ANTONIO, TEX.	2739.	3420.	3501.	3385.	3501.	3394.	99.0	101.4	100.3	100.3
53	LEXINGTON, KY.	2738.	4936.	5676.	4996.	5590.	4801.	98.8	115.0	113.2	97.3
43	COLUMBUS, GA.-ALA.	2731.	4996.	4720.	4511.	4538.	4480.	100.7	100.6	100.6	99.3
116	SPRINGFIELD, MO.	2715.	4481.	4634.	4477.	4691.	4424.	99.1	100.6	104.6	98.8
92	GRAND FORKS, N. D.	2708.	4477.	3811.	3553.	3830.	3536.	100.7	108.3	107.7	98.8
33	SAVANNAH, GA.	2706.	3553.	4291.	3971.	3998.	3997.	99.1	99.8	107.3	99.9
93	MINOT, N. D.	2700.	3971.	5304.	3998.	4291.	4666.	100.7	108.3	113.9	100.0
97	FAR-MOOR, N. D.-MINN.	2699.	3998.	5825.	5166.	5304.	5644.	100.1	100.5	102.3	99.1
65	CLARKSBURG, W. VA.	2683.	4593.	5655.	5723.	5983.	5538.	100.5	102.4	105.8	97.9
51	BRISTOL, VA.-TENN.	2652.	5696.	4734.	4702.	4703.	4654.	100.1	100.7	100.7	99.0
143	CORPUS CHRISTI, TEX.	2641.	5427.	4008.	4029.	3989.	3997.	99.9	100.1	99.5	99.7
131	TEXARKANA, TEX.-ARK.	2635.	4702.	4069.	4426.	4364.	4032.	100.6	108.8	108.8	99.4
52	HUNT-ASH, W.VA.-KY.-OHIO	2631.	4680.	5138.	5194.	5151.	5107.	101.4	100.3	100.3	99.1
27	ASHEVILLE, N. C.	2626.	4003.	4159.	4120.	4328.	4121.	102.4	101.1	105.1	99.1
96	BISMARCK, N. D.	2590.	4063.	5607.	5676.	5896.	5502.	99.6	101.2	101.8	98.1
115	PADUCAH, KY.	2590.	5138.	5529.	5607.	4672.	4623.	100.0	101.2	103.9	98.1
50	KNOXVILLE, TENN.	2563.	4136.	4837.	4816.	5027.	4688.	99.7	104.4	104.2	97.3
132	SHREVEPORT, LA.	2557.	5529.	4412.	4525.	4719.	4451.	99.9	101.7	101.7	100.2
31	CHARLESTON, S. C.	2555.	4391.	3503.	3499.	3479.	3499.	97.2	99.6	106.0	98.8
40	MONTGOMERY, ALA.	2521.	4496.	3956.	3959.	4308.	3909.	99.8	101.7	106.0	100.0
41	ALBANY, GA.	2508.	4837.	3559.	3663.	4085.	3559.	99.6	101.7	108.9	99.6
23	RALEIGH, N. C.	2518.	4412.	3807.	3612.	3876.	3791.	97.2	114.8	101.8	98.7
118	FORT SMITH, ARK.-OKLA.	2428.	3559.	4805.	4785.	4859.	4722.	99.6	100.0	114.7	101.5
134	GREENVILLE, MISS.	2306.	3807.	3552.	3552.	3939.	3392.	96.3	99.6	115.1	99.3
136	MERIDIAN, MISS.	2294.	4805.	3926.	3422.	3939.	4193.	100.0	114.9	115.1	99.3
139	LAKE CHARLES, LA.	2235.	3552.	4389.	4224.	4491.	3225.	99.9	100.6	106.3	99.9
30	FLORENCE, S. C.	2199.	4226.	3248.	3228.	3291.	4015.	98.1	101.9	101.9	96.6
133	MONROE, LA.	2127.	3230.	4201.	4156.	4235.	3236.	99.1	99.1	106.1	100.1
144	BROWN-HARL-S BENITO, TEX	1975.	2814.	2753.	2634.	2922.	2646.	93.6	104.5	111.0	100.5

Primary system are Honolulu; Lubbock, Texas; and Pensacola, Florida. Honolulu does not receive any new highways under the Extended Highway system. When benefit is measured by percent change in per capita income, the areas that gain the most from the Extended Primary system are Lexington, Kentucky; Albany, Georgia; and Greenville, Mississippi. The areas that lose the most in terms of per capita income are Cincinnati; Peoria, Illinois; and Youngstown, Ohio.

Economic Development vs.
Completed Interstate

The low income economic areas are definitely helped by the Economic Development system. Fifty-eight out of the poorest 60 areas show some income improvement under this system. Many areas that show improvement under the Economic Development system also show improvement under the Extended Primary system. The links of the highway system in certain areas, measured by population, also gained with the Economic Development system. The East-South Central and the West-South Central census regions gain the most under the Economic Development system, and the Pacific region loses the most relatively.

Comparing 1990 projections by the percent population change, the areas that gain under the economic Development system are San Angelo, Texas; Clarksburg, West Virginia; and Minot, North Dakota. Areas made worse off are Honolulu, Omaha, and Spokane. When measured by percent change in per capita income, the areas with the largest gains are Albany, Georgia; Greenville, Mississippi; and Minot, North Dakota. The areas with large losses in per capita income are Omaha, Indianapolis, and Toledo, Ohio.

Urban vs. Completed Interstate

The Urban system does not benefit many areas, since only 29 areas received construction expenditures under this alternative. The percent changes in population and economic variables are not as high under this alternative as they were in the previous alternatives, since the Urban system affects areas with large economic bases. The Urban system definitely helps the larger areas and the highest income areas. The Mid-Atlantic region is the largest gainer in terms of percent change in population, and New England and the East-North Central region also show slight gains. All other census regions show relative losses.

Comparing 1990 projections by percent population change, the areas which show the largest increases due to the Urban system are Erie, Pennsylvania; Washington, D.C.; and New York City. The areas with the largest percent drops in population are Eureka, Redding, and Fresno, all in California. When measured by percent change in per capita income, the areas with the largest percent gain are Chicago, Eureka, California; and Detroit. The areas with the largest percent drop in per capita income are Columbus, Ohio; Syracuse, New York; and

Indianapolis. The changes in Eureka show an interesting anomaly. Eureka is expected to lose 6.3 percent of its population and at the same time have a 3.9 percent increase in its per capita income. As a result of the Urban system, Eureka shows a drop in employment in some of the low wage industries.

SUMMARY OF TRANSPORTATION STATISTICS

Table 5-6 gives summary statistics from the linear transportation algorithms. These statistics represent the total interarea shipments, and the transportation and mileage associated with the shipments. The linear programming algorithm assumes that all interarea flows are optimal and that there are no cross-hauls involved. The modal split between rail and truck as given in the table may not be realistic, since actual trade flows are not optimal and other modes of transportation are not given. The table excludes intraarea shipments, since in the linear programming algorithm they are assumed to be zero. Because the average radius of an economic area is approximately 50-60 miles, most intraarea shipments would go by truck.

The numbers in the table comparing one alternative to another go in the right direction, although their magnitudes of change are not very large. The percentage of interarea shipments going by truck goes up as highways are added, and the truck transport cost per dollar of shipment goes down. The data also reveal that total interarea shipments go up as highways are added. This implies that because of the transport rate savings, the transport costs are less important in industry location, therefore there is less incentive for industry to move closer to its markets.

The percent of interarea shipments by truck show an increase from 31 percent to 33 percent between 1970 and 1990 under the Base Year alternative. The 1990 Base Year alternative assumes that the Interstate construction stopped in 1970. The data also show that there was a 4.1 percent drop in the truck transport costs per dollar of shipment between 1970 and 1990 in the Base Year alternative. The percent decrease was 7.1 percent for manufacturing commodities. Since a large portion of the Interstate system was completed by 1970, the changes in the Base Year alternatives partially reflect changes that are due to the Interstate highway system.

When the Completed Interstate system is compared with the Base Year system in 1990, the percent of interarea shipments going by truck increased from 33 to 34 percent. The truck transport costs per dollar of output decreased 1.2 percent.

When the highway links of the Extended Primary system and the Economic Development system are added to the Completed Interstate system, there is further savings in truck transport costs per dollar of output. There is an additional 1.2 percent savings with the Economic Development system and a 0.6 percent savings with the Extended Primary system. These additional highway

	VALUE OF INTER-AREA SHIPMENTS (BILLIONS)	%	VALUE-MILES (BILLIONS)	%	TRANSPORT COST (MILLIONS)	%	AVERAGE MILES SHIPPED (2)/(1)	TRANSPORT COST PER DOLLAR SHIPPED (3)/(1)
BASE YEAR (1970)								
ALL COMMODITIES:								
MOTOR	62.	31	41989.	28	1802.	13	682.	.02925
RAIL	135.	69	106910.	72	11834.	87	789.	.08737
TOTAL	197.	100	148896.	100	13636.	100	756.	.06920
MANUFACTURED COMMODITIES:								
MOTOR	61.	36	41894.	33	1731.	21	688.	.02845
RAIL	108.	64	85154.	67	6675.	79	785.	.06153
TOTAL	169.	100	127045.	100	8405.	100	750.	.04964
COMPLETED INTERSTATE (1990)								
ALL COMMODITIES:								
MOTOR	218.	34	122627.	30	6041.	16	562.	.02769
RAIL	423.	66	282010.	70	32160.	84	666.	.07599
TOTAL	641.	100	404637.	100	38201.	100	631.	.05956
MANUFACTURED COMMODITIES:								
MOTOR	214.	38	121858.	34	5592.	22	569.	.02609
RAIL	351.	62	237660.	66	19638.	78	678.	.05599
TOTAL	565.	100	359518.	100	25230.	100	636.	.04465
BASE YEAR (1990)								
ALL COMMODITIES:								
MOTOR	214.	33	120668.	30	5989.	16	565.	.02804
RAIL	426.	67	284150.	70	31913.	84	667.	.07487
TOTAL	640.	100	404818.	100	37902.	100	633.	.05923
MANUFACTURED COMMODITIES:								
MOTOR	210.	37	119898.	33	5540.	22	571.	.02641
RAIL	354.	63	239980.	67	19737.	78	678.	.05577
TOTAL	564.	100	359878.	100	25276.	100	638.	.04484
EXTENDED PRIMARY (1990)								
ALL COMMODITIES:								
MOTOR	221.	34	123564.	30	6076.	16	560.	.02753
RAIL	425.	66	281730.	70	31516.	84	663.	.07418
TOTAL	646.	100	405304.	100	37593.	100	628.	.05823

MANUFACTURED COMMODITIES:

MOTOR	217.	38	122775.	34	5631.	22	566.	.02597
RAIL	352.	62	237670.	66	19492.	78	675.	.05539
TOTAL	569.	100	360455.	100	25122.	100	634.	.04417

ECONOMIC DEVELOPMENT (1990)

ALL COMMODITIES:

MOTOR	271.	34	123428.	31	6041.	16	559.	.02735
RAIL	426.	66	280520.	69	31183.	84	659.	.07323
TOTAL	647.	100	403948.	100	37224.	100	625.	.05756

MANUFACTURED COMMODITIES:

MOTOR	217.	38	122656.	34	5602.	22	565.	.02582
RAIL	353.	62	236590.	66	19508.	78	670.	.05527
TOTAL	570.	100	359246.	100	25110.	100	630.	.04406

URBAN (1990)

ALL COMMODITIES:

MOTOR	218.	34	122627.	30	6041.	16	562.	.02769
RAIL	423.	66	282010.	70	32160.	84	666.	.07599
TOTAL	641.	100	404637.	100	38201.	100	631.	.05956

MANUFACTURED COMMODITIES:

MOTOR	214.	38	121858.	34	5592.	22	569.	.02609
RAIL	351.	62	237660.	66	19638.	78	678.	.05599
TOTAL	565.	100	359518.	100	25230.	100	636.	.04465

systems, however, do not change the percentage of total shipments going by truck.

The numbers in Table 5-6 for the Urban system are identical with those for the Completed Interstate system. Under the Urban system, as defined in this study, there are no interarea highways; therefore, there were no changes in the transport costs between the areas. The Urban system, however, does show regional economic effects that stem from the lowering of the highway congestion index below what it would have been under the Interstate system.

Chapter Six

Energy Requirements and Pollution Emissions

In recent years there has been much concern about the environmental quality of our air and water. Currently there is a great deal of concern about the availability of energy and other resources. If for any reason shortages occur, or if pollution is controlled, then regional economies will certainly be affected. Pollution control may impede the growth of some regions while encouraging it in other regions. If energy resources are insufficient, the regions who depend on them the most will suffer more than other regions.

It would be useful to know energy requirements and pollution emission in each region. With this information incorporated in the Multiregional, Multi-Industry Forecasting Model it would be possible to find the regional impacts of resource restrictions and pollution control. This chapter reports on the first step in this direction. Using preliminary data available at the national level, energy coefficients are developed by user sector; pollution emission coefficients are developed by the polluter sector. Although there may be regional variations in these coefficients, only national coefficients are used in this study. However, the application of national coefficients to regional data should produce fairly close approximations of the regional energy requirements and pollution emissions. As the model now stands there is no feedback of energy limitations or pollution controls on the economic forecasts. That is, the economic forecasts were made assuming no limitations on growth.

Energy sources are classified by user sector, with special emphasis on the transportation sector, using a national input-output model. Pollution data were obtained with special emphasis on air pollution, since it is most relevant to the transportation sectors. The energy and pollution coefficients are applied to the 1990 forecasts made with the regional forecasting model under alternative assumptions as to the transportation system.

ENERGY REQUIREMENTS

In the 99 industry sector classifications used in the regional forecasting model there are two fuel mining sectors—coal and petroleum (and gas), and three fuel processing sectors—petroleum refining, electric utility, and gas utility. Energy can be used directly from mining sectors; however, energy user sectors buy most of their Btu's from the processing industries.

The regional forecasting model makes use of a national input-output model consistent with its 99 industry sector classifications.[a] In order to have more relevant detail for computing energy coefficients associated with transportation it was necessary to augment the input-output model to include extra sectors. The maintenance construction industry sector was divided into four sectors, including maintenance construction for three types of highways. New highway construction was already one final demand sector in the model; however, it was divided into five sectors that classify highway construction by type of highway. The transportation industry sector was divided into five modes of transportation. In addition, the gasoline and jet fuel production activity of the petroleum refining industry was separated out, and the production of tires and tubes was separated from the rubber and plastics industry. The methods used to augment the input-output model will be explained below.

For each of the energy sectors data are available on the amount of Btu's produced.[b] The input-output model is used to convert resource data by source industry to data by user sector. Coefficients for each energy source industry were developed, which are the number of Btu's used in the United States divided by the available supply. The available supply of each resource is equal to the dollar value of domestic output plus imports minus exports and minus the intrasector transaction in the input-output table.[c] These coefficients were then applied to the dollar transactions from the energy source industries to the user sectors, using a two-price system. Data were available on the fuel source of Btu's used by the electric utility industry, and since the electric utility industry is one of the major buyers of energy resources, it was assumed that it paid a lower price than other buyers.

The 1970 energy requirements by user sector and source are given in Table 6-1. Most of the industry sectors have been aggregated into broader classifications, although detail is maintained in the sectors that are related with transportation. Energy originated from four sources—coal mining, petroleum and gas mining, nuclear power, and hydropower. Btu's originating in the mining

[a]Obtained from Professor Clopper Almon of the University of Maryland.

[b]U.S. Bureau of Mines data as reported in *Population, Resources, and the Environment*, the Commission on Population Growth and the American Future, Vol. 3, edited by Ronald G. Ridker, Washington, D.C.: U.S. Government Printing Office, 1972.

[c]The intrasector transactions were subtracted since they largely represent transactions between firms within an industry and do not reflect the creation of available supply.

TARIF 6.1

ENERGY REQUIREMENTS BY USER SECTOR AND SOURCE, 1970

UNITED STATES

TRANSPORTATION SYSTEM ALTERNATIVE: BASE YEAR

ENERGY SOURCE (BILLIONS OF BTU'S)

USER SECTOR	COAL MINING	GAS&OIL MINING	ELECTRIC UTILITY	GAS UTILITY	PETROLEUM REFINING	BTU TOTAL
1 AGRICULTURE	31769	0	45899	9876	2439691	2527235
2 MINING	47183	0	92733	18106	317485	475507
3 CONSTRUCTION	0	0	63323	22245	4495341	4580909
3.1 HIGHWAY CONSTRUCTION	0	0	2382	919	869635	872936
3.1.1 INTERSTATE, RURAL	0	0	448	218	226975	227640
3.1.2 INTERSTATE, URBAN	0	0	481	236	55657	56374
3.1.3 PRIMARY, RURAL	0	0	445	191	213930	214567
3.1.4 PRIMARY, URBAN	0	0	386	101	74789	75276
3.1.5 LOCAL	0	0	622	173	298285	299079
3.2 HIGHWAY MAINTENANCE	0	0	2902	1025	228281	232208
3.2.1 INTERSTATE	0	0	731	53	12327	13112
3.2.2 PRIMARY	0	0	493	480	81268	82241
3.2.3 LOCAL	0	0	1677	492	134686	136855
4 MANUFACTURING	4834170	43869354	985234	998111	4256418	11109096
4.1 MOTOR VEHICLES	50758	0	25173	9440	116735	202106
4.2 OTHER TRANSPORTATION EQUIPMENT	15835	0	29410	7231	150413	202889
4.3 PETROLEUM REFINING	20331	43834141	38876	144437	0	203644
4.3.1 GASOLINE AND JET FUEL	11751	41642434	30168	137215	0	179133
4.4 RUBBER AND PLASTIC PRODUCTS	54157	0	38919	10177	56301	159554
4.4.1 TIRES AND TUBES	20634	0	14828	3877	21451	60790
5 UTILITIES	7870258	8225568	11786377	3943226	2438251	12137381
6 TRANSPORTATION	23061	68078	33972	23725	3625772	3774608
6.1 RAILROAD	18864	0	0	4864	449596	473323
6.2 TRUCK	4197	0	0	5670	837553	847421
6.3 BUS AND TAXI	0	0	33972	807	340823	375601
6.4 AIRLINE	0	0	0	3772	1450309	1454081
6.5 OTHER	0	68078	0	8612	547492	624182
7 SERVICES	86408	0	1391318	532305	7061217	9071248
8 PERSONAL CONSUMPTION	606424	0	2151939	2325522	16700607	21784492
8.1 USER-OPERATED TRANSPORTATION	0	0	0	0	12936958	12936958
9 GOVERNMENT	292780	0	416209	141183	2499359	3349531
9.1 USER-OPERATED TRANSPORTATION	0	0	0	0	1993589	1993589
TOTAL	13792003	52163000	16967004	8014299	43834140	68810006

sectors are reported separately in the table, but the nuclear and hydropower generation is assumed to be created within the electric utility industry. In 1970 nuclear and hydropower accounted for 2,855 trillion Btu's.

It should be noted that there is considerable loss of Btu's when they are converted to electricity and transmitted to users. In 1970 the electric utility industry either created or acquired nearly 17,000 trillion Btu's, but the users of electricity used only approximately 5,000 trillion. The total Btu's consumed by user sector, as given in the last column of Table 6-1, excludes the Btu's lost in electricity generation. The loss is recorded in the "utilities" row of the last column.

In order to avoid double counting, the total Btu column in Table 6-1 is not the sum of the five energy columns in each of the rows. For example, in the manufacturing row there is an entry that records the sale of crude petroleum to the petroleum refining industry. This transaction is not counted as total Btu's in the manufacturing row since the refining industry processes the oil and distributes it to the users. Thus the Btu's transferred from the oil mining sector to the oil refining sector are accounted for in other rows in the table.

The numbers associated with the transportation industry are only for commercial common carriers. If a manufacturing firm were to own its own trucks, the energy required to run these trucks would be part of the total energy required by the manufacturing industry. Common carrier trucks account for approximately one-third of the total truck traffic.

Table 6-2 shows the 1990 energy requirements under the Completed Interstate system alternative. Since the national economic projections are the same for all alternative highway systems. there would not be much variation in the 1990 energy requirements by alternative. The other systems require the construction of new highways of interstate quality; however, there would be fewer new highways of lower quality. Although the construction of a mile of the Interstate highway system requires more energy than a mile of primary or local highway, it is possible to build more miles of primary local highway for the same amount of dollars. The energy requirements for highway construction includes the Btu equivalent of the bitumens used for paving.

A word of caution is required in evaluating the 1990 resource requirements. The forecasts are made simply by applying the 1970 coefficients to the appropriate 1990 data, and as a result the resource forecasts are probably on the high side. Also, there are no adjustments for the energy saving practices adopted in the 1973-74 energy crisis. This procedure entails several underlying assumptions. It assumes that the growth rate in energy requirements will be the same as the growth rate in the corresponding user sectors; therefore it assumes that there will be no increase in efficiency in resource production and no changes in the conservation practices or life style of the users. Historical data show that the long term growth in energy use was slower than GNP, although between 1965 and 1973 it was faster. The procedure also assumes that the

TABLE 6.2

ENERGY REQUIREMENTS BY USER SECTOR AND SOURCE, 1990

UNITED STATES

TRANSPORTATION SYSTEM ALTERNATIVE: COMPLETED INTERSTATE

ENERGY SOURCE (BILLIONS OF BTU'S)

USER SECTOR	COAL MINING	GAS/OIL MINING	ELECTRIC UTILITY	GAS UTILITY	PETROLEUM REFINING	BTU TOTAL
1 AGRICULTURE	55952.	0.	79257.	17097.	4140492.	4292798.
2 MINING	93175.	0.	202282.	52233.	706038.	1053728.
3 CONSTRUCTION	0.	0.	118738.	41489.	7842860.	8003086.
3.1 HIGHWAY CONSTRUCTION	0.	0.	7702.	863.	1087998.	1091564.
3.1.1 INTERSTATE, RURAL	0.	0.	0.	0.	0.	0.
3.1.2 INTERSTATE, URBAN	0.	0.	0.	0.	0.	0.
3.1.3 PRIMARY, RURAL	0.	0.	620.	352.	393889.	395061.
3.1.4 PRIMARY, URBAN	0.	0.	731.	191.	141601.	142523.
3.1.5 LOCAL	0.	0.	1152.	320.	552509.	553980.
3.2 HIGHWAY MAINTENANCE	0.	0.	3881.	1241.	275990.	281113.
3.2.1 INTERSTATE	0.	0.	1344.	98.	22653.	24095.
3.2.2 PRIMARY	0.	0.	587.	571.	96742.	97900.
3.2.3 LOCAL	0.	0.	1950.	572.	156595.	159117.
4 MANUFACTURING	9617761.	8803241.	2166157.	2119903.	9373804.	23501062.
4.1 MOTOR VEHICLES	144892.	0.	71858.	26947.	333228.	576925.
4.2 OTHER TRANSPORTATION EQUIPMENT	38151.	0.	73459.	17841.	376618.	506069.
4.3 PETROLEUM REFINING	40818.	8803803.	78050.	289980.	0.	408845.
4.3.1 GASOLINE AND JET FUEL	23593.	83603612.	60566.	275481.	0.	359637.
4.4 RUBBER AND PLASTIC PRODUCTS	122041.	0.	87703.	22934.	126873.	359551.
4.4.1 TIRES AND TUBES	46498.	0.	33415.	8738.	48339.	136989.
5 UTILITIES	17342648.	16920039.	25979103.	8688597.	5338773.	26707235.
6 TRANSPORTATION	46739.	143887.	71802.	49942.	7666094.	7978465.
6.1 RAILROAD	37581.	0.	0.	9689.	895695.	942966.
6.2 TRUCK	9158.	0.	0.	12373.	1825566.	1849097.
6.3 BUS AND TAXI	0.	0.	71802.	1705.	720351.	793858.
6.4 AIRLINE	0.	0.	0.	7973.	3065322.	3073295.
6.5 OTHER	0.	143887.	0.	18202.	1157159.	1319249.
7 SERVICES	188224.	0.	3067191.	1172389.	15363039.	19790842.
8 PERSONAL CONSUMPTION	0.	0.	4995548.	4515382.	34998989.	44508919.
8.1 USER-OPERATED TRANSPORTATION	0.	0.	0.	0.	27111616.	27111616.
9 GOVERNMENT	463183.	0.	691408.	246547.	37666226.	5167361.
9.1 USER-OPERATED TRANSPORTATION	0.	0.	0.	0.	3151262.	3151262.
TOTAL	27951682.	105147166.	37370485.	16903576.	89196313.	141003496.

sources of energy in 1990 will be supplied to each user sector in the same proportion as in 1970, and that the loss rate in converting fuels to electricity will not change. Undoubtedly there will be changes in the source mix, and total Btu requirements will change if some sources are more efficient than others.

Summary data and forecasts of energy use by OBE economic areas are given in the Appendix.

The Augmented Input-Output Model

In order to obtain energy requirements relevant to transportation it was necessary to expand the national input-output model beyond the sectoring used for the regional economic projections. Some additional detail was readily available, but other required considerable effort to obtain.

Some of the additional sectors were available from a larger Almon input-output model. These are: (1) the transportation service industry divided into five modes of transportation; (2) the separation of the tire and tube production from the rubber and plastics industry; and (3) the separation of the gasoline and jet fuel production from the petroleum refining industry.

User Operated Transportation Expenditures. The private use of cars and other motor vehicles by consumers requires more energy than any other transportation activity. In order to estimate the energy used for personal transportation it is necessary to break out the personal consumption from the total personal consumption expenditure (PCE) final demand column in the national input-output table.

The use of motor vehicles by governments is also classified in the user operated category. Once the input-output coefficients were developed for consumers by type of transportation expenditure they are also applied to governmental expenditures in order to derive the government's use of energy for transportation purposes.

The Bureau of Economic Analysis (BEA) in its *Survey of Current Business* publishes annual data on personal consumption expenditures by type of product, including user operated transportation. In order to derive the PCE vector for their national input-output, BEA converts the expenditures by type of product to industry sector.[d] Using BEA's 1963 conversion table (the latest available), PCE coefficients vectors were derived classified by our industry sectors for four types of expenditures on user operated transportation. The results are shown in Table 6-3, along with the 1970 total expenditures.

Highway Construction. The national input-output table used in the regional forecasting model already includes new highway construction as a final

[d]U.S. Department of Commerce, Office of Business Economics, *Input-Output Structure of the U.S. Economy: 1963*. A supplement to the *Survey of Current Business*, 1969.

Table 6-3. Industry Distribution of Consumers Expenditures on
User Operated Transportation

No.	Industry Name	New Cars	Tires & Parts	Gasoline & Oil	Auto Repair & Other
25	Rugs & tire cord		.005		
27	Household textiles		.112		
35	Basic chemicals		.028		
37	Drugs & cleaning items		.008		
39	Petroleum refining			.451	
40	Rubber & plastic products		.399		
52	Hardware & wire		.003		
60	Machine shops		.001		
62	Service industry mach.		.020		
65	Electric lights & wiring		.010		
66	Communication equip.		.036		
68	Batteries & elec. equip.		.077		
69	Motor vehicles	.688	.013		
71	Ships, trains, trailers, cycles	.027			
75	Transportation: railroad	.009	.007	.007	.043
75	Transportation: truck	.009	.010	.008	
75	Transportation: water	.001		.015	
75	Transportation: pipeline			.013	
81	Wholesale trade	.023	.094	.300	.273
82	Finance & insurance				
86	Auto repair service				.684
92	Auto dealers	.226	.138		
93	Gasoline stations		.139	.206	
	Imports	.017			
	Total	1.000	1.000	1.000	1.000
	1970 expenditures (millions of dollars)	$31,595	$5,702	$22,211	$12,742

demand sector. However, since it was possible to obtain cost data by type of highway, this sector was divided into five new sectors, namely: (1) rural interstate, (2) urban interstate, (3) rural primary, (4) urban primary, and (5) local highway construction.

In determining the dollar coefficients by industry sector and by type of highway, cost data by type of material were obtained from several sources including several state highway agencies or state departments of transportation and the National Highway Users Federation for Safety and Mobility. All indications were that the best available data were those provided by the states to the Federal Highway Administration for the purposes of administering federal aid monies. Such data are used in compiling the tables presented in the annual publication, *Highway Statistics*, Federal Highway Administration, U.S. Department of Transportation.

Additional cost data were obtained from the Federal Highway Administration, including detailed summaries of the PR-47 forms for eight states and totals for each state. These summaries were used to supplement the figures in *Highway Statistics.*

A detailed sample of individual construction site figures were obtained for two states, California and North Carolina. These data, showing quantities of resources required for each specific project, the length of the project, and costs, were very helpful in obtaining the final set of data for estimating the dollar coefficients by type of highway.

The dollar coefficients for the different highway classifications are given in Table 6-4. Labor costs and depreciation of construction equipment are included in value added. Equipment purchases and right-of-way costs are not included in the figures shown.

Highway Maintenance. The highway maintenance data from several states and local agencies were analyzed and subsequently incorporated with the highway construction data.[e] Although some variation was found, the total maintenance costs are distributed approximately as follows:

Labor	56%
Equipment	23%
Material	21%

The data allow highways to be divided into three types: (1) interstate, (2) primary, and (3) local. As a general rule, the labor proportion of the cost for local roads was higher than the percentage shown above.

Maintenance costs are generally summarized in a format that identifies the labor, equipment, and material costs for various maintenance activities. These activities include tasks such as "spot premix patching," "mowing," "centerline painting," etc. Approximately 60 activity descriptions are required to identify the variety of highway maintenance functions performed by state and local agencies.

Material costs for the maintenance activities were analyzed by type of highway with respect to their components by industry sectors. For example, the material costs for the activity "major premix patching" were assigned to five industry sectors in the following percentages:

Stone and Clay Products	45%
Petroleum Refining	35%
Electric Utility	2%
Water Utility	2%
Gas Utility	1%

[e]Data were obtained from (1) Roy Jorgensen Associates, Inc., Gaithersburg, Maryland, maintenance cost reports for Tennessee, Alabama and Virginia; (2) West Virginia Highway Department; (3) Virginia Highway Department; and (4) *Highway Statistics,* Federal Highway Administration.

Approximately 85 percent of the maintenance material costs were easily assigned to industries in this manner. The remaining 15 percent of the costs were distributed among all industry sectors having a recognizable maintenance material cost element.

Equipment purchases were examined for the purpose of obtaining the depreciation component of value added. Cognizant practitioners in the highway maintenance field indicated that, on a long term basis, the total annual depreciation of all maintenance equipment is approximately equivalent to the cost of new equipment expenditures in any specific year. The latter values, which are reflected in state summaries of annual maintenance equipment costs, were used in our analyses.

The other major costs associated with equipment are replacement parts, fuel, lubricants, and tires. These were assigned to industry sectors in a manner similar to that used for material costs. Maintenance material and equipment related costs were combined and summarized by highway type and industry sector. The labor costs were identified for each highway and classified into value added. The dollar coefficients are given in Table 6-5.

POLLUTION EMISSIONS

It is very difficult to measure the environmental damage caused by pollution. The damage depends not only on the amount of emissions but also on ability of the air or water to cleanse itself of the pollution. However, except for a few types of pollution such as pesticides and radiation, pollution emissions have short lives. That is, most pollutants will eventually disappear even though they may do some immediate damage to the environment. The total amount of emissions does not measure the concentration level of pollution, but in any area, given its prevailing wind currents or water flow, it would be a fairly good approximation to say that if the amount of pollution emissions were to double, the amount of pollution concentration would also double. Therefore, even though emissions do not measure environmental damage, they do serve as an index of change in environmental damage.

Pollution emissions for 1970 were derived from various sources. In general they are the amount of emissions after having been treated with average 1970 techniques. The emissions are converted into coefficients by polluter sector so that they can be applied to economic variables forecasts for future years.

The projections show the approximate amount of pollution that would occur in 1990 if there were no change in the average treatment as defined in 1970. More likely, the actual amount of pollution in 1990 would be less than the estimates given by applying 1970 coefficients. First of all, it is possible that better treatment facilities will be available. Even in 1970 some polluters used better treatment facilities than others, and even though no new treatment facilities are invented or applied, it is quite possible that the polluters who are

Table 6-4. New Highway Construction Input-Output Coefficients by Type of Highway, 1970

Industry No.	Industry Name	Interstate		Primary		Local	Total
		Rural	Urban	Rural	Urban		
2	Crops	.00030	.00058	.00034	.00057	.00015	.00032
9	Minerals mining	.07736	.07013	.07220	.07955	.06392	.07061
12	Maintenance construction	.00021	.00029	.00019	.00023	.00013	.00019
22	Misc. food products	.00005	.00005	.00005	.00005	.00005	.00005
25	Rugs, tire cord, misc. textiles	.00001	.00001	.00001	.00001	.00001	.00001
26	Apparel	.00054	.00055	.00052	.00055	.00041	.00049
28	Lumber and prod. exc. containers	.01008	.01362	.01007	.01179	.01110	.01116
32	Paper and prod. exc. containers	.00003	.00003	.00003	.00003	.00003	.00003
33	Paper containers	.00002	.00002	.00002	.00002	.00002	.00002
34	Printing and publishing	.00003	.00003	.00003	.00003	.00003	.00003
35	Basic chemicals	.00784	.00387	.00636	.00437	.00480	.00549
37	Drugs, cleaning and toilet items	.00004	.00004	.00004	.00004	.00004	.00004
38	Paint and allied products	.00365	.00472	.00403	.00471	.00499	.00449
39	Petroleum refining	.06307	.02156	.06805	.03743	.04342	.04778
40	Rubber and plastic products	.00316	.00383	.00351	.00378	.00283	.00326
41	Leather tanning	.00005	.00005	.00005	.00005	.00005	.00005
44	Stone and clay products	.08823	.06740	.08402	.08135	.06923	.07661
45	Iron and steel	.06390	.07268	.04807	.05983	.04578	.05514
48	Other nonferrous metals	.00112	.00030	.00093	.00049	.00072	.00075
50	Heating, plumbing, struc. metal	.04988	.10067	.04404	.05176	.04929	.05611
51	Stampings, screw mach. prod.	.00015	.00022	.00015	.00023	.00010	.00015
52	Hardward, plating, wire prod.	.00913	.01110	.01005	.01259	.00820	.00960
54	Farm machinery and equipment	.00007	.00007	.00007	.00007	.00007	.00007
55	Construction and mining mach.	.00771	.00403	.00817	.00437	.01070	.00802
60	Machine shops and misc. mach.	.00120	.00176	.00133	.00182	.00088	.00125
61	Office and computing machines	.00003	.00003	.00003	.00003	.00003	.00003
63	Electric apparatus and motors	.00001	.00001	.00001	.00001	.00001	.00001
65	Electric light and wiring equipment	.00966	.01818	.01035	.01820	.00450	.00999
66	Communication equipment	.00205	.00318	.00222	.00318	.00140	.00212
68	Batteries and engine elec. equipment	.00128	.00200	.00141	.00199	.00082	.00131

69 Motor vehicles	.00267	.00420	.00289	.00506	.00177	.00285
71 Ships, trains, trailers, cycles	.00078	.00090	.00077	.00093	.00043	.00068
72 Instruments and clocks	.00001	.00001	.00001	.00001	.00001	.00001
73 Optical and photographic equip.	.00012	.00018	.00012	.00010	.00005	.00010
74 Misc. manufactured products	.00368	.00479	.00405	.00475	.00506	.00454
75 Transportation	.05745	.09360	.06230	.09354	.03583	.05927
76 Communication	.00177	.00342	.00195	.00326	.00084	.00185
78 Electric utility	.00114	.00170	.00130	.00177	.00083	.00120
79 Gas utility	.00012	.00018	.00012	.00010	.00005	.00010
80 Water utility	.00209	.00396	.00227	.00382	.00098	.00216
81 Wholesale trade	.06859	.10139	.07476	.10110	.04942	.07069
82 Finance and insurance	.01023	.01359	.01012	.01189	.01115	.01122
83 Real estate and rental	.00322	.00638	.00282	.00627	.00535	.00474
85 Business services	.12907	.08794	.12118	.11314	.14916	.12765
86 Automobiles repair services	.00563	.00878	.00614	.00877	.00395	.00588
88 Medical and educational instit.	.00257	.00489	.00278	.00489	.00121	.00268
Value Added	.31000	.26308	.33007	.26147	.41020	.33920
Total	1.00000	1.00000	1.00000	1.00000	1.00000	1.00000

Table 6–5. Highway Maintenance Construction Input-Output Coefficients by Type of Highway, 1970

Industry No.	Industry Name	Interstate	Primary	Local	Total
2	Crops	.00141	.00144	.00002	.00063
9	Minerals mining	.01241	.01484	.01598	.01530
12	Maintenance construction	.00003	.00003	.00003	.00003
22	Misc. food products	.00001	.00001	.00001	.00001
25	Rugs, tire cord, misc. textiles	.00051	.00049	.00051	.00050
26	Apparel	.00003	.00003	.00004	.00003
28	Lumber & prod. exc. containers	.01032	.00862	.00648	.00753
32	Paper & prod. exc. containers	.00016	.00014	.00001	.00007
33	Paper containers	.00001	.00001	.00001	.00001
34	Printing & publishing	.00001	.00001	.00001	.00001
35	Basic chemicals	.02698	.02030	.01425	.01738
37	Drugs, cleaning & toilet items	.00001	.00001	.00001	.00001
38	Paint & allied products	.03521	.03177	.01517	.02260
39	Petroleum refining	.05051	.07399	.07598	.07328
40	Rubber & plastic products	.01534	.01466	.01519	.01501
41	Leather tanning	.00001	.00001	.00000	.00001
44	Stone & clay products	.01648	.02485	.05815	.04313
45	Iron & steel	.01699	.01143	.01281	.01265
48	Other nonferrous metals	.00758	.00613	.00411	.00510
50	Heating, plumbing, struc. metal	.00630	.00612	.00675	.00649
51	Stampings, screw mach. prod.	.00161	.00016	.00002	.00019
52	Hardware plating wire prod.	.00587	.00621	.00690	.00658
54	Farm machinery & equipment	.00321	.00309	.00323	.00318
55	Construction & mining mach.	.00562	.00541	.00564	.00556
60	Machine shops & misc. mach.	.00534	.00514	.00538	.00529
61	Office & computing machines	.00001	.00001	.00001	.00001
63	Electric apparatus & motors	.00881	.00076	.00001	.00097
65	Elec. light & wiring equipment	.00811	.00152	.00073	.00159
66	Communication equipment	.00346	.00277	.00286	.00287
68	Batteries & engine elec. equip.	.00535	.00583	.00652	.00619
69	Motor vehicles	.00289	.00278	.00291	.00286
71	Ships, trains, trailers, cycles	.00596	.00575	.00600	.00591

72	Instruments & clocks	.00001	.00028	.00046	.00036
73	Optical & photographic equip.	.00002	.00001	.00002	.00002
74	Misc. manufactured products	.00554	.00535	.00562	.00552
75	Transportation	.00839	.00813	.00885	.00856
76	Communication	.00012	.00012	.00013	.00013
78	Electric utility	.00670	.00100	.00211	.00208
79	Gas utility	.00288	.00571	.00363	.00431
80	Water utility	.00453	.00234	.00273	.00274
81	Wholesale trade	.00716	.00716	.00805	.00767
82	Finance & insurance	.00072	.00070	.00082	.00077
83	Real estate & rental	.00300	.00300	.00300	.00300
85	Business services	.06000	.06000	.06000	.06000
86	Automobile repair services	.00826	.00878	.00973	.00928
88	Medical & educational instit.	.00017	.00017	.00020	.00018
V.A.	Value added	.63599	.64295	.62889	.63441
	Total	1.00000	1.00000	1.00000	1.00000

TABLE 6.6

POLLUTION EMISSIONS, 1970
(THOUSANDS OF TONS)

UNITED STATES

TRANSPORTATION SYSTEM ALTERNATIVE: BASE YEAR

AIR POLLUTION

SOURCE	SO	PART.	CO	HC	NO
TRANSPORTATION					
RAILROADS	124.	47.	100.	93.	142.
MOTOR VEHICLES	300.	400.	96600.	16700.	9100.
AIRCRAFT	100.	49.	3000.	420.	364.
OTHER	460.	159.	11200.	2317.	2082.
ELECTRIC UTILITY	19400.	3700.	162.	140.	4710.
INDUSTRIAL	6030.	13300.	11400.	9530.	199.
SPACE HEATING	7100.	3150.	628.	475.	5290.
BURNING AND INCINERATION	104.	4765.	23820.	5015.	802.
TOTAL	33618.	25570.	146910.	34690.	22689.

WATER POLLUTION

CHEMICAL OXYGEN DEMAND	44744.
BIOCHEMICAL OXYGEN DEMAND	111930.

LAND POLLUTION

SOLID WASTE	160500

using average or less than average treatment facilities in 1970 will be using the 1970 "best-practice" treatment facilities in 1990.

Another problem occurs because the coefficients are applied to aggregated industry classifications. If the product mix or input mix within an industry were to change, then the amount of emission would also change. Moreover, new technological processes in 1990 probably will produce less pollution than the processes used in 1970. Finally, the amount of pollution in 1990 could be greatly reduced if more stringent pollution controls were instituted.

The 1970 pollution emissions are shown in Table 6-6. The data for air pollution emissions were obtained from the U.S. Environmental Protection Agency.[f] The data for the water pollution were obtained from Professor John H. Cumberland of the University of Maryland,[g] and the data for the solid waste

[f]*Nationwide Air Pollutant Emissions Trends, 1940-1970*, January 1973.
[g]John H. Cumberland and Bruce N. Stram, "Empirical Results from Application of Input-Output Models to Environmental Problems," Sixth International Conference on Input-Output Techniques, Vienna, April 1974.

TABLF 6.7

POLLUTION EMISSIONS, 1990
(THOUSANDS OF TONS)

UNITED STATES

TRANSPORTATION SYSTEM ALTERNATIVF: COMPLETED INTERSTATE

AIR POLLUTION

SOURCE	SO	PART.	CO	HC	NO
TRANSPORTATION					
RAILROADS	247.	94.	199.	185.	283.
MOTOR VEHICLFS	637.	847.	202511.	35006.	19183.
AIRCRAFT	211.	104.	6341.	888.	769.
OTHER	895.	285.	19151.	3945.	3487.
FLECTRIC UTILITY	42764.	8156.	357.	309.	0382.
INDUSTRIAL	12879.	25627.	22051.	19929.	437.
SPACE HEATING	15928.	7067.	1409.	1066.	11868.
BURNING AND INCINFRATION	217.	9034.	43994.	9256.	1561.
TOTAL	73779.	51213.	296013.	70584.	47971.

WATER POLLUTION

CHEMICAL OXYGEN DFMAND	82631.
BIOCHEMICAL OXYGEN DEMAND	198721.

LAND POLLUTION

SOLID WASTE	213028.

pollution were obtained from the Commission on Population Growth and the American Future.[h] The air and water pollution data were available by polluter sector, and the numbers in Table 6-6 are based on a more detailed set of data. Table 6-7 shows the 1990 pollution emissions, assuming 1970 coefficients, that would occur under the Completed Interstate system alternative.

[h]*Population, Resources, and the Environment*, op. cit.

Chapter Seven

Conclusion

Before the concluding remarks are made, this chapter reports on a test of the accuracy of the regional forecasting model and mentions other possible applications of the model.

ACCURACY OF THE FORECASTS

In the runs of the forecasting model, the coefficients in the equations were estimated using data for 1965 and 1966; but since partial data were available for 1970, the year 1970 was used as the "take-off" or "base year" in making the projections. The model could have used 1966 as the base year, but the year 1970 was preferred since it is more recent, and other 1970 data were available on highway systems. However, making 1970 forecasts from a 1966 base offers an opportunity to test how well the model performs.

Actual or estimated 1970 data were available for (1) employment by 103 sectors, (2) population by eight age-race groups, and (3) personal income by four components. The predicted 1970 values were compared with the actual 1970 values for each of these sectors using a simple linear regression equation

$$A_j = a + bP_j,$$

where A_j is the actual 1970 value for region j and P_j is the predicted (forecast) 1970 value for region j.

If the forecasting model did a perfect job in forecasting the 1970 values, then the intercept "a" would be 0, the coefficient "b" would be 1 and the coefficient of determination (R^2), which is a measure of the overall fit, would be 1. Therefore, the closer that the coefficients b and R^2 are to 1, the better the forecast. In interpreting the intercept term, it must be remembered that if the variable in question, such as personal income, contains large numbers,

159

then the intercept itself could be a large number but not significantly different from 0 if the standard error is also large.

The results of this test are presented in Table 7-1. In 65 out of the 103 employment sectors, over 90 percent of the regional variation in the actual number of jobs was explained by the forecast of the number of jobs. The R^2 was greater than 80 percent for 83 of the sectors. There were only two sectors in which the R^2 was less than 50 percent. The forecast accuracy in the agricultural sectors was low, but in these sectors there is some question about the 1970 figures since they were estimated and not actual data.

Table 7-1.   Measurement of Accuracy of Forecasting Model
$A = a + bP$

Jobs by Sector	Intercept a	Coefficient b	R^2
1. Livestock	4350	.56489	.4521
2. Crops	2474	.72571	.5863
3. Forestry & fishery products	51	.79132	.8524
4. Agricultural services	61	.96298	.9044
5. Iron ore mining	−91	1.12114	.8602
6. Nonferrous ore mining	−37	1.03910	.8538
7. Coal mining	−20	1.00836	.9774
8. Petroleum mining	48	.97569	.8976
9. Minerals mining	118	.80965	.6641
*10. Chemical mining	245	.52740	.5601
11. New construction	−1408	1.06992	.9424
12. Maintenance construction	−384	1.21490	.9088
13. Ordnance	747	.77046	.9440
*14. Meat packing	55	.97951	.8651
15. Dairy Products	108	.92453	.9118
*16. Canned and frozen foods	114	.93376	.7943
*17. Grain mill products	32	.96469	.8122
18. Bakery products	174	.90670	.9713
*19. Sugar	315	.59648	.8597
*20. Candy	−51	1.05497	.9425
21. Beverages	181	.87075	.8552
*22. Misc. food products	−75	1.08140	.8892
23; Tobacco	19	1.11828	.5984
24. Fabrics & yarn	446	.95649	.9306
25. Rugs, tire cord, misc. textiles	25	1.05267	.7999
26. Apparel	564	.94641	.9916
27. Household textiles & upholst.	−11	1.01311	.9643
*28 Lumber & prod. exc. containers	98	.97244	.9328
*29. Wooden containers	78	.73957	.5474
30. Household furniture	24	1.02897	.9226
31. Office furniture	116	.91018	.9038
*32. Paper & prod. exc. containers	264	.93182	.9404
*33. Paper containers	426	.80283	.9435
34. Printing & publishing	156	.97818	.9918
*35. Basic chemicals	108	.97191	.9187
36. Plastics & synthetics	660	.74502	.6489
37. Drugs, cleaning & toilet items	−81	1.08579	.9759

Table 7-1 continued

Jobs by Sector		Intercept *a*	Coefficient *b*	R^2
38.	Paint & allied products	67	.92435	.9242
*39	Petroleum refining	72	.94042	.8665
40.	Rubber & plastic products	170	.95165	.9541
41.	Leather tanning	66	.88973	.8638
42.	Shoes & other leather products	582	.81077	.9497
43.	Glass & glass products	124	.92216	.8917
*44.	Stone & clay products	209	.92223	.8963
*45.	Iron & steel	−877	1.09991	.9659
46.	Copper	272	.80639	.6637
47.	Aluminum	558	.65030	.5960
48.	Other nonferrous metals	174	.89453	.9049
49.	Metal containers	215	.81361	.7710
50.	Heating, plumbing, struc. metal	374	.87805	.9435
51.	Stampings, screw mach. prod.	58	.97940	.9670
52.	Hardware, plating, wire prod.	272	.91990	.9799
53.	Engines & turbines	581	.72186	.5463
54.	Farm machinery & equipment	214	.82473	.7460
55.	Construction & mining mach.	−33	1.02584	.7635
56.	Material handling equipment	172	.87195	.8284
57.	Metalworking mach. & equip.	60	.98494	.9510
58.	Special industrial mach.	−18	1.02439	.9294
59.	General industrial mach.	390	.86748	.9191
60.	Machine shops & misc. mach.	215	.87481	.9183
61.	Office & computing machines	329	.96587	.6556
62.	Service industry machines	438	.75430	.6628
63.	Electric apparatus & motors	625	.85405	.8021
64.	Household appliances	370	.87596	.7588
65.	Electric light & wiring equipment	201	.90068	.9271
66.	Communication equipment	1019	.87479	.9003
67.	Electronic components	−183	1.08060	.9111
68.	Batteries & engine elec. equipment	199	.96100	.5436
69.	Motor vehicles	627	.91449	.9784
70.	Aircraft & parts	858	.86768	.8702
71.	Ships, trains, trailers, cycles	1369	.41646	.3287
72.	Instruments & clocks	42	.95630	.9351
73.	Optical & photographic equip.	−21	1.05333	.9389
74.	Misc. manufactured products	−303	1.10615	.9663
*75.	Transportation	−1173	1.07103	.9932
76.	Communication	−413	1.07448	.9483
77.	Radio, TV broadcasting	147	.82429	.8645
*78.	Electric utility	342	.86998	.8764
79.	Gas utility	69	.93752	.7491
80.	Water utility	43	.83600	.8117
81.	Wholesale trade	711	.97189	.9961
82.	Finance & insurance	−204	1.01137	.9967
83.	Real estate & rental	−21	1.00432	.9880
84.	Hotels, personal & repair svc.	1236	.91938	.9822
*85.	Business services	1856	.88876	.9914
86.	Automobile repair services	124	.95957	.9636
87.	Amusements & recreation	352	.91639	.9629

(Continued)

Table 7-1 continued

Jobs by Sector	Intercept a	Coefficient b	R^2
88. Medical & educational instit.	−411	1.01291	.9966
89. Lumber, houseware, farm equip. stores	−176	1.05528	.9664
90. General merchandise stores	26	.99816	.9936
91. Food stores	19	.99832	.9954
92. Automotive dealers	−113	1.01674	.9851
93. Gasoline service stations	−200	1.04309	.9889
94. Apparel, accessory stores	136	.97502	.9959
95. Furniture stores	28	.99110	.9928
96. Eating, drinking places	636	.96304	.9909
97. Drug and proprietary stores	−104	1.03380	.9825
98. Other retail stores	−127	1.02310	.9928
99. Nonstore retailers	1	.99890	.9779
100. Federal civilian government	1494	.90628	.9805
101. State and local government	−688	1.01200	.9780
102. Domestic services	−547	1.04625	.9981
103. Armed forces	−361	1.03435	.9764
Total jobs	−2981	1.00622	.9983
Population by Age-Race Group			
1. White under 14	3139	.98891	.9977
2. White 15–34	1850	.99389	.9963
3. White 35–64	−4126	1.01232	.9990
4. White over 64	−12	1.00012	.9967
5. Nonwhite under 14	−3433	1.06647	.9823
6. Nonwhite 15–34	−1547	1.03367	.9870
7. Nonwhite 35–64	−368	1.00920	.9943
8. Nonwhite over 64	−431	1.04278	.9844
Total population	−11759	1.01001	.9991
Personal Income by Sector			
1. Transfer payments	−13347	1.03040	.9981
2. Social insurance payments	7624	.95059	.9965
3. Property income	−2099	1.00337	.9986
4. Earnings	253763	.92895	.9896
Total personal income	233912	.94812	.9937

*Indicates that transportation costs are greater than 4% of output value.

While the forecast for a few individual sectors was not as accurate as could be hoped for, the forecast accuracy of the total jobs, total population, and total personal income was very high. For these three items the correlation coefficients were: .9983 for total jobs, .9991 for total population, and .9937 for total personal income. The 1970 forecast of total population had the greatest accuracy of any of the items tested. Even the forecast of the components of population achieved a high degree of accuracy. Also, the accuracy of the components of personal income was high.

Good or poor forecasts for 1970, however, does not necessarily mean that the 1990 forecasts will be good or poor. The year-to-year forecasts do not follow any smooth trend line, and low forecast in the early years may be offset by high forecast in later years, or vice versa.

FUTURE RESEARCH

The regional forecasting model was applied to a set of 173 economic areas. Each area is a group of counties containing at least one central city and supporting suburban and rural counties. The model is not restricted to geographic units of this size, however. It has already been applied at the county level and if data were available it could be applied even at the city level. The redistribution effects within a state or an economic area or even within a metropolitan area could be evaluated. Thus it would be possible to study the central city versus the suburban effects of alternative highways—although, given the lack of local area data, it might be more meaningful to use a metropolitan land use model with the control table taken from the regional forecasting model.

The model could be expanded to study the effects of alternative highway systems on passenger travel. By attaching components concerned with passenger travel and time savings of passenger travel, it would be possible to attain a more complete measure of the overall effects of the alternative highway systems. This would be especially important for intrametropolitan area studies.

In Chapter Six it was shown how energy requirements and environmental effects can be attached to the model. Resources are required not only to build the highways, but if highways cause geographic redistributions of industry, then the resource requirements and environmental effects of particular regions will change. If an area's economy is stimulated, additional resources would be required in that area and environmental problems would increase. With appropriate modifications in the model it would be possible to impose limits on growth in any one area due to the lack of resources or because the growth would violate environmental standards. If resource constraints were specified in the model, then the forecast growth of some areas could be restricted.

The regional forecasting model can measure regional economic impact in many other applications. Any variable, or the rate of change of any variable, can be predetermined in any time period. For example, the model can be used to study the location of a new plant or the shutting down of an old one. Indeed, the viability of a whole new town can be evaluated. The model can be used to study the effects of alternative governmental expenditures, such as defense or educational expenditures. With additional information on state and local governmental revenues and expenditures the fiscal impact of alternative governmental plans or policies could be measured, and with the addition of monetary variables the impact on financial institutions could be measured.

CONCLUDING REMARKS

There is little doubt that past highway systems have been beneficial to the nation's economy. They have reduced the time and cost of moving people and goods between regions, and therefore they have increased the efficiency of the economy. Many prices would probably be higher if this increase in efficiency had not occurred. Moreover, construction of highways often has come at a time when there has been wide unemployment, thus adding jobs and income to the nation's economy.

Will future highway systems contribute as much? After the completion of the Interstate system, additional highway systems may add little to the efficiency of the nation's economy. If we have a full employment economy, then money spent on highways is money that cannot be spent on other items, such as other government programs and consumer goods. Moreover, further use of highways will use value energy resources and increase environmental damage.

In this study, a full employment economy was assumed. It was also assumed that the total money spent for highway construction would be the same under all alternative highway systems considered. The different systems, then, really specify a redistribution of highway money from one region to another. Under these assumptions very little improvement in the efficiency of the nation's economy is shown. The cost of shipping goods went down as additional highways were added, but the amount of this change was very small.

If improvements in overall national efficiency are small as new highway systems are added, then it is necessary to look at the regional redistribution effects of these systems in order to evaluate their benefits. This study has shown that regional economies can be stimulated by the construction of highway systems. Highways located in one area and not in another gave the area with the highways a competitive advantage over the one without. Industries are attracted to areas because of the low transportation costs and low levels of congestion. Moreover, an area's economy is stimulated by highway construction expenditures.

Stimulating regional economies may be a worthwhile goal for transportation planners. The redistribution goals of the hypothetical highway systems considered in this study were met. The Economic Development system was designed to help low income areas, and the results show that it would help low income areas. The Extended Primary system did help small areas, and the Urban system did stimulate growth in large urban areas.

Whatever the regional redistributional goals, it seems that construction of highway systems could be a contributing factor toward achieving the goals.

Appendix Tables

SUMMARY PROJECTIONS BY ORE ECONOMIC AREA UNDER FIVE ALTERNATIVE HIGHWAY SYSTEMS

1 BANGOR, MAINE

	1970	1990 BASE YEAR	1990 COMPLETED INTERSTATE	1990 EXTENDED PRIMARY	1990 ECONOMIC DEVELOPMENT	1990 URBAN	PERCENT CI/BY	EP/CI	ED/CI	U/CI
JOBS BY INDUSTRY			(THOUSANDS)							
NATURAL RESOURCES (1-10)	7.2	5.6	5.6	5.9	5.5	5.6	100	107	100	101
CONSTRUCTION (11,12)	3.4	3.7	3.7	5.5	2.9	3.1	98	151	78	85
MANUFACTURING (13-74)	28.5	42.5	41.9	43.8	40.2	41.2	99	105	96	98
TRANSPORTATION INDUSTRY (75)	3.3	2.3	2.3	2.5	2.3	2.3	99	109	97	98
PUBLIC UTILITIES (76-80)	2.1	1.5	1.5	2.5	1.2	1.4	97	169	81	93
TRADE (81,86,89-99)	22.3	32.4	32.1	35.9	30.5	31.8	99	112	95	99
SERVICES (82-85,87-88,102)	27.2	30.5	31.0	30.8	30.6	31.0	102	99	99	100
STATE & LOCAL GOVT. (101)	15.6	19.2	19.1	20.0	18.5	18.9	100	104	97	99
FEDERAL GOVERNMENT (100,103)	8.8	8.9	8.9	9.1	8.8	8.9	100	102	99	100
TOTAL JOBS	118.4	146.7	146.1	156.1	140.5	144.2	100	107	96	99
CIVILIAN PERSONS EMPLOYED	113.6	141.1	140.6	150.1	135.3	138.1	100	107	96	99
CIVILIAN UNEMPLOYMENT RATE	5.2	5.1	.5	.5	U	.5				
POPULATION	321.9	338.2	336.5	360.3	322.7	334.1	99	107	96	99
PER CAPITA INCOME	2906.3	5331.3	5319.3	5441.6	5218.3	5258.8	100	102	98	99
ENERGY USER SECTOR			(TRILLIONS OF BTU'S)							
NATURAL RESOURCES	1.7	1.3	1.2	1.8	1.2	1.3	96	148	98	108
CONSTRUCTION	5.0	8.5	8.6	15.0	4.2	4.4	101	174	48	51
MANUFACTURING	13.4	26.5	26.2	27.4	25.6	25.9	99	105	97	99
TRANSPORTATION INDUSTRY	2.1	5.0	5.0	5.8	4.6	4.9	99	116	72	99
PUBLIC UTILITIES	15.6	53.4	52.2	82.8	43.7	56.6	98	159	84	108
TRADE AND SERVICES	6.8	14.9	14.9	16.9	14.0	14.9	100	113	94	100
GOVERNMENT, EXC. TRANSPORTATION	.8	1.3	1.3	1.4	1.2	1.2	99	107	95	98
CONSUMERS, EXC. TRANSPORTATION	10.2	18.3	18.2	19.2	17.6	18.0	100	106	97	99
USER-OPERATED TRANSPORTATION	20.4	39.7	39.6	41.8	38.7	39.1	100	106	97	99
TRANSPORTATION AIR POLLUTION			(THOUSANDS OF TONS)							
SULFUR OXIDES	.7	1.4	1.4	1.6	1.3	1.4	99	111	94	99
PARTICULATE MATTER	.6	1.2	1.2	1.3	1.2	1.2	99	108	96	99
CARBON MONOXIDE	151.7	290.1	288.8	305.5	278.8	285.6	100	106	97	99
HYDROCARBONS	26.4	50.3	50.0	52.9	48.3	49.5	100	106	97	99
NITROGEN OXIDES	13.7	25.9	25.8	27.5	24.8	25.5	100	107	96	99
OTHER AIR POLLUTION										
SULFUR OXIDES	28.6	90.5	88.6	139.1	74.5	95.8	98	157	84	108
PARTICULATE MATTER	19.5	38.1	37.4	54.1	34.2	39.6	98	145	91	104
CARBON MONOXIDE	30.2	40.8	39.4	47.6	40.5	40.5	97	121	104	103
HYDROCARBONS	5.5	12.1	10.7	13.1	8.6	8.7	88	122	80	81
NITROGEN OXIDES	8.6	23.6	23.1	35.7	19.7	24.9	98	155	86	108
WATER OXYGEN DEMAND	87.3	164.6	163.7	167.8	164.6	164.6	99	101	101	101
LAND SOLID WASTE	254.3	267.2	265.8	284.1	255.0	263.9	99	107	96	99

2 PORTLAND, MAINE

	1970	1990 BASE YEAR	1990 COMPLETED INTERSTATE	1990 EXTENDED PRIMARY	1990 ECONOMIC DEVELOPMENT	1990 URBAN	CI/BY	EP/CI	ED/CI	U/CI
JOBS BY INDUSTRY			(THOUSANDS)							
NATURAL RESOURCES (1-10)	10.3	4.7	4.5	4.8	4.8	4.5	96	105	106	99
CONSTRUCTION (11-12)	13.9	6.9	7.0	7.2	7.0	7.0	101	103	101	100
MANUFACTURING (13-74)	95.2	122.7	122.3	127.2	126.0	121.3	100	104	103	99
TRANSPORTATION INDUSTRY (75)	6.2	4.3	4.2	4.4	4.3	4.1	98	105	104	99
PUBLIC UTILITIES (76-80)	5.7	2.7	1.9	3.3	3.2	1.6	70	172	168	82
TRADE (81,86,89-99)	59.0	58.4	56.7	60.2	59.7	55.8	97	106	105	98
SERVICES (82-85,87,88,102)	74.7	111.3	111.5	111.6	111.6	111.5	100	100	100	100
STATE & LOCAL GOVT. (101)	36.0	41.7	41.5	42.5	42.3	41.4	100	102	102	100
FEDERAL GOVERNMENT (100,103)	14.4	15.3	15.2	15.4	15.4	15.2	100	101	101	100
TOTAL JOBS	315.3	368.0	364.8	376.7	374.3	362.3	99	103	103	99
CIVILIAN PERSONS EMPLOYED	305.4	355.4	352.3	363.6	361.4	349.9	99	103	103	99
CIVILIAN UNEMPLOYMENT RATE	4.9	.5	.5	.5	.5	.5				
POPULATION	740.6	759.3	755.6	772.4	765.8	756.9	100	101	101	100
PER CAPITA INCOME	3310.7	5754.5	5731.0	5848.4	5841.8	5677.6	100	102	102	99
ENERGY USER SECTOR			(TRILLIONS OF BTU'S)							
NATURAL RESOURCES	2.9	5.8	5.4	5.7	5.7	5.3	93	105	106	98
CONSTRUCTION	11.0	18.2	17.7	18.5	18.4	17.6	98	104	103	99
MANUFACTURING	31.7	87.6	87.2	89.2	88.7	86.8	100	102	102	100
TRANSPORTATION INDUSTRY	6.3	14.1	13.6	14.5	14.4	13.4	97	107	106	98
PUBLIC UTILITIES	41.0	116.4	96.2	120.4	118.9	89.4	83	125	124	93
TRADE AND SERVICES	20.9	46.5	45.0	47.3	47.0	44.4	97	105	104	99
GOVERNMENT, EXC. TRANSPORTATION	1.7	2.4	2.4	2.5	2.5	2.4	99	105	103	99
CONSUMERS, EXC. TRANSPORTATION	33.9	54.4	54.1	55.3	55.0	53.9	100	102	102	100
USER-OPERATED TRANSPORTATION	68.2	130.5	130.0	132.5	132.0	129.5	100	102	101	100
TRANSPORTATION AIR POLLUTION			(THOUSANDS OF TONS)							
SULFUR OXIDES	2.1	4.3	4.2	4.4	4.3	4.1	98	104	104	99
PARTICULATE MATTER	2.0	3.9	3.8	3.9	3.9	3.8	99	103	102	99
CARBON MONOXIDE	499.5	957.5	953.2	971.9	967.9	949.6	100	102	102	100
HYDROCARBONS	86.6	165.8	165.1	168.3	167.6	164.4	100	102	102	100
NITROGEN OXIDES	43.5	83.7	83.3	85.3	84.9	82.9	99	102	102	100
OTHER AIR POLLUTION										
SULFUR OXIDES	89.7	246.8	212.9	253.3	250.6	201.7	86	119	118	95
PARTICULATE MATTER	58.6	145.0	134.2	147.0	145.9	131.0	93	110	109	98
CARBON MONOXIDE	80.0	183.9	175.7	182.9	182.5	173.3	96	104	104	99
HYDROCARBONS	12.4	20.0	20.7	24.1	23.5	19.6	103	116	114	95
NITROGEN OXIDES	24.8	66.8	58.1	68.4	67.7	55.3	87	118	116	95
WATER OXYGEN DEMAND	202.0	214.3	214.1	214.5	214.4	213.8	100	100	100	100
LAND SOLID WASTE	585.0	599.8	596.9	610.2	605.0	598.0	100	102	101	100

SUMMARY PROJECTIONS BY OBE ECONOMIC AREA UNDER FIVE ALTERNATIVE HIGHWAY SYSTEMS

3 BURLINGTON, VT.

	1970	1990 BASE YEAR	1990 COMPLETED INTERSTATE	1990 EXTENDED PRIMARY	1990 ECONOMIC DEVELOPMENT	1990 URBAN	CI/BY	P E R C E N T EP/CI	ED/CI	U/CI
JOBS BY INDUSTRY										
NATURAL RESOURCES (1-10)	13.1	2.3	3.0	3.1	4.9	2.9	134	103	163	97
CONSTRUCTION (11,12)	8.0	10.1	10.2	10.5	13.3	10.0	101	102	129	98
MANUFACTURING (13-74)	48.5	56.9	93.8	97.6	107.7	91.7	165	104	115	98
TRANSPORTATION INDUSTRY (75)	3.9	4.9	6.4	6.6	7.4	6.3	130	104	117	98
PUBLIC UTILITIES (76-80)	4.0	1.0	3.7	5.2	11.5	3.3	360	141	310	88
TRADE (81,86,89-99)	36.4	24.7	50.1	54.3	67.2	48.2	202	108	134	96
SERVICES (82-85,87,88,102)	49.6	67.7	70.9	71.0	71.6	70.9	105	100	101	100
STATE & LOCAL GOVT. (101)	24.0	26.3	33.8	34.6	37.9	33.3	129	103	112	99
FEDERAL GOVERNMENT (100,103)	4.5	4.1	5.8	6.0	6.7	5.7	140	103	116	98
TOTAL JOBS	191.9	198.1	277.7	289.0	328.2	272.2	140	104	118	98
CIVILIAN PERSONS EMPLOYED	187.4	193.4	269.5	280.3	317.8	264.3	139	104	118	98
CIVILIAN UNEMPLOYMENT RATE	4.9	4.9	3.5	2.8	2.7	3.7	123	101	113	99
POPULATION	502.1	580.5	713.5	721.6	803.4	709.4	123	101	113	99
PER CAPITA INCOME	3263.1	4790.5	5787.5	5982.4	6204.4	5696.9	121	103	107	98
ENERGY USER SECTOR (TRILLIONS OF BTU'S)										
NATURAL RESOURCES	4.8	3.4	4.1	4.1	5.9	4.0	121	99	143	98
CONSTRUCTION	11.1	12.7	17.5	18.3	30.2	17.1	138	104	173	98
MANUFACTURING	18.2	28.5	46.2	47.7	54.7	44.9	162	103	118	97
TRANSPORTATION INDUSTRY	4.2	6.3	13.9	15.0	18.4	13.4	220	108	132	96
PUBLIC UTILITIES	43.1	37.7	161.0	190.2	313.1	149.1	427	118	194	93
TRADE AND SERVICES	16.3	29.2	44.6	47.2	56.3	43.5	153	106	126	97
GOVERNMENT, EXC. TRANSPORTATION	1.3	1.8	2.6	2.7	3.0	2.5	146	104	117	98
CONSUMERS, EXC. TRANSPORTATION	21.4	32.3	43.6	45.1	50.7	42.8	135	104	116	98
USER-OPERATED TRANSPORTATION	38.8	71.1	89.1	91.5	100.2	87.9	125	103	112	99
TRANSPORTATION AIR POLLUTION (THOUSANDS OF TONS)										
SULFUR OXIDES	1.4	2.1	2.6	3.8	4.5	3.5	170	105	125	97
PARTICULATE MATTER	1.2	2.0	2.9	3.0	3.4	2.8	144	104	119	98
CARBON MONOXIDE	285.5	515.5	650.3	668.8	734.4	641.5	126	103	113	99
HYDROCARBONS	49.6	89.4	112.6	115.8	127.1	111.1	126	103	113	99
NITROGEN OXIDES	25.6	44.8	59.0	61.0	67.8	58.0	132	103	115	98
OTHER AIR POLLUTION										
SULFUR OXIDES	79.1	89.4	296.6	344.9	549.2	276.9	332	116	185	93
PARTICULATE MATTER	58.7	93.7	176.1	189.7	259.2	170.6	188	108	147	97
CARBON MONOXIDE	28.2	21.7	34.9	34.0	69.9	33.8	160	97	200	97
HYDROCARBONS	6.3	8.3	18.5	18.9	36.3	15.1	222	102	197	82
NITROGEN OXIDES	22.7	33.1	86.1	98.1	150.0	81.2	260	114	174	94
WATER OXYGEN DEMAND	634.2	343.1	347.1	348.0	351.0	346.8	101	100	101	100
LAND SOLID WASTE	396.7	458.6	563.6	570.1	634.7	560.4	123	101	113	99

SUMMARY PROJECTIONS BY ORE ECONOMIC AREA UNDER FIVE ALTERNATIVE HIGHWAY SYSTEMS

4   BOSTON, MASS.

	1970	1990 BASE YEAR	1990 COMPLETED INTERSTATE	1990 EXTENDED PRIMARY	1990 ECONOMIC DEVELOPMENT	1990 URBAN	CI/BY	EP/CI	ED/CI	U/CI
JOBS BY INDUSTRY			(THOUSANDS)					P E R	C E N T	
NATURAL RESOURCES (1-10)	23.9	9.2	9.5	9.6	8.2	10.0	103	101	86	106
CONSTRUCTION (11-12)	106.6	99.7	100.0	97.2	94.5	100.9	100	97	95	101
MANUFACTURING (13-74)	794.4	831.3	875.2	901.3	874.5	878.8	105	103	100	101
TRANSPORTATION INDUSTRY (75)	75.9	92.0	93.1	93.6	92.5	93.6	101	101	100	100
PUBLIC UTILITIES (76-80)	59.1	41.1	44.4	45.3	37.6	46.4	108	101	85	105
TRADE (81,86,89-99)	609.2	792.0	814.3	824.7	805.0	821.0	103	101	99	101
SERVICES (82-85,87,88,102)	654.4	959.2	961.2	961.5	960.7	961.7	100	100	100	100
STATE & LOCAL GOVT. (101)	289.2	347.1	355.3	358.8	352.5	356.8	102	101	99	100
FEDERAL GOVERNMENT (100,103)	108.9	113.7	115.5	116.3	114.9	115.8	102	101	99	100
TOTAL JOBS	2721.6	3285.2	3368.4	3408.4	3340.3	3385.0	103	101	99	100
CIVILIAN PERSONS EMPLOYED	2512.6	3049.9	3127.4	3165.5	3102.3	3142.1	103	101	99	100
CIVILIAN UNEMPLOYMENT RATE	4.5	4.1	4.0	4.1	4.1	3.9	101	101	100	100
POPULATION	6339.0	7771.1	7883.1	7933.8	7847.1	7919.5	101	101	100	100
PER CAPITA INCOME	4086.2	6484.6	6570.1	6610.8	6538.3	6576.9	101	101	100	100
ENERGY USER SECTOR			(TRILLIONS OF BTU'S)							
NATURAL RESOURCES	30.8	71.5	71.8	71.4	70.1	72.6	100	99	98	101
CONSTRUCTION	151.9	234.9	244.5	247.0	232.4	270.0	104	101	95	110
MANUFACTURING	266.1	570.1	593.2	608.6	592.0	596.6	104	103	100	101
TRANSPORTATION INDUSTRY	115.1	227.2	233.8	236.6	231.3	235.6	103	101	99	101
PUBLIC UTILITIES	533.7	1320.7	1349.7	1355.8	1284.4	1361.8	102	100	95	103
TRADE AND SERVICES	329.5	654.8	667.1	672.4	661.1	670.2	102	101	99	102
GOVERNMENT, EXC. TRANSPORTATION	29.7	45.8	46.7	47.1	46.4	46.9	102	101	99	102
CONSUMERS, EXC. TRANSPORTATION	349.0	575.1	586.8	592.3	582.6	589.4	102	101	99	102
USER-OPERATED TRANSPORTATION	504.2	968.8	987.2	995.8	980.7	991.3	102	101	99	100
TRANSPORTATION AIR POLLUTION			(THOUSANDS OF TONS)							
SULFUR OXIDES	26.7	52.0	53.1	53.5	52.5	53.5	102	101	99	101
PARTICULATE MATTER	18.7	36.2	37.1	37.5	36.8	37.3	102	101	99	99
CARBON MONOXIDE	3637.1	7041.5	7178.5	7242.5	7129.3	7209.8	102	101	99	101
HYDROCARBONS	630.3	1219.3	1242.7	1253.4	1233.9	1248.1	102	101	99	100
NITROGEN OXIDES	346.3	669.6	685.4	693.7	681.2	688.7	102	101	99	100
OTHER AIR POLLUTION										
SULFUR OXIDES	1191.4	2701.5	2750.0	2755.5	2642.5	2769.6	102	100	96	102
PARTICULATE MATTER	744.6	1774.0	1779.8	1781.6	1746.4	1787.9	100	100	98	100
CARBON MONOXIDE	800.8	1946.6	1917.0	1909.3	1898.0	1922.0	98	100	99	98
HYDROCARBONS	246.2	374.0	444.8	453.5	469.7	470.7	119	121	106	121
NITROGEN OXIDES	375.6	838.9	849.7	851.8	822.3	855.1	101	100	97	101
WATER OXYGEN DEMAND	801.3	735.5	722.9	720.2	724.5	723.2	98	100	96	98
LAND SOLID WASTE	5007.8	6139.2	6227.6	6267.7	6199.2	6256.3	101	101	100	101

SUMMARY PROJECTIONS BY ORE ECONOMIC AREA UNDER FIVE ALTERNATIVE HIGHWAY SYSTEMS

5 HARTFORD, CONN.

	1970	1990 BASE YEAR	1990 COMPLETED INTERSTATE	1990 EXTENDED PRIMARY	1990 ECONOMIC DEVELOPMENT	1990 URBAN	CI/BY	PERCENT EP/BY	PERCENT ED/CI	PERCENT U/CI
JOBS BY INDUSTRY			(THOUSANDS)							
NATURAL RESOURCES (1-10)	17.2	6.3	6.1	6.1	6.1	6.2	99	99	99	100
CONSTRUCTION (11,12)	51.5	51.4	51.4	49.8	48.1	51.4	101	97	94	100
MANUFACTURING (13-74)	427.7	520.7	558.2	558.5	544.8	547.5	107	100	98	98
TRANSPORTATION INDUSTRY (75)	27.8	38.5	39.7	39.3	38.7	39.3	103	99	98	99
PUBLIC UTILITIES (76-80)	25.8	18.0	19.6	16.2	13.2	17.7	109	83	67	90
TRADE (81,86,89-99)	252.7	428.5	450.7	447.5	436.5	443.0	105	99	97	98
SERVICES (82-85,87,88,102)	279.4	541.5	544.3	544.0	543.4	544.0	101	100	100	100
STATE & LOCAL GOVT. (101)	136.4	188.3	194.8	194.1	190.9	192.6	103	103	98	99
FEDERAL GOVERNMENT (100,103)	32.9	38.8	40.2	40.1	39.4	39.7	104	100	98	99
TOTAL JOBS	1251.3	1831.7	1905.2	1895.6	1861.2	1881.4	104	99	98	99
CIVILIAN PERSONS EMPLOYED	1209.0	1769.0	1839.1	1830.1	1797.2	1816.3	104	100	98	99
CIVILIAN UNEMPLOYMENT RATE	5.3	5.8	6.0	6.0	6.1	6.3				
POPULATION	2966.6	4647.6	4777.5	4747.9	4703.0	4767.7	103	99	99	100
PER CAPITA INCOME	4468.0	6655.3	6727.1	6731.8	6667.0	6653.9	101	100	99	99
ENERGY USER SECTOR			(TRILLIONS OF BTU'S)							
NATURAL RESOURCES	12.5	12.1	12.3	12.2	12.1	12.3	102	99	99	100
CONSTRUCTION	65.1	113.3	117.0	116.6	104.6	106.1	103	100	89	91
MANUFACTURING	162.2	378.7	392.9	394.4	387.9	388.0	104	100	99	99
TRANSPORTATION INDUSTRY	35.7	86.6	92.9	91.9	88.8	91.1	107	99	96	98
PUBLIC UTILITIES	203.9	504.1	529.4	491.3	449.7	504.2	105	93	85	95
TRADE AND SERVICES	120.6	268.3	279.8	277.2	270.2	275.7	104	99	97	99
GOVERNMENT, EXC. TRANSPORTATION	10.5	18.9	19.6	19.5	19.2	19.4	104	100	98	99
CONSUMERS, EXC. TRANSPORTATION	144.0	278.0	288.2	286.7	281.5	284.7	104	99	98	99
USER-OPERATED TRANSPORTATION	225.1	496.3	512.3	510.0	502.0	506.9	103	100	98	99
TRANSPORTATION AIR POLLUTION			(THOUSANDS OF TONS)							
SULFUR OXIDES	9.9	22.0	23.2	22.9	22.3	22.8	105	99	96	98
PARTICULATE MATTER	7.7	16.8	17.6	17.5	17.1	17.4	105	99	97	99
CARBON MONOXIDE	1654.3	3612.5	3732.1	3714.1	3653.6	3691.9	103	98	98	99
HYDROCARBONS	287.8	626.2	646.7	643.5	633.1	639.8	103	99	98	99
NITROGEN OXIDES	154.1	332.6	345.6	344.4	337.8	341.6	104	100	98	99
OTHER AIR POLLUTION										
SULFUR OXIDES	937.5	2604.8	2647.1	2584.7	2516.7	2605.7	102	98	95	98
PARTICULATE MATTER	314.7	804.4	813.4	797.9	780.7	804.0	101	98	96	99
CARBON MONOXIDE	295.9	621.1	610.2	609.8	611.8	613.1	98	100	100	100
HYDROCARBONS	117.2	224.2	258.6	285.9	265.3	239.0	115	111	103	92
NITROGEN OXIDES	147.2	406.7	416.6	401.2	384.5	406.6	102	96	92	98
WATER OXYGEN DEMAND	786.0	699.2	691.8	689.6	689.1	692.9	99	100	100	100
LAND SOLID WASTE	2343.6	3671.6	3774.2	3750.8	3715.3	3766.5	103	99	98	100

SUMMARY PROJECTIONS BY ORE ECONOMIC AREA UNDER FIVE ALTERNATIVE HIGHWAY SYSTEMS

6 ALB.-SCHEN.-TROY. N. Y.

	1970	1990 BASE YEAR	1990 COMPLETED INTERSTATE	1990 EXTENDED PRIMARY	1990 ECONOMIC DEVELOPMENT	1990 URBAN	CI/BY	EP/CI	ED/CI	U/CI
							PER CENT			
JOBS BY INDUSTRY			(THOUSANDS)							
NATURAL RESOURCES (1-10)	13.9	4.2	4.3	4.5	4.2	4.2	103	106	99	100
CONSTRUCTION (11-12)	19.8	27.2	27.3	26.8	26.0	27.4	101	98	95	100
MANUFACTURING (13-74)	131.5	118.2	123.2	127.9	119.2	120.7	104	104	97	98
TRANSPORTATION INDUSTRY (75)	12.8	14.7	14.9	15.2	14.7	14.8	101	102	99	99
PUBLIC UTILITIES (76-80)	11.7	1.6	2.2	3.0	2.0	1.9	138	137	92	87
TRADE (81,86,89-99)	101.7	132.8	137.0	142.0	134.5	135.1	103	104	98	99
SERVICES (82-85,87,88,102)	106.5	179.0	179.5	179.6	179.3	179.4	100	100	100	100
STATE & LOCAL GOVT. (101)	100.7	120.6	121.7	122.7	120.9	121.2	101	101	99	100
FEDERAL GOVERNMENT (100,103)	16.0	16.2	16.4	16.6	16.2	16.3	102	101	99	99
TOTAL JOBS	514.7	614.3	626.5	638.4	617.1	621.0	102	102	98	99
CIVILIAN PERSONS EMPLOYED	449.6	542.7	553.3	564.0	545.4	548.3	102	102	99	99
CIVILIAN UNEMPLOYMENT RATE	8.3	7.4	7.5	6.8	7.2	7.5				
POPULATION	1331.8	1677.0	1695.4	1704.3	1677.3	1685.0	101	101	99	99
PER CAPITA INCOME	3627.7	5559.9	5617.7	5696.6	5589.2	5597.6	101	101	99	100
ENERGY USER SECTOR			(TRILLIONS OF BTU'S)							
NATURAL RESOURCES	7.6	9.2	9.6	10.3	9.4	9.6	105	107	98	99
CONSTRUCTION	24.9	35.3	36.7	38.0	32.2	32.0	104	104	88	87
MANUFACTURING	64.0	146.3	149.2	152.1	146.7	148.2	102	102	98	99
TRANSPORTATION INDUSTRY	13.6	24.2	25.5	26.8	24.7	25.0	105	105	97	98
PUBLIC UTILITIES	74.1	50.9	86.5	125.3	77.3	79.1	170	145	89	91
TRADE AND SERVICES	48.6	84.2	87.4	90.7	85.9	86.3	104	104	98	98
GOVERNMENT. EXC. TRANSPORTATION	4.7	6.8	6.9	7.1	6.9	6.9	102	102	99	99
CONSUMERS. EXC. TRANSPORTATION	48.2	81.1	82.8	84.4	81.5	82.0	102	102	98	99
USER-OPERATED TRANSPORTATION	88.8	169.8	172.4	174.9	170.5	171.2	102	101	99	99
TRANSPORTATION AIR POLLUTION			(THOUSANDS OF TONS)							
SULFUR OXIDES	3.7	6.6	6.8	7.1	6.6	6.7	104	103	97	99
PARTICULATE MATTER	2.9	5.4	5.5	5.7	5.4	5.4	103	103	98	99
CARBON MONOXIDE	640.4	1211.9	1232.5	1252.1	1217.2	1223.1	102	102	99	99
HYDROCARBONS	111.3	210.1	213.7	217.0	211.0	212.1	102	102	99	99
NITROGEN OXIDES	59.2	109.7	112.2	114.6	110.6	111.2	102	102	99	99
OTHER AIR POLLUTION										
SULFUR OXIDES	147.4	166.7	226.8	291.7	210.5	214.5	136	129	93	95
PARTICULATE MATTER	179.1	405.1	426.3	447.6	413.3	421.3	105	105	97	99
CARBON MONOXIDE	67.1	124.6	131.3	133.8	127.4	128.4	105	102	97	98
HYDROCARBONS	17.3	22.9	24.8	28.2	23.5	23.8	108	114	95	96
NITROGEN OXIDES	45.2	72.5	87.7	103.8	83.0	84.5	121	118	95	96
WATER OXYGEN DEMAND	822.3	1692.3	1703.5	1709.1	1689.6	1700.3	101	100	99	100
LAND SOLID WASTE	1052.1	1324.8	1339.3	1346.4	1325.0	1331.2	101	101	99	99

SUMMARY PROJECTIONS BY ORE ECONOMIC AREA UNDER FIVE ALTERNATIVE HIGHWAY SYSTEMS

7 SYRACUSE, N. Y.

	1970	1990 BASE YEAR	1990 COMPLETED INTERSTATE	1990 EXTENDED PRIMARY	1990 ECONOMIC DEVELOPMENT	1990 URBAN	P E R C E N T CI/BY	EP/CI	ED/CI	U/CI
JOBS BY INDUSTRY			(THOUSANDS)							
NATURAL RESOURCES (1-10)	23.0	6.3	5.9	6.2	5.7	5.6	94	105	96	96
CONSTRUCTION (11,12)	16.7	23.3	23.3	22.6	21.7	22.6	100	97	93	97
MANUFACTURING (13-74)	146.2	199.6	183.2	188.2	175.3	167.5	92	103	96	91
TRANSPORTATION INDUSTRY (75)	13.3	21.9	21.5	21.8	21.3	21.1	99	101	99	98
PUBLIC UTILITIES (76-80)	12.8	1.5	1.4	2.1	1.4	1.3	89	150	81	92
TRADE (81,86,89-99)	108.4	156.3	149.2	153.5	144.4	141.9	95	103	97	95
SERVICES (82-85,87,88,102)	109.2	151.6	151.5	151.6	151.2	151.3	100	100	100	100
STATE & LOCAL GOVT. (101)	87.9	109.0	106.4	107.4	104.9	104.1	98	101	99	98
FEDERAL GOVERNMENT (100,103)	17.7	19.0	18.4	18.6	18.0	17.9	97	101	98	97
TOTAL JOBS	535.2	688.6	660.8	672.0	643.6	633.2	96	102	97	96
CIVILIAN PERSONS EMPLOYED	484.0	626.0	600.7	611.2	585.5	575.3	96	102	97	96
CIVILIAN UNEMPLOYMENT RATE	5.6	4.4	4.6	4.7	4.7	5.4	98	100	98	99
POPULATION	1444.7	1873.7	1831.9	1837.8	1803.8	1811.8	98	100	98	99
PER CAPITA INCOME	3291.7	5345.5	5218.7	5286.7	5134.8	5028.2	98	101	98	96
ENERGY USER SECTOR			(TRILLIONS OF BTU'S)							
NATURAL RESOURCES	12.8	19.9	18.3	18.6	17.3	17.2	92	102	95	94
CONSTRUCTION	30.4	56.6	55.2	44.8	34.1	34.1	98	81	62	62
MANUFACTURING	58.2	126.0	118.6	119.9	114.4	111.7	94	101	96	94
TRANSPORTATION INDUSTRY	17.4	33.2	31.2	32.3	29.8	29.3	94	104	96	94
PUBLIC UTILITIES	122.7	217.9	195.3	241.0	136.0	177.7	90	123	70	91
TRADE AND SERVICES	50.6	95.9	92.6	95.1	90.4	89.5	97	103	98	97
GOVERNMENT, EXC. TRANSPORTATION	5.6	9.0	8.7	8.8	8.5	8.4	97	101	98	97
CONSUMERS, EXC. TRANSPORTATION	40.1	76.8	73.0	74.3	70.4	69.3	95	102	96	95
USER-OPERATED TRANSPORTATION	76.8	155.8	149.8	151.8	145.8	144.0	96	101	97	96
TRANSPORTATION AIR POLLUTION			(THOUSANDS OF TONS)							
SULFUR OXIDES	4.3	7.9	7.5	7.7	7.2	7.1	94	103	96	95
PARTICULATE MATTER	3.0	5.6	5.4	5.5	5.2	5.1	95	102	97	95
CARBON MONOXIDE	557.0	1111.0	1066.6	1082.8	1036.3	1023.7	96	102	97	96
HYDROCARBONS	97.1	192.8	185.1	187.9	179.8	177.7	96	102	97	96
NITROGEN OXIDES	54.7	105.9	101.7	103.9	98.7	97.5	96	102	97	96
OTHER AIR POLLUTION										
SULFUR OXIDES	341.4	523.3	485.3	561.8	386.2	455.9	93	116	80	94
PARTICULATE MATTER	130.8	244.3	233.7	255.1	205.7	225.1	96	109	88	96
CARBON MONOXIDE	88.5	148.7	143.7	145.1	141.3	139.0	97	101	98	97
HYDROCARBONS	29.8	79.5	70.3	63.4	62.1	62.3	88	90	88	89
NITROGEN OXIDES	69.6	141.4	131.5	150.3	106.5	123.8	93	114	81	94
WATER OXYGEN DEMAND	1390.7	2813.4	2814.4	2818.9	2804.4	2812.7	100	100	100	100
LAND SOLID WASTE	1141.3	1480.3	1447.2	1451.9	1425.0	1431.4	98	100	99	99

SUMMARY PROJECTIONS BY ORE ECONOMIC AREA UNDER FIVE ALTERNATIVE HIGHWAY SYSTEMS

8 ROCHESTER, N. Y.

	1970	1990 BASE YEAR	1990 COMPLETED INTERSTATE	1990 EXTENDED PRIMARY	1990 ECONOMIC DEVELOPMENT	1990 URBAN	CI/BY	EP/CI	ED/CI	U/CI
								PER CENT		
JOBS BY INDUSTRY			(THOUSANDS)							
NATURAL RESOURCES (1-10)	10.2	3.3	3.3	3.2	3.3	3.2	98	99	102	99
CONSTRUCTION (11,12)	14.3	19.9	19.9	19.2	18.5	19.2	100	97	97	100
MANUFACTURING (13-74)	160.6	192.5	180.5	175.8	183.2	175.4	94	97	102	97
TRANSPORTATION INDUSTRY (75)	6.7	10.3	9.9	10.0	10.0	9.7	97	98	100	98
PUBLIC UTILITIES (76-80)	7.6	1.8	1.3	1.1	1.4	1.2	72	87	111	92
TRADE (81,86,89-99)	83.1	152.9	144.3	140.4	146.4	140.1	94	97	101	97
SERVICES (82-85,87,88,102)	81.4	145.7	145.4	145.3	145.5	145.4	100	100	100	100
STATE & LOCAL GOVT. (101)	58.1	72.7	70.5	69.7	71.2	69.6	97	99	101	99
FEDERAL GOVERNMENT (100,103)	6.8	7.5	7.0	6.8	7.2	6.8	93	98	102	97
TOTAL JOBS	428.8	606.6	582.0	571.3	586.8	571.1	96	98	101	98
CIVILIAN PERSONS EMPLOYED	403.5	571.3	548.2	538.2	552.8	537.9	96	98	101	98
CIVILIAN UNEMPLOYMENT RATE	3.0	.3	.3	.3	.3	.3				
POPULATION	1016.4	1349.2	1311.7	1307.6	1331.5	1312.3	97	100	102	100
PER CAPITA INCOME	3935.5	6952.8	6847.6	6741.8	6808.5	6715.4	98	98	99	98
ENERGY USER SECTOR			(TRILLIONS OF BTU'S)							
NATURAL RESOURCES	11.2	12.6	12.3	12.0	12.4	12.1	97	98	101	99
CONSTRUCTION	20.2	41.5	40.0	35.8	34.8	33.3	96	90	87	83
MANUFACTURING	50.1	111.4	107.0	105.6	108.4	105.1	96	99	101	98
TRANSPORTATION INDUSTRY	9.0	20.4	18.4	17.5	18.9	17.5	90	95	103	95
PUBLIC UTILITIES	63.2	137.5	96.0	64.9	96.9	81.9	70	68	101	85
TRADE AND SERVICES	39.1	83.4	79.7	77.9	80.6	77.9	96	98	101	98
GOVERNMENT, EXC. TRANSPORTATION	3.8	6.1	6.0	6.0	6.1	5.9	99	99	101	98
CONSUMERS, EXC. TRANSPORTATION	30.8	64.5	61.0	59.7	61.8	59.7	95	98	101	98
USER-OPERATED TRANSPORTATION	59.7	132.8	127.5	125.3	128.6	125.2	96	98	101	98
TRANSPORTATION AIR POLLUTION			(THOUSANDS OF TONS)							
SULFUR OXIDES	3.1	6.0	5.6	5.4	5.7	5.4	93	96	101	97
PARTICULATE MATTER	2.4	4.7	4.5	4.3	4.5	4.3	95	97	101	98
CARBON MONOXIDE	461.1	979.4	939.7	922.5	947.6	922.9	96	98	101	98
HYDROCARBONS	81.5	171.2	164.3	161.3	165.6	161.4	96	98	101	98
NITROGEN OXIDES	46.7	93.4	89.5	87.7	90.4	87.7	96	98	101	98
OTHER AIR POLLUTION										
SULFUR OXIDES	120.2	272.4	203.0	151.0	204.5	179.4	75	74	101	88
PARTICULATE MATTER	88.1	247.2	229.9	213.8	229.6	223.8	93	93	100	97
CARBON MONOXIDE	199.5	645.6	647.3	643.9	644.3	647.7	100	99	100	100
HYDROCARBONS	55.1	190.0	186.9	185.9	188.8	187.0	-100	99	101	100
NITROGEN OXIDES	45.2	125.4	108.3	95.2	108.6	102.5	86	88	100	95
WATER OXYGEN DEMAND	489.4	1173.6	1169.4	1161.4	1167.5	1168.6	100	99	100	100
LAND SOLID WASTE	803.0	1065.9	1036.2	1033.0	1051.9	1036.7	97	100	102	100

SUMMARY PROJECTIONS BY ORE ECONOMIC AREA UNDER FIVE ALTERNATIVE HIGHWAY SYSTEMS

9   BUFFALO, N. Y.

	1970	1990 BASE YEAR	1990 COMPLETED INTERSTATE	1990 EXTENDED PRIMARY	1990 ECONOMIC DEVELOPMENT	1990 URBAN	CI/BY	EP/CI	ED/CI	U/CI
JOBS BY INDUSTRY			(THOUSANDS)							
NATURAL RESOURCES (1-10)	18.1	7.4	6.8	8.1	6.7	6.6	92	119	99	98
CONSTRUCTION (11,12)	22.9	26.8	26.4	29.3	25.2	26.3	99	111	95	100
MANUFACTURING (13-74)	225.5	342.9	298.2	332.4	310.5	291.5	87	111	104	98
TRANSPORTATION INDUSTRY (75)	24.4	29.7	28.2	30.0	28.6	27.9	95	106	101	99
PUBLIC UTILITIES (76-80)	13.7	10.7	8.4	17.2	7.9	7.2	79	205	95	86
TRADE (81,86,89-99)	147.0	232.3	206.5	234.6	212.5	201.7	89	114	103	98
SERVICES (82-85,87,88,102)	127.1	216.6	212.2	215.6	212.9	211.7	98	102	100	98
STATE & LOCAL GOVT. (101)	101.1	132.7	124.5	132.6	126.3	123.2	94	107	102	99
FEDERAL GOVERNMENT (100,103)	13.4	16.2	14.4	16.2	14.8	14.1	89	113	103	98
TOTAL JOBS	693.4	1015.2	925.5	1015.8	945.4	910.4	91	110	102	98
CIVILIAN PERSONS EMPLOYED	658.9	965.0	879.9	965.6	898.8	865.5	91	110	102	98
CIVILIAN UNEMPLOYMENT RATE	5.2	1.7	1.3	1.6	1.2	1.5				
POPULATION	1789.4	2319.1	2088.9	2302.0	2122.6	2070.7	90	110	102	99
PER CAPITA INCOME	3633.3	6688.2	6671.2	6730.4	6722.5	6611.7	100	101	101	99
ENERGY USER SECTOR			(TRILLIONS OF BTU'S)							
NATURAL RESOURCES	10.7	14.9	13.9	14.9	13.7	13.8	94	107	99	99
CONSTRUCTION	30.5	64.9	53.6	67.8	51.2	48.1	83	126	96	90
MANUFACTURING	147.5	314.2	295.3	312.0	299.2	292.6	94	106	102	99
TRANSPORTATION INDUSTRY	28.1	63.3	56.0	63.9	57.8	54.7	88	114	103	98
PUBLIC UTILITIES	88.1	290.7	253.3	381.0	254.8	237.0	87	150	101	94
TRADE AND SERVICES	74.1	161.7	148.0	164.9	151.0	145.4	92	111	102	98
GOVERNMENT. EXC. TRANSPORTATION	6.8	11.7	10.8	11.7	11.0	10.7	92	108	102	99
CONSUMERS. EXC. TRANSPORTATION	55.2	119.2	105.8	119.0	108.6	103.7	89	112	103	98
USER-OPERATED TRANSPORTATION	94.2	213.7	192.9	213.4	197.3	189.7	90	111	102	98
TRANSPORTATION AIR POLLUTION			(THOUSANDS OF TONS)							
SULFUR OXIDES	6.5	14.0	12.4	14.0	12.8	12.2	89	112	103	98
PARTICULATE MATTER	4.2	9.0	8.1	9.1	8.3	7.9	90	112	102	98
CARBON MONOXIDE	701.0	1562.3	1407.9	1562.3	1440.5	1383.5	90	111	102	98
HYDROCARBONS	122.5	271.3	244.6	271.2	250.2	240.4	90	111	102	98
NITROGEN OXIDES	72.7	156.8	141.8	158.3	145.4	139.2	90	112	103	98
OTHER AIR POLLUTION										
SULFUR OXIDES	250.5	820.3	758.1	967.7	760.6	731.5	92	128	100	96
PARTICULATE MATTER	297.4	711.9	697.2	753.1	698.4	689.7	98	108	100	99
CARBON MONOXIDE	242.5	474.7	476.4	472.7	471.1	476.3	100	99	99	100
HYDROCARBONS	82.0	224.7	176.6	220.0	181.7	172.5	79	125	103	98
NITROGEN OXIDES	61.3	225.0	209.9	261.4	210.2	203.3	93	125	100	97
WATER OXYGEN DEMAND	770.2	1579.5	1581.8	1598.1	1580.3	1579.7	100	101	100	100
LAND SOLID WASTE	1413.6	1832.1	1650.2	1818.6	1676.8	1635.9	90	110	102	99

SUMMARY PROJECTIONS BY ORE ECONOMIC AREA UNDER FIVE ALTERNATIVE HIGHWAY SYSTEMS

10 ERIE, PA.

	1970	1990 BASE YEAR	1990 COMPLETED INTERSTATE	1990 EXTENDED PRIMARY	1990 ECONOMIC DEVELOPMENT	1990 URBAN	CI/BY	EP/CI	ED/CI	U/CI
JOBS BY INDUSTRY		(THOUSANDS)						P E R C E N T		
NATURAL RESOURCES (1-10)	7.2	2.1	2.1	2.1	2.0	2.4	100	99	98	115
CONSTRUCTION (11,12)	5.4	7.0	7.0	6.2	5.9	7.0	100	88	85	100
MANUFACTURING (13-74)	68.0	80.9	75.0	70.6	71.3	76.7	93	94	95	102
TRANSPORTATION INDUSTRY (75)	4.6	4.8	4.4	3.9	4.0	4.7	92	88	90	107
PUBLIC UTILITIES (76-80)	4.7	2.2	2.0	1.9	2.0	6.0	94	96	98	296
TRADE (81,86,89-99)	34.2	28.4	24.0	21.7	22.1	28.8	85	90	92	120
SERVICES (82-85,87,88,102)	29.6	45.5	44.6	44.3	44.2	44.9	98	99	99	101
STATE & LOCAL GOVT. (101)	19.4	20.1	18.9	18.0	18.1	19.9	94	95	96	105
FEDERAL GOVERNMENT (100,103)	2.1	1.4	1.2	1.2	1.2	1.3	89	100	100	109
TOTAL JOBS	175.1	192.4	179.2	169.8	170.9	191.6	93	95	95	107
CIVILIAN PERSONS EMPLOYED	167.8	184.0	171.5	162.5	163.5	183.4	93	95	95	107
CIVILIAN UNEMPLOYMENT RATE	4.0	4.2	4.3	3.6	3.5	3.7				
POPULATION	460.0	553.1	527.7	495.8	500.1	545.5	95	94	95	103
PER CAPITA INCOME	3550.2	5041.2	4893.2	4858.3	4853.6	5073.6	97	99	99	104
ENERGY USER SECTOR		(TRILLIONS OF BTU'S)								
NATURAL RESOURCES	2.9	3.3	3.1	2.8	2.8	3.7	95	90	90	119
CONSTRUCTION	8.7	13.1	12.6	7.6	7.8	13.6	96	61	62	108
MANUFACTURING	42.3	65.2	61.3	59.6	60.0	63.2	94	97	98	103
TRANSPORTATION INDUSTRY	3.7	5.5	4.1	3.3	3.4	5.5	75	81	83	134
PUBLIC UTILITIES	18.2	22.9	18.5	16.4	16.7	60.5	81	88	90	326
TRADE AND SERVICES	12.9	23.5	20.7	19.4	19.6	24.8	88	93	94	120
GOVERNMENT. EXC. TRANSPORTATION	1.6	2.0	1.9	1.8	1.8	2.0	94	95	95	105
CONSUMERS. EXC. TRANSPORTATION	20.5	34.6	32.8	31.4	31.5	34.4	95	96	96	105
USER-OPERATED TRANSPORTATION	31.0	54.1	51.3	49.1	49.3	53.8	95	96	96	105
TRANSPORTATION AIR POLLUTION		(THOUSANDS OF TONS)								
SULFUR OXIDES	1.2	1.8	1.5	1.3	1.3	1.8	85	88	90	119
PARTICULATE MATTER	1.0	1.6	1.5	1.3	1.3	1.6	91	93	94	111
CARBON MONOXIDE	225.5	386.8	365.7	348.5	350.5	385.8	95	95	96	105
HYDROCARBONS	39.4	67.1	63.5	60.5	60.9	67.0	95	95	96	106
NITROGEN OXIDES	21.0	34.3	32.1	30.3	30.5	34.4	93	95	95	107
OTHER AIR POLLUTION										
SULFUR OXIDES	93.4	211.0	203.1	197.9	198.3	273.6	96	97	98	135
PARTICULATE MATTER	41.8	66.3	64.7	62.1	62.1	88.0	98	96	96	136
CARBON MONOXIDE	104.3	163.2	165.8	164.0	163.8	174.3	102	99	99	105
HYDROCARBONS	30.3	47.7	47.0	45.4	45.4	47.6	99	96	96	101
NITROGEN OXIDES	12.2	20.7	18.9	17.1	17.0	37.0	91	90	90	196
WATER OXYGEN DEMAND	228.7	484.9	485.0	475.2	473.9	496.8	100	98	98	102
LAND SOLID WASTE	363.4	437.0	416.9	391.7	395.1	431.0	95	94	95	103

SUMMARY PROJECTIONS BY OBE ECONOMIC AREA UNDER FIVE ALTERNATIVE HIGHWAY SYSTEMS

11 WILLIAMSPORT, PA.

	1970	1990 BASE YEAR	1990 COMPLETED INTERSTATE	1990 EXTENDED PRIMARY	1990 ECONOMIC DEVELOPMENT	1990 URBAN	P E R C E N T			
							CI/BY	EP/CI	ED/CI	U/CI
JOBS BY INDUSTRY		(THOUSANDS)								
NATURAL RESOURCES (1-10)	8.0	5.1	4.0	5.4	3.6	3.9	78	135	89	98
CONSTRUCTION (11,12)	5.6	7.4	6.9	7.9	6.3	6.8	93	116	92	99
MANUFACTURING (13-74)	56.4	71.1	66.4	72.4	66.1	65.7	93	109	100	99
TRANSPORTATION INDUSTRY (75)	5.6	9.4	9.2	9.6	9.2	9.1	98	105	100	99
PUBLIC UTILITIES (76-80)	2.9	.8	.8	2.7	.8	.8	99	344	101	99
TRADE (81,86,89-99)	26.7	33.5	30.6	36.7	30.3	30.0	92	120	99	98
SERVICES (82-85,87,88,102)	23.5	28.9	28.7	28.9	28.7	28.7	99	101	100	100
STATE & LOCAL GOVT. (101)	24.3	29.1	28.1	29.7	27.9	28.0	96	106	99	100
FEDERAL GOVERNMENT (100,103)	2.0	1.8	1.6	2.0	1.6	1.6	87	122	98	99
TOTAL JOBS	155.0	187.1	176.2	195.2	174.3	174.5	94	111	99	99
CIVILIAN PERSONS EMPLOYED	131.6	161.0	151.7	168.1	150.2	150.2	94	111	99	99
CIVILIAN UNEMPLOYMENT RATE	5.0	2.1	2.2	1.5	2.1	2.3				
POPULATION	419.4	490.7	471.2	491.8	468.2	474.0	96	104	99	101
PER CAPITA INCOME	3303.5	5521.1	5352.6	5746.3	5314.6	5279.0	97	107	99	99
ENERGY USER SECTOR		(TRILLIONS OF BTU'S)								
NATURAL RESOURCES	2.8	4.1	2.8	4.5	2.6	2.7	68	161	94	99
CONSTRUCTION	8.5	16.6	10.8	18.2	9.5	7.5	65	169	88	69
MANUFACTURING	29.7	72.6	69.9	74.8	69.3	69.3	96	107	99	99
TRANSPORTATION INDUSTRY	3.9	8.3	7.4	9.3	7.2	7.2	89	125	98	98
PUBLIC UTILITIES	21.5	16.2	16.0	51.4	16.3	15.7	99	321	102	98
TRADE AND SERVICES	9.0	17.3	15.7	19.7	15.5	15.4	91	125	98	98
GOVERNMENT, EXC. TRANSPORTATION	2.9	4.0	3.9	4.0	3.8	3.9	97	104	100	100
CONSUMERS, EXC. TRANSPORTATION	16.6	27.7	26.2	28.7	25.9	26.0	94	110	99	99
USER-OPERATED TRANSPORTATION	24.2	45.5	43.0	47.0	42.6	42.8	95	109	99	99
TRANSPORTATION AIR POLLUTION		(THOUSANDS OF TONS)								
SULFUR OXIDES	1.0	2.0	1.9	2.2	1.8	1.8	91	120	98	98
PARTICULATE MATTER	.8	1.5	1.4	1.6	1.4	1.4	93	116	99	99
CARBON MONOXIDE	169.6	321.2	303.0	334.2	299.7	300.8	94	110	99	99
HYDROCARBONS	29.5	55.6	52.5	57.9	51.9	52.1	94	110	99	99
NITROGEN OXIDES	15.9	29.7	27.9	31.5	27.6	27.7	94	113	99	99
OTHER AIR POLLUTION										
SULFUR OXIDES	127.1	280.8	280.4	337.8	280.9	280.0	100	120	100	98
PARTICULATE MATTER	64.9	148.4	149.0	171.4	145.0	147.4	100	115	97	99
CARBON MONOXIDE	60.1	192.6	194.0	199.6	193.5	193.7	101	103	100	100
HYDROCARBONS	15.1	56.3	52.7	63.1	52.6	52.6	94	120	100	100
NITROGEN OXIDES	12.6	14.8	14.7	28.8	14.8	14.6	100	195	101	99
WATER OXYGEN DEMAND	209.4	481.5	482.8	492.8	477.1	481.1	100	102	100	100
LAND SOLID WASTE	331.3	387.6	372.2	388.5	369.9	374.5	96	104	99	101

12 BINGHAMTON, N. Y. - PA.

	1970	1990 BASE YEAR	1990 COMPLETED INTERSTATE	1990 EXTENDED PRIMARY	1990 ECONOMIC DEVELOPMENT	1990 URBAN	CI/BY	EP/BY	PERCENT ED/CI	U/CI
JOBS BY INDUSTRY			(THOUSANDS)							
NATURAL RESOURCES (1-10)	17.8	5.0	5.0	5.2	5.1	4.9	99	101	102	99
CONSTRUCTION (11,12)	8.6	5.9	5.6	5.2	5.1	4.7	95	93	90	84
MANUFACTURING (13-74)	101.0	85.4	84.5	85.0	86.9	79.9	99	101	103	95
TRANSPORTATION INDUSTRY (75)	6.9	11.0	10.7	10.9	11.2	10.4	100	102	105	100
PUBLIC UTILITIES (76-80)	5.7	10.7	10.7	10.9	11.2	10.4	97	100	101	98
TRADE (81,86,89-99)	50.9	51.4	60.9	61.1	61.6	59.9	99	101	101	98
SERVICES (82-85,87,88,102)	44.2	21.2	21.2	21.2	21.2	21.1	100	101	101	100
STATE & LOCAL GOVT. (101)	47.4	45.0	44.7	44.7	45.0	43.9	99	101	101	98
FEDERAL GOVERNMENT (100,103)	3.7	1.9	1.9	1.9	1.9	1.9	100	100	100	100
TOTAL JOBS	286.3	237.8	235.4	235.9	238.9	227.6	99	100	101	97
CIVILIAN PERSONS EMPLOYED	273.8	227.1	224.9	225.4	228.2	217.4	99	100	101	97
CIVILIAN UNEMPLOYMENT RATE	4.7	4.3	4.5	4.4	4.0	4.7				
POPULATION	765.4	749.2	742.8	737.6	737.6	727.1	99	99	99	98
PER CAPITA INCOME	4291.7	6607.1	6604.5	6677.7	6723.1	6524.6	100	101	102	99
ENERGY USER SECTOR			(TRILLIONS OF BTU'S)							
NATURAL RESOURCES	7.3	15.1	15.0	14.9	15.0	14.9	99	100	100	100
CONSTRUCTION	48.2	81.0	81.1	78.4	76.7	70.2	100	97	95	87
MANUFACTURING	32.2	56.1	55.5	56.0	56.8	54.7	99	101	102	98
TRANSPORTATION INDUSTRY	3.7	2.5	2.5	2.6	2.5	2.5	99	101	102	98
PUBLIC UTILITIES	46.2	155.6	148.1	142.4	147.4	145.5	95	96	99	98
TRADE AND SERVICES	40.3	65.6	64.8	64.9	65.3	64.0	99	100	101	99
GOVERNMENT, EXC. TRANSPORTATION	2.8	3.0	2.9	2.9	3.0	2.8	99	100	101	97
CONSUMERS, EXC. TRANSPORTATION	19.8	21.9	21.7	21.6	21.9	20.7	99	100	101	95
USER-OPERATED TRANSPORTATION	38.3	50.7	50.1	50.0	50.7	48.0	99	100	101	96
TRANSPORTATION AIR POLLUTION			(THOUSANDS OF TONS)							
SULFUR OXIDES	1.4	1.4	1.4	1.4	1.4	1.4	99	100	101	98
PARTICULATE MATTER	1.2	1.4	1.4	1.4	1.4	1.4	99	100	101	97
CARBON MONOXIDE	274.2	359.2	355.1	354.6	359.3	340.9	99	100	101	96
HYDROCARBONS	48.0	62.8	62.1	62.0	62.8	59.6	99	100	101	96
NITROGEN OXIDES	25.5	32.2	31.9	31.9	32.2	30.7	99	100	101	96
OTHER AIR POLLUTION										
SULFUR OXIDES	105.2	288.8	276.3	266.7	274.8	272.0	96	97	99	98
PARTICULATE MATTER	37.4	114.1	111.1	109.2	110.9	110.3	97	98	100	99
CARBON MONOXIDE	39.1	92.1	91.0	90.8	91.2	90.6	99	100	100	100
HYDROCARBONS	12.1	20.4	19.5	20.9	25.3	18.8	96	107	130	97
NITROGEN OXIDES	34.3	75.6	72.5	70.2	72.2	71.5	96	97	99	96
WATER OXYGEN DEMAND	1133.2	2344.3	2342.8	2341.9	2343.1	2342.6	100	100	100	100
LAND SOLID WASTE	604.7	591.9	586.8	580.3	582.7	574.4	99	99	99	98

SUMMARY PROJECTIONS BY ORE ECONOMIC AREA UNDER FIVE ALTERNATIVE HIGHWAY SYSTEMS

13 WIL-BARRE-HAZLE, PA.

	1970	1990 BASE YEAR	1990 COMPLETED INTERSTATE	1990 EXTENDED PRIMARY	1990 ECONOMIC DEVELOPMENT	1990 URBAN	P E R C E N T CI/BY	EP/CI	ED/CI	U/CI
JOBS BY INDUSTRY		(THOUSANDS)								
NATURAL RESOURCES (1-10)	8.6	3.5	3.3	3.0	2.9	2.9	95	90	87	86
CONSTRUCTION (11,12)	10.4	9.9	9.5	9.2	9.0	9.4	95	97	95	99
MANUFACTURING (13-74)	103.5	123.3	120.9	120.7	120.9	116.1	98	100	100	96
TRANSPORTATION INDUSTRY (75)	8.3	7.7	7.6	7.6	7.6	7.5	99	100	100	98
PUBLIC UTILITIES (76-80)	5.7	6.0	5.3	5.8	5.5	5.0	89	108	102	94
TRADE (81,86,89-99)	51.1	55.9	53.9	54.1	53.7	51.4	96	100	100	95
SERVICES (82-85,87,88,102)	42.1	68.8	68.6	68.6	68.6	68.5	100	100	100	100
STATE & LOCAL GOVT. (101)	26.0	30.6	29.8	29.8	29.7	28.9	97	100	100	97
FEDERAL GOVERNMENT (100,103)	5.0	5.1	4.9	4.9	4.9	4.7	96	100	100	96
TOTAL JOBS	260.7	310.9	303.8	303.7	302.8	294.4	98	100	100	97
CIVILIAN PERSONS EMPLOYED	249.0	297.0	290.3	290.1	289.3	281.3	98	100	100	97
CIVILIAN UNEMPLOYMENT RATE	6.4	3.4	3.5	3.5	3.1	3.6				
POPULATION	692.0	782.0	760.8	756.1	751.5	741.4	97	99	99	97
PER CAPITA INCOME	3044.3	5287.4	5256.2	5281.2	5292.8	5177.3	99	100	101	98
ENERGY USER SECTOR		(TRILLIONS OF BTU'S)								
NATURAL RESOURCES	3.0	4.2	3.9	3.7	3.6	3.7	95	94	92	93
CONSTRUCTION	15.0	24.9	24.5	22.6	24.5	18.0	99	92	100	73
MANUFACTURING	21.7	48.9	47.5	47.1	47.0	44.8	97	99	99	94
TRANSPORTATION INDUSTRY	6.9	12.4	11.8	11.8	11.7	11.1	95	100	99	94
PUBLIC UTILITIES	35.4	111.7	98.6	103.4	97.4	93.5	88	105	99	95
TRADE AND SERVICES	17.3	30.3	28.9	29.1	28.6	27.6	95	101	99	96
GOVERNMENT, EXC. TRANSPORTATION	5.8	7.8	7.7	7.7	7.7	7.7	99	100	100	99
CONSUMERS, EXC. TRANSPORTATION	32.2	54.0	52.9	52.8	52.7	51.5	98	100	100	97
USER-OPERATED TRANSPORTATION	38.2	70.7	68.9	68.8	68.6	66.8	97	100	100	97
TRANSPORTATION AIR POLLUTION		(THOUSANDS OF TONS)								
SULFUR OXIDES	1.7	3.0	2.9	2.9	2.9	2.8	95	99	99	95
PARTICULATE MATTER	1.2	2.3	2.2	2.2	2.2	2.1	97	100	99	96
CARBON MONOXIDE	249.7	473.3	460.0	459.6	457.8	444.5	97	100	100	97
HYDROCARBONS	43.4	82.0	79.7	79.6	79.3	77.0	97	100	100	97
NITROGEN OXIDES	23.7	43.9	42.6	42.7	42.4	41.1	97	100	100	96
OTHER AIR POLLUTION										
SULFUR OXIDES	71.1	195.9	174.6	182.3	172.4	166.4	89	104	99	95
PARTICULATE MATTER	35.7	87.8	82.7	84.1	81.2	80.6	94	102	98	97
CARBON MONOXIDE	34.6	55.1	54.2	52.5	51.7	53.4	98	97	95	99
HYDROCARBONS	15.3	26.5	23.0	17.4	17.3	11.9	87	76	75	51
NITROGEN OXIDES	23.2	51.1	45.9	47.7	45.3	43.9	90	104	99	96
WATER OXYGEN DEMAND	271.8	549.2	547.9	549.0	547.5	547.5	100	100	100	100
LAND SOLID WASTE	546.7	617.8	601.0	597.3	593.6	585.7	97	99	97	97

SUMMARY PROJECTIONS BY OBE ECONOMIC AREA UNDER FIVE ALTERNATIVE HIGHWAY SYSTEMS

14 NEW YORK, N. Y.

	1970	1990 BASE YEAR	1990 COMPLETED INTERSTATE	1990 EXTENDED PRIMARY	1990 ECONOMIC DEVELOPMENT	1990 URBAN	PERCENT CI/BY	PERCENT EP/CI	PERCENT ED/CI	PERCENT U/CI
JOBS BY INDUSTRY		(THOUSANDS)								
NATURAL RESOURCES (1-10)	36.2	31.7	30.8	30.2	30.7	32.4	97	98	100	105
CONSTRUCTION (11,12)	288.2	267.5	269.5	260.2	252.9	275.5	101	97	94	102
MANUFACTURING (13-74)	2042.4	2426.1	2374.3	2263.9	2285.4	2565.9	98	95	96	108
TRANSPORTATION INDUSTRY (75)	391.8	425.7	424.6	420.6	421.2	431.6	100	99	99	102
PUBLIC UTILITIES (76-80)	214.5	79.5	74.3	68.0	70.4	85.6	93	91	95	115
TRADE (81,86,89-99)	1801.6	2653.6	2621.8	2564.4	2575.8	2725.4	99	98	98	104
SERVICES (82-85,87,88,102)	2271.3	4020.0	4018.2	4016.1	4017.0	4021.7	100	100	100	100
STATE & LOCAL GOVT. (101)	949.3	1232.6	1222.6	1204.5	1207.2	1253.2	99	99	99	103
FEDERAL GOVERNMENT (100,103)	215.4	247.0	244.8	240.8	241.5	251.6	99	98	99	103
TOTAL JOBS	8210.7	11383.8	11281.0	11068.6	11102.6	11642.8	99	98	98	103
CIVILIAN PERSONS EMPLOYED	7583.5	10570.9	10475.1	10280.3	10313.2	10808.5	99	98	98	103
CIVILIAN UNEMPLOYMENT RATE	4.8	3.0	3.0	3.1	3.2	2.7				
POPULATION	18228.3	22848.1	22673.4	22505.2	22538.9	23125.4	99	99	99	102
PER CAPITA INCOME	4589.3	8365.8	8355.1	8268.1	8281.2	8446.2	100	99	99	101
ENERGY USER SECTOR		(TRILLIONS OF BTU'S)								
NATURAL RESOURCES	28.7	63.3	61.6	58.7	58.9	65.8	97	95	96	107
CONSTRUCTION	525.1	858.9	857.0	742.3	736.8	1153.1	100	87	86	135
MANUFACTURING	643.2	1404.9	1385.5	1320.0	1331.3	1474.0	99	95	96	106
TRANSPORTATION INDUSTRY	676.7	1322.4	1312.6	1297.7	1301.4	1340.1	99	99	99	102
PUBLIC UTILITIES	1056.2	2705.4	2609.9	2486.2	2531.1	2762.4	96	96	97	106
TRADE AND SERVICES	1282.9	2513.3	2492.8	2464.4	2471.8	2543.6	99	99	99	102
GOVERNMENT, EXC. TRANSPORTATION	87.1	145.2	144.2	142.2	142.6	147.5	99	99	99	102
CONSUMERS, EXC. TRANSPORTATION	763.9	1484.2	1469.6	1441.2	1445.8	1519.8	99	98	98	103
USER-OPERATED TRANSPORTATION	1109.1	2412.2	2389.3	2344.7	2352.0	2467.6	99	98	98	103
TRANSPORTATION AIR POLLUTION		(THOUSANDS OF TONS)								
SULFUR OXIDES	127.9	252.1	248.8	244.4	245.8	254.5	99	98	99	102
PARTICULATE MATTER	68.1	137.7	136.7	134.9	135.2	140.2	99	99	99	103
CARBON MONOXIDE	8401.5	18153.0	17988.4	17664.3	17716.9	18571.1	99	98	98	103
HYDROCARBONS	1451.2	3133.2	3102.9	3045.0	3055.0	3203.6	99	98	98	103
NITROGEN OXIDES	964.0	2014.2	2007.7	1985.7	1986.2	2066.7	100	99	99	103
OTHER AIR POLLUTION										
SULFUR OXIDES	3704.5	6891.7	6734.1	6531.0	6605.4	6984.4	97	95	96	104
PARTICULATE MATTER	1726.1	2843.5	2813.8	2758.1	2773.0	2888.8	98	98	99	103
CARBON MONOXIDE	1158.6	1777.9	1794.7	1778.7	1774.4	1812.6	101	99	99	101
HYDROCARBONS	837.0	1547.1	1520.9	1119.6	1176.6	1775.8	98	74	77	117
NITROGEN OXIDES	1527.2	2463.4	2425.2	2374.6	2392.9	2487.9	98	99	99	103
WATER OXYGEN DEMAND	1680.8	3247.5	3262.0	3261.3	3258.9	3267.0	100	100	100	100
LAND SOLID WASTE	14400.3	18049.9	17911.9	17779.1	17805.7	18269.0	99	99	99	102

	1970	1990 BASE YEAR	1990 COMPLETED INTERSTATE	1990 EXTENDED PRIMARY	1990 ECONOMIC DEVELOPMENT	1990 URBAN	PERCENT CI/BY	PERCENT EP/CI	PERCENT ED/CI	PERCENT U/CI
JOBS BY INDUSTRY			(THOUSANDS)							
NATURAL RESOURCES (1-10)	39.0	15.4	17.5	15.2	15.1	23.6	114	87	86	135
CONSTRUCTION (11,12)	134.4	134.1	135.1	131.2	127.6	137.1	101	97	94	101
MANUFACTURING (13-74)	922.4	1201.0	1294.5	1279.0	1281.0	1329.4	108	99	99	103
TRANSPORTATION INDUSTRY (75)	103.8	85.1	88.1	86.9	86.9	89.9	104	99	99	102
PUBLIC UTILITIES (76-80)	60.4	37.8	41.7	33.0	32.7	46.5	110	79	78	112
TRADE (81,86,89-99)	636.7	803.6	857.3	839.0	839.6	885.2	107	98	98	103
SERVICES (82-85,87,88,102)	679.6	1188.5	1192.7	1191.7	1192.0	1193.8	100	100	100	100
STATE & LOCAL GOVT. (101)	302.3	366.1	382.8	377.8	377.7	390.6	105	99	99	102
FEDERAL GOVERNMENT (100,103)	165.4	173.8	177.5	176.4	176.4	179.3	102	99	99	101
TOTAL JOBS	3044.1	4005.6	4187.1	4130.1	4128.9	4275.4	105	99	99	102
CIVILIAN PERSONS EMPLOYED	2866.7	3788.3	3961.8	3907.4	3906.3	4046.2	105	99	99	102
CIVILIAN UNEMPLOYMENT RATE	4.6	3.9	3.5	4.1	3.8	3.4				
POPULATION	7281.8	9459.7	9671.5	9639.1	9617.6	9774.1	102	100	99	101
PER CAPITA INCOME	4015.1	6370.1	6543.3	6472.4	6482.9	6624.3	103	99	99	101
ENERGY USER SECTOR			(TRILLIONS OF BTU'S)							
NATURAL RESOURCES	34.2	70.8	76.2	73.4	73.4	85.3	108	96	96	112
CONSTRUCTION	152.5	239.2	252.2	244.1	237.2	304.5	105	97	94	121
MANUFACTURING	598.4	1387.9	1432.4	1424.7	1423.7	1455.9	103	99	99	102
TRANSPORTATION INDUSTRY	134.5	283.4	298.8	294.0	294.3	306.3	105	98	98	103
PUBLIC UTILITIES	384.0	574.0	632.1	524.4	526.8	699.0	110	83	83	111
TRADE AND SERVICES	341.9	684.8	712.2	701.2	701.8	726.2	104	98	99	102
GOVERNMENT, EXC. TRANSPORTATION	98.5	135.6	137.4	136.8	136.8	138.2	101	100	100	101
CONSUMERS, EXC. TRANSPORTATION	334.9	594.1	619.8	612.2	611.8	632.2	104	99	99	102
USER-OPERATED TRANSPORTATION	643.3	1165.5	1205.5	1193.5	1193.0	1225.1	103	99	99	102
TRANSPORTATION AIR POLLUTION			(THOUSANDS OF TONS)							
SULFUR OXIDES	30.7	63.8	66.6	65.3	65.5	68.1	104	98	98	102
PARTICULATE MATTER	20.2	41.4	43.3	42.7	42.7	44.2	105	99	99	102
CARBON MONOXIDE	3566.3	7170.2	7469.5	7380.3	7376.3	7615.9	104	99	99	102
HYDROCARBONS	620.3	1247.0	1298.3	1282.4	1281.9	1323.6	104	99	99	102
NITROGEN OXIDES	356.6	722.0	755.0	748.1	746.7	770.1	105	99	99	102
OTHER AIR POLLUTION										
SULFUR OXIDES	1156.3	2203.6	2300.2	2123.4	2127.1	2410.2	104	92	92	105
PARTICULATE MATTER	971.4	2337.3	2361.9	2315.4	2315.7	2395.6	101	98	98	101
CARBON MONOXIDE	1641.9	4286.6	4273.8	4270.2	4267.7	4285.3	100	100	100	100
HYDROCARBONS	814.4	2151.4	2311.9	2297.4	2282.3	2465.9	107	99	99	107
NITROGEN OXIDES	397.4	823.3	847.4	803.3	804.1	875.9	103	95	95	103
WATER OXYGEN DEMAND	1731.9	4183.5	4174.7	4156.1	4155.0	4186.3	100	100	100	100
LAND SOLID WASTE	5752.6	7473.2	7640.5	7614.8	7597.8	7721.5	102	99	99	101

SUMMARY PROJECTIONS BY OBE ECONOMIC AREA UNDER FIVE ALTERNATIVE HIGHWAY SYSTEMS

16 HARRISBURG, PA.

	1970	1990 BASE YEAR	1990 COMPLETED INTERSTATE	1990 EXTENDED PRIMARY	1990 ECONOMIC DEVELOPMENT	1990 URBAN	P E R C E N T CI/BY	EP/CI	ED/CI	U/CI
JOBS BY INDUSTRY			(THOUSANDS)							
NATURAL RESOURCES (1-10)	34.3	9.9	9.0	8.8	8.1	8.0	91	98	90	89
CONSTRUCTION (11,12)	34.3	44.2	44.4	43.4	42.0	44.2	100	98	95	100
MANUFACTURING (13-74)	242.2	332.4	325.8	328.4	320.7	311.2	98	101	98	96
TRANSPORTATION INDUSTRY (75)	29.9	15.3	15.1	15.2	14.6	14.6	99	101	97	97
PUBLIC UTILITIES (76-80)	12.5	19.2	17.1	21.2	14.4	15.3	89	124	84	90
TRADE (81,86,89-99)	144.4	210.8	206.0	209.9	200.7	196.6	98	102	97	95
SERVICES (82-85,87,88,102)	121.9	214.6	214.6	214.7	214.4	214.3	100	100	100	100
STATE & LOCAL GOVT. (101)	82.0	107.5	105.9	106.9	104.4	103.4	99	101	99	98
FEDERAL GOVERNMENT (100,103)	26.8	30.8	30.5	30.7	30.1	29.9	99	101	99	98
TOTAL JOBS	728.5	984.8	968.3	979.3	949.4	937.4	98	101	98	97
CIVILIAN PERSONS EMPLOYED	673.9	912.5	897.3	907.7	880.1	868.5	98	101	98	97
CIVILIAN UNEMPLOYMENT RATE	3.9	3.9	4.3	4.3	4.5	4.3				
POPULATION	1723.5	2399.2	2384.9	2394.6	2362.7	2365.7	99	100	99	99
PER CAPITA INCOME	3499.2	5635.8	5557.8	5601.0	5472.3	5394.3	99	101	98	97
ENERGY USER SECTOR			(TRILLIONS OF BTU'S)							
NATURAL RESOURCES	18.2	29.8	28.6	28.2	26.8	26.6	96	99	94	93
CONSTRUCTION	34.0	66.1	65.5	61.7	50.8	47.3	99	94	77	72
MANUFACTURING	102.7	226.1	221.5	222.4	217.1	212.4	98	100	98	96
TRANSPORTATION INDUSTRY	28.7	64.0	62.5	63.6	61.0	60.1	98	102	98	96
PUBLIC UTILITIES	103.8	351.4	322.4	372.0	288.1	301.5	92	115	89	94
TRADE AND SERVICES	53.8	117.5	114.3	117.6	110.6	109.8	97	103	97	96
GOVERNMENT, EXC. TRANSPORTATION	8.1	12.5	12.9	12.4	12.1	12.0	99	101	99	98
CONSUMERS, EXC. TRANSPORTATION	75.2	146.0	143.7	145.0	141.0	139.5	99	101	98	97
USER-OPERATED TRANSPORTATION	136.3	286.8	283.2	285.4	279.1	276.8	99	101	99	98
TRANSPORTATION AIR POLLUTION			(THOUSANDS OF TONS)							
SULFUR OXIDES	7.3	15.0	14.7	14.8	14.3	14.2	98	101	98	97
PARTICULATE MATTER	5.2	10.6	10.5	10.6	10.3	10.2	98	101	98	97
CARBON MONOXIDE	1007.1	2096.0	2069.7	2086.7	2038.1	2021.3	99	101	98	98
HYDROCARBONS	175.7	363.4	358.7	361.6	353.2	350.3	99	101	98	98
NITROGEN OXIDES	98.3	199.1	196.8	199.2	193.8	191.9	99	101	98	97
OTHER AIR POLLUTION										
SULFUR OXIDES	236.9	766.8	718.2	801.3	661.1	683.4	94	112	92	95
PARTICULATE MATTER	210.0	525.2	512.9	539.8	497.0	503.5	98	105	97	98
CARBON MONOXIDE	203.1	268.8	268.1	273.8	267.0	267.6	100	102	100	100
HYDROCARBONS	54.9	119.1	95.8	82.0	73.8	66.3	80	86	77	69
NITROGEN OXIDES	63.8	199.0	187.0	207.7	172.8	178.5	94	111	92	95
WATER OXYGEN DEMAND	1728.1	3508.8	3503.6	3514.4	3500.6	3501.7	100	100	100	100
LAND SOLID WASTE	1361.6	1895.3	1884.0	1891.7	1866.5	1868.9	99	100	99	99

SUMMARY PROJECTIONS BY OBE ECONOMIC AREA UNDER FIVE ALTERNATIVE HIGHWAY SYSTEMS

17 BALTIMORE, MD.

	1970	1990 BASE YEAR	1990 COMPLETED INTERSTATE	1990 EXTENDED PRIMARY	1990 ECONOMIC DEVELOPMENT	1990 URBAN	CI/BY	EP/CI	ED/CI	U/CI
								PER	CENT	
JOBS BY INDUSTRY				(THOUSANDS)						
NATURAL RESOURCES (1-10)	26.4	6.4	6.7	7.0	9.4	6.6	104	105	141	99
CONSTRUCTION (11-12)	58.8	62.9	63.3	61.9	59.9	63.7	101	98	95	101
MANUFACTURING (13-74)	265.4	343.9	371.1	382.5	414.5	365.0	108	103	112	98
TRANSPORTATION INDUSTRY (75)	43.5	35.9	36.8	37.3	38.8	36.7	103	101	101	100
PUBLIC UTILITIES (76-80)	25.8	31.8	36.1	39.2	49.9	34.8	114	109	138	96
TRADE (81,86,89-99)	230.4	378.4	396.3	405.4	430.8	392.4	105	102	109	99
SERVICES (82-85,87-88,102)	249.1	484.0	485.1	485.4	486.5	485.0	100	100	100	100
STATE & LOCAL GOVT. (101)	131.0	172.9	179.1	181.6	189.0	177.9	104	101	106	99
FEDERAL GOVERNMENT (100,103)	109.2	118.5	119.9	120.4	122.1	119.6	101	100	102	100
TOTAL JOBS	1139.5	1634.8	1694.3	1720.7	1800.8	1681.9	104	102	106	99
CIVILIAN PERSONS EMPLOYED	1047.0	1519.8	1576.7	1601.9	1678.8	1564.8	104	102	106	99
CIVILIAN UNEMPLOYMENT RATE	4.8	2.1	1.9	1.5	1.4	1.7				
POPULATION	2670.2	3413.6	3469.1	3492.5	3587.3	3475.0	102	101	103	100
PER CAPITA INCOME	4400.3	7176.0	7368.0	7451.7	7655.8	7297.1	103	101	104	99
ENERGY USER SECTOR			(TRILLIONS	OF BTU'S)						
NATURAL RESOURCES	32.6	82.7	84.1	84.9	88.3	84.0	102	101	105	100
CONSTRUCTION	63.7	121.8	125.6	127.6	132.5	126.1	103	102	105	100
MANUFACTURING	137.8	268.6	284.1	292.4	310.7	281.0	106	103	109	99
TRANSPORTATION INDUSTRY	46.6	108.6	113.8	116.3	123.2	112.9	105	102	108	99
PUBLIC UTILITIES	404.9	245.1	240.4	242.2	245.8	235.2	98	101	102	98
TRADE AND SERVICES	106.7	273.4	285.4	291.2	308.7	283.2	104	102	108	99
GOVERNMENT, EXC. TRANSPORTATION	9.7	15.5	16.2	16.4	17.2	16.0	104	101	107	99
CONSUMERS, EXC. TRANSPORTATION	134.0	243.5	252.4	256.4	268.4	250.7	104	102	106	99
USER-OPERATED TRANSPORTATION	186.2	378.5	392.6	398.6	417.4	389.9	104	102	106	99
TRANSPORTATION AIR POLLUTION			(THOUSANDS	OF TONS)						
SULFUR OXIDES	12.2	28.4	29.4	29.8	31.3	29.2	103	101	106	99
PARTICULATE MATTER	8.3	18.6	19.3	19.6	20.5	19.1	104	102	106	99
CARBON MONOXIDE	1446.2	3025.8	3131.5	3178.1	3319.8	3111.6	103	101	106	99
HYDROCARBONS	254.2	534.5	552.6	560.5	585.2	549.2	103	101	106	99
NITROGEN OXIDES	149.7	326.7	338.5	344.3	358.5	336.5	104	102	106	99
OTHER AIR POLLUTION										
SULFUR OXIDES	836.3	981.0	976.0	980.2	990.0	967.4	99	100	101	99
PARTICULATE MATTER	416.2	901.6	923.3	938.6	990.5	920.2	102	102	107	100
CARBON MONOXIDE	425.3	1071.3	1080.8	1093.1	1147.8	1081.3	101	101	106	100
HYDROCARBONS	130.2	263.6	298.2	341.7	389.0	281.3	113	115	130	94
NITROGEN OXIDES	244.5	425.7	425.8	427.7	433.8	423.6	100	100	102	99
WATER OXYGEN DEMAND	2236.9	4584.0	4600.1	4611.6	4649.9	4599.7	100	100	101	100
LAND SOLID WASTE	2109.4	2696.3	2740.6	2759.1	2833.9	2745.3	102	101	103	100

SUMMARY PROJECTIONS BY ORE ECONOMIC AREA UNDER FIVE ALTERNATIVE HIGHWAY SYSTEMS

18   WASH., D. C. - MD. - VA.

	1970	1990 BASE YEAR	1990 COMPLETED INTERSTATE	1990 EXTENDED PRIMARY	1990 ECONOMIC DEVELOPMENT	1990 URBAN	CI/BY	EP/CI	ED/CI	U/CI
							PER CENT			
JOBS BY INDUSTRY		(THOUSANDS)								
NATURAL RESOURCES (1-10)	15.0	9.9	10.5	9.5	9.8	11.8	106	90	93	112
CONSTRUCTION (11,12)	73.9	93.8	92.7	93.0	90.5	96.4	99	100	93	104
MANUFACTURING (13-74)	63.9	135.4	140.3	131.5	132.8	154.7	104	94	95	110
TRANSPORTATION INDUSTRY (75)	33.1	58.8	59.1	58.2	58.3	60.3	100	98	99	102
PUBLIC UTILITIES (76-80)	31.8	55.2	57.7	50.8	51.9	65.9	104	88	90	114
TRADE (81,86,89-99)	268.8	463.3	469.5	455.3	457.1	488.3	101	97	97	104
SERVICES (82-85,87,88,102)	388.6	843.1	843.6	843.1	843.2	844.3	100	100	100	100
STATE & LOCAL GOVT. (101)	155.1	226.9	228.4	225.2	225.4	233.8	101	99	99	102
FEDERAL GOVERNMENT (100,103)	421.3	473.8	474.1	473.4	473.5	475.3	100	100	100	100
TOTAL JOBS	1451.6	2360.4	2376.0	2340.1	2342.5	2430.7	101	98	99	102
CIVILIAN PERSONS EMPLOYED	1390.4	2273.2	2288.0	2253.9	2256.5	2340.3	101	99	99	102
CIVILIAN UNEMPLOYMENT RATE	2.1	1.0	1.1	1.0	1.0	1.2				
POPULATION	3090.2	4776.6	4810.2	4734.4	4719.8	4962.6	101	98	98	103
PER CAPITA INCOME	4235.4	6733.0	6738.9	6713.4	6735.5	6736.8	100	100	100	100
ENERGY USER SECTOR		(TRILLIONS OF BTU'S)								
NATURAL RESOURCES	9.0	22.3	23.8	22.1	22.2	25.1	107	93	93	105
CONSTRUCTION	86.5	190.3	191.8	188.7	189.3	246.6	101	98	99	129
MANUFACTURING	23.9	66.3	69.1	64.6	65.7	76.5	104	93	95	111
TRANSPORTATION INDUSTRY	46.8	128.7	130.7	126.9	127.6	136.0	102	97	98	104
PUBLIC UTILITIES	100.0	601.3	631.7	518.9	531.3	751.9	105	82	84	119
TRADE AND SERVICES	192.7	487.1	492.2	483.1	484.8	504.9	101	98	98	103
GOVERNMENT, EXC. TRANSPORTATION	15.8	26.0	26.2	25.8	25.9	26.8	101	99	99	102
CONSUMERS, EXC. TRANSPORTATION	120.9	278.0	280.1	274.8	274.9	288.7	101	98	98	103
USER-OPERATED TRANSPORTATION	237.6	550.6	554.0	545.8	545.9	567.3	101	99	99	102
TRANSPORTATION AIR POLLUTION		(THOUSANDS OF TONS)								
SULFUR OXIDES	11.6	30.4	30.7	29.8	29.9	31.7	101	97	98	104
PARTICULATE MATTER	8.5	21.0	21.3	20.9	20.9	21.9	101	98	98	103
CARBON MONOXIDE	1717.4	3988.0	4015.1	3951.8	3953.4	4115.7	101	98	98	103
HYDROCARBONS	298.2	692.9	697.4	686.2	686.6	714.8	101	98	98	103
NITROGEN OXIDES	162.2	386.7	390.8	385.0	384.9	401.4	101	99	98	103
OTHER AIR POLLUTION										
SULFUR OXIDES	472.3	1973.9	2023.9	1838.8	1858.8	2221.2	103	91	92	110
PARTICULATE MATTER	251.6	847.0	872.9	811.0	815.1	930.1	103	93	93	107
CARBON MONOXIDE	146.9	468.9	490.3	461.9	460.3	489.9	105	94	94	100
HYDROCARBONS	82.5	232.0	238.3	237.8	245.7	263.3	103	100	103	111
NITROGEN OXIDES	275.5	996.9	1010.4	963.7	968.7	1059.1	101	95	96	105
WATER OXYGEN DEMAND	216.4	248.5	246.5	241.9	241.0	246.6	99	98	98	100
LAND SOLID WASTE	2441.2	3773.5	3800.0	3740.2	3728.6	3920.4	101	98	98	103

SUMMARY PROJECTIONS BY ORE ECONOMIC AREA UNDER FIVE ALTERNATIVE HIGHWAY SYSTEMS

19 STAUNTON, VA.

	1970	1990 BASE YEAR	1990 COMPLETED INTERSTATE	1990 EXTENDED PRIMARY	1990 ECONOMIC DEVELOPMENT	1990 URBAN	PERCENT CI/BY	EP/CI	ED/CI	U/CI
JOBS BY INDUSTRY			(THOUSANDS)							
NATURAL RESOURCES (1-10)	15.5	14.5	14.5	14.5	15.0	14.5	100	99	103	100
CONSTRUCTION (11,12)	7.4	7.1	7.1	6.9	8.8	7.1	100	96	123	100
MANUFACTURING (13-74)	46.1	55.9	55.5	53.8	58.0	53.8	99	97	105	97
TRANSPORTATION INDUSTRY (75)	4.8	8.1	8.1	8.1	8.3	8.1	100	99	102	99
PUBLIC UTILITIES (76-80)	2.2	.7	.7	.7	1.0	.7	99	102	138	97
TRADE (81,86,89-99)	25.9	35.1	34.9	34.1	37.3	34.0	99	98	107	98
SERVICES (82-85,87,88,102)	26.0	36.4	36.5	36.5	36.6	36.4	100	100	100	100
STATE & LOCAL GOVT. (101)	16.7	20.8	20.7	20.4	21.6	20.4	100	98	104	99
FEDERAL GOVERNMENT (100,103)	3.6	4.0	4.0	3.9	4.2	3.9	100	98	105	98
TOTAL JOBS	148.2	182.6	182.0	178.8	190.7	179.0	100	98	105	98
CIVILIAN PERSONS EMPLOYED	131.4	162.9	162.4	159.6	170.2	159.7	100	98	105	98
CIVILIAN UNEMPLOYMENT RATE	5.4	9.1	9.0	9.0	8.9	9.3				
POPULATION	395.1	541.4	540.7	529.3	556.0	531.0	100	98	103	98
PER CAPITA INCOME	3065.2	4415.3	4402.3	4374.3	4581.5	4377.4	100	99	104	99
ENERGY USER SECTOR			(TRILLIONS OF BTUS)							
NATURAL RESOURCES	12.9	33.7	33.4	33.0	34.5	33.2	99	99	103	100
CONSTRUCTION	7.1	11.9	11.6	7.1	16.7	7.3	101	62	144	63
MANUFACTURING	20.6	40.8	40.5	39.2	42.8	39.8	99	97	106	98
TRANSPORTATION INDUSTRY	5.4	11.7	11.7	11.4	12.3	11.4	99	98	106	98
PUBLIC UTILITIES	12.2	7.4	7.2	7.3	16.0	7.1	98	101	221	98
TRADE AND SERVICES	9.4	20.5	20.4	20.0	21.6	20.0	98	98	105	98
GOVERNMENT, EXC. TRANSPORTATION	.8	1.2	1.2	1.1	1.3	1.1	99	97	108	97
CONSUMERS, EXC. TRANSPORTATION	13.4	24.0	23.9	23.4	25.3	23.4	100	98	106	98
USER-OPERATED TRANSPORTATION	24.3	47.9	47.7	46.9	49.9	47.0	100	98	105	98
TRANSPORTATION AIR POLLUTION			(THOUSANDS OF TONS)							
SULFUR OXIDES	2.0	4.6	4.6	4.5	4.8	4.6	99	98	103	99
PARTICULATE MATTER	1.4	3.2	3.2	3.1	3.3	3.1	100	99	103	99
CARBON MONOXIDE	224.0	476.2	474.9	468.1	492.0	469.4	100	99	104	99
HYDROCARBONS	40.4	88.7	86.5	85.3	89.5	85.5	100	99	103	99
NITROGEN OXIDES	25.6	57.5	57.5	56.8	59.3	56.9	100	99	103	99
OTHER AIR POLLUTION										
SULFUR OXIDES	25.8	21.0	20.8	20.8	35.1	20.5	99	100	169	99
PARTICULATE MATTER	76.4	99.1	95.5	87.4	110.5	94.0	96	91	116	98
CARBON MONOXIDE	92.2	196.7	191.9	187.7	204.3	190.5	98	98	106	98
HYDROCARBONS	21.8	47.6	47.9	46.0	59.3	46.4	101	96	124	97
NITROGEN OXIDES	10.6	10.2	10.0	9.9	13.9	9.9	98	99	140	99
WATER OXYGEN DEMAND	651.2	1066.7	1065.6	1065.3	1065.9	1065.5	100	100	100	100
LAND SOLID WASTE	312.1	427.7	427.1	418.2	439.2	419.5	100	98	103	98

20 ROANOKE, VA.

	1970	1990 BASE YEAR	1990 COMPLETED INTERSTATE	1990 EXTENDED PRIMARY	1990 ECONOMIC DEVELOPMENT	1990 URBAN	CI/BY	EP/CI	ED/CI	U/CI
							\<--	PER C	ENT --\>	
JOBS BY INDUSTRY			(THOUSANDS)							
NATURAL RESOURCES (1-10)	29.8	13.3	13.2	13.2	13.4	13.2	99	100	102	100
CONSTRUCTION (11,12)	16.6	17.1	17.3	17.1	16.9	17.4	101	99	109	100
MANUFACTURING (13-74)	124.4	186.8	185.4	186.6	189.6	183.5	99	101	102	99
TRANSPORTATION INDUSTRY (75)	13.2	18.1	18.1	18.2	18.5	18.0	100	101	102	99
PUBLIC UTILITIES (76-80)	5.4	2.6	2.4	3.0	5.9	2.2	95	124	243	89
TRADE (81,86,89-99)	56.9	76.3	75.4	77.3	81.9	74.0	99	102	109	98
SERVICES (82-85,87,88,102)	58.6	87.6	87.7	87.7	88.0	87.6	100	100	100	100
STATE & LOCAL GOVT. (101)	59.6	75.8	75.5	75.9	77.1	75.1	100	101	102	100
FEDERAL GOVERNMENT (100,103)	5.6	6.3	6.3	6.4	6.6	6.2	99	102	106	99
TOTAL JOBS										
CIVILIAN PERSONS EMPLOYED	370.0	483.9	481.3	485.8	499.9	477.2	99	101	104	99
CIVILIAN UNEMPLOYMENT RATE	322.5	422.2	419.9	424.0	436.3	416.2	99	101	104	99
POPULATION	2.2	8.4	8.6	8.5	8.1	8.4	99	101	102	99
PER CAPITA INCOME	831.3	1260.4	1253.6	1262.1	1277.3	1240.0	99	101	104	99
	3321.9	4531.3	4518.6	4548.7	4677.1	4508.1	100	101	104	100
ENERGY USER SECTOR			(TRILLIONS OF BTU'S)							
NATURAL RESOURCES	6.9	5.1	4.8	4.9	5.2	4.8	96	102	108	99
CONSTRUCTION	12.7	21.6	21.7	22.3	24.9	15.7	100	103	115	72
MANUFACTURING	97.4	226.6	225.6	228.5	230.6	224.1	100	101	102	99
TRANSPORTATION INDUSTRY	9.6	20.5	20.2	20.7	21.9	19.9	99	102	108	98
PUBLIC UTILITIES	39.6	29.4	27.7	39.2	83.4	27.2	94	141	301	98
TRADE AND SERVICES	20.3	40.2	39.7	40.7	43.8	39.1	99	102	110	98
GOVERNMENT, EXC. TRANSPORTATION	1.9	3.1	3.1	3.1	3.3	3.0	99	102	106	99
CONSUMERS, EXC. TRANSPORTATION	29.8	55.4	55.0	55.7	57.6	54.4	99	102	105	99
USER-OPERATED TRANSPORTATION	56.4	114.5	113.9	114.9	118.0	112.9	99	101	104	99
TRANSPORTATION AIR POLLUTION			(THOUSANDS OF TONS)							
SULFUR OXIDES	2.7	5.2	5.1	5.2	5.4	5.0	99	102	106	99
PARTICULATE MATTER	2.1	4.0	3.9	4.0	4.1	3.9	99	102	105	99
CARBON MONOXIDE	430.6	850.5	845.7	853.9	876.6	838.5	99	101	104	99
HYDROCARBONS	75.1	147.4	146.5	147.9	151.9	145.3	99	101	104	99
NITROGEN OXIDES	40.9	78.3	77.9	79.0	81.2	77.2	100	101	104	99
OTHER AIR POLLUTION										
SULFUR OXIDES	108.6	133.6	130.8	149.7	222.9	129.9	98	114	170	99
PARTICULATE MATTER	71.8	108.6	103.4	113.7	139.4	101.5	95	110	135	98
CARBON MONOXIDE	96.6	140.4	138.7	140.1	147.6	139.7	99	101	106	101
HYDROCARBONS	84.1	266.3	262.9	288.7	291.2	250.5	99	110	111	95
NITROGEN OXIDES	33.5	40.1	39.4	44.1	62.4	39.2	98	112	158	100
WATER OXYGEN DEMAND	346.0	304.5	303.4	304.7	306.1	304.0	100	101	101	100
LAND SOLID WASTE	656.7	995.7	989.9	997.1	1009.0	979.6	99	101	102	99

SUMMARY PROJECTIONS BY ORE ECONOMIC AREA UNDER FIVE ALTERNATIVE HIGHWAY SYSTEMS

21 RICHMOND, VA.

	1970	1990 BASE YEAR	1990 COMPLETED INTERSTATE	1990 EXTENDED PRIMARY	1990 ECONOMIC DEVELOPMENT	1990 URBAN	CI/BY	EP/CI	ED/CI	U/CI
							P E R C E N T			
JOBS BY INDUSTRY			(THOUSANDS)							
NATURAL RESOURCES (1-10)	22.6	10.9	11.5	11.8	11.3	11.3	105	103	98	98
CONSTRUCTION (11,12)	27.8	29.7	30.0	29.5	28.5	30.1	101	103	95	100
MANUFACTURING (13-74)	100.3	96.9	102.6	106.2	102.4	101.7	106	103	100	99
TRANSPORTATION INDUSTRY (75)	15.5	17.4	18.6	18.9	18.5	18.4	107	102	100	99
PUBLIC UTILITIES (76-80)	10.1	17.6	21.5	24.9	20.7	20.0	122	116	97	93
TRADE (81,86,89-99)	89.1	98.6	106.0	111.6	105.3	104.0	108	105	99	98
SERVICES (82-85,87,88,102)	93.3	170.5	170.9	171.1	170.9	170.9	100	105	100	100
STATE & LOCAL GOVT. (101)	46.3	54.3	56.6	57.9	56.3	56.1	104	100	100	99
FEDERAL GOVERNMENT (100,103)	32.7	33.2	33.7	34.0	33.6	33.6	102	101	100	100
TOTAL JOBS	437.6	529.1	551.4	565.8	547.6	546.2	104	103	99	99
CIVILIAN PERSONS EMPLOYED	433.1	525.6	546.9	560.8	543.5	541.8	104	103	99	99
CIVILIAN UNEMPLOYMENT RATE	1.7	1.5	1.9	1.9	1.7	2.0				
POPULATION	1009.3	1258.8	1323.2	1358.3	1308.9	1317.4	105	103	99	100
PER CAPITA INCOME	3995.2	5866.2	5881.7	5907.5	5892.6	5845.1	100	100	100	99
ENERGY USER SECTOR			(TRILLIONS OF BTU'S)							
NATURAL RESOURCES	5.8	14.2	15.0	15.8	14.9	14.9	106	105	99	99
CONSTRUCTION	20.0	31.8	35.5	38.2	33.9	32.9	112	108	95	93
MANUFACTURING	47.3	83.9	86.4	88.8	86.7	85.8	103	103	100	99
TRANSPORTATION INDUSTRY	13.7	16.1	18.2	19.7	17.9	17.7	113	108	99	97
PUBLIC UTILITIES	67.3	209.6	264.1	307.0	252.7	247.6	126	116	96	94
TRADE AND SERVICES	40.9	76.3	81.5	85.4	80.8	80.0	107	105	99	98
GOVERNMENT, EXC. TRANSPORTATION	3.1	4.4	4.7	4.8	4.7	4.6	106	103	99	99
CONSUMERS, EXC. TRANSPORTATION	51.4	82.7	86.0	88.1	85.4	85.3	104	102	99	99
USER-OPERATED TRANSPORTATION	77.3	144.1	149.3	152.6	148.5	148.2	104	102	99	99
TRANSPORTATION AIR POLLUTION			(THOUSANDS OF TONS)							
SULFUR OXIDES	3.6	4.9	5.3	5.5	5.2	5.2	108	105	99	98
PARTICULATE MATTER	2.7	4.3	4.6	4.7	4.5	4.5	106	104	99	99
CARBON MONOXIDE	578.9	1050.2	1089.3	1113.8	1082.9	1080.9	104	102	99	99
HYDROCARBONS	100.6	182.0	188.7	192.9	187.6	187.2	104	102	99	99
NITROGEN OXIDES	54.0	92.5	96.7	99.5	96.1	95.8	105	103	99	99
OTHER AIR POLLUTION										
SULFUR OXIDES	156.6	497.2	587.1	657.0	568.1	560.1	118	112	97	95
PARTICULATE MATTER	82.1	213.2	239.2	262.2	235.2	232.7	112	110	98	97
CARBON MONOXIDE	76.1	276.6	287.3	302.5	285.8	286.1	104	105	99	100
HYDROCARBONS	32.7	64.9	72.2	84.2	77.6	69.0	111	117	107	95
NITROGEN OXIDES	49.2	178.3	200.9	218.8	196.2	194.2	113	109	98	97
WATER OXYGEN DEMAND	308.3	271.4	269.3	270.0	268.6	269.4	99	100	100	100
LAND SOLID WASTE	797.4	994.4	1045.3	1073.0	1034.0	1040.8	105	103	99	100

SUMMARY PROJECTIONS BY ORE ECONOMIC AREA UNDER FIVE ALTERNATIVE HIGHWAY SYSTEMS

22 NORF--PORTS., VA.

	1970	1990 BASE YEAR	1990 COMPLETED INTERSTATE	1990 EXTENDED PRIMARY	1990 ECONOMIC DEVELOPMENT	1990 URBAN	CI/BY	EP/CI	ED/CI	U/CI
JOBS BY INDUSTRY			(THOUSANDS)							
NATURAL RESOURCES (1-10)	12.8	5.3	5.2	5.5	5.3	5.5	98	106	101	104
CONSTRUCTION (11,12)	26.8	28.8	29.1	28.6	27.7	29.4	101	98	95	101
MANUFACTURING (13-74)	67.8	48.8	48.3	50.5	48.7	48.2	99	105	101	100
TRANSPORTATION INDUSTRY (75)	15.8	29.7	29.4	29.6	29.4	29.4	99	101	100	100
PUBLIC UTILITIES (76-80)	6.9	9.8	8.1	10.0	7.5	9.4	82	124	93	116
TRADE (81,86,89-99)	89.3	98.3	95.8	99.1	95.6	96.7	97	103	100	101
SERVICES (82-85,87,88,102)	85.4	191.4	191.5	191.7	191.4	191.6	100	100	100	100
STATE & LOCAL GOVT. (101)	47.4	55.4	55.9	55.6	54.7	55.2	99	101	100	100
FEDERAL GOVERNMENT (100,103)	100.7	105.1	105.0	105.2	105.0	105.1	100	100	100	100
TOTAL JOBS	453.0	572.7	567.3	575.7	565.3	570.3	99	101	100	101
CIVILIAN PERSONS EMPLOYED	376.4	489.8	484.8	492.6	483.0	487.5	99	102	100	101
CIVILIAN UNEMPLOYMENT RATE	3.5	3.5								
POPULATION	1225.9	1539.0	1518.3	1550.9	1513.2	1536.0	99	102	100	101
PER CAPITA INCOME	3630.9	5145.4	5158.2	5125.0	5141.4	5138.2	100	99	100	100
ENERGY USER SECTOR			(TRILLIONS OF BTU'S)							
NATURAL RESOURCES	3.6	2.1	2.1	2.2	2.1	2.1	99	105	101	101
CONSTRUCTION	25.0	41.8	41.1	42.3	41.4	42.1	98	103	101	102
MANUFACTURING	29.0	41.8	41.4	42.7	41.7	41.5	99	103	101	100
TRANSPORTATION INDUSTRY	14.8	30.1	29.4	30.3	29.3	29.7	98	103	100	101
PUBLIC UTILITIES	43.5	175.9	147.0	181.2	140.3	167.9	84	123	95	114
TRADE AND SERVICES	30.5	71.9	69.9	72.5	69.5	71.0	97	104	99	102
GOVERNMENT, EXC. TRANSPORTATION	4.0	6.1	6.0	6.2	6.0	6.0	99	101	100	101
CONSUMERS, EXC. TRANSPORTATION	42.7	58.7	58.1	58.9	57.8	58.5	99	101	100	101
USER-OPERATED TRANSPORTATION	80.2	145.0	143.8	145.4	143.2	144.6	99	101	100	101
TRANSPORTATION AIR POLLUTION			(THOUSANDS OF TONS)							
SULFUR OXIDES	3.8	7.2	7.0	7.1	7.0	7.1	98	102	99	101
PARTICULATE MATTER	2.9	5.2	5.1	5.2	5.1	5.2	99	102	100	101
CARBON MONOXIDE	595.1	1067.8	1058.9	1071.4	1054.6	1064.5	99	101	100	101
HYDROCARBONS	103.4	184.9	183.3	185.4	182.5	184.3	99	101	100	101
NITROGEN OXIDES	55.7	99.6	98.8	100.4	98.5	99.4	99	102	100	101
OTHER AIR POLLUTION										
SULFUR OXIDES	107.0	342.4	294.9	351.9	284.2	329.9	86	119	96	112
PARTICULATE MATTER	75.0	114.3	105.1	116.7	103.2	112.0	92	111	98	107
CARBON MONOXIDE	64.0	87.1	86.7	87.4	87.1	87.4	100	101	100	100
HYDROCARBONS	22.2	42.7	42.1	47.3	44.3	42.6	99	112	105	101
NITROGEN OXIDES	43.4	110.7	99.0	113.1	96.3	107.7	89	114	97	109
WATER OXYGEN DEMAND	99.9	125.0	124.0	123.8	123.9	124.0	99	100	100	100
LAND SOLID WASTE	968.5	1215.8	1199.4	1225.2	1195.4	1213.5	99	102	100	101

SUMMARY PROJECTIONS BY ORE ECONOMIC AREA UNDER FIVE ALTERNATIVE HIGHWAY SYSTEMS

23 RALEIGH, N. C.

	1970	1990 BASE YEAR	1990 COMPLETED INTERSTATE	1990 EXTENDED PRIMARY	1990 ECONOMIC DEVELOPMENT	1990 URBAN	PER CENT CI/BY	EP/CI	ED/CI	U/CI
JOBS BY INDUSTRY		(THOUSANDS)								
NATURAL RESOURCES (1-10)	74.1	29.7	29.6	29.9	30.5	29.6	100	101	103	100
CONSTRUCTION (11.12)	35.0	41.9	42.1	41.2	45.6	42.3	101	98	108	100
MANUFACTURING (13-74)	136.2	190.1	172.5	172.3	179.6	168.8	91	100	104	98
TRANSPORTATION INDUSTRY (75)	10.3	15.1	14.5	14.5	15.0	14.3	96	100	104	99
PUBLIC UTILITIES (76-80)	10.3	4.5	4.1	4.1	7.0	3.7	91	100	170	90
TRADE (81.86.89-99)	120.0	134.5	124.2	124.4	131.9	121.9	92	100	106	98
SERVICES (82-85.87.88.102)	125.3	196.9	195.7	195.7	196.0	195.6	99	100	100	100
STATE & LOCAL GOVT. (101)	93.1	113.1	110.5	110.4	112.6	109.8	98	100	102	99
FEDERAL GOVERNMENT (100.103)	77.6	76.3	75.7	75.7	76.2	75.5	99	100	101	100
TOTAL JOBS	681.8	802.0	769.0	768.3	794.2	761.5	96	100	103	99
CIVILIAN PERSONS EMPLOYED	518.2	622.9	595.9	595.7	617.6	589.5	96	100	104	99
CIVILIAN UNEMPLOYMENT RATE	5.9	7.3	6.4	6.4	6.6	6.6				
POPULATION	1621.2	2066.4	1943.2	1934.0	2017.1	1915.3	94	100	104	99
PER CAPITA INCOME	2508.4	3816.8	3807.3	3812.1	3875.8	3791.0	100	100	102	100
ENERGY USER SECTOR		(TRILLIONS OF BTU'S)								
NATURAL RESOURCES	20.0	12.9	12.7	13.2	14.1	12.7	98	104	111	100
CONSTRUCTION	24.6	43.2	42.0	40.1	64.9	34.8	97	96	154	83
MANUFACTURING	39.7	88.3	82.3	82.3	86.5	81.1	93	100	105	99
TRANSPORTATION INDUSTRY	9.4	23.4	20.4	20.4	22.4	19.7	87	100	110	97
PUBLIC UTILITIES	81.0	190.8	178.6	173.8	221.8	167.1	94	97	124	94
TRADE AND SERVICES	44.0	105.2	99.6	99.6	104.5	98.1	95	100	105	98
GOVERNMENT, EXC. TRANSPORTATION	4.3	6.3	6.0	6.0	6.3	6.0	96	100	104	99
CONSUMERS, EXC. TRANSPORTATION	59.6	108.6	104.4	104.3	108.0	103.3	96	100	103	99
USER-OPERATED TRANSPORTATION	104.4	205.9	199.3	199.1	204.9	197.5	97	100	103	99
TRANSPORTATION AIR POLLUTION		(THOUSANDS OF TONS)								
SULFUR OXIDES	4.6	7.5	6.9	6.9	7.3	6.8	92	100	106	98
PARTICULATE MATTER	3.9	6.5	6.2	6.2	6.4	6.1	95	100	104	99
CARBON MONOXIDE	838.7	1528.6	1479.3	1477.7	1521.0	1465.4	97	100	103	99
HYDROCARBONS	148.5	265.9	257.4	257.1	264.6	255.0	97	100	103	99
NITROGEN OXIDES	82.7	138.1	133.1	133.1	137.4	131.7	96	100	103	99
OTHER AIR POLLUTION										
SULFUR OXIDES	159.3	364.1	343.7	335.6	415.0	324.5	94	98	121	94
PARTICULATE MATTER	160.6	194.7	190.9	189.1	209.5	186.6	98	99	110	98
CARBON MONOXIDE	164.1	125.9	128.7	128.8	129.8	130.0	102	100	101	101
HYDROCARBONS	44.8	45.7	44.8	44.7	59.8	44.9	98	100	134	100
NITROGEN OXIDES	54.0	114.6	109.7	107.7	127.4	105.1	96	98	116	96
WATER OXYGEN DEMAND	256.0	238.7	240.6	240.4	243.0	240.8	101	100	101	100
LAND SOLID WASTE	1280.8	1632.5	1535.1	1527.9	1593.5	1513.0	94	100	104	99

SUMMARY PROJECTIONS BY OBE ECONOMIC AREA UNDER FIVE ALTERNATIVE HIGHWAY SYSTEMS

24 WILMINGTON, N. C.

	1970	1990 BASE YEAR	1990 COMPLETED INTERSTATE	1990 EXTENDED PRIMARY	1990 ECONOMIC DEVELOPMENT	1990 URBAN	CI/BY	EPCI	ED/CI	U/CI
			(THOUSANDS)					P E R C E N T		
JOBS BY INDUSTRY										
NATURAL RESOURCES (1-10)	19.5	8.2	8.2	8.3	8.2	8.2	100	101	101	100
CONSTRUCTION (11-12)	8.8	9.6	9.6	9.9	11.9	9.8	102	102	123	101
MANUFACTURING (13-74)	32.3	44.9	44.0	47.8	47.5	43.7	98	109	108	99
TRANSPORTATION INDUSTRY (75)	5.3	8.5	8.4	8.6	8.6	8.4	99	103	103	100
PUBLIC UTILITIES (76-80)	2.8	.7	.7	.9	.7	.7	97	119	120	103
TRADE (81,86,89-99)	30.4	27.8	26.9	30.2	30.1	26.6	97	112	112	99
SERVICES (82-85,87,88,102)	25.8	48.6	48.6	49.0	48.9	48.6	100	101	101	100
STATE & LOCAL GOVT. (101)	17.3	17.5	17.2	18.0	18.2	17.2	98	105	105	100
FEDERAL GOVERNMENT (100,103)	48.3	47.3	47.3	47.4	47.5	47.2	100	100	100	100
TOTAL JOBS	190.3	213.2	210.9	220.1	221.7	210.4	99	104	105	100
CIVILIAN PERSONS EMPLOYED	139.5	161.1	159.0	167.4	168.8	158.5	99	105	106	100
CIVILIAN UNEMPLOYMENT RATE	6.4	6.9	7.4	6.8	6.7	6.5				
POPULATION	482.1	608.2	601.2	627.9	635.7	589.6	99	104	106	98
PER CAPITA INCOME	2780.5	3523.3	3504.0	3574.5	3586.9	3552.1	99	102	102	101
ENERGY USER SECTOR			(TRILLIONS OF BTU'S)							
NATURAL RESOURCES	5.2	2.5	2.3	2.9	2.7	2.3	96	124	115	100
CONSTRUCTION	6.7	10.0	8.3	10.8	18.3	7.9	83	130	221	95
MANUFACTURING	16.7	34.6	33.8	35.9	35.7	33.7	98	106	105	100
TRANSPORTATION INDUSTRY	4.3	7.0	6.7	7.6	7.6	6.7	97	113	112	99
PUBLIC UTILITIES	23.3	18.9	15.8	30.0	26.9	16.5	84	190	170	98
TRADE AND SERVICES	10.1	16.9	16.4	18.2	18.1	16.3	99	110	110	99
GOVERNMENT, EXC. TRANSPORTATION	2.1	2.6	2.6	2.7	2.7	2.6	99	103	104	100
CONSUMERS, EXC. TRANSPORTATION	13.6	20.9	20.7	21.5	21.7	20.6	99	104	105	100
USER-OPERATED TRANSPORTATION	24.2	40.3	39.8	41.6	42.1	39.6	99	105	106	100
TRANSPORTATION AIR POLLUTION			(THOUSANDS OF TONS)							
SULFUR OXIDES	1.4	1.9	1.8	2.0	2.0	1.8	97	108	109	99
PARTICULATE MATTER	1.1	1.5	1.4	1.5	1.5	1.4	98	107	107	99
CARBON MONOXIDE	197.6	304.6	301.0	314.9	318.1	299.7	99	105	106	100
HYDROCARBONS	35.0	53.0	52.4	54.8	55.3	52.2	99	105	106	100
NITROGEN OXIDES	20.4	28.7	28.3	29.9	30.1	28.2	99	105	106	100
OTHER AIR POLLUTION										
SULFUR OXIDES	45.3	39.3	33.6	59.9	53.9	32.9	86	178	160	98
PARTICULATE MATTER	28.3	24.8	22.8	32.8	29.8	22.6	92	144	131	99
CARBON MONOXIDE	53.4	39.9	37.7	50.3	45.4	37.7	94	133	121	100
HYDROCARBONS	13.6	9.9	9.7	14.6	17.5	9.7	98	151	180	100
NITROGEN OXIDES	15.5	14.0	12.2	20.5	18.4	11.9	87	168	151	98
WATER OXYGEN DEMAND	95.5	71.7	71.2	73.7	73.0	71.1	99	103	102	100
LAND SOLID WASTE	380.8	480.5	474.9	496.0	502.2	465.8	99	104	106	98

SUMMARY PROJECTIONS BY ORE ECONOMIC AREA UNDER FIVE ALTERNATIVE HIGHWAY SYSTEMS

25 GR-WINS SALEM-H PT. N.C.

	1970	1990 BASE YEAR	1990 COMPLETED INTERSTATE	1990 EXTENDED PRIMARY	1990 ECONOMIC DEVELOPMENT	1990 URBAN	CI/BY	EP/CI	ED/CI	U/CI
							PERCENT			
JOBS BY INDUSTRY (THOUSANDS)										
NATURAL RESOURCES (1-10)	42.0	17.3	17.3	17.3	17.3	17.3	100	100	100	100
CONSTRUCTION (11,12)	31.2	31.4	31.7	30.9	30.0	31.9	101	97	95	100
MANUFACTURING (13-74)	225.1	381.1	385.7	380.6	381.8	378.8	101	99	99	98
TRANSPORTATION INDUSTRY (75)	16.3	27.1	27.3	27.1	27.1	27.0	101	99	99	99
PUBLIC UTILITIES (76-80)	16.7	2.2	2.3	2.3	2.3	2.1	103	100	100	91
TRADE (81,86,89-99)	96.4	110.6	112.2	110.6	111.0	109.3	101	99	99	97
SERVICES (82-85,87,88,102)	87.5	174.9	175.5	175.0	175.0	174.9	100	100	100	100
STATE & LOCAL GOVT. (101)	41.6	60.1	61.0	60.2	60.3	59.9	101	99	99	98
FEDERAL GOVERNMENT (100,103)	5.2	7.3	7.5	7.4	7.4	7.3	103	99	99	97
TOTAL JOBS	552.1	812.1	820.5	811.3	812.1	808.4	101	99	99	99
CIVILIAN PERSONS EMPLOYED	521.6	765.8	773.7	765.1	765.9	762.3	101	99	99	99
CIVILIAN UNEMPLOYMENT RATE	3.2	3.3	3.3	3.5	3.3	3.3				
POPULATION	1142.7	1747.3	1759.4	1746.6	1744.2	1746.4	101	99	99	99
PER CAPITA INCOME	3335.1	5500.4	5547.5	5503.7	5515.5	5471.9	101	99	99	99
ENERGY USER SECTOR (TRILLIONS OF BTU'S)										
NATURAL RESOURCES	8.8	4.0	4.0	4.0	4.0	4.0	100	100	100	100
CONSTRUCTION	20.5	37.7	38.2	36.1	34.5	34.2	101	94	90	90
MANUFACTURING	51.6	117.7	120.0	117.5	118.3	115.5	102	98	99	96
TRANSPORTATION INDUSTRY	26.0	51.2	51.7	51.2	51.4	50.9	101	99	99	98
PUBLIC UTILITIES	73.5	43.7	43.0	43.3	43.9	42.0	98	101	102	98
TRADE AND SERVICES	34.9	71.4	72.2	71.4	71.5	70.9	101	99	99	98
GOVERNMENT, EXC. TRANSPORTATION	3.3	6.2	6.3	6.2	6.2	6.2	101	99	99	99
CONSUMERS, EXC. TRANSPORTATION	43.0	91.7	92.9	91.7	91.8	91.2	101	99	99	98
USER-OPERATED TRANSPORTATION	81.9	188.3	190.3	188.4	188.5	187.6	101	99	99	99
TRANSPORTATION AIR POLLUTION (THOUSANDS OF TONS)										
SULFUR OXIDES	6.0	11.4	11.5	11.3	11.3	11.3	101	99	99	99
PARTICULATE MATTER	3.8	7.6	7.7	7.7	7.7	7.7	101	100	100	100
CARBON MONOXIDE	643.1	1414.1	1428.6	1415.2	1416.1	1408.8	101	99	99	99
HYDROCARBONS	112.3	245.0	247.4	245.0	245.2	243.9	101	99	99	99
NITROGEN OXIDES	66.3	137.1	138.9	138.0	138.0	137.0	101	99	99	99
OTHER AIR POLLUTION										
SULFUR OXIDES	143.1	168.3	167.0	166.5	167.5	165.3	99	100	100	99
PARTICULATE MATTER	96.5	184.9	184.5	177.4	177.5	182.8	100	96	96	99
CARBON MONOXIDE	61.0	46.2	46.1	46.0	46.1	46.1	100	100	100	100
HYDROCARBONS	56.7	83.9	96.1	91.6	100.0	62.9	115	95	104	65
NITROGEN OXIDES	47.2	89.4	89.1	88.4	88.7	88.6	100	99	99	99
WATER OXYGEN DEMAND	512.6	392.7	392.5	391.1	391.0	392.3	100	100	100	100
LAND SOLID WASTE	902.7	1380.4	1389.9	1379.8	1377.9	1379.6	101	99	99	99

SUMMARY PROJECTIONS BY ORE ECONOMIC AREA UNDER FIVE ALTERNATIVE HIGHWAY SYSTEMS

26 CHARLOTTE, N. C.

	1970	1990 BASE YEAR	1990 COMPLETED INTERSTATE	1990 EXTENDED PRIMARY	1990 ECONOMIC DEVELOPMENT	1990 URBAN	CI/BY	EP/CI	ED/CI	U/CI
								P E R C E N T		
JOBS BY INDUSTRY			(THOUSANDS)							
NATURAL RESOURCES (1-10)	31.7	13.8	13.6	14.2	13.5	13.4	99	104	99	99
CONSTRUCTION (11.12)	40.7	40.3	40.7	40.3	38.5	40.8	101	99	95	100
MANUFACTURING (13-74)	303.5	485.6	486.6	491.4	486.6	483.6	100	101	100	100
TRANSPORTATION INDUSTRY (75)	24.3	43.3	43.2	43.5	43.1	43.1	100	101	100	100
PUBLIC UTILITIES (76-80)	13.0	4.0	3.5	5.0	2.8	3.0	88	141	81	84
TRADE (81,86,89-99)	132.1	171.2	190.0	195.0	187.8	187.5	99	103	99	99
SERVICES (82-85,87,88,102)	118.5	241.0	241.1	241.3	241.1	241.1	100	100	100	100
STATE & LOCAL GOVT. (101)	54.6	83.2	83.1	84.5	82.7	82.5	100	102	100	99
FEDERAL GOVERNMENT (100,103)	11.8	15.5	15.5	15.8	15.4	15.3	100	102	99	99
TOTAL JOBS	730.2	1117.8	1117.2	1130.9	1111.6	1110.3	100	101	99	99
CIVILIAN PERSONS EMPLOYED	662.3	1018.2	1017.6	1030.3	1012.0	1011.2	100	101	100	99
CIVILIAN UNEMPLOYMENT RATE	3.5	2.5	2.5	2.2	2.6	2.5	100	101	100	100
POPULATION	1496.4	2224.2	2225.1	2245.6	2225.9	2229.1	100	101	100	100
PER CAPITA INCOME	3164.9	5797.3	5790.3	5838.0	5748.5	5734.8	100	101	99	99
ENERGY USER SECTOR			(TRILLIONS OF BTU'S)							
NATURAL RESOURCES	8.0	11.8	11.9	12.0	11.9	11.8	100	101	100	99
CONSTRUCTION	24.7	53.7	53.6	55.4	53.5	48.3	100	103	100	90
MANUFACTURING	96.6	256.2	256.1	258.7	255.8	254.5	100	101	100	99
TRANSPORTATION INDUSTRY	35.5	85.1	84.8	86.4	84.4	84.0	100	102	100	99
PUBLIC UTILITIES	175.5	404.4	387.0	433.5	365.0	366.7	96	112	94	95
TRADE AND SERVICES	64.9	161.7	160.7	164.6	159.3	159.0	99	102	99	99
GOVERNMENT, EXC. TRANSPORTATION	3.7	7.7	7.7	7.8	7.6	7.6	100	102	99	99
CONSUMERS, EXC. TRANSPORTATION	69.9	162.2	162.1	164.1	161.5	161.2	100	101	100	99
USER-OPERATED TRANSPORTATION	118.4	281.9	281.7	284.8	280.7	280.3	100	101	100	99
TRANSPORTATION AIR POLLUTION			(THOUSANDS OF TONS)							
SULFUR OXIDES	7.9	18.3	18.2	18.4	18.0	18.0	99	101	99	99
PARTICULATE MATTER	5.2	11.9	11.9	12.1	11.9	11.8	100	102	100	99
CARBON MONOXIDE	912.9	2137.4	2136.3	2160.0	2128.9	2125.3	100	101	100	99
HYDROCARBONS	158.4	369.7	369.4	373.4	368.0	367.5	100	101	100	99
NITROGEN OXIDES	90.6	209.0	209.4	212.7	209.0	208.2	100	102	100	99
OTHER AIR POLLUTION										
SULFUR OXIDES	328.7	805.8	777.1	853.3	740.9	743.9	96	110	95	96
PARTICULATE MATTER	144.8	259.9	253.9	271.0	245.8	246.8	98	107	97	97
CARBON MONOXIDE	66.4	82.6	82.4	83.3	82.2	82.0	100	101	100	99
HYDROCARBONS	33.5	46.4	46.8	55.4	49.1	45.2	101	118	105	97
NITROGEN OXIDES	95.1	254.2	247.2	266.1	238.2	239.0	97	108	96	97
WATER OXYGEN DEMAND	727.4	649.7	649.2	648.7	647.5	649.0	100	100	100	100
LAND SOLID WASTE	1182.1	1757.1	1757.8	1774.0	1758.5	1761.0	100	101	100	99

	1970	1990 BASE YEAR	1990 COMPLETED INTERSTATE	1990 EXTENDED PRIMARY	1990 ECONOMIC DEVELOPMENT	1990 URBAN	CI/BY	EP/CI	ED/CI	U/CI
							P E R C E N T			
JOBS BY INDUSTRY			(THOUSANDS)							
NATURAL RESOURCES (1-10)	19.1	7.9	7.9	7.9	8.0	7.9	100	100	101	100
CONSTRUCTION (11,12)	8.2	5.2	4.9	4.1	5.2	3.9	95	83	107	81
MANUFACTURING (13-74)	50.8	59.3	59.3	57.4	62.5	57.6	100	97	105	97
TRANSPORTATION INDUSTRY (75)	2.2	1.4	1.4	1.3	1.6	1.3	100	94	116	96
PUBLIC UTILITIES (76-80)	2.7	.8	.8	.8	1.8	.8	98	101	226	95
TRADE (81,86,89-99)	23.8	26.0	26.0	25.1	29.0	25.2	100	96	112	97
SERVICES (82-85,87,88,102)	27.0	60.4	60.4	60.2	60.9	60.3	100	100	101	100
STATE & LOCAL GOVT. (101)	14.7	18.0	18.0	17.6	18.7	17.7	100	98	104	98
FEDERAL GOVERNMENT (100,103)	3.6	4.0	4.0	3.9	4.1	3.9	100	98	104	98
TOTAL JOBS	152.1	182.9	182.6	178.2	191.7	178.6	100	98	105	98
CIVILIAN PERSONS EMPLOYED	140.2	168.2	167.9	163.9	176.3	162.2	100	98	105	98
CIVILIAN UNEMPLOYMENT RATE	5.1	6.3	5.9	6.1	5.6	5.5				
POPULATION	391.6	527.3	523.5	512.1	534.7	512.9	99	98	102	98
PER CAPITA INCOME	2625.6	4135.7	4159.3	4119.8	4327.8	4120.6	101	99	104	99
ENERGY USER SECTOR			(TRILLIONS OF BTU'S)							
NATURAL RESOURCES	4.1	5.1	5.2	5.1	5.4	5.2	101	97	104	100
CONSTRUCTION	7.0	12.5	12.7	9.7	15.8	8.4	101	76	125	67
MANUFACTURING	23.3	47.2	47.2	46.0	49.7	46.3	100	97	105	98
TRANSPORTATION INDUSTRY	3.0	6.6	6.6	6.2	7.5	6.3	100	94	114	96
PUBLIC UTILITIES	27.7	19.4	18.2	18.3	44.9	17.8	94	101	247	98
TRADE AND SERVICES	8.5	21.8	21.8	21.2	23.7	21.4	100	97	109	98
GOVERNMENT, EXC. TRANSPORTATION	1.0	1.5	1.5	1.5	1.6	1.5	100	97	105	98
CONSUMERS, EXC. TRANSPORTATION	13.8	25.2	25.2	24.7	26.4	24.7	100	98	105	98
USER-OPERATED TRANSPORTATION	23.5	48.3	48.2	47.4	50.0	47.4	100	98	104	98
TRANSPORTATION AIR POLLUTION			(THOUSANDS OF TONS)							
SULFUR OXIDES	1.1	1.9	1.9	1.8	2.1	1.8	100	97	109	97
PARTICULATE MATTER	1.6	1.6	1.6	1.5	1.7	1.5	100	97	107	98
CARBON MONOXIDE	183.0	356.7	356.3	349.8	370.3	350.1	100	98	104	98
HYDROCARBONS	32.2	61.9	61.9	60.7	64.3	60.8	100	98	104	98
NITROGEN OXIDES	17.7	32.3	32.4	31.7	33.9	31.7	100	98	105	98
OTHER AIR POLLUTION										
SULFUR OXIDES	56.0	69.3	67.5	66.2	113.8	66.7	97	98	169	99
PARTICULATE MATTER	37.0	43.5	44.1	41.7	61.0	43.6	101	95	138	99
CARBON MONOXIDE	33.7	34.5	36.0	33.1	40.0	35.8	104	92	111	99
HYDROCARBONS	7.1	9.5	9.7	9.4	15.3	9.7	102	96	157	99
NITROGEN OXIDES	18.7	35.5	35.2	34.1	47.7	35.0	99	97	136	99
WATER OXYGEN DEMAND	195.6	134.2	134.6	133.5	136.3	134.7	100	99	101	100
LAND SOLID WASTE	309.4	416.6	413.5	404.5	422.4	405.2	99	98	102	98

28 GREENVILLE, S. C.

	1970	1990 BASE YEAR	1990 COMPLETED INTERSTATE	1990 EXTENDED PRIMARY	1990 ECONOMIC DEVELOPMENT	1990 URBAN	CI/BY	EP/CI	ED/CI	U/CI
JOBS BY INDUSTRY		(THOUSANDS)								
NATURAL RESOURCES (1-10)	13.8	13.5	13.4	13.5	13.5	13.4	100	100	100	100
CONSTRUCTION (11-12)	20.4	19.8	20.0	19.5	19.0	20.1	101	98	95	100
MANUFACTURING (13-74)	163.5	188.9	187.3	186.3	186.0	185.9	99	99	99	99
TRANSPORTATION INDUSTRY (75)	6.4	11.8	11.7	11.6	11.6	11.6	99	100	100	99
PUBLIC UTILITIES (76-80)	6.7	.6	.7	.5	.5	.5	87	103	101	95
TRADE (81,86,89-99)	59.1	99.7	97.7	97.0	96.8	96.6	98	99	99	99
SERVICES (82-85,87,88,102)	61.3	89.0	88.8	88.7	88.7	88.8	100	100	100	100
STATE & LOCAL GOVT. (101)	33.9	45.3	44.9	44.6	44.6	44.6	99	99	99	99
FEDERAL GOVERNMENT (100,103)	2.9	3.6	3.5	3.5	3.5	3.5	98	99	98	98
TOTAL JOBS	367.9	472.1	467.9	465.4	464.1	465.1	99	99	99	99
CIVILIAN PERSONS EMPLOYED	353.7	453.1	449.2	446.7	445.5	446.4	99	99	99	99
CIVILIAN UNEMPLOYMENT RATE	4.5	4.3	3.9	4.2	4.1	4.3				
POPULATION	817.7	1125.9	1111.0	1107.1	1107.2	1109.1	99	100	100	100
PER CAPITA INCOME	3331.3	5256.6	5266.5	5246.9	5229.0	5236.1	100	100	99	99
ENERGY USER SECTOR		(TRILLIONS OF BTU'S)								
NATURAL RESOURCES	6.9	16.5	16.4	16.3	16.2	16.3	99	99	99	100
CONSTRUCTION	9.3	17.5	17.2	16.7	17.3	13.7	98	97	101	79
MANUFACTURING	56.1	167.1	165.2	163.7	163.2	163.7	97	99	98	99
TRANSPORTATION INDUSTRY	6.2	17.6	17.0	16.8	16.7	16.7	97	99	98	98
PUBLIC UTILITIES	54.2	43.3	34.3	35.2	35.0	33.5	79	103	102	98
TRADE AND SERVICES	21.9	51.7	50.0	49.6	49.4	49.4	97	99	99	99
GOVERNMENT, EXC. TRANSPORTATION	1.6	2.9	2.9	2.9	2.9	2.9	99	99	99	99
CONSUMERS, EXC. TRANSPORTATION	26.2	50.5	49.9	49.5	49.5	49.5	99	99	99	99
USER-OPERATED TRANSPORTATION	53.6	112.7	111.8	111.3	111.0	111.2	99	100	99	100
TRANSPORTATION AIR POLLUTION		(THOUSANDS OF TONS)								
SULFUR OXIDES	2.1	5.3	5.2	5.1	5.1	5.1	98	99	98	99
PARTICULATE MATTER	1.8	4.1	4.1	4.1	4.0	4.1	99	99	99	99
CARBON MONOXIDE	406.6	870.7	863.3	859.0	857.0	858.7	99	100	99	99
HYDROCARBONS	71.0	152.3	151.0	150.2	149.9	150.2	99	99	99	99
NITROGEN OXIDES	37.5	83.1	82.4	82.0	81.7	81.9	99	100	99	99
OTHER AIR POLLUTION										
SULFUR OXIDES	103.6	95.6	80.0	80.8	80.2	78.5	84	101	100	98
PARTICULATE MATTER	73.9	160.6	153.1	149.4	147.2	151.1	95	98	96	99
CARBON MONOXIDE	35.7	126.9	124.0	123.3	123.2	123.3	98	99	99	99
HYDROCARBONS	20.3	49.8	47.6	44.6	45.3	37.1	96	94	95	78
NITROGEN OXIDES	31.9	36.5	32.3	32.2	31.9	31.9	89	100	99	99
WATER OXYGEN DEMAND	969.7	1637.0	1634.1	1632.9	1632.6	1633.8	100	99	100	100
LAND SOLID WASTE	646.0	889.5	877.7	874.6	874.7	876.2	99	100	100	100

193

SUMMARY PROJECTIONS BY OBE ECONOMIC AREA UNDER FIVE ALTERNATIVE HIGHWAY SYSTEMS

29 COLUMBIA, S. C.

	1970	1990 BASE YEAR	1990 COMPLETED INTERSTATE	1990 EXTENDED PRIMARY	1990 ECONOMIC DEVELOPMENT	1990 URBAN	CI/BY	EP/CI	ED/CI	U/CI
							P E R C E N T			
JOBS BY INDUSTRY				(THOUSANDS)						
NATURAL RESOURCES (1-10)	13.9	10.1	10.0	10.0	10.0	10.0	99	100	100	100
CONSTRUCTION (11,12)	14.3	15.4	15.5	15.2	14.8	15.5	101	98	95	100
MANUFACTURING (13-74)	50.2	79.5	79.1	78.9	78.3	77.7	99	100	99	98
TRANSPORTATION INDUSTRY (75)	4.3	7.4	7.4	7.4	7.3	7.3	99	100	100	99
PUBLIC UTILITIES (76-80)	5.5	8.5	8.4	8.5	8.5	8.4	89	100	109	99
TRADE (81,86,89-99)	46.3	85.5	84.1	84.2	83.7	83.0	98	100	100	99
SERVICES (82-85,87,88,102)	48.5	73.8	73.7	73.6	73.4	73.4	100	100	100	100
STATE & LOCAL GOVT. (101)	37.5	49.9	49.7	49.6	49.4	49.4	100	100	99	99
FEDERAL GOVERNMENT (100,103)	36.6	37.1	37.0	37.0	37.0	37.0	100	100	100	100
TOTAL JOBS	257.2	359.1	356.9	356.3	354.3	353.6	99	100	99	99
CIVILIAN PERSONS EMPLOYED	199.1	290.4	288.4	288.0	286.3	285.4	99	100	99	99
CIVILIAN UNEMPLOYMENT RATE	5.8	8.0	7.8	7.3	7.9	7.2				
POPULATION	610.8	974.4	978.4	966.7	971.1	956.7	100	99	99	98
PER CAPITA INCOME	2807.5	3897.2	3848.9	3866.7	3814.1	3866.8	99	100	100	100
ENERGY USER SECTOR			(TRILLIONS OF BTU'S)							
NATURAL RESOURCES	15.5	37.8	37.6	37.4	37.3	37.5	99	100	99	100
CONSTRUCTION	8.7	16.7	16.6	16.7	16.7	13.0	99	101	101	79
MANUFACTURING	19.1	52.5	51.7	51.2	50.6	50.7	99	99	98	98
TRANSPORTATION INDUSTRY	4.6	10.7	10.4	10.3	10.2	10.2	97	99	98	98
PUBLIC UTILITIES	26.2	16.1	15.8	16.0	16.2	15.5	98	101	102	98
TRADE AND SERVICES	16.7	35.5	34.3	34.3	34.0	33.9	97	100	100	99
GOVERNMENT, EXC. TRANSPORTATION	1.2	2.2	2.2	2.2	2.2	2.2	99	100	98	99
CONSUMERS, EXC. TRANSPORTATION	21.0	41.4	41.1	40.9	40.6	40.5	99	99	99	99
USER-OPERATED TRANSPORTATION	42.3	89.7	89.3	89.0	88.6	88.4	100	100	99	99
TRANSPORTATION AIR POLLUTION			(THOUSANDS OF TONS)							
SULFUR OXIDES	2.3	5.7	5.6	5.6	5.6	5.6	99	99	99	99
PARTICULATE MATTER	1.9	4.4	4.4	4.4	4.4	4.4	99	100	99	99
CARBON MONOXIDE	362.7	804.5	800.9	798.1	794.7	794.2	100	100	99	99
HYDROCARBONS	64.9	145.0	144.3	143.8	143.2	143.2	100	100	99	99
NITROGEN OXIDES	38.0	88.2	87.8	87.6	87.2	87.2	100	100	99	99
OTHER AIR POLLUTION										
SULFUR OXIDES	49.9	58.6	57.7	57.5	57.3	57.0	98	100	100	99
PARTICULATE MATTER	52.7	112.3	108.5	104.8	101.3	107.0	97	97	93	99
CARBON MONOXIDE	100.6	246.3	243.2	240.9	240.4	242.1	99	99	98	100
HYDROCARBONS	29.2	69.9	69.8	68.8	68.5	61.3	100	99	98	88
NITROGEN OXIDES	18.2	35.1	34.5	34.1	33.8	34.2	98	99	98	99
WATER OXYGEN DEMAND	1110.4	1819.9	1818.3	1817.8	1817.9	1818.0	100	100	99	100
LAND SOLID WASTE	482.5	769.8	773.0	763.7	767.2	755.8	100	99	99	98

194

SUMMARY PROJECTIONS BY ORE ECONOMIC AREA UNDER FIVE ALTERNATIVE HIGHWAY SYSTEMS

30 FLORENCE, S. C.

	1970	1990 BASE YEAR	1990 COMPLETED INTERSTATE	1990 EXTENDED PRIMARY	1990 ECONOMIC DEVELOPMENT	1990 URBAN	CI/BY	EP/CI	ED/CI	U/CI
							PERCENT			
JOBS BY INDUSTRY			(THOUSANDS)							
NATURAL RESOURCES (1-10)	19.6	8.9	9.0	9.0	9.1	9.0	101	100	101	100
CONSTRUCTION (11.12)	7.2	9.4	9.5	9.6	15.0	9.4	101	102	159	99
MANUFACTURING (13-74)	45.0	76.5	73.8	74.4	79.3	71.4	96	101	108	97
TRANSPORTATION INDUSTRY (75)	2.7	3.4	3.3	3.4	3.6	3.2	99	101	108	97
PUBLIC UTILITIES (76-80)	2.0	3.4	3.3	3.4	3.3	3.3	93	103	171	75
TRADE (81,86,89-99)	24.9	42.4	41.2	42.1	45.7	39.8	97	102	111	96
SERVICES (82-85,87,88,102)	26.6	52.4	52.3	52.4	52.6	52.3	100	100	101	100
STATE & LOCAL GOVT. (101)	14.6	21.1	20.6	20.8	22.1	20.1	97	101	107	98
FEDERAL GOVERNMENT (100,103)	3.9	4.6	4.4	4.5	4.8	4.3	97	101	108	98
TOTAL JOBS	146.6	219.1	214.5	217.0	232.9	209.8	98	101	109	98
CIVILIAN PERSONS EMPLOYED	120.6	180.8	177.0	179.1	192.4	173.0	98	101	109	98
CIVILIAN UNEMPLOYMENT RATE	6.4	5.2	5.1	4.7	5.0	5.3				
POPULATION	400.7	537.8	524.5	530.2	564.5	520.4	98	101	108	99
PER CAPITA INCOME	2198.8	4235.4	4156.4	4200.7	4408.3	4014.6	98	101	106	97
ENERGY USER SECTOR		(TRILLIONS OF BTU'S)								
NATURAL RESOURCES	22.7	59.9	59.8	59.9	60.1	59.7	100	100	100	100
CONSTRUCTION	7.3	16.0	15.9	16.3	34.3	11.1	100	102	216	70
MANUFACTURING	31.9	74.3	72.9	74.0	76.7	71.6	98	101	105	98
TRANSPORTATION INDUSTRY	1.9	6.0	5.7	5.9	6.8	5.3	95	104	120	94
PUBLIC UTILITIES	10.3	6.4	6.3	6.9	13.1	6.2	98	110	208	98
TRADE AND SERVICES	10.1	27.8	27.2	27.6	29.5	26.6	98	101	108	98
GOVERNMENT, EXC. TRANSPORTATION	0.7	1.4	1.3	1.4	1.5	1.3	96	102	112	96
CONSUMERS, EXC. TRANSPORTATION	11.8	26.2	25.4	25.8	28.0	24.6	97	102	110	97
USER-OPERATED TRANSPORTATION	21.1	48.9	47.6	48.2	51.6	46.4	97	101	108	97
TRANSPORTATION AIR POLLUTION		(THOUSANDS OF TONS)								
SULFUR OXIDES	2.4	6.7	6.6	6.6	6.8	6.5	99	101	104	99
PARTICULATE MATTER	1.8	4.8	4.7	4.7	4.9	4.7	99	101	104	99
CARBON MONOXIDE	257.6	645.3	635.8	640.8	666.1	626.8	99	101	105	99
HYDROCARBONS	48.5	122.5	120.8	121.7	126.1	119.3	99	101	104	99
NITROGEN OXIDES	34.3	89.7	88.9	89.4	91.9	88.0	99	101	103	99
OTHER AIR POLLUTION										
SULFUR OXIDES	24.3	35.9	35.4	36.8	47.4	35.1	104	101	134	99
PARTICULATE MATTER	57.4	125.6	125.2	126.4	130.7	124.9	101	101	104	100
CARBON MONOXIDE	194.9	495.6	496.5	496.6	498.7	496.4	100	100	100	100
HYDROCARBONS	36.0	102.9	100.0	104.9	116.0	98.8	105	105	116	99
NITROGEN OXIDES	11.0	25.4	25.2	25.7	28.6	25.0	99	102	114	99
WATER OXYGEN DEMAND	530.2	946.8	941.3	944.4	948.3	940.2	100	100	101	100
LAND SOLID WASTE	316.6	424.9	414.3	418.8	446.0	411.2	98	101	108	99

SUMMARY PROJECTIONS BY OBE ECONOMIC AREA UNDER FIVE ALTERNATIVE HIGHWAY SYSTEMS

31 CHARLESTON, S. C.

	1970	1990 BASE YEAR	1990 COMPLETED INTERSTATE	1990 EXTENDED PRIMARY	1990 ECONOMIC DEVELOPMENT	1990 ECONOMIC URBAN	PERCENT CI/BY	PERCENT EP/CI	PERCENT ED/CI	PERCENT U/CI
JOBS BY INDUSTRY		(THOUSANDS)								
NATURAL RESOURCES (1-10)	6.2	4.7	4.7	4.7	4.7	4.7	99	100	100	100
CONSTRUCTION (11,12)	8.8	11.7	11.6	11.3	11.2	11.6	98	97	97	100
MANUFACTURING (13-74)	22.3	21.8	21.4	21.1	21.4	21.1	98	99	100	99
TRANSPORTATION INDUSTRY (75)	4.2	6.8	6.8	6.7	6.8	6.5	100	100	100	99
PUBLIC UTILITIES (76-80)	2.4	2.8	2.8	2.8	2.8	2.8	82	78	97	77
TRADE (81,86,89-99)	29.2	52.7	51.9	51.1	52.0	51.2	98	98	100	99
SERVICES (82-85,87,88,102)	30.4	52.0	51.9	51.8	51.9	51.9	100	100	100	100
STATE & LOCAL GOVT. (101)	19.1	24.1	24.1	23.9	24.1	24.0	99	100	100	99
FEDERAL GOVERNMENT (100,103)	40.0	41.6	41.6	41.5	41.5	41.5	100	100	100	100
TOTAL JOBS	162.5	216.5	214.6	212.6	214.3	213.3	99	99	100	99
CIVILIAN PERSONS EMPLOYED	127.0	177.4	175.7	173.9	175.5	174.5	99	99	100	99
CIVILIAN UNEMPLOYMENT RATE	6.1	6.1	5.9	5.7	5.6	5.7				
POPULATION	430.8	614.9	605.7	596.0	602.0	597.6	98	98	99	99
PER CAPITA INCOME	2554.9	3503.2	3493.2	3479.2	3499.1	3499.3	100	100	100	100
ENERGY USER SECTOR		(TRILLIONS OF BTU'S)								
NATURAL RESOURCES	5.2	11.8	11.5	11.3	11.5	11.4	97	99	100	100
CONSTRUCTION	10.3	21.2	21.2	19.4	22.1	18.0	100	91	104	85
MANUFACTURING	11.2	26.2	25.3	24.3	25.2	24.9	96	96	100	99
TRANSPORTATION INDUSTRY	4.6	11.1	10.9	10.7	10.9	10.8	98	98	100	99
PUBLIC UTILITIES	15.2	10.6	10.0	10.1	10.2	10.2	94	101	102	98
TRADE AND SERVICES	10.4	26.1	25.7	25.4	25.7	25.4	99	99	100	99
GOVERNMENT, EXC. TRANSPORTATION	2.0	2.9	2.9	2.9	2.9	2.9	99	99	100	100
CONSUMERS, EXC. TRANSPORTATION	10.0	17.4	17.1	16.8	17.0	16.9	98	98	100	99
USER-OPERATED TRANSPORTATION	22.4	42.0	41.5	40.9	41.4	41.2	99	99	100	99
TRANSPORTATION AIR POLLUTION		(THOUSANDS OF TONS)								
SULFUR OXIDES	1.4	3.2	3.2	3.1	3.1	3.1	98	98	100	99
PARTICULATE MATTER	.9	2.1	2.1	2.1	2.1	2.1	99	99	100	99
CARBON MONOXIDE	165.5	337.8	333.6	328.9	332.8	330.9	99	99	100	99
HYDROCARBONS	29.3	60.2	59.4	58.6	59.3	59.0	99	99	100	99
NITROGEN OXIDES	17.4	37.7	37.3	36.8	37.2	37.0	99	99	100	99
OTHER AIR POLLUTION										
SULFUR OXIDES	40.1	78.7	76.8	76.0	76.9	76.1	98	99	100	99
PARTICULATE MATTER	45.9	101.9	94.7	88.1	93.5	92.7	93	93	99	98
CARBON MONOXIDE	47.1	103.5	97.7	96.6	98.1	97.4	94	99	100	99
HYDROCARBONS	12.1	26.6	24.4	24.1	26.2	24.3	92	99	108	100
NITROGEN OXIDES	17.7	50.6	49.5	48.9	49.5	49.3	98	99	100	99
WATER OXYGEN DEMAND	332.6	547.6	545.0	543.9	544.9	544.6	100	100	100	100
LAND SOLID WASTE	340.3	485.8	478.5	470.9	475.9	472.1	98	98	99	99

SUMMARY PROJECTIONS BY ORE ECONOMIC AREA UNDER FIVE ALTERNATIVE HIGHWAY SYSTEMS

32   AUGUSTA, GA.

	1970	1990 BASE YEAR	1990 COMPLETED INTERSTATE	1990 EXTENDED PRIMARY	1990 ECONOMIC DEVELOPMENT	1990 URBAN	PER CENT CI/BY	EP/CI	ED/CI	U/CI
JOBS BY INDUSTRY		(THOUSANDS)								
NATURAL RESOURCES (1-10)	10.5	2.7	2.6	2.6	2.7	2.6	99	99	103	100
CONSTRUCTION (11-12)	8.8	8.4	8.5	8.3	10.4	8.5	101	97	123	100
MANUFACTURING (13-74)	52.2	69.7	68.8	67.8	72.3	67.6	99	99	105	98
TRANSPORTATION INDUSTRY (75)	3.2	3.2	3.2	3.1	3.4	3.1	99	99	106	98
PUBLIC UTILITIES (76-80)	2.7	2.1	1.9	1.9	3.0	1.9	91	102	160	99
TRADE (81,86,89-99)	26.5	42.7	42.1	41.7	45.4	41.3	99	99	108	98
SERVICES (82-85,87,88,102)	29.8	56.6	56.6	56.6	56.7	56.6	100	100	100	100
STATE & LOCAL GOVT. (101)	22.3	28.0	27.8	27.6	28.7	27.6	99	99	103	99
FEDERAL GOVERNMENT (100,103)	29.1	29.2	29.1	29.1	29.3	29.1	100	100	101	100
TOTAL JOBS	185.0	241.7	240.0	238.0	251.0	237.6	99	99	105	99
CIVILIAN PERSONS EMPLOYED	154.4	207.8	206.2	204.4	216.6	204.0	99	99	105	99
CIVILIAN UNEMPLOYMENT RATE	4.9	1.1	1.1	.9	1.1	.9				
POPULATION	461.5	583.2	574.5	571.5	606.0	570.6	99	99	105	99
PER CAPITA INCOME	2936.0	4539.9	4560.2	4513.0	4631.7	4522.7	100	100	102	99
ENERGY USER SECTOR		(TRILLIONS OF BTUS)								
NATURAL RESOURCES	12.3	30.3	30.2	30.1	30.5	30.2	100	99	101	100
CONSTRUCTION	6.1	10.9	10.8	10.1	22.3	8.1	100	93	206	75
MANUFACTURING	37.1	102.3	101.5	100.6	103.6	100.9	99	99	102	99
TRANSPORTATION INDUSTRY	2.2	5.8	5.7	5.5	6.5	5.5	97	97	114	96
PUBLIC UTILITIES	18.0	18.7	13.4	13.5	27.8	13.1	72	101	207	98
TRADE AND SERVICES	9.8	24.7	24.4	24.2	26.1	24.1	99	99	107	98
GOVERNMENT, EXC. TRANSPORTATION	1.5	2.3	2.3	2.3	2.4	2.3	99	99	104	99
CONSUMERS, EXC. TRANSPORTATION	13.3	24.4	24.1	23.8	25.7	23.8	99	99	107	99
USER-OPERATED TRANSPORTATION	21.8	41.6	41.3	40.7	43.7	40.7	99	99	106	99
TRANSPORTATION AIR POLLUTION		(THOUSANDS OF TONS)								
SULFUR OXIDES	1.5	3.8	3.7	3.7	3.9	3.7	99	99	105	99
PARTICULATE MATTER	1.2	2.8	2.7	2.7	2.9	2.7	99	99	104	99
CARBON MONOXIDE	200.0	425.7	422.6	418.4	441.7	418.5	99	99	105	99
HYDROCARBONS	36.4	78.5	78.0	77.2	81.3	77.3	99	99	104	99
NITROGEN OXIDES	22.9	52.7	52.4	52.0	54.4	51.9	99	99	104	99
OTHER AIR POLLUTION										
SULFUR OXIDES	41.1	53.3	44.5	44.7	68.1	44.0	84	100	153	99
PARTICULATE MATTER	55.7	123.5	118.9	115.0	130.9	117.5	96	97	110	99
CARBON MONOXIDE	88.1	242.7	242.1	241.5	244.7	242.0	100	100	101	100
HYDROCARBONS	39.1	112.4	110.9	111.5	113.1	110.3	99	100	102	99
NITROGEN OXIDES	14.6	20.7	18.5	18.6	24.3	18.4	90	100	131	99
WATER OXYGEN DEMAND	608.9	1267.4	1264.0	1258.8	1272.0	1262.4	100	100	101	100
LAND SOLID WASTE	364.5	460.7	453.9	451.5	478.7	450.8	99	99	105	99

SUMMARY PROJECTIONS BY ORE ECONOMIC AREA UNDER FIVE ALTERNATIVE HIGHWAY SYSTEMS

33 SAVANNAH, GA.

	1970	1990 BASE YEAR	1990 COMPLETED INTERSTATE	1990 EXTENDED PRIMARY	1990 ECONOMIC DEVELOPMENT	1990 URBAN	CI/BY	EP/CI	ED/CI	U/CI
JOBS BY INDUSTRY		(THOUSANDS)								
NATURAL RESOURCES (1-10)	10.8	3.2	3.2	3.2	3.3	3.2	100	100	105	100
CONSTRUCTION (11,12)	9.2	10.6	10.3	10.0	15.4	10.2	98	97	149	98
MANUFACTURING (13-74)	35.8	32.9	33.7	33.2	37.8	33.4	102	99	112	99
TRANSPORTATION INDUSTRY (75)	8.9	11.6	11.7	11.7	11.9	11.6	100	100	102	100
PUBLIC UTILITIES (76-80)	2.2	1.3	1.3	1.3	1.8	1.3	99	103	140	101
TRADE (81,86,89-99)	31.1	50.7	51.2	50.9	55.0	50.9	101	99	107	99
SERVICES (82-85,87,88,102)	29.5	53.0	53.0	53.0	53.2	53.0	101	100	100	100
STATE & LOCAL GOVT. (101)	20.3	25.8	26.0	25.8	27.5	25.9	101	100	106	100
FEDERAL GOVERNMENT (100,103)	13.3	13.6	13.7	13.6	14.0	13.6	100	100	102	100
TOTAL JOBS	160.9	202.8	204.1	202.8	220.1	203.2	101	99	108	100
CIVILIAN PERSONS EMPLOYED	131.0	168.1	169.2	168.1	183.0	168.3	101	99	108	99
CIVILIAN UNEMPLOYMENT RATE	4.8	7.0	6.4	6.3	6.6	6.3				
POPULATION	417.8	586.3	589.8	582.9	617.3	585.9	101	100	105	99
PER CAPITA INCOME	2706.5	3970.7	3997.7	3990.6	4290.6	3996.8	101	100	107	100
ENERGY USER SECTOR		(TRILLIONS OF BTU'S)								
NATURAL RESOURCES	15.4	40.0	40.1	39.8	40.4	40.0	100	99	101	100
CONSTRUCTION	6.2	9.1	9.1	9.1	34.1	9.1	100	99	373	100
MANUFACTURING	30.7	87.9	88.7	88.1	91.0	88.4	101	99	103	100
TRANSPORTATION INDUSTRY	5.8	13.9	14.1	14.0	15.1	14.0	101	99	107	99
PUBLIC UTILITIES	5.6	3.5	3.5	3.5	6.1	3.4	98	101	178	98
TRADE AND SERVICES	12.3	29.3	29.7	29.5	31.7	29.5	101	99	107	99
GOVERNMENT, EXC. TRANSPORTATION	2.2	3.2	3.3	3.2	3.4	3.3	101	99	105	99
CONSUMERS, EXC. TRANSPORTATION	14.5	27.8	28.0	27.8	30.5	27.9	101	99	109	99
USER-OPERATED TRANSPORTATION	28.6	55.9	56.3	55.9	60.2	56.1	101	99	107	100
TRANSPORTATION AIR POLLUTION		(THOUSANDS OF TONS)								
SULFUR OXIDES	2.6	6.5	6.5	6.5	6.8	6.5	100	99	103	100
PARTICULATE MATTER	1.8	4.4	4.4	4.4	4.5	4.4	101	99	104	100
CARBON MONOXIDE	263.3	590.2	593.4	589.5	622.4	591.6	101	99	105	100
HYDROCARBONS	48.3	109.6	110.2	109.4	115.2	109.8	101	99	105	100
NITROGEN OXIDES	32.6	77.9	78.4	78.0	81.4	78.2	101	100	104	100
OTHER AIR POLLUTION										
SULFUR OXIDES	18.9	26.2	26.1	26.2	30.4	26.0	100	100	116	100
PARTICULATE MATTER	47.7	99.3	101.2	99.9	112.8	100.8	102	99	111	99
CARBON MONOXIDE	147.4	397.3	397.6	396.1	402.5	397.4	100	100	101	100
HYDROCARBONS	45.3	133.7	136.9	136.9	140.0	135.8	102	100	102	99
NITROGEN OXIDES	9.2	13.7	13.7	13.7	14.9	13.7	100	100	109	100
WATER OXYGEN DEMAND	174.6	180.4	180.4	180.3	181.1	180.4	100	99	100	100
LAND SOLID WASTE	330.0	463.1	466.0	460.5	487.7	462.9	101	99	105	99

SUMMARY PROJECTIONS BY OBE ECONOMIC AREA UNDER FIVE ALTERNATIVE HIGHWAY SYSTEMS

34 JACKSONVILLE, FLA.

	1970	1990 BASE YEAR	1990 COMPLETED INTERSTATE	1990 EXTENDED PRIMARY	1990 ECONOMIC DEVELOPMENT	1990 URBAN	CI/BY	EP/BY	ED/CI	U/CI
			(THOUSANDS)					PER CENT		
JOBS BY INDUSTRY										
NATURAL RESOURCES (1-10)	22.6	9.3	9.3	9.4	9.5	9.3	100	100	101	100
CONSTRUCTION (11,12)	22.9	26.9	27.4	26.7	25.7	27.1	102	97	94	99
MANUFACTURING (13-74)	55.6	73.5	67.7	65.7	66.6	63.5	92	97	98	94
TRANSPORTATION INDUSTRY (75)	18.0	30.4	30.3	30.3	30.4	30.1	100	100	100	99
PUBLIC UTILITIES (76-80)	9.3	3.4	2.5	2.2	2.5	2.1	74	87	100	82
TRADE (81,86,89-99)	95.9	158.2	156.1	155.2	156.4	153.4	99	99	100	98
SERVICES (82-85,87,88,102)	95.2	184.1	184.1	184.0	184.1	184.0	100	100	100	100
STATE & LOCAL GOVT. (101)	63.2	86.3	85.1	84.6	84.8	84.2	99	99	100	99
FEDERAL GOVERNMENT (100,103)	25.6	28.8	28.5	28.4	28.5	28.3	99	99	100	99
TOTAL JOBS	408.4	600.9	591.0	586.5	588.3	581.6	98	99	100	98
CIVILIAN PERSONS EMPLOYED	377.2	558.6	549.3	545.9	546.8	540.6	98	98	100	98
CIVILIAN UNEMPLOYMENT RATE	2.6	5.4	4.9	5.1	4.7	4.8				
POPULATION	1051.3	1654.3	1629.9	1624.4	1621.8	1614.0	99	100	100	99
PER CAPITA INCOME	3379.9	5105.5	5048.3	5003.7	5028.5	4982.2	99	99	100	99
ENERGY USER SECTOR		(TRILLIONS OF BTU'S)								
NATURAL RESOURCES	7.3	9.3	9.3	9.2	9.6	9.0	99	101	105	98
CONSTRUCTION	28.3	57.3	57.7	48.4	49.2	34.7	101	84	85	60
MANUFACTURING	49.7	114.3	108.8	106.8	107.4	103.3	95	98	99	95
TRANSPORTATION INDUSTRY	17.0	36.0	35.4	35.1	35.4	34.7	98	98	100	98
PUBLIC UTILITIES	48.0	35.6	35.6	40.7	52.2	35.1	100	114	147	98
TRADE AND SERVICES	54.0	111.8	110.7	110.3	111.0	109.5	99	100	100	99
GOVERNMENT, EXC. TRANSPORTATION	3.4	6.3	6.2	6.1	6.1	6.1	98	99	99	98
CONSUMERS, EXC. TRANSPORTATION	45.9	96.8	95.0	94.2	94.4	93.4	98	98	99	98
USER-OPERATED TRANSPORTATION	97.0	212.1	209.2	208.0	208.4	206.7	99	99	100	99
TRANSPORTATION AIR POLLUTION		(THOUSANDS OF TONS)								
SULFUR OXIDES	4.5	9.2	9.0	8.9	9.0	8.8	98	98	100	98
PARTICULATE MATTER	3.5	7.1	7.0	7.0	7.0	6.9	99	99	100	99
CARBON MONOXIDE	728.0	1559.0	1538.5	1529.7	1532.8	1520.1	99	99	99	99
HYDROCARBONS	126.6	270.0	266.4	264.9	265.4	263.2	99	99	100	99
NITROGEN OXIDES	68.3	142.3	140.6	140.1	140.3	138.8	99	99	100	99
OTHER AIR POLLUTION										
SULFUR OXIDES	118.3	178.1	178.0	186.4	205.8	176.7	100	105	116	99
PARTICULATE MATTER	123.6	170.4	170.5	172.7	179.2	169.9	100	101	105	100
CARBON MONOXIDE	143.5	297.3	297.8	299.1	306.8	299.1	100	100	103	100
HYDROCARBONS	79.9	277.1	216.7	191.6	196.2	148.0	78	88	91	68
NITROGEN OXIDES	50.5	107.8	107.7	109.9	115.1	107.4	100	102	107	100
WATER OXYGEN DEMAND	399.4	384.4	386.1	386.6	386.7	388.9	100	100	100	101
LAND SOLID WASTE	830.5	1306.9	1287.6	1283.3	1281.2	1275.0	99	100	100	99

SUMMARY PROJECTIONS BY ORE ECONOMIC AREA UNDER FIVE ALTERNATIVE HIGHWAY SYSTEMS

35 ORLANDO, FLA.

	1970	1990 BASE YEAR	1990 COMPLETED INTERSTATE	1990 EXTENDED PRIMARY	1990 ECONOMIC DEVELOPMENT	1990 URBAN	PER CENT CI/BY	EP/CI	ED/CI	U/CI
JOBS BY INDUSTRY			(THOUSANDS)							
NATURAL RESOURCES (1-10)	17.7	7.2	7.2	7.2	7.2	7.1	100	100	100	100
CONSTRUCTION (11,12)	23.3	19.5	19.7	19.1	18.6	19.6	101	97	94	100
MANUFACTURING (13-74)	47.8	41.1	38.0	37.7	37.5	37.2	92	99	99	98
TRANSPORTATION INDUSTRY (75)	7.0	9.1	8.1	7.9	7.8	7.7	89	98	96	95
PUBLIC UTILITIES (76-80)	8.6	2.9	2.1	1.9	1.9	1.8	72	93	90	88
TRADE (81,86,89-99)	79.9	89.8	84.7	84.0	83.6	82.5	94	99	99	97
SERVICES (82-85,87,88,102)	91.1	131.4	131.3	131.3	131.3	131.3	100	100	100	100
STATE & LOCAL GOVT. (101)	40.2	44.1	43.1	42.9	42.8	42.7	98	100	100	99
FEDERAL GOVERNMENT (100,103)	24.2	24.0	23.7	23.7	23.7	23.7	99	100	100	100
TOTAL JOBS	339.9	369.1	357.9	355.7	354.3	353.7	97	99	99	99
CIVILIAN PERSONS EMPLOYED	323.9	353.2	342.4	340.4	339.0	338.4	97	99	99	99
CIVILIAN UNEMPLOYMENT RATE	3.6	6.3	6.6	6.0	6.4	6.4				
POPULATION	941.4	1163.3	1135.6	1118.2	1128.7	1117.0	98	98	98	98
PER CAPITA INCOME	3393.1	4661.1	4614.4	4646.7	4602.1	4631.0	99	101	100	100
ENERGY USER SECTOR			(TRILLIONS OF BTU'S)							
NATURAL RESOURCES	3.3	2.2	2.2	2.2	2.2	2.2	100	100	100	100
CONSTRUCTION	18.8	28.0	27.3	24.4	24.1	20.3	97	89	88	74
MANUFACTURING	14.9	29.6	27.1	26.9	26.6	26.5	92	99	98	98
TRANSPORTATION INDUSTRY	7.3	9.3	8.3	8.1	8.0	7.9	89	98	97	95
PUBLIC UTILITIES	63.2	113.8	82.5	72.0	65.9	70.4	73	87	80	85
TRADE AND SERVICES	34.2	57.3	54.8	54.7	54.5	54.0	96	100	99	99
GOVERNMENT, EXC. TRANSPORTATION	5.7	7.8	7.7	7.7	7.7	7.6	98	100	100	100
CONSUMERS, EXC. TRANSPORTATION	48.5	84.2	82.6	82.3	82.3	82.0	98	100	100	99
USER-OPERATED TRANSPORTATION	89.7	163.2	160.8	160.3	160.3	159.9	99	100	100	99
TRANSPORTATION AIR POLLUTION			(THOUSANDS OF TONS)							
SULFUR OXIDES	2.6	3.9	3.7	3.7	3.6	3.6	95	99	98	98
PARTICULATE MATTER	2.5	4.1	4.0	4.0	4.0	4.0	97	99	99	99
CARBON MONOXIDE	614.1	1123.0	1104.8	1101.1	1101.0	1097.7	98	100	100	99
HYDROCARBONS	106.8	194.7	191.5	190.9	190.8	190.3	98	100	100	99
NITROGEN OXIDES	54.3	95.7	93.9	93.6	93.5	93.1	98	100	100	99
OTHER AIR POLLUTION										
SULFUR OXIDES	135.8	210.4	159.6	142.7	132.6	140.1	76	89	83	88
PARTICULATE MATTER	60.3	100.8	88.1	83.7	80.1	83.0	87	95	91	94
CARBON MONOXIDE	30.5	17.9	16.9	17.1	17.1	17.1	95	101	101	101
HYDROCARBONS	13.9	29.2	14.7	14.4	13.8	12.7	50	99	94	86
NITROGEN OXIDES	49.9	64.0	51.6	47.5	45.1	46.9	81	92	87	91
WATER OXYGEN DEMAND	144.6	104.8	102.3	102.0	102.0	101.8	98	98	100	100
LAND SOLID WASTE	743.7	919.0	897.1	883.4	891.6	882.4	98	98	99	98

36 MIAMI, FLA.

	1970	1990 BASE YEAR	1990 COMPLETED INTERSTATE	1990 EXTENDED PRIMARY	1990 ECONOMIC DEVELOPMENT	1990 ECONOMIC URBAN	CI/BY	EP/CI	ED/CI	U/CI
JOBS BY INDUSTRY		(THOUSANDS)								
NATURAL RESOURCES (1-10)	16.2	5.2	5.2	5.2	5.3	5.1	99	101	102	99
CONSTRUCTION (11-12)	86.0	107.2	107.7	104.6	102.4	108.3	100	97	95	101
MANUFACTURING (13-74)	123.5	214.6	169.7	154.8	153.0	174.2	79	91	90	103
TRANSPORTATION INDUSTRY (75)	51.9	95.6	94.3	93.4	93.3	94.6	99	99	99	99
PUBLIC UTILITIES (76-80)	24.0	12.5	8.6	4.2	4.3	9.8	68	49	47	115
TRADE (81,86,89-99)	274.8	577.7	552.9	539.9	539.2	555.1	96	98	98	100
SERVICES (82-85,87,88,102)	304.6	635.0	633.7	633.0	633.0	634.0	100	100	100	100
STATE & LOCAL GOVT. (101)	112.5	189.6	180.9	177.2	176.7	182.1	95	98	98	101
FEDERAL GOVERNMENT (100,103)	30.1	42.2	40.3	39.5	39.3	40.6	95	98	98	101
TOTAL JOBS	1023.4	1879.8	1793.3	1751.7	1746.3	1803.9	95	98	97	101
CIVILIAN PERSONS EMPLOYED	1003.8	1829.2	1746.5	1706.8	1701.8	1756.6	95	98	97	101
CIVILIAN UNEMPLOYMENT RATE	3.2									
POPULATION	2430.5	3902.2	3735.5	3671.2	3640.6	3780.2	96	98	97	101
PER CAPITA INCOME	4064.9	7411.1	7317.4	7248.1	7275.5	7286.9	99	99	99	100
ENERGY USER SECTOR		(TRILLIONS OF BTU'S)								
NATURAL RESOURCES	3.7	2.1	2.0	2.0	2.1	2.0	99	100	100	99
CONSTRUCTION	99.7	255.0	251.1	228.4	223.4	255.4	98	91	89	102
MANUFACTURING	40.8	84.4	66.6	60.5	60.2	67.2	79	91	90	101
TRANSPORTATION INDUSTRY	98.0	241.0	233.9	230.2	229.9	234.8	97	98	98	101
PUBLIC UTILITIES	170.3	294.5	225.3	131.9	127.1	245.2	77	59	56	109
TRADE AND SERVICES	117.9	309.1	295.7	286.7	286.1	297.9	96	97	97	101
GOVERNMENT, EXC. TRANSPORTATION	9.9	21.5	20.6	20.1	20.1	20.7	96	98	98	101
CONSUMERS, EXC. TRANSPORTATION	99.4	263.5	250.1	244.0	242.9	251.9	95	98	98	101
USER-OPERATED TRANSPORTATION	203.6	521.8	500.8	491.3	489.8	503.6	96	98	98	101
TRANSPORTATION AIR POLLUTION		(THOUSANDS OF TONS)								
SULFUR OXIDES	19.2	47.2	45.5	44.6	44.6	45.7	96	98	98	100
PARTICULATE MATTER	10.9	27.1	26.3	25.8	25.8	26.4	97	98	98	101
CARBON MONOXIDE	1561.6	3981.7	3828.3	3758.6	3746.9	3848.7	96	98	98	101
HYDROCARBONS	249.8	687.4	660.6	648.2	646.4	664.1	96	98	98	101
NITROGEN OXIDES	167.1	421.1	407.7	402.4	400.4	409.7	97	99	98	100
OTHER AIR POLLUTION										
SULFUR OXIDES	565.2	1685.2	1571.2	1418.7	1411.2	1603.5	93	90	90	102
PARTICULATE MATTER	308.5	739.2	718.5	688.2	686.7	724.9	97	96	96	101
CARBON MONOXIDE	190.9	380.1	393.6	396.8	396.7	394.7	104	101	101	100
HYDROCARBONS	96.4	293.2	237.3	213.9	215.1	228.1	81	90	91	96
NITROGEN OXIDES	288.8	1029.8	1002.2	964.8	963.1	1010.1	97	96	96	101
WATER OXYGEN DEMAND	183.0	229.2	237.5	240.0	239.9	238.2	104	101	101	100
LAND SOLID WASTE	1920.4	3082.7	2951.0	2900.2	2876.2	2986.3	96	98	97	101

SUMMARY PROJECTIONS BY OBE ECONOMIC AREA UNDER FIVE ALTERNATIVE HIGHWAY SYSTEMS

37 TAMPA-ST. PETE. FLA.

	1970	1990 BASE YEAR	1990 COMPLETED INTERSTATE	1990 EXTENDED PRIMARY	1990 ECONOMIC DEVELOPMENT	1990 URBAN	PERCENT CI/BY	PERCENT EP/CI	PERCENT ED/CI	PERCENT U/CI
JOBS BY INDUSTRY			(THOUSANDS)							
NATURAL RESOURCES (1-10)	33.6	14.8	14.8	14.5	14.6	14.6	100	98	99	99
CONSTRUCTION (11.12)	51.1	51.2	51.6	50.0	48.9	51.6	101	97	95	100
MANUFACTURING (13-74)	88.4	113.7	117.8	108.3	110.6	109.7	104	92	94	93
TRANSPORTATION INDUSTRY (75)	15.6	16.6	16.7	16.2	16.4	16.4	101	97	98	98
PUBLIC UTILITIES (76-80)	15.4	22.7	22.6	18.7	20.2	21.1	100	83	89	94
TRADE (81.86.89-99)	163.6	265.9	268.5	260.8	264.1	262.3	101	97	98	98
SERVICES (82-85.87.88.102)	150.7	296.6	296.9	296.4	296.6	296.7	100	100	100	100
STATE & LOCAL GOVT. (101)	84.1	116.4	117.2	114.6	115.3	115.4	101	98	98	98
FEDERAL GOVERNMENT (100.103)	18.4	21.7	21.9	21.3	21.5	21.5	101	97	98	98
TOTAL JOBS	620.9	919.6	928.1	900.9	908.1	909.4	101	97	98	98
CIVILIAN PERSONS EMPLOYED	612.3	902.1	910.1	884.2	891.2	892.2	101	97	98	98
CIVILIAN UNEMPLOYMENT RATE	3.7	4.7	4.8	4.6	4.5	4.6				
POPULATION	1797.8	2695.0	2710.7	2659.2	2664.8	2667.7	101	98	98	98
PER CAPITA INCOME	3355.0	5302.9	5329.2	5244.2	5276.4	5283.2	100	98	99	99
ENERGY USER SECTOR			(TRILLIONS OF BTU'S)							
NATURAL RESOURCES	10.2	16.5	16.2	14.8	15.5	15.5	98	92	96	96
CONSTRUCTION	49.6	104.4	105.3	96.3	100.3	90.3	101	91	95	86
MANUFACTURING	59.2	114.0	115.9	110.7	112.3	110.7	102	96	97	95
TRANSPORTATION INDUSTRY	17.2	47.4	48.1	45.9	46.6	46.6	101	95	97	97
PUBLIC UTILITIES	172.0	624.1	623.6	563.3	591.4	598.6	100	90	95	96
TRADE AND SERVICES	60.7	148.0	149.2	143.7	145.7	146.2	101	96	98	98
GOVERNMENT. EXC. TRANSPORTATION	6.2	11.0	11.1	10.8	10.9	10.9	101	98	98	98
CONSUMERS. EXC. TRANSPORTATION	83.7	180.2	181.5	177.3	178.3	178.5	101	98	98	98
USER-OPERATED TRANSPORTATION	153.2	335.1	337.1	330.7	332.2	332.4	101	98	99	99
TRANSPORTATION AIR POLLUTION			(THOUSANDS OF TONS)							
SULFUR OXIDES	5.3	12.8	12.9	12.4	12.5	12.6	101	96	97	98
PARTICULATE MATTER	4.6	10.5	10.6	10.3	10.4	10.4	101	97	98	98
CARBON MONOXIDE	1108.8	2422.1	2437.3	2389.6	2401.2	2402.8	101	98	99	99
HYDROCARBONS	192.4	419.4	421.9	413.6	415.7	416.0	101	98	99	99
NITROGEN OXIDES	98.7	216.8	218.8	214.3	215.4	215.4	101	98	98	98
OTHER AIR POLLUTION										
SULFUR OXIDES	367.0	1322.2	1321.4	1221.1	1267.9	1279.8	100	92	96	97
PARTICULATE MATTER	214.6	580.1	580.2	551.9	564.4	569.9	100	95	97	98
CARBON MONOXIDE	158.5	435.4	432.4	432.2	433.1	433.3	99	100	100	100
HYDROCARBONS	122.0	278.7	283.3	255.2	265.2	241.6	102	90	94	85
NITROGEN OXIDES	130.3	480.3	480.0	455.3	466.8	469.9	100	95	97	98
WATER OXYGEN DEMAND	467.4	597.7	599.1	600.0	599.9	600.6	100	100	100	100
LAND SOLID WASTE	1420.2	2129.0	2141.4	2100.7	2105.2	2107.5	101	98	98	98

SUMMARY PROJECTIONS BY ONE ECONOMIC AREA UNDER FIVE ALTERNATIVE HIGHWAY SYSTEMS

38 TALLAHASSEE, FLA.

	1970	1990 BASE YEAR	1990 COMPLETED INTERSTATE	1990 EXTENDED PRIMARY	1990 ECONOMIC DEVELOPMENT	1990 URBAN	PERCENT CI/BY	EP/CI	ED/CI	U/CI
JOBS BY INDUSTRY		**(THOUSANDS)**								
NATURAL RESOURCES (1-10)	14.8	5.8	5.9	6.0	6.0	5.9	101	102	102	100
CONSTRUCTION (11-12)	5.8	3.0	3.2	3.1	4.7	3.0	108	98	146	95
MANUFACTURING (13-74)	13.5	17.8	18.8	20.4	20.7	18.7	106	108	110	100
TRANSPORTATION INDUSTRY (75)	2.7	4.9	5.3	5.5	5.5	5.2	106	104	105	100
PUBLIC UTILITIES (76-80)	2.5	0.9	1.2	2.3	2.1	1.2	129	186	177	97
TRADE (81,86,89-99)	23.9	31.1	32.7	34.9	35.4	32.5	105	107	108	99
SERVICES (82-85,87,88,102)	19.9	32.4	32.7	32.8	32.9	32.7	101	100	101	100
STATE & LOCAL GOVT. (101)	34.6	42.1	42.7	43.5	43.6	42.7	102	100	102	100
FEDERAL GOVERNMENT (100-103)	8.3	8.2	8.4	8.5	8.5	8.4	102	102	102	100
TOTAL JOBS	126.0	146.3	150.9	157.1	159.5	150.3	103	104	106	100
CIVILIAN PERSONS EMPLOYED	105.6	123.9	127.8	133.2	135.3	127.2	103	104	106	100
CIVILIAN UNEMPLOYMENT RATE	3.7	6.1	6.8	6.0	6.0	6.4				
POPULATION	344.5	418.4	437.7	447.9	454.6	434.1	105	102	104	99
PER CAPITA INCOME	3338.7	4759.0	4828.4	5013.4	5016.7	4839.9	101	104	104	100
ENERGY USER SECTOR		**(TRILLIONS OF BTU*S)**								
NATURAL RESOURCES	3.2	1.7	2.5	3.0	3.2	2.4	143	122	126	95
CONSTRUCTION	4.7	6.0	6.9	6.9	20.0	6.4	108	108	311	99
MANUFACTURING	9.4	21.4	21.7	22.6	22.6	21.7	102	104	104	100
TRANSPORTATION INDUSTRY	4.5	4.8	4.8	5.4	5.5	4.8	108	111	113	99
PUBLIC UTILITIES	22.2	13.7	23.8	45.4	44.0	23.2	174	191	185	97
TRADE AND SERVICES	7.8	15.7	16.3	17.6	17.7	16.3	104	107	108	100
GOVERNMENT, EXC. TRANSPORTATION	1.5	1.5	1.5	1.6	1.5	1.5	105	105	106	100
CONSUMERS, EXC. TRANSPORTATION	13.2	21.9	22.9	24.0	24.3	22.8	105	105	106	100
USER-OPERATED TRANSPORTATION	23.6	42.7	44.3	46.0	46.5	44.1	104	104	105	100
TRANSPORTATION AIR POLLUTION		**(THOUSANDS OF TONS)**								
SULFUR OXIDES	0.8	1.4	1.5	1.6	1.6	1.5	105	109	109	99
PARTICULATE MATTER	0.7	1.3	1.3	1.4	1.4	1.3	105	107	107	100
CARBON MONOXIDE	173.4	307.5	319.0	331.8	335.2	317.7	104	104	105	100
HYDROCARBONS	30.2	53.3	55.3	57.5	58.1	55.1	104	104	105	100
NITROGEN OXIDES	15.7	27.1	28.2	29.5	29.8	28.1	104	105	106	100
OTHER AIR POLLUTION										
SULFUR OXIDES	40.9	36.6	55.3	91.4	89.2	54.1	151	165	161	98
PARTICULATE MATTER	29.5	28.0	37.6	48.9	49.6	36.5	134	130	132	97
CARBON MONOXIDE	48.9	41.5	58.1	69.8	72.4	55.5	140	120	125	96
HYDROCARBONS	11.1	11.7	15.1	22.0	21.9	14.5	129	146	145	96
NITROGEN OXIDES	13.5	15.8	22.1	31.5	31.2	21.6	140	143	141	98
WATER OXYGEN DEMAND	294.4	177.8	177.9	177.9	178.1	177.9	100	100	100	100
LAND SOLID WASTE	272.1	330.5	345.8	353.8	359.1	342.9	105	102	104	99

SUMMARY PROJECTIONS BY ORE ECONOMIC AREA UNDER FIVE ALTERNATIVE HIGHWAY SYSTEMS

39 PENSACOLA, FLA.

	1970	1990 BASE YEAR	1990 COMPLETED INTERSTATE	1990 EXTENDED PRIMARY	1990 ECONOMIC DEVELOPMENT	1990 URBAN	CI/BY	EP/CI	ED/CI	U/CI
							P E R C E N T			
JOBS BY INDUSTRY			(THOUSANDS)							
NATURAL RESOURCES (1-10)	6.2	3.2	3.0	2.8	3.1	3.0	94	91	103	100
CONSTRUCTION (11,12)	8.8	3.6	3.2	2.7	3.0	2.7	90	82	93	84
MANUFACTURING (13-74)	17.2	15.2	15.4	14.7	16.0	15.1	101	95	103	98
TRANSPORTATION INDUSTRY (75)	2.5	3.4	3.2	2.5	3.3	3.1	96	77	103	97
PUBLIC UTILITIES (76-80)	2.9	4.0	3.8	2.0	5.0	3.7	96	53	131	97
TRADE (81,86,89-99)	25.6	31.4	30.9	28.3	32.5	30.5	98	92	105	99
SERVICES (82-85,87,88,102)	23.0	32.5	32.5	32.4	32.6	32.5	100	100	100	100
STATE & LOCAL GOVT. (101)	15.4	16.6	16.5	15.6	16.8	16.3	99	95	102	99
FEDERAL GOVERNMENT (100,103)	46.4	46.5	46.5	46.3	46.5	46.4	100	100	100	100
TOTAL JOBS	147.8	156.5	155.2	147.3	158.8	153.5	99	95	102	99
CIVILIAN PERSONS EMPLOYED	110.8	119.7	118.5	111.0	122.0	116.9	99	94	103	99
CIVILIAN UNEMPLOYMENT RATE	4.5	4.5	4.1	3.3	4.6	4.0				
POPULATION	382.3	426.6	417.2	381.4	431.6	409.9	98	91	103	98
PER CAPITA INCOME	3088.6	4492.8	4538.3	4563.6	4522.1	4550.4	101	101	100	100
ENERGY USER SECTOR			(TRILLIONS OF BTU'S)							
NATURAL RESOURCES	1.2	1.1	1.0	.7	1.1	1.0	91	69	112	100
CONSTRUCTION	7.6	11.8	11.7	9.6	12.3	9.0	99	82	106	78
MANUFACTURING	21.3	26.5	26.4	26.4	27.0	26.5	100	99	101	100
TRANSPORTATION INDUSTRY	2.1	2.8	2.7	2.0	3.1	2.6	96	76	114	97
PUBLIC UTILITIES	32.4	131.5	122.5	119.5	145.3	119.7	93	76	119	98
TRADE AND SERVICES	9.0	19.3	19.3	17.4	20.4	19.1	98	90	106	99
GOVERNMENT, EXC. TRANSPORTATION	1.5	2.1	2.1	2.0	2.1	2.1	99	95	102	99
CONSUMERS, EXC. TRANSPORTATION	13.3	21.2	21.0	19.8	21.5	20.8	99	94	102	99
USER-OPERATED TRANSPORTATION	21.8	36.9	36.6	34.6	37.4	36.2	99	95	102	99
TRANSPORTATION AIR POLLUTION			(THOUSANDS OF TONS)							
SULFUR OXIDES	.7	1.0	1.0	.9	1.1	1.0	98	86	107	98
PARTICULATE MATTER	.6	1.0	1.0	.9	1.0	1.0	99	91	104	99
CARBON MONOXIDE	156.9	262.2	260.0	245.4	265.9	257.3	99	94	102	99
HYDROCARBONS	27.3	45.5	45.1	42.5	46.1	44.6	99	94	102	99
NITROGEN OXIDES	14.0	22.6	22.4	21.0	23.1	22.1	99	94	103	99
OTHER AIR POLLUTION										
SULFUR OXIDES	60.6	223.3	208.3	160.8	246.0	203.6	93	77	118	98
PARTICULATE MATTER	32.3	65.2	61.8	50.9	70.2	60.8	95	82	114	98
CARBON MONOXIDE	22.3	36.8	35.2	29.3	38.1	35.0	96	83	108	100
HYDROCARBONS	7.4	8.2	7.9	7.0	9.5	7.9	97	88	119	99
NITROGEN OXIDES	18.3	57.1	53.3	41.5	62.7	52.2	93	78	117	98
WATER OXYGEN DEMAND	112.5	84.4	84.3	84.0	84.7	84.3	100	100	100	100
LAND SOLID WASTE	302.0	337.0	329.6	301.3	341.0	323.9	98	91	103	98

40 MONTGOMERY, ALA.

	1970	1990 BASE YEAR	1990 COMPLETED INTERSTATE	1990 EXTENDED PRIMARY	1990 ECONOMIC DEVELOPMENT	1990 URBAN	CI/BY	EP/CI	ED/CI	U/CI
							\[PERCENT\]			
JOBS BY INDUSTRY			(THOUSANDS)							
NATURAL RESOURCES (1-10)	19.1	15.6	15.6	16.5	15.8	15.6	100	106	101	100
CONSTRUCTION (11,12)	12.7	13.9	14.0	17.0	23.1	14.1	101	121	165	100
MANUFACTURING (13-74)	54.7	79.7	78.9	90.0	85.3	77.5	99	114	108	98
TRANSPORTATION INDUSTRY (75)	9.1	15.2	15.2	16.0	15.7	15.1	100	106	103	99
PUBLIC UTILITIES (76-80)	4.6	2.0	1.7	5.5	2.3	1.6	89	313	133	94
TRADE (81,86,89-99)	45.1	63.0	62.1	75.9	69.1	60.5	99	122	111	98
SERVICES (82-85,87,88,102)	58.6	106.4	106.3	107.2	106.7	106.3	100	101	100	100
STATE & LOCAL GOVT. (101)	32.5	42.7	42.5	45.9	45.0	42.2	99	108	106	99
FEDERAL GOVERNMENT (100,103)	30.8	32.0	31.9	32.7	32.5	31.9	100	102	102	100
TOTAL JOBS	267.2	370.6	368.4	406.8	395.5	364.8	99	110	107	99
CIVILIAN PERSONS EMPLOYED	219.4	313.0	311.0	344.9	335.1	307.8	99	111	108	99
CIVILIAN UNEMPLOYMENT RATE	4.1	4.1	4.4	3.5	4.1	4.1				
POPULATION	686.9	962.3	950.9	1000.4	985.1	947.3	99	105	104	100
PER CAPITA INCOME	2521.3	3958.6	3956.2	4417.6	4307.8	3909.1	100	112	109	99
ENERGY USER SECTOR			(TRILLIONS OF BTU'S)							
NATURAL RESOURCES	8.4	6.8	6.7	8.3	7.0	6.7	99	123	104	99
CONSTRUCTION	8.5	15.7	15.5	23.7	48.4	11.4	99	152	312	73
MANUFACTURING	14.0	22.7	22.1	28.9	25.1	21.3	97	130	114	96
TRANSPORTATION INDUSTRY	9.0	18.0	17.7	21.5	19.5	17.3	99	121	110	98
PUBLIC UTILITIES	48.5	57.8	42.2	193.3	73.8	36.5	73	458	175	86
TRADE AND SERVICES	17.6	40.1	39.6	48.6	43.3	38.9	99	123	109	98
GOVERNMENT, EXC. TRANSPORTATION	3.4	5.1	5.1	5.5	5.4	5.1	99	107	105	99
CONSUMERS, EXC. TRANSPORTATION	23.5	46.6	46.2	51.8	50.3	45.7	99	112	109	99
USER-OPERATED TRANSPORTATION	26.4	53.6	53.0	61.6	59.3	52.2	99	116	112	99
TRANSPORTATION AIR POLLUTION			(THOUSANDS OF TONS)							
SULFUR OXIDES	2.2	3.8	3.8	4.5	4.1	3.7	98	119	110	98
PARTICULATE MATTER	1.4	2.4	2.3	2.8	2.6	2.3	99	119	111	98
CARBON MONOXIDE	198.5	375.0	370.4	435.5	416.5	364.3	99	118	112	98
HYDROCARBONS	35.2	65.2	64.3	75.6	72.3	63.3	99	117	112	98
NITROGEN OXIDES	22.8	39.0	38.6	45.6	43.2	38.0	99	118	112	98
OTHER AIR POLLUTION										
SULFUR OXIDES	85.9	117.6	91.2	344.1	143.8	81.4	78	377	158	89
PARTICULATE MATTER	40.6	48.6	41.1	126.7	58.8	38.6	84	308	143	94
CARBON MONOXIDE	55.9	48.6	48.2	77.9	54.4	48.7	99	162	113	101
HYDROCARBONS	15.1	23.8	22.3	32.5	24.5	21.2	93	146	110	95
NITROGEN OXIDES	25.1	41.3	34.5	99.4	47.9	32.0	84	289	139	93
WATER OXYGEN DEMAND	717.0	1158.7	1157.7	1161.4	1158.4	1158.0	100	100	100	100
LAND SOLID WASTE	542.7	760.2	751.2	790.3	778.2	748.3	99	105	104	100

SUMMARY PROJECTIONS BY ORE ECONOMIC AREA UNDER FIVE ALTERNATIVE HIGHWAY SYSTEMS

41 ALBANY, GA.

	1970	1990 BASE YEAR	1990 COMPLETED INTERSTATE	1990 EXTENDED PRIMARY	1990 ECONOMIC DEVELOPMENT	1990 URBAN	CI/BY	EP/CI	ED/CI	U/CI
								PERCENT		
JOBS BY INDUSTRY			(THOUSANDS)							
NATURAL RESOURCES (1-10)	16.2	5.0	5.0	5.1	5.0	5.0	99	103	103	100
CONSTRUCTION (11,12)	8.7	10.0	10.0	13.7	20.9	10.1	101	136	208	101
MANUFACTURING (13-74)	37.5	46.9	44.8	52.7	52.3	44.5	95	118	117	99
TRANSPORTATION INDUSTRY (75)	2.9	3.6	3.2	4.4	4.2	3.1	88	140	133	98
PUBLIC UTILITIES (76-80)	2.6	1.4	1.1	2.0	1.3	1.0	77	191	127	95
TRADE (81,86,89-99)	32.3	38.7	37.4	43.6	43.5	37.0	97	117	116	99
SERVICES (82-85,87,88,.02)	29.7	48.5	48.5	49.1	49.0	48.5	100	101	101	100
STATE & LOCAL GOVT. (101)	21.4	25.9	25.3	27.8	28.2	25.2	98	110	112	100
FEDERAL GOVERNMENT (100,103)	8.9	9.1	8.9	9.5	9.6	8.9	100	106	107	100
TOTAL JOBS	160.4	189.1	184.2	208.0	214.1	183.2	97	113	116	100
CIVILIAN PERSONS EMPLOYED	139.7	165.3	160.2	182.0	187.4	160.0	97	113	117	99
CIVILIAN UNEMPLOYMENT RATE	5.4	6.2	6.0	5.6	5.5	5.5	97	93	92	92
POPULATION	460.8	580.7	566.3	611.1	628.3	560.9	98	108	111	99
PER CAPITA INCOME	2514.5	3662.6	3559.3	4085.4	4136.1	3559.5	97	115	116	100
ENERGY USER SECTOR			(TRILLIONS OF BTU'S)							
NATURAL RESOURCES	35.1	95.4	95.3	96.1	95.6	95.2	100	101	100	100
CONSTRUCTION	5.2	10.0	7.4	18.0	40.0	6.8	74	243	540	92
MANUFACTURING	13.7	21.6	20.8	23.4	23.2	20.8	97	112	111	100
TRANSPORTATION INDUSTRY	7.0	2.4	2.1	3.5	3.4	2.1	88	162	160	97
PUBLIC UTILITIES	17.8	10.9	10.8	21.0	12.6	10.6	99	195	117	98
TRADE AND SERVICES	9.1	16.3	15.8	18.4	18.1	15.7	97	117	115	99
GOVERNMENT, EXC. TRANSPORTATION	1.3	2.0	1.9	2.2	2.2	1.9	97	114	117	100
CONSUMERS, EXC. TRANSPORTATION	12.4	22.8	21.9	25.9	26.8	21.7	96	119	122	99
USER-OPERATED TRANSPORTATION	21.8	40.3	38.8	45.1	46.5	38.6	96	116	120	99
TRANSPORTATION AIR POLLUTION			(THOUSANDS OF TONS)							
SULFUR OXIDES	3.5	9.0	8.9	9.2	9.2	8.9	99	104	104	100
PARTICULATE MATTER	2.5	6.3	6.3	6.5	6.5	6.3	99	104	104	100
CARBON MONOXIDE	323.5	751.0	740.3	788.4	796.4	738.1	99	106	108	100
HYDROCARBONS	62.3	147.4	145.6	154.0	155.3	145.2	99	106	107	100
NITROGEN OXIDES	47.6	118.3	117.3	122.1	122.6	117.1	99	104	105	100
OTHER AIR POLLUTION										
SULFUR OXIDES	34.9	36.3	35.8	55.7	40.5	35.2	99	156	113	98
PARTICULATE MATTER	65.4	142.3	142.1	153.8	145.2	141.8	100	108	102	100
CARBON MONOXIDE	266.9	707.7	707.9	718.1	710.5	707.5	100	101	100	100
HYDROCARBONS	56.3	155.4	152.6	157.8	159.6	152.5	98	103	105	98
NITROGEN OXIDES	16.3	31.2	31.0	37.7	33.0	30.7	99	122	107	99
WATER OXYGEN DEMAND	196.2	123.3	123.8	123.1	123.1	123.8	100	99	99	100
LAND SOLID WASTE	364.1	458.7	447.4	482.7	496.4	443.1	98	108	111	99

42 MACON, GA.

	1970	1990 BASE YEAR	1990 COMPLETED INTERSTATE	1990 EXTENDED PRIMARY	1990 ECONOMIC DEVELOPMENT	1990 URBAN	CI/BY	EP/CI	ED/CI	U/CI
								P E R C E N T		
JOBS BY INDUSTRY			(THOUSANDS)							
NATURAL RESOURCES (1-10)	13.8	4.5	4.5	4.5	4.5	4.5	100	100	100	100
CONSTRUCTION (11-12)	7.0	9.0	9.1	8.9	12.5	9.1	101	97	137	99
MANUFACTURING (13-74)	36.5	57.2	55.0	53.8	58.4	53.7	96	98	106	98
TRANSPORTATION INDUSTRY (75)	3.3	4.2	4.1	4.1	4.3	4.1	99	99	105	99
PUBLIC UTILITIES (76-80)	3.6	1.5	1.4	1.4	2.1	1.3	94	101	150	93
TRADE (81,86,89-99)	31.3	41.3	39.5	38.8	43.3	38.5	96	98	109	97
SERVICES (82-85,87,88,102)	36.7	53.0	53.0	52.9	53.2	53.0	100	100	100	100
STATE & LOCAL GOVT. (101)	25.1	31.5	30.8	30.5	32.1	30.5	98	99	104	99
FEDERAL GOVERNMENT (100,103)	26.0	28.5	28.3	28.2	28.6	28.2	99	100	101	100
TOTAL JOBS	183.3	230.7	225.8	223.0	238.9	222.9	98	99	106	99
CIVILIAN PERSONS EMPLOYED,	171.6	216.6	211.9	209.3	224.4	209.2	98	99	106	99
CIVILIAN UNEMPLOYMENT RATE	4.4	4.7	4.9	4.7	4.4	5.1				
POPULATION	496.2	653.1	636.8	631.8	653.3	635.2	98	99	103	100
PER CAPITA INCOME	2866.2	4329.2	4260.7	4192.5	4543.7	4179.1	98	98	107	98
ENERGY USER SECTOR		(TRILLIONS OF BTU'S)								
NATURAL RESOURCES	21.0	47.7	47.5	47.4	47.8	47.5	100	100	101	100
CONSTRUCTION	7.1	13.3	13.2	10.9	24.1	8.8	99	83	183	67
MANUFACTURING	13.6	28.9	27.3	26.4	29.2	26.7	94	97	107	98
TRANSPORTATION INDUSTRY	2.2	3.9	3.5	3.3	4.3	3.3	91	95	121	94
PUBLIC UTILITIES	35.6	32.2	27.4	27.6	49.0	26.8	85	101	179	98
TRADE AND SERVICES	10.5	20.8	20.2	19.9	21.6	19.8	97	98	107	98
GOVERNMENT, EXC. TRANSPORTATION	2.0	3.0	2.9	2.9	3.1	2.9	98	99	105	99
CONSUMERS, EXC. TRANSPORTATION	18.8	36.5	35.5	35.0	37.7	35.0	97	99	106	99
USER-OPERATED TRANSPORTATION	35.1	70.0	68.4	67.6	71.8	67.7	98	99	105	99
TRANSPORTATION AIR POLLUTION		(THOUSANDS OF TONS)								
SULFUR OXIDES	2.3	5.5	5.5	5.4	5.6	5.4	98	99	103	99
PARTICULATE MATTER	1.9	4.4	4.3	4.3	4.4	4.3	99	99	103	99
CARBON MONOXIDE	334.4	729.1	718.1	711.7	743.3	712.1	98	99	104	99
HYDROCARBONS	61.0	134.7	132.8	131.6	137.2	131.7	99	99	103	99
NITROGEN OXIDES	38.0	88.1	87.1	86.4	89.5	86.5	99	99	103	99
OTHER AIR POLLUTION										
SULFUR OXIDES	64.6	76.0	67.9	67.6	104.4	66.7	89	100	154	98
PARTICULATE MATTER	76.6	141.6	141.4	136.6	156.0	139.7	98	97	110	99
CARBON MONOXIDE	133.1	346.3	345.7	344.9	348.7	345.4	100	101	101	100
HYDROCARBONS	31.8	93.0	81.0	78.7	84.7	77.6	87	97	105	96
NITROGEN OXIDES	21.2	35.5	33.4	32.9	42.8	33.0	94	99	128	99
WATER OXYGEN DEMAND	151.5	100.0	100.1	100.1	100.2	100.0	100	100	100	100
LAND SOLID WASTE	392.0	515.9	503.0	499.1	516.1	501.8	98	99	103	100

SUMMARY PROJECTIONS BY ORE ECONOMIC AREA UNDER FIVE ALTERNATIVE HIGHWAY SYSTEMS

43 COLUMBUS, GA.-ALA.

	1970	1990 BASE YEAR	1990 COMPLETED INTERSTATE	1990 EXTENDED PRIMARY	1990 ECONOMIC DEVELOPMENT	1990 URBAN	CI/BY	EP/CI	ED/CI	U/CI
							P	E R C	E N T	
JOBS BY INDUSTRY (THOUSANDS)										
NATURAL RESOURCES (1-10)	7.0	1.6	1.6	1.6	1.7	1.6	100	101	106	100
CONSTRUCTION (11-12)	9.1	10.0	9.8	10.1	8.9	9.8	98	103	91	101
MANUFACTURING (13-74)	54.7	84.0	85.4	87.3	89.9	84.8	102	102	105	99
TRANSPORTATION INDUSTRY (75)	3.2	5.3	5.3	5.3	5.6	5.3	100	101	106	99
PUBLIC UTILITIES (76-80)	2.9	1.0	1.0	1.0	2.4	0.9	98	104	251	97
TRADE (81,86,89-99)	29.1	43.6	43.6	44.7	49.2	43.0	102	103	113	99
SERVICES (82-85,87,88,102)	37.1	65.7	65.7	65.7	66.0	65.7	100	100	100	100
STATE & LOCAL GOVT. (101)	22.8	29.9	29.9	30.4	31.0	29.8	101	102	104	100
FEDERAL GOVERNMENT (100,103)	39.9	40.0	40.0	40.1	40.2	40.0	100	100	101	100
TOTAL JOBS	205.8	279.9	282.2	286.3	294.9	280.8	101	101	105	100
CIVILIAN PERSONS EMPLOYED	150.5	217.0	218.9	222.6	230.2	217.7	101	102	105	99
CIVILIAN UNEMPLOYMENT RATE	3.8	2.0	2.1	2.6	1.8	2.4				
POPULATION	488.1	638.7	644.2	659.6	660.6	644.8	101	102	103	100
PER CAPITA INCOME	2731.0	4481.3	4511.1	4537.8	4720.2	4480.4	101	101	105	99
ENERGY USER SECTOR (TRILLIONS OF BTU'S)										
NATURAL RESOURCES	5.2	12.3	12.3	12.4	12.9	12.3	100	101	105	100
CONSTRUCTION	6.4	10.7	10.8	10.9	11.7	10.7	101	102	108	99
MANUFACTURING	19.2	38.3	39.0	40.6	43.0	38.5	102	104	110	99
TRANSPORTATION INDUSTRY	2.5	4.8	4.9	5.1	6.2	4.8	102	105	126	98
PUBLIC UTILITIES	25.3	20.9	19.9	20.9	56.0	19.5	95	105	281	98
TRADE AND SERVICES	10.4	23.0	23.3	23.6	25.7	23.1	101	101	110	100
GOVERNMENT, EXC. TRANSPORTATION	1.5	2.4	2.4	2.5	2.5	2.4	101	102	105	100
CONSUMERS, EXC. TRANSPORTATION	12.9	25.7	26.0	26.8	27.8	25.9	101	103	107	99
USER-OPERATED TRANSPORTATION	19.3	39.1	39.6	40.8	42.4	39.4	101	103	107	99
TRANSPORTATION AIR POLLUTION (THOUSANDS OF TONS)										
SULFUR OXIDES	1.0	2.3	2.3	2.4	2.6	2.3	101	102	111	99
PARTICULATE MATTER	0.8	1.8	1.8	1.8	2.0	1.8	101	102	109	99
CARBON MONOXIDE	152.6	328.2	332.5	340.8	354.9	330.6	101	103	107	99
HYDROCARBONS	27.2	58.9	59.7	61.1	63.6	59.3	101	102	107	99
NITROGEN OXIDES	15.9	35.4	35.9	36.7	38.4	35.7	101	102	107	99
OTHER AIR POLLUTION										
SULFUR OXIDES	50.3	57.6	56.1	57.9	117.0	55.2	97	103	209	98
PARTICULATE MATTER	36.7	58.8	59.6	60.8	86.7	57.8	102	102	145	97
CARBON MONOXIDE	43.0	93.0	92.9	93.0	101.1	92.5	100	100	109	100
HYDROCARBONS	15.4	29.0	32.1	43.3	42.4	30.9	111	135	132	96
NITROGEN OXIDES	17.4	26.7	26.5	26.9	42.4	26.1	99	102	160	99
WATER OXYGEN DEMAND	219.5	170.2	170.3	170.3	175.3	170.0	100	100	103	100
LAND SOLID WASTE	385.6	504.6	508.9	521.1	521.9	509.4	101	102	103	100

44 ATLANTA, GA.

	1970	1990 BASE YEAR	1990 COMPLETED INTERSTATE	1990 EXTENDED PRIMARY	1990 ECONOMIC DEVELOPMENT	1990 URBAN	CI/BY	EP/CI	ED/CI	U/CI
JOBS BY INDUSTRY			(THOUSANDS)							
NATURAL RESOURCES (1-10)	33.4	25.2	24.7	24.0	23.6	24.5	98	97	95	99
CONSTRUCTION (11,12)	56.7	56.6	56.9	55.4	53.8	57.2	101	97	94	101
MANUFACTURING (13-74)	252.6	303.4	302.3	297.9	294.1	294.5	100	99	97	97
TRANSPORTATION INDUSTRY (75)	45.4	77.9	77.9	77.7	77.5	77.6	100	100	100	100
PUBLIC UTILITIES (76-80)	23.9	12.1	11.7	11.9	11.8	11.3	97	101	101	97
TRADE (81,86,89-99)	243.6	414.8	413.6	410.3	407.7	408.5	100	99	99	99
SERVICES (82-85,87,88,102)	230.4	386.0	386.0	385.7	385.4	385.9	100	100	100	100
STATE & LOCAL GOVT. (101)	122.2	166.4	166.1	165.2	164.4	164.8	100	99	99	99
FEDERAL GOVERNMENT (100,103)	38.4	44.9	44.8	44.6	44.4	44.5	100	99	99	99
TOTAL JOBS	1046.6	1487.2	1484.1	1472.7	1462.9	1469.0	100	99	99	99
CIVILIAN PERSONS EMPLOYED	967.4	1379.3	1376.3	1366.1	1357.1	1362.2	100	99	99	99
CIVILIAN UNEMPLOYMENT RATE	3.5	2.2	2.0	2.2	2.3	2.3	100	100	100	100
POPULATION	2296.7	3199.8	3194.7	3199.9	3181.7	3194.0	100	100	100	100
PER CAPITA INCOME	3683.4	6074.3	6068.5	6001.6	5982.1	5994.6	100	99	99	99
ENERGY USER SECTOR			(TRILLIONS OF BTU'S)							
NATURAL RESOURCES	13.1	24.1	23.6	22.2	21.8	23.3	98	94	93	99
CONSTRUCTION	52.0	109.2	109.4	107.3	100.4	105.8	100	98	92	97
MANUFACTURING	104.1	186.6	186.6	186.2	183.3	178.6	100	99	98	96
TRANSPORTATION INDUSTRY	75.8	160.4	160.0	159.2	158.7	158.7	100	99	99	99
PUBLIC UTILITIES	141.3	90.3	88.4	88.6	89.4	86.4	98	100	101	98
TRADE AND SERVICES	133.0	283.0	282.3	281.0	279.8	279.9	100	100	99	99
GOVERNMENT, EXC. TRANSPORTATION	24.8	36.1	36.1	36.0	35.9	36.0	100	100	99	100
CONSUMERS, EXC. TRANSPORTATION	100.5	219.9	219.5	218.0	216.5	217.4	100	99	99	99
USER-OPERATED TRANSPORTATION	193.3	390.0	389.3	386.9	384.7	386.1	100	99	99	99
TRANSPORTATION AIR POLLUTION			(THOUSANDS OF TONS)							
SULFUR OXIDES	15.5	32.5	32.2	31.9	31.8	32.0	99	99	99	99
PARTICULATE MATTER	8.9	18.7	18.7	18.6	18.5	18.5	100	99	99	99
CARBON MONOXIDE	1247.5	2688.5	2684.0	2667.2	2650.4	2660.1	100	99	99	99
HYDROCARBONS	216.9	465.5	465.5	462.4	459.6	461.4	100	99	99	99
NITROGEN OXIDES	136.9	291.0	291.8	291.4	289.1	289.3	100	100	99	99
OTHER AIR POLLUTION										
SULFUR OXIDES	348.8	592.7	589.6	590.1	591.6	586.5	99	100	100	99
PARTICULATE MATTER	256.6	432.9	429.7	424.1	420.8	428.4	99	98	98	98
CARBON MONOXIDE	145.8	384.3	379.7	368.0	362.0	379.2	99	97	95	97
HYDROCARBONS	121.2	283.8	287.6	295.5	277.3	220.0	101	103	96	76
NITROGEN OXIDES	127.9	341.0	339.9	339.3	339.3	339.0	100	100	100	100
WATER OXYGEN DEMAND	806.6	533.0	532.5	532.8	532.9	532.6	100	100	100	100
LAND SOLID WASTE	1814.4	2527.9	2523.8	2527.9	2513.6	2523.3	100	100	100	100

SUMMARY PROJECTIONS BY ORE ECONOMIC AREA UNDER FIVE ALTERNATIVE HIGHWAY SYSTEMS

45 BIRMINGHAM, ALA.

	1970	1990 BASE YEAR	1990 COMPLETED INTERSTATE	1990 EXTENDED PRIMARY	1990 ECONOMIC DEVELOPMENT	1990 URBAN	CI/BY	EP/CI	ED/CI	U/CI
JOBS BY INDUSTRY		(THOUSANDS)								
NATURAL RESOURCES (1-10)	47.9	38.1	38.3	38.0	39.9	38.1	100	99	104	100
CONSTRUCTION (11,12)	31.1	29.4	29.7	28.8	31.4	29.8	101	97	106	100
MANUFACTURING (13-74)	181.4	261.7	260.5	256.4	271.8	252.8	100	98	104	97
TRANSPORTATION INDUSTRY (75)	17.4	13.0	13.0	12.6	13.7	12.7	100	97	106	98
PUBLIC UTILITIES (76-80)	13.8	7.9	7.7	6.0	11.9	7.4	98	78	154	96
TRADE (81,86,89-99)	122.6	198.9	197.8	192.1	211.1	193.0	100	97	107	98
SERVICES (82-85,87,88,102)	132.2	288.5	288.6	288.3	289.0	288.5	100	100	100	100
STATE & LOCAL GOVT. (101)	81.4	111.1	110.9	109.7	114.1	109.7	100	99	103	99
FEDERAL GOVERNMENT (100,103)	26.6	30.2	30.2	29.9	30.9	29.9	100	99	102	99
TOTAL JOBS	654.3	978.6	976.7	961.9	1013.8	961.9	100	98	104	98
CIVILIAN PERSONS EMPLOYED	575.7	869.7	867.9	855.1	901.6	854.1	100	99	104	98
CIVILIAN UNEMPLOYMENT RATE	5.4	3.5	3.5	3.6	3.3	4.2				
POPULATION	1725.3	2310.8	2306.7	2287.5	2366.6	2305.0	100	99	103	100
PER CAPITA INCOME	2816.5	4999.1	4990.3	4923.4	5129.0	4893.5	100	99	103	98
ENERGY USER SECTOR		(TRILLIONS OF BTU'S)								
NATURAL RESOURCES	17.5	15.4	15.4	15.2	17.1	15.3	100	99	111	99
CONSTRUCTION	26.1	46.1	46.3	40.4	58.2	39.1	100	87	126	84
MANUFACTURING	163.7	184.5	183.5	180.4	189.2	178.9	99	95	103	97
TRANSPORTATION INDUSTRY	17.5	31.6	31.4	29.9	34.4	30.4	99	95	110	95
PUBLIC UTILITIES	130.7	357.7	350.2	305.5	417.6	338.1	98	87	119	87
TRADE AND SERVICES	51.3	111.3	110.2	107.0	117.7	108.6	99	97	106	98
GOVERNMENT. EXC. TRANSPORTATION	8.1	12.7	12.6	12.5	13.0	12.5	100	99	103	99
CONSUMERS. EXC. TRANSPORTATION	74.1	158.2	157.8	155.8	163.2	155.8	100	99	103	99
USER-OPERATED TRANSPORTATION	85.8	191.2	190.6	187.4	198.8	187.6	100	98	104	98
TRANSPORTATION AIR POLLUTION		(THOUSANDS OF TONS)								
SULFUR OXIDES	4.7	8.2	8.1	7.8	8.7	7.9	99	96	107	97
PARTICULATE MATTER	3.4	6.4	6.3	6.2	6.7	6.2	100	97	106	98
CARBON MONOXIDE	647.5	1380.1	1376.1	1351.7	1437.2	1353.6	100	98	104	98
HYDROCARBONS	113.3	239.3	238.6	234.3	249.1	234.7	100	98	104	98
NITROGEN OXIDES	63.8	126.7	126.5	124.2	132.9	124.3	100	98	105	98
OTHER AIR POLLUTION										
SULFUR OXIDES	260.2	658.5	646.3	573.1	756.0	626.6	98	89	117	97
PARTICULATE MATTER	295.7	523.8	521.6	502.1	553.9	516.5	100	96	106	99
CARBON MONOXIDE	445.3	268.6	268.5	267.9	271.0	268.5	100	100	101	100
HYDROCARBONS	95.9	122.4	111.4	94.6	112.5	92.7	91	85	101	83
NITROGEN OXIDES	76.8	177.5	174.6	156.4	201.9	169.7	98	90	116	97
WATER OXYGEN DEMAND	1711.7	2698.5	2700.0	2699.4	2704.1	2699.7	100	100	100	100
LAND SOLID WASTE	1363.0	1825.5	1822.3	1807.1	1869.6	1820.9	100	99	103	100

46 MEMPHIS, TENN.-ARK.

	1970	1990 BASE YEAR	1990 COMPLETED INTERSTATE	1990 EXTENDED PRIMARY	1990 ECONOMIC DEVELOPMENT	1990 URBAN	CI/BY	EP/CI	ED/CI	U/CI
							| P E R C E N T			
JOBS BY INDUSTRY										
NATURAL RESOURCES (1-10)	62.4	39.2	38.8	39.8	39.0	38.6	99	103	101	100
CONSTRUCTION (11,12)	26.9	33.4	33.5	33.6	35.2	33.4	100	100	105	100
MANUFACTURING (13-74)	147.2	270.0	262.1	269.2	269.1	253.0	97	103	103	97
TRANSPORTATION INDUSTRY (75)	21.3	36.2	35.9	36.5	36.3	35.5	99	102	101	99
PUBLIC UTILITIES (76-80)	7.9	4.2	2.8	7.0	3.8	2.5	68	249	136	88
TRADE (81,86,89-99)	137.8	162.5	156.5	165.2	160.8	151.4	96	106	103	97
SERVICES (82-85,87,88,102)	141.1	248.7	248.5	248.9	248.6	248.1	100	100	100	100
STATE & LOCAL GOVT. (101)	65.1	87.7	85.9	88.0	87.3	84.4	98	102	102	98
FEDERAL GOVERNMENT (100,103)	29.9	31.9	31.5	31.9	31.8	31.1	99	101	101	99
TOTAL JOBS	639.5	913.7	895.2	920.2	911.9	878.0	98	103	102	98
CIVILIAN PERSONS EMPLOYED	590.7	846.3	829.0	852.5	844.8	812.9	98	103	102	98
CIVILIAN UNEMPLOYMENT RATE	4.5	2.6	2.8	2.7	2.7	3.1				
POPULATION	1700.5	2200.6	2179.8	2200.9	2185.1	2175.5	99	101	100	100
PER CAPITA INCOME	2819.8	5081.1	4988.6	5114.7	5113.5	4866.3	98	103	103	98
ENERGY USER SECTOR (TRILLIONS OF BTUS)										
NATURAL RESOURCES	51.0	26.8	26.2	27.0	26.2	25.9	98	103	100	99
CONSTRUCTION	37.7	70.2	69.4	71.3	81.2	57.3	99	103	117	83
MANUFACTURING	60.4	142.5	138.5	141.8	141.5	131.1	97	102	102	95
TRANSPORTATION INDUSTRY	24.1	49.7	47.9	50.6	49.6	46.3	96	106	103	97
PUBLIC UTILITIES	28.3	108.9	82.3	140.4	88.2	72.8	76	171	107	88
TRADE AND SERVICES	73.3	159.0	155.0	162.0	158.2	151.9	97	105	102	98
GOVERNMENT, EXC. TRANSPORTATION	4.5	8.0	7.8	8.0	8.0	7.6	98	103	102	98
CONSUMERS, EXC. TRANSPORTATION	38.2	81.7	79.1	82.3	81.6	76.7	97	104	103	97
USER-OPERATED TRANSPORTATION	94.1	205.4	201.3	206.4	205.2	197.5	98	103	102	98
TRANSPORTATION AIR POLLUTION (THOUSANDS OF TONS)										
SULFUR OXIDES	9.4	12.9	12.4	12.9	12.7	12.1	97	104	102	98
PARTICULATE MATTER	6.4	8.9	8.7	9.0	8.8	8.5	98	103	102	98
CARBON MONOXIDE	929.4	1610.3	1579.5	1618.3	1608.8	1550.9	98	102	102	98
HYDROCARBONS	169.7	282.1	276.7	283.5	281.8	271.8	98	102	102	98
NITROGEN OXIDES	114.3	162.8	160.0	164.7	163.1	157.0	98	103	102	98
OTHER AIR POLLUTION										
SULFUR OXIDES	93.3	251.6	207.8	303.5	218.0	192.3	83	146	105	93
PARTICULATE MATTER	177.7	144.6	154.7	178.3	157.5	151.2	94	115	102	98
CARBON MONOXIDE	400.2	321.4	318.0	331.5	319.6	317.4	99	104	101	100
HYDROCARBONS	126.1	230.8	219.6	208.4	217.5	154.3	95	95	99	70
NITROGEN OXIDES	38.1	71.4	60.4	84.9	63.2	56.6	85	140	105	94
WATER OXYGEN DEMAND	757.1	1322.4	1321.9	1330.0	1325.1	1322.0	100	101	100	100
LAND SOLID WASTE	1343.4	1738.4	1722.0	1738.7	1726.2	1718.6	99	101	100	100

SUMMARY PROJECTIONS BY ORE ECONOMIC AREA UNDER FIVE ALTERNATIVE HIGHWAY SYSTEMS

47   HUNTSVILLE, ALA

	1970	1990 BASE YEAR	1990 COMPLETED INTERSTATE	1990 EXTENDED PRIMARY	1990 ECONOMIC DEVELOPMENT	1990 URBAN	PERCENT CI/BY	EP/CI	ED/CI	U/CI
JOBS BY INDUSTRY			(THOUSANDS)							
NATURAL RESOURCES (1-10)	20.5	16.8	16.6	16.8	16.7	16.6	99	101	101	100
CONSTRUCTION (11,12)	11.5	7.5	6.8	6.8	7.3	6.2	91	100	108	91
MANUFACTURING (13-74)	68.3	106.4	102.4	108.7	109.9	100.6	96	106	107	98
TRANSPORTATION INDUSTRY (75)	3.0	5.7	5.5	5.9	5.9	5.4	97	106	106	98
PUBLIC UTILITIES (76-80)	2.9	1.7	1.1	2.2	1.6	.9	66	202	145	85
TRADE (81,84,89-99)	39.8	76.8	72.7	79.1	79.0	70.8	95	109	109	97
SERVICES (82-85,87,88,102)	41.0	86.3	86.1	86.4	86.4	86.1	100	100	100	100
STATE & LOCAL GOVT. (101)	25.0	35.7	34.7	36.2	36.1	34.2	97	104	104	99
FEDERAL GOVERNMENT (100,103)	30.9	35.0	34.8	35.1	35.1	34.7	99	101	101	100
TOTAL JOBS	243.0	371.8	360.7	377.1	378.1	355.4	97	105	105	99
CIVILIAN PERSONS EMPLOYED	233.9	357.6	346.9	362.7	363.6	341.9	97	105	105	99
CIVILIAN UNEMPLOYMENT RATE	4.8	2.5	2.6	2.1	2.3	2.8				
POPULATION	671.3	955.4	934.1	951.6	965.0	933.6	98	102	103	100
PER CAPITA INCOME	2930.5	5144.6	5067.2	5254.5	5207.9	4981.8	98	104	103	98
ENERGY USER SECTOR			(TRILLIONS OF BTU'S)							
NATURAL RESOURCES	8.1	6.5	6.4	6.6	6.4	6.3	98	104	101	99
CONSTRUCTION	9.3	20.4	19.7	21.1	27.4	17.5	97	107	139	89
MANUFACTURING	33.5	82.6	79.7	83.6	83.8	78.7	96	105	105	99
TRANSPORTATION INDUSTRY	2.9	9.2	8.2	9.7	9.7	7.8	89	118	117	95
PUBLIC UTILITIES	7.9	24.1	12.9	23.7	18.0	10.0	54	184	139	78
TRADE AND SERVICES	15.5	40.7	38.3	41.9	41.2	37.3	94	110	108	98
GOVERNMENT, EXC. TRANSPORTATION	1.5	2.9	2.8	3.0	3.0	2.8	96	106	106	98
CONSUMERS, EXC. TRANSPORTATION	18.4	40.8	39.3	41.5	41.7	38.6	96	106	106	98
USER-OPERATED TRANSPORTATION	29.9	70.7	68.3	71.8	72.1	67.2	97	106	106	98
TRANSPORTATION AIR POLLUTION			(THOUSANDS OF TONS)							
SULFUR OXIDES	1.4	2.7	2.5	2.8	2.8	2.4	93	111	111	97
PARTICULATE MATTER	1.1	2.3	2.2	2.3	2.3	2.1	95	108	108	98
CARBON MONOXIDE	239.3	518.0	500.1	526.5	528.7	492.0	97	105	106	98
HYDROCARBONS	42.4	90.1	87.0	91.5	91.9	85.6	97	105	106	98
NITROGEN OXIDES	23.9	47.2	45.4	48.2	48.4	44.6	96	106	107	98
OTHER AIR POLLUTION										
SULFUR OXIDES	66.3	134.4	114.4	133.8	124.2	109.3	85	117	109	96
PARTICULATE MATTER	76.0	137.9	124.9	142.5	141.1	122.4	91	114	113	98
CARBON MONOXIDE	54.7	73.1	69.9	72.9	69.9	70.1	96	104	100	100
HYDROCARBONS	18.9	40.6	38.8	41.6	40.0	37.4	96	107	103	96
NITROGEN OXIDES	11.3	41.3	36.0	41.4	39.0	34.8	87	115	108	97
WATER OXYGEN DEMAND	637.6	1063.2	1059.0	1060.8	1060.8	1058.8	100	100	100	100
LAND SOLID WASTE	530.4	754.8	737.9	751.7	762.4	737.6	98	102	103	100

48 CHATTANOOGA, TENN.--GA.

	1970	1990 BASE YEAR	1990 COMPLETED INTERSTATE	1990 EXTENDED PRIMARY	1990 ECONOMIC DEVELOPMENT	1990 URBAN	CI/BY	EP/CI	ED/CI	U/CI
JOBS BY INDUSTRY		(THOUSANDS)								
NATURAL RESOURCES (1-10)	16.5	5.6	5.7	5.6	5.7	5.7	101	99	100	100
CONSTRUCTION (11,12)	11.6	15.3	14.9	15.8	13.7	15.0	98	106	92	100
MANUFACTURING (13-74)	119.8	134.5	142.2	143.2	145.3	140.1	106	101	102	99
TRANSPORTATION INDUSTRY (75)	5.7	5.3	5.4	5.4	5.5	5.4	106	97	99	98
PUBLIC UTILITIES (76-80)	3.4	2.0	3.4	2.4	2.8	3.0	170	71	82	88
TRADE (81,86,89-99)	49.8	56.4	62.8	60.0	62.3	60.7	111	96	99	97
SERVICES (82-85,87,88,102)	44.8	81.5	81.8	81.6	81.8	81.8	100	100	100	100
STATE & LOCAL GOVT. (101)	22.4	27.5	29.2	29.1	29.3	28.8	107	100	100	98
FEDERAL GOVERNMENT (100,103)	6.3	6.9	7.3	7.2	7.3	7.2	106	100	100	99
TOTAL JOBS	280.3	334.9	352.8	350.3	353.6	347.5	105	99	100	98
CIVILIAN PERSONS EMPLOYED	266.3	317.8	334.7	332.4	335.5	329.7	105	99	100	98
CIVILIAN UNEMPLOYMENT RATE	4.7	4.2	3.9	3.9	3.4	4.2				
POPULATION	718.2	922.9	951.6	950.0	945.2	950.5	103	100	99	100
PER CAPITA INCOME	2911.3	4726.9	4902.3	4887.2	4954.0	4822.2	104	100	101	98
ENERGY USER SECTOR		(TRILLIONS OF BTUS)								
NATURAL RESOURCES	6.1	6.8	7.0	7.1	7.2	7.0	103	101	102	100
CONSTRUCTION	10.8	18.1	19.5	18.7	19.1	19.1	108	96	98	98
MANUFACTURING	61.2	128.0	131.8	131.7	133.6	130.3	103	100	101	99
TRANSPORTATION INDUSTRY	5.2	9.1	11.1	10.3	10.9	10.3	121	93	99	95
PUBLIC UTILITIES	18.1	14.3	51.0	28.2	36.8	40.9	358	55	72	80
TRADE AND SERVICES	20.6	42.4	46.9	44.3	45.9	45.6	111	95	98	97
GOVERNMENT, EXC. TRANSPORTATION	2.6	4.0	4.2	4.1	4.1	4.1	105	100	100	99
CONSUMERS, EXC. TRANSPORTATION	26.0	49.4	52.0	51.8	52.1	51.3	105	100	100	99
USER-OPERATED TRANSPORTATION	37.6	74.6	78.6	78.3	78.8	77.5	105	100	100	99
TRANSPORTATION AIR POLLUTION		(THOUSANDS OF TONS)								
SULFUR OXIDES	1.6	2.6	3.0	2.9	3.0	2.9	114	95	102	96
PARTICULATE MATTER	1.3	2.2	2.4	2.4	2.4	2.4	110	98	98	98
CARBON MONOXIDE	266.9	519.5	549.8	546.6	551.1	541.6	106	99	100	99
HYDROCARBONS	46.7	90.1	95.3	94.8	95.6	93.9	106	99	100	99
NITROGEN OXIDES	25.4	46.6	49.9	49.5	50.0	49.0	107	99	100	98
OTHER AIR POLLUTION										
SULFUR OXIDES	66.0	146.5	206.9	169.1	183.6	190.4	141	82	89	92
PARTICULATE MATTER	77.3	133.9	148.6	133.1	141.2	144.3	111	90	95	97
CARBON MONOXIDE	82.8	119.2	112.9	112.8	112.7	113.0	95	95	100	100
HYDROCARBONS	43.7	103.6	107.0	120.3	126.9	101.0	103	112	119	94
NITROGEN OXIDES	18.4	46.7	61.5	51.6	55.5	57.4	131	84	90	93
WATER OXYGEN DEMAND	619.5	410.5	407.4	406.2	406.9	407.3	99	100	100	100
LAND SOLID WASTE	567.4	729.1	751.8	750.5	746.7	750.9	103	100	99	100

SUMMARY PROJECTIONS BY ORE ECONOMIC AREA UNDER FIVE ALTERNATIVE HIGHWAY SYSTEMS

49 NASHVILLE, TENN.

	1970	1990 BASE YEAR	1990 COMPLETED INTERSTATE	1990 EXTENDED PRIMARY	1990 ECONOMIC DEVELOPMENT	1990 URBAN	P E R C E N T			
							CI/BY	EP/CI	ED/CI	U/CI
JOBS BY INDUSTRY		(THOUSANDS)								
NATURAL RESOURCES (1-10)	61.8	53.5	53.7	53.9	53.8	53.6	101	100	100	98
CONSTRUCTION (11,12)	28.7	37.1	37.5	36.9	36.1	37.5	101	98	96	98
MANUFACTURING (13-74)	153.9	217.6	222.1	221.5	223.6	212.9	102	100	101	96
TRANSPORTATION INDUSTRY (75)	13.9	9.6	9.8	9.9	9.9	9.4	102	101	102	97
PUBLIC UTILITIES (76-80)	8.6	3.4	3.8	4.6	4.6	3.3	112	123	122	87
TRADE (81,86,89-99)	116.4	170.5	174.0	176.4	177.2	168.4	102	101	101	97
SERVICES (82-85,87,88,102)	118.4	204.8	205.5	205.5	205.6	205.3	100	100	100	100
STATE & LOCAL GOVT. (101)	79.8	104.2	105.1	105.3	105.4	103.7	101	100	100	99
FEDERAL GOVERNMENT (100,103)	40.3	42.3	42.5	42.5	42.5	42.2	100	100	100	99
TOTAL JOBS	621.8	842.9	853.9	856.5	858.9	836.3	101	100	101	98
CIVILIAN PERSONS EMPLOYED	545.9	750.2	760.0	762.5	764.9	743.9	101	100	101	98
CIVILIAN UNEMPLOYMENT RATE	4.3	1.6	1.4	1.3	1.2	1.7				
POPULATION	1426.8	1754.7	1761.2	1766.2	1762.5	1762.1	100	100	100	100
PER CAPITA INCOME	2920.4	5335.5	5411.7	5410.7	5444.3	5249.8	101	101	101	97
ENERGY USER SECTOR		(TRILLIONS OF BTU'S)								
NATURAL RESOURCES	16.6	18.6	18.9	19.1	19.1	18.3	101	101	101	97
CONSTRUCTION	25.4	50.5	51.6	52.6	53.4	40.2	102	102	103	78
MANUFACTURING	51.0	109.2	111.2	110.7	111.8	106.9	103	102	101	96
TRANSPORTATION INDUSTRY	16.4	35.5	36.6	37.2	37.4	35.0	103	102	102	96
PUBLIC UTILITIES	42.4	137.7	153.7	181.6	180.1	136.5	112	118	117	89
TRADE AND SERVICES	49.3	115.5	117.8	119.7	120.0	114.7	102	102	102	97
GOVERNMENT, EXC. TRANSPORTATION	3.5	5.9	6.0	6.0	6.0	5.9	102	100	101	97
CONSUMERS, EXC. TRANSPORTATION	59.1	120.1	121.5	121.8	122.1	119.1	101	100	101	98
USER-OPERATED TRANSPORTATION	100.4	214.4	216.6	217.0	217.5	212.9	101	100	100	98
TRANSPORTATION AIR POLLUTION		(THOUSANDS OF TONS)								
SULFUR OXIDES	5.0	9.4	9.5	9.5	9.7	9.2	102	101	101	97
PARTICULATE MATTER	3.9	7.3	7.4	7.5	7.5	7.3	102	101	101	98
CARBON MONOXIDE	785.9	1592.2	1609.3	1613.2	1617.0	1581.2	101	100	100	98
HYDROCARBONS	137.9	276.3	279.2	279.8	280.5	274.3	101	100	100	98
NITROGEN OXIDES	76.6	146.3	148.4	149.3	149.6	145.5	101	101	101	98
OTHER AIR POLLUTION										
SULFUR OXIDES	98.1	329.1	355.2	400.8	398.2	327.1	108	113	112	92
PARTICULATE MATTER	90.4	251.5	261.7	276.7	275.2	253.5	104	106	105	97
CARBON MONOXIDE	119.4	222.8	228.0	232.6	231.5	227.2	102	102	102	100
HYDROCARBONS	55.4	139.8	135.4	124.6	131.6	116.8	97	92	97	86
NITROGEN OXIDES	36.1	129.9	136.6	148.1	147.4	129.6	105	108	108	95
WATER OXYGEN DEMAND	1358.4	2249.7	2249.7	2250.1	2250.9	2251.0	100	100	100	100
LAND SOLID WASTE	1127.1	1386.2	1391.4	1395.3	1392.4	1392.1	100	100	100	100

50 KNOXVILLE, TENN.

	1970	1990 BASE YEAR	1990 COMPLETED INTERSTATE	1990 EXTENDED PRIMARY	1990 ECONOMIC DEVELOPMENT	1990 URBAN	CI/BY	EP/BY	ED/CI	U/CI
							PERCENT			
JOBS BY INDUSTRY		(THOUSANDS)								
NATURAL RESOURCES (1-10)	32.2	25.8	25.7	26.3	27.5	25.0	100	102	107	97
CONSTRUCTION (11,12)	14.8	18.9	19.1	19.9	25.6	19.0	101	104	134	100
MANUFACTURING (13-74)	86.9	89.4	87.5	93.2	94.9	84.5	98	107	109	97
TRANSPORTATION INDUSTRY (75)	7.6	9.5	9.4	10.1	10.1	9.2	99	108	107	98
PUBLIC UTILITIES (76-80)	3.7	2.1	1.7	6.3	3.6	1.5	81	370	210	86
TRADE (81,86,89-99)	62.9	103.9	100.3	115.0	112.4	96.4	97	115	112	96
SERVICES (82-85,87,88,102)	58.1	114.1	114.3	114.5	114.6	114.3	100	100	100	100
STATE & LOCAL GOVT. (101)	23.2	29.0	28.3	31.0	31.5	27.5	98	110	111	97
FEDERAL GOVERNMENT (100,103)	8.6	9.7	9.5	10.2	10.3	9.4	98	106	107	98
TOTAL JOBS	298.1	402.3	395.9	426.5	430.4	386.8	98	108	109	98
CIVILIAN PERSONS EMPLOYED	296.3	397.5	391.3	420.6	424.4	382.6	98	107	108	98
CIVILIAN UNEMPLOYMENT RATE	5.5	5.5	5.3	5.1	4.7	5.3				
POPULATION	904.8	1026.9	1007.9	1067.5	1094.8	1003.6	98	106	109	100
PER CAPITA INCOME	2563.2	4836.6	4815.6	5027.4	5016.1	4687.7	100	104	104	97
ENERGY USER SECTOR		(TRILLIONS OF BTU'S)								
NATURAL RESOURCES	8.0	14.5	14.1	15.8	16.6	13.3	97	112	118	94
CONSTRUCTION	13.4	26.6	26.2	29.6	51.9	19.5	98	113	198	75
MANUFACTURING	52.0	80.7	79.4	84.1	84.3	78.4	98	106	106	99
TRANSPORTATION INDUSTRY	6.6	16.4	15.7	18.8	18.4	14.9	96	120	118	95
PUBLIC UTILITIES	15.0	43.9	28.6	106.4	65.1	23.4	65	371	227	82
TRADE AND SERVICES	22.7	55.8	54.0	62.5	60.8	52.2	97	116	112	97
GOVERNMENT, EXC. TRANSPORTATION	5.8	8.2	8.1	8.4	8.5	8.0	99	104	104	99
CONSUMERS, EXC. TRANSPORTATION	20.7	41.3	40.3	44.7	45.7	39.1	98	111	113	97
USER-OPERATED TRANSPORTATION	55.1	112.4	110.9	117.7	119.3	108.9	99	106	108	98
TRANSPORTATION AIR POLLUTION		(THOUSANDS OF TONS)								
SULFUR OXIDES	2.1	4.4	4.3	4.9	4.8	4.1	96	114	113	96
PARTICULATE MATTER	1.8	3.6	3.5	3.8	3.8	3.4	98	110	110	97
CARBON MONOXIDE	396.5	801.9	790.3	841.9	852.4	775.7	99	107	108	98
HYDROCARBONS	69.2	139.0	137.0	145.9	147.7	134.5	99	106	108	98
NITROGEN OXIDES	36.8	72.6	71.5	77.2	77.8	70.0	98	108	109	98
OTHER AIR POLLUTION										
SULFUR OXIDES	46.5	132.9	107.8	235.1	167.8	99.2	81	218	156	92
PARTICULATE MATTER	52.9	107.8	99.1	145.1	124.3	95.6	92	146	125	96
CARBON MONOXIDE	51.4	55.5	51.7	63.6	56.8	51.5	93	123	110	100
HYDROCARBONS	51.0	54.7	53.0	59.2	68.2	52.7	97	112	129	100
NITROGEN OXIDES	17.5	52.6	46.2	78.5	61.6	44.1	88	170	133	95
WATER OXYGEN DEMAND	470.3	766.1	764.7	767.2	766.3	764.5	100	100	100	100
LAND SOLID WASTE	714.8	811.2	795.8	843.3	864.9	792.8	98	106	109	100

SUMMARY PROJECTIONS BY OBE ECONOMIC AREA UNDER FIVE ALTERNATIVE HIGHWAY SYSTEMS

51 BRISTOL, VA.-TENN.

	1970	1990 BASE YEAR	1990 COMPLETED INTERSTATE	1990 EXTENDED PRIMARY	1990 ECONOMIC DEVELOPMENT	1990 URBAN	CI/BY	EP/CI	ED/CI	U/CI
							P E R C E N T			
JOBS BY INDUSTRY		(THOUSANDS)								
NATURAL RESOURCES (1-10)	48.6	26.2	26.7	26.1	25.9	26.3	102	98	97	99
CONSTRUCTION (11,12)	11.8	13.1	13.3	13.2	13.2	13.2	101	99	100	99
MANUFACTURING (13-74)	71.5	94.8	92.6	97.8	96.1	90.3	98	106	104	98
TRANSPORTATION INDUSTRY (75)	7.8	10.6	10.6	10.9	10.9	10.5	100	103	103	99
PUBLIC UTILITIES (76-80)	4.0	3.8	3.4	7.0	5.6	3.1	90	207	164	92
TRADE (81,86,89-99)	46.0	60.1	59.0	64.8	62.7	57.3	100	110	106	97
SERVICES (82-85,87,88,102)	38.2	66.9	67.0	67.5	67.1	67.0	100	101	100	100
STATE & LOCAL GOVT. (101)	23.4	26.6	26.2	27.7	26.6	25.7	98	106	102	98
FEDERAL GOVERNMENT (100,103)	4.2	4.2	4.1	4.4	4.2	4.0	98	108	102	97
TOTAL JOBS	255.6	306.3	302.7	319.3	312.3	297.3	99	105	103	98
CIVILIAN PERSONS EMPLOYED	232.6	277.5	274.3	289.2	282.9	269.3	99	105	103	98
CIVILIAN UNEMPLOYMENT RATE	6.2	3.5	3.2	3.6	3.3	3.2	98	106	103	99
POPULATION	762.2	833.7	816.0	862.7	843.7	804.3	98	106	103	99
PER CAPITA INCOME	2652.4	4679.7	4701.9	4733.9	4702.6	4653.8	100	101	100	99
ENERGY USER SECTOR		(TRILLIONS OF BTUS)								
NATURAL RESOURCES	21.3	23.1	23.0	22.5	22.5	22.5	100	98	98	98
CONSTRUCTION	13.2	22.9	22.9	20.9	24.3	15.9	100	91	106	69
MANUFACTURING	59.2	121.8	120.9	123.5	122.3	120.3	99	102	101	99
TRANSPORTATION INDUSTRY	6.7	12.1	11.7	13.3	12.7	11.3	97	114	109	97
PUBLIC UTILITIES	33.4	36.9	30.3	40.3	42.8	29.7	82	133	141	98
TRADE AND SERVICES	19.6	38.2	37.4	42.4	40.4	36.6	98	113	108	98
GOVERNMENT, EXC. TRANSPORTATION	11.7	15.4	15.4	15.5	15.4	15.3	100	101	100	100
CONSUMERS, EXC. TRANSPORTATION	17.8	31.9	31.4	33.5	32.5	30.6	98	107	104	98
USER-OPERATED TRANSPORTATION	40.2	77.9	77.0	80.4	78.8	75.8	99	104	102	98
TRANSPORTATION AIR POLLUTION		(THOUSANDS OF TONS)								
SULFUR OXIDES	2.1	3.3	3.2	3.5	3.4	3.1	97	109	106	97
PARTICULATE MATTER	1.6	2.6	2.6	2.8	2.7	2.5	98	107	104	98
CARBON MONOXIDE	315.7	579.1	572.6	597.8	586.4	563.6	99	104	102	98
HYDROCARBONS	55.4	100.6	99.4	103.7	101.8	97.9	99	104	102	98
NITROGEN OXIDES	31.0	53.1	52.5	55.3	54.1	51.6	99	105	103	98
OTHER AIR POLLUTION										
SULFUR OXIDES	75.9	118.7	108.3	126.6	129.9	107.4	91	117	120	99
PARTICULATE MATTER	50.3	60.5	58.7	69.0	65.9	58.6	97	118	112	100
CARBON MONOXIDE	55.4	74.9	74.7	85.0	78.6	74.8	100	114	105	100
HYDROCARBONS	45.7	98.3	97.3	99.8	100.2	96.0	99	103	103	99
NITROGEN OXIDES	22.5	43.9	41.7	47.5	47.6	41.5	95	114	114	100
WATER OXYGEN DEMAND	479.9	311.2	311.4	314.1	313.2	311.5	100	101	101	100
LAND SOLID WASTE	602.1	658.6	644.7	681.5	666.5	635.4	98	106	103	99

SUMMARY PROJECTIONS BY OBE ECONOMIC AREA UNDER FIVE ALTERNATIVE HIGHWAY SYSTEMS

52   HUNT-ASH, W.VA.-KY.-OHIO

	1970	1990 BASE YEAR	1990 COMPLETED INTERSTATE	1990 EXTENDED PRIMARY	1990 ECONOMIC DEVELOPMENT	1990 URBAN	P E R C E N T			
							CI/BY	EP/CI	ED/CI	U/CI
JOBS BY INDUSTRY	(THOUSANDS)									
NATURAL RESOURCES (1-10)	58.8	28.0	30.2	30.5	29.8	30.7	108	108	99	102
CONSTRUCTION (11,12)	20.2	25.7	23.0	25.9	19.4	23.1	89	113	85	100
MANUFACTURING (13-74)	72.8	92.8	97.1	100.2	99.8	96.1	105	103	103	99
TRANSPORTATION INDUSTRY (75)	17.9	10.8	11.2	11.1	11.2	11.1	103	99	100	100
PUBLIC UTILITIES (76-80)	12.7	24.3	27.9	27.1	28.8	26.8	115	97	103	96
TRADE (81,86,89-99)	78.6	130.7	136.5	136.3	137.6	135.3	104	100	101	99
SERVICES (82-85,87,88,102)	68.7	141.1	141.3	141.3	141.3	141.3	100	100	100	100
STATE & LOCAL GOVT. (101)	57.5	71.4	72.8	73.6	72.9	72.6	102	101	100	100
FEDERAL GOVERNMENT (100,103)	8.1	8.9	9.2	9.4	9.2	9.1	104	102	100	99
TOTAL JOBS	395.2	533.9	549.1	555.5	550.0	546.1	103	101	100	99
CIVILIAN PERSONS EMPLOYED	370.9	500.5	514.8	520.9	515.0	511.9	103	101	100	99
CIVILIAN UNEMPLOYMENT RATE	8.6	.9	.9	1.1	1.0	1.1				
POPULATION	1310.0	1408.4	1461.4	1469.0	1459.2	1461.1	104	101	100	100
PER CAPITA INCOME	2631.1	5142.1	5138.3	5196.5	5151.3	5107.3	100	101	100	99
ENERGY USER SECTOR	(TRILLIONS OF BTU'S)									
NATURAL RESOURCES	40.2	101.5	104.0	104.5	103.8	104.8	102	101	100	101
CONSTRUCTION	20.7	29.3	30.6	30.4	30.6	30.3	105	99	100	99
MANUFACTURING	128.2	312.0	316.0	317.8	318.3	314.9	101	101	101	100
TRANSPORTATION INDUSTRY	12.5	34.8	36.5	36.4	36.7	36.2	105	100	101	99
PUBLIC UTILITIES	107.5	327.0	367.9	346.6	363.4	356.2	113	94	99	97
TRADE AND SERVICES	30.2	95.1	99.1	98.5	99.4	98.3	104	99	100	99
GOVERNMENT, EXC. TRANSPORTATION	79.6	105.3	105.4	105.5	105.4	105.4	100	100	100	100
CONSUMERS, EXC. TRANSPORTATION	54.1	111.2	113.4	114.5	113.5	113.0	102	101	100	100
USER-OPERATED TRANSPORTATION	66.6	135.1	138.6	140.2	138.7	138.0	103	101	100	100
TRANSPORTATION AIR POLLUTION	(THOUSANDS OF TONS)									
SULFUR OXIDES	4.7	12.6	12.9	12.8	12.9	12.8	102	100	100	100
PARTICULATE MATTER	3.4	8.4	8.6	8.7	8.6	8.6	102	100	100	100
CARBON MONOXIDE	575.6	1268.3	1295.2	1306.4	1296.6	1290.7	102	101	100	100
HYDROCARBONS	103.4	230.0	234.6	236.5	234.8	233.8	102	101	100	100
NITROGEN OXIDES	64.1	151.6	154.8	155.9	155.2	154.3	102	101	100	100
OTHER AIR POLLUTION										
SULFUR OXIDES	239.7	692.7	760.0	725.0	752.4	740.9	110	95	99	97
PARTICULATE MATTER	192.4	511.7	530.4	520.3	528.5	525.6	104	98	100	99
CARBON MONOXIDE	386.9	981.9	982.0	980.1	981.8	982.3	100	100	100	100
HYDROCARBONS	178.8	497.6	533.1	552.3	557.3	523.3	107	104	105	104
NITROGEN OXIDES	72.3	197.5	214.1	205.4	212.1	209.5	108	96	99	98
WATER OXYGEN DEMAND	1021.4	2140.8	2145.1	2140.6	2143.9	2144.7	100	100	100	100
LAND SOLID WASTE	1034.9	1112.6	1154.5	1160.5	1152.7	1154.3	104	101	100	99

SUMMARY PROJECTIONS BY ORE ECONOMIC AREA UNDER FIVE ALTERNATIVE HIGHWAY SYSTEMS

53 LEXINGTON, KY.

	1970	1990 BASE YEAR	1990 COMPLETED INTERSTATE	1990 EXTENDED PRIMARY	1990 ECONOMIC DEVELOPMENT	1990 URBAN	CI/BY	EP/CI	ED/CI	U/CI
								P E R C E N T		
JOBS BY INDUSTRY		(THOUSANDS)								
NATURAL RESOURCES (1-10)	44.9	32.1	31.9	32.1	33.9	31.3	99	100	106	98
CONSTRUCTION (11,12)	12.1	14.6	14.8	15.9	24.7	14.7	101	107	167	99
MANUFACTURING (13-74)	52.0	100.3	95.7	117.7	116.4	91.5	95	123	122	96
TRANSPORTATION INDUSTRY (75)	5.6	3.0	2.9	1.8	1.7	.9	85	206	195	102
PUBLIC UTILITIES (76-80)	5.3	3.3	2.9	8.8	5.9	2.7	89	303	203	91
TRADE (81,86,89-99)	51.9	48.8	46.5	63.3	62.0	43.7	95	136	133	94
SERVICES (82-85,87,88,102)	50.7	92.1	92.1	92.8	92.8	92.0	100	101	101	100
STATE & LOCAL GOVT. (101)	41.4	52.5	51.7	56.4	56.7	51.0	98	109	110	99
FEDERAL GOVERNMENT (100,103)	10.3	11.6	11.4	12.5	12.6	11.3	98	109	110	99
TOTAL JOBS	274.2	356.4	347.9	401.4	406.7	339.0	98	115	117	97
CIVILIAN PERSONS EMPLOYED	253.9	330.1	322.3	371.3	376.3	314.1	98	115	117	97
CIVILIAN UNEMPLOYMENT RATE	5.8	3.0	2.9	2.0	2.2	3.3	98	106	111	100
POPULATION	753.4	849.7	829.1	882.2	919.0	826.2	98	106	111	97
PER CAPITA INCOME	2737.8	4996.0	4936.1	5676.1	5589.5	4800.8	99	115	113	97
ENERGY USER SECTOR		(TRILLIONS OF BTU'S)								
NATURAL RESOURCES	16.5	14.1	13.5	14.0	15.7	12.8	96	104	116	95
CONSTRUCTION	11.8	20.1	19.9	24.0	51.3	12.9	99	120	258	65
MANUFACTURING	15.3	35.9	33.9	41.8	44.1	31.2	94	123	130	92
TRANSPORTATION INDUSTRY	2.8	5.1	4.3	9.0	8.5	3.5	85	207	196	81
PUBLIC UTILITIES	57.2	111.1	106.3	233.7	187.6	95.4	96	220	176	90
TRADE AND SERVICES	19.0	39.1	37.7	46.9	45.2	36.3	96	124	120	96
GOVERNMENT, EXC. TRANSPORTATION	3.7	5.2	5.2	5.7	5.7	5.1	98	110	111	99
CONSUMERS, EXC. TRANSPORTATION	33.9	69.0	67.7	75.4	76.5	66.6	98	111	113	98
USER-OPERATED TRANSPORTATION	44.3	89.9	87.8	99.8	101.4	86.1	98	114	115	98
TRANSPORTATION AIR POLLUTION		(THOUSANDS OF TONS)								
SULFUR OXIDES	2.1	2.6	2.4	3.3	3.3	2.2	94	138	136	93
PARTICULATE MATTER	1.8	2.6	2.5	3.1	3.1	2.4	96	123	123	96
CARBON MONOXIDE	374.0	665.7	650.7	740.4	751.1	637.9	98	114	115	98
HYDROCARBONS	66.8	116.1	113.5	129.0	130.9	111.3	98	114	115	98
NITROGEN OXIDES	38.3	59.0	57.5	66.8	67.4	56.1	97	116	117	98
OTHER AIR POLLUTION										
SULFUR OXIDES	102.4	190.0	182.1	392.0	316.2	164.0	96	215	174	90
PARTICULATE MATTER	57.6	66.5	65.1	121.7	101.1	61.4	98	187	155	94
CARBON MONOXIDE	94.2	62.4	64.1	62.1	63.4	65.4	103	97	99	102
HYDROCARBONS	23.7	27.5	23.3	30.7	46.3	21.8	85	132	199	94
NITROGEN OXIDES	30.3	50.2	48.4	99.9	81.3	44.1	96	206	168	91
WATER OXYGEN DEMAND	807.5	1314.8	1313.6	1320.6	1317.9	1313.6	100	100	100	100
LAND SOLID WASTE	595.2	671.2	655.0	697.0	726.0	652.7	98	106	111	100

54 LOUISVILLE, KY.-IND.

	1970	1990 BASE YEAR	1990 COMPLETED INTERSTATE	1990 EXTENDED PRIMARY	1990 ECONOMIC DEVELOPMENT	1990 URBAN	CI/BY	EP/CI	ED/CI	U/CI
			(THOUSANDS)				P E R C E N T			
JOBS BY INDUSTRY										
NATURAL RESOURCES (1-10)	27.7	15.0	14.7	14.4	14.4	15.1	98	98	98	102
CONSTRUCTION (11-12)	21.6	28.4	28.6	27.9	27.2	28.8	101	97	95	101
MANUFACTURING (13-74)	143.3	161.1	161.9	154.6	157.3	160.7	101	95	97	99
TRANSPORTATION INDUSTRY (75)	18.3	30.7	30.7	30.4	30.5	30.6	100	99	99	100
PUBLIC UTILITIES (76-80)	9.5	2.5	2.2	2.2	2.2	2.5	91	98	99	110
TRADE (81,86,89-99)	110.9	101.3	100.8	95.1	96.6	100.5	99	94	96	100
SERVICES (82-85,87,88,102)	98.0	137.8	137.8	137.5	137.6	137.8	100	100	100	100
STATE & LOCAL GOVT. (101)	47.4	51.2	51.3	50.1	50.5	51.2	100	98	98	100
FEDERAL GOVERNMENT (100,103)	43.5	42.9	43.0	42.7	42.8	42.9	100	99	100	100
TOTAL JOBS	520.4	570.9	570.9	554.8	559.2	570.0	100	97	98	100
CIVILIAN PERSONS EMPLOYED	488.1	539.1	539.2	523.9	528.1	538.3	100	97	98	100
CIVILIAN UNEMPLOYMENT RATE	3.8	6.8	5.8	5.8	6.6	6.7				
POPULATION	1220.9	1597.8	1584.5	1540.2	1566.9	1593.9	99	97	99	101
PER CAPITA INCOME	3699.9	4936.3	4982.9	4984.6	4949.5	4942.3	101	100	99	99
ENERGY USER SECTOR			(TRILLIONS OF BTU'S)							
NATURAL RESOURCES	10.8	12.2	12.0	11.3	11.4	12.1	99	94	94	101
CONSTRUCTION	18.2	26.3	26.3	22.6	23.6	26.7	100	86	90	101
MANUFACTURING	81.1	171.7	171.7	168.2	170.8	169.8	100	98	99	99
TRANSPORTATION INDUSTRY	20.6	41.5	41.4	39.8	40.3	41.3	100	96	97	100
PUBLIC UTILITIES	143.5	86.0	84.4	84.8	85.9	82.5	98	101	102	98
TRADE AND SERVICES	42.5	82.6	82.3	79.8	80.6	82.3	100	97	98	100
GOVERNMENT. EXC. TRANSPORTATION	3.4	4.6	4.6	4.5	4.5	4.6	100	98	98	100
CONSUMERS. EXC. TRANSPORTATION	42.0	69.0	69.1	67.2	67.9	69.0	100	97	98	100
USER-OPERATED TRANSPORTATION	99.3	182.8	182.9	180.0	181.0	182.6	100	98	99	100
TRANSPORTATION AIR POLLUTION			(THOUSANDS OF TONS)							
SULFUR OXIDES	5.5	9.9	9.8	9.5	9.6	9.8	99	96	94	100
PARTICULATE MATTER	4.0	7.0	7.0	6.8	6.9	7.0	100	98	90	100
CARBON MONOXIDE	769.8	1386.4	1386.6	1363.4	1371.3	1385.1	100	98	99	100
HYDROCARBONS	134.5	240.5	240.5	236.4	237.8	240.2	100	98	99	100
NITROGEN OXIDES	75.2	131.9	132.1	129.8	130.5	132.0	100	98	99	100
OTHER AIR POLLUTION										
SULFUR OXIDES	262.1	185.2	182.3	181.5	183.6	179.6	98	100	101	99
PARTICULATE MATTER	157.1	175.1	172.1	158.6	160.2	173.8	98	92	93	101
CARBON MONOXIDE	90.1	81.0	80.4	75.6	75.3	80.4	99	94	94	100
HYDROCARBONS	179.2	254.2	262.1	270.2	289.3	235.6	103	103	110	90
NITROGEN OXIDES	76.6	63.1	62.2	60.9	61.5	61.7	99	98	99	99
WATER OXYGEN DEMAND	849.7	1707.0	1700.0	1680.8	1682.9	1704.1	100	100	99	100
LAND SOLID WASTE	964.5	1262.2	1251.8	1216.8	1237.9	1259.1	99	97	99	101

55 EVANSVILLE, IND.-KY.

	1970	1990 BASE YEAR	1990 COMPLETED INTERSTATE	1990 EXTENDED PRIMARY	1990 ECONOMIC DEVELOPMENT	1990 URBAN	PER CENT CI/BY	EP/CI	ED/CI	U/CI
JOBS BY INDUSTRY			(THOUSANDS)							
NATURAL RESOURCES (1-10)	37.1	10.3	10.6	11.6	11.8	10.6	103	110	111	100
CONSTRUCTION (11-12)	13.5	16.0	16.1	16.2	17.1	16.1	101	101	106	100
MANUFACTURING (13-74)	75.7	134.4	130.4	138.4	141.3	128.0	97	106	108	98
TRANSPORTATION INDUSTRY (75)	7.4	4.1	4.0	4.8	5.0	3.8	96	120	128	97
PUBLIC UTILITIES (76-80)	6.0	3.4	3.9	11.3	13.7	3.5	114	292	352	90
TRADE (81,86,89-99)	59.2	84.5	81.2	94.2	98.9	78.8	96	116	122	97
SERVICES (82-85,87,88,102)	50.4	88.4	87.2	87.7	88.0	87.1	99	101	101	100
STATE & LOCAL GOVT. (101)	29.5	35.9	35.2	38.2	39.2	34.7	98	109	111	99
FEDERAL GOVERNMENT (100,103)	11.1	12.1	11.9	12.6	12.8	11.8	99	106	108	99
TOTAL JOBS	289.8	389.1	380.4	414.9	427.7	374.4	98	109	112	98
CIVILIAN PERSONS EMPLOYED	286.9	382.3	374.0	407.0	419.3	368.3	98	109	112	98
CIVILIAN UNEMPLOYMENT RATE	4.2	4.5	4.5	4.5	4.5	4.5				
POPULATION	771.0	875.7	854.5	927.9	951.5	850.2	98	109	111	100
PER CAPITA INCOME	3096.7	5948.1	5930.1	6076.6	6156.5	5850.0	100	102	104	99
ENERGY USER SECTOR			(TRILLIONS OF BTU'S)							
NATURAL RESOURCES	27.5	50.7	50.9	51.7	52.0	51.0	100	102	102	100
CONSTRUCTION	13.5	23.5	23.4	27.3	28.9	20.3	100	116	123	87
MANUFACTURING	29.5	73.9	70.6	75.9	77.7	69.2	95	108	110	98
TRANSPORTATION INDUSTRY	6.0	15.8	14.9	18.3	19.6	14.2	94	123	132	96
PUBLIC UTILITIES	43.6	78.0	92.1	189.0	222.3	84.0	118	205	241	91
TRADE AND SERVICES	23.1	59.0	57.2	65.6	68.5	56.0	97	115	120	98
GOVERNMENT, EXC. TRANSPORTATION	32.4	43.1	43.1	43.4	43.5	43.0	100	101	101	100
CONSUMERS, EXC. TRANSPORTATION	33.8	69.6	68.4	73.3	75.1	67.6	98	107	110	99
USER-OPERATED TRANSPORTATION	50.3	105.0	103.0	110.6	113.5	101.8	98	107	110	99
TRANSPORTATION AIR POLLUTION			(THOUSANDS OF TONS)							
SULFUR OXIDES	3.1	7.5	7.3	8.0	8.3	7.2	97	109	113	98
PARTICULATE MATTER	2.4	5.6	5.5	5.9	6.1	5.4	98	107	110	99
CARBON MONOXIDE	439.4	961.0	946.7	1005.5	1027.9	937.2	99	106	109	99
HYDROCARBONS	79.0	173.7	171.2	181.4	185.2	169.6	99	106	108	99
NITROGEN OXIDES	47.7	108.4	107.0	113.6	115.8	106.0	99	106	108	99
OTHER AIR POLLUTION										
SULFUR OXIDES	85.7	188.3	211.4	370.1	424.7	198.0	112	175	201	94
PARTICULATE MATTER	110.7	222.7	230.4	274.9	289.5	227.0	103	119	126	98
CARBON MONOXIDE	214.8	559.9	561.4	569.1	569.9	562.1	100	101	102	100
HYDROCARBONS	75.5	179.0	180.6	188.9	189.4	179.8	101	105	105	100
NITROGEN OXIDES	30.0	77.4	83.3	122.8	136.2	80.0	108	147	164	96
WATER OXYGEN DEMAND	934.1	1983.3	1988.1	2006.0	2011.4	1986.9	100	101	101	100
LAND SOLID WASTE	609.1	691.8	674.7	733.0	751.7	671.6	98	109	111	100

SUMMARY PROJECTIONS BY ORE ECONOMIC AREA UNDER FIVE ALTERNATIVE HIGHWAY SYSTEMS

58 CHAMPAIGN-URBANA, ILL.

	1970	1990 BASE YEAR	1990 COMPLETED INTERSTATE	1990 EXTENDED PRIMARY	1990 ECONOMIC DEVELOPMENT	1990 URBAN	CI/BY	EP/CI	ED/CI	U/CI
							|———— PER CENT ————|			
JOBS BY INDUSTRY			(THOUSANDS)							
NATURAL RESOURCES (1-10)	10.4	3.3	3.3	3.3	3.3	3.3	101	99	99	100
CONSTRUCTION (11,12)	5.5	6.4	6.4	6.2	6.1	6.4	100	99	99	100
MANUFACTURING (13-74)	30.9	32.2	32.5	31.6	32.0	31.6	101	97	98	97
TRANSPORTATION INDUSTRY (75)	4.5	5.0	5.0	4.9	4.9	4.9	99	98	99	97
PUBLIC UTILITIES (76-80)	3.1	2.8	2.3	1.9	2.0	2.1	81	85	88	92
TRADE (81,86,89-99)	30.5	33.7	33.0	31.3	31.5	32.3	98	95	96	98
SERVICES (82-85,87,88,102)	25.0	55.7	55.7	55.6	55.6	55.7	100	100	100	100
STATE & LOCAL GOVT. (101)	27.0	29.3	29.2	28.9	28.9	29.0	100	100	100	100
FEDERAL GOVERNMENT (100,103)	16.1	15.3	15.3	15.2	15.2	15.2	100	100	100	100
TOTAL JOBS	153.1	183.7	182.6	178.9	179.5	180.5	99	98	98	99
CIVILIAN PERSONS EMPLOYED	129.6	158.1	157.1	153.8	154.4	155.2	99	98	98	99
CIVILIAN UNEMPLOYMENT RATE	4.4	1.4	1.3	1.3	1.4	1.4				
POPULATION	390.4	431.6	427.9	423.7	424.1	428.2	99	99	99	100
PER CAPITA INCOME	3907.9	5769.2	5773.3	5701.9	5714.3	5688.0	100	99	99	98
ENERGY USER SECTOR			(TRILLIONS OF BTU'S)							
NATURAL RESOURCES	22.2	59.6	59.5	59.3	59.3	59.5	100	100	100	100
CONSTRUCTION	5.7	8.7	8.4	7.3	7.4	7.6	96	87	89	90
MANUFACTURING	17.8	30.7	30.6	29.7	30.0	30.0	100	97	98	98
TRANSPORTATION INDUSTRY	2.9	6.9	6.7	6.3	6.4	6.5	97	94	95	96
PUBLIC UTILITIES	30.4	80.5	45.3	24.4	26.5	33.2	56	54	58	73
TRADE AND SERVICES	17.7	42.2	41.9	41.2	41.3	41.4	99	98	99	99
GOVERNMENT, EXC. TRANSPORTATION	1.2	1.5	1.4	1.4	1.4	1.4	99	98	98	99
CONSUMERS, EXC. TRANSPORTATION	14.7	22.8	22.6	22.2	22.2	22.3	99	98	98	99
USER-OPERATED TRANSPORTATION	24.9	40.9	40.6	39.9	40.0	40.2	99	98	98	99
TRANSPORTATION AIR POLLUTION			(THOUSANDS OF TONS)							
SULFUR OXIDES	2.6	6.6	6.5	6.4	6.5	6.5	99	98	99	99
PARTICULATE MATTER	1.9	4.6	4.5	4.5	4.5	4.5	99	99	99	99
CARBON MONOXIDE	280.4	581.6	579.1	572.6	573.5	575.3	99	98	99	99
HYDROCARBONS	52.4	111.2	110.8	109.6	109.8	110.1	100	99	99	99
NITROGEN OXIDES	36.3	84.2	83.9	83.2	83.3	83.5	100	99	99	99
OTHER AIR POLLUTION										
SULFUR OXIDES	61.6	165.2	106.5	70.5	74.1	86.4	64	66	70	81
PARTICULATE MATTER	55.5	147.5	131.0	116.6	117.7	125.3	89	89	90	96
CARBON MONOXIDE	175.1	455.3	455.2	453.4	453.4	454.7	100	100	100	100
HYDROCARBONS	42.8	101.8	101.4	100.7	100.7	101.2	100	99	99	100
NITROGEN OXIDES	19.4	55.3	40.7	31.3	32.2	35.8	74	77	79	88
WATER OXYGEN DEMAND	394.6	774.5	771.0	766.5	768.6	770.2	100	99	99	100
LAND SOLID WASTE	308.4	341.0	338.0	334.8	335.0	338.3	99	99	99	98

SUMMARY PROJECTIONS BY ORE ECONOMIC AREA UNDER FIVE ALTERNATIVE HIGHWAY SYSTEMS

59 LAFAY-W. LAFAY, IND.

	1970	1990 BASE YEAR	1990 COMPLETED INTERSTATE	1990 EXTENDED PRIMARY	1990 ECONOMIC DEVELOPMENT	1990 URBAN	PERCENT CI/BY	PERCENT EP/CI	PERCENT ED/CI	PERCENT U/CI
JOBS BY INDUSTRY		(THOUSANDS)								
NATURAL RESOURCES (1-10)	8.0	2.1	2.1	2.1	2.1	2.1	100	101	100	100
CONSTRUCTION (11-12)	3.1	4.1	4.1	4.1	3.7	4.1	100	101	90	100
MANUFACTURING (13-74)	24.5	45.5	44.8	46.4	44.2	44.5	99	103	99	99
TRANSPORTATION INDUSTRY (75)	2.6	1.4	1.4	1.5	1.4	1.4	97	107	97	99
PUBLIC UTILITIES (76-80)	1.5	.6	.6	.6	.6	.6	93	103	104	96
TRADE (81,86,89-99)	20.4	30.4	29.7	31.3	29.3	29.4	98	105	98	99
SERVICES (82-85,87,88,102)	15.1	23.4	23.3	23.4	23.2	23.3	100	101	100	100
STATE & LOCAL GOVT. (101)	17.0	19.3	19.2	19.5	19.0	19.1	99	102	99	100
FEDERAL GOVERNMENT (100,103)	1.2	.8	.8	.8	.7	.8	96	110	94	98
TOTAL JOBS	93.4	127.6	125.9	129.8	124.1	125.1	99	103	99	99
CIVILIAN PERSONS EMPLOYED	94.2	127.4	125.7	129.5	124.0	125.0	99	103	99	99
CIVILIAN UNEMPLOYMENT RATE	3.2	.8	.8	.8	.8	.8				
POPULATION	250.8	317.3	315.1	325.1	310.8	315.3	99	103	99	99
PER CAPITA INCOME	3684.4	5832.4	5780.0	5912.3	5727.6	5742.9	99	101	100	99
ENERGY USER SECTOR		(TRILLIONS OF BTUS)								
NATURAL RESOURCES	10.9	27.4	27.3	27.5	27.2	27.2	100	101	100	100
CONSTRUCTION	4.2	6.7	6.6	7.6	6.0	5.9	98	114	91	89
MANUFACTURING	13.1	31.3	30.9	32.1	30.6	30.6	99	104	99	99
TRANSPORTATION INDUSTRY	12.4	4.4	4.2	4.6	4.1	4.1	95	110	97	98
PUBLIC UTILITIES	12.9	8.9	8.2	8.3	8.4	8.0	92	101	102	98
TRADE AND SERVICES	7.8	17.1	16.7	17.4	16.5	16.6	98	104	99	99
GOVERNMENT, EXC. TRANSPORTATION	10.7	20.3	20.0	20.6	19.7	19.9	98	105	97	99
CONSUMERS, EXC. TRANSPORTATION	16.2	31.4	31.0	31.9	30.5	30.8	99	103	98	100
USER-OPERATED TRANSPORTATION										
TRANSPORTATION AIR POLLUTION		(THOUSANDS OF TONS)								
SULFUR OXIDES	1.3	3.3	3.2	3.3	3.2	3.2	98	103	99	99
PARTICULATE MATTER	1.0	2.4	2.4	2.4	2.3	2.3	99	102	99	100
CARBON MONOXIDE	161.7	351.8	348.4	356.2	344.2	347.1	99	102	99	100
HYDROCARBONS	29.7	65.5	64.9	66.2	64.1	64.6	99	102	99	100
NITROGEN OXIDES	19.5	45.2	44.8	45.8	44.4	44.7	99	102	99	100
OTHER AIR POLLUTION										
SULFUR OXIDES	28.2	38.7	36.5	38.1	35.9	35.9	94	104	98	98
PARTICULATE MATTER	34.0	71.3	68.5	73.9	66.4	67.3	96	108	97	98
CARBON MONOXIDE	83.3	210.3	210.4	211.5	209.7	209.9	100	101	100	100
HYDROCARBONS	19.6	54.6	55.3	58.7	54.1	52.2	101	106	98	94
NITROGEN OXIDES	8.6	14.4	13.7	14.6	13.3	13.4	95	107	98	98
WATER OXYGEN DEMAND	444.0	884.5	880.4	887.2	878.0	878.9	100	101	100	100
LAND SOLID WASTE	198.1	250.7	249.0	256.8	245.6	249.1	99	103	99	100

SUMMARY PROJECTIONS BY ORE ECONOMIC AREA UNDER FIVE ALTERNATIVE HIGHWAY SYSTEMS

60   INDIANAPOLIS, IND.

	1970	1990 BASE YEAR	1990 COMPLETED INTERSTATE	1990 EXTENDED PRIMARY	1990 ECONOMIC DEVELOPMENT	1990 URBAN	PERCENT CI/BY	EP/CI	ED/CI	U/CI
JOBS BY INDUSTRY		(THOUSANDS)								
NATURAL RESOURCES (1-10)	24.1	7.8	7.4	7.2	6.8	7.1	94	99	93	97
CONSTRUCTION (11,12)	31.0	40.9	41.2	40.1	38.9	41.0	101	97	94	100
MANUFACTURING (13-74)	203.2	281.7	271.8	264.8	256.7	252.8	96	97	94	93
TRANSPORTATION INDUSTRY (75)	22.3	20.7	20.4	20.1	19.7	19.9	96	99	96	98
PUBLIC UTILITIES (76-80)	13.9	5.7	4.9	4.4	3.2	4.0	86	89	64	80
TRADE (81,86,89-99)	158.5	260.9	254.4	250.8	243.2	245.6	98	99	96	97
SERVICES (82-85,87,88,102)	129.1	313.6	313.2	313.0	312.2	312.8	100	100	100	100
STATE & LOCAL GOVT. (101)	84.2	108.4	106.4	105.2	103.2	103.3	98	99	97	97
FEDERAL GOVERNMENT (100,103)	26.2	28.9	28.4	28.1	27.7	27.7	98	99	97	98
TOTAL JOBS	692.5	1068.7	1048.1	1033.8	1012.0	1014.3	98	99	97	97
CIVILIAN PERSONS EMPLOYED	732.4	1104.8	1084.9	1071.6	1051.0	1052.5	98	99	97	97
CIVILIAN UNEMPLOYMENT RATE	2.6									
POPULATION	1613.2	2200.9	2176.3	2184.5	2160.9	2172.3	99	100	99	100
PER CAPITA INCOME	3980.9	7117.7	7089.2	6949.1	6849.8	6832.5	99	98	97	96
ENERGY USER SECTOR		(TRILLIONS OF BTU'S)								
NATURAL RESOURCES	19.1	51.6	51.3	51.2	50.9	51.2	99	100	99	100
CONSTRUCTION	37.4	76.1	75.1	68.6	58.9	59.5	99	91	78	79
MANUFACTURING	83.0	176.9	173.4	169.5	166.4	164.1	98	98	96	95
TRANSPORTATION INDUSTRY	29.8	68.9	67.0	66.1	64.0	64.6	97	99	96	96
PUBLIC UTILITIES	113.3	221.8	189.2	179.7	112.5	169.0	85	95	59	89
TRADE AND SERVICES	77.1	186.2	182.0	180.2	174.6	177.3	98	99	96	97
GOVERNMENT, EXC. TRANSPORTATION	5.7	9.4	9.2	9.0	8.8	8.8	98	99	96	96
CONSUMERS, EXC. TRANSPORTATION	81.5	176.1	172.9	170.9	167.7	168.0	98	99	97	97
USER-OPERATED TRANSPORTATION	134.8	302.3	297.4	294.2	289.2	289.7	98	99	97	97
TRANSPORTATION AIR POLLUTION		(THOUSANDS OF TONS)								
SULFUR OXIDES	8.1	19.1	18.6	18.4	18.0	18.1	98	99	96	97
PARTICULATE MATTER	5.7	13.4	13.1	13.0	12.8	12.8	98	99	97	98
CARBON MONOXIDE	1050.5	2420.4	2383.9	2360.7	2322.5	2327.2	98	99	97	98
HYDROCARBONS	184.4	425.9	419.5	415.3	408.8	409.6	98	99	97	98
NITROGEN OXIDES	106.1	248.0	244.8	243.1	238.7	239.2	99	99	98	98
OTHER AIR POLLUTION										
SULFUR OXIDES	370.4	749.2	695.1	679.7	567.5	661.7	93	98	82	95
PARTICULATE MATTER	211.1	385.5	372.7	369.8	342.9	365.0	97	99	92	98
CARBON MONOXIDE	326.8	500.5	497.4	496.9	493.3	496.1	99	100	99	100
HYDROCARBONS	130.8	241.9	234.5	203.4	196.3	178.5	97	87	84	76
NITROGEN OXIDES	92.6	265.6	252.1	248.3	220.4	243.8	95	98	87	97
WATER OXYGEN DEMAND	1128.7	2162.3	2157.5	2157.6	2146.9	2155.5	100	100	100	100
LAND SOLID WASTE	1274.4	1738.7	1719.3	1725.8	1707.1	1716.1	99	100	99	100

SUMMARY PROJECTIONS BY ORE ECONOMIC AREA UNDER FIVE ALTERNATIVE HIGHWAY SYSTEMS

61 MUNCIE, IND.

	1970	1990 BASE YEAR	1990 COMPLETED INTERSTATE	1990 EXTENDED PRIMARY	1990 ECONOMIC DEVELOPMENT	1990 URBAN	CI/BY	EP/CI	ED/CI	U/CI
							PERCENT			
JOBS BY INDUSTRY			(THOUSANDS)							
NATURAL RESOURCES (1-10)	10.2	2.4	2.4	2.4	2.4	2.4	100	100	99	100
CONSTRUCTION (11-12)	6.6	8.9	8.9	8.7	8.9	8.9	98	98	95	100
MANUFACTURING (13-74)	91.2	104.3	103.6	104.6	104.1	101.4	99	101	100	98
TRANSPORTATION INDUSTRY (75)	4.0	6.6	6.6	6.6	6.5	6.5	99	101	100	98
PUBLIC UTILITIES (76-80)	2.7	.2	.2	.2	.2	.2	96	104	107	95
TRADE (81,86,89-99)	42.5	64.9	64.3	64.9	64.3	63.1	99	101	100	98
SERVICES (82-85,87,88,102)	31.8	60.6	60.5	60.5	60.4	60.1	100	100	100	100
STATE & LOCAL GOVT. (101)	22.0	25.2	25.2	25.2	25.1	24.8	99	101	100	99
FEDERAL GOVERNMENT (100,103)	2.8	2.5	2.5	2.5	2.5	2.4	99	101	100	97
TOTAL JOBS	213.9	275.7	274.0	275.7	273.9	270.1	99	101	100	99
CIVILIAN PERSONS EMPLOYED	219.4	280.7	279.0	280.7	279.0	275.3	99	101	100	99
CIVILIAN UNEMPLOYMENT RATE	3.2	1.5	1.7	1.5	2.0	2.0				
POPULATION	551.7	681.5	678.4	679.3	676.8	680.6	100	100	100	100
PER CAPITA INCOME	3739.3	6653.2	6646.5	6667.8	6650.6	6543.0	100	100	100	98
ENERGY USER SECTOR			(TRILLIONS OF BTU'S)							
NATURAL RESOURCES	7.8	20.0	19.9	19.9	19.6	19.8	100	100	99	100
CONSTRUCTION	7.4	12.3	12.2	11.4	9.7	9.7	99	93	80	80
MANUFACTURING	47.6	95.3	94.8	95.6	94.7	93.6	99	101	100	99
TRANSPORTATION INDUSTRY	4.6	9.3	9.2	9.3	9.1	8.9	98	101	99	97
PUBLIC UTILITIES	15.2	9.2	8.8	8.9	9.0	8.6	95	101	98	98
TRADE AND SERVICES	13.8	26.3	26.3	26.5	26.2	25.9	99	101	100	99
GOVERNMENT, EXC. TRANSPORTATION	1.6	2.4	2.4	2.4	2.4	2.4	99	101	100	99
CONSUMERS, EXC. TRANSPORTATION	23.9	47.5	47.6	47.8	47.6	47.2	100	100	100	99
USER-OPERATED TRANSPORTATION	34.3	71.5	71.6	71.4	71.0	70.5	100	100	100	99
TRANSPORTATION AIR POLLUTION			(THOUSANDS OF TONS)							
SULFUR OXIDES	1.8	4.0	3.9	3.9	3.9	3.9	99	100	99	99
PARTICULATE MATTER	1.4	3.1	3.1	3.1	3.1	3.0	99	100	99	99
CARBON MONOXIDE	274.9	597.8	594.8	596.5	592.6	589.7	99	100	100	99
HYDROCARBONS	48.7	106.5	105.9	106.2	105.5	105.0	99	100	100	99
NITROGEN OXIDES	27.9	62.1	61.8	62.0	61.5	61.3	100	100	100	98
OTHER AIR POLLUTION										
SULFUR OXIDES	68.8	125.4	124.0	124.0	122.8	123.5	99	100	99	100
PARTICULATE MATTER	63.9	130.4	125.9	125.4	115.1	129.1	97	100	91	99
CARBON MONOXIDE	85.4	193.4	192.8	192.7	191.0	192.5	100	100	99	100
HYDROCARBONS	16.1	36.3	36.1	36.1	35.6	35.9	99	100	99	100
NITROGEN OXIDES	11.8	20.5	19.7	19.7	18.6	19.5	96	100	94	99
WATER OXYGEN DEMAND	449.2	897.8	893.2	892.4	882.5	891.6	99	100	99	100
LAND SOLID WASTE	435.9	538.4	535.9	536.7	534.7	537.6	100	100	100	100

62 CIN., OHIO-KY.-IND.

	1970	1990 BASE YEAR	1990 COMPLETED INTERSTATE	1990 EXTENDED PRIMARY	1990 ECONOMIC DEVELOPMENT	1990 URBAN	CI/BY	PERCENT EP/CI	ED/CI	U/CI
JOBS BY INDUSTRY		(THOUSANDS)								
NATURAL RESOURCES (1-10)	29.7	9.7	9.8	9.1	9.7	10.5	101	92	99	107
CONSTRUCTION (11,12)	31.0	38.0	38.2	37.0	36.6	38.5	105	97	96	101
MANUFACTURING (13-74)	223.1	331.4	349.1	333.9	356.4	350.9	105	96	102	101
TRANSPORTATION INDUSTRY (75)	27.4	25.0	25.5	24.4	25.5	25.8	102	96	100	101
PUBLIC UTILITIES (76-80)	14.1	23.5	24.7	17.4	24.6	26.5	105	70	99	107
TRADE (81,86,89-99)	163.5	284.8	294.8	277.5	296.4	298.9	103	94	101	101
SERVICES (82-85,87,88,102)	135.6	257.1	259.4	256.8	257.4	257.6	100	100	100	100
STATE & LOCAL GOVT. (101)	81.7	109.3	112.8	108.5	113.8	113.8	103	96	101	101
FEDERAL GOVERNMENT (100,103)	17.7	21.0	21.8	20.8	22.0	22.0	104	96	101	101
TOTAL JOBS	723.7	1099.8	1134.1	1085.3	1142.6	1144.5	103	96	101	101
CIVILIAN PERSONS EMPLOYED	749.3	1118.7	1151.4	1105.0	1160.0	1161.2	103	96	101	101
CIVILIAN UNEMPLOYMENT RATE	4.2	2.6	2.4	2.7	2.3	2.3				
POPULATION	1889.0	2655.8	2697.2	2668.3	2701.4	2718.4	102	99	100	101
PER CAPITA INCOME	3901.5	6661.9	6779.9	6550.7	6822.2	6792.2	102	97	101	100
ENERGY USER SECTOR		(TRILLIONS OF BTU'S)								
NATURAL RESOURCES	13.5	33.5	34.2	32.8	33.7	34.9	102	96	99	102
CONSTRUCTION	38.8	76.8	81.6	75.4	79.6	87.6	106	92	98	107
MANUFACTURING	128.7	253.4	264.0	255.5	268.0	265.7	104	97	102	101
TRANSPORTATION INDUSTRY	34.3	85.6	88.6	84.0	89.3	89.7	103	95	101	101
PUBLIC UTILITIES	143.4	537.5	561.9	450.7	566.3	590.5	105	80	101	105
TRADE AND SERVICES	93.1	285.2	290.8	280.0	291.9	293.4	102	96	100	100
GOVERNMENT, EXC. TRANSPORTATION	22.2	31.9	32.3	31.8	32.4	32.4	101	99	100	100
CONSUMERS, EXC. TRANSPORTATION	83.8	185.9	190.8	184.0	191.9	192.4	103	96	100	101
USER-OPERATED TRANSPORTATION	155.3	317.0	324.8	314.1	326.5	327.3	102	97	101	101
TRANSPORTATION AIR POLLUTION		(THOUSANDS OF TONS)								
SULFUR OXIDES	8.2	19.9	20.4	19.4	20.5	20.6	103	95	100	101
PARTICULATE MATTER	5.4	12.7	13.1	12.6	13.2	13.2	103	96	101	101
CARBON MONOXIDE	920.2	2110.9	2169.4	2087.7	2181.6	2188.6	103	96	101	101
HYDROCARBONS	160.9	369.0	379.0	364.7	381.0	382.3	103	96	101	101
NITROGEN OXIDES	94.4	219.7	226.4	218.4	228.0	228.4	103	96	101	101
OTHER AIR POLLUTION										
SULFUR OXIDES	329.4	1102.5	1143.3	958.4	1150.8	1191.6	104	84	101	104
PARTICULATE MATTER	169.5	465.9	478.7	421.2	477.1	495.2	103	88	100	103
CARBON MONOXIDE	234.9	563.2	566.6	552.1	559.1	566.7	101	97	99	100
HYDROCARBONS	120.9	306.0	359.0	337.1	380.9	363.4	117	94	107	102
NITROGEN OXIDES	101.0	348.7	359.0	312.7	360.5	370.9	103	87	100	103
WATER OXYGEN DEMAND	825.6	1662.0	1666.8	1644.1	1667.3	1671.4	100	99	100	100
LAND SOLID WASTE	1492.3	2098.1	2130.8	2108.0	2133.8	2147.5	102	99	101	101

SUMMARY PROJECTIONS BY ORE ECONOMIC AREA UNDER FIVE ALTERNATIVE HIGHWAY SYSTEMS

63   DAYTON, OHIO

	1970	1990 BASE YEAR	1990 COMPLETED INTERSTATE	1990 EXTENDED PRIMARY	1990 ECONOMIC DEVELOPMENT	1990 URBAN	CI/BY	EP/CI	ED/CI	U/CI
								P E R C E N T		
JOBS BY INDUSTRY		(THOUSANDS)								
NATURAL RESOURCES (1-10)	14.6	5.0	4.6	3.9	4.0	4.5	91	87	87	99
CONSTRUCTION (11-12)	15.9	21.4	21.4	20.6	20.2	21.4	100	99	95	100
MANUFACTURING (13-74)	167.6	276.3	270.6	267.4	270.6	261.5	98	99	100	97
TRANSPORTATION INDUSTRY (75)	9.8	19.5	19.3	18.8	18.9	19.0	98	98	98	98
PUBLIC UTILITIES (76-80)	8.0	10.0	7.9	3.1	3.5	7.2	79	39	44	91
TRADE (81,86,89-99)	96.9	181.4	176.5	169.2	170.9	171.2	97	96	97	97
SERVICES (82-85,87,88,102)	74.2	105.3	105.1	104.7	104.9	104.9	100	100	100	100
STATE & LOCAL GOVT. (101)	47.5	71.5	70.3	68.6	69.2	68.7	98	98	98	98
FEDERAL GOVERNMENT (100,103)	42.2	48.1	47.8	47.5	47.6	47.5	99	99	99	99
TOTAL JOBS	476.7	738.6	723.5	704.0	709.8	705.8	98	97	98	98
CIVILIAN PERSONS EMPLOYED	429.3	673.5	659.5	642.1	647.6	642.8	98	97	98	97
CIVILIAN UNEMPLOYMENT RATE	3.3	4.0	3.8	4.0	4.3	4.5				
POPULATION	1159.8	1780.0	1769.7	1745.3	1750.9	1768.0	99	99	99	100
PER CAPITA INCOME	3805.3	6577.6	6485.0	6395.0	6429.1	6317.7	99	99	99	97
ENERGY USER SECTOR		(TRILLIONS OF BTU'S)								
NATURAL RESOURCES	11.7	30.5	30.0	29.2	29.2	29.9	98	97	97	100
CONSTRUCTION	19.5	49.0	47.9	42.9	43.4	47.4	98	90	91	99
MANUFACTURING	67.3	146.1	145.2	143.1	144.5	141.2	99	97	100	97
TRANSPORTATION INDUSTRY	14.7	48.7	47.3	45.3	45.8	45.8	96	96	97	94
PUBLIC UTILITIES	87.3	214.4	176.0	78.8	90.0	165.5	82	45	51	98
TRADE AND SERVICES	45.6	166.2	162.8	157.2	158.3	160.3	98	97	97	98
GOVERNMENT. EXC. TRANSPORTATION	5.0	9.2	9.0	8.8	8.9	8.8	98	98	99	98
CONSUMERS. EXC. TRANSPORTATION	45.0	111.7	109.7	106.8	107.6	107.2	98	97	98	98
USER-OPERATED TRANSPORTATION	76.8	185.6	182.4	178.0	179.2	178.6	98	98	98	98
TRANSPORTATION AIR POLLUTION		(THOUSANDS OF TONS)								
SULFUR OXIDES	4.2	12.7	12.3	11.9	12.0	12.1	97	96	97	98
PARTICULATE MATTER	3.0	8.5	8.3	8.1	8.2	8.2	98	97	98	98
CARBON MONOXIDE	575.3	1455.0	1430.9	1396.6	1405.6	1402.4	98	98	98	98
HYDROCARBONS	101.1	256.0	251.7	245.7	247.3	246.8	98	98	98	98
NITROGEN OXIDES	57.9	152.2	150.0	146.6	147.4	147.1	99	98	98	98
OTHER AIR POLLUTION										
SULFUR OXIDES	179.8	502.3	438.7	277.2	295.9	421.2	87	63	67	96
PARTICULATE MATTER	125.9	347.7	327.4	277.7	282.1	323.0	94	85	86	99
CARBON MONOXIDE	192.8	474.7	467.5	460.2	459.3	469.0	98	98	98	100
HYDROCARBONS	91.5	186.7	189.0	186.5	190.8	178.4	101	99	101	94
NITROGEN OXIDES	62.4	196.1	180.1	139.8	144.4	175.9	92	78	80	98
WATER OXYGEN DEMAND	768.3	1582.1	1573.4	1559.0	1560.5	1573.8	99	99	99	100
LAND SOLID WASTE	916.3	1406.2	1398.0	1378.7	1383.2	1396.7	99	99	99	100

SUMMARY PROJECTIONS BY ORE ECONOMIC AREA UNDER FIVE ALTERNATIVE HIGHWAY SYSTEMS

64   COLUMBUS, OHIO

	1970	1990 BASE YEAR (THOUSANDS)	1990 COMPLETED INTERSTATE	1990 EXTENDED PRIMARY	1990 ECONOMIC DEVELOPMENT	1990 URBAN	CI/BY	EP/CI PERCENT	ED/CI	U/CI
JOBS BY INDUSTRY										
NATURAL RESOURCES (1-10)	29.5	12.7	10.2	9.8	10.6	9.3	81	96	103	90
CONSTRUCTION (11-12)	28.4	37.3	37.7	36.4	35.7	37.1	101	97	95	98
MANUFACTURING (13-74)	183.5	259.5	235.4	230.1	237.6	219.6	91	99	101	93
TRANSPORTATION INDUSTRY (75)	21.5	15.9	14.5	14.3	14.9	13.9	91	99	103	95
PUBLIC UTILITIES (76-80)	16.1	23.1	20.4	21.5	26.2	19.1	88	105	128	93
TRADE (81,86,89-99)	153.5	256.3	240.3	238.9	248.4	228.9	94	100	103	95
SERVICES (82-85,87,88,102)	130.4	178.2	177.5	177.5	177.8	177.2	100	100	100	100
STATE & LOCAL GOVT. (101)	92.9	118.7	113.7	113.3	115.2	111.0	96	100	101	98
FEDERAL GOVERNMENT (100,103)	25.5	26.2	25.1	25.0	25.4	24.5	96	100	101	98
TOTAL JOBS	681.4	927.4	874.9	866.9	891.9	840.6	94	99	102	96
CIVILIAN PERSONS EMPLOYED	620.8	849.0	801.0	793.9	817.1	769.3	94	99	102	96
CIVILIAN UNEMPLOYMENT RATE	4.5	3.1	3.0	3.3	2.9	3.6				
POPULATION	1763.0	2268.7	2194.9	2205.8	2205.6	2184.6	97	100	100	100
PER CAPITA INCOME	3429.4	5911.4	5707.6	5621.0	5791.2	5489.2	97	98	101	96
ENERGY USER SECTOR (TRILLIONS OF BTU'S)										
NATURAL RESOURCES	17.8	51.5	47.8	47.0	47.5	46.8	93	98	99	98
CONSTRUCTION	48.4	100.6	98.9	76.7	79.7	69.8	98	78	81	71
MANUFACTURING	119.7	291.9	276.8	273.7	277.7	268.4	95	99	100	97
TRANSPORTATION INDUSTRY	23.9	63.8	59.1	58.8	61.3	56.2	93	99	104	95
PUBLIC UTILITIES	135.4	527.3	487.2	512.0	570.2	475.2	92	105	117	98
TRADE AND SERVICES	68.9	215.4	206.7	206.9	212.5	201.6	96	100	103	98
GOVERNMENT, EXC. TRANSPORTATION	11.0	11.0	10.4	10.4	10.6	10.1	95	100	102	97
CONSUMERS, EXC. TRANSPORTATION	107.3	220.5	213.0	212.1	215.2	208.5	97	100	101	98
USER-OPERATED TRANSPORTATION	121.9	255.9	244.1	242.5	247.4	237.1	95	99	101	97
TRANSPORTATION AIR POLLUTION (THOUSANDS OF TONS)										
SULFUR OXIDES	6.7	17.0	16.0	15.9	16.4	15.4	94	99	102	96
PARTICULATE MATTER	4.9	11.7	11.1	11.1	11.3	10.8	95	100	102	97
CARBON MONOXIDE	944.6	2064.4	1977.3	1965.8	2003.6	1924.1	96	99	101	99
HYDROCARBONS	165.6	363.0	347.9	345.8	352.4	338.7	96	99	101	97
NITROGEN OXIDES	93.4	213.1	204.6	204.0	208.0	199.0	96	100	102	97
OTHER AIR POLLUTION										
SULFUR OXIDES	282.1	969.3	903.1	943.3	1038.0	883.7	93	104	115	98
PARTICULATE MATTER	271.2	696.9	683.0	696.0	721.7	678.6	98	102	106	99
CARBON MONOXIDE	212.9	480.5	488.7	488.5	487.9	490.0	102	100	100	100
HYDROCARBONS	94.4	302.5	210.0	183.1	192.6	172.2	69	87	92	82
NITROGEN OXIDES	93.7	282.1	266.1	276.0	299.3	261.4	94	104	112	98
WATER OXYGEN DEMAND	1083.7	2213.1	2215.4	2218.8	2225.7	2216.1	100	100	100	100
LAND SOLID WASTE	1392.8	1792.3	1733.9	1742.6	1742.4	1725.8	97	100	100	100

SUMMARY PROJECTIONS BY ORE ECONOMIC AREA UNDER FIVE ALTERNATIVE HIGHWAY SYSTEMS

65 CLARKSBURG, W. VA.

	1970	1990 BASE YEAR	1990 COMPLETED INTERSTATE	1990 EXTENDED PRIMARY	1990 ECONOMIC DEVELOPMENT	1990 URBAN	P E R C E N T			
							CI/BY	EP/CI	ED/CI	U/CI
JOBS BY INDUSTRY (THOUSANDS)										
NATURAL RESOURCES (1-10)	16.0	5.6	5.8	6.0	8.1	5.9	104	102	140	101
CONSTRUCTION (11,12)	4.3	4.8	5.0	6.0	12.0	4.8	104	120	239	96
MANUFACTURING (13-74)	21.3	31.0	34.4	37.2	41.9	32.8	111	108	122	96
TRANSPORTATION INDUSTRY (75)	3.4	1.9	2.1	2.3	2.7	2.0	110	111	128	97
PUBLIC UTILITIES (76-80)	4.8	8.8	10.5	13.0	14.4	10.2	119	124	137	97
TRADE (81,86,89-99)	18.9	31.7	35.4	39.1	44.6	34.3	112	110	126	97
SERVICES (82-85,87,88,102)	18.5	33.6	34.8	35.0	35.2	34.3	103	101	101	99
STATE & LOCAL GOVT. (101)	19.1	24.3	25.7	26.9	29.0	25.3	106	105	113	98
FEDERAL GOVERNMENT (100,103)	2.7	3.0	3.3	3.6	4.1	3.2	111	108	122	97
TOTAL JOBS	109.0	144.8	157.1	169.1	191.9	152.9	109	108	122	97
CIVILIAN PERSONS EMPLOYED	100.0	133.6	144.2	155.3	176.1	140.3	108	108	122	97
CIVILIAN UNEMPLOYMENT RATE	5.9	5.9	.6	-.6	1.1	.6				
POPULATION	326.8	351.3	382.4	412.5	471.7	376.2	109	108	123	98
PER CAPITA INCOME	2683.1	5427.0	5665.3	5793.2	5983.3	5537.6	104	102	106	98
ENERGY USER SECTOR (TRILLIONS OF BTUS)										
NATURAL RESOURCES	15.8	31.9	32.2	32.6	35.2	32.3	101	101	109	100
CONSTRUCTION	6.3	7.0	10.1	13.5	49.9	7.7	143	134	496	76
MANUFACTURING	8.4	19.6	21.1	23.0	24.9	20.4	108	109	118	97
TRANSPORTATION INDUSTRY	7.4	5.8	6.9	7.9	9.3	6.6	118	114	134	96
PUBLIC UTILITIES	54.2	237.6	267.8	294.4	310.4	261.5	113	110	116	98
TRADE AND SERVICES	7.1	19.9	22.2	24.4	27.1	21.6	112	110	122	97
GOVERNMENT, EXC. TRANSPORTATION	3.5	4.7	4.9	5.0	4.8	4.8	103	103	107	99
CONSUMERS, EXC. TRANSPORTATION	16.0	33.1	35.2	37.2	40.8	34.6	107	105	116	98
USER-OPERATED TRANSPORTATION	17.0	35.7	39.0	42.0	47.6	38.0	109	108	122	97
TRANSPORTATION AIR POLLUTION (THOUSANDS OF TONS)										
SULFUR OXIDES	1.4	3.6	3.8	4.0	4.3	3.7	106	105	114	98
PARTICULATE MATTER	1.0	2.5	2.7	2.8	3.0	2.6	106	105	113	98
CARBON MONOXIDE	166.7	380.3	405.4	427.6	468.6	397.8	107	105	116	98
HYDROCARBONS	30.5	70.3	74.7	78.5	85.6	73.3	106	105	115	98
NITROGEN OXIDES	19.7	47.8	50.4	52.7	56.6	49.7	105	105	112	99
OTHER AIR POLLUTION										
SULFUR OXIDES	94.3	402.1	451.0	494.1	520.0	440.7	112	110	115	98
PARTICULATE MATTER	35.6	114.4	124.7	136.7	142.7	122.6	109	110	114	98
CARBON MONOXIDE	72.1	187.8	188.0	189.5	190.0	188.6	100	100	101	100
HYDROCARBONS	16.7	44.6	49.8	56.8	59.3	47.3	112	114	119	95
NITROGEN OXIDES	24.9	100.0	111.9	122.3	128.6	109.4	112	109	115	98
WATER OXYGEN DEMAND	542.7	1114.7	1118.6	1121.6	1123.2	1118.5	100	100	100	100
LAND SOLID WASTE	258.2	277.5	302.1	325.9	372.6	297.2	109	108	123	98

SUMMARY PROJECTIONS BY ORE ECONOMIC AREA UNDER FIVE ALTERNATIVE HIGHWAY SYSTEMS

66 PITTSBURGH, PA.

	1970	1990 BASE YEAR	1990 COMPLETED INTERSTATE	1990 EXTENDED PRIMARY	1990 ECONOMIC DEVELOPMENT	1990 URBAN	P E R C E N T			
							CI/BY	EP/CI	ED/CI	U/CI
JOBS BY INDUSTRY			(THOUSANDS)							
NATURAL RESOURCES (1-10)	60.0	27.7	28.8	30.1	25.7	27.5	104	105	89	96
CONSTRUCTION (11-12)	63.6	62.6	63.0	61.5	59.3	63.1	101	98	94	100
MANUFACTURING (13-74)	418.7	443.2	445.5	463.0	443.4	433.1	101	104	100	97
TRANSPORTATION INDUSTRY (75)	57.5	51.7	51.8	52.4	51.3	51.4	101	101	99	99
PUBLIC UTILITIES (76-80)	30.8	30.9	31.0	35.6	26.2	29.0	100	115	84	94
TRADE (81,86,89-99)	300.9	367.3	368.1	379.3	360.1	362.0	100	103	98	98
SERVICES (82-85,87,88,102)	277.1	387.3	387.3	387.7	387.0	387.2	100	100	100	100
STATE & LOCAL GOVT. (101)	150.5	161.9	162.3	165.8	160.2	160.2	100	102	99	99
FEDERAL GOVERNMENT (100,103)	25.7	22.0	22.1	22.9	21.7	21.7	100	104	98	98
TOTAL JOBS	1384.9	1554.5	1560.0	1598.3	1535.0	1535.3	100	102	98	98
CIVILIAN PERSONS EMPLOYED	1346.4	1512.5	1517.7	1554.4	1493.9	1494.0	100	102	98	98
CIVILIAN UNEMPLOYMENT RATE	5.5	2.3	2.5	2.1	2.7	2.8				
POPULATION	3716.2	3783.3	3778.3	3843.9	3767.1	3783.1	100	102	100	100
PER CAPITA INCOME	3657.5	6456.8	6490.1	6541.8	6404.8	6376.8	101	101	99	98
ENERGY USER SECTOR			(TRILLIONS OF BTU'S)							
NATURAL RESOURCES	32.3	82.7	83.8	85.1	79.5	82.9	101	102	95	99
CONSTRUCTION	63.8	113.5	113.9	117.1	101.9	102.3	100	103	89	90
MANUFACTURING	626.1	1186.9	1188.3	1199.8	1187.0	1182.7	100	101	100	100
TRANSPORTATION INDUSTRY	57.2	117.6	117.8	121.0	115.7	116.1	100	103	98	99
PUBLIC UTILITIES	211.1	637.7	630.4	681.8	571.1	606.6	99	108	91	96
TRADE AND SERVICES	144.0	288.2	288.3	295.3	283.0	284.8	100	102	98	99
GOVERNMENT, EXC. TRANSPORTATION	19.6	26.1	26.2	26.6	26.0	26.0	100	101	99	99
CONSUMERS, EXC. TRANSPORTATION	160.5	282.3	283.0	288.3	279.7	279.6	100	102	99	99
USER-OPERATED TRANSPORTATION	215.0	374.6	375.7	383.9	370.5	370.6	100	102	99	99
TRANSPORTATION AIR POLLUTION			(THOUSANDS OF TONS)							
SULFUR OXIDES	13.2	26.7	26.6	27.2	26.1	26.3	100	102	98	98
PARTICULATE MATTER	8.7	17.0	17.1	17.5	16.8	16.9	100	102	99	99
CARBON MONOXIDE	1565.3	2837.7	2848.4	2910.5	2809.1	2810.4	100	102	99	99
HYDROCARBONS	272.2	495.2	496.6	507.1	489.7	490.0	100	102	99	99
NITROGEN OXIDES	155.7	292.7	294.5	301.9	290.8	290.7	101	103	99	99
OTHER AIR POLLUTION										
SULFUR OXIDES	586.0	1697.4	1685.3	1769.6	1588.0	1646.2	99	105	94	98
PARTICULATE MATTER	734.2	1757.7	1756.0	1782.3	1724.5	1745.2	100	101	98	99
CARBON MONOXIDE	1627.3	3539.2	3538.7	3541.2	3517.0	3538.7	100	100	99	100
HYDROCARBONS	378.5	765.1	774.7	843.1	785.7	759.9	101	109	101	98
NITROGEN OXIDES	174.4	581.8	578.8	599.8	554.0	569.3	99	104	96	98
WATER OXYGEN DEMAND	1015.8	2204.8	2203.4	2209.7	2194.8	2203.9	100	100	100	100
LAND SOLID WASTE	2935.8	2988.8	2984.9	3036.7	2976.0	2988.6	100	102	100	100

SUMMARY PROJECTIONS BY ORE ECONOMIC AREA UNDER FIVE ALTERNATIVE HIGHWAY SYSTEMS

67 YOUNGSTOWN-WARREN, OHIO

	1970	1990 BASE YEAR	1990 COMPLETED INTERSTATE	1990 EXTENDED PRIMARY	1990 ECONOMIC DEVELOPMENT	1990 URBAN	PERCENT CI/BY	EP/CI	ED/CI	U/CI
JOBS BY INDUSTRY (THOUSANDS)										
NATURAL RESOURCES (1-10)	7.0	2.8	2.1	1.8	1.8	1.9	77	84	84	91
CONSTRUCTION (11,12)	12.3	12.0	12.1	11.6	11.3	12.0	101	96	93	99
MANUFACTURING (13-74)	118.6	138.6	135.0	130.9	131.8	131.0	97	97	98	97
TRANSPORTATION INDUSTRY (75)	9.9	14.8	14.6	14.5	14.5	14.5	99	99	99	99
PUBLIC UTILITIES (76-80)	4.9	1.9	1.3	.9	.9	.9	65	73	74	70
TRADE (81,86,89-99)	59.7	82.1	79.9	77.5	77.7	78.1	97	97	97	98
SERVICES (82-85,87,88,102)	46.4	74.5	74.4	74.3	74.3	74.4	100	100	100	100
STATE & LOCAL GOVT. (101)	25.1	28.8	28.1	27.4	27.5	27.5	98	97	98	98
FEDERAL GOVERNMENT (100,103)	3.0	2.7	2.5	2.4	2.4	2.4	94	94	95	94
TOTAL JOBS	286.7	358.1	350.2	341.3	342.3	342.7	98	98	98	98
CIVILIAN PERSONS EMPLOYED	278.5	347.6	340.0	331.5	332.6	332.8	98	98	98	98
CIVILIAN UNEMPLOYMENT RATE	3.9	2.2	2.0	2.5	2.5	2.4				
POPULATION	770.6	918.6	907.8	905.3	904.7	909.6	99	100	100	100
PER CAPITA INCOME	3667.1	6299.9	6239.8	6101.4	6122.2	6092.3	99	98	98	98
ENERGY USER SECTOR (TRILLIONS OF BTU'S)										
NATURAL RESOURCES	2.8	6.7	6.1	5.7	5.7	5.9	91	93	93	97
CONSTRUCTION	14.6	28.8	28.6	21.0	21.2	21.3	99	73	74	74
MANUFACTURING	191.0	364.0	362.2	360.4	360.7	360.6	100	100	100	100
TRANSPORTATION INDUSTRY	9.1	23.0	22.3	21.7	21.8	21.8	97	97	98	98
PUBLIC UTILITIES	53.1	32.0	31.2	31.2	31.7	30.3	97	100	102	97
TRADE AND SERVICES	27.8	83.6	82.1	81.0	81.1	81.1	98	99	99	99
GOVERNMENT, EXC. TRANSPORTATION	2.1	3.2	3.1	3.1	3.1	3.1	98	98	98	98
CONSUMERS, EXC. TRANSPORTATION	21.7	39.9	38.8	37.6	37.8	37.8	97	97	97	97
USER-OPERATED TRANSPORTATION	20.1	36.9	35.3	33.4	33.6	33.7	96	95	95	96
TRANSPORTATION AIR POLLUTION (THOUSANDS OF TONS)										
SULFUR OXIDES	1.9	4.6	4.4	4.3	4.3	4.3	97	96	97	97
PARTICULATE MATTER	1.1	2.4	2.4	2.3	2.3	2.3	97	96	97	97
CARBON MONOXIDE	146.6	286.9	274.7	260.0	261.3	262.9	96	95	95	96
HYDROCARBONS	25.6	50.1	48.0	45.4	45.6	46.0	96	95	95	96
NITROGEN OXIDES	16.4	34.8	33.7	32.3	32.4	32.5	97	96	96	96
OTHER AIR POLLUTION										
SULFUR OXIDES	175.2	188.3	186.9	186.2	187.0	185.6	99	100	100	99
PARTICULATE MATTER	201.7	388.7	386.0	379.0	379.8	384.4	99	98	98	100
CARBON MONOXIDE	413.5	777.3	777.0	775.8	775.9	776.8	100	100	100	100
HYDROCARBONS	54.8	111.0	107.3	105.9	105.9	106.2	97	99	99	99
NITROGEN OXIDES	31.4	38.1	37.4	36.7	36.9	37.0	98	98	99	99
WATER OXYGEN DEMAND	180.7	371.2	366.1	356.8	358.0	364.7	99	97	98	100
LAND SOLID WASTE	608.7	725.7	717.2	715.2	714.7	718.6	99	100	100	100

SUMMARY PROJECTIONS BY ORE ECONOMIC AREA UNDER FIVE ALTERNATIVE HIGHWAY SYSTEMS

68   CLEVELAND, OHIO

	1970	1990 BASE YEAR	1990 COMPLETED INTERSTATE	1990 EXTENDED PRIMARY	1990 ECONOMIC DEVELOPMENT	1990 URBAN	PERCENT CI/BY	EP/CI	ED/CI	U/CI
JOBS BY INDUSTRY		(THOUSANDS)								
NATURAL RESOURCES (1-10)	38.5	17.3	16.0	13.2	13.2	15.8	92	83	83	99
CONSTRUCTION (11,12)	68.0	66.3	66.7	63.7	61.9	67.1	101	95	93	101
MANUFACTURING (13-74)	640.4	806.4	790.3	747.5	757.2	775.8	98	95	96	98
TRANSPORTATION INDUSTRY (75)	62.5	87.6	87.0	84.9	85.2	86.9	99	98	98	100
PUBLIC UTILITIES (76-80)	35.2	52.9	50.2	42.1	42.9	51.1	95	84	86	102
TRADE (81,86,89-99)	381.8	657.8	645.0	609.9	615.8	641.9	98	95	95	100
SERVICES (82-85,87,88,102)	307.1	462.1	461.6	460.3	460.6	461.6	100	100	100	100
STATE & LOCAL GOVT. (101)	169.6	227.4	223.7	214.7	216.3	222.2	98	96	97	99
FEDERAL GOVERNMENT (100,103)	31.7	38.1	37.2	35.2	35.6	36.9	98	95	96	99
TOTAL JOBS	1734.8	2416.0	2377.7	2271.5	2288.9	2359.4	98	96	96	99
CIVILIAN PERSONS EMPLOYED	1620.4	2263.4	2227.7	2128.9	2145.5	2209.9	98	96	96	99
CIVILIAN UNEMPLOYMENT RATE	3.7	4.7	5.0	4.9	5.3	5.1				
POPULATION	4255.6	6231.6	6146.4	5960.1	6005.6	6161.4	99	97	98	100
PER CAPITA INCOME	3882.6	6230.9	6213.1	6119.8	6122.3	6143.2	100	98	99	99
ENERGY USER SECTOR		(TRILLIONS OF BTU'S)								
NATURAL RESOURCES	25.4	77.5	74.6	68.9	68.8	75.8	96	92	92	102
CONSTRUCTION	92.1	188.7	187.4	150.0	148.6	192.0	99	80	79	102
MANUFACTURING	460.0	969.8	962.4	936.0	941.6	949.3	99	97	98	99
TRANSPORTATION INDUSTRY	86.5	228.7	224.8	215.4	217.2	223.8	98	96	97	100
PUBLIC UTILITIES	246.8	760.9	711.8	603.2	616.6	736.8	94	85	87	104
TRADE AND SERVICES	208.0	684.4	676.6	658.2	661.5	675.7	99	97	98	100
GOVERNMENT, EXC. TRANSPORTATION	21.0	33.8	33.4	32.4	32.6	33.2	99	97	98	99
CONSUMERS, EXC. TRANSPORTATION	185.6	407.4	401.8	387.3	389.7	399.6	99	96	97	99
USER-OPERATED TRANSPORTATION	257.3	560.3	551.7	528.8	532.5	548.2	98	96	97	99
TRANSPORTATION AIR POLLUTION		(THOUSANDS OF TONS)								
SULFUR OXIDES	19.0	49.0	48.0	45.9	46.4	47.8	98	96	97	100
PARTICULATE MATTER	11.7	29.0	28.6	27.5	27.7	28.5	99	96	97	100
CARBON MONOXIDE	1857.3	4277.3	4213.4	4042.0	4069.4	4189.2	99	96	97	99
HYDROCARBONS	323.8	746.6	735.2	705.3	710.2	731.0	98	96	97	99
NITROGEN OXIDES	195.1	465.4	460.5	444.3	446.4	458.2	99	96	97	99
OTHER AIR POLLUTION										
SULFUR OXIDES	750.0	2003.4	1922.8	1744.0	1765.4	1964.5	96	91	92	102
PARTICULATE MATTER	614.1	1235.5	1216.0	1167.8	1172.9	1223.0	98	96	96	101
CARBON MONOXIDE	755.1	1464.3	1463.3	1459.9	1460.2	1468.5	100	100	100	100
HYDROCARBONS	394.2	859.0	846.6	688.8	717.5	763.3	99	81	85	90
NITROGEN OXIDES	186.0	423.6	403.6	359.3	364.5	414.2	95	89	90	103
WATER OXYGEN DEMAND	1234.3	2494.3	2488.3	2469.9	2470.9	2496.3	100	99	99	100
LAND SOLID WASTE	3361.9	4923.0	4855.7	4708.4	4744.4	4873.0	99	97	98	100

SUMMARY PROJECTIONS BY ORE ECONOMIC AREA UNDER FIVE ALTERNATIVE HIGHWAY SYSTEMS

69 LIMA, OHIO

	1970	1990 BASE YEAR	1990 COMPLETED INTERSTATE	1990 EXTENDED PRIMARY	1990 ECONOMIC DEVELOPMENT	1990 URBAN	CI/BY	EP/CI	ED/CI	U/CI
							P E R C E N T			
JOBS BY INDUSTRY			(THOUSANDS)							
NATURAL RESOURCES (1-10)	9.5	2.5	2.5	2.6	2.8	2.5	98	104	111	99
CONSTRUCTION (11,12)	4.2	4.8	4.8	4.8	5.0	4.8	100	100	103	100
MANUFACTURING (13-74)	35.7	37.8	36.9	38.0	39.9	36.3	98	103	108	98
TRANSPORTATION INDUSTRY (75)	2.7	.9	.9	.9	1.0	.8	99	105	117	98
PUBLIC UTILITIES (76-80)	1.5	1.2	1.5	1.9	3.3	1.2	123	131	221	79
TRADE (81,86,89-99)	21.2	27.2	26.7	27.8	30.5	26.2	98	104	114	98
SERVICES (82-85,87,88,102)	14.1	17.9	17.9	17.9	17.9	17.9	100	100	100	100
STATE & LOCAL GOVT. (101)	10.2	10.4	10.3	10.5	11.1	10.2	99	100	108	99
FEDERAL GOVERNMENT (100,103)	1.0	.6	.5	.5	.6	.5	95	101	121	100
TOTAL JOBS	100.2	103.2	101.9	104.9	112.0	100.4	99	103	110	98
CIVILIAN PERSONS EMPLOYED	98.6	101.7	100.4	103.3	110.1	99.0	99	103	110	99
CIVILIAN UNEMPLOYMENT RATE	4.4	1.5	1.3	1.5	1.5	1.4				
POPULATION	276.2	303.2	298.3	307.7	327.2	296.6	98	103	110	99
PER CAPITA INCOME	3408.8	5456.0	5468.4	5437.7	5467.7	5441.3	100	99	100	100
ENERGY USER SECTOR			(TRILLIONS OF BTU'S)							
NATURAL RESOURCES	8.7	23.1	23.1	23.2	23.4	23.0	100	100	101	100
CONSTRUCTION	4.9	8.4	8.0	8.7	9.4	6.5	95	110	118	82
MANUFACTURING	17.8	35.6	34.7	35.7	36.5	34.3	97	103	105	99
TRANSPORTATION INDUSTRY	2.6	5.6	5.4	5.7	6.4	5.2	97	106	119	97
PUBLIC UTILITIES	13.4	28.3	30.5	38.3	60.4	25.9	108	126	198	85
TRADE AND SERVICES	10.7	27.8	27.8	28.3	29.9	27.2	99	103	108	99
GOVERNMENT, EXC. TRANSPORTATION	1.0	1.3	1.3	1.3	1.4	1.3	99	102	108	99
CONSUMERS, EXC. TRANSPORTATION	11.8	20.5	20.3	20.7	21.6	20.2	99	102	107	99
USER-OPERATED TRANSPORTATION	17.7	31.2	30.9	31.5	33.0	30.7	99	102	107	99
TRANSPORTATION AIR POLLUTION			(THOUSANDS OF TONS)							
SULFUR OXIDES	1.3	3.1	3.0	3.1	3.2	3.0	99	102	107	99
PARTICULATE MATTER	1.0	2.2	2.2	2.2	2.3	2.1	99	102	106	99
CARBON MONOXIDE	159.7	324.0	321.7	326.2	338.4	319.8	99	101	105	99
HYDROCARBONS	29.0	59.8	59.4	60.1	62.3	59.0	99	101	105	99
NITROGEN OXIDES	18.3	40.6	40.4	40.9	42.3	40.1	99	101	105	99
OTHER AIR POLLUTION										
SULFUR OXIDES	27.1	52.7	56.2	68.9	104.8	48.8	107	123	186	87
PARTICULATE MATTER	20.6	47.5	48.4	52.0	59.9	46.8	102	107	124	97
CARBON MONOXIDE	89.3	200.4	202.3	202.2	203.5	201.4	101	100	101	100
HYDROCARBONS	39.1	66.4	65.4	70.1	68.4	64.3	99	107	105	98
NITROGEN OXIDES	8.3	16.9	17.9	20.9	29.7	16.0	105	117	166	90
WATER OXYGEN DEMAND	442.3	897.0	898.2	900.0	906.6	897.5	100	100	101	100
LAND SOLID WASTE	218.2	239.5	235.7	243.1	258.5	234.3	98	103	110	99

SUMMARY PROJECTIONS BY OBE ECONOMIC AREA UNDER FIVE ALTERNATIVE HIGHWAY SYSTEMS

70   TOLEDO, OHIO

	1970	1990 BASE YEAR	1990 COMPLETED INTERSTATE	1990 EXTENDED PRIMARY	1990 ECONOMIC DEVELOPMENT	1990 URBAN	CI/BY	EP/CI	ED/CI	U/CI
JOBS BY INDUSTRY (THOUSANDS)										
NATURAL RESOURCES (1-10)	18.6	5.1	5.1	5.1	5.0	5.0	99	101	98	99
CONSTRUCTION (11,12)	18.5	18.5	18.8	18.3	17.3	18.6	101	98	92	99
MANUFACTURING (13-74)	131.6	180.4	193.6	196.3	178.8	183.3	107	101	92	95
TRANSPORTATION INDUSTRY (75)	13.8	16.3	16.7	16.8	16.0	16.3	103	101	96	98
PUBLIC UTILITIES (76-80)	7.0	4.4	4.7	5.7	3.0	3.6	106	121	64	77
TRADE (81,86,89-99)	90.0	149.6	157.1	159.7	145.5	151.0	105	102	93	96
SERVICES (82-85,87,88,102)	65.8	103.2	104.8	104.8	104.1	104.5	101	100	99	100
STATE & LOCAL GOVT. (101)	43.7	55.7	58.1	58.8	55.1	56.3	104	101	95	97
FEDERAL GOVERNMENT (100,103)	4.1	4.6	5.1	5.3	4.4	4.7	112	103	87	92
TOTAL JOBS	393.1	537.8	563.8	570.9	529.3	543.4	105	101	94	96
CIVILIAN PERSONS EMPLOYED	370.8	507.2	531.6	538.3	499.3	512.3	105	101	94	96
CIVILIAN UNEMPLOYMENT RATE	4.3	1.6	1.7	1.7	1.9	1.7	106	100	112	100
POPULATION	1054.3	1324.4	1385.2	1393.9	1323.0	1359.9	105	101	96	98
PER CAPITA INCOME	3648.2	6516.2	6553.6	6592.2	6419.1	6458.6	101	101	98	99
ENERGY USER SECTOR (TRILLIONS OF BTU'S)										
NATURAL RESOURCES	18.5	48.3	48.1	47.9	47.2	47.4	100	100	98	99
CONSTRUCTION	32.1	63.2	64.9	63.1	53.5	54.3	103	97	83	84
MANUFACTURING	67.6	139.6	143.3	143.5	136.9	137.9	103	100	96	96
TRANSPORTATION INDUSTRY	14.4	40.3	42.5	43.2	39.4	40.8	105	102	93	96
PUBLIC UTILITIES	65.8	123.6	133.8	151.9	82.7	122.2	108	114	62	91
TRADE AND SERVICES	42.5	131.1	134.8	136.5	129.3	131.8	103	101	96	98
GOVERNMENT, EXC. TRANSPORTATION	12.8	18.1	18.3	18.4	18.0	18.1	101	101	98	99
CONSUMERS, EXC. TRANSPORTATION	51.7	106.1	109.9	110.9	105.0	106.9	104	101	95	97
USER-OPERATED TRANSPORTATION	91.1	176.1	182.0	183.5	174.3	177.4	103	101	96	97
TRANSPORTATION AIR POLLUTION (THOUSANDS OF TONS)										
SULFUR OXIDES	4.7	12.4	12.8	12.9	12.2	12.5	103	101	95	98
PARTICULATE MATTER	3.3	8.3	8.6	8.7	8.2	8.4	103	101	95	98
CARBON MONOXIDE	577.3	1302.3	1346.4	1357.8	1287.7	1312.1	103	101	96	97
HYDROCARBONS	102.7	233.2	240.7	242.7	230.5	234.8	103	101	96	98
NITROGEN OXIDES	62.1	148.0	152.8	154.4	146.8	149.3	103	101	96	98
OTHER AIR POLLUTION (THOUSANDS OF TONS)										
SULFUR OXIDES	172.9	371.7	388.4	418.0	304.6	369.6	104	108	78	95
PARTICULATE MATTER	170.4	302.5	306.8	315.3	282.8	304.4	101	103	92	99
CARBON MONOXIDE	205.8	551.8	551.6	551.5	548.4	549.7	100	100	99	100
HYDROCARBONS	127.4	357.3	359.1	350.3	338.2	324.5	101	98	94	90
NITROGEN OXIDES	43.4	97.1	101.3	108.6	80.1	96.4	104	107	79	95
WATER OXYGEN DEMAND	654.9	1338.6	1339.4	1341.3	1332.6	1338.6	100	100	99	100
LAND SOLID WASTE	832.9	1046.2	1094.3	1101.2	1045.2	1067.2	105	101	96	98

	1970	1990 BASE YEAR	1990 COMPLETED INTERSTATE	1990 EXTENDED PRIMARY	1990 ECONOMIC DEVELOPMENT	1990 URBAN	CI/BY	EP/CI	ED/CI	U/CI
JOBS BY INDUSTRY		(THOUSANDS)								
NATURAL RESOURCES (1-10)	25.0	11.9	11.6	10.2	10.6	12.6	97	88	91	109
CONSTRUCTION (11,12)	79.4	87.0	86.8	84.0	82.0	89.2	100	97	94	103
MANUFACTURING (13-74)	705.7	981.6	990.6	976.8	983.5	1048.1	101	99	99	106
TRANSPORTATION INDUSTRY (75)	54.8	103.4	103.5	102.3	102.6	105.9	100	99	99	102
PUBLIC UTILITIES (76-80)	44.3	80.6	79.5	73.4	75.5	85.3	99	92	95	107
TRADE (81,86,89-99)	457.4	912.6	913.6	894.5	899.5	951.1	100	98	98	104
SERVICES (82-85,87,88,102)	410.3	757.5	757.6	756.8	757.1	759.2	100	100	100	100
STATE & LOCAL GOVT. (101)	238.1	338.3	339.4	334.9	336.2	350.4	100	99	99	103
FEDERAL GOVERNMENT (100,103)	38.8	51.2	51.5	50.5	50.7	53.9	100	98	99	105
TOTAL JOBS	2053.8	3324.2	3334.1	3283.4	3297.6	3455.7	100	98	99	104
CIVILIAN PERSONS EMPLOYED	2114.0	3356.0	3365.1	3317.3	3331.6	3481.2	100	99	99	103
CIVILIAN UNEMPLOYMENT RATE	3.6	.4	.5	.5						
POPULATION	5207.8	7260.4	7272.8	7260.8	7259.7	7327.7	100	100	100	101
PER CAPITA INCOME	4373.1	8211.8	8221.5	8121.0	8152.8	8448.1	100	99	99	103
ENERGY USER SECTOR		(TRILLIONS OF BTU'S)								
NATURAL RESOURCES	12.0	29.4	28.8	26.2	26.4	31.5	98	91	92	109
CONSTRUCTION	102.5	231.0	231.5	230.6	222.2	324.8	100	95	96	140
MANUFACTURING	444.4	986.7	991.9	987.1	990.4	1028.2	101	100	100	104
TRANSPORTATION INDUSTRY	85.6	276.1	276.4	271.5	273.1	286.5	100	98	98	104
PUBLIC UTILITIES	322.7	1124.1	1100.0	982.2	1005.2	1203.5	98	89	91	109
TRADE AND SERVICES	268.9	787.9	787.8	776.5	779.7	807.5	100	99	99	102
GOVERNMENT, EXC. TRANSPORTATION	21.9	39.4	39.5	39.0	39.2	40.7	100	99	99	103
CONSUMERS, EXC. TRANSPORTATION	255.9	595.9	597.3	590.4	592.1	615.2	100	99	99	103
USER-OPERATED TRANSPORTATION	347.0	843.8	846.0	835.0	837.7	874.0	100	99	99	103
TRANSPORTATION AIR POLLUTION		(THOUSANDS OF TONS)								
SULFUR OXIDES	19.5	58.5	58.3	57.0	57.5	60.4	100	98	99	104
PARTICULATE MATTER	13.3	36.8	36.9	36.4	36.5	38.2	100	99	99	103
CARBON MONOXIDE	2484.9	6245.3	6261.7	6178.8	6199.4	6471.3	100	99	99	103
HYDROCARBONS	4431.0	1081.4	1083.8	1069.1	1072.8	1120.1	100	99	99	103
NITROGEN OXIDES	240.8	626.3	630.0	623.3	624.5	651.3	101	99	99	103
OTHER AIR POLLUTION										
SULFUR OXIDES	917.9	3151.1	3111.5	2917.8	2954.8	3281.5	99	94	95	105
PARTICULATE MATTER	560.5	1558.7	1545.9	1479.0	1488.8	1607.1	99	96	96	104
CARBON MONOXIDE	717.7	1384.1	1373.7	1331.4	1335.1	1411.1	99	97	97	104
HYDROCARBONS	339.2	500.2	528.8	538.6	550.8	810.6	106	102	104	153
NITROGEN OXIDES	257.2	990.1	980.0	930.5	939.8	1023.7	99	95	96	104
WATER OXYGEN DEMAND	746.0	1548.0	1541.6	1517.1	1520.0	1564.8	100	98	99	102
LAND SOLID WASTE	4114.1	5735.7	5745.5	5736.0	5735.1	5788.8	100	100	100	101

SUMMARY PROJECTIONS BY ORE ECONOMIC AREA UNDER FIVE ALTERNATIVE HIGHWAY SYSTEMS

72 SAGINAW, MICH.

	1970	1990 BASE YEAR	1990 COMPLETED INTERSTATE	1990 EXTENDED PRIMARY	1990 ECONOMIC DEVELOPMENT	1990 URBAN	PERCENT CI/BY	PERCENT EP/CI	PERCENT ED/CI	PERCENT U/CI
JOBS BY INDUSTRY		(THOUSANDS)								
NATURAL RESOURCES (1-10)	24.9	5.9	5.8	5.9	5.9	5.7	98	102	103	99
CONSTRUCTION (11,12)	8.8	12.8	12.9	12.6	12.1	12.9	100	98	94	100
MANUFACTURING (13-74)	74.9	84.1	83.7	85.3	85.4	83.1	100	102	102	99
TRANSPORTATION INDUSTRY (75)	9.2	9.2	9.2	9.3	9.4	9.2	100	101	102	100
PUBLIC UTILITIES (76-80)	5.6	3.5	3.0	3.8	4.3	2.9	84	130	145	96
TRADE (81,86,89-99)	52.7	74.5	73.4	75.5	75.9	72.7	98	103	104	99
SERVICES (82-85,87,88,102)	44.0	78.4	78.3	78.4	78.4	78.3	100	100	100	100
STATE & LOCAL GOVT. (101)	35.3	40.5	40.3	40.7	40.7	40.2	99	101	101	100
FEDERAL GOVERNMENT (100,103)	10.8	10.1	10.1	10.2	10.2	10.1	100	101	101	100
TOTAL JOBS	262.3	319.1	316.6	321.7	322.3	315.0	99	102	102	99
CIVILIAN PERSONS EMPLOYED	255.1	310.3	307.9	312.8	313.4	306.3	99	102	102	99
CIVILIAN UNEMPLOYMENT RATE	5.9	4.9	4.9	5.3	5.4	5.0				
POPULATION	798.4	1019.7	1014.1	1027.7	1031.2	1013.1	99	101	102	100
PER CAPITA INCOME	3207.4	5170.1	5163.7	5160.4	5148.4	5150.9	100	100	100	100
ENERGY USER SECTOR		(TRILLIONS OF BTU'S)								
NATURAL RESOURCES	16.0	25.5	25.0	25.5	25.5	25.0	98	102	102	100
CONSTRUCTION	10.0	17.1	16.8	18.2	17.6	14.7	98	109	105	87
MANUFACTURING	84.1	172.5	172.4	173.3	173.3	172.0	100	101	101	100
TRANSPORTATION INDUSTRY	6.4	15.8	15.5	16.1	16.2	15.3	98	104	105	99
PUBLIC UTILITIES	44.3	54.0	35.0	57.3	62.8	34.4	65	164	179	98
TRADE AND SERVICES	22.2	54.0	53.3	54.6	55.0	53.0	99	102	103	99
GOVERNMENT, EXC. TRANSPORTATION	3.1	4.4	4.4	4.5	4.5	4.4	99	101	101	100
CONSUMERS, EXC. TRANSPORTATION	35.2	63.1	62.8	63.4	63.4	62.6	99	101	101	100
USER-OPERATED TRANSPORTATION	60.4	120.4	119.9	120.8	120.9	119.6	100	101	101	100
TRANSPORTATION AIR POLLUTION		(THOUSANDS OF TONS)								
SULFUR OXIDES	2.9	6.1	6.0	6.1	6.1	5.7	99	102	102	99
PARTICULATE MATTER	2.4	4.8	4.8	4.8	4.8	4.7	99	101	102	100
CARBON MONOXIDE	483.4	964.6	960.5	968.2	969.1	958.1	100	101	101	100
HYDROCARBONS	85.9	170.6	169.9	171.2	171.4	169.5	100	101	101	100
NITROGEN OXIDES	49.1	96.8	96.4	97.4	97.5	96.1	100	101	101	100
OTHER AIR POLLUTION										
SULFUR OXIDES	95.5	152.7	120.6	158.0	167.1	119.3	79	131	139	99
PARTICULATE MATTER	113.2	175.8	168.0	177.0	179.0	167.7	96	105	107	100
CARBON MONOXIDE	220.5	583.6	577.5	582.8	583.4	578.2	99	101	101	100
HYDROCARBONS	88.0	279.2	278.2	281.7	281.3	277.4	100	101	101	100
NITROGEN OXIDES	27.6	58.7	50.3	59.9	62.2	49.9	86	119	124	99
WATER OXYGEN DEMAND	623.7	1350.0	1344.1	1348.4	1349.7	1343.1	100	100	100	100
LAND SOLID WASTE	630.7	805.6	801.2	811.9	814.6	800.3	99	101	102	100

SUMMARY PROJECTIONS BY OBE ECONOMIC AREA UNDER FIVE ALTERNATIVE HIGHWAY SYSTEMS

73   GRAND RAPIDS, MICH.

	1970	1990 BASE YEAR	1990 COMPLETED INTERSTATE	1990 EXTENDED PRIMARY	1990 ECONOMIC DEVELOPMENT	1990 URBAN	CI/BY	EP/CI	ED/CI	U/CI
								P E R C E N T		
JOBS BY INDUSTRY			(THOUSANDS)							
NATURAL RESOURCES (1-10)	24.8	6.3	6.3	6.3	6.3	6.3	100	100	100	100
CONSTRUCTION (11,12)	14.9	20.3	20.3	20.0	19.3	20.2	100	99	95	100
MANUFACTURING (13-74)	134.5	266.8	265.0	271.3	267.1	256.9	99	102	101	97
TRANSPORTATION INDUSTRY (75)	9.7	8.5	8.4	8.5	8.4	8.2	99	101	99	98
PUBLIC UTILITIES (76-80)	7.7	4.2	3.6	3.6	3.5	3.3	85	101	99	92
TRADE (81,86,89-99)	88.5	131.6	130.0	132.2	129.7	126.5	99	102	100	97
SERVICES (82-85,87,88,102)	77.8	131.1	131.0	131.1	130.9	130.8	100	102	100	100
STATE & LOCAL GOVT. (101)	42.6	61.2	60.6	61.6	60.7	59.3	99	102	100	98
FEDERAL GOVERNMENT (100,103)	5.1	7.2	7.1	7.3	7.1	6.8	98	103	100	96
TOTAL JOBS	405.6	637.2	632.2	641.9	633.0	618.3	99	102	100	98
CIVILIAN PERSONS EMPLOYED	419.1	645.4	640.6	650.0	641.6	627.2	99	101	100	98
CIVILIAN UNEMPLOYMENT RATE	4.5	4.0	4.2	4.1	4.1	4.1				
POPULATION	1124.1	1690.8	1684.1	1690.6	1679.2	1676.2	100	100	100	100
PER CAPITA INCOME	3326.5	5948.9	5916.9	5996.7	5939.8	5794.2	99	101	100	98
ENERGY USER SECTOR			(TRILLIONS OF BTU'S)							
NATURAL RESOURCES	12.0	20.0	19.8	19.8	19.7	19.8	99	100	99	100
CONSTRUCTION	18.7	36.2	35.8	36.5	32.7	30.4	99	102	91	85
MANUFACTURING	65.3	139.6	138.5	140.6	137.9	135.2	99	102	100	98
TRANSPORTATION INDUSTRY	13.1	28.8	28.3	28.9	28.2	27.4	98	102	100	97
PUBLIC UTILITIES	46.2	73.4	44.0	44.4	36.2	33.6	60	101	82	76
TRADE AND SERVICES	39.0	80.1	79.3	80.3	79.1	77.7	99	101	100	98
GOVERNMENT, EXC. TRANSPORTATION	5.8	9.5	9.4	9.5	9.4	9.3	99	101	100	98
CONSUMERS, EXC. TRANSPORTATION	47.1	108.8	107.9	109.4	108.0	105.9	99	101	100	98
USER-OPERATED TRANSPORTATION	81.3	189.4	188.1	190.4	188.2	184.9	99	101	100	98
TRANSPORTATION AIR POLLUTION			(THOUSANDS OF TONS)							
SULFUR OXIDES	4.0	8.7	8.5	8.6	8.5	8.3	98	101	100	98
PARTICULATE MATTER	3.0	6.7	6.7	6.8	6.7	6.5	99	101	100	98
CARBON MONOXIDE	591.2	1392.2	1382.7	1399.1	1382.5	1358.8	99	101	100	98
HYDROCARBONS	104.0	243.7	242.0	244.8	241.9	237.9	99	101	100	98
NITROGEN OXIDES	58.9	133.9	133.1	134.9	133.1	130.8	99	101	100	98
OTHER AIR POLLUTION										
SULFUR OXIDES	121.3	218.2	168.5	169.3	154.9	151.1	77	100	92	90
PARTICULATE MATTER	89.9	202.1	187.3	186.8	177.1	182.3	93	100	95	97
CARBON MONOXIDE	143.3	278.0	277.0	275.7	275.5	277.7	100	101	99	100
HYDROCARBONS	60.1	100.8	99.3	109.7	98.9	82.8	98	110	100	83
NITROGEN OXIDES	32.1	80.9	68.7	68.8	65.0	64.5	85	100	95	94
WATER OXYGEN DEMAND	713.0	1459.2	1455.3	1453.9	1449.6	1454.7	100	100	100	100
LAND SOLID WASTE	888.1	1335.7	1330.5	1335.6	1326.6	1324.2	100	100	100	100

SUMMARY PROJECTIONS BY ORE ECONOMIC AREA UNDER FIVE ALTERNATIVE HIGHWAY SYSTEMS

74   LANSING, MICH.

	1970	1990 BASE YEAR	1990 COMPLETED INTERSTATE	1990 EXTENDED PRIMARY	1990 ECONOMIC DEVELOPMENT	1990 URBAN	PERCENT CI/BY	PERCENT EP/CI	PERCENT ED/CI	PERCENT U/CI
JOBS BY INDUSTRY			(THOUSANDS)							
NATURAL RESOURCES (1-10)	21.5	5.0	5.0	5.0	4.9	5.0	99	100	99	99
CONSTRUCTION (11,12)	14.4	19.8	19.8	19.4	18.9	19.8	100	98	95	100
MANUFACTURING (13-74)	123.7	191.3	193.5	194.5	190.5	189.0	101	101	98	98
TRANSPORTATION INDUSTRY (75)	6.3	12.8	12.9	12.8	12.7	12.8	100	100	99	99
PUBLIC UTILITIES (76-80)	8.8	1.9	1.9	2.0	2.0	1.8	102	103	104	95
TRADE (81,86,89-99)	79.4	165.4	165.9	166.1	164.1	163.8	100	100	99	99
SERVICES (82-85,87,88,102)	70.4	137.7	137.8	137.7	137.6	137.7	100	100	100	100
STATE & LOCAL GOVT. (101)	70.8	96.0	96.3	96.5	95.7	95.5	100	100	99	99
FEDERAL GOVERNMENT (100,103)	7.4	9.6	9.7	9.7	9.6	9.5	101	100	99	98
TOTAL JOBS	402.8	639.5	642.7	643.7	636.1	634.9	100	100	99	99
CIVILIAN PERSONS EMPLOYED	385.0	609.7	612.7	613.7	606.5	605.3	100	100	99	99
CIVILIAN UNEMPLOYMENT RATE	4.1	4.1	3.5	3.6	4.0	4.2				
POPULATION	1034.6	1634.7	1637.6	1636.6	1629.0	1637.8	100	100	99	100
PER CAPITA INCOME	3647.9	6049.7	6071.9	6090.2	6040.7	5991.2	100	100	99	99
ENERGY USER SECTOR			(TRILLIONS OF BTU'S)							
NATURAL RESOURCES	10.3	18.2	18.1	17.9	17.6	18.0	100	99	98	99
CONSTRUCTION	17.7	34.1	34.2	34.3	32.0	32.1	100	100	93	94
MANUFACTURING	67.0	166.3	166.6	166.5	164.8	165.3	100	100	99	99
TRANSPORTATION INDUSTRY	8.1	29.4	29.6	29.6	29.1	29.1	100	100	98	98
PUBLIC UTILITIES	96.6	57.4	56.3	56.8	57.6	55.1	98	101	102	96
TRADE AND SERVICES	34.3	91.2	91.4	91.5	90.6	90.6	100	100	99	99
GOVERNMENT, EXC. TRANSPORTATION	3.2	5.9	6.0	6.0	5.9	5.9	101	100	99	99
CONSUMERS, EXC. TRANSPORTATION	44.7	99.2	99.7	99.9	98.8	98.6	100	100	99	99
USER-OPERATED TRANSPORTATION	79.8	187.9	188.6	188.9	187.2	186.9	100	100	99	99
TRANSPORTATION AIR POLLUTION			(THOUSANDS OF TONS)							
SULFUR OXIDES	3.1	8.6	8.6	8.6	8.5	8.5	100	100	98	99
PARTICULATE MATTER	2.7	6.8	6.8	6.8	6.7	6.7	100	100	99	99
CARBON MONOXIDE	607.8	1426.3	1431.3	1433.1	1420.3	1418.7	100	100	99	99
HYDROCARBONS	106.6	249.1	249.9	250.2	247.9	247.7	100	100	99	99
NITROGEN OXIDES	57.2	135.3	135.9	136.3	134.8	134.7	101	100	99	99
OTHER AIR POLLUTION										
SULFUR OXIDES	185.5	199.0	196.9	197.1	197.5	194.6	99	100	100	99
PARTICULATE MATTER	226.5	599.1	597.8	594.0	586.4	595.3	100	99	98	100
CARBON MONOXIDE	111.6	195.8	195.0	194.3	193.6	194.8	100	100	99	100
HYDROCARBONS	27.2	49.3	49.6	49.9	48.7	48.2	100	101	98	99
NITROGEN OXIDES	55.4	89.7	89.1	88.9	88.6	88.4	99	100	99	99
WATER OXYGEN DEMAND	642.8	1379.7	1377.4	1373.7	1368.2	1375.8	100	100	99	100
LAND SOLID WASTE	817.4	1291.4	1293.9	1292.9	1286.9	1293.9	100	100	99	100

SUMMARY PROJECTIONS BY ORE ECONOMIC AREA UNDER FIVE ALTERNATIVE HIGHWAY SYSTEMS

75 FORT WAYNE, IND.

	1970	1990 BASE YEAR	1990 COMPLETED INTERSTATE	1990 EXTENDED PRIMARY	1990 ECONOMIC DEVELOPMENT	1990 URBAN	CI/BY	EP/CI	ED/CI	U/CI
								P E R C E N T		
JOBS BY INDUSTRY		(THOUSANDS)								
NATURAL RESOURCES (1-10)	16.2	4.0	4.0	4.0	4.0	4.0	100	100	99	100
CONSTRUCTION (11,12)	9.6	12.2	12.1	11.9	11.5	12.1	99	98	95	100
MANUFACTURING (13-74)	94.3	113.8	109.1	112.0	109.9	107.5	96	103	101	99
TRANSPORTATION INDUSTRY (75)	7.8	13.6	13.5	13.6	13.5	13.4	99	101	100	100
PUBLIC UTILITIES (76-80)	5.0	0.9	0.7	0.8	0.8	0.7	80	118	106	97
TRADE (81,86,89-99)	58.8	100.1	97.1	98.5	96.2	96.2	97	101	100	99
SERVICES (82-85,87,88,102)	40.6	93.4	93.2	93.2	93.1	93.1	100	100	100	100
STATE & LOCAL GOVT. (101)	23.2	31.0	30.2	30.6	30.2	30.0	97	102	100	99
FEDERAL GOVERNMENT (100,103)	2.6	3.2	3.0	3.1	3.0	3.0	94	103	100	98
TOTAL JOBS	258.1	372.2	362.9	367.8	362.7	360.1	98	101	100	99
CIVILIAN PERSONS EMPLOYED	266.4	378.7	369.8	374.8	369.7	367.1	98	101	100	99
CIVILIAN UNEMPLOYMENT RATE	2.4	1.8	1.9	1.7	1.6	2.1				
POPULATION	597.4	867.4	856.2	865.3	852.2	859.3	99	100	100	100
PER CAPITA INCOME	3763.1	6533.6	6448.1	6473.9	6472.1	6372.9	99	100	100	99
ENERGY USER SECTOR		(TRILLIONS OF BTU'S)								
NATURAL RESOURCES	13.0	34.3	34.1	34.1	33.9	34.1	100	100	99	100
CONSTRUCTION	10.1	20.9	17.1	19.0	15.5	15.3	82	111	90	89
MANUFACTURING	40.5	92.0	88.1	89.6	87.4	87.4	96	102	99	99
TRANSPORTATION INDUSTRY	9.6	24.3	23.4	23.8	23.3	23.2	96	102	100	99
PUBLIC UTILITIES	23.1	19.3	14.6	17.2	14.9	14.3	75	118	102	98
TRADE AND SERVICES	22.6	63.1	61.3	62.0	61.1	61.0	97	101	100	99
GOVERNMENT, EXC. TRANSPORTATION	1.9	3.3	3.2	3.2	3.2	3.2	97	102	100	99
CONSUMERS, EXC. TRANSPORTATION	25.8	59.1	57.9	58.6	57.8	57.5	98	101	100	99
USER-OPERATED TRANSPORTATION	40.8	94.7	92.7	93.8	92.7	92.2	98	101	100	99
TRANSPORTATION AIR POLLUTION		(THOUSANDS OF TONS)								
SULFUR OXIDES	3.0	7.8	7.6	7.6	7.5	7.5	97	99	99	99
PARTICULATE MATTER	2.1	5.3	5.2	5.2	5.1	5.1	98	100	100	99
CARBON MONOXIDE	350.3	843.9	828.8	836.6	827.0	824.4	98	101	100	99
HYDROCARBONS	62.5	151.1	148.5	149.8	148.1	147.7	98	101	100	99
NITROGEN OXIDES	38.5	95.2	93.7	94.7	93.5	93.3	98	101	100	100
OTHER AIR POLLUTION										
SULFUR OXIDES	89.5	179.1	170.4	174.5	169.3	169.6	95	102	99	100
PARTICULATE MATTER	109.3	256.0	247.0	246.6	233.2	244.2	97	100	94	99
CARBON MONOXIDE	113.4	265.0	264.1	263.9	262.5	263.8	100	100	99	100
HYDROCARBONS	36.7	95.6	69.0	79.6	71.6	66.9	72	115	104	97
NITROGEN OXIDES	17.4	37.6	35.0	35.9	33.9	34.7	93	103	97	99
WATER OXYGEN DEMAND	725.1	1443.6	1437.0	1435.5	1426.3	1435.1	100	100	99	100
LAND SOLID WASTE	471.9	685.3	676.4	683.6	673.2	678.8	99	100	100	100

76 SOUTH BEND, IND.

	1970	1990 BASE YEAR	1990 COMPLETED INTERSTATE	1990 EXTENDED PRIMARY	1990 ECONOMIC DEVELOPMENT	1990 URBAN	CI/BY	EP/CI	ED/CI	U/CI
							\ P E R C E N T \			
JOBS BY INDUSTRY			(THOUSANDS)							
NATURAL RESOURCES (1-10)	16.1	3.7	3.7	3.6	3.6	3.7	100	100	99	100
CONSTRUCTION (11,12)	11.1	10.8	10.8	10.8	10.1	10.8	100	100	94	100
MANUFACTURING (13-74)	125.4	183.9	180.0	180.6	177.8	174.6	98	100	99	97
TRANSPORTATION INDUSTRY (75)	6.8	11.3	11.1	11.1	11.0	11.0	99	100	99	97
PUBLIC UTILITIES (76-80)	5.6	.5	.5	.6	.6	.5	98	105	109	99
TRADE (81,86,89-99)	65.1	107.7	104.8	105.1	103.6	102.1	97	100	99	97
SERVICES (82-85,87,88,102)	54.9	71.6	71.6	71.4	71.3	71.4	100	100	100	100
STATE & LOCAL GOVT. (101)	26.6	33.1	32.4	32.5	32.0	31.6	98	100	99	98
FEDERAL GOVERNMENT (100,103)	2.6	2.7	2.5	2.5	2.4	2.3	94	101	97	94
TOTAL JOBS	314.0	425.2	417.2	417.9	412.5	408.0	98	100	99	98
CIVILIAN PERSONS EMPLOYED	303.0	409.1	401.5	402.1	396.9	392.6	98	100	99	98
CIVILIAN UNEMPLOYMENT RATE	4.1	1.4	1.5	1.5	1.7	1.8				
POPULATION	747.1	966.6	955.3	956.6	950.7	955.7	99	100	100	100
PER CAPITA INCOME	3525.1	6429.8	6376.0	6383.3	6331.7	6223.6	99	100	99	98
ENERGY USER SECTOR			(TRILLIONS OF BTU'S)							
NATURAL RESOURCES	11.2	24.9	24.8	24.7	24.6	24.8	100	99	99	100
CONSTRUCTION	12.4	23.3	23.0	22.3	20.1	20.0	99	97	87	87
MANUFACTURING	55.2	120.0	117.4	117.4	115.8	115.2	98	100	98	98
TRANSPORTATION INDUSTRY	8.8	17.4	16.7	16.7	16.4	16.1	96	100	98	96
PUBLIC UTILITIES	33.8	19.9	19.9	19.8	20.0	19.1	98	101	102	98
TRADE AND SERVICES	29.0	57.8	56.6	56.7	56.1	55.6	98	100	99	98
GOVERNMENT, EXC. TRANSPORTATION	2.4	3.9	3.9	3.8	3.7	3.7	98	100	99	98
CONSUMERS, EXC. TRANSPORTATION	34.7	70.8	69.7	69.8	69.1	68.5	98	100	99	98
USER-OPERATED TRANSPORTATION	55.2	121.2	119.6	119.8	118.6	117.7	99	100	99	98
TRANSPORTATION AIR POLLUTION			(THOUSANDS OF TONS)							
SULFUR OXIDES	3.0	6.3	6.1	6.1	6.0	6.0	97	100	98	98
PARTICULATE MATTER	2.3	4.9	4.9	4.8	4.8	4.7	98	99	99	99
CARBON MONOXIDE	443.9	980.3	967.5	968.4	959.5	953.7	98	100	99	99
HYDROCARBONS	78.4	173.1	170.9	171.0	169.5	168.5	99	100	99	99
NITROGEN OXIDES	44.7	98.0	96.8	96.9	95.9	95.4	99	100	99	99
OTHER AIR POLLUTION										
SULFUR OXIDES	75.8	110.8	108.9	108.3	108.0	107.9	98	99	99	99
PARTICULATE MATTER	66.8	146.4	140.5	133.3	128.1	138.3	96	95	91	98
CARBON MONOXIDE	116.9	249.7	248.9	248.1	247.5	248.7	100	100	99	100
HYDROCARBONS	32.1	59.4	56.8	60.0	57.8	54.7	95	106	102	96
NITROGEN OXIDES	23.9	51.1	50.4	49.9	49.6	50.1	99	99	98	99
WATER OXYGEN DEMAND	707.0	1449.5	1441.6	1436.3	1432.4	1440.0	99	99	99	100
LAND SOLID WASTE	590.2	763.6	754.7	755.7	751.0	755.0	99	100	100	100

SUMMARY PROJECTIONS BY ORE ECONOMIC AREA UNDER FIVE ALTERNATIVE HIGHWAY SYSTEMS

77 CHICAGO, ILL.

	1970	1990 BASE YEAR	1990 COMPLETED INTERSTATE	1990 EXTENDED PRIMARY	1990 ECONOMIC DEVELOPMENT	1990 URBAN	PERCENT CI/BY	EP/CI	ED/CI	U/CI
JOBS BY INDUSTRY			(THOUSANDS)							
NATURAL RESOURCES (1-10)	35.3	14.1	14.1	11.8	11.8	18.8	100	84	84	133
CONSTRUCTION (11,12)	159.2	150.1	150.7	146.5	142.3	153.9	100	97	94	102
MANUFACTURING (13-74)	1167.1	1711.8	1749.3	1741.1	1746.1	1900.1	102	100	100	109
TRANSPORTATION INDUSTRY (75)	174.6	210.1	211.3	210.4	210.6	217.4	101	100	100	103
PUBLIC UTILITIES (76-80)	71.3	71.3	72.3	64.6	65.0	87.8	101	89	90	121
TRADE (81,86,89-99)	889.0	1107.2	1130.4	1113.4	1114.4	1232.1	102	98	99	109
SERVICES (82-85,87,88,102)	823.2	1334.9	1336.1	1335.1	1335.6	1339.6	100	100	100	100
STATE & LOCAL GOVT. (101)	350.4	437.8	444.8	440.9	441.2	472.4	102	99	99	106
FEDERAL GOVERNMENT (100,103)	114.6	120.8	122.4	121.5	121.6	128.5	101	99	99	105
TOTAL JOBS	3784.8	5158.1	5231.3	5185.2	5188.3	5550.6	101	99	99	106
CIVILIAN PERSONS EMPLOYED	3802.7	5156.8	5226.3	5183.1	5187.1	5531.0	101	99	99	106
CIVILIAN UNEMPLOYMENT RATE	3.0	3.1	2.9	3.0	3.1	2.3				
POPULATION	8194.0	11176.1	11259.7	11192.5	11190.7	11473.9	101	99	99	102
PER CAPITA INCOME	4599.6	7584.3	7634.8	7616.4	7623.1	7943.3	101	100	100	104
ENERGY USER SECTOR			(TRILLIONS OF BTU'S)							
NATURAL RESOURCES	49.2	122.7	123.7	121.5	121.6	131.4	101	98	98	106
CONSTRUCTION	203.8	321.7	325.6	320.6	309.0	482.9	101	98	95	148
MANUFACTURING	922.7	1818.4	1838.9	1843.4	1844.2	1940.6	101	100	100	106
TRANSPORTATION INDUSTRY	240.9	463.8	470.7	466.7	467.3	497.9	101	99	99	106
PUBLIC UTILITIES	417.6	1010.4	1027.9	896.4	900.5	1259.9	102	87	88	123
TRADE AND SERVICES	535.9	1018.1	1029.9	1019.5	1020.6	1081.8	101	99	99	105
GOVERNMENT, EXC. TRANSPORTATION	54.3	81.3	82.1	81.6	81.7	85.0	101	99	100	104
CONSUMERS, EXC. TRANSPORTATION	459.3	896.4	906.5	900.5	900.8	950.7	101	99	99	105
USER-OPERATED TRANSPORTATION	654.0	1350.7	1366.6	1356.8	1357.4	1435.7	101	99	99	105
TRANSPORTATION AIR POLLUTION			(THOUSANDS OF TONS)							
SULFUR OXIDES	51.6	104.1	105.0	103.7	104.1	110.5	101	99	99	105
PARTICULATE MATTER	30.9	64.4	65.2	64.8	64.8	68.5	101	99	99	105
CARBON MONOXIDE	4682.6	10141.1	10262.6	10189.9	10193.6	10781.0	101	99	99	105
HYDROCARBONS	816.1	1772.3	1792.6	1779.3	1780.3	1882.2	101	99	99	105
NITROGEN OXIDES	501.4	1076.5	1093.1	1089.1	1087.8	1146.7	102	100	100	105
OTHER AIR POLLUTION										
SULFUR OXIDES	1443.8	3007.0	3037.1	2819.5	2825.6	3418.9	101	93	93	113
PARTICULATE MATTER	1345.5	2712.8	2717.2	2665.1	2666.0	2812.4	100	98	98	104
CARBON MONOXIDE	2156.9	4695.2	4674.6	4678.0	4676.8	4661.9	100	100	100	100
HYDROCARBONS	1214.2	1986.2	2063.9	2178.2	2181.1	2717.8	104	106	106	132
NITROGEN OXIDES	535.6	999.8	1006.3	952.9	954.4	1100.1	101	95	95	109
WATER OXYGEN DEMAND	2087.7	4425.5	4415.0	4398.1	4398.9	4424.2	100	99	99	100
LAND SOLID WASTE	6473.2	8829.1	8895.1	8842.1	8840.7	9064.3	101	99	99	102

SUMMARY PROJECTIONS BY ORE ECONOMIC AREA UNDER FIVE ALTERNATIVE HIGHWAY SYSTEMS

78 PEORIA, ILL.

	1970	1990 BASE YEAR	1990 COMPLETED INTERSTATE	1990 EXTENDED PRIMARY	1990 ECONOMIC DEVELOPMENT	1990 URBAN	CI/BY	EP/CI	ED/CI	U/CI
								P E R C E N T		
JOBS BY INDUSTRY (THOUSANDS)										
NATURAL RESOURCES (1-10)	15.3	4.4	4.7	4.2	4.1	4.6	108	89	88	98
CONSTRUCTION (11,12)	10.2	11.3	11.0	11.0	10.3	11.0	97	101	94	100
MANUFACTURING (13-74)	70.3	76.2	80.1	79.0	78.5	78.3	105	99	98	98
TRANSPORTATION INDUSTRY (75)	7.6	7.0	7.1	6.8	6.9	7.0	102	96	96	99
PUBLIC UTILITIES (76-80)	5.4	6.6	7.8	3.9	4.3	6.9	119	49	55	88
TRADE (81,86,89-99)	60.0	75.6	78.6	73.5	73.7	77.3	104	94	94	98
SERVICES (82-85,87,88,102)	50.9	81.3	81.4	81.2	81.2	81.4	100	100	100	100
STATE & LOCAL GOVT. (101)	37.3	40.6	41.3	40.4	40.4	40.9	102	98	98	99
FEDERAL GOVERNMENT (100,103)	3.3	2.1	2.3	2.1	2.1	2.2	108	92	91	97
TOTAL JOBS	260.3	305.0	314.4	302.2	301.5	309.7	103	96	96	99
CIVILIAN PERSONS EMPLOYED	233.3	274.1	282.4	271.8	271.3	278.1	103	96	96	98
CIVILIAN UNEMPLOYMENT RATE	3.7	1.4	1.0	1.6	1.6	1.4				
POPULATION	628.6	704.0	712.0	710.0	705.2	714.8	101	100	99	100
PER CAPITA INCOME	3983.6	6585.3	6701.8	6485.5	6507.8	6581.3	102	97	97	98
ENERGY USER SECTOR (TRILLIONS OF BTU'S)										
NATURAL RESOURCES	25.7	69.2	69.9	69.1	69.0	69.9	101	99	99	100
CONSTRUCTION	12.9	20.6	21.2	19.7	19.9	20.8	103	93	94	98
MANUFACTURING	86.3	154.1	155.4	154.0	154.0	154.8	101	99	99	100
TRANSPORTATION INDUSTRY	6.4	9.3	10.2	8.9	8.9	9.8	109	87	88	96
PUBLIC UTILITIES	57.0	178.0	196.3	113.9	123.9	181.3	110	58	63	92
TRADE AND SERVICES	32.3	65.9	67.8	63.8	64.3	66.8	103	94	95	98
GOVERNMENT, EXC. TRANSPORTATION	2.8	3.5	3.6	3.5	3.5	3.6	102	97	97	99
CONSUMERS, EXC. TRANSPORTATION	24.7	44.2	45.4	44.0	43.8	44.8	103	97	97	99
USER-OPERATED TRANSPORTATION	43.0	78.9	80.6	78.5	78.2	79.8	102	97	97	99
TRANSPORTATION AIR POLLUTION (THOUSANDS OF TONS)										
SULFUR OXIDES	3.4	7.5	7.7	7.4	7.4	7.6	102	96	97	99
PARTICULATE MATTER	2.5	5.6	5.7	5.5	5.5	5.6	102	97	97	99
CARBON MONOXIDE	413.4	857.4	871.1	853.1	851.8	864.5	102	98	98	99
HYDROCARBONS	75.3	158.9	161.8	158.1	157.9	160.1	101	98	98	99
NITROGEN OXIDES	48.5	107.4	109.0	106.9	106.9	108.3	101	98	98	99
OTHER AIR POLLUTION										
SULFUR OXIDES	121.0	356.8	387.3	250.3	266.9	362.4	109	65	69	94
PARTICULATE MATTER	155.3	400.6	410.6	368.2	373.6	403.6	102	90	91	98
CARBON MONOXIDE	315.8	724.0	725.9	712.2	713.8	724.6	100	98	98	100
HYDROCARBONS	69.5	147.4	149.2	147.2	147.4	148.5	101	99	99	100
NITROGEN OXIDES	32.9	109.5	117.1	82.7	86.9	111.0	107	71	74	95
WATER OXYGEN DEMAND	1079.8	2173.6	2175.3	2165.9	2168.8	2173.6	100	100	100	100
LAND SOLID WASTE	496.6	556.2	562.5	560.9	557.1	564.7	101	100	99	100

SUMMARY PROJECTIONS BY ORE ECONOMIC AREA UNDER FIVE ALTERNATIVE HIGHWAY SYSTEMS

79 DAV-R IS-MOL. IOWA-ILL.

	1970	1990 BASE YEAR	1990 COMPLETED INTERSTATE	1990 EXTENDED PRIMARY	1990 ECONOMIC DEVELOPMENT	1990 URBAN	CI/BY	EP/CI	ED/CI	U/CI
JOBS BY INDUSTRY			(THOUSANDS)							
NATURAL RESOURCES (1-10)	16.3	3.7	3.4	3.5	3.3	3.3	99	102	98	99
CONSTRUCTION (11-12)	11.1	11.7	11.6	11.4	10.9	11.6	99	98	94	100
MANUFACTURING (13-74)	69.6	83.6	82.2	82.5	81.0	80.6	98	100	99	98
TRANSPORTATION INDUSTRY (75)	6.7	6.8	6.8	6.8	6.7	6.7	99	101	98	98
PUBLIC UTILITIES (76-80)	4.2	3.7	3.3	3.6	2.6	3.1	88	108	80	95
TRADE (81,86,89-99)	57.6	53.0	51.8	52.3	49.7	49.7	98	101	96	96
SERVICES (82-85,87,88,102)	43.8	61.2	61.0	61.1	60.9	61.0	100	100	100	100
STATE & LOCAL GOVT. (101)	23.9	23.8	23.4	23.5	22.9	23.0	98	100	98	98
FEDERAL GOVERNMENT (100,103)	11.5	11.4	11.3	11.3	11.2	11.2	99	100	99	99
TOTAL JOBS	244.6	259.0	254.9	255.9	249.3	250.2	98	100	98	98
CIVILIAN PERSONS EMPLOYED	250.0	266.0	262.1	263.2	256.6	257.6	99	100	98	98
CIVILIAN UNEMPLOYMENT RATE	3.3	5.1	4.6	4.9	4.4	5.0				
POPULATION	605.2	738.6	720.5	723.8	702.3	712.0	98	100	97	99
PER CAPITA INCOME	3692.7	5420.9	5461.2	5452.6	5460.1	5414.2	101	100	100	99
ENERGY USER SECTOR			(TRILLIONS OF BTUS)							
NATURAL RESOURCES	18.0	44.1	43.8	43.9	43.6	43.7	99	100	100	100
CONSTRUCTION	14.2	23.6	23.4	22.4	17.9	18.0	99	96	76	77
MANUFACTURING	46.3	76.9	75.9	75.7	73.9	73.3	99	100	97	97
TRANSPORTATION INDUSTRY	5.8	11.7	11.3	11.4	10.8	10.7	97	102	96	95
PUBLIC UTILITIES	42.7	109.3	88.7	97.2	56.4	80.3	81	110	64	91
TRADE AND SERVICES	24.2	50.8	50.1	50.4	49.2	49.0	99	101	98	98
GOVERNMENT, EXC. TRANSPORTATION	1.7	2.2	2.2	2.2	2.2	2.2	99	100	100	98
CONSUMERS, EXC. TRANSPORTATION	21.7	36.8	36.2	36.3	35.3	35.5	98	100	97	98
USER-OPERATED TRANSPORTATION	39.5	71.0	70.1	70.3	68.8	69.0	99	100	98	98
TRANSPORTATION AIR POLLUTION			(THOUSANDS OF TONS)							
SULFUR OXIDES	2.5	5.6	5.5	5.5	5.4	5.4	98	100	98	98
PARTICULATE MATTER	1.9	4.1	4.0	4.0	3.9	4.0	99	100	98	98
CARBON MONOXIDE	339.9	672.0	664.9	666.6	654.6	656.7	99	100	98	99
HYDROCARBONS	60.9	122.0	120.7	121.0	118.9	119.3	99	100	98	99
NITROGEN OXIDES	36.6	77.7	77.0	77.3	75.9	76.1	99	100	99	99
OTHER AIR POLLUTION										
SULFUR OXIDES	89.7	230.0	195.2	209.4	140.8	181.2	85	107	72	93
PARTICULATE MATTER	154.0	183.5	173.3	177.9	156.5	169.7	94	103	90	98
CARBON MONOXIDE	137.6	279.3	275.4	277.1	273.9	275.1	99	101	99	100
HYDROCARBONS	38.8	101.2	95.4	86.6	79.5	72.7	94	91	83	76
NITROGEN OXIDES	23.8	59.4	50.7	54.3	37.0	47.3	85	107	73	93
WATER OXYGEN DEMAND	1880.0	3797.0	3792.6	3793.7	3786.0	3791.3	100	100	100	100
LAND SOLID WASTE	478.1	583.5	569.2	571.8	554.8	562.4	98	100	97	99

SUMMARY PROJECTIONS BY ORE ECONOMIC AREA UNDER FIVE ALTERNATIVE HIGHWAY SYSTEMS

80   CEDAR RAPIDS, IOWA

	1970	1990 BASE YEAR	1990 COMPLETED INTERSTATE	1990 EXTENDED PRIMARY	1990 ECONOMIC DEVELOPMENT	1990 URBAN	CI/BY	EP/CI	ED/CI	U/CI
JOBS BY INDUSTRY			(THOUSANDS)							
NATURAL RESOURCES (1-10)	14.0	4.5	4.4	3.9	4.0	4.4	100	89	91	98
CONSTRUCTION (11,12)	5.9	7.6	7.3	7.4	6.9	7.3	96	101	94	100
MANUFACTURING (13-74)	32.8	42.1	40.9	40.6	39.9	40.1	97	99	97	98
TRANSPORTATION INDUSTRY (75)	2.6	5.1	5.0	4.8	4.8	4.9	98	96	96	99
PUBLIC UTILITIES (76-80)	2.5	6.5	6.0	3.1	3.5	5.5	92	52	58	92
TRADE (81,86,89-99)	36.8	39.2	37.7	35.0	35.1	37.1	96	93	93	98
SERVICES (82-85,87,88,102)	28.9	48.1	48.0	47.8	47.8	48.0	100	100	100	100
STATE & LOCAL GOVT. (101)	27.0	22.2	21.9	21.3	21.2	21.7	98	97	97	99
FEDERAL GOVERNMENT (100,103)	2.4	1.4	1.3	1.2	1.2	1.2	94	93	93	97
TOTAL JOBS	147.8	176.7	172.5	165.1	164.3	170.2	98	96	95	99
CIVILIAN PERSONS EMPLOYED	146.9	174.7	170.7	163.6	163.0	168.5	98	96	95	99
CIVILIAN UNEMPLOYMENT RATE	1.6	.4	.4	.4	.4	.4				
POPULATION	330.1	344.9	335.3	323.6	319.6	334.2	97	97	95	100
PER CAPITA INCOME	4260.1	7009.1	7004.3	6921.2	6951.0	6918.0	100	99	99	99
ENERGY USER SECTOR			(TRILLIONS OF BTU'S)							
NATURAL RESOURCES	12.7	33.1	33.1	32.9	32.9	33.0	100	99	100	100
CONSTRUCTION	5.6	10.9	10.5	9.4	9.6	10.3	96	90	91	98
MANUFACTURING	14.2	38.2	37.4	36.5	36.4	37.0	98	97	97	99
TRANSPORTATION INDUSTRY	2.5	8.8	8.3	7.3	7.3	8.1	94	88	89	97
PUBLIC UTILITIES	14.7	95.6	82.3	39.8	45.8	75.6	86	48	56	92
TRADE AND SERVICES	12.1	35.2	34.0	31.1	31.3	33.4	96	92	92	98
GOVERNMENT. EXC. TRANSPORTATION	.9	.8	.8	.8	.8	.8				
CONSUMERS. EXC. TRANSPORTATION	13.4	21.2	20.6	19.7	19.5	20.3	95	93	92	99
USER-OPERATED TRANSPORTATION	17.8	28.4	27.5	26.0	25.8	27.0	97	95	94	98
TRANSPORTATION AIR POLLUTION			(THOUSANDS OF TONS)							
SULFUR OXIDES	1.2	3.4	3.3	3.1	3.1	3.3	97	94	94	99
PARTICULATE MATTER	.9	2.2	2.2	2.1	2.1	2.2	98	95	95	99
CARBON MONOXIDE	159.5	305.5	298.3	285.5	284.9	294.6	98	96	96	99
HYDROCARBONS	28.8	56.3	55.0	52.9	52.7	54.4	98	96	96	99
NITROGEN OXIDES	17.9	39.5	38.7	37.4	37.2	38.3	98	96	96	99
OTHER AIR POLLUTION			(THOUSANDS OF TONS)							
SULFUR OXIDES	34.3	201.4	179.3	109.3	119.2	168.2	89	61	66	94
PARTICULATE MATTER	98.3	356.5	350.9	331.7	334.2	347.8	98	95	95	99
CARBON MONOXIDE	53.6	149.7	149.2	148.0	148.1	148.9	100	99	99	100
HYDROCARBONS	13.3	37.7	37.8	37.4	37.2	37.5	100	99	98	99
NITROGEN OXIDES	14.3	74.0	68.5	51.1	53.6	65.8	93	75	78	96
WATER OXYGEN DEMAND	1487.6	3048.3	3043.8	3034.2	3036.8	3042.4	100	100	100	100
LAND SOLID WASTE	260.8	272.5	264.9	255.6	252.5	264.0	97	97	95	99

SUMMARY PROJECTIONS BY ORE ECONOMIC AREA UNDER FIVE ALTERNATIVE HIGHWAY SYSTEMS

81   DUBUQUE, IOWA

	1970	1990 BASE YEAR	1990 COMPLETED INTERSTATE	1990 EXTENDED PRIMARY	1990 ECONOMIC DEVELOPMENT	1990 URBAN	CI/BY	EP/CI	ED/CI	U/CI
JOBS BY INDUSTRY				(THOUSANDS)					P E R C E N T	
NATURAL RESOURCES (1-10)	23.2	5.6	5.5	5.8	5.8	5.5	98	105	106	100
CONSTRUCTION (11,12)	4.3	3.2	3.4	9.3	7.1	3.0	105	273	209	87
MANUFACTURING (13-74)	20.2	40.4	39.9	44.1	45.3	39.5	99	110	113	99
TRANSPORTATION INDUSTRY (75)	2.6	2.9	2.9	3.2	3.2	2.9	102	108	109	99
PUBLIC UTILITIES (76-80)	1.5	4.1	5.1	5.8	6.0	4.9	124	114	116	96
TRADE (81,86,89-99)	24.2	18.2	18.7	22.1	22.4	18.3	103	118	119	98
SERVICES (82-85,87,88,102)	19.8	31.3	30.5	31.3	31.2	30.4	97	102	102	100
STATE & LOCAL GOVT. (101)	9.9	11.4	11.2	12.8	12.7	11.1	99	114	113	99
FEDERAL GOVERNMENT (100,103)	1.3	1.1	1.1	1.4	1.4	1.0	97	133	131	97
TOTAL JOBS	107.1	118.2	118.5	135.9	135.1	116.6	100	115	114	98
CIVILIAN PERSONS EMPLOYED	109.4	120.5	120.5	137.2	136.5	118.8	100	114	113	99
CIVILIAN UNEMPLOYMENT RATE	3.6	4.0	3.7	3.4	3.3	3.9				
POPULATION	301.9	362.1	361.1	387.8	384.4	358.3	100	107	106	99
PER CAPITA INCOME	2963.3	5062.7	5063.3	5505.9	5535.5	5019.2	100	109	109	99
ENERGY USER SECTOR				(TRILLIONS OF BTU'S)						
NATURAL RESOURCES	11.0	29.5	29.1	29.8	29.8	29.2	99	102	102	100
CONSTRUCTION	6.6	14.2	10.5	23.8	17.4	9.1	74	227	166	87
MANUFACTURING	8.8	21.6	21.4	23.7	25.3	21.2	99	111	118	99
TRANSPORTATION INDUSTRY	2.6	6.6	6.4	7.8	7.9	6.6	103	115	116	98
PUBLIC UTILITIES	15.0	116.1	135.5	162.3	165.6	131.2	117	120	122	97
TRADE AND SERVICES	7.8	21.4	21.9	23.8	23.9	21.6	102	109	109	99
GOVERNMENT, EXC. TRANSPORTATION		1.2	1.2	1.3	1.3	1.1	98	115	114	99
CONSUMERS, EXC. TRANSPORTATION	9.4	17.8	17.8	20.4	20.3	17.5	100	115	114	99
USER-OPERATED TRANSPORTATION	15.3	30.5	30.4	34.4	34.3	30.0	100	113	113	99
TRANSPORTATION AIR POLLUTION				(THOUSANDS OF TONS)						
SULFUR OXIDES	.9	2.3	2.3	2.6	2.3	2.3	101	110	102	99
PARTICULATE MATTER	.7	1.6	1.6	1.8	1.8	1.6	101	110	110	99
CARBON MONOXIDE	125.9	268.7	269.0	298.9	298.4	266.0	100	111	111	99
HYDROCARBONS	22.4	48.2	48.3	53.4	53.4	47.8	100	111	111	99
NITROGEN OXIDES	13.2	30.1	30.3	33.3	33.3	30.0	101	110	110	99
OTHER AIR POLLUTION										
SULFUR OXIDES	27.9	204.3	236.7	281.4	287.1	229.6	116	119	121	97
PARTICULATE MATTER	13.4	73.4	82.8	93.7	95.0	81.3	113	113	115	98
CARBON MONOXIDE	30.9	101.8	103.7	106.4	106.8	104.0	102	103	103	100
HYDROCARBONS	8.6	29.7	25.9	37.1	55.5	25.9	87	143	214	100
NITROGEN OXIDES	8.4	57.1	65.1	76.5	78.0	63.4	114	117	120	97
WATER OXYGEN DEMAND	1947.2	3951.0	3955.3	3961.1	3965.2	3954.1	100	100	100	100
LAND SOLID WASTE	238.5	286.0	285.3	306.4	303.7	283.1	100	107	106	99

	1970	1990 BASE YEAR	1990 COMPLETED INTERSTATE	1990 EXTENDED PRIMARY	1990 ECONOMIC DEVELOPMENT	1990 URBAN	CI/BY	EP/BY	ED/CI	U/CI
JOBS BY INDUSTRY			(THOUSANDS)						P E R C E N T	
NATURAL RESOURCES (1-10)	12.9	2.8	2.8	3.2	2.9	2.8	100	117	104	100
CONSTRUCTION (11,12)	8.8	9.8	9.8	11.6	9.8	9.8	100	118	99	100
MANUFACTURING (13-74)	93.4	132.1	127.1	146.6	138.0	122.4	96	115	109	96
TRANSPORTATION INDUSTRY (75)	4.5	7.3	7.2	7.9	7.5	7.1	98	110	104	99
PUBLIC UTILITIES (76-80)	4.1	1.1	1.0	4.8	2.4	.9	91	502	250	96
TRADE (81,86,89-99)	46.7	59.2	56.4	69.6	62.8	54.5	95	123	111	97
SERVICES (82-85,87,88,102)	37.8	60.5	60.4	61.1	60.7	60.3	100	101	101	100
STATE & LOCAL GOVT. (101)	21.1	26.1	25.3	29.1	27.2	24.7	97	115	107	98
FEDERAL GOVERNMENT (100,103)	2.1	2.1	1.9	2.8	2.3	1.8	91	144	122	93
TOTAL JOBS	231.3	301.0	291.9	336.8	313.7	284.4	97	115	107	97
CIVILIAN PERSONS EMPLOYED	229.6	297.3	288.6	331.4	309.4	281.4	97	115	107	98
CIVILIAN UNEMPLOYMENT RATE	3.1	2.2	2.3	1.0	1.7	2.6				
POPULATION	560.4	757.0	740.8	776.7	757.6	737.3	98	105	102	100
PER CAPITA INCOME	3982.0	6650.2	6600.4	7198.9	6894.8	6477.0	99	109	104	98
ENERGY USER SECTOR			(TRILLIONS OF BTU'S)							
NATURAL RESOURCES	12.7	31.5	31.4	32.1	31.7	31.3	100	102	101	100
CONSTRUCTION	9.3	17.7	15.6	19.9	15.7	13.7	88	128	101	88
MANUFACTURING	33.7	68.9	66.0	75.5	71.4	64.0	96	114	108	97
TRANSPORTATION INDUSTRY	6.2	12.3	11.6	14.8	13.1	11.1	94	128	113	96
PUBLIC UTILITIES	48.7	29.4	28.4	88.8	43.3	27.8	96	313	153	98
TRADE AND SERVICES	18.5	36.6	35.5	42.2	38.5	34.8	97	119	107	98
GOVERNMENT, EXC. TRANSPORTATION	1.7	2.9	2.8	3.2	3.0	2.7	97	115	107	98
CONSUMERS, EXC. TRANSPORTATION	19.5	41.1	39.8	45.7	42.6	38.9	97	115	107	98
USER-OPERATED TRANSPORTATION	39.6	84.8	82.9	92.1	87.3	81.5	98	111	105	98
TRANSPORTATION AIR POLLUTION			(THOUSANDS OF TONS)							
SULFUR OXIDES	2.3	5.2	5.0	5.7	5.3	4.9	97	113	106	98
PARTICULATE MATTER	1.7	3.9	3.8	4.3	4.1	3.8	98	111	105	98
CARBON MONOXIDE	326.8	727.3	712.7	782.5	745.9	702.0	98	110	105	99
HYDROCARBONS	58.1	130.0	127.5	139.6	133.2	125.6	98	109	105	99
NITROGEN OXIDES	34.0	77.5	76.1	83.5	79.6	75.1	98	110	105	99
OTHER AIR POLLUTION										
SULFUR OXIDES	92.9	78.2	75.9	177.9	101.9	74.7	97	234	134	98
PARTICULATE MATTER	66.4	106.5	104.3	133.4	114.3	103.3	98	128	110	99
CARBON MONOXIDE	74.5	173.5	172.8	180.7	175.2	172.5	100	105	101	100
HYDROCARBONS	39.8	70.8	55.6	92.2	76.9	51.5	79	166	138	92
NITROGEN OXIDES	27.0	32.4	31.4	57.7	38.6	31.0	97	184	123	99
WATER OXYGEN DEMAND	1194.4	2430.5	2425.6	2444.6	2437.5	2423.9	100	101	100	100
LAND SOLID WASTE	442.7	598.0	585.2	613.6	598.5	582.5	98	105	102	100

SUMMARY PROJECTIONS BY ORE ECONOMIC AREA UNDER FIVE ALTERNATIVE HIGHWAY SYSTEMS

83 MADISON, WIS.

	1970	1990 BASE YEAR	1990 COMPLETED INTERSTATE	1990 EXTENDED PRIMARY	1990 ECONOMIC DEVELOPMENT	1990 URBAN	P E R C E N T			
							CI/BY	EP/CI	ED/CI	U/CI
JOBS BY INDUSTRY			(THOUSANDS)							
NATURAL RESOURCES (1-10)	20.5	4.3	4.2	4.6	5.0	4.2	99	109	109	117
CONSTRUCTION (11,12)	9.0	11.1	11.2	11.1	11.1	11.2	100	99	99	101
MANUFACTURING (13-74)	29.7	50.4	49.0	52.5	53.3	47.8	97	107	109	97
TRANSPORTATION INDUSTRY (75)	3.8	4.8	4.7	5.0	5.1	4.6	98	107	109	99
PUBLIC UTILITIES (76-80)	4.7	5.1	3.0	8.4	9.4	2.8	59	280	313	93
TRADE (81,86,89-99)	42.5	51.7	49.5	55.0	56.4	48.9	96	111	114	99
SERVICES (82-85,87,88,102)	39.1	78.3	78.0	78.3	78.4	77.8	100	100	101	99
STATE & LOCAL GOVT. (101)	45.9	56.8	56.2	57.5	57.8	56.0	99	102	103	100
FEDERAL GOVERNMENT (100,103)	4.7	2.7	2.7	2.7	2.7	2.7	100	100	100	100
TOTAL JOBS	200.0	265.2	258.4	275.1	279.3	256.1	97	106	108	99
CIVILIAN PERSONS EMPLOYED	180.2	238.9	232.9	247.9	251.7	230.7	97	106	108	99
CIVILIAN UNEMPLOYMENT RATE	3.2	4.3	4.3	3.4	2.9	4.4				
POPULATION	455.6	607.7	593.3	606.8	606.7	591.8	98	102	102	100
PER CAPITA INCOME	3844.7	5873.2	5817.3	6113.4	6222.1	5763.2	99	105	107	99
ENERGY USER SECTOR			(TRILLIONS OF BTU'S)							
NATURAL RESOURCES	8.1	14.6	14.9	15.0	15.3	14.4	99	105	105	100
CONSTRUCTION	8.6	18.0	17.3	19.0	19.2	17.2	96	110	111	100
MANUFACTURING	16.6	38.9	37.4	40.1	41.0	36.9	96	107	115	99
TRANSPORTATION INDUSTRY		13.1	12.4	13.9	14.3	12.3	95	112	115	99
PUBLIC UTILITIES	34.8	83.6	41.7	110.6	129.5	44.2	50	265	311	106
TRADE AND SERVICES	15.8	43.3	41.7	45.4	46.5	41.4	96	110	112	99
GOVERNMENT, EXC. TRANSPORTATION	2.4	4.3	4.2	4.4	4.5	4.2	98	104	104	100
CONSUMERS, EXC. TRANSPORTATION	20.5	38.2	37.2	39.4	40.0	36.9	97	106	107	99
USER-OPERATED TRANSPORTATION	31.1	59.7	58.2	61.6	62.4	57.6	97	106	107	99
TRANSPORTATION AIR POLLUTION			(THOUSANDS OF TONS)							
SULFUR OXIDES	1.5	3.5	3.4	3.7	3.7	3.3	96	109	112	99
PARTICULATE MATTER	1.2	2.5	2.5	2.6	2.7	2.4	97	107	110	99
CARBON MONOXIDE	249.5	494.1	481.9	508.7	515.8	478.1	98	106	107	99
HYDROCARBONS	43.8	86.4	84.3	88.9	90.2	83.6	98	106	107	99
NITROGEN OXIDES	24.2	48.5	47.2	50.3	51.0	46.9	98	106	108	99
OTHER AIR POLLUTION										
SULFUR OXIDES	74.5	196.1	126.1	241.2	273.4	130.4	64	191	217	103
PARTICULATE MATTER	40.1	89.5	70.2	105.4	119.4	71.6	78	150	170	102
CARBON MONOXIDE	37.0	66.8	64.4	74.5	77.5	64.9	96	116	120	100
HYDROCARBONS	22.2	66.2	57.2	62.9	65.1	53.5	86	110	114	93
NITROGEN OXIDES	24.1	74.2	56.7	85.8	94.1	57.8	76	151	166	102
WATER OXYGEN DEMAND	1142.8	2361.6	2355.7	2368.9	2377.0	2356.2	100	101	101	100
LAND SOLID WASTE	360.0	480.1	468.7	479.4	479.3	467.5	98	102	102	100

SUMMARY PROJECTIONS BY ORE ECONOMIC AREA UNDER FIVE ALTERNATIVE HIGHWAY SYSTEMS

84 MILWAUKEE, WIS.

	1970	1990 BASE YEAR	1990 COMPLETED INTERSTATE	1990 EXTENDED PRIMARY	1990 ECONOMIC DEVELOPMENT	1990 URBAN	PERCENT CI/BY	EP/CI	ED/CI	U/CI
JOBS BY INDUSTRY			(THOUSANDS)							
NATURAL RESOURCES (1-10)	25.8	6.6	6.2	5.2	5.0	6.0	94	83	80	97
CONSTRUCTION (11,12)	33.7	32.6	31.5	31.5	30.6	32.5	100	96	93	97
MANUFACTURING (13-74)	315.5	445.4	431.6	424.6	423.7	415.7	97	98	98	96
TRANSPORTATION INDUSTRY (75)	25.3	39.8	39.3	39.0	39.0	38.8	99	99	99	99
PUBLIC UTILITIES (76-80)	17.1	7.4	6.0	4.3	4.3	5.4	82	71	72	90
TRADE (81,86,89-99)	206.4	243.3	234.8	229.0	227.6	226.1	97	98	97	96
SERVICES (82-85,87,88,102)	183.2	321.7	321.0	320.6	320.7	320.8	100	100	100	100
STATE & LOCAL GOVT. (101)	79.1	96.5	94.0	92.4	92.1	91.5	97	98	98	98
FEDERAL GOVERNMENT (100,103)	13.7	14.3	13.7	13.4	13.3	13.2	96	97	97	96
TOTAL JOBS	899.7	1207.5	1179.4	1160.1	1156.2	1149.9	98	98	98	98
CIVILIAN PERSONS EMPLOYED	914.8	1218.4	1191.4	1173.3	1169.7	1163.2	98	98	98	98
CIVILIAN UNEMPLOYMENT RATE	3.3	3.9	4.5	4.7	4.5	4.4				
POPULATION	2066.2	2778.2	2743.5	2732.9	2723.0	2734.1	99	100	99	100
PER CAPITA INCOME	3922.7	6570.6	6488.7	6404.1	6405.5	6336.0	99	99	99	98
ENERGY USER SECTOR			(TRILLIONS OF BTU'S)							
NATURAL RESOURCES	11.4	22.2	21.8	21.0	20.9	21.6	98	96	96	99
CONSTRUCTION	40.4	72.3	71.4	61.8	57.1	56.8	99	87	80	79
MANUFACTURING	160.6	357.6	352.9	348.3	347.6	343.6	97	98	98	97
TRANSPORTATION INDUSTRY	33.1	73.1	70.7	69.2	68.8	68.3	97	98	97	97
PUBLIC UTILITIES	80.3	55.4	54.1	53.5	54.1	52.7	98	99	100	97
TRADE AND SERVICES	87.5	187.2	182.6	179.9	179.3	178.4	98	99	98	98
GOVERNMENT, EXC. TRANSPORTATION	7.6	12.6	12.3	12.1	12.1	12.0	98	99	99	98
CONSUMERS, EXC. TRANSPORTATION	107.9	209.1	205.2	202.7	202.2	201.2	98	99	99	98
USER-OPERATED TRANSPORTATION	146.9	313.5	307.4	303.4	302.6	301.1	98	99	99	98
TRANSPORTATION AIR POLLUTION			(THOUSANDS OF TONS)							
SULFUR OXIDES	8.0	17.3	16.8	16.4	16.3	16.3	97	98	97	97
PARTICULATE MATTER	5.7	12.1	11.8	11.6	11.6	11.5	98	98	98	98
CARBON MONOXIDE	1089.7	2336.1	2290.7	2260.6	2253.8	2243.8	98	99	98	98
HYDROCARBONS	189.5	405.6	397.6	392.3	391.2	389.5	98	99	98	98
NITROGEN OXIDES	105.4	224.6	220.5	217.9	216.9	215.7	98	99	98	98
OTHER AIR POLLUTION										
SULFUR OXIDES	272.6	296.1	294.2	293.5	294.3	292.3	99	100	100	99
PARTICULATE MATTER	204.8	458.6	453.1	439.1	436.9	449.1	99	97	96	99
CARBON MONOXIDE	188.5	348.5	344.8	334.1	334.1	343.5	99	97	97	100
HYDROCARBONS	94.6	183.1	178.2	143.8	147.4	125.2	97	81	83	70
NITROGEN OXIDES	68.8	126.9	126.1	125.0	125.1	125.4	99	99	99	99
WATER OXYGEN DEMAND	1485.0	3074.5	3068.1	3061.1	3057.5	3061.3	100	100	100	100
LAND SOLID WASTE	1632.3	2194.7	2167.4	2158.9	2151.2	2160.0	99	100	99	100

85 GREEN BAY, WIS.

	1970	1990 BASE YEAR	1990 COMPLETED INTERSTATE (THOUSANDS)	1990 EXTENDED PRIMARY	1990 ECONOMIC DEVELOPMENT	1990 URBAN	CI/BY	EP/CI	ED/CI	U/CI
JOBS BY INDUSTRY										
NATURAL RESOURCES (1-10)	35.7	8.9	8.6	9.3	9.1	8.6	97	108	105	99
CONSTRUCTION (11,12)	14.0	16.4	16.2	17.5	17.0	16.3	99	108	104	100
MANUFACTURING (13-74)	97.6	139.3	129.0	139.1	136.0	128.1	93	108	105	99
TRANSPORTATION INDUSTRY (75)	8.9	15.4	15.1	15.7	15.5	15.0	98	104	103	99
PUBLIC UTILITIES (76-80)	6.3	6.4	4.8	11.0	10.0	4.4	75	228	207	92
TRADE (81,86,89-99)	74.4	117.9	112.5	122.1	119.7	111.3	95	108	106	99
SERVICES (82-85,87,88,102)	55.7	89.4	89.1	89.5	89.4	89.1	100	100	100	100
STATE & LOCAL GOVT. (101)	44.6	55.7	53.6	56.3	55.6	53.4	96	105	104	100
FEDERAL GOVERNMENT (100,103)	8.1	8.2	7.8	8.4	8.2	7.7	94	108	106	99
TOTAL JOBS	345.2	457.6	436.8	468.9	460.5	433.9	95	107	105	99
CIVILIAN PERSONS EMPLOYED	336.0	443.9	424.0	454.7	446.8	421.3	96	107	105	99
CIVILIAN UNEMPLOYMENT RATE	4.5	2.1	2.6	1.7	2.8	2.8				
POPULATION	926.1	1147.2	1117.6	1136.6	1127.8	1122.0	97	102	101	100
PER CAPITA INCOME	3051.1	5602.5	5419.0	5789.9	5707.7	5363.5	97	107	105	99
ENERGY USER SECTOR (TRILLIONS OF BTU'S)										
NATURAL RESOURCES	21.8	40.4	39.3	41.2	41.6	38.9	97	105	106	99
CONSTRUCTION	15.6	32.5	24.7	36.5	34.1	22.9	76	148	138	93
MANUFACTURING	66.2	173.5	169.4	173.6	172.2	169.0	98	102	102	100
TRANSPORTATION INDUSTRY	8.5	20.0	18.4	20.9	20.3	18.2	92	114	110	99
PUBLIC UTILITIES	57.5	151.8	127.3	210.4	191.3	113.7	84	165	150	89
TRADE AND SERVICES	26.7	63.2	60.0	66.1	64.7	59.6	95	110	108	99
GOVERNMENT, EXC. TRANSPORTATION	3.0	4.9	4.7	5.0	4.9	4.7	96	106	105	100
CONSUMERS, EXC. TRANSPORTATION	33.6	68.7	65.6	70.0	68.8	65.3	95	107	105	99
USER-OPERATED TRANSPORTATION	54.1	116.0	111.1	118.0	116.1	110.6	96	106	105	100
TRANSPORTATION AIR POLLUTION (THOUSANDS OF TONS)										
SULFUR OXIDES	2.5	5.5	5.1	5.6	5.5	5.1	94	110	107	99
PARTICULATE MATTER	1.9	4.2	3.9	4.3	4.2	3.9	95	108	106	99
CARBON MONOXIDE	405.8	867.0	831.0	883.4	869.0	826.7	96	106	105	99
HYDROCARBONS	70.9	151.0	144.8	153.8	151.4	144.0	96	106	105	99
NITROGEN OXIDES	38.7	81.9	78.5	84.1	82.5	78.0	96	107	105	99
OTHER AIR POLLUTION										
SULFUR OXIDES	110.9	314.0	272.9	411.2	379.2	250.3	87	151	139	92
PARTICULATE MATTER	92.0	223.4	211.0	253.1	243.2	204.7	94	120	115	97
CARBON MONOXIDE	160.3	326.0	318.2	333.2	332.5	316.0	98	105	105	99
HYDROCARBONS	31.0	66.5	49.6	58.2	55.9	48.6	75	117	113	98
NITROGEN OXIDES	39.3	110.9	100.2	135.3	127.6	94.5	90	135	127	94
WATER OXYGEN DEMAND	1490.7	3085.3	3083.0	3092.8	3090.8	3081.4	100	100	100	100
LAND SOLID WASTE	731.7	906.3	883.1	897.9	891.0	886.4	97	102	101	100

PERCENT columns: CI/BY, EP/CI, ED/CI, U/CI

SUMMARY PROJECTIONS BY ORE ECONOMIC AREA UNDER FIVE ALTERNATIVE HIGHWAY SYSTEMS

86   WAUSAU, WIS.

	1970	1990 BASE YEAR	1990 COMPLETED INTERSTATE	1990 EXTENDED PRIMARY	1990 ECONOMIC DEVELOPMENT	1990 URBAN	CI/BY	EP/CI	ED/CI	U/CI
							P E R C E N T			
JOBS BY INDUSTRY (THOUSANDS)										
NATURAL RESOURCES (1-10)	20.6	4.8	4.8	4.9	4.8	4.8	101	101	101	100
CONSTRUCTION (11,12)	3.6	4.5	4.5	5.7	5.6	4.5	100	126	124	100
MANUFACTURING (13-74)	35.1	38.6	37.4	40.1	39.5	37.2	97	107	106	100
TRANSPORTATION INDUSTRY (75)	3.5	6.2	6.1	6.3	6.2	6.1	99	102	102	100
PUBLIC UTILITIES (76-80)	2.0	1.1	1.1	1.3	1.1	1.0	90	128	110	98
TRADE (81,86,89-99)	26.1	31.6	30.8	32.7	32.2	30.6	97	106	105	99
SERVICES (82-85,87,88,102)	24.8	42.3	42.1	42.2	42.2	42.0	99	100	100	100
STATE & LOCAL GOVT. (101)	16.1	19.8	19.5	20.2	20.0	19.5	99	103	103	100
FEDERAL GOVERNMENT (100,103)	1.7	1.6	1.5	1.7	1.7	1.5	96	109	107	100
TOTAL JOBS	133.5	150.5	147.7	154.9	153.3	147.3	98	105	104	100
CIVILIAN PERSONS EMPLOYED	124.7	139.9	137.3	143.9	142.5	136.9	98	105	104	100
CIVILIAN UNEMPLOYMENT RATE	4.4	8.0	7.5	8.2	8.2	7.5				
POPULATION	350.3	461.6	456.5	473.9	470.1	453.1	99	104	103	99
PER CAPITA INCOME	2909.5	4798.1	4743.1	4830.2	4812.2	4764.0	99	102	101	100
ENERGY USER SECTOR (TRILLIONS OF BTU'S)										
NATURAL RESOURCES	7.6	12.7	12.5	12.9	12.7	12.4	98	103	102	100
CONSTRUCTION	4.1	8.3	6.9	11.5	11.0	6.5	83	167	159	95
MANUFACTURING	28.1	75.5	75.0	76.2	76.2	75.0	99	102	102	100
TRANSPORTATION INDUSTRY	3.0	7.5	7.2	7.8	7.6	7.2	97	107	105	99
PUBLIC UTILITIES	12.9	9.9	8.2	11.8	9.3	8.0	83	145	114	98
TRADE AND SERVICES	10.0	24.0	23.5	24.5	24.2	23.4	98	104	104	100
GOVERNMENT, EXC. TRANSPORTATION	1.1	1.8	1.8	1.9	1.9	1.8	98	104	103	100
CONSUMERS, EXC. TRANSPORTATION	12.5	24.5	24.1	25.2	24.9	24.1	98	104	103	100
USER-OPERATED TRANSPORTATION	22.3	46.3	45.6	47.2	46.9	45.5	99	104	103	100
TRANSPORTATION AIR POLLUTION (THOUSANDS OF TONS)										
SULFUR OXIDES	1.2	2.4	2.3	2.4	2.4	2.3	97	105	104	100
PARTICULATE MATTER	0.9	1.8	1.8	1.9	1.9	1.8	98	104	103	100
CARBON MONOXIDE	179.1	363.4	358.2	370.8	368.1	357.3	99	104	103	100
HYDROCARBONS	31.7	63.9	63.0	65.2	64.8	62.9	99	103	103	100
NITROGEN OXIDES	18.2	36.0	35.5	36.9	36.6	35.4	99	104	103	100
OTHER AIR POLLUTION										
SULFUR OXIDES	27.0	37.4	34.1	40.8	36.6	33.6	91	120	107	99
PARTICULATE MATTER	34.5	61.6	59.3	62.8	61.1	59.1	96	106	103	100
CARBON MONOXIDE	63.5	121.4	116.8	123.1	120.4	116.6	96	105	103	100
HYDROCARBONS	11.4	15.9	15.4	19.2	21.6	15.4	97	125	140	100
NITROGEN OXIDES	9.3	17.3	16.1	18.3	17.1	15.9	93	114	106	99
WATER OXYGEN DEMAND	950.3	1960.0	1955.1	1960.2	1960.1	1953.7	100	100	100	100
LAND SOLID WASTE	276.7	364.7	360.6	374.4	371.4	358.0	99	104	103	99

87 DULUTH-SUP. MINN.-WIS.

	1970	1990 BASE YEAR	1990 COMPLETED INTERSTATE	1990 EXTENDED PRIMARY	1990 ECONOMIC DEVELOPMENT	1990 URBAN	CI/BY	EP/CI	ED/CI	U/CI
								PER CENT		
JOBS BY INDUSTRY										
NATURAL RESOURCES (1-10)	21.9	9.2	9.1	9.6	10.3	8.9	99	105	113	97
CONSTRUCTION (11-12)	4.9	5.8	5.8	8.1	7.6	5.7	99	141	132	99
MANUFACTURING (13-74)	25.5	34.5	33.7	35.9	36.8	33.1	98	107	109	98
TRANSPORTATION INDUSTRY (75)	7.0	8.0	8.0	8.2	8.3	7.9	100	103	104	99
PUBLIC UTILITIES (76-80)	3.4	11.0	11.0	12.6	13.0	10.6	100	114	119	96
TRADE (81,86,89-99)	33.7	46.3	45.5	48.7	50.3	44.6	100	107	110	98
SERVICES (82-85,87,88,102)	28.3	38.3	38.1	38.9	38.6	38.1	100	102	101	100
STATE & LOCAL GOVT. (101)	23.5	27.0	26.8	27.9	28.2	26.6	99	104	105	99
FEDERAL GOVERNMENT (100,103)	5.3	5.0	5.0	5.2	5.3	4.9	99	105	106	99
TOTAL JOBS	153.4	185.2	183.0	195.1	198.4	180.5	99	107	108	99
CIVILIAN PERSONS EMPLOYED	149.5	180.4	178.3	189.9	193.1	175.5	99	107	108	99
CIVILIAN UNEMPLOYMENT RATE	5.3	5.3	.5	.5	.5	.5				
POPULATION	429.0	435.7	429.7	457.8	462.7	427.5	99	107	108	99
PER CAPITA INCOME	3139.2	6190.6	6192.8	6278.2	6332.1	6132.7	100	101	102	99
ENERGY USER SECTOR (TRILLIONS OF BTU'S)										
NATURAL RESOURCES	35.5	67.1	66.9	68.4	71.8	65.8	100	102	107	98
CONSTRUCTION	4.6	10.2	10.1	18.7	13.9	7.1	99	185	137	70
MANUFACTURING	22.5	39.9	39.4	40.5	42.5	39.1	99	103	108	97
TRANSPORTATION INDUSTRY	3.2	7.8	7.6	8.5	8.9	7.4	97	111	116	97
PUBLIC UTILITIES	41.8	255.3	246.8	280.8	301.7	238.4	97	114	122	97
TRADE AND SERVICES	14.4	40.7	40.3	42.2	42.9	39.8	99	105	106	99
GOVERNMENT, EXC. TRANSPORTATION	2.1	3.3	3.3	3.3	3.4	3.2	99	104	105	99
CONSUMERS, EXC. TRANSPORTATION	16.4	29.6	29.3	31.1	31.5	29.0	99	106	108	99
USER-OPERATED TRANSPORTATION	27.7	53.9	53.4	56.2	56.9	52.8	99	105	107	99
TRANSPORTATION AIR POLLUTION (THOUSANDS OF TONS)										
SULFUR OXIDES	1.0	2.3	2.2	2.4	2.5	2.2	98	108	112	98
PARTICULATE MATTER	1.8	1.8	1.8	1.9	1.9	1.7	99	107	109	98
CARBON MONOXIDE	191.8	386.3	382.2	403.4	408.8	378.3	99	106	107	99
HYDROCARBONS	33.4	67.3	66.6	70.2	71.2	65.9	99	105	107	99
NITROGEN OXIDES	17.4	36.0	35.7	37.9	38.5	35.3	99	106	108	99
OTHER AIR POLLUTION										
SULFUR OXIDES	93.2	445.3	430.9	487.6	522.4	417.1	97	113	121	97
PARTICULATE MATTER	78.9	201.7	198.3	213.8	226.4	193.6	98	108	114	98
CARBON MONOXIDE	204.4	386.8	387.0	391.3	404.7	381.6	100	101	105	99
HYDROCARBONS	53.0	91.2	88.5	91.9	116.3	87.3	97	104	131	99
NITROGEN OXIDES	36.9	138.4	134.8	149.2	159.1	131.0	97	111	118	97
WATER OXYGEN DEMAND	225.9	473.8	472.8	475.6	477.4	472.0	100	101	101	100
LAND SOLID WASTE	338.9	344.2	339.4	361.6	365.5	337.7	99	107	108	99

88 EAU CLAIRE, WIS.

	1970	1990 BASE YEAR	1990 COMPLETED INTERSTATE	1990 EXTENDED PRIMARY	1990 ECONOMIC DEVELOPMENT	1990 URBAN	CI/BY	EP/CI	ED/CI	U/CI
			(THOUSANDS)							
JOBS BY INDUSTRY										
NATURAL RESOURCES (1-10)	14.8	2.6	2.6	2.6	2.7	2.6	100	102	106	100
CONSTRUCTION (11,12)	2.5	3.3	3.0	3.9	6.2	3.0	93	129	203	97
MANUFACTURING (13-74)	17.0	31.6	30.2	31.6	34.0	29.7	95	105	113	97
TRANSPORTATION INDUSTRY (75)	1.9	1.7	1.7	1.8	1.9	1.7	98	105	113	99
PUBLIC UTILITIES (76-80)	1.5	1.8	1.5	1.8	1.5	1.4	64	162	304	88
TRADE (81-86,89-99)	17.1	17.0	16.3	17.5	19.7	16.0	96	107	121	98
SERVICES (82-85,87,88,102)	13.1	18.9	18.8	18.8	19.0	18.8	100	100	101	100
STATE & LOCAL GOVT. (101)	12.7	15.5	15.2	15.6	16.4	15.1	98	103	108	100
FEDERAL GOVERNMENT (100,103)	1.0	1.0	.9	1.0	1.2	.9	93	110	129	98
TOTAL JOBS	81.7	92.3	89.2	93.7	102.6	88.2	97	105	115	99
CIVILIAN PERSONS EMPLOYED	79.1	88.8	85.8	90.1	98.7	84.9	97	105	115	99
CIVILIAN UNEMPLOYMENT RATE	5.5	8.8	8.5	8.2	8.2	8.9				
POPULATION	219.9	281.6	272.0	283.0	302.3	271.1	97	104	111	100
PER CAPITA INCOME	2869.8	4617.2	4577.0	4659.8	4900.6	4540.0	99	102	107	99
			(TRILLIONS OF BTU'S)							
ENERGY USER SECTOR										
NATURAL RESOURCES	3.8	7.5	7.4	7.8	8.0	7.4	99	105	109	99
CONSTRUCTION	4.2	7.7	6.2	8.2	12.9	3.9	81	131	206	62
MANUFACTURING	8.1	18.0	17.3	18.2	19.3	17.1	96	105	112	99
TRANSPORTATION INDUSTRY	1.6	3.2	2.9	3.3	3.9	2.8	93	112	132	97
PUBLIC UTILITIES	19.6	29.1	24.7	41.8	71.6	23.2	85	169	289	94
TRADE AND SERVICES	6.3	14.0	13.6	14.2	15.3	13.4	97	104	113	99
GOVERNMENT, EXC. TRANSPORTATION	1.9	2.7	2.7	2.8	2.8	2.7	99	102	105	99
CONSUMERS, EXC. TRANSPORTATION	9.5	18.3	17.8	18.4	19.8	17.7	97	104	111	100
USER-OPERATED TRANSPORTATION	17.9	35.4	34.7	35.7	37.8	34.5	98	103	109	99
			(THOUSANDS OF TONS)							
TRANSPORTATION AIR POLLUTION										
SULFUR OXIDES	.6	1.1	1.1	1.1	1.3	1.0	95	107	120	98
PARTICULATE MATTER	.5	1.0	1.0	1.0	1.1	1.0	97	105	114	99
CARBON MONOXIDE	123.1	247.7	242.4	250.1	266.1	240.8	98	103	110	99
HYDROCARBONS	21.5	43.1	42.2	43.5	46.3	41.9	98	103	110	99
NITROGEN OXIDES	11.2	22.2	21.7	22.5	24.1	21.5	98	104	111	99
OTHER AIR POLLUTION										
SULFUR OXIDES	33.3	49.2	42.0	70.1	119.6	39.5	85	167	285	94
PARTICULATE MATTER	24.0	44.6	43.2	54.8	69.8	41.5	97	127	162	96
CARBON MONOXIDE	13.7	21.9	20.8	27.1	31.7	20.3	95	130	152	98
HYDROCARBONS	4.0	9.4	4.9	7.1	8.2	4.8	52	144	166	98
NITROGEN OXIDES	8.8	12.5	10.7	17.8	30.2	10.1	86	166	282	94
WATER OXYGEN DEMAND	735.4	1494.1	1493.8	1498.0	1503.3	1492.7	100	100	101	100
LAND SOLID WASTE	173.7	222.5	214.9	223.6	238.8	214.2	97	104	111	100

SUMMARY PROJECTIONS BY OBE ECONOMIC AREA UNDER FIVE ALTERNATIVE HIGHWAY SYSTEMS

89 LA CROSSE, WIS.

	1970	1990 BASE YEAR	1990 COMPLETED INTERSTATE	1990 EXTENDED PRIMARY	1990 ECONOMIC DEVELOPMENT	1990 URBAN	CI/BY	EP/CI	ED/CI	U/CI
								PER	CENT	
JOBS BY INDUSTRY			(THOUSANDS)							
NATURAL RESOURCES (1-10)	18.3	3.2	3.2	3.1	3.8	3.2	100	97	118	100
CONSTRUCTION (11-12)	3.2	4.1	4.2	4.1	4.6	4.2	101	98	111	99
MANUFACTURING (13-74)	19.7	24.4	24.7	24.2	28.8	23.3	101	98	116	94
TRANSPORTATION INDUSTRY (75)	2.9	.6	.6	.5	.7	.6	99	95	126	96
PUBLIC UTILITIES (76-80)	2.1	2.0	1.8	1.5	4.3	1.7	93	84	235	93
TRADE (81,86,89-99)	21.5	21.2	20.9	20.1	26.0	20.1	98	96	125	96
SERVICES (82-85,87,88,102)	17.3	29.1	28.9	28.8	29.2	28.9	100	100	101	100
STATE & LOCAL GOVT. (101)	10.8	11.6	11.7	11.4	12.6	11.4	100	98	108	97
FEDERAL GOVERNMENT (100,103)	3.2	3.1	3.1	3.0	3.3	3.0	100	98	107	98
TOTAL JOBS	99.1	99.3	99.1	96.9	113.3	96.3	98	98	114	97
CIVILIAN PERSONS EMPLOYED	99.1	99.3	99.1	97.0	112.7	96.5	100	98	114	97
CIVILIAN UNEMPLOYMENT RATE	5.8	8.4	7.4	7.0	6.6	8.3				
POPULATION	269.5	312.6	309.1	297.6	328.1	305.2	99	96	106	99
PER CAPITA INCOME	3007.0	4434.3	4518.8	4560.0	4859.1	4396.6	102	101	108	97
ENERGY USER SECTOR			(TRILLIONS OF BTU'S)							
NATURAL RESOURCES	5.6	10.8	10.8	10.5	11.5	10.8	100	97	106	100
CONSTRUCTION	4.4	7.0	7.0	6.6	9.4	4.7	100	94	134	67
MANUFACTURING	9.5	17.6	17.5	16.9	20.0	17.1	99	96	114	98
TRANSPORTATION INDUSTRY	2.7	5.0	4.9	4.6	6.2	4.7	98	96	127	96
PUBLIC UTILITIES	25.4	57.1	51.4	42.3	113.2	48.1	90	82	220	94
TRADE AND SERVICES	6.9	14.8	14.6	14.1	17.3	14.2	98	97	119	98
GOVERNMENT, EXC. TRANSPORTATION	1.1	1.6	1.6	1.6	1.7	1.6	100	98	107	98
CONSUMERS, EXC. TRANSPORTATION	10.6	18.0	18.1	17.8	19.8	17.6	100	98	109	98
USER-OPERATED TRANSPORTATION	19.2	34.7	34.8	34.3	37.4	34.1	100	99	107	98
TRANSPORTATION AIR POLLUTION			(THOUSANDS OF TONS)							
SULFUR OXIDES	.9	1.6	1.5	1.5	1.8	1.5	99	98	117	97
PARTICULATE MATTER	2.7	1.2	1.2	1.2	1.4	1.2	100	98	112	98
CARBON MONOXIDE	142.6	260.6	261.2	256.8	282.0	256.1	100	98	108	98
HYDROCARBONS	25.0	45.6	45.8	45.0	49.4	44.9	100	98	108	98
NITROGEN OXIDES	13.7	25.0	25.0	24.6	27.4	24.5	100	98	109	98
OTHER AIR POLLUTION										
SULFUR OXIDES	43.8	99.9	90.4	74.6	193.2	85.0	90	83	214	94
PARTICULATE MATTER	32.3	61.8	59.0	48.9	92.7	58.1	95	83	157	99
CARBON MONOXIDE	23.4	40.3	40.8	35.7	50.6	41.3	101	88	124	101
HYDROCARBONS	6.3	10.3	10.3	9.6	15.3	10.2	100	93	149	100
NITROGEN OXIDES	12.2	28.0	25.6	21.3	51.5	24.4	91	83	201	95
WATER OXYGEN DEMAND	1001.0	2024.3	2023.1	2016.9	2033.3	2023.0	100	100	101	100
LAND SOLID WASTE	212.9	246.9	244.2	235.1	259.2	241.1	99	96	106	99

SUMMARY PROJECTIONS BY ORE ECONOMIC AREA UNDER FIVE ALTERNATIVE HIGHWAY SYSTEMS

90 ROCHESTER, MINN.

	1970	1990 BASE YEAR (THOUSANDS)	1990 COMPLETED INTERSTATE	1990 EXTENDED PRIMARY	1990 ECONOMIC DEVELOPMENT	1990 URBAN	P E R C E N T CI/BY	EP/CI	ED/CI	U/CI
JOBS BY INDUSTRY										
NATURAL RESOURCES (1-10)	13.6	3.9	3.9	3.8	4.0	4.0	101	96	99	100
CONSTRUCTION (11-12)	3.7	5.2	5.3	5.1	4.7	5.2	101	96	90	99
MANUFACTURING (13-74)	21.4	31.3	30.1	28.4	29.8	28.6	96	95	99	95
TRANSPORTATION INDUSTRY (75)	2.3	3.9	3.9	3.8	3.9	3.8	99	98	101	98
PUBLIC UTILITIES (76-80)	1.6	2.2	2.4	1.6	2.3	2.3	107	68	95	98
TRADE (81,86,89-99)	21.4	24.0	23.3	22.3	23.2	22.3	97	96	103	96
SERVICES (82-85,87,88,102)	23.1	26.4	26.3	26.2	26.2	26.2	99	100	100	100
STATE & LOCAL GOVT. (101)	11.3	12.7	12.6	12.3	12.7	12.3	99	97	100	98
FEDERAL GOVERNMENT (100-103)	1.0	.8	.8	.7	.8	.7	96	96	101	98
TOTAL JOBS	99.5	110.5	108.5	104.0	108.2	105.5	98	96	100	97
CIVILIAN PERSONS EMPLOYED	96.5	106.7	104.8	100.6	104.5	101.9	98	96	100	97
CIVILIAN UNEMPLOYMENT RATE	5.1	3.1	3.2	2.9	3.0	3.4				
POPULATION	245.1	263.5	261.1	250.6	258.7	257.2	99	96	99	99
PER CAPITA INCOME	3641.8	6358.4	6350.1	6342.4	6426.7	6243.0	100	100	101	98
ENERGY USER SECTOR	(TRILLIONS OF BTU'S)									
NATURAL RESOURCES	8.5	20.8	20.9	20.7	20.8	20.9	100	99	100	100
CONSTRUCTION	5.2	10.4	10.5	6.4	7.8	6.7	101	61	75	64
MANUFACTURING	6.7	14.7	14.2	13.6	14.4	13.5	96	96	102	96
TRANSPORTATION INDUSTRY	2.3	4.9	4.7	4.3	4.8	4.4	95	93	104	93
PUBLIC UTILITIES	3.6	9.5	11.0	7.1	11.5	10.4	116	64	104	94
TRADE AND SERVICES	9.9	26.7	26.3	25.3	26.5	25.8	99	96	101	98
GOVERNMENT, EXC. TRANSPORTATION	.9	1.4	1.3	1.3	1.4	1.3	99	97	100	98
CONSUMERS, EXC. TRANSPORTATION	9.2	17.1	16.9	16.3	16.9	16.5	99	97	100	97
USER-OPERATED TRANSPORTATION	16.8	31.5	31.3	30.3	31.3	30.6	99	97	100	98
TRANSPORTATION AIR POLLUTION	(THOUSANDS OF TONS)									
SULFUR OXIDES	1.0	2.4	2.3	2.3	2.4	2.3	98	97	101	97
PARTICULATE MATTER	.8	1.8	1.8	1.7	1.7	1.7	99	98	101	98
CARBON MONOXIDE	143.0	292.5	290.5	283.6	291.1	285.4	99	98	100	98
HYDROCARBONS	25.6	53.1	52.7	51.5	52.8	51.8	99	98	100	98
NITROGEN OXIDES	15.4	33.7	33.5	32.8	33.6	32.9	99	98	100	98
OTHER AIR POLLUTION										
SULFUR OXIDES	7.9	23.6	26.0	19.3	26.7	25.0	110	74	103	96
PARTICULATE MATTER	15.7	38.0	39.0	35.1	38.5	39.4	103	90	99	101
CARBON MONOXIDE	38.2	112.2	113.0	109.6	111.8	113.9	101	97	99	101
HYDROCARBONS	8.9	27.5	25.8	23.6	24.6	24.1	94	92	95	93
NITROGEN OXIDES	3.8	12.4	13.0	11.1	13.1	12.8	104	86	101	99
WATER OXYGEN DEMAND	981.1	1942.2	1942.6	1940.2	1942.6	1942.6	100	100	100	100
LAND SOLID WASTE	193.6	208.2	206.3	198.0	204.4	203.2	99	96	99	99

SUMMARY PROJECTIONS BY OBE ECONOMIC AREA UNDER FIVE ALTERNATIVE HIGHWAY SYSTEMS

91 MINN.-ST. PAUL, MINN.

	1970	1990 BASE YEAR	1990 COMPLETED INTERSTATE	1990 EXTENDED PRIMARY	1990 ECONOMIC DEVELOPMENT	1990 URBAN	PERCENT CI/BY	EP/CI	ED/CI	U/CI
JOBS BY INDUSTRY			(THOUSANDS)							
NATURAL RESOURCES (1-10)	91.7	22.3	22.2	22.1	22.0	21.8	99	100	99	98
CONSTRUCTION (11-12)	57.6	54.4	55.0	53.6	50.8	54.8	101	98	92	100
MANUFACTURING (13-74)	280.6	520.1	506.2	514.1	515.4	474.1	97	102	102	94
TRANSPORTATION INDUSTRY (75)	49.8	85.9	85.4	85.7	85.9	84.3	100	100	100	99
PUBLIC UTILITIES (76-80)	23.5	31.7	30.1	29.6	30.1	27.0	95	98	100	90
TRADE (81,86,89-99)	321.5	376.7	368.7	370.9	371.9	352.9	98	101	101	96
SERVICES (82-85,87,88,102)	288.0	485.3	484.8	484.6	484.4	484.4	100	100	100	100
STATE & LOCAL GOVT. (101)	144.6	196.9	194.7	195.4	195.6	189.6	99	100	100	97
FEDERAL GOVERNMENT (100,103)	27.0	31.4	30.9	31.0	31.1	29.7	98	101	101	96
TOTAL JOBS	1284.3	1804.8	1778.0	1787.2	1787.6	1718.6	99	101	101	97
CIVILIAN PERSONS EMPLOYED	1220.9	1712.6	1687.1	1696.1	1696.6	1630.7	99	101	101	97
CIVILIAN UNEMPLOYMENT RATE	4.1	3.1	3.0	2.9	2.9	3.7				
POPULATION	2935.4	3819.0	3782.2	3779.0	3777.1	3762.7	99	100	100	99
PER CAPITA INCOME	3835.7	7042.3	6995.7	7043.7	7047.3	6779.6	99	101	101	97
ENERGY USER SECTOR		(TRILLIONS OF BTU'S)								
NATURAL RESOURCES	55.4	136.3	135.7	135.4	135.0	134.5	100	100	100	99
CONSTRUCTION	66.6	113.1	112.5	113.9	95.3	87.5	100	101	85	78
MANUFACTURING	124.7	265.8	261.7	262.9	263.2	249.5	98	100	101	95
TRANSPORTATION INDUSTRY	52.6	117.2	114.9	115.7	116.2	110.3	98	101	101	96
PUBLIC UTILITIES	143.4	426.1	403.0	391.8	406.6	379.0	95	97	101	94
TRADE AND SERVICES	159.7	362.2	357.6	358.5	359.7	349.3	99	100	101	98
GOVERNMENT, EXC. TRANSPORTATION	14.6	25.0	24.8	24.8	24.9	24.2	99	100	100	98
CONSUMERS, EXC. TRANSPORTATION	143.9	309.0	305.2	306.5	306.4	297.2	99	100	100	97
USER-OPERATED TRANSPORTATION	244.7	536.1	530.3	532.1	532.1	517.8	99	100	100	98
TRANSPORTATION AIR POLLUTION		(THOUSANDS OF TONS)								
SULFUR OXIDES	15.1	35.2	34.6	34.7	34.8	33.7	98	100	101	97
PARTICULATE MATTER	10.6	24.7	24.4	24.5	24.6	23.9	99	100	101	98
CARBON MONOXIDE	1911.0	4348.7	4305.0	4319.6	4320.0	4212.1	99	100	100	98
HYDROCARBONS	337.1	770.1	762.4	764.7	764.9	746.4	99	100	100	98
NITROGEN OXIDES	197.9	458.9	455.3	457.8	457.6	445.8	99	101	100	98
OTHER AIR POLLUTION										
SULFUR OXIDES	320.5	779.1	741.8	723.2	747.1	703.2	95	97	101	95
PARTICULATE MATTER	363.5	752.0	743.6	740.5	745.7	732.5	99	100	100	99
CARBON MONOXIDE	373.9	911.7	908.5	907.0	905.8	902.5	100	100	101	99
HYDROCARBONS	169.3	374.0	369.4	371.8	374.7	342.4	99	101	101	93
NITROGEN OXIDES	121.8	229.7	226.3	215.7	221.3	210.4	96	98	100	95
WATER OXYGEN DEMAND	5338.9	10826.1	10822.1	10820.0	10825.7	10819.2	100	100	100	100
LAND SOLID WASTE	2319.0	3017.0	2987.9	2985.4	2983.9	2972.6	99	100	100	99

SUMMARY PROJECTIONS BY OBE ECONOMIC AREA UNDER FIVE ALTERNATIVE HIGHWAY SYSTEMS

92 GRAND FORKS, N. D.

	1970	1990 BASE YEAR	1990 COMPLETED INTERSTATE	1990 EXTENDED PRIMARY	1990 ECONOMIC DEVELOPMENT	1990 URBAN	CI/BY	EP/CI	ED/CI	U/CI
JOBS BY INDUSTRY			(THOUSANDS)							
NATURAL RESOURCES (1-10)	18.1	5.6	5.6	5.9	5.9	5.6	99	106	106	106
CONSTRUCTION (11,12)	2.6	1.0	.9	2.0	1.1	.6	90	222	122	67
MANUFACTURING (13-74)	6.4	13.2	12.9	15.1	15.4	12.6	98	117	119	98
TRANSPORTATION INDUSTRY (75)	2.4	4.0	3.9	4.1	4.1	3.9	99	105	105	100
PUBLIC UTILITIES (76-80)	1.3	1.0	1.0	2.7	2.8	1.0	96	271	285	101
TRADE (81,86-89,99)	21.4	19.0	18.8	21.4	21.2	18.6	99	114	113	99
SERVICES (82-85,87,88,102)	16.2	17.1	17.1	17.1	17.1	17.1	100	100	100	100
STATE & LOCAL GOVT. (101)	11.6	11.5	11.4	12.0	12.1	11.3	99	106	106	99
FEDERAL GOVERNMENT (100,103)	8.1	7.3	7.2	7.4	7.4	7.2	100	102	102	100
TOTAL JOBS	88.0	79.6	78.8	87.8	87.0	77.9	99	111	110	99
CIVILIAN PERSONS EMPLOYED	78.0	69.6	68.8	77.2	76.6	68.0	99	112	111	99
CIVILIAN UNEMPLOYMENT RATE	6.4	10.7	10.6	9.2	9.2	10.8				
POPULATION	220.5	238.3	235.8	250.9	251.2	232.4	99	106	107	99
PER CAPITA INCOME	2707.6	3552.6	3538.1	3830.0	3810.8	3535.6	100	108	108	100
ENERGY USER SECTOR			(TRILLIONS OF BTU'S)							
NATURAL RESOURCES	23.4	41.0	40.9	41.4	41.4	40.9	100	101	101	100
CONSTRUCTION	3.0	4.9	4.9	14.6	5.8	2.8	100	299	119	57
MANUFACTURING	5.6	15.1	14.8	16.0	16.4	14.8	98	108	111	99
TRANSPORTATION INDUSTRY	1.0	2.9	2.8	3.7	3.6	2.8	98	129	127	98
PUBLIC UTILITIES	8.8	31.2	28.2	57.1	58.8	28.0	91	202	208	99
TRADE AND SERVICES	6.1	15.1	15.0	17.1	17.1	19.9	99	114	114	99
GOVERNMENT, EXC. TRANSPORTATION	2.5	3.2	3.2	3.3	3.3	3.2	100	102	102	100
CONSUMERS, EXC. TRANSPORTATION	6.5	9.5	9.4	10.5	10.4	9.3	99	111	111	99
USER-OPERATED TRANSPORTATION	17.0	26.9	26.7	28.4	28.3	26.5	99	106	106	99
TRANSPORTATION AIR POLLUTION			(THOUSANDS OF TONS)							
SULFUR OXIDES	2.3	4.0	4.0	4.1	4.1	4.0	100	104	104	100
PARTICULATE MATTER	1.6	2.8	2.8	2.9	2.9	2.8	100	103	103	100
CARBON MONOXIDE	209.4	354.1	352.9	366.0	365.6	351.5	100	104	104	100
HYDROCARBONS	40.4	68.2	68.0	70.3	70.2	67.8	100	103	103	100
NITROGEN OXIDES	30.7	52.4	52.2	53.7	53.7	52.1	100	103	103	100
OTHER AIR POLLUTION										
SULFUR OXIDES	16.1	57.0	52.0	100.1	102.9	51.7	91	192	198	99
PARTICULATE MATTER	39.5	98.0	96.6	114.0	113.9	96.6	99	118	118	100
CARBON MONOXIDE	164.1	294.6	294.2	303.4	302.3	294.2	100	103	103	100
HYDROCARBONS	34.3	63.4	61.1	64.7	68.6	61.0	96	106	112	100
NITROGEN OXIDES	8.0	22.7	21.4	33.7	34.3	21.3	94	157	160	100
WATER OXYGEN DEMAND	433.3	906.0	905.4	910.9	911.3	905.3	100	101	101	100
LAND SOLID WASTE	174.2	188.2	186.3	198.2	198.4	183.6	99	106	107	99

257

SUMMARY PROJECTIONS BY ORE ECONOMIC AREA UNDER FIVE ALTERNATIVE HIGHWAY SYSTEMS

93   MINOT. N. D.

	1970	1990 BASE YEAR	1990 COMPLETED INTERSTATE	1990 EXTENDED PRIMARY	1990 ECONOMIC DEVELOPMENT	1990 URBAN	PERCENT CI/BY	EP/CI	ED/CI	U/CI
JOBS BY INDUSTRY			(THOUSANDS)							
NATURAL RESOURCES (1-10)	15.7	4.9	5.2	5.5	5.6	5.1	106	107	109	99
CONSTRUCTION (11.12)	3.0	2.9	2.3	6.3	8.5	2.3	78	277	377	100
MANUFACTURING (13-74)	2.1	5.8	6.4	9.1	9.8	6.1	110	142	153	95
TRANSPORTATION INDUSTRY (75)	2.0	2.6	2.8	3.0	3.0	2.7	105	108	110	98
PUBLIC UTILITIES (76-80)	1.2	1.8	2.3	3.1	3.2	2.7	125	135	142	93
TRADE (81,86,89-99)	17.5	14.0	14.8	17.5	18.2	14.4	106	119	123	98
SERVICES (82-85,87,88,102)	14.0	22.5	22.6	22.7	22.8	22.6	100	101	101	100
STATE & LOCAL GOVT. (101)	7.9	8.9	8.9	10.2	10.6	8.8	100	114	120	99
FEDERAL GOVERNMENT (100,103)	9.1	8.6	8.6	8.9	9.0	8.6	100	103	105	100
TOTAL JOBS	72.4	72.0	73.7	86.2	90.8	72.6	102	117	123	99
CIVILIAN PERSONS EMPLOYED	66.1	65.8	67.4	79.5	83.8	66.5	102	118	124	99
CIVILIAN UNEMPLOYMENT RATE	6.5	11.6	9.9	10.2	9.0	9.9				
POPULATION	182.2	209.6	208.3	239.2	247.5	204.0	99	115	119	98
PER CAPITA INCOME	2699.7	4592.6	4658.1	5166.2	5304.3	4666.1	101	111	114	100
ENERGY USER SECTOR			(TRILLIONS OF BTU'S)							
NATURAL RESOURCES	18.1	33.5	33.7	34.2	34.3	33.6	100	102	102	100
CONSTRUCTION	2.7	4.4	3.2	13.8	13.8	2.7	74	426	425	84
MANUFACTURING	1.5	6.1	6.5	7.7	8.2	6.4	107	118	126	98
TRANSPORTATION INDUSTRY	0.9	2.0	2.2	3.0	3.2	2.1	112	134	143	96
PUBLIC UTILITIES	9.7	56.0	68.3	89.1	97.2	64.7	122	130	142	95
TRADE AND SERVICES	6.2	14.6	15.1	16.6	16.9	14.9	103	109	112	99
GOVERNMENT. EXC. TRANSPORTATION	2.3	3.1	3.1	3.2	3.3	3.1	100	104	106	100
CONSUMERS. EXC. TRANSPORTATION	6.1	11.8	11.8	13.8	14.3	11.7	100	117	121	99
USER-OPERATED TRANSPORTATION	17.0	31.8	31.9	35.3	36.4	31.6	100	111	114	99
TRANSPORTATION AIR POLLUTION			(THOUSANDS OF TONS)							
SULFUR OXIDES	1.7	3.2	3.3	3.4	3.5	3.2	101	105	107	99
PARTICULATE MATTER	1.3	2.4	2.4	2.6	2.6	2.4	101	105	107	99
CARBON MONOXIDE	182.6	353.0	354.3	379.7	387.1	352.3	100	107	109	99
HYDROCARBONS	34.4	66.5	66.7	71.1	72.4	66.4	100	107	109	99
NITROGEN OXIDES	24.5	46.9	47.1	49.6	50.3	46.9	101	105	107	100
OTHER AIR POLLUTION										
SULFUR OXIDES	17.2	95.6	116.1	150.4	164.1	110.0	121	130	141	95
PARTICULATE MATTER	28.8	72.8	79.9	89.2	93.5	78.2	110	112	117	98
CARBON MONOXIDE	117.3	221.8	224.9	228.2	228.2	224.2	101	101	102	100
HYDROCARBONS	24.9	48.0	47.2	51.0	50.3	47.1	98	108	107	100
NITROGEN OXIDES	7.3	29.5	34.6	43.2	46.7	33.1	118	125	135	96
WATER OXYGEN DEMAND	403.8	835.4	838.2	840.7	843.6	837.5	100	100	101	100
LAND SOLID WASTE	143.9	165.6	164.6	189.0	195.5	161.1	99	99	119	98

SUMMARY PROJECTIONS BY ORE ECONOMIC AREA UNDER FIVE ALTERNATIVE HIGHWAY SYSTEMS

94 GREAT FALLS, MONT.

	1970	1990 BASE YEAR	1990 COMPLETED INTERSTATE	1990 EXTENDED PRIMARY	1990 ECONOMIC DEVELOPMENT	1990 URBAN	CI/BY	EP/CI	ED/CI	U/CI
JOBS BY INDUSTRY		(THOUSANDS)							PERCENT	
NATURAL RESOURCES (1-10)	10.9	5.7	5.8	6.1	6.3	5.8	101	105	109	100
CONSTRUCTION (11-12)	3.3	4.4	4.1	8.0	4.8	3.9	93	196	118	96
MANUFACTURING (13-74)	4.8	9.4	11.0	15.6	16.1	10.5	116	142	146	96
TRANSPORTATION INDUSTRY (75)	3.7	6.4	6.4	6.8	6.1	6.4	106	106	106	100
PUBLIC UTILITIES (76-80)	2.4	.7	.9	1.9	3.0	.8	131	220	342	96
TRADE (81,86,89-99)	19.7	20.9	21.7	27.0	28.0	21.5	104	124	129	99
SERVICES (82-85,87,88,102)	17.9	30.7	30.8	31.1	31.2	30.8	100	101	101	100
STATE & LOCAL GOVT. (101)	13.4	15.0	15.4	17.1	17.0	15.3	103	111	110	99
FEDERAL GOVERNMENT (100,103)	10.1	9.8	9.9	10.3	10.3	9.9	101	104	104	100
TOTAL JOBS	86.2	102.9	106.0	123.9	123.4	104.9	103	117	116	99
CIVILIAN PERSONS EMPLOYED	79.4	95.6	98.5	115.6	115.2	97.4	103	117	117	99
CIVILIAN UNEMPLOYMENT RATE	5.1	4.6	4.6	3.7	3.9	4.6				
POPULATION	222.6	277.6	291.1	318.9	319.5	288.4	105	110	110	99
PER CAPITA INCOME	3454.2	4924.6	4958.3	5545.1	5484.3	4933.4	101	112	111	99
ENERGY USER SECTOR		(TRILLIONS OF BTU'S)								
NATURAL RESOURCES	14.4	37.8	38.0	38.4	39.0	37.9	101	102	103	100
CONSTRUCTION	3.8	3.7	3.9	3.9	8.0	3.9	105	644	204	99
MANUFACTURING	3.4	9.1	9.8	12.6	13.3	9.6	108	129	136	98
TRANSPORTATION INDUSTRY	2.1	4.9	5.1	6.6	6.9	5.1	106	128	134	99
PUBLIC UTILITIES	8.0	6.6	8.0	25.7	40.3	7.9	121	320	501	98
TRADE AND SERVICES	8.5	18.2	18.6	22.4	23.6	18.6	103	119	126	99
GOVERNMENT, EXC. TRANSPORTATION	1.0	1.4	1.4	1.6	1.6	1.4	103	113	112	99
CONSUMERS, EXC. TRANSPORTATION	11.2	20.4	21.1	23.8	23.7	20.9	103	113	112	99
USER-OPERATED TRANSPORTATION	16.0	28.9	29.9	34.2	34.0	29.6	103	114	114	99
TRANSPORTATION AIR POLLUTION		(THOUSANDS OF TONS)								
SULFUR OXIDES	1.6	4.2	4.2	4.6	4.2	4.2	101	108	109	100
PARTICULATE MATTER	1.2	2.9	3.0	3.2	3.2	2.9	102	107	108	100
CARBON MONOXIDE	174.9	380.5	388.2	421.4	421.1	386.1	102	109	108	99
HYDROCARBONS	32.6	72.3	73.6	79.4	79.4	73.3	102	108	108	100
NITROGEN OXIDES	22.7	53.8	54.6	58.1	58.3	54.4	102	106	107	100
OTHER AIR POLLUTION										
SULFUR OXIDES	119.6	305.4	308.0	338.8	363.6	307.7	101	110	118	100
PARTICULATE MATTER	40.5	95.6	98.8	120.3	134.7	98.6	103	122	136	100
CARBON MONOXIDE	108.0	273.3	274.1	276.6	281.0	273.9	100	101	103	100
HYDROCARBONS	28.0	72.9	75.5	84.0	80.0	74.3	104	111	106	98
NITROGEN OXIDES	8.0	17.5	18.3	26.8	33.4	18.2	105	147	183	100
WATER OXYGEN DEMAND	519.8	1045.7	1050.4	1065.9	1073.8	1050.1	100	101	102	100
LAND SOLID WASTE	175.8	219.3	230.0	252.0	252.4	227.8	105	110	110	99

SUMMARY PROJECTIONS BY OBE ECONOMIC AREA UNDER FIVE ALTERNATIVE HIGHWAY SYSTEMS

95 BILLINGS, MONT.

	1970	1990 BASE YEAR	1990 COMPLETED INTERSTATE	1990 EXTENDED PRIMARY	1990 ECONOMIC DEVELOPMENT	1990 URBAN	CI/BY	PER CENT EP/CI	ED/CI	U/CI
JOBS BY INDUSTRY		(THOUSANDS)								
NATURAL RESOURCES (1-10)	14.2	15.5	16.2	16.7	16.7	16.1	105	103	103	100
CONSTRUCTION (11,12)	3.8	.8	1.1	2.9	1.4	1.0	141	262	126	91
MANUFACTURING (13-74)	6.4	9.3	13.2	18.6	15.7	12.9	141	141	119	98
TRANSPORTATION INDUSTRY (75)	4.8	6.7	7.2	7.5	7.4	7.1	106	105	103	99
PUBLIC UTILITIES (76-80)	2.0	1.4	3.5	4.7	5.0	3.2	248	137	143	93
TRADE (81,86,89-99)	24.0	22.3	26.9	32.0	30.4	26.4	121	119	113	98
SERVICES (82-85,87,88,102)	20.5	39.2	38.8	39.4	38.9	38.8	99	101	100	100
STATE & LOCAL GOVT. (101)	14.3	15.2	16.4	17.7	17.1	16.3	107	108	105	99
FEDERAL GOVERNMENT (100,103)	3.4	3.0	3.3	3.6	3.5	3.3	108	109	105	99
TOTAL JOBS	93.5	113.5	126.5	143.1	136.2	125.1	111	113	108	99
CIVILIAN PERSONS EMPLOYED	91.0	110.3	122.7	138.6	132.0	121.4	111	113	108	99
CIVILIAN UNEMPLOYMENT RATE	5.2	2.8	3.4	2.8	2.9	3.4				
POPULATION	246.9	261.1	293.0	324.9	313.3	290.4	112	111	107	99
PER CAPITA INCOME	3205.3	4942.3	5078.8	5395.6	5239.8	5055.5	103	106	103	100
ENERGY USER SECTOR		(TRILLIONS OF BTU'S)								
NATURAL RESOURCES	13.1	31.1	32.3	32.9	33.0	32.2	104	102	102	100
CONSTRUCTION	4.1	2.2	3.4	3.4	4.2	3.3	153	654	124	96
MANUFACTURING	5.8	8.7	11.1	14.4	12.9	10.9	127	130	116	98
TRANSPORTATION INDUSTRY	3.3	5.4	6.8	8.1	7.7	6.7	125	120	114	98
PUBLIC UTILITIES	14.3	31.3	81.2	119.6	134.5	75.4	260	147	166	93
TRADE AND SERVICES	8.7	15.8	18.7	21.4	20.6	18.3	119	114	111	98
GOVERNMENT, EXC. TRANSPORTATION	.9	1.2	1.3	1.5	1.4	1.3	110	111	106	99
CONSUMERS, EXC. TRANSPORTATION	12.2	21.4	23.1	25.3	24.4	22.9	108	110	106	99
USER-OPERATED TRANSPORTATION	20.0	35.6	38.2	41.7	40.3	38.0	107	109	105	99
TRANSPORTATION AIR POLLUTION		(THOUSANDS OF TONS)								
SULFUR OXIDES	1.5	3.1	3.4	3.6	3.6	3.3	109	108	106	99
PARTICULATE MATTER	1.1	2.2	2.4	2.6	2.5	2.4	107	107	105	99
CARBON MONOXIDE	179.1	355.2	375.9	402.5	392.1	373.7	106	107	104	99
HYDROCARBONS	32.4	65.1	68.7	73.3	71.5	68.3	106	107	104	99
NITROGEN OXIDES	20.3	42.9	45.3	48.2	47.1	45.0	106	106	104	99
OTHER AIR POLLUTION										
SULFUR OXIDES	27.6	54.3	135.9	199.2	223.6	126.3	250	147	164	93
PARTICULATE MATTER	25.2	71.8	96.3	114.3	120.3	93.8	134	119	125	97
CARBON MONOXIDE	77.8	205.2	206.7	206.7	207.2	206.5	101	100	100	100
HYDROCARBONS	32.9	61.6	64.5	81.0	68.5	63.8	105	126	106	99
NITROGEN OXIDES	9.0	18.8	38.6	54.0	59.9	36.3	205	140	155	94
WATER OXYGEN DEMAND	817.1	1579.8	1590.4	1595.8	1597.7	1589.5	101	100	100	100
LAND SOLID WASTE	195.0	206.3	231.5	256.6	247.5	229.4	112	111	107	99

SUMMARY PROJECTIONS BY ORE ECONOMIC AREA UNDER FIVE ALTERNATIVE HIGHWAY SYSTEMS

96   BISMARCK, N. D.

	1970	1990 BASE YEAR	1990 COMPLETED INTERSTATE	1990 EXTENDED PRIMARY	1990 ECONOMIC DEVELOPMENT	1990 URBAN	CI/BY	EP/CI	ED/CI	U/CI
JOBS BY INDUSTRY			(THOUSANDS)						P E R C E N T	
NATURAL RESOURCES (1-10)	11.9	7.7	7.6	7.7	7.8	7.6	99	101	103	99
CONSTRUCTION (11-12)	2.6	1.9	1.7	1.8	2.5	1.3	89	105	146	80
MANUFACTURING (13-74)	2.0	9.0	8.3	8.7	9.5	8.1	92	105	114	98
TRANSPORTATION INDUSTRY (75)	2.5	2.7	2.7	2.7	2.8	2.7	100	100	103	99
PUBLIC UTILITIES (76-80)	1.4	2.2	2.5	2.4	2.7	2.5	114	97	108	98
TRADE (81,86,89-99)	14.9	15.0	14.9	15.0	16.1	14.7	100	101	108	99
SERVICES (82-85,87,88,102)	12.8	18.0	17.9	17.9	18.0	17.9	100	100	100	100
STATE & LOCAL GOVT. (101)	7.9	9.7	9.4	9.6	9.9	9.3	97	101	106	99
FEDERAL GOVERNMENT (100,103)	1.7	1.7	1.6	1.6	1.7	1.6	96	102	107	98
TOTAL JOBS	56.8	67.8	66.7	67.4	71.0	65.7	98	101	106	99
CIVILIAN PERSONS EMPLOYED	53.1	64.0	62.9	63.6	66.9	62.0	98	101	106	99
CIVILIAN UNEMPLOYMENT RATE	5.1	4.7	3.4	3.6	3.6	3.6				
POPULATION	144.9	159.5	150.0	152.0	159.5	147.9	94	101	106	99
PER CAPITA INCOME	2595.6	5528.9	5606.7	5676.4	5895.9	5502.3	101	101	105	98
ENERGY USER SECTOR			(TRILLIONS OF BTU'S)							
NATURAL RESOURCES	10.1	15.2	14.9	15.1	15.3	14.8	98	101	102	99
CONSTRUCTION	2.2	5.3	4.9	6.3	11.3	3.3	93	127	230	67
MANUFACTURING	1.3	6.1	6.1	6.3	6.8	6.1	100	102	110	100
TRANSPORTATION INDUSTRY	2.9	3.2	3.2	3.2	3.5	3.1	99	101	110	98
PUBLIC UTILITIES	9.1	68.3	76.6	71.7	83.2	76.6	112	94	109	100
TRADE AND SERVICES	5.2	15.1	15.1	15.1	15.7	14.9	100	100	104	99
GOVERNMENT, EXC. TRANSPORTATION	2.1	2.9	2.9	2.9	2.9	2.9	99	101	102	99
CONSUMERS, EXC. TRANSPORTATION	4.4	9.7	9.2	9.4	9.9	9.0	96	102	107	98
USER-OPERATED TRANSPORTATION	13.7	26.3	25.8	26.1	27.1	25.4	98	101	105	99
TRANSPORTATION AIR POLLUTION			(THOUSANDS OF TONS)							
SULFUR OXIDES	1.0	1.6	1.6	1.6	1.7	1.6	99	100	104	99
PARTICULATE MATTER	0.7	1.2	1.2	1.2	1.3	1.2	99	101	104	99
CARBON MONOXIDE	110.8	204.9	201.3	203.3	210.9	198.7	98	101	105	99
HYDROCARBONS	20.6	37.2	36.5	36.9	38.2	36.1	98	101	105	99
NITROGEN OXIDES	14.0	23.5	23.2	23.4	24.1	23.0	99	101	104	99
OTHER AIR POLLUTION										
SULFUR OXIDES	16.6	113.6	127.2	119.1	138.0	127.2	112	94	108	100
PARTICULATE MATTER	14.0	39.5	43.1	41.1	45.7	43.2	109	95	106	100
CARBON MONOXIDE	58.9	68.8	69.1	68.9	69.3	69.1	100	100	100	100
HYDROCARBONS	15.6	18.4	18.6	20.2	22.3	18.6	101	109	120	100
NITROGEN OXIDES	5.7	29.3	32.6	30.7	35.2	32.6	111	94	108	100
WATER OXYGEN DEMAND	568.4	1141.8	1142.6	1141.3	1143.6	1142.7	100	100	100	100
LAND SOLID WASTE	114.5	126.0	118.5	120.1	126.0	116.8	94	101	106	99

SUMMARY PROJECTIONS BY ORE ECONOMIC AREA UNDER FIVE ALTERNATIVE HIGHWAY SYSTEMS

97   FAR-MOOR, N. D.--MINN.

	1970	1990 BASE YEAR	1990 COMPLETED INTERSTATE	1990 EXTENDED PRIMARY	1990 ECONOMIC DEVELOPMENT	1990 URBAN	CI/BY	EP/CI	ED/CI	U/CI
JOBS BY INDUSTRY			(THOUSANDS)					(P E R C E N T)		
NATURAL RESOURCES (1-10)	25.0	9.0	9.0	9.0	9.1	9.0	100	100	101	100
CONSTRUCTION (11,12)	6.6	4.2	3.9	3.9	4.4	3.7	93	99	112	95
MANUFACTURING (13-74)	6.5	18.1	17.8	18.1	19.1	17.4	98	101	107	98
TRANSPORTATION INDUSTRY (75)	4.1	7.4	7.4	7.4	7.5	7.3	100	101	101	100
PUBLIC UTILITIES (76-80)	2.9	9.5	9.4	9.5	9.9	9.2	99	101	106	98
TRADE (81,86-89,99)	35.9	45.0	44.8	44.8	46.1	44.5	100	100	103	99
SERVICES (82-85,87,88,102)	30.6	31.3	31.2	31.1	31.2	31.2	100	100	100	100
STATE & LOCAL GOVT. (101)	17.6	20.9	20.9	20.8	21.2	20.7	100	100	102	99
FEDERAL GOVERNMENT (100,103)	3.6	3.4	3.4	3.4	3.5	3.3	100	100	102	99
TOTAL JOBS	133.0	148.8	147.8	148.1	151.9	146.8	99	100	103	99
CIVILIAN PERSONS EMPLOYED	129.5	144.1	143.1	143.4	147.0	141.8	99	100	103	99
CIVILIAN UNEMPLOYMENT RATE	5.5	3.5	3.7	3.8	3.3	3.7				
POPULATION	335.4	335.1	333.5	332.5	339.1	332.1	100	100	102	100
PER CAPITA INCOME	2698.9	5710.1	5696.3	5723.4	5825.1	5643.7	100	100	102	99
ENERGY USER SECTOR			(TRILLIONS OF BTU'S)							
NATURAL RESOURCES	23.2	40.5	40.5	40.4	40.5	40.4	100	100	100	100
CONSTRUCTION	5.4	9.5	10.3	10.1	15.9	9.2	108	98	154	89
MANUFACTURING	3.4	15.7	15.8	15.8	16.5	15.7	101	100	104	99
TRANSPORTATION INDUSTRY	2.6	8.4	8.3	8.3	8.7	8.2	99	100	104	99
PUBLIC UTILITIES	17.0	164.9	162.3	162.1	168.6	161.9	98	100	104	100
TRADE AND SERVICES	13.7	35.6	35.4	35.4	36.2	35.2	100	100	102	99
GOVERNMENT, EXC. TRANSPORTATION	1.3	2.0	2.0	2.0	2.0	2.0	100	100	102	99
CONSUMERS, EXC. TRANSPORTATION	12.7	24.7	24.6	24.6	25.2	24.4	100	100	103	99
USER-OPERATED TRANSPORTATION	27.1	55.1	54.9	54.9	55.9	54.5	100	100	102	99
TRANSPORTATION AIR POLLUTION			(THOUSANDS OF TONS)							
SULFUR OXIDES	7.5	4.8	4.8	4.8	4.9	4.8	100	100	101	100
PARTICULATE MATTER	1.8	3.5	3.5	3.5	3.6	3.5	100	100	101	100
CARBON MONOXIDE	287.5	556.1	554.7	555.2	562.2	552.2	100	100	101	100
HYDROCARBONS	53.4	102.0	101.8	101.8	103.1	101.4	100	100	101	100
NITROGEN OXIDES	36.0	67.3	67.2	67.4	68.0	67.0	100	100	101	100
OTHER AIR POLLUTION										
SULFUR OXIDES	31.6	286.6	282.3	281.9	292.6	281.7	99	100	104	100
PARTICULATE MATTER	35.4	134.6	133.7	133.8	136.2	133.8	99	100	102	100
CARBON MONOXIDE	142.1	249.5	249.0	248.9	249.3	248.8	100	100	100	100
HYDROCARBONS	30.4	54.3	55.5	55.3	59.4	55.0	102	100	107	99
NITROGEN OXIDES	12.2	82.0	80.9	80.7	83.4	80.8	99	100	103	100
WATER OXYGEN DEMAND	1157.9	2394.2	2393.0	2392.2	2393.8	2393.0	100	100	100	100
LAND SOLID WASTE	265.0	264.7	263.4	262.6	267.9	262.4	100	100	102	102

SUMMARY PROJECTIONS BY ORE ECONOMIC AREA UNDER FIVE ALTERNATIVE HIGHWAY SYSTEMS

98 ABERDEEN, S. D.

	1970	1990 BASE YEAR	1990 COMPLETED INTERSTATE	1990 EXTENDED PRIMARY	1990 ECONOMIC DEVELOPMENT	1990 URBAN	CI/BY	EP/CI	ED/CI	U/CI
								P E R C E N T		
JOBS BY INDUSTRY			(THOUSANDS)							
NATURAL RESOURCES (1-10)	12.8	4.0	3.9	4.0	4.0	3.9	100	101	101	100
CONSTRUCTION (11,12)	1.4	2.1	1.9	2.0	4.7	1.9	89	108	249	100
MANUFACTURING (13-74)	2.6	7.7	8.0	9.4	10.1	7.9	104	116	126	98
TRANSPORTATION INDUSTRY (75)	1.1	2.2	2.2	2.2	2.3	2.2	101	101	103	99
PUBLIC UTILITIES (76-80)	1.7	2.3	2.3	2.4	2.4	2.2	98	103	106	96
TRADE (81,86,89-99)	14.1	10.5	10.5	10.9	11.5	10.4	100	104	109	99
SERVICES (82-85,87,88,102)	11.3	14.3	14.3	14.3	14.3	14.3	100	100	100	100
STATE & LOCAL GOVT. (101)	8.8	10.2	10.3	10.6	10.9	10.3	101	102	106	100
FEDERAL GOVERNMENT (100,103)	1.6	1.4	1.5	1.5	1.6	1.5	102	104	109	100
TOTAL JOBS	54.5	54.8	55.0	57.3	61.8	54.5	100	104	113	99
CIVILIAN PERSONS EMPLOYED	54.7	55.0	55.1	57.3	61.7	54.7	100	104	112	99
CIVILIAN UNEMPLOYMENT RATE	4.6	2.9	2.9	3.0	2.6	3.1				
POPULATION	132.9	120.5	127.7	131.4	137.6	127.9	106	103	108	100
PER CAPITA INCOME	2862.5	5630.9	5461.8	5645.7	5908.8	5406.5	97	103	108	99
ENERGY USER SECTOR			(TRILLIONS OF BTU'S)							
NATURAL RESOURCES	9.5	24.7	24.7	24.7	24.7	24.7	100	100	100	100
CONSTRUCTION	1.3	2.0	2.0	2.1	9.5	2.0	101	104	464	99
MANUFACTURING	3.0	8.5	8.6	9.1	9.3	8.5	101	106	108	99
TRANSPORTATION INDUSTRY	.5	2.4	2.4	2.5	2.7	2.3	101	106	113	98
PUBLIC UTILITIES	3.0	33.6	33.0	33.3	33.8	32.3	98	101	102	98
TRADE AND SERVICES	3.9	11.3	11.3	11.5	11.8	11.1	100	102	105	99
GOVERNMENT, EXC. TRANSPORTATION	.4	.5	.5	.6	.6	.5	102	105	112	99
CONSUMERS, EXC. TRANSPORTATION	5.2	9.4	9.6	10.0	10.6	9.6	102	104	110	99
USER-OPERATED TRANSPORTATION	11.3	21.6	21.8	22.4	23.3	21.8	101	103	107	100
TRANSPORTATION AIR POLLUTION			(THOUSANDS OF TONS)							
SULFUR OXIDES	.8	2.3	2.3	2.3	2.4	2.3	100	101	103	100
PARTICULATE MATTER	.7	1.7	1.7	1.7	1.8	1.7	100	103	103	100
CARBON MONOXIDE	114.6	252.6	254.2	258.4	265.1	253.6	101	102	104	100
HYDROCARBONS	21.1	47.3	47.5	48.2	49.4	47.4	101	102	104	100
NITROGEN OXIDES	13.6	32.9	33.0	33.4	34.0	32.9	100	101	103	100
OTHER AIR POLLUTION										
SULFUR OXIDES	6.1	56.0	55.1	55.4	56.2	53.9	98	101	102	98
PARTICULATE MATTER	14.2	57.7	57.0	56.4	57.0	56.6	99	99	100	99
CARBON MONOXIDE	53.5	145.3	145.2	145.1	145.2	145.1	100	100	100	100
HYDROCARBONS	11.1	30.8	32.0	35.6	36.7	31.6	104	111	114	99
NITROGEN OXIDES	2.8	16.7	16.5	16.5	16.7	16.2	99	100	102	98
WATER OXYGEN DEMAND	794.2	1642.2	1641.0	1640.2	1641.2	1640.6	100	100	100	100
LAND SOLID WASTE	105.0	95.2	100.9	103.8	108.7	101.1	106	103	108	100

SUMMARY PROJECTIONS BY ORE ECONOMIC AREA UNDER FIVE ALTERNATIVE HIGHWAY SYSTEMS

99 SIOUX FALLS, S. D.

	1970	1990 BASE YEAR	1990 COMPLETED INTERSTATE	1990 EXTENDED PRIMARY	1990 ECONOMIC DEVELOPMENT	1990 URBAN	CI/BY	EP/CI	ED/CI	U/CI
									PERCENT	
JOBS BY INDUSTRY		(THOUSANDS)								
NATURAL RESOURCES (1-10)	30.6	10.1	10.0	10.2	10.2	10.0	99	102	102	99
CONSTRUCTION (11,12)	6.0	7.4	7.5	9.2	8.2	7.5	101	123	109	100
MANUFACTURING (13-74)	13.4	25.7	25.5	26.7	26.2	25.1	99	105	103	99
TRANSPORTATION INDUSTRY (75)	4.2	8.8	8.8	8.9	8.9	8.8	100	101	101	100
PUBLIC UTILITIES (76-80)	2.7	9.0	9.0	9.5	9.5	8.6	99	106	105	96
TRADE (81,86,89-99)	40.4	52.8	52.6	53.7	53.3	52.2	99	102	101	99
SERVICES (82-85,87,88,102)	31.6	37.5	37.5	37.5	37.5	37.5	100	100	100	100
STATE & LOCAL GOVT. (101)	16.1	19.9	19.8	20.3	20.1	19.7	100	102	101	99
FEDERAL GOVERNMENT (100,103)	3.7	3.8	3.8	3.9	3.8	3.7	100	103	102	99
TOTAL JOBS	148.7	175.1	174.5	179.9	177.6	173.1	100	103	102	99
CIVILIAN PERSONS EMPLOYED	150.1	175.4	174.8	179.9	177.8	173.4	100	103	102	99
CIVILIAN UNEMPLOYMENT RATE	3.9	.5	.5	.5	.5	.5				
POPULATION	365.0	349.4	347.7	357.4	351.9	347.8	100	103	101	100
PER CAPITA INCOME	3131.5	6853.9	6849.0	6922.6	6913.7	6791.3	100	101	101	99
ENERGY USER SECTOR		(TRILLIONS OF BTU'S)								
NATURAL RESOURCES	23.4	59.5	59.4	59.4	59.5	59.4	100	100	100	100
CONSTRUCTION	5.2	11.1	11.1	11.9	13.0	9.2	100	135	117	83
MANUFACTURING	5.8	25.0	24.9	25.7	25.3	24.7	99	103	102	99
TRANSPORTATION INDUSTRY	4.1	16.5	16.4	16.7	16.6	16.3	99	102	101	99
PUBLIC UTILITIES	12.9	138.1	136.2	140.0	139.4	133.5	99	103	102	98
TRADE AND SERVICES	14.2	45.7	45.5	46.1	45.9	45.1	100	101	101	99
GOVERNMENT. EXC. TRANSPORTATION	1.0	1.8	1.8	1.8	1.8	1.7	100	103	102	99
CONSUMERS. EXC. TRANSPORTATION	12.6	24.6	24.5	25.3	24.9	24.3	100	103	102	99
USER-OPERATED TRANSPORTATION	22.8	46.4	46.2	47.4	46.9	45.9	100	103	101	99
TRANSPORTATION AIR POLLUTION		(THOUSANDS OF TONS)								
SULFUR OXIDES	2.1	6.6	6.5	6.6	6.6	6.5	100	101	101	100
PARTICULATE MATTER	1.5	4.2	4.2	4.2	4.2	4.2	100	101	101	100
CARBON MONOXIDE	231.3	535.6	534.2	543.3	539.4	532.2	100	102	101	100
HYDROCARBONS	42.5	99.5	99.3	100.8	100.1	98.9	100	102	101	100
NITROGEN OXIDES	28.4	72.5	72.5	73.5	73.1	72.3	100	101	101	100
OTHER AIR POLLUTION										
SULFUR OXIDES	24.4	230.7	227.6	233.8	232.8	223.1	99	103	102	98
PARTICULATE MATTER	40.0	146.1	144.9	147.1	146.4	143.8	99	102	101	99
CARBON MONOXIDE	100.9	301.3	300.6	300.8	301.0	300.3	100	100	100	100
HYDROCARBONS	22.5	66.8	66.3	71.0	68.1	65.7	99	107	103	99
NITROGEN OXIDES	9.6	64.4	63.6	65.1	64.9	62.5	99	102	102	98
WATER OXYGEN DEMAND	2791.1	5833.1	5831.2	5831.6	5833.1	5830.6	100	100	100	100
LAND SOLID WASTE	288.3	276.0	274.6	282.3	278.0	274.8	100	103	101	100

SUMMARY PROJECTIONS BY ORE ECONOMIC AREA UNDER FIVE ALTERNATIVE HIGHWAY SYSTEMS

100 RAPID CITY, S. D.

	1970	1990 BASE YEAR	1990 COMPLETED INTERSTATE	1990 EXTENDED PRIMARY	1990 ECONOMIC DEVELOPMENT	1990 URBAN	CI/BY	EP/CI	ED/CI	U/CI
JOBS BY INDUSTRY			(THOUSANDS)							
NATURAL RESOURCES (1-10)	17.6	9.0	8.7	8.9	9.3	8.7	98	102	106	99
CONSTRUCTION (11,12)	3.7	1.5	1.5	2.4	1.8	1.4	101	155	120	93
MANUFACTURING (13-74)	3.3	11.3	12.0	13.4	13.1	11.6	106	112	110	97
TRANSPORTATION INDUSTRY (75)	1.8	3.4	3.4	3.5	3.4	3.4	100	100	100	99
PUBLIC UTILITIES (76-80)	1.7	4.6	4.5	4.7	4.8	4.3	98	104	106	96
TRADE (81,86,89-99)	21.5	13.7	13.5	14.5	14.3	13.3	99	107	106	99
SERVICES (82-85,87,88,102)	19.4	16.7	16.6	16.6	16.6	16.6	99	102	106	100
STATE & LOCAL GOVT. (101)	14.0	14.6	14.6	15.0	14.9	14.5	100	102	102	99
FEDERAL GOVERNMENT (100,103)	10.7	10.4	10.4	10.4	10.4	10.4	100	101	101	100
TOTAL JOBS	93.8	85.0	85.2	89.4	88.7	84.2	100	105	104	99
CIVILIAN PERSONS EMPLOYED	84.9	76.2	76.4	80.4	79.8	75.5	100	105	104	99
CIVILIAN UNEMPLOYMENT RATE	4.9	4.3	4.4	4.1	3.7	4.6				
POPULATION	231.9	213.6	215.4	220.3	219.5	214.6	101	102	102	100
PER CAPITA INCOME	3134.8	4873.1	4868.9	5505.6	5503.1	4812.3	100	104	103	99
ENERGY USER SECTOR			(TRILLIONS OF BTU'S)							
NATURAL RESOURCES	12.3	32.8	32.5	32.5	33.0	32.5	99	100	102	100
CONSTRUCTION	3.2	3.6	3.6	11.5	3.7	3.5	99	320	104	99
MANUFACTURING	1.0	6.3	6.6	7.3	7.1	6.4	103	111	109	98
TRANSPORTATION INDUSTRY	1.6	5.7	5.6	5.9	5.9	5.5	99	105	105	99
PUBLIC UTILITIES	7.7	81.6	79.9	81.3	82.4	78.2	98	102	103	98
TRADE AND SERVICES	6.1	17.1	17.0	17.5	17.5	16.8	99	103	103	99
GOVERNMENT, EXC. TRANSPORTATION	1.7	2.1	2.1	2.1	2.1	2.1	100	102	102	100
CONSUMERS, EXC. TRANSPORTATION	7.8	11.9	12.0	12.5	12.4	11.8	101	105	104	99
USER-OPERATED TRANSPORTATION	18.8	30.9	31.0	31.8	31.7	30.8	100	103	103	99
TRANSPORTATION AIR POLLUTION			(THOUSANDS OF TONS)							
SULFUR OXIDES	1.1	3.0	3.0	3.1	3.1	3.0	99	102	102	100
PARTICULATE MATTER	0.9	2.1	2.1	2.2	2.2	2.1	100	102	102	100
CARBON MONOXIDE	158.2	312.0	312.4	318.8	318.2	311.0	100	102	102	100
HYDROCARBONS	28.7	57.7	57.7	58.8	58.7	57.5	100	102	102	100
NITROGEN OXIDES	17.7	39.5	39.5	40.2	40.2	39.4	100	102	102	100
OTHER AIR POLLUTION										
SULFUR OXIDES	14.5	135.2	132.4	134.6	136.5	129.6	98	102	103	98
PARTICULATE MATTER	13.7	68.3	67.5	68.5	69.3	67.0	99	101	103	99
CARBON MONOXIDE	51.0	148.8	147.7	148.0	148.4	148.3	99	100	100	100
HYDROCARBONS	11.7	35.1	36.7	41.6	39.7	36.2	104	114	108	98
NITROGEN OXIDES	5.5	36.7	35.9	36.5	36.9	35.3	98	102	103	98
WATER OXYGEN DEMAND	1134.6	2352.2	2348.9	2348.9	2351.5	2349.0	100	100	100	100
LAND SOLID WASTE	183.2	168.7	170.1	174.0	173.4	169.8	101	102	102	100

SUMMARY PROJECTIONS BY OBE ECONOMIC AREA UNDER FIVE ALTERNATIVE HIGHWAY SYSTEMS

101   SCOTTSBLUFF, NEBR.

	1970	1990 BASE YEAR	1990 COMPLETED INTERSTATE	1990 EXTENDED PRIMARY	1990 ECONOMIC DEVELOPMENT	1990 URBAN	PERCENT CI/BY	EP/CI	ED/CI	U/CI
JOBS BY INDUSTRY			(THOUSANDS)							
NATURAL RESOURCES (1-10)	8.5	6.1	6.1	6.2	6.0	6.0	100	103	98	100
CONSTRUCTION (11,12)	1.3	1.0	1.1	2.9	.9	1.0	106	273	85	91
MANUFACTURING (13-74)	4.0	8.4	8.1	9.7	7.9	7.9	96	120	98	97
TRANSPORTATION INDUSTRY (75)	1.9	3.1	3.1	3.2	3.1	3.1	100	104	99	100
PUBLIC UTILITIES (76-80)	1.6	1.6	1.6	2.0	1.5	1.5	98	129	81	98
TRADE (81,86,89-99)	11.3	11.0	10.8	12.1	10.4	10.7	99	112	96	99
SERVICES (82-85,87,88,102)	7.6	10.9	10.8	11.0	10.8	10.8	99	101	100	100
STATE & LOCAL GOVT. (101)	5.6	6.0	6.0	6.4	5.9	5.9	99	107	98	98
FEDERAL GOVERNMENT (100,103)	.8	.5	.5	.6	.5	.5	98	120	95	98
TOTAL JOBS	41.5	48.6	48.0	54.1	46.7	47.4	99	113	97	99
CIVILIAN PERSONS EMPLOYED	41.2	48.0	47.4	53.3	46.2	46.9	99	112	97	99
CIVILIAN UNEMPLOYMENT RATE	3.9	1.0	1.0	1.0	.9	1.1				
POPULATION	105.7	109.3	108.0	120.6	104.1	107.8	99	112	96	100
PER CAPITA INCOME	3539.4	6020.7	5996.5	6113.4	6038.7	5927.8	100	102	101	99
ENERGY USER SECTOR			(TRILLIONS OF BTU'S)							
NATURAL RESOURCES	11.9	29.7	29.7	29.8	29.7	29.7	100	100	100	100
CONSTRUCTION	1.8	1.9	2.3	10.0	1.8	1.9	119	432	77	81
MANUFACTURING	3.4	5.4	5.4	6.2	5.2	5.3	100	116	96	98
TRANSPORTATION INDUSTRY	1.0	2.7	2.6	3.1	2.5	2.6	98	116	95	98
PUBLIC UTILITIES	4.5	39.6	38.5	47.5	33.1	38.0	97	123	86	99
TRADE AND SERVICES	3.6	9.1	9.0	9.8	8.7	9.0	99	109	96	99
GOVERNMENT, EXC. TRANSPORTATION	.4	.5	.5	.6	.5	.5	99	109	98	99
CONSUMERS, EXC. TRANSPORTATION	7.7	12.7	12.6	13.3	12.4	12.5	99	106	99	99
USER-OPERATED TRANSPORTATION	14.5	28.2	28.0	29.2	27.8	27.9	100	104	99	100
TRANSPORTATION AIR POLLUTION			(THOUSANDS OF TONS)							
SULFUR OXIDES	1.2	3.0	3.0	3.1	3.0	3.0	99	103	99	100
PARTICULATE MATTER	.9	2.2	2.2	2.3	2.2	2.2	100	103	99	100
CARBON MONOXIDE	150.4	332.0	330.9	339.9	329.0	329.7	100	103	99	100
HYDROCARBONS	27.7	62.1	61.9	63.5	61.6	61.7	100	103	99	100
NITROGEN OXIDES	18.1	43.1	43.0	43.9	42.7	42.9	100	102	100	100
OTHER AIR POLLUTION										
SULFUR OXIDES	7.8	65.1	63.2	78.0	54.4	62.5	97	123	86	99
PARTICULATE MATTER	18.0	66.1	65.2	69.6	62.2	65.0	99	107	95	100
CARBON MONOXIDE	66.7	180.4	180.3	180.6	180.1	180.2	100	100	100	100
HYDROCARBONS	14.2	38.3	39.7	44.6	39.4	38.9	103	112	99	98
NITROGEN OXIDES	3.6	19.7	19.2	22.9	17.0	19.0	97	119	89	99
WATER OXYGEN DEMAND	646.9	1330.5	1329.1	1330.7	1328.4	1329.2	100	100	100	100
LAND SOLID WASTE	83.5	86.4	85.4	95.3	82.2	85.1	99	112	96	100

266

SUMMARY PROJECTIONS BY ORE ECONOMIC AREA UNDER FIVE ALTERNATIVE HIGHWAY SYSTEMS

102 GRAND ISLAND, NEBR.

	1970	1990 BASE YEAR	1990 COMPLETED INTERSTATE	1990 EXTENDED PRIMARY	1990 ECONOMIC DEVELOPMENT	1990 URBAN	CI/BY	P E R C E N T EP/CI	ED/CI	U/CI
JOBS BY INDUSTRY			(THOUSANDS)							
NATURAL RESOURCES (1-10)	27.0	21.4	21.4	21.5	21.3	21.4	100	100	99	100
CONSTRUCTION (11,12)	5.2	6.6	6.0	8.1	5.6	6.0	91	135	94	100
MANUFACTURING (13-74)	14.9	24.8	22.6	23.8	22.0	22.2	91	105	97	98
TRANSPORTATION INDUSTRY (75)	4.7	7.6	7.5	7.6	7.4	7.5	99	101	99	99
PUBLIC UTILITIES (76-80)	2.0	5.4	5.4	5.8	4.4	5.1	97	108	82	96
TRADE (81,86,89-99)	33.8	34.4	33.4	34.3	31.6	33.0	97	103	94	99
SERVICES (82-85,87,88,102)	25.4	31.3	31.1	31.4	31.1	31.3	100	101	100	99
STATE & LOCAL GOVT. (101)	17.6	19.1	18.7	19.2	18.3	18.6	98	103	98	100
FEDERAL GOVERNMENT (100,103)	2.8	1.9	1.8	1.9	1.7	1.8	95	106	95	99
TOTAL JOBS	133.5	152.5	148.0	153.6	143.4	146.7	97	104	97	99
CIVILIAN PERSONS EMPLOYED	125.2	142.6	138.4	143.6	134.2	137.2	97	104	97	99
CIVILIAN UNEMPLOYMENT RATE	4.1									
POPULATION	323.8	321.3	316.6	327.8	305.2	315.9	99	104	96	100
PER CAPITA INCOME	3442.8	6062.9	5914.5	6017.7	5895.1	5863.6	98	102	100	99
ENERGY USER SECTOR			(TRILLIONS OF BTU'S)							
NATURAL RESOURCES	30.3	77.3	77.3	77.3	77.1	77.2	100	100	100	100
CONSTRUCTION	5.0	10.8	8.9	14.2	6.1	6.5	83	159	69	72
MANUFACTURING	5.0	12.2	11.3	11.6	10.7	11.2	93	102	94	98
TRANSPORTATION INDUSTRY	2.3	7.3	7.0	7.3	6.6	6.9	96	103	93	98
PUBLIC UTILITIES	7.7	80.5	79.9	83.1	69.1	77.8	99	104	87	97
TRADE AND SERVICES	11.8	31.5	31.0	31.5	29.8	30.8	98	102	96	99
GOVERNMENT, EXC. TRANSPORTATION	1.1	1.5	1.5	1.6	1.5	1.5	97	104	97	99
CONSUMERS, EXC. TRANSPORTATION	21.7	34.6	33.9	34.8	33.3	33.7	98	103	98	99
USER-OPERATED TRANSPORTATION	40.3	77.6	76.6	77.9	75.7	76.3	99	102	99	100
TRANSPORTATION AIR POLLUTION			(THOUSANDS OF TONS)							
SULFUR OXIDES	3.0	7.7	7.6	7.7	7.5	7.6	99	101	99	100
PARTICULATE MATTER	2.4	5.8	5.7	5.8	5.7	5.7	99	101	99	100
CARBON MONOXIDE	409.0	887.2	879.8	889.5	872.5	877.4	99	101	99	100
HYDROCARBONS	75.2	165.2	163.9	165.6	162.7	163.5	99	101	99	100
NITROGEN OXIDES	48.2	112.7	112.0	112.9	111.2	111.7	99	101	99	100
OTHER AIR POLLUTION										
SULFUR OXIDES	14.6	134.6	133.4	138.4	115.7	129.9	99	104	87	97
PARTICULATE MATTER	49.0	128.7	127.9	127.9	121.3	126.3	99	100	95	99
CARBON MONOXIDE	170.4	452.8	452.6	452.7	452.2	452.4	100	100	100	100
HYDROCARBONS	36.8	101.8	98.2	99.4	97.3	97.6	97	101	99	99
NITROGEN OXIDES	8.2	44.1	43.6	44.8	39.2	42.8	99	103	90	98
WATER OXYGEN DEMAND	2025.2	4167.6	4165.9	4164.9	4163.1	4164.7	100	100	100	100
LAND SOLID WASTE	255.8	253.8	250.1	259.0	241.1	249.6	99	104	96	100

SUMMARY PROJECTIONS BY ORE ECONOMIC AREA UNDER FIVE ALTERNATIVE HIGHWAY SYSTEMS

103 SIOUX CITY, IOWA-NEBR.

	1970	1990 BASE YEAR	1990 COMPLETED INTERSTATE	1990 EXTENDED PRIMARY	1990 ECONOMIC DEVELOPMENT	1990 URBAN	CI/BY	EP/CI	P E R C E N T ED/CI	U/CI
JOBS BY INDUSTRY										
NATURAL RESOURCES (1-10)	39.5	17.0	17.0	17.5	17.3	17.0	100	103	102	100
CONSTRUCTION (11-12)	7.3	9.6	9.5	11.2	9.5	9.4	100	118	100	100
MANUFACTURING (13-74)	19.4	38.5	37.1	39.4	37.7	35.4	96	106	102	95
TRANSPORTATION INDUSTRY (75)	5.1	11.2	11.2	11.5	11.3	11.2	100	102	101	99
PUBLIC UTILITIES (76-80)	2.9	2.1	2.1	4.4	3.2	2.2	111	188	141	95
TRADE (81,86,89-99)	45.7	67.9	67.8	71.0	68.6	66.7	100	105	102	99
SERVICES (82-85,87,88,102)	34.7	56.7	56.2	56.7	56.1	56.0	99	101	100	100
STATE & LOCAL GOVT. (101)	21.0	24.7	24.1	25.2	24.3	23.8	99	104	101	99
FEDERAL GOVERNMENT (100,103)	3.5	3.1	3.1	3.3	3.1	3.0	98	108	102	98
TOTAL JOBS	179.0	230.7	228.3	240.1	231.5	224.8	99	105	101	98
CIVILIAN PERSONS EMPLOYED	175.6	224.3	222.0	233.3	225.1	218.7	99	105	101	98
CIVILIAN UNEMPLOYMENT RATE	3.0	.4	.4	.4	.4	.4				
POPULATION	454.2	485.6	481.2	504.5	485.5	478.0	99	105	101	99
PER CAPITA INCOME	3190.5	6021.5	5987.6	6122.5	6034.7	5914.3	99	102	101	99
ENERGY USER SECTOR		(TRILLIONS OF BTU'S)								
NATURAL RESOURCES	32.9	79.5	79.5	79.6	79.6	79.5	100	100	100	100
CONSTRUCTION	8.3	17.2	17.3	19.6	17.9	12.4	101	113	103	72
MANUFACTURING	8.9	35.5	35.1	36.6	35.4	34.3	99	104	101	98
TRANSPORTATION INDUSTRY	4.6	18.8	18.7	19.6	19.1	18.4	100	105	102	98
PUBLIC UTILITIES	20.6	101.5	104.6	127.2	115.3	101.2	103	122	110	97
TRADE AND SERVICES	20.7	60.8	60.7	62.9	61.6	60.1	100	104	101	99
GOVERNMENT, EXC. TRANSPORTATION	1.7	2.4	2.4	2.5	2.4	2.4	100	105	101	99
CONSUMERS, EXC. TRANSPORTATION	19.9	36.5	36.2	37.9	36.6	35.7	99	105	101	99
USER-OPERATED TRANSPORTATION	35.2	70.4	69.8	72.5	70.5	69.1	99	104	101	99
TRANSPORTATION AIR POLLUTION		(THOUSANDS OF TONS)								
SULFUR OXIDES	2.7	8.2	8.1	8.3	8.2	8.1	100	102	101	99
PARTICULATE MATTER	2.1	5.5	5.5	5.6	5.5	5.4	100	102	101	99
CARBON MONOXIDE	342.1	766.7	762.8	783.5	768.2	757.3	99	103	103	99
HYDROCARBONS	62.4	141.4	140.7	144.2	141.6	139.7	100	103	101	99
NITROGEN OXIDES	40.0	98.3	98.1	100.3	98.8	97.5	100	102	101	99
OTHER AIR POLLUTION										
SULFUR OXIDES	37.9	174.1	179.2	216.0	196.6	173.6	103	121	110	97
PARTICULATE MATTER	51.7	158.8	160.1	170.9	165.2	158.8	101	107	103	99
CARBON MONOXIDE	127.5	344.6	344.7	345.4	345.1	344.5	100	100	100	100
HYDROCARBONS	31.6	89.7	90.0	94.4	89.8	86.8	100	105	100	97
NITROGEN OXIDES	13.5	52.4	53.6	62.8	58.0	52.3	102	117	108	97
WATER OXYGEN DEMAND	4407.2	9160.3	9159.3	9163.0	9163.6	9158.1	100	100	100	100
LAND SOLID WASTE	358.8	383.6	380.1	398.6	383.7	377.6	99	105	101	99

SUMMARY PROJECTIONS BY OBE ECONOMIC AREA UNDER FIVE ALTERNATIVE HIGHWAY SYSTEMS

104 FORT DODGE, IOWA

	1970	1990 BASE YEAR	1990 COMPLETED INTERSTATE	1990 EXTENDED PRIMARY	1990 ECONOMIC DEVELOPMENT	1990 URBAN	CI/BY	EP/CI	ED/CI	U/CI
								P E R C E N T		
JOBS BY INDUSTRY										
NATURAL RESOURCES (1-10)	23.0	7.5	7.5	7.3	7.3	7.4	100	97	97	99
CONSTRUCTION (11,12)	4.2	5.3	4.9	5.6	4.9	4.9	94	113	97	99
MANUFACTURING (13-74)	14.6	27.2	24.8	25.4	24.8	23.7	91	102	100	95
TRANSPORTATION INDUSTRY (75)	2.8	5.0	4.9	4.9	4.9	4.9	99	100	99	99
PUBLIC UTILITIES (76-80)	1.6	4.4	4.4	4.1	4.0	4.5	106	89	85	97
TRADE (81,86,89-99)	26.9	28.6	28.0	27.6	27.1	27.3	98	99	97	98
SERVICES (82-85,87,88,102)	18.1	34.8	34.8	34.7	34.7	34.8	100	100	100	100
STATE & LOCAL GOVT. (101)	11.8	14.0	13.6	13.7	13.5	13.4	97	100	99	98
FEDERAL GOVERNMENT (100,103)	1.3	1.1	1.0	1.0	1.0	0.9	92	101	96	95
TOTAL JOBS	104.2	127.8	124.2	124.3	122.0	121.9	97	100	98	98
CIVILIAN PERSONS EMPLOYED	103.6	125.9	122.4	122.5	120.4	120.2	97	100	98	98
CIVILIAN UNEMPLOYMENT RATE	2.7	2.7	2.5	2.5	2.5	2.9				
POPULATION	266.1	276.5	267.5	266.9	261.0	265.5	97	100	97	99
PER CAPITA INCOME	3326.8	7030.1	6997.9	7056.6	7046.8	6887.0	100	101	101	98
ENERGY USER SECTOR		(TRILLIONS OF BTU'S)								
NATURAL RESOURCES	32.7	85.8	85.6	85.5	85.6	85.6	100	100	100	100
CONSTRUCTION	4.5	10.9	9.9	11.0	7.4	7.0	91	111	75	71
MANUFACTURING	7.5	22.4	21.7	21.8	21.5	21.3	97	101	99	98
TRANSPORTATION INDUSTRY	2.2	7.2	7.0	6.9	6.8	6.8	97	98	96	97
PUBLIC UTILITIES	10.2	85.7	90.8	79.6	77.2	89.3	106	88	85	98
TRADE AND SERVICES	9.7	31.0	30.7	30.3	30.0	30.4	99	99	98	99
GOVERNMENT, EXC. TRANSPORTATION	0.8	1.3	1.2	1.2	1.2	1.2	97	100	99	98
CONSUMERS, EXC. TRANSPORTATION	13.0	25.9	25.4	25.4	25.1	25.0	98	100	99	99
USER-OPERATED TRANSPORTATION	20.3	42.4	41.6	41.7	41.1	41.0	98	100	99	99
TRANSPORTATION AIR POLLUTION		(THOUSANDS OF TONS)								
SULFUR OXIDES	2.8	7.8	7.7	7.7	7.7	7.7	99	100	99	99
PARTICULATE MATTER	2.0	6.4	5.3	5.3	5.3	5.3	99	100	99	99
CARBON MONOXIDE	271.6	660.4	654.3	654.7	650.5	649.8	99	100	99	99
HYDROCARBONS	51.7	127.3	126.2	126.3	125.6	125.8	99	100	99	99
NITROGEN OXIDES	38.0	98.5	98.0	98.1	97.6	97.6	99	100	100	100
OTHER AIR POLLUTION										
SULFUR OXIDES	18.4	146.7	155.0	136.5	132.5	152.6	106	88	86	98
PARTICULATE MATTER	91.5	282.4	285.8	280.0	279.1	285.0	101	98	98	100
CARBON MONOXIDE	185.8	507.8	508.1	507.6	507.7	507.9	100	100	100	100
HYDROCARBONS	40.1	111.7	109.5	110.7	108.0	108.2	98	101	99	99
NITROGEN OXIDES	9.2	49.9	52.0	47.3	46.3	51.4	104	91	89	99
WATER OXYGEN DEMAND	2176.6	4425.9	4426.8	4423.8	4425.3	4425.7	100	100	100	100
LAND SOLID WASTE	210.2	218.0	211.7	210.8	206.2	209.9	97	100	97	99

SUMMARY PROJECTIONS BY ORE ECONOMIC AREA UNDER FIVE ALTERNATIVE HIGHWAY SYSTEMS

105   WATERLOO, IOWA

	1970	1990 BASE YEAR	1990 COMPLETED INTERSTATE	1990 EXTENDED PRIMARY	1990 ECONOMIC DEVELOPMENT	1990 URBAN	CI/BY	EP/CI	ED/CI	U/CI
									PERCENT	
JOBS BY INDUSTRY										
NATURAL RESOURCES (1-10)	28.5	8.0	7.9	7.9	7.9	7.8	98	100	100	99
CONSTRUCTION (11,12)	6.4	7.2	7.9	7.1	7.1	6.8	102	101	87	93
MANUFACTURING (13-74)	34.2	65.5	66.0	66.6	67.3	63.6	101	101	102	96
TRANSPORTATION INDUSTRY (75)	4.0	6.8	6.8	6.7	6.7	6.6	100	100	100	98
PUBLIC UTILITIES (76-80)	2.4	5.3	4.7	4.7	4.6	4.5	88	100	97	95
TRADE (81,86,89-99)	43.2	35.7	34.9	35.0	35.2	33.9	98	100	101	97
SERVICES (82-85,87,88,102)	30.1	22.3	22.2	22.2	22.2	22.2	99	100	100	100
STATE & LOCAL GOVT. (101)	18.8	20.4	20.4	20.4	20.4	19.9	100	100	100	98
FEDERAL GOVERNMENT (100,103)	2.0	1.1	1.1	1.1	1.1	1.0	99	101	101	92
TOTAL JOBS	169.6	172.5	171.4	171.7	171.9	166.3	99	100	100	97
CIVILIAN PERSONS EMPLOYED	170.7	173.8	172.7	173.1	173.3	167.8	99	100	100	97
CIVILIAN UNEMPLOYMENT RATE	2.8	3.9	3.9	3.5	4.2	4.2				
POPULATION	426.3	455.1	454.9	454.1	453.4	451.4	100	100	100	99
PER CAPITA INCOME	3476.1	6212.1	6193.8	6210.8	6219.8	6044.7	100	100	100	98
ENERGY USER SECTOR (TRILLIONS OF BTU'S)										
NATURAL RESOURCES	28.2	72.1	72.0	72.0	72.1	72.1	100	100	100	100
CONSTRUCTION	9.5	14.0	13.8	13.8	12.5	11.0	98	101	91	80
MANUFACTURING	14.4	34.2	33.9	34.0	34.3	33.2	99	100	101	98
TRANSPORTATION INDUSTRY	3.1	9.0	8.7	8.7	8.8	8.3	97	100	101	96
PUBLIC UTILITIES	19.4	114.6	96.4	92.7	96.2	92.4	84	96	100	96
TRADE AND SERVICES	14.4	34.8	34.0	34.1	34.2	33.3	98	100	100	98
GOVERNMENT, EXC. TRANSPORTATION	1.2	1.8	1.8	1.8	1.8	1.7	100	100	100	97
CONSUMERS, EXC. TRANSPORTATION	19.2	33.2	33.1	33.2	33.1	32.4	100	100	100	98
USER-OPERATED TRANSPORTATION	33.8	65.3	65.2	65.3	65.2	64.1	100	100	100	98
TRANSPORTATION AIR POLLUTION (THOUSANDS OF TONS)										
SULFUR OXIDES	2.6	7.0	6.9	6.9	6.9	6.8	99	100	100	99
PARTICULATE MATTER	2.0	5.0	5.0	5.0	5.0	5.0	100	100	100	99
CARBON MONOXIDE	338.6	744.9	743.2	743.7	743.7	734.8	100	100	100	99
HYDROCARBONS	62.2	138.7	138.4	138.5	138.5	137.0	100	100	100	99
NITROGEN OXIDES	40.2	95.9	95.7	95.8	95.8	94.8	100	100	100	99
OTHER AIR POLLUTION										
SULFUR OXIDES	35.9	194.5	164.6	158.5	164.3	158.2	85	96	100	96
PARTICULATE MATTER	78.4	174.8	168.0	166.8	168.2	166.6	96	99	100	99
CARBON MONOXIDE	140.5	385.7	385.0	384.9	385.1	384.8	100	100	100	100
HYDROCARBONS	31.8	89.0	88.6	88.6	89.5	88.4	100	100	101	100
NITROGEN OXIDES	13.6	58.2	50.7	49.2	50.7	49.2	87	97	101	97
WATER OXYGEN DEMAND	2607.8	5346.3	5340.3	5339.2	5341.5	5339.4	100	100	100	100
LAND SOLID WASTE	336.7	359.5	359.4	358.7	358.2	356.6	100	100	100	99

SUMMARY PROJECTIONS BY ORE ECONOMIC AREA UNDER FIVE ALTERNATIVE HIGHWAY SYSTEMS

106   DES MOINES, IOWA

	1970	1990 BASE YEAR	1990 COMPLETED INTERSTATE	1990 EXTENDED PRIMARY	1990 ECONOMIC DEVELOPMENT	1990 URBAN	CI/BY	EP/BY	ED/CI	U/CI
							PERCENT			
JOBS BY INDUSTRY		(THOUSANDS)								
NATURAL RESOURCES (1-10)	40.9	9.6	9.5	9.5	9.6	9.5	99	100	100	100
CONSTRUCTION (11,12)	15.4	19.7	19.4	19.2	17.9	19.4	99	99	92	99
MANUFACTURING (13-74)	56.8	81.4	76.7	78.8	79.0	74.8	94	103	103	98
TRANSPORTATION INDUSTRY (75)	9.8	17.6	17.4	17.6	17.6	17.3	99	101	101	99
PUBLIC UTILITIES (76-80)	7.7	3.3	2.6	3.2	4.3	2.2	77	123	169	86
TRADE (81-86,89-99)	94.3	72.0	68.8	70.4	71.2	67.2	95	102	104	98
SERVICES (82-85,87,88,102)	83.7	120.3	119.7	119.8	119.9	119.7	100	100	100	100
STATE & LOCAL GOVT. (101)	47.9	51.7	50.7	51.0	51.1	50.3	98	101	101	99
FEDERAL GOVERNMENT (100,103)	8.1	6.8	6.6	6.7	6.7	6.5	97	101	102	99
TOTAL JOBS	364.7	382.4	371.4	376.2	377.4	366.4	97	101	102	99
CIVILIAN PERSONS EMPLOYED	357.4	374.3	363.7	368.4	369.4	359.4	97	101	102	99
CIVILIAN UNEMPLOYMENT RATE	2.2	3.5	3.4	3.2	3.4	3.5				
POPULATION	782.8	861.9	845.7	852.7	848.0	843.8	98	101	100	100
PER CAPITA INCOME	3617.0	5718.7	5620.6	5663.2	5701.6	5552.0	98	101	101	99
ENERGY USER SECTOR		(TRILLIONS OF BTU'S)								
NATURAL RESOURCES	33.5	87.4	87.0	87.1	87.1	86.9	100	100	100	100
CONSTRUCTION	16.9	33.6	29.9	33.5	25.7	22.8	89	112	86	76
MANUFACTURING	24.0	65.0	59.9	62.3	61.5	57.9	92	104	103	97
TRANSPORTATION INDUSTRY	10.0	25.9	24.7	25.3	25.6	24.1	95	103	104	98
PUBLIC UTILITIES	44.0	100.3	83.0	91.2	111.1	75.0	83	110	134	90
TRADE AND SERVICES	36.3	86.3	83.9	85.1	86.3	82.7	97	101	103	99
GOVERNMENT, EXC. TRANSPORTATION	2.5	3.1	3.0	3.1	3.1	3.0	97	101	102	99
CONSUMERS, EXC. TRANSPORTATION	41.7	73.9	72.4	73.1	73.1	71.8	98	101	101	99
USER-OPERATED TRANSPORTATION	62.1	113.3	110.9	111.9	112.0	110.0	98	101	101	99
TRANSPORTATION AIR POLLUTION		(THOUSANDS OF TONS)								
SULFUR OXIDES	4.5	11.4	11.1	11.2	11.3	11.0	98	101	101	99
PARTICULATE MATTER	3.3	7.8	7.7	7.8	7.8	7.7	98	101	101	99
CARBON MONOXIDE	566.5	1162.9	1145.1	1153.4	1154.8	1137.7	98	101	101	99
HYDROCARBONS	102.3	213.1	210.0	211.4	211.6	208.7	98	101	101	99
NITROGEN OXIDES	63.9	143.5	141.8	142.9	143.1	140.9	99	101	101	99
OTHER AIR POLLUTION										
SULFUR OXIDES	93.4	254.6	226.3	239.8	272.5	213.1	89	106	120	94
PARTICULATE MATTER	99.2	249.3	242.7	246.6	255.0	239.2	97	102	105	99
CARBON MONOXIDE	179.6	490.8	490.5	490.8	491.4	490.1	100	100	100	100
HYDROCARBONS	59.8	190.3	146.7	165.6	150.9	134.8	77	113	103	92
NITROGEN OXIDES	36.0	113.8	106.7	110.1	118.2	103.4	94	103	111	97
WATER OXYGEN DEMAND	2773.3	5698.1	5695.5	5696.7	5701.3	5693.7	100	100	100	100
LAND SOLID WASTE	618.4	680.9	668.1	673.6	669.9	666.6	98	101	100	100

SUMMARY PROJECTIONS BY ORE ECONOMIC AREA UNDER FIVE ALTERNATIVE HIGHWAY SYSTEMS

107   OMAHA, NEBR.-IOWA

	1970	1990 BASE YEAR	1990 COMPLETED INTERSTATE	1990 EXTENDED PRIMARY	1990 ECONOMIC DEVELOPMENT	1990 ECONOMIC URBAN	PERCENT CI/BY	PERCENT EP/CI	PERCENT ED/CI	PERCENT U/CI
JOBS BY INDUSTRY		(THOUSANDS)								
NATURAL RESOURCES (1-10)	28.6	11.3	10.9	11.4	10.1	10.8	97	104	92	98
CONSTRUCTION (11,12)	18.8	21.1	21.2	20.8	19.9	21.2	100	98	94	100
MANUFACTURING (13-74)	56.5	73.7	58.9	62.6	49.4	55.2	80	106	84	94
TRANSPORTATION INDUSTRY (75)	17.3	28.2	27.2	27.6	26.5	27.0	97	101	97	99
PUBLIC UTILITIES (76-80)	7.2	6.9	5.6	7.7	3.5	4.8	82	136	63	85
TRADE (81,86,89-99)	98.9	114.9	103.5	108.1	95.2	100.1	90	105	92	97
SERVICES (82-85,87,88,102)	88.1	105.3	103.0	103.3	101.4	102.8	98	103	98	100
STATE & LOCAL GOVT. (101)	38.1	41.6	38.5	39.6	36.0	37.7	93	103	94	98
FEDERAL GOVERNMENT (100,103)	21.5	20.5	19.8	20.0	19.3	19.6	97	101	97	99
TOTAL JOBS	375.0	423.5	388.9	401.3	361.3	379.1	92	103	93	97
CIVILIAN PERSONS EMPLOYED	358.7	406.6	373.5	385.4	347.3	364.2	92	103	93	98
CIVILIAN UNEMPLOYMENT RATE	2.8	4.3	4.3	4.0	4.6	5.0	95	102	94	99
POPULATION	794.2	990.5	940.2	955.7	881.0	928.5	95	102	94	99
PER CAPITA INCOME	3516.5	5255.6	4929.1	5050.8	4704.8	4821.5	94	102	95	98
ENERGY USER SECTOR		(TRILLIONS OF BTU'S)								
NATURAL RESOURCES	28.0	71.2	70.8	71.0	70.4	70.7	99	100	99	100
CONSTRUCTION	18.8	32.7	31.4	30.3	21.5	22.2	96	97	68	71
MANUFACTURING	31.1	75.7	70.1	72.0	66.3	68.6	93	103	95	98
TRANSPORTATION INDUSTRY	10.2	21.7	18.5	19.9	16.3	17.5	85	108	88	95
PUBLIC UTILITIES	15.2	16.9	16.5	22.6	15.9	16.2	98	137	96	98
TRADE AND SERVICES	47.1	101.4	95.2	98.4	91.1	93.1	94	103	96	98
GOVERNMENT, EXC. TRANSPORTATION	2.7	3.6	3.3	3.4	3.0	3.2	91	103	92	97
CONSUMERS, EXC. TRANSPORTATION	45.9	81.8	77.0	78.6	72.8	75.6	94	102	95	98
USER-OPERATED TRANSPORTATION	69.6	133.7	126.1	128.7	119.7	124.0	94	102	95	98
TRANSPORTATION AIR POLLUTION		(THOUSANDS OF TONS)								
SULFUR OXIDES	4.2	9.8	9.1	9.4	8.7	8.9	93	103	95	98
PARTICULATE MATTER	3.2	7.2	6.8	7.0	6.6	6.7	95	102	96	98
CARBON MONOXIDE	596.7	1235.8	1178.8	1199.1	1130.7	1162.5	95	102	96	99
HYDROCARBONS	106.6	223.1	213.2	216.7	204.9	210.4	96	102	96	99
NITROGEN OXIDES	63.4	139.1	133.3	135.7	128.5	131.5	96	102	96	99
OTHER AIR POLLUTION										
SULFUR OXIDES	95.4	183.5	183.3	192.6	182.7	182.9	100	105	100	100
PARTICULATE MATTER	118.8	343.7	342.8	350.0	334.5	341.7	100	102	98	100
CARBON MONOXIDE	179.1	557.2	563.5	562.7	564.1	565.1	101	100	100	100
HYDROCARBONS	50.3	163.3	160.3	160.5	157.5	158.1	98	100	98	99
NITROGEN OXIDES	23.8	38.2	38.2	40.7	37.4	38.2	100	106	98	100
WATER OXYGEN DEMAND	2802.5	5719.9	5718.8	5722.6	5713.3	5718.9	100	100	100	100
LAND SOLID WASTE	627.4	782.5	742.8	755.0	696.0	733.5	95	102	94	99

SUMMARY PROJECTIONS BY ORE ECONOMIC AREA UNDER FIVE ALTERNATIVE HIGHWAY SYSTEMS

108   LINCOLN, NEBR.

	1970	1990 BASE YEAR	1990 COMPLETED INTERSTATE	1990 EXTENDED PRIMARY	1990 ECONOMIC DEVELOPMENT	1990 URBAN	CI/BY	EP/CI	ED/CI	U/CI
							\ P E R C E N T \			
JOBS BY INDUSTRY		(THOUSANDS)								
NATURAL RESOURCES (1-10)	18.7	16.0	16.0	16.0	16.0	15.9	100	100	100	100
CONSTRUCTION (11,12)	7.9	9.7	9.7	9.5	9.2	9.7	100	102	95	100
MANUFACTURING (13-74)	16.9	23.5	22.3	23.5	22.2	21.8	95	105	100	98
TRANSPORTATION INDUSTRY (75)	4.9	7.6	7.5	7.5	7.5	7.4	99	101	100	99
PUBLIC UTILITIES (76-80)	3.3	6.5	6.2	6.4	5.9	5.9	95	104	95	96
TRADE (81,86,89-99)	35.9	32.2	31.7	32.2	31.3	31.3	98	102	99	99
SERVICES (82-85,87,88,102)	33.4	46.4	46.1	46.1	46.1	46.1	100	100	100	99
STATE & LOCAL GOVT. (101)	28.2	33.3	33.0	33.2	32.9	32.9	99	101	100	100
FEDERAL GOVERNMENT (100,103)	3.3	2.9	2.9	2.9	2.8	2.8	98	101	99	99
TOTAL JOBS	152.5	178.0	175.4	177.8	174.0	174.2	99	101	99	99
CIVILIAN PERSONS EMPLOYED	143.7	167.7	165.3	167.6	164.0	164.1	99	101	99	99
CIVILIAN UNEMPLOYMENT RATE	3.4	.5	.5	.5	.5	.5				
POPULATION	324.0	301.7	296.3	300.3	292.8	296.1	98	101	99	100
PER CAPITA INCOME	3854.4	7741.2	7719.8	7734.6	7730.5	7673.3	100	100	100	99
ENERGY USER SECTOR		(TRILLIONS OF BTU'S)								
NATURAL RESOURCES	18.5	48.2	48.2	48.2	48.1	48.2	100	100	100	100
CONSTRUCTION	5.8	12.9	12.1	14.1	10.5	10.2	94	116	87	85
MANUFACTURING	6.8	19.6	19.1	19.4	18.9	18.9	97	102	98	98
TRANSPORTATION INDUSTRY	2.4	7.1	6.9	7.1	6.8	6.8	97	102	98	98
PUBLIC UTILITIES	4.1	43.1	42.3	42.7	42.9	41.3	98	101	101	98
TRADE AND SERVICES	11.4	28.3	27.7	28.0	27.3	27.4	98	101	99	99
GOVERNMENT, EXC. TRANSPORTATION	2.9	1.2	1.2	1.2	1.2	1.2	98	102	99	99
CONSUMERS, EXC. TRANSPORTATION	22.6	41.9	41.5	41.8	41.3	41.4	99	102	100	99
USER-OPERATED TRANSPORTATION	30.2	58.1	57.4	57.9	57.1	57.2	99	101	99	100
TRANSPORTATION AIR POLLUTION		(THOUSANDS OF TONS)								
SULFUR OXIDES	2.1	5.5	5.5	5.5	5.4	5.4	99	100	99	100
PARTICULATE MATTER	1.7	4.1	4.1	4.1	4.0	4.0	99	101	100	100
CARBON MONOXIDE	293.3	630.8	626.1	629.7	623.5	624.3	99	101	100	100
HYDROCARBONS	53.6	116.8	115.9	116.6	115.5	115.6	99	101	100	100
NITROGEN OXIDES	33.8	78.7	78.3	78.7	78.0	78.1	99	101	100	100
OTHER AIR POLLUTION										
SULFUR OXIDES	13.8	102.4	101.2	101.7	102.3	99.7	99	100	101	98
PARTICULATE MATTER	57.6	217.5	217.1	217.0	213.9	216.2	100	100	99	100
CARBON MONOXIDE	109.8	298.2	298.1	298.1	297.8	298.0	100	100	100	100
HYDROCARBONS	25.3	73.4	70.0	71.4	71.1	68.8	95	102	102	98
NITROGEN OXIDES	9.3	47.9	47.5	47.6	47.6	47.1	99	100	100	99
WATER OXYGEN DEMAND	1039.9	2137.8	2136.9	2136.3	2134.7	2136.3	100	100	100	100
LAND SOLID WASTE	255.9	238.3	234.1	237.2	231.3	233.9	98	101	99	99

	1970	1990 BASE YEAR	1990 COMPLETED INTERSTATE	1990 EXTENDED PRIMARY	1990 ECONOMIC DEVELOPMENT	1990 URBAN	CI/BY	EP/CI	ED/CI	U/CI
JOBS BY INDUSTRY			(THOUSANDS)							
NATURAL RESOURCES (1-10)	31.1	24.6	24.7	24.6	24.7	24.6	100	100	100	100
CONSTRUCTION (11-12)	5.8	5.7	5.5	5.3	4.9	5.4	96	96	89	98
MANUFACTURING (13-74)	10.0	19.9	19.9	18.0	20.2	18.6	100	90	102	93
TRANSPORTATION INDUSTRY (75)	4.6	7.3	7.2	7.0	7.2	7.1	99	97	100	99
PUBLIC UTILITIES (76-80)	3.4	2.8	2.8	1.0	2.3	2.0	99	84	41	87
TRADE (81,86,89-99)	35.0	32.2	31.6	28.8	31.6	30.8	98	91	96	98
SERVICES (82-85,87,88,102)	26.3	34.9	34.6	34.5	34.6	34.6	99	100	100	98
STATE & LOCAL GOVT. (101)	18.8	21.4	21.2	20.6	21.2	20.9	99	97	100	98
FEDERAL GOVERNMENT (100,103)	2.5	1.5	1.5	1.3	1.5	1.4	97	90	100	95
TOTAL JOBS	137.6	150.3	148.5	141.0	148.2	145.5	99	95	100	98
CIVILIAN PERSONS EMPLOYED	135.9	148.2	146.5	139.4	146.3	143.7	99	95	100	98
CIVILIAN UNEMPLOYMENT RATE	2.6	3.2	3.3	3.3	3.1	3.1				
POPULATION	349.0	367.0	362.6	347.4	361.1	357.1	99	96	100	98
PER CAPITA INCOME	3581.8	5859.8	5852.8	5756.6	5864.0	5776.4	100	98	100	99
ENERGY USER SECTOR			(TRILLIONS OF BTU'S)							
NATURAL RESOURCES	26.8	58.2	58.1	57.7	58.2	58.1	100	99	100	100
CONSTRUCTION	5.4	7.6	7.5	6.8	6.7	5.1	98	91	90	69
MANUFACTURING	3.8	12.2	12.2	11.2	12.7	11.8	100	92	100	97
TRANSPORTATION INDUSTRY	3.1	6.6	6.4	5.6	6.4	6.2	97	88	100	97
PUBLIC UTILITIES	24.9	69.0	59.3	30.4	59.8	55.9	86	51	101	94
TRADE AND SERVICES	13.8	29.4	28.7	27.0	28.8	28.3	98	94	100	98
GOVERNMENT, EXC. TRANSPORTATION	1.4	2.2	2.2	2.1	2.2	2.2	99	97	100	98
CONSUMERS, EXC. TRANSPORTATION	20.8	36.6	36.3	35.3	36.3	35.8	99	97	100	99
USER-OPERATED TRANSPORTATION	33.5	62.2	61.8	60.2	61.8	61.0	99	97	100	99
TRANSPORTATION AIR POLLUTION			(THOUSANDS OF TONS)							
SULFUR OXIDES	2.7	5.9	5.8	5.7	5.8	5.8	99	97	100	99
PARTICULATE MATTER	2.1	4.4	4.4	4.3	4.4	4.3	100	98	100	99
CARBON MONOXIDE	342.0	681.8	678.9	666.5	678.7	673.0	100	98	100	99
HYDROCARBONS	62.9	126.4	125.9	123.8	125.9	124.9	100	98	100	99
NITROGEN OXIDES	41.1	85.2	85.0	83.7	85.0	84.4	100	98	100	99
OTHER AIR POLLUTION										
SULFUR OXIDES	43.2	116.8	100.9	53.6	101.7	95.5	86	53	101	95
PARTICULATE MATTER	44.1	118.3	115.0	102.1	114.6	114.1	97	89	100	99
CARBON MONOXIDE	167.2	358.9	359.4	359.3	359.0	360.2	100	100	100	100
HYDROCARBONS	47.8	89.9	89.9	89.3	89.9	89.6	100	100	100	100
NITROGEN OXIDES	14.7	37.9	34.0	22.4	34.2	32.8	90	66	100	96
WATER OXYGEN DEMAND	1503.6	2454.3	2453.7	2452.2	2453.9	2453.9	100	100	100	100
LAND SOLID WASTE	275.7	289.9	286.5	274.4	285.3	282.1	99	96	100	98

SUMMARY PROJECTIONS BY ORE ECONOMIC AREA UNDER FIVE ALTERNATIVE HIGHWAY SYSTEMS

110 WICHITA, KANS.

	1970	1990 BASE YEAR	1990 COMPLETED INTERSTATE	1990 EXTENDED PRIMARY	1990 ECONOMIC DEVELOPMENT	1990 URBAN	CI/BY	EP/CI	ED/CI	U/CI
							\	P E R	C E N	T
							CI/BY	EP/CI	ED/CI	U/CI
JOBS BY INDUSTRY			(THOUSANDS)							
NATURAL RESOURCES (1-10)	29.4	23.7	23.4	23.9	23.9	23.2	101	102	102	99
CONSTRUCTION (11,12)	15.5	15.3	15.5	18.0	14.2	15.5	101	116	92	100
MANUFACTURING (13-74)	63.4	88.9	86.7	92.4	89.1	84.1	98	107	103	97
TRANSPORTATION INDUSTRY (75)	10.4	18.3	18.0	18.4	18.2	17.9	99	102	103	97
PUBLIC UTILITIES (76-80)	7.4	2.4	1.8	4.1	3.4	1.6	73	231	193	88
TRADE (81,86,89-99)	79.1	79.4	77.5	83.2	80.5	76.2	98	107	104	98
SERVICES (82-85,87,88,102)	67.4	84.4	84.3	84.4	84.4	84.3	100	100	100	100
STATE & LOCAL GOVT. (101)	37.3	42.8	42.3	43.9	42.9	41.8	99	104	102	99
FEDERAL GOVERNMENT (100,103)	15.2	14.0	13.8	14.2	14.0	13.7	99	103	101	99
TOTAL JOBS	325.0	369.2	363.3	382.5	370.6	358.3	98	105	102	99
CIVILIAN PERSONS EMPLOYED	314.1	358.4	352.8	371.2	359.9	348.0	98	105	102	99
CIVILIAN UNEMPLOYMENT RATE	3.5	3.4	3.4	3.1	3.1	3.5				
POPULATION	728.3	890.5	880.9	908.4	890.7	872.7	99	103	101	99
PER CAPITA INCOME	3850.4	5746.2	5704.4	5873.8	5758.3	5659.7	99	103	101	99
ENERGY USER SECTOR			(TRILLIONS OF BTU'S)							
NATURAL RESOURCES	26.9	58.2	57.9	58.4	58.3	57.9	100	101	101	100
CONSTRUCTION	12.6	18.5	18.2	27.4	17.3	14.7	98	150	95	81
MANUFACTURING	27.3	63.2	62.2	67.8	63.8	59.9	98	109	102	96
TRANSPORTATION INDUSTRY	8.7	16.8	16.2	17.7	17.0	15.8	97	109	105	98
PUBLIC UTILITIES	40.5	29.5	26.0	43.0	36.5	25.3	88	166	141	97
TRADE AND SERVICES	31.1	63.4	62.1	65.5	64.1	61.5	98	105	103	99
GOVERNMENT, EXC. TRANSPORTATION	5.8	8.3	8.3	8.4	8.3	8.2	99	102	101	99
CONSUMERS, EXC. TRANSPORTATION	38.4	69.5	68.7	71.3	69.6	67.9	99	104	101	99
USER-OPERATED TRANSPORTATION	65.0	117.3	116.4	120.2	117.5	114.9	99	104	101	99
TRANSPORTATION AIR POLLUTION			(THOUSANDS OF TONS)							
SULFUR OXIDES	3.9	8.0	7.9	8.2	8.1	7.8	98	104	102	99
PARTICULATE MATTER	2.9	5.9	5.9	6.1	6.0	5.8	99	103	102	99
CARBON MONOXIDE	515.3	1005.3	995.8	1027.0	1007.3	987.3	99	103	101	99
HYDROCARBONS	92.7	182.0	180.3	185.7	182.3	178.9	99	103	101	99
NITROGEN OXIDES	56.9	114.5	113.6	116.9	115.0	112.7	99	103	101	99
OTHER AIR POLLUTION										
SULFUR OXIDES	87.7	85.5	80.3	107.2	96.5	79.5	94	134	120	99
PARTICULATE MATTER	99.3	178.8	174.9	185.9	182.9	173.7	98	106	105	99
CARBON MONOXIDE	200.8	495.3	497.0	496.2	495.6	497.4	100	100	100	100
HYDROCARBONS	112.6	312.5	311.9	365.4	317.1	286.5	100	117	102	92
NITROGEN OXIDES	27.2	27.8	26.6	33.1	30.5	26.5	96	124	114	99
WATER OXYGEN DEMAND	1558.0	2570.8	2562.6	2566.6	2572.4	2562.7	100	100	100	100
LAND SOLID WASTE	575.3	703.5	695.9	717.6	703.6	689.5	99	103	101	99

SUMMARY PROJECTIONS BY OBE ECONOMIC AREA UNDER FIVE ALTERNATIVE HIGHWAY SYSTEMS

111 KANSAS CITY, MO.-KANS.

	1970	1990 BASE YEAR	1990 COMPLETED INTERSTATE	1990 EXTENDED PRIMARY	1990 ECONOMIC DEVELOPMENT	1990 URBAN	PERCENT CI/BY	EP/CI	ED/CI	U/CI
JOBS BY INDUSTRY			(THOUSANDS)							
NATURAL RESOURCES (1-10)	64.2	23.9	24.0	24.0	24.1	23.9	101	100	100	100
CONSTRUCTION (11,12)	48.1	45.3	45.6	44.3	43.0	45.7	101	97	94	100
MANUFACTURING (13-74)	181.9	241.9	251.2	252.1	253.7	243.1	104	100	101	97
TRANSPORTATION INDUSTRY (75)	51.0	85.8	86.0	86.0	86.0	85.6	100	100	100	99
PUBLIC UTILITIES (76-80)	23.1	32.7	33.4	31.2	30.8	31.4	102	94	92	94
TRADE (81,86,89-99)	246.4	282.0	287.0	284.3	284.4	281.8	102	99	99	98
SERVICES (82-85,87,88,102)	211.1	385.4	385.8	385.6	385.7	385.6	100	100	100	100
STATE & LOCAL GOVT. (101)	112.6	135.5	137.2	136.7	137.0	135.6	101	100	100	99
FEDERAL GOVERNMENT (100,103)	71.7	73.1	73.4	73.3	73.4	73.1	101	100	100	100
TOTAL JOBS	1010.0	1305.6	1323.6	1317.5	1318.1	1305.8	101	100	100	99
CIVILIAN PERSONS EMPLOYED	1004.1	1298.5	1315.6	1310.1	1310.9	1298.5	101	100	100	99
CIVILIAN UNEMPLOYMENT RATE	3.8	4.7	5.0	5.1	4.6	5.1				
POPULATION	2249.2	3184.0	3215.4	3192.0	3180.5	3187.6	101	99	99	99
PER CAPITA INCOME	3878.1	5701.1	5739.7	5749.6	5770.7	5697.2	101	101	101	99
ENERGY USER SECTOR			(TRILLIONS OF BTU'S)							
NATURAL RESOURCES	40.2	85.4	86.1	85.7	86.1	85.8	101	99	100	100
CONSTRUCTION	53.4	88.0	89.3	88.9	83.0	80.8	101	100	93	91
MANUFACTURING	112.5	260.9	266.5	268.1	269.7	261.7	102	101	101	98
TRANSPORTATION INDUSTRY	59.4	125.6	127.2	126.7	126.9	125.5	101	100	101	99
PUBLIC UTILITIES	132.4	480.7	491.8	459.6	462.2	469.7	102	93	94	96
TRADE AND SERVICES	127.8	279.3	282.3	280.5	281.0	278.8	101	99	100	99
GOVERNMENT, EXC. TRANSPORTATION	10.5	15.0	15.2	15.2	15.2	15.0	101	100	100	99
CONSUMERS, EXC. TRANSPORTATION	117.5	229.4	231.9	231.9	231.1	229.4	101	100	100	99
USER-OPERATED TRANSPORTATION	160.6	319.5	323.5	322.2	322.2	319.6	101	100	100	99
TRANSPORTATION AIR POLLUTION			(THOUSANDS OF TONS)							
SULFUR OXIDES	14.3	29.9	30.1	29.8	29.9	29.7	101	99	100	99
PARTICULATE MATTER	8.8	18.2	18.4	18.3	18.3	18.2	101	100	100	99
CARBON MONOXIDE	1304.3	2654.0	2688.3	2674.7	2674.6	2654.8	101	100	100	99
HYDROCARBONS	230.3	468.6	473.6	471.8	471.8	468.5	101	100	100	99
NITROGEN OXIDES	146.0	299.0	303.1	303.1	302.7	300.0	101	100	100	99
OTHER AIR POLLUTION										
SULFUR OXIDES	304.2	970.3	988.8	935.7	939.9	953.0	102	95	95	96
PARTICULATE MATTER	340.5	657.8	663.2	649.7	651.0	654.7	101	98	98	99
CARBON MONOXIDE	333.3	737.2	734.9	731.6	733.2	736.3	100	100	100	100
HYDROCARBONS	165.3	373.2	399.3	421.9	438.3	377.5	107	106	110	95
NITROGEN OXIDES	108.1	299.2	303.7	290.4	291.5	295.0	102	96	96	97
WATER OXYGEN DEMAND	3302.1	6723.3	6722.5	6716.5	6717.1	6720.2	100	100	100	100
LAND SOLID WASTE	1776.9	2515.3	2540.2	2521.7	2512.6	2518.2	101	99	99	99

SUMMARY PROJECTIONS BY ORE ECONOMIC AREA UNDER FIVE ALTERNATIVE HIGHWAY SYSTEMS

112 COLUMBIA, MO.

	1970	1990 BASE YEAR	1990 COMPLETED INTERSTATE	1990 EXTENDED PRIMARY	1990 ECONOMIC DEVELOPMENT	1990 URBAN	PERCENT CI/BY	EP/BY	ED/CI	U/CI
JOBS BY INDUSTRY			(THOUSANDS)							
NATURAL RESOURCES (1-10)	28.6	6.2	6.1	7.0	7.3	6.1	99	113	118	99
CONSTRUCTION (11,12)	5.4	6.9	6.7	8.1	12.3	6.7	97	121	183	100
MANUFACTURING (13-74)	21.2	30.0	26.3	33.4	36.2	25.3	88	127	138	96
TRANSPORTATION INDUSTRY (75)	4.2	6.8	6.7	7.0	7.2	6.7	98	104	107	99
PUBLIC UTILITIES (76-80)	3.0	6.9	6.9	2.0	2.5	.8	94	232	285	96
TRADE (81,86,89-99)	28.9	35.4	34.1	38.5	40.7	33.5	96	113	119	98
SERVICES (82-85,87,88,102)	26.6	43.0	43.0	43.2	43.4	42.9	100	101	101	100
STATE & LOCAL GOVT. (101)	36.2	44.6	43.8	45.3	46.4	43.6	98	104	106	100
FEDERAL GOVERNMENT (100,103)	2.8	2.7	2.6	2.9	3.1	2.5	94	113	123	98
TOTAL JOBS	157.0	176.7	170.1	187.5	199.0	168.1	96	110	117	99
CIVILIAN PERSONS EMPLOYED	129.6	144.5	139.3	153.4	162.7	137.6	96	110	117	99
CIVILIAN UNEMPLOYMENT RATE	3.8	4.7	4.3	4.8	4.9	4.5				
POPULATION	397.1	462.1	439.4	484.3	516.0	435.5	95	110	117	99
PER CAPITA INCOME	2979.5	5314.1	5245.3	5408.0	5470.7	5234.5	99	103	104	99
ENERGY USER SECTOR			(TRILLIONS OF BTU'S)							
NATURAL RESOURCES	14.1	29.0	28.8	29.3	29.5	28.7	99	102	102	100
CONSTRUCTION	7.2	12.6	11.0	14.1	21.9	8.5	87	128	199	77
MANUFACTURING	9.8	23.9	22.1	25.9	27.3	21.6	93	117	124	98
TRANSPORTATION INDUSTRY	3.5	7.1	6.7	7.9	8.5	6.5	94	118	127	97
PUBLIC UTILITIES	26.8	17.5	16.8	32.0	41.9	16.4	96	191	250	98
TRADE AND SERVICES	11.0	21.4	20.7	23.1	24.3	20.4	97	112	117	99
GOVERNMENT, EXC. TRANSPORTATION	1.0	1.1	1.1	1.2	1.3	1.0	93	116	127	98
CONSUMERS, EXC. TRANSPORTATION	14.3	24.2	23.0	25.6	27.3	22.7	95	111	118	99
USER-OPERATED TRANSPORTATION	28.2	57.1	55.3	59.3	61.9	54.8	97	107	112	99
TRANSPORTATION AIR POLLUTION			(THOUSANDS OF TONS)							
SULFUR OXIDES	1.7	3.3	3.2	3.5	3.6	3.2	97	108	113	99
PARTICULATE MATTER	1.3	2.6	2.5	2.7	2.8	2.5	98	107	111	99
CARBON MONOXIDE	247.5	494.4	481.6	511.9	531.5	478.1	97	106	110	99
HYDROCARBONS	44.4	88.4	86.2	91.9	94.9	85.6	98	106	110	99
NITROGEN OXIDES	26.6	52.2	51.1	54.2	56.1	50.7	98	106	110	99
OTHER AIR POLLUTION										
SULFUR OXIDES	48.7	47.4	47.0	72.8	89.7	46.4	99	155	191	99
PARTICULATE MATTER	95.1	199.2	204.6	219.7	227.3	203.6	103	107	111	100
CARBON MONOXIDE	75.4	129.3	131.8	134.9	136.4	132.2	102	102	104	100
HYDROCARBONS	22.0	51.2	36.2	45.5	46.8	34.6	71	126	129	96
NITROGEN OXIDES	16.3	24.3	24.7	31.7	36.1	24.6	102	128	146	99
WATER OXYGEN DEMAND	1385.0	2815.9	2822.1	2830.8	2836.0	2821.6	100	100	100	100
LAND SOLID WASTE	313.7	365.0	347.1	382.6	407.7	344.0	95	110	117	99

113 QUINCY, ILL.

	1970	1990 BASE YEAR	1990 COMPLETED INTERSTATE	1990 EXTENDED PRIMARY	1990 ECONOMIC DEVELOPMENT	1990 URBAN	PERCENT CI/BY	EP/CI	ED/CI	U/CI
JOBS BY INDUSTRY			(THOUSANDS)							
NATURAL RESOURCES (1-10)	15.6	4.4	4.4	4.5	4.5	4.4	99	101	101	99
CONSTRUCTION (11-12)	4.6	5.9	5.8	8.7	6.4	5.9	100	149	109	100
MANUFACTURING (13-74)	30.8	43.7	41.3	47.5	45.3	40.7	95	115	110	99
TRANSPORTATION INDUSTRY (75)	3.1	5.3	5.2	5.5	5.2	5.2	98	106	104	99
PUBLIC UTILITIES (76-80)	1.7	4.7	4.7	6.3	6.2	4.3	100	134	132	92
TRADE (81,86,89-99)	25.6	30.4	29.3	32.9	31.7	28.8	96	112	108	98
SERVICES (82-85,87,88,102)	22.3	28.6	28.6	28.7	28.7	28.5	100	101	100	100
STATE & LOCAL GOVT. (101)	11.8	13.3	12.8	14.4	13.7	12.7	97	112	107	99
FEDERAL GOVERNMENT (100,103)	1.6	1.4	1.3	1.7	1.5	1.3	93	125	114	98
TOTAL JOBS	116.8	137.6	133.5	150.1	143.3	131.8	97	112	107	99
CIVILIAN PERSONS EMPLOYED	114.5	134.2	130.3	146.2	139.6	128.7	97	112	107	99
CIVILIAN UNEMPLOYMENT RATE	2.8	.3	.3	.3	.3	.3				
POPULATION	299.1	317.1	309.4	327.8	318.6	311.0	98	106	103	101
PER CAPITA INCOME	3250.4	6349.0	6255.9	6807.0	6593.1	6149.6	99	109	105	98
ENERGY USER SECTOR			(TRILLIONS OF BTU'S)							
NATURAL RESOURCES	16.2	42.5	42.4	42.5	42.5	42.4	100	100	100	100
CONSTRUCTION	5.3	10.6	8.7	19.8	11.3	8.1	83	227	130	93
MANUFACTURING	18.8	42.0	40.3	47.8	44.1	39.5	96	119	109	98
TRANSPORTATION INDUSTRY	2.3	6.0	5.6	6.9	6.4	5.4	93	123	115	97
PUBLIC UTILITIES	12.2	90.4	92.1	121.1	115.3	86.3	102	132	125	94
TRADE AND SERVICES	10.9	25.8	25.2	27.9	27.1	24.7	97	111	108	98
GOVERNMENT, EXC. TRANSPORTATION	1.0	1.4	1.3	1.5	1.4	1.3	97	112	107	99
CONSUMERS, EXC. TRANSPORTATION	10.8	20.1	19.5	22.0	20.8	19.3	97	113	107	99
USER-OPERATED TRANSPORTATION	21.3	42.7	41.7	45.5	43.8	41.4	98	109	105	99
TRANSPORTATION AIR POLLUTION			(THOUSANDS OF TONS)							
SULFUR OXIDES	1.8	4.6	4.5	4.8	4.7	4.5	98	104	104	99
PARTICULATE MATTER	1.3	3.3	3.3	3.4	3.2	3.2	99	103	103	99
CARBON MONOXIDE	212.9	482.7	475.1	504.2	491.7	472.6	98	106	104	99
HYDROCARBONS	39.2	90.0	88.7	93.8	91.6	88.3	99	106	103	100
NITROGEN OXIDES	25.8	62.7	61.9	64.9	63.7	61.6	99	105	103	100
OTHER AIR POLLUTION										
SULFUR OXIDES	24.4	159.2	161.8	210.2	200.7	152.2	102	130	124	94
PARTICULATE MATTER	56.3	104.1	104.1	116.8	114.9	102.1	100	112	110	98
CARBON MONOXIDE	115.7	297.7	296.7	297.9	298.0	296.3	100	100	100	100
HYDROCARBONS	70.1	140.2	126.7	210.4	162.0	116.4	90	166	128	92
NITROGEN OXIDES	10.0	47.8	48.3	60.4	58.1	45.9	101	125	120	95
WATER OXYGEN DEMAND	1015.5	2091.6	2090.3	2094.3	2095.0	2089.4	100	100	100	100
LAND SOLID WASTE	236.3	250.5	244.4	259.0	251.7	245.7	98	106	105	101

SUMMARY PROJECTIONS BY ORE ECONOMIC AREA UNDER FIVE ALTERNATIVE HIGHWAY SYSTEMS

114   ST. LOUIS, MO.-ILL.

	1970	1990 BASE YEAR	1990 COMPLETED INTERSTATE	1990 EXTENDED PRIMARY	1990 ECONOMIC DEVELOPMENT	1990 URBAN	PER CENT CI/BY	EP/BY	ED/CI	U/CI
JOBS BY INDUSTRY										
NATURAL RESOURCES (1-10)	72.0	30.3	30.6	26.9	26.9	31.0	101	88	88	101
CONSTRUCTION (11,12)	55.7	55.2	55.5	54.0	52.4	55.8	101	97	94	101
MANUFACTURING (13-74)	340.4	465.0	471.2	460.6	457.9	467.5	101	98	97	99
TRANSPORTATION INDUSTRY (75)	54.8	88.7	88.8	88.0	88.0	88.7	100	99	99	100
PUBLIC UTILITIES (76-80)	26.9	17.2	16.9	11.7	11.6	17.3	98	69	69	103
TRADE (81-86,89-99)	291.8	238.2	240.9	227.8	226.1	241.2	101	95	94	100
SERVICES (82-85,87,88,102)	278.9	544.5	544.5	543.9	543.9	544.6	100	100	100	100
STATE & LOCAL GOVT. (101)	133.4	150.0	151.1	147.6	147.0	151.0	101	98	97	100
FEDERAL GOVERNMENT (100,103)	79.9	80.6	80.8	80.4	79.9	80.8	100	99	99	100
TOTAL JOBS	1333.8	1669.5	1680.3	1640.7	1633.6	1678.0	101	98	97	100
CIVILIAN PERSONS EMPLOYED	1339.7	1676.5	1686.6	1649.1	1642.7	1684.2	101	98	97	100
CIVILIAN UNEMPLOYMENT RATE	4.0	2.4	2.2	2.5	2.5	2.2				
POPULATION	3248.2	3997.1	4012.1	3959.0	3941.1	4033.6	100	99	98	101
PER CAPITA INCOME	3647.2	6077.7	6101.3	6017.8	6013.5	6061.3	100	99	99	99
ENERGY USER SECTOR (TRILLIONS OF BTU'S)										
NATURAL RESOURCES	52.0	138.6	139.1	132.9	133.1	139.6	100	96	96	100
CONSTRUCTION	56.4	71.9	72.7	68.8	62.2	73.8	101	95	86	102
MANUFACTURING	204.1	461.4	466.4	461.7	459.1	464.3	101	98	98	100
TRANSPORTATION INDUSTRY	65.6	128.9	129.8	126.0	125.5	129.6	101	97	97	100
PUBLIC UTILITIES	194.6	518.5	514.3	421.1	413.7	516.2	99	82	80	100
TRADE AND SERVICES	159.2	331.1	332.5	323.3	322.6	332.2	100	97	97	100
GOVERNMENT, EXC. TRANSPORTATION	31.5	42.2	42.3	41.9	41.9	42.3	100	99	99	100
CONSUMERS, EXC. TRANSPORTATION	123.3	233.9	235.4	229.9	228.8	235.2	100	98	97	100
USER-OPERATED TRANSPORTATION	235.8	450.4	452.8	444.1	442.5	452.5	101	98	98	100
TRANSPORTATION AIR POLLUTION (THOUSANDS OF TONS)										
SULFUR OXIDES	16.4	34.4	34.5	33.6	33.5	34.4	100	97	96	100
PARTICULATE MATTER	10.5	22.3	22.4	22.0	21.9	22.4	101	98	98	100
CARBON MONOXIDE	1706.8	3539.1	3557.2	3491.4	3479.1	3554.5	101	98	98	100
HYDROCARBONS	300.5	627.2	630.1	618.6	616.5	629.7	100	98	98	100
NITROGEN OXIDES	183.0	389.6	392.4	386.4	384.7	392.1	101	98	98	100
OTHER AIR POLLUTION										
SULFUR OXIDES	554.9	1358.3	1351.5	1196.1	1183.6	1354.9	99	89	88	100
PARTICULATE MATTER	450.8	858.3	857.6	807.3	804.5	860.0	100	94	94	100
CARBON MONOXIDE	726.0	1184.8	1186.2	1152.2	1154.1	1189.9	100	97	97	100
HYDROCARBONS	355.5	538.0	563.7	553.3	538.0	553.0	105	98	95	98
NITROGEN OXIDES	165.6	335.5	334.1	294.2	291.2	335.2	100	88	87	100
WATER OXYGEN DEMAND	2379.0	4697.7	4698.1	4679.4	4678.2	4699.7	100	100	100	100
LAND SOLID WASTE	2566.1	3157.7	3169.5	3127.6	3113.5	3186.6	100	99	98	101

SUMMARY PROJECTIONS BY ORE ECONOMIC AREA UNDER FIVE ALTERNATIVE HIGHWAY SYSTEMS

115   PADUCAH, KY.

	1970	1990 BASE YEAR	1990 COMPLETED INTERSTATE	1990 EXTENDED PRIMARY	1990 ECONOMIC DEVELOPMENT	1990 URBAN	PERCENT CI/BY	PERCENT EP/CI	PERCENT ED/CI	PERCENT U/CI
JOBS BY INDUSTRY		(THOUSANDS)								
NATURAL RESOURCES (1-10)	29.1	11.2	11.7	12.6	12.6	11.5	105	105	107	98
CONSTRUCTION (11-12)	9.4	12.5	12.7	14.5	17.4	12.5	102	114	137	98
MANUFACTURING (13-74)	39.3	59.3	63.1	67.1	68.7	61.2	106	106	109	97
TRANSPORTATION INDUSTRY (75)	5.9	1.8	1.9	2.2	2.3	1.9	108	113	117	97
PUBLIC UTILITIES (76-80)	3.6	.6	.7	.7	.7	1.1	218	209	207	83
TRADE (81,86,89-99)	39.2	40.5	45.3	50.5	52.5	43.5	112	112	116	96
SERVICES (82-85,87,88,102)	29.5	74.9	75.7	76.4	76.5	75.4	101	101	101	100
STATE & LOCAL GOVT. (101)	24.0	29.1	30.3	31.6	32.3	29.8	104	104	107	98
FEDERAL GOVERNMENT (100,103)	3.8	3.8	4.0	4.3	4.5	3.9	107	107	111	97
TOTAL JOBS	183.8	233.6	246.1	262.0	269.5	240.9	105	106	110	98
CIVILIAN PERSONS EMPLOYED	169.3	214.0	225.2	239.8	246.6	220.5	105	106	110	98
CIVILIAN UNEMPLOYMENT RATE	7.0	5.4	5.4	5.7	5.2	5.4				
POPULATION	558.5	676.3	705.1	747.5	769.0	694.7	104	106	109	99
PER CAPITA INCOME	2590.1	4391.5	4496.3	4623.5	4672.1	4451.3	102	103	104	99
ENERGY USER SECTOR		(TRILLIONS OF BTU'S)								
NATURAL RESOURCES	26.5	40.3	41.9	43.6	43.7	41.2	104	104	104	98
CONSTRUCTION	11.8	16.3	18.4	26.7	44.1	16.2	113	145	240	88
MANUFACTURING	23.9	40.8	43.4	45.6	46.2	42.3	106	105	106	97
TRANSPORTATION INDUSTRY	4.6	9.7	11.1	13.4	13.0	10.6	114	112	117	95
PUBLIC UTILITIES	43.3	79.0	109.8	139.4	145.9	104.2	139	127	133	95
TRADE AND SERVICES	14.5	35.4	38.7	41.9	42.9	37.7	109	108	111	97
GOVERNMENT, EXC. TRANSPORTATION	1.4	2.1	2.2	2.4	2.4	2.2	106	107	110	98
CONSUMERS, EXC. TRANSPORTATION	19.3	36.1	37.8	40.2	41.3	37.1	105	106	109	98
USER-OPERATED TRANSPORTATION	34.7	70.1	72.7	76.5	78.3	71.7	104	105	108	99
TRANSPORTATION AIR POLLUTION		(THOUSANDS OF TONS)								
SULFUR OXIDES	3.3	5.4	5.6	5.9	6.0	5.5	105	105	107	98
PARTICULATE MATTER	2.4	4.0	4.2	4.3	4.4	4.1	104	104	106	99
CARBON MONOXIDE	370.5	673.0	699.5	721.9	735.1	685.4	103	103	106	99
HYDROCARBONS	68.5	122.4	125.9	130.8	133.1	124.6	103	104	106	99
NITROGEN OXIDES	46.1	77.8	80.2	83.2	84.4	79.3	103	104	105	99
OTHER AIR POLLUTION										
SULFUR OXIDES	80.7	152.6	203.5	252.3	263.2	194.2	133	124	129	95
PARTICULATE MATTER	70.8	108.2	121.2	135.5	138.3	119.2	112	112	114	98
CARBON MONOXIDE	194.6	306.2	305.2	308.3	308.5	306.0	100	101	101	100
HYDROCARBONS	59.2	101.5	109.0	114.2	114.8	103.7	107	105	105	95
NITROGEN OXIDES	25.8	52.4	64.8	77.0	79.7	62.6	124	119	123	97
WATER OXYGEN DEMAND	628.0	1293.7	1295.7	1299.3	1300.2	1295.8	100	100	100	100
LAND SOLID WASTE	441.2	534.3	557.0	590.5	607.5	548.8	104	106	109	99

SUMMARY PROJECTIONS BY OBE ECONOMIC AREA UNDER FIVE ALTERNATIVE HIGHWAY SYSTEMS

116 SPRINGFIELD, MO.

	1970	1990 BASE YEAR	1990 COMPLETED INTERSTATE	1990 EXTENDED PRIMARY	1990 ECONOMIC DEVELOPMENT	1990 URBAN	CI/BY	EP/CI	ED/CI	U/CI
							PERCENT			
JOBS BY INDUSTRY		(THOUSANDS)								
NATURAL RESOURCES (1-10)	58.0	22.3	22.2	22.6	22.5	22.0	99	102	102	99
CONSTRUCTION (11,12)	10.4	12.9	13.0	15.8	19.9	13.0	101	122	152	100
MANUFACTURING (13-74)	68.1	103.5	100.6	106.2	107.8	98.2	97	106	107	98
TRANSPORTATION INDUSTRY (75)	10.4	17.1	17.0	17.3	17.4	16.9	99	102	102	99
PUBLIC UTILITIES (76-80)	5.4	1.4	1.4	2.9	1.2	1.2	94	217	183	85
TRADE (81,86,89-99)	63.1	67.3	66.0	71.6	71.9	64.5	98	108	109	98
SERVICES (82-85,87,88,102)	49.9	79.5	79.4	79.6	79.6	79.7	100	100	100	100
STATE & LOCAL GOVT. (101)	35.9	43.7	43.1	44.7	45.3	42.7	99	104	105	99
FEDERAL GOVERNMENT (100,103)	5.2	5.2	5.1	5.4	5.6	5.0	98	107	109	98
TOTAL JOBS	306.3	353.0	347.8	366.2	372.5	342.7	99	107	107	99
CIVILIAN PERSONS EMPLOYED	286.4	328.1	323.3	340.2	346.1	318.6	99	107	107	99
CIVILIAN UNEMPLOYMENT RATE	4.8	5.8	5.5	5.2	5.6	5.7				
POPULATION	830.4	1035.5	1023.8	1052.3	1065.3	1016.7	99	103	104	99
PER CAPITA INCOME	2715.2	4518.7	4476.9	4633.8	4694.2	4423.7	99	104	105	99
ENERGY USER SECTOR		(TRILLIONS OF BTU'S)								
NATURAL RESOURCES	17.2	32.8	32.3	33.2	32.9	31.7	99	103	102	98
CONSTRUCTION	10.4	17.1	17.0	22.5	32.0	11.5	100	132	188	67
MANUFACTURING	26.9	59.4	58.1	60.7	61.5	57.1	98	104	106	98
TRANSPORTATION INDUSTRY	10.1	19.4	19.0	20.4	20.5	18.6	98	108	108	98
PUBLIC UTILITIES	45.0	29.5	27.6	64.7	54.2	27.1	94	234	196	98
TRADE AND SERVICES	21.7	42.1	41.4	44.7	44.4	40.7	98	107	107	98
GOVERNMENT. EXC. TRANSPORTATION	2.5	3.7	3.7	3.8	3.9	3.6	98	106	106	98
CONSUMERS. EXC. TRANSPORTATION	28.2	50.0	49.2	51.7	52.7	48.4	98	104	107	98
USER-OPERATED TRANSPORTATION	49.5	100.2	99.0	102.8	104.5	97.8	99	104	106	99
TRANSPORTATION AIR POLLUTION		(THOUSANDS OF TONS)								
SULFUR OXIDES	3.2	6.1	6.0	6.3	6.3	5.9	98	106	106	99
PARTICULATE MATTER	2.3	4.4	4.4	4.6	4.6	4.3	99	105	105	99
CARBON MONOXIDE	406.2	817.7	808.1	838.4	849.5	799.3	99	104	105	99
HYDROCARBONS	72.0	144.6	142.9	148.2	150.1	141.4	99	105	105	99
NITROGEN OXIDES	42.6	84.4	83.6	87.0	87.8	82.7	99	104	105	99
OTHER AIR POLLUTION										
SULFUR OXIDES	85.6	60.5	57.4	118.2	100.9	56.5	95	206	176	98
PARTICULATE MATTER	105.2	168.1	166.3	184.9	179.2	165.6	99	111	108	100
CARBON MONOXIDE	107.2	194.5	195.4	198.9	195.7	196.0	100	102	100	100
HYDROCARBONS	51.2	84.7	81.9	83.7	88.7	80.0	97	108	108	98
NITROGEN OXIDES	26.2	22.4	21.7	36.5	32.2	21.5	97	168	148	99
WATER OXYGEN DEMAND	1980.2	4057.2	4053.3	4066.3	4064.1	4052.2	100	100	100	100
LAND SOLID WASTE	656.0	818.1	808.8	831.3	841.5	803.2	99	103	104	99

SUMMARY PROJECTIONS BY ORE ECONOMIC AREA UNDER FIVE ALTERNATIVE HIGHWAY SYSTEMS

117   L ROCK-N L ROCK, ARK.

	1970	1990 BASE YEAR	1990 COMPLETED INTERSTATE	1990 EXTENDED PRIMARY	1990 ECONOMIC DEVELOPMENT	1990 URBAN	CI/BY	EP/CI	ED/CI	U/CI
								PERCENT		
JOBS BY INDUSTRY			(THOUSANDS)							
NATURAL RESOURCES (1-10)	39.3	33.7	33.2	34.0	33.7	33.0	98	103	102	99
CONSTRUCTION (11,12)	14.6	19.7	19.9	21.4	20.8	19.9	101	108	105	100
MANUFACTURING (13-74)	66.1	79.0	77.7	80.7	79.8	75.4	98	104	103	97
TRANSPORTATION INDUSTRY (75)	9.9	16.2	16.1	16.4	16.3	15.9	99	102	103	99
PUBLIC UTILITIES (76-80)	7.7	3.0	2.3	4.4	3.7	2.0	75	192	163	86
TRADE (81,86,89-99)	68.5	73.6	71.9	76.6	75.1	69.8	98	107	104	97
SERVICES (82-85,87,88,102)	70.3	171.1	171.0	171.1	171.1	170.9	100	100	100	100
STATE & LOCAL GOVT. (101)	42.4	56.3	55.8	57.0	56.7	55.4	99	102	101	99
FEDERAL GOVERNMENT (100,103)	17.3	19.1	19.0	19.2	19.1	18.9	99	101	101	100
TOTAL JOBS	336.0	471.7	466.8	480.9	476.3	461.1	99	103	102	99
CIVILIAN PERSONS EMPLOYED	306.3	432.8	428.2	441.3	437.1	423.0	99	103	102	99
CIVILIAN UNEMPLOYMENT RATE	5.5	5.6	6.2	6.0	6.3					
POPULATION	864.5	1262.2	1254.7	1279.5	1273.4	1250.7	99	102	101	100
PER CAPITA INCOME	2811.0	4474.0	4436.7	4523.1	4484.9	4390.0	99	102	101	99
ENERGY USER SECTOR			(TRILLIONS OF BTU'S)							
NATURAL RESOURCES	21.9	13.7	13.4	13.9	13.6	13.3	98	103	101	99
CONSTRUCTION	13.4	24.7	24.7	28.3	27.5	18.6	99	115	111	75
MANUFACTURING	38.1	80.6	79.5	81.7	81.1	76.9	99	103	102	97
TRANSPORTATION INDUSTRY	8.1	16.0	15.5	16.8	16.3	14.9	97	108	105	96
PUBLIC UTILITIES	43.5	36.6	29.9	59.2	48.5	29.3	82	198	162	98
TRADE AND SERVICES	25.0	59.1	57.7	60.8	59.8	56.6	98	105	104	98
GOVERNMENT, EXC. TRANSPORTATION	1.9	3.2	3.2	3.3	3.3	3.1	98	104	103	99
CONSUMERS, EXC. TRANSPORTATION	39.3	81.9	81.2	83.1	82.4	80.5	99	102	102	99
USER-OPERATED TRANSPORTATION	57.5	125.3	124.2	127.1	126.1	123.1	99	102	102	99
TRANSPORTATION AIR POLLUTION			(THOUSANDS OF TONS)							
SULFUR OXIDES	3.7	5.1	5.0	5.2	5.1	4.9	98	105	103	98
PARTICULATE MATTER	2.8	4.2	4.2	4.3	4.3	4.1	99	104	104	98
CARBON MONOXIDE	508.4	948.5	940.3	962.5	955.2	932.1	99	102	102	99
HYDROCARBONS	91.2	165.5	164.1	167.9	166.6	162.7	99	102	102	99
NITROGEN OXIDES	55.1	87.9	87.2	89.6	88.8	86.2	99	103	102	99
OTHER AIR POLLUTION										
SULFUR OXIDES	91.9	132.8	121.4	169.5	152.0	120.2	91	140	125	99
PARTICULATE MATTER	96.2	156.8	150.4	166.3	160.5	148.3	96	111	107	99
CARBON MONOXIDE	165.7	179.3	180.0	181.2	180.4	180.3	100	101	101	100
HYDROCARBONS	56.2	89.4	86.2	89.6	89.2	67.9	97	104	103	79
NITROGEN OXIDES	33.3	69.7	66.7	78.7	74.3	66.3	96	118	111	99
WATER OXYGEN DEMAND	932.7	1571.9	1570.8	1570.4	1570.9	1570.9	100	100	100	100
LAND SOLID WASTE	683.0	997.1	991.2	1010.8	1006.0	988.0	99	102	101	100

SUMMARY PROJECTIONS BY ORE ECONOMIC AREA UNDER FIVE ALTERNATIVE HIGHWAY SYSTEMS

118 FORT SMITH, ARK.-OKLA.

	1970	1990 BASE YEAR	1990 COMPLETED INTERSTATE	1990 EXTENDED PRIMARY	1990 ECONOMIC DEVELOPMENT	1990 URBAN	PER CENT CI/BY	EP/CI	ED/CI	U/CI
JOBS BY INDUSTRY				(THOUSANDS)						
NATURAL RESOURCES (1-10)	18.7	20.1	20.1	20.1	20.2	20.0	100	100	100	99
CONSTRUCTION (11,12)	4.9	5.8	5.9	6.0	6.8	5.9	101	101	115	100
MANUFACTURING (13-74)	25.8	46.3	46.0	46.0	46.4	45.5	99	100	101	99
TRANSPORTATION INDUSTRY (75)	2.0	3.3	3.3	3.3	3.4	3.3	100	100	102	99
PUBLIC UTILITIES (76-80)	1.8	3.7	3.7	3.7	3.8	3.6	96	101	111	88
TRADE (81,86,89-99)	18.7	32.0	31.8	31.9	32.7	31.0	100	100	103	98
SERVICES (82-85,87,88,102)	16.3	38.0	38.0	38.0	38.1	38.0	100	100	100	100
STATE & LOCAL GOVT. (101)	12.0	17.7	17.6	17.6	17.9	17.0	99	100	102	99
FEDERAL GOVERNMENT (100,103)	5.7	7.1	7.0	7.0	7.1	7.0	100	100	101	99
TOTAL JOBS	106.0	171.1	170.4	170.7	173.3	168.6	100	100	102	99
CIVILIAN PERSONS EMPLOYED	98.5	158.6	157.9	158.2	160.7	156.2	100	100	102	99
CIVILIAN UNEMPLOYMENT RATE	8.3	2.6	2.5	2.6	2.3	2.5				
POPULATION	289.3	405.9	403.8	403.8	407.9	401.9	99	100	101	100
PER CAPITA INCOME	2427.8	4804.7	4785.1	4786.5	4858.6	4721.8	100	100	102	99
ENERGY USER SECTOR				(TRILLIONS OF BTU'S)						
NATURAL RESOURCES	4.4	7.1	7.0	6.9	7.2	6.6	98	99	104	95
CONSTRUCTION	4.7	9.3	9.3	9.5	13.8	6.3	100	102	148	68
MANUFACTURING	7.0	15.6	15.3	15.5	15.7	15.0	99	101	102	98
TRANSPORTATION INDUSTRY	2.1	5.8	5.8	5.8	6.0	5.6	99	100	104	97
PUBLIC UTILITIES	13.3	9.1	8.3	8.4	9.9	8.1	91	101	119	98
TRADE AND SERVICES	6.7	17.5	17.4	17.4	17.8	17.0	99	100	102	98
GOVERNMENT, EXC. TRANSPORTATION	1.0	1.8	1.8	1.8	1.8	1.7	99	100	102	99
CONSUMERS, EXC. TRANSPORTATION	10.6	25.0	24.9	24.9	25.3	24.6	99	100	102	99
USER-OPERATED TRANSPORTATION	14.1	35.1	34.9	34.9	35.5	34.4	99	100	102	99
TRANSPORTATION AIR POLLUTION				(THOUSANDS OF TONS)						
SULFUR OXIDES	.6	1.5	1.5	1.5	1.5	1.5	99	100	103	97
PARTICULATE MATTER	.5	1.2	1.2	1.2	1.2	1.1	99	100	103	98
CARBON MONOXIDE	107.5	255.2	253.5	253.7	258.5	250.1	99	100	102	99
HYDROCARBONS	18.8	44.3	43.9	44.0	44.8	43.4	99	100	102	99
NITROGEN OXIDES	10.3	23.4	23.3	23.4	23.8	22.9	99	100	102	98
OTHER AIR POLLUTION										
SULFUR OXIDES	23.8	23.1	21.4	21.8	24.6	20.9	92	102	115	98
PARTICULATE MATTER	13.7	12.4	11.6	11.8	13.2	11.4	93	102	114	99
CARBON MONOXIDE	21.9	16.3	15.9	15.9	16.0	15.8	97	100	101	100
HYDROCARBONS	6.6	10.9	8.4	8.4	10.3	6.8	78	122	122	80
NITROGEN OXIDES	7.7	10.3	9.6	9.8	10.7	9.4	94	102	111	98
WATER OXYGEN DEMAND	681.4	1127.3	1125.8	1125.6	1126.2	1125.7	100	100	100	100
LAND SOLID WASTE	228.6	320.6	319.0	319.0	322.3	317.5	99	100	101	100

SUMMARY PROJECTIONS BY ORE ECONOMIC AREA UNDER FIVE ALTERNATIVE HIGHWAY SYSTEMS

119   TULSA, OKLA.

	1970	1990 BASE YEAR	1990 COMPLETED INTERSTATE	1990 EXTENDED PRIMARY	1990 ECONOMIC DEVELOPMENT	1990 URBAN	CI/BY	EP/CI	ED/CI	U/CI
JOBS BY INDUSTRY		(THOUSANDS)						PER CENT		
NATURAL RESOURCES (1-10)	47.3	49.4	49.3	49.2	49.3	49.2	100	100	100	100
CONSTRUCTION (11,12)	19.3	20.0	19.8	19.2	18.9	19.7	99	97	96	96
MANUFACTURING (13-74)	85.1	102.5	99.6	98.8	101.0	95.4	97	99	101	96
TRANSPORTATION INDUSTRY (75)	16.6	32.9	32.5	32.4	32.6	32.3	99	100	100	99
PUBLIC UTILITIES (76-80)	9.8	4.3	3.2	2.9	3.9	3.0	76	89	121	91
TRADE (81,84,89-99)	87.6	103.3	99.4	97.3	101.1	96.0	96	98	102	97
SERVICES (82-85,87,88,102)	81.3	180.6	180.2	180.0	180.3	179.9	100	100	100	100
STATE & LOCAL GOVT. (101)	41.6	54.9	53.9	53.4	54.3	52.9	98	99	101	98
FEDERAL GOVERNMENT (100,103)	8.4	9.9	9.7	9.6	9.8	9.5	98	99	101	98
TOTAL JOBS	396.9	557.8	547.7	542.8	551.2	537.8	98	99	101	98
CIVILIAN PERSONS EMPLOYED	384.8	539.5	529.8	525.1	533.2	520.4	98	99	101	98
CIVILIAN UNEMPLOYMENT RATE	4.9	5.1	4.5	4.8	4.7	5.2				
POPULATION	1014.4	1387.4	1360.2	1356.2	1366.7	1353.1	98	100	100	99
PER CAPITA INCOME	3250.0	5346.7	5326.6	5264.6	5334.1	5221.7	100	100	100	98
ENERGY USER SECTOR		(TRILLIONS OF BTU'S)								
NATURAL RESOURCES	17.2	34.6	34.4	34.2	34.4	33.7	99	100	100	98
CONSTRUCTION	20.5	35.9	35.1	34.9	36.1	28.9	98	100	103	82
MANUFACTURING	30.5	56.5	55.0	54.4	55.7	53.5	97	99	101	97
TRANSPORTATION INDUSTRY	27.3	56.1	54.9	54.4	55.5	54.0	98	99	101	98
PUBLIC UTILITIES	58.2	89.0	57.7	40.7	67.9	45.0	65	71	118	78
TRADE AND SERVICES	35.4	74.3	71.7	70.3	72.8	69.8	96	98	102	97
GOVERNMENT, EXC. TRANSPORTATION	4.9	7.4	7.3	7.2	7.3	7.2	99	99	101	99
CONSUMERS, EXC. TRANSPORTATION	42.1	86.2	84.7	83.9	85.2	83.2	98	99	100	98
USER-OPERATED TRANSPORTATION	44.4	91.9	89.6	88.3	90.2	87.3	98	99	101	97
TRANSPORTATION AIR POLLUTION		(THOUSANDS OF TONS)								
SULFUR OXIDES	5.4	10.6	10.3	10.2	10.4	10.1	97	100	101	98
PARTICULATE MATTER	2.9	5.6	5.5	5.4	5.5	5.4	98	99	101	98
CARBON MONOXIDE	331.0	673.7	656.7	646.5	661.5	638.9	97	98	101	98
HYDROCARBONS	57.9	116.5	113.5	111.6	114.2	110.4	97	98	101	97
NITROGEN OXIDES	40.6	78.4	77.0	76.4	77.9	75.2	98	99	101	98
OTHER AIR POLLUTION										
SULFUR OXIDES	140.0	203.8	152.8	125.9	169.7	132.7	75	82	111	87
PARTICULATE MATTER	86.7	148.1	133.1	124.5	137.8	127.2	90	94	104	96
CARBON MONOXIDE	98.0	74.8	74.6	74.4	74.7	74.4	100	100	100	100
HYDROCARBONS	62.8	53.5	50.4	50.1	51.2	46.4	94	99	102	92
NITROGEN OXIDES	43.6	50.4	38.0	31.5	42.1	33.1	75	83	111	87
WATER OXYGEN DEMAND	1741.9	2829.7	2827.7	2827.4	2828.5	2827.4	100	100	100	100
LAND SOLID WASTE	801.4	1096.5	1074.6	1071.4	1079.7	1068.9	98	100	100	99

SUMMARY PROJECTIONS BY ORE ECONOMIC AREA UNDER FIVE ALTERNATIVE HIGHWAY SYSTEMS

120   OKLAHOMA CITY, OKLA.

	1970	1990 BASE YEAR	1990 COMPLETED INTERSTATE	1990 EXTENDED PRIMARY	1990 ECONOMIC DEVELOPMENT	1990 URBAN	CI/BY	EP/CI	ED/CI	U/CI
								P E R C E N T		
JOBS BY INDUSTRY			(THOUSANDS)							
NATURAL RESOURCES (1-10)	58.3	45.7	45.5	45.2	45.2	45.3	99	99	100	100
CONSTRUCTION (11,12)	25.2	14.5	14.4	14.2	13.3	14.4	99	98	92	100
MANUFACTURING (13-74)	54.9	63.5	61.0	58.0	56.2	59.0	96	95	92	97
TRANSPORTATION INDUSTRY (75)	16.8	28.2	28.1	27.7	27.5	27.9	99	99	98	99
PUBLIC UTILITIES (76-80)	9.6	10.6	8.9	5.5	3.6	7.9	84	62	40	89
TRADE (81,86,89-99)	112.8	154.5	150.9	145.1	141.6	148.5	98	96	94	98
SERVICES (82-85,87,88,102)	103.0	224.9	224.7	224.5	224.4	224.7	100	100	100	100
STATE & LOCAL GOVT. (101)	63.1	81.7	81.0	79.9	79.3	80.5	99	99	98	99
FEDERAL GOVERNMENT (100,103)	47.1	52.1	51.9	51.7	51.5	51.8	100	100	99	100
TOTAL JOBS	491.0	675.7	666.2	651.7	642.5	660.0	99	98	96	99
CIVILIAN PERSONS EMPLOYED	460.7	636.7	627.7	614.0	605.3	621.8	99	98	96	99
CIVILIAN UNEMPLOYMENT RATE	4.2	6.6	6.7	6.2	6.5	6.9				
POPULATION	1156.8	1674.3	1661.0	1637.2	1616.3	1653.0	99	99	97	100
PER CAPITA INCOME	3260.2	4882.9	4849.3	4791.6	4769.9	4815.0	99	99	98	99
ENERGY USER SECTOR			(TRILLIONS OF BTU'S)							
NATURAL RESOURCES	27.0	19.2	19.2	19.0	19.0	19.1	100	99	99	100
CONSTRUCTION	20.0	27.9	27.3	26.3	20.8	23.9	98	96	76	87
MANUFACTURING	15.3	31.0	29.7	28.2	27.5	29.1	96	95	92	98
TRANSPORTATION INDUSTRY	24.1	47.5	46.5	44.9	44.0	45.9	98	97	95	99
PUBLIC UTILITIES	42.5	189.1	164.8	116.8	82.1	153.4	87	71	50	93
TRADE AND SERVICES	48.2	107.0	104.6	100.6	98.0	103.2	98	96	94	99
GOVERNMENT, EXC. TRANSPORTATION	7.2	10.6	10.5	10.4	10.3	10.4	99	99	98	99
CONSUMERS, EXC. TRANSPORTATION	54.6	109.8	108.8	107.1	106.0	108.0	99	98	97	99
USER-OPERATED TRANSPORTATION	98.3	198.6	197.0	194.3	192.5	195.7	99	99	98	99
TRANSPORTATION AIR POLLUTION			(THOUSANDS OF TONS)							
SULFUR OXIDES	6.7	11.1	10.9	10.6	10.4	10.8	98	97	95	99
PARTICULATE MATTER	4.5	7.6	7.5	7.4	7.3	7.5	99	98	97	99
CARBON MONOXIDE	752.4	1429.8	1417.4	1396.6	1383.2	1407.4	99	99	98	99
HYDROCARBONS	133.2	248.5	246.3	242.6	240.4	244.5	99	99	98	99
NITROGEN OXIDES	80.8	139.5	138.4	136.4	134.8	137.4	99	99	97	99
OTHER AIR POLLUTION										
SULFUR OXIDES	99.4	349.9	310.0	230.8	173.0	291.3	89	74	56	94
PARTICULATE MATTER	105.4	171.8	160.8	142.4	129.6	156.2	94	89	81	97
CARBON MONOXIDE	141.5	89.9	89.2	87.1	86.5	88.7	99	99	97	100
HYDROCARBONS	46.8	59.7	59.3	58.8	57.4	57.9	99	99	97	98
NITROGEN OXIDES	41.0	103.2	93.3	73.6	59.3	88.7	90	79	64	95
WATER OXYGEN DEMAND	1678.0	2714.3	2712.1	2710.9	2710.8	2711.4	100	100	100	100
LAND SOLID WASTE	913.9	1322.7	1312.2	1293.4	1276.9	1305.8	99	99	97	99

285

SUMMARY PROJECTIONS BY ORE ECONOMIC AREA UNDER FIVE ALTERNATIVE HIGHWAY SYSTEMS

121   WICHITA FALLS, TEX.

	1970	1990 BASE YEAR	1990 COMPLETED INTERSTATE	1990 EXTENDED PRIMARY	1990 ECONOMIC DEVELOPMENT	1990 URBAN	CI/BY	PERCENT EP/CI	ED/CI	U/CI
JOBS BY INDUSTRY		(THOUSANDS)								
NATURAL RESOURCES (1-10)	25.6	22.0	22.0	22.1	22.4	21.9	100	101	102	100
CONSTRUCTION (11,12)	5.2	1.5	1.9	1.7	2.1	.6	60	187	230	72
MANUFACTURING (13-74)	13.7	17.8	17.0	18.4	19.0	17.0	95	108	111	100
TRANSPORTATION INDUSTRY (75)	3.2	4.2	3.9	4.3	4.4	3.9	92	110	112	99
PUBLIC UTILITIES (76-80)	3.1	1.0	1.0	1.3	2.1	.9	98	141	217	97
TRADE (81,86,89-99)	32.3	31.6	30.6	32.1	33.0	30.4	97	105	108	99
SERVICES (82-85,87,88,102)	27.8	55.1	55.1	55.2	55.2	55.1	100	100	100	100
STATE & LOCAL GOVT. (101)	18.7	19.6	19.3	19.7	20.0	19.3	99	102	104	100
FEDERAL GOVERNMENT (100,103)	49.1	47.9	47.9	48.0	48.0	47.9	100	100	100	100
TOTAL JOBS	178.8	200.8	197.7	202.8	206.1	197.0	98	103	104	100
CIVILIAN PERSONS EMPLOYED	127.3	148.9	146.0	150.7	153.8	145.4	98	103	105	100
CIVILIAN UNEMPLOYMENT RATE	5.8	8.6	9.1	8.9	8.8	8.8	98	102	104	98
POPULATION	455.8	589.8	579.1	589.4	599.5	570.3	98	102	104	98
PER CAPITA INCOME	3076.3	3773.0	3761.5	3823.3	3842.7	3798.5	100	102	102	101
ENERGY USER SECTOR		(TRILLIONS OF BTU'S)								
NATURAL RESOURCES	17.6	18.1	17.8	18.0	18.2	17.8	99	101	102	100
CONSTRUCTION	7.4	11.6	6.9	12.3	12.8	5.6	59	179	186	82
MANUFACTURING	4.2	6.3	5.6	6.6	7.2	5.5	89	119	130	99
TRANSPORTATION INDUSTRY	3.1	4.0	3.7	4.1	4.4	3.7	92	112	119	99
PUBLIC UTILITIES	30.8	18.3	18.0	18.1	20.8	17.6	98	101	116	98
TRADE AND SERVICES	12.6	22.2	21.7	22.6	23.4	21.6	97	104	108	100
GOVERNMENT, EXC. TRANSPORTATION	3.9	5.1	5.1	5.2	5.2	5.1	99	101	101	100
CONSUMERS, EXC. TRANSPORTATION	16.9	28.1	27.7	28.4	28.8	27.6	99	102	104	100
USER-OPERATED TRANSPORTATION	30.9	50.6	50.0	51.0	51.6	49.8	99	102	103	100
TRANSPORTATION AIR POLLUTION		(THOUSANDS OF TONS)								
SULFUR OXIDES	1.9	1.7	1.7	1.8	1.8	1.7	96	105	108	99
PARTICULATE MATTER	1.5	1.5	1.5	1.6	1.6	1.5	98	103	105	100
CARBON MONOXIDE	253.3	355.4	350.7	358.3	363.3	349.4	98	102	104	100
HYDROCARBONS	46.0	62.4	61.6	62.9	63.8	61.4	99	102	104	100
NITROGEN OXIDES	28.7	33.4	32.9	33.7	34.2	32.7	99	103	104	100
OTHER AIR POLLUTION										
SULFUR OXIDES	55.6	34.6	34.4	34.4	38.6	33.5	98	101	113	98
PARTICULATE MATTER	39.8	20.7	20.6	21.8	22.9	20.5	99	106	111	100
CARBON MONOXIDE	93.0	46.3	46.3	47.9	48.0	46.6	100	103	104	101
HYDROCARBONS	23.9	23.9	21.0	28.0	32.3	21.1	88	133	153	101
NITROGEN OXIDES	17.7	10.9	10.8	10.9	12.0	10.7	99	101	111	99
WATER OXYGEN DEMAND	737.3	1191.8	1190.3	1190.3	1191.0	1190.4	100	100	100	100
LAND AND SOLID WASTE	360.1	465.9	457.5	465.6	473.6	450.5	98	102	104	98

SUMMARY PROJECTIONS BY ORE ECONOMIC AREA UNDER FIVE ALTERNATIVE HIGHWAY SYSTEMS

122 AMARILLO, TEX.

	1970	1990 BASE YEAR	1990 COMPLETED INTERSTATE	1990 EXTENDED PRIMARY	1990 ECONOMIC DEVELOPMENT	1990 URBAN	P E R C E N T CI/BY	EP/CI	ED/CI	U/CI
JOBS BY INDUSTRY		(THOUSANDS)								
NATURAL RESOURCES (1-10)	25.6	23.6	23.8	23.7	24.4	23.7	101	100	102	99
CONSTRUCTION (11-12)	9.1	2.9	2.8	3.0	3.0	2.6	96	109	111	93
MANUFACTURING (13-74)	15.7	17.8	17.9	20.0	19.9	17.7	101	112	111	99
TRANSPORTATION INDUSTRY (75)	6.4	6.0	6.1	6.1	6.9	6.0	101	101	104	99
PUBLIC UTILITIES (76-80)	5.0	4.3	5.3	5.1	8.6	4.8	124	95	161	90
TRADE (81,86-89-99)	38.9	33.0	34.0	34.5	38.2	33.3	103	102	112	98
SERVICES (82-85,87,88,102)	28.1	41.8	41.7	41.7	41.9	41.7	100	100	100	100
STATE & LOCAL GOVT. (101)	39.8	45.3	45.5	45.7	46.3	45.3	100	100	102	100
FEDERAL GOVERNMENT (100,103)	15.5	13.6	13.6	13.7	13.8	13.6	100	100	101	100
TOTAL JOBS	184.1	188.2	190.7	193.5	202.4	188.7	101	101	106	99
CIVILIAN PERSONS EMPLOYED	137.0	144.2	146.0	148.5	155.6	144.4	101	102	107	99
CIVILIAN UNEMPLOYMENT RATE	4.0	4.4	4.4	4.4	4.4	4.4				
POPULATION	437.0	432.8	436.0	438.7	444.7	437.4	101	101	102	100
PER CAPITA INCOME	3470.3	5034.8	5074.0	5144.6	5327.7	4999.6	101	101	105	99
ENERGY USER SECTOR		(TRILLIONS OF BTU'S)								
NATURAL RESOURCES	28.5	23.9	24.2	24.5	24.6	24.1	101	101	102	100
CONSTRUCTION	8.4	8.2	8.5	8.5	9.3	8.4	103	100	109	98
MANUFACTURING	13.6	17.0	17.2	17.9	18.0	17.1	104	104	105	99
TRANSPORTATION INDUSTRY	5.3	7.2	7.5	7.6	8.6	7.3	104	102	115	98
PUBLIC UTILITIES	35.3	26.0	39.9	37.7	75.2	34.4	142	95	189	86
TRADE AND SERVICES	15.5	27.9	28.7	28.7	31.6	28.2	103	100	110	98
GOVERNMENT, EXC. TRANSPORTATION	2.0	2.8	2.8	2.9	2.9	2.8	101	101	103	99
CONSUMERS, EXC. TRANSPORTATION	24.4	40.4	40.7	41.1	42.0	40.5	101	101	103	99
USER-OPERATED TRANSPORTATION	40.7	69.9	70.3	70.9	72.4	69.9	101	101	103	99
TRANSPORTATION AIR POLLUTION		(THOUSANDS OF TONS)								
SULFUR OXIDES	3.3	3.0	3.0	3.0	3.2	3.0	102	101	107	99
PARTICULATE MATTER	2.4	2.5	2.6	2.6	2.7	2.6	101	101	105	99
CARBON MONOXIDE	402.8	561.5	565.0	569.4	581.1	562.2	101	101	103	100
HYDROCARBONS	73.6	98.8	99.4	100.1	102.1	98.9	101	101	103	100
NITROGEN OXIDES	47.4	53.7	54.2	54.6	56.0	53.9	101	101	103	99
OTHER AIR POLLUTION										
SULFUR OXIDES	73.0	66.5	86.0	82.4	143.6	77.0	129	96	167	90
PARTICULATE MATTER	63.4	72.6	77.9	77.1	91.4	75.6	107	99	117	97
CARBON MONOXIDE	201.4	157.8	160.1	160.7	162.4	159.1	101	100	101	99
HYDROCARBONS	82.5	68.6	69.6	71.4	71.1	69.3	101	103	102	100
NITROGEN OXIDES	24.2	29.4	29.4	28.5	43.7	27.1	120	97	149	92
WATER OXYGEN DEMAND	1139.2	1851.9	1852.2	1852.2	1853.2	1852.1	100	100	100	100
LAND SOLID WASTE	345.8	341.9	344.5	346.6	351.3	345.5	101	101	102	100

SUMMARY PROJECTIONS BY ORE ECONOMIC AREA UNDER FIVE ALTERNATIVE HIGHWAY SYSTEMS

123 LUBBOCK, TEX.

	1970	1990 BASE YEAR	1990 COMPLETED INTERSTATE	1990 EXTENDED PRIMARY	1990 ECONOMIC DEVELOPMENT	1990 URBAN	CI/BY	EP/CI	ED/CI	U/CI
							PERCENT			
JOBS BY INDUSTRY		(THOUSANDS)								
NATURAL RESOURCES (1-10)	14.2	10.4	10.3	9.9	10.7	10.2	99	96	104	100
CONSTRUCTION (11,12)	5.9	3.7	3.5	3.1	3.9	3.1	94	88	110	88
MANUFACTURING (13-74)	8.4	9.8	8.6	7.6	9.6	8.4	88	87	112	97
TRANSPORTATION INDUSTRY (75)	3.6	.7	.7	.7	.8	.7	99	91	110	99
PUBLIC UTILITIES (76-80)	3.2	4.2	4.1	2.3	6.4	3.9	98	54	155	94
TRADE (81,86,89-99)	31.0	28.2	27.7	25.3	30.6	27.2	98	91	111	98
SERVICES (82-85,87,88,102)	23.8	36.7	36.6	36.4	36.7	36.6	100	100	100	100
STATE & LOCAL GOVT. (101)	12.4	13.5	13.1	12.4	13.8	12.9	97	95	105	98
FEDERAL GOVERNMENT (100,103)	6.2	5.0	4.9	4.8	5.1	4.9	98	97	103	99
TOTAL JOBS	108.8	112.4	109.7	102.4	117.8	108.0	98	93	107	98
CIVILIAN PERSONS EMPLOYED	95.5	99.0	96.6	90.1	103.9	95.0	98	93	108	98
CIVILIAN UNEMPLOYMENT RATE	4.4	6.6	6.3	4.7	5.9	6.2				
POPULATION	328.7	376.5	361.8	325.7	387.7	354.2	96	90	107	98
PER CAPITA INCOME	3184.3	4964.5	4965.7	5119.2	4983.6	4975.3	100	103	100	100
ENERGY USER SECTOR		(TRILLIONS OF BTU'S)								
NATURAL RESOURCES	37.4	23.8	23.8	23.4	24.1	23.8	100	98	101	100
CONSTRUCTION	5.7	11.0	10.9	10.3	12.0	8.7	99	94	110	80
MANUFACTURING	3.8	7.8	7.6	7.0	8.3	7.3	96	92	110	96
TRANSPORTATION INDUSTRY	4.4	8.2	8.1	7.4	8.9	7.9	98	91	110	98
PUBLIC UTILITIES	32.5	33.5	33.5	21.5	69.0	30.5	101	64	206	91
TRADE AND SERVICES	13.0	26.8	26.4	24.4	28.8	26.1	99	92	109	99
GOVERNMENT, EXC. TRANSPORTATION	1.1	1.8	1.7	1.6	1.8	1.7	97	96	104	99
CONSUMERS, EXC. TRANSPORTATION	18.0	33.9	33.3	32.2	34.5	33.0	98	97	103	99
USER-OPERATED TRANSPORTATION	29.2	55.2	54.2	52.5	56.0	53.8	98	97	103	99
TRANSPORTATION AIR POLLUTION		(THOUSANDS OF TONS)								
SULFUR OXIDES	4.1	3.4	3.4	3.2	3.5	3.3	98	96	105	99
PARTICULATE MATTER	2.9	2.6	2.6	2.5	2.7	2.6	99	97	104	99
CARBON MONOXIDE	390.8	488.6	481.8	469.3	495.5	478.3	99	97	103	99
HYDROCARBONS	74.1	87.2	86.0	83.8	88.4	85.4	99	97	103	99
NITROGEN OXIDES	54.4	51.6	51.0	49.8	52.5	50.7	99	98	103	99
OTHER AIR POLLUTION										
SULFUR OXIDES	62.3	81.1	81.5	61.8	140.6	76.6	101	76	173	94
PARTICULATE MATTER	69.5	63.1	63.6	55.8	77.6	62.5	101	88	122	98
CARBON MONOXIDE	265.8	171.0	172.2	166.3	174.4	172.4	101	97	101	100
HYDROCARBONS	57.9	45.2	45.2	43.1	42.4	42.4	100	95	102	94
NITROGEN OXIDES	21.8	31.4	31.7	26.4	46.4	30.5	101	83	146	96
WATER OXYGEN DEMAND	404.9	671.9	672.1	671.8	673.2	672.1	100	100	100	100
LAND SOLID WASTE	259.7	297.4	285.8	257.3	306.3	279.9	96	90	107	98

124 ODESSA, TEX.

	1970	1990 BASE YEAR	1990 COMPLETED INTERSTATE	1990 EXTENDED PRIMARY	1990 ECONOMIC DEVELOPMENT	1990 URBAN	P E R C E N T			
							CI/BY	EP/CI	ED/CI	U/CI
JOBS BY INDUSTRY			(THOUSANDS)							
NATURAL RESOURCES (1-10)	28.3	17.1	17.2	17.2	17.4	17.2	101	100	101	100
CONSTRUCTION (11,12)	7.0	2.9	2.7	2.6	2.2	2.7	95	59	82	98
MANUFACTURING (13-74)	8.0	9.7	12.3	13.3	13.5	12.0	126	108	110	98
TRANSPORTATION INDUSTRY (75)	4.5	2.5	2.6	2.6	2.9	2.6	106	99	109	99
PUBLIC UTILITIES (76-80)	3.0	3.4	4.4	3.1	3.9	3.9	131	71	179	90
TRADE (81,86,89-99)	28.2	9.2	10.2	9.8	12.0	9.9	111	97	119	97
SERVICES (82-85,87,88,102)	21.4	32.0	31.4	31.4	31.4	31.4	98	100	100	100
STATE & LOCAL GOVT (101+)	23.4	24.5	24.8	24.7	25.5	24.7	101	99	103	100
FEDERAL GOVERNMENT (100,103)	5.9	4.7	4.7	4.7	4.9	4.7	101	100	103	100
TOTAL JOBS	129.7	105.9	110.4	108.5	117.8	109.2	104	98	107	99
CIVILIAN PERSONS EMPLOYED	106.6	88.8	92.5	91.0	98.9	91.5	104	98	107	99
CIVILIAN UNEMPLOYMENT RATE	5.5	17.2	16.8	16.8	14.1	15.9	103	99	102	97
POPULATION	319.2	333.1	342.4	337.5	350.2	333.1	103	99	102	100
PER CAPITA INCOME	3740.6	4607.0	4680.6	4686.9	4927.9	4739.7	102	100	105	101
ENERGY USER SECTOR			(TRILLIONS OF BTU'S)							
NATURAL RESOURCES	18.4	11.7	11.9	12.2	12.2	11.9	102	102	102	100
CONSTRUCTION	4.8	1.6	1.9	2.6	1.3	1.7	126	78	163	91
MANUFACTURING	10.0	19.5	20.7	21.3	22.0	20.5	106	103	106	99
TRANSPORTATION INDUSTRY	6.2	5.6	6.3	6.1	7.3	6.1	112	97	117	98
PUBLIC UTILITIES	25.9	37.3	48.5	30.5	92.7	43.3	130	63	191	89
TRADE AND SERVICES	11.4	12.7	13.8	12.9	16.3	13.4	109	94	119	97
GOVERNMENT, EXC. TRANSPORTATION	1.2	1.6	1.6	1.6	1.7	1.6	102	99	105	99
CONSUMERS, EXC. TRANSPORTATION	17.6	27.5	28.0	27.9	29.1	27.8	102	99	104	99
USER-OPERATED TRANSPORTATION	24.8	37.7	38.6	38.3	40.2	38.3	102	99	104	99
TRANSPORTATION AIR POLLUTION			(THOUSANDS OF TONS)							
SULFUR OXIDES	2.0	1.7	1.8	1.8	2.0	1.8	107	98	110	98
PARTICULATE MATTER	1.3	1.4	1.8	1.4	1.5	1.4	105	99	107	99
CARBON MONOXIDE	217.9	290.9	298.2	296.1	310.9	295.8	103	99	104	99
HYDROCARBONS	39.0	50.9	52.1	51.7	54.3	51.7	102	99	104	99
NITROGEN OXIDES	24.4	27.6	28.6	28.4	30.1	28.3	103	99	105	99
OTHER AIR POLLUTION										
SULFUR OXIDES	50.2	66.2	84.3	54.9	155.8	75.9	127	65	185	90
PARTICULATE MATTER	30.1	36.2	40.2	33.9	57.6	38.5	111	84	143	96
CARBON MONOXIDE	87.2	99.9	100.0	100.2	99.6	100.0	100	100	100	100
HYDROCARBONS	46.8	54.5	59.2	66.0	62.9	58.2	109	111	106	98
NITROGEN OXIDES	15.5	21.2	25.6	18.5	42.9	23.6	121	72	168	92
WATER OXYGEN DEMAND	274.6	473.3	474.8	474.4	475.9	474.7	100	100	100	100
LAND SOLID WASTE	252.2	263.1	270.5	266.6	276.6	263.2	103	99	102	97

SUMMARY PROJECTIONS BY ORE ECONOMIC AREA UNDER FIVE ALTERNATIVE HIGHWAY SYSTEMS

125 ABILENE, TEX.

	1970	1990 BASE YEAR	1990 COMPLETED INTERSTATE	1990 EXTENDED PRIMARY	1990 ECONOMIC DEVELOPMENT	1990 URBAN	CI/BY	EP/CI	ED/CI	U/CI
JOBS BY INDUSTRY			(THOUSANDS)				PERCENT			
NATURAL RESOURCES (1-10)	19.2	16.4	16.3	16.1	16.4	16.2	99	99	101	100
CONSTRUCTION (11,12)	3.9	1.4	.9	.7	2.6	.0	65	76	295	0
MANUFACTURING (13-74)	9.8	20.0	18.8	18.4	20.1	18.0	94	98	107	96
TRANSPORTATION INDUSTRY (75)	2.3	.2	.3	.2	.2	.2	89	106	119	105
PUBLIC UTILITIES (76-80)	3.1	1.4	1.3	1.0	1.9	1.2	90	82	146	96
TRADE (81,86,89-99)	20.6	12.0	11.5	11.2	12.4	11.2	95	98	109	97
SERVICES (82-85,87,88,102)	17.7	13.9	13.9	13.9	14.0	13.9	100	100	100	100
STATE & LOCAL GOVT. (101)	33.7	39.8	39.6	39.5	39.0	39.5	100	100	101	100
FEDERAL GOVERNMENT (100,103)	7.0	6.2	6.2	6.1	6.2	6.1	99	100	101	99
TOTAL JOBS	117.3	111.3	108.6	107.3	113.9	106.4	98	99	105	98
CIVILIAN PERSONS EMPLOYED	80.0	79.8	78.0	77.3	81.9	76.4	98	99	105	98
CIVILIAN UNEMPLOYMENT RATE	5.5	9.9	9.2	9.3	9.2	9.3				
POPULATION	264.8	280.1	271.6	267.5	285.7	265.2	97	98	105	98
PER CAPITA INCOME	3090.6	4092.3	4078.2	4085.8	4103.6	4074.6	100	100	101	100
ENERGY USER SECTOR			(TRILLIONS OF BTU'S)							
NATURAL RESOURCES	11.0	10.2	10.1	10.0	10.3	10.1	99	99	101	100
CONSTRUCTION	4.4	3.4	3.4	3.5	5.8	1.3	101	102	172	38
MANUFACTURING	4.6	7.3	6.8	6.5	7.4	6.5	93	96	108	95
TRANSPORTATION INDUSTRY	2.3	1.8	1.6	1.5	1.9	1.5	89	94	120	93
PUBLIC UTILITIES	37.8	22.5	22.1	22.2	22.7	21.6	98	100	103	98
TRADE AND SERVICES	7.3	7.7	7.3	7.1	8.1	7.2	95	97	110	97
GOVERNMENT, EXC. TRANSPORTATION	1.0	1.2	1.2	1.2	1.2	1.2	98	99	103	99
CONSUMERS, EXC. TRANSPORTATION	16.2	28.6	28.3	28.2	28.8	28.0	99	100	102	99
USER-OPERATED TRANSPORTATION	24.0	41.8	41.3	41.1	42.2	40.9	99	100	102	99
TRANSPORTATION AIR POLLUTION			(THOUSANDS OF TONS)							
SULFUR OXIDES	1.3	1.2	1.1	1.1	1.2	1.1	96	99	106	98
PARTICULATE MATTER	1.1	1.1	1.1	1.2	1.2	1.1	98	99	103	99
CARBON MONOXIDE	207.9	318.3	314.5	313.1	321.0	311.8	99	100	102	99
HYDROCARBONS	37.2	55.6	55.0	54.7	56.1	54.5	99	100	102	99
NITROGEN OXIDES	21.8	28.3	27.9	27.7	28.5	27.6	99	100	102	99
OTHER AIR POLLUTION										
SULFUR OXIDES	64.6	38.6	38.0	38.3	38.8	37.2	98	101	102	98
PARTICULATE MATTER	49.4	36.3	35.9	35.2	36.8	35.7	99	98	102	99
CARBON MONOXIDE	65.2	59.6	58.9	56.4	60.8	58.7	99	96	103	100
HYDROCARBONS	17.1	14.8	13.8	13.4	14.0	12.8	93	97	102	93
NITROGEN OXIDES	18.4	12.2	12.0	12.0	12.3	11.8	98	100	102	98
WATER OXYGEN DEMAND	485.2	785.1	784.0	783.0	785.0	783.8	100	100	100	100
LAND SOLID WASTE	209.2	221.3	214.6	211.3	225.7	209.5	97	98	105	98

SUMMARY PROJECTIONS BY ORE ECONOMIC AREA UNDER FIVE ALTERNATIVE HIGHWAY SYSTEMS

126   SAN ANGELO, TEX.

	1970	1990 BASE YEAR	1990 COMPLETED INTERSTATE	1990 EXTENDED PRIMARY	1990 ECONOMIC DEVELOPMENT	1990 URBAN	CI/BY	EP/CI	ED/CI	U/CI
JOBS BY INDUSTRY		(THOUSANDS)							PERCENT	
NATURAL RESOURCES (1-10)	7.5	7.7	7.7	7.7	7.7	7.7	100	100	100	100
CONSTRUCTION (11,12)	2.0	2.2	2.0	3.3	7.2	2.0	91	163	351	100
MANUFACTURING (13-74)	4.0	6.0	6.0	7.3	8.2	5.9	100	122	138	98
TRANSPORTATION INDUSTRY (75)	4.8	6.0	5.9	6.4	6.8	5.8	98	108	116	99
PUBLIC UTILITIES (76-80)	1.7	1.9	1.4	3.2	4.5	1.3	74	225	318	95
TRADE (81,86,89-99)	9.9	11.4	11.0	12.5	14.0	10.9	97	113	127	99
SERVICES (82-85,87,88,102)	9.4	10.7	10.7	10.8	11.1	10.7	100	105	103	100
STATE & LOCAL GOVT. (101)	6.6	7.5	7.4	7.8	8.5	7.4	99	105	115	100
FEDERAL GOVERNMENT (100,103)	4.0	3.8	3.7	3.8	4.0	3.7	100	102	106	100
TOTAL JOBS	45.8	51.4	50.5	56.0	64.2	50.2	98	111	127	99
CIVILIAN PERSONS EMPLOYED	35.7	41.0	40.3	44.8	51.5	40.1	98	111	128	99
CIVILIAN UNEMPLOYMENT RATE	4.7	4.3	4.4	5.0	5.6	4.1				
POPULATION	125.0	143.2	141.7	157.8	185.4	140.6	99	111	131	100
PER CAPITA INCOME	3036.9	4446.5	4431.9	4477.0	4517.5	4432.8	100	101	102	100
ENERGY USER SECTOR		(TRILLIONS OF BTU'S)								
NATURAL RESOURCES	4.0	5.8	5.7	5.8	5.9	5.7	98	102	104	99
CONSTRUCTION	1.6	1.8	1.7	7.2	18.1	1.6	94	434	1090	99
MANUFACTURING	1.8	4.6	4.3	5.3	5.7	4.1	94	123	134	96
TRANSPORTATION INDUSTRY	1.7	1.9	1.3	1.7	2.1	1.3	93	130	162	98
PUBLIC UTILITIES	11.1	6.7	6.6	13.7	19.0	6.4	98	208	289	98
TRADE AND SERVICES	4.5	9.4	9.1	10.1	11.1	9.0	97	111	122	99
GOVERNMENT, EXC. TRANSPORTATION	.4	.6	.6	.6	.7	.6	99	107	121	100
CONSUMERS, EXC. TRANSPORTATION	7.7	14.1	14.0	14.7	15.8	13.9	99	105	113	100
USER-OPERATED TRANSPORTATION	9.0	16.4	16.3	17.3	19.0	16.2	99	106	117	100
TRANSPORTATION AIR POLLUTION		(THOUSANDS OF TONS)								
SULFUR OXIDES	.4	.5	.5	.6	.7	.5	96	115	134	99
PARTICULATE MATTER	.3	.5	.5	.5	.6	.5	98	110	123	99
CARBON MONOXIDE	72.4	121.8	120.9	128.6	141.0	120.4	99	106	117	100
HYDROCARBONS	12.8	21.2	21.0	22.4	24.5	21.0	99	107	116	100
NITROGEN OXIDES	7.1	10.8	10.7	11.5	12.7	10.7	99	107	118	100
OTHER AIR POLLUTION										
SULFUR OXIDES	19.6	11.9	11.8	23.7	32.9	11.5	98	201	279	98
PARTICULATE MATTER	11.6	16.1	12.1	15.8	22.4	11.1	75	130	185	91
CARBON MONOXIDE	14.3	10.1	10.5	10.5	10.0	10.6	103	100	95	101
HYDROCARBONS	3.6	3.7	4.7	11.6	9.2	4.4	130	245	195	94
NITROGEN OXIDES	5.7	3.6	3.6	6.6	9.0	3.6	99	183	249	99
WATER OXYGEN DEMAND	514.3	838.3	836.3	835.9	836.2	836.3	100	100	100	100
LAND SOLID WASTE	98.7	113.1	112.0	124.6	146.5	111.1	99	111	131	99

291

SUMMARY PROJECTIONS BY ORE ECONOMIC AREA UNDER FIVE ALTERNATIVE HIGHWAY SYSTEMS

127 DALLAS. TEX.

	1970	1990 BASE YEAR (THOUSANDS)	1990 COMPLETED INTERSTATE	1990 EXTENDED PRIMARY	1990 ECONOMIC DEVELOPMENT	1990 URBAN	CI/BY	EP/CI (PERCENT)	ED/CI	U/CI
JOBS BY INDUSTRY										
NATURAL RESOURCES (1-10)	50.7	49.2	48.5	47.5	47.6	48.3	99	98	98	99
CONSTRUCTION (11-12)	67.7	42.9	43.3	41.5	40.1	43.0	101	96	93	99
MANUFACTURING (13-74)	308.1	368.3	359.8	346.1	347.8	344.2	98	96	97	96
TRANSPORTATION INDUSTRY (75)	48.8	84.0	83.8	83.3	83.4	83.1	100	99	100	99
PUBLIC UTILITIES (76-80)	26.2	8.6	8.5	8.8	9.0	8.2	99	103	105	96
TRADE (81,86,89-99)	310.3	418.4	414.3	405.5	406.6	403.8	99	98	98	97
SERVICES (82-85,87,88,102)	296.9	485.7	485.2	484.7	485.0	485.0	100	100	100	100
STATE & LOCAL GOVT. (101)	106.2	134.1	132.5	130.0	130.4	129.8	99	98	98	98
FEDERAL GOVERNMENT (100,103)	41.4	44.1	43.7	43.2	43.3	43.1	99	99	99	99
TOTAL JOBS	1256.4	1635.2	1619.6	1590.6	1593.2	1588.5	99	98	98	98
CIVILIAN PERSONS EMPLOYED	1154.2	1513.0	1498.4	1471.7	1474.2	1469.3	99	98	98	98
CIVILIAN UNEMPLOYMENT RATE	4.1	4.7	4.5	5.0	4.6	4.7				
POPULATION	2736.5	3815.7	3777.9	3754.4	3742.1	3745.8	99	99	99	99
PER CAPITA INCOME	3903.4	5846.0	5831.3	5745.7	5778.0	5744.1	100	99	99	99
ENERGY USER SECTOR			(TRILLIONS OF BTU'S)							
NATURAL RESOURCES	19.8	32.1	30.9	29.2	29.4	30.0	96	95	95	97
CONSTRUCTION	75.9	135.5	135.5	110.9	105.9	104.4	100	82	78	77
MANUFACTURING	129.8	253.9	249.0	236.4	238.8	233.6	98	95	96	94
TRANSPORTATION INDUSTRY	75.1	160.4	159.0	156.7	157.1	156.0	99	99	99	98
PUBLIC UTILITIES	217.2	128.8	126.6	127.6	129.4	123.8	98	101	102	98
TRADE AND SERVICES	159.6	325.1	322.7	318.9	319.6	317.6	99	99	99	98
GOVERNMENT, EXC. TRANSPORTATION	20.8	30.2	30.0	29.8	29.8	29.7	99	99	99	99
CONSUMERS, EXC. TRANSPORTATION	132.0	271.7	269.5	265.7	266.1	265.1	99	99	99	99
USER-OPERATED TRANSPORTATION	225.3	440.2	436.6	430.7	431.4	429.8	99	99	99	98
TRANSPORTATION AIR POLLUTION			(THOUSANDS OF TONS)							
SULFUR OXIDES	16.1	32.7	32.3	31.6	31.7	31.7	99	98	98	98
PARTICULATE MATTER	9.8	19.7	19.6	19.3	19.3	19.2	99	99	99	98
CARBON MONOXIDE	1566.3	3127.7	3102.3	3058.6	3063.8	3050.9	99	99	99	98
HYDROCARBONS	272.3	540.9	536.3	528.6	529.5	527.4	99	99	99	98
NITROGEN OXIDES	163.1	321.2	319.9	316.7	316.6	314.5	100	99	99	98
OTHER AIR POLLUTION										
SULFUR OXIDES	533.5	624.1	619.8	620.5	623.5	614.9	99	100	101	99
PARTICULATE MATTER	361.7	550.1	544.4	529.7	531.4	539.7	99	97	98	99
CARBON MONOXIDE	158.6	161.0	155.0	136.0	138.3	150.1	96	88	89	97
HYDROCARBONS	146.1	285.6	268.4	177.8	199.9	154.3	94	66	74	58
NITROGEN OXIDES	200.7	342.0	340.3	339.1	340.1	338.7	99	100	100	100
WATER OXYGEN DEMAND	1304.2	2072.0	2070.9	2070.4	2071.2	2070.6	100	100	100	100
LAND SOLID WASTE	2161.8	3012.8	2984.5	2966.0	2956.2	2959.2	99	99	99	99

SUMMARY PROJECTIONS BY ORE ECONOMIC AREA UNDER FIVE ALTERNATIVE HIGHWAY SYSTEMS

128 WACO, TEX.

	1970	1990 BASE YEAR	1990 COMPLETED INTERSTATE	1990 EXTENDED PRIMARY	1990 ECONOMIC DEVELOPMENT	1990 URBAN	CI/BY	EP/CI PERCENT	ED/CI	U/CI
JOBS BY INDUSTRY			**(THOUSANDS)**							
NATURAL RESOURCES (1-10)	15.1	12.9	12.9	12.9	13.1	12.9	100	100	101	99
CONSTRUCTION (11,12)	6.5	2.7	2.9	2.3	2.2	2.2	92	94	128	89
MANUFACTURING (13-74)	19.2	31.7	31.6	31.2	34.4	31.2	101	99	109	99
TRANSPORTATION INDUSTRY (75)	2.5	6.2	6.2	6.2	6.4	6.2	100	100	102	100
PUBLIC UTILITIES (76-80)	2.5	0.8	0.8	0.9	1.4	0.8	99	103	166	98
TRADE (81,86,89-99)	28.8	27.1	27.2	27.1	29.3	26.9	100	99	107	99
SERVICES (82-85,87,88,102)	28.9	50.2	50.4	50.4	50.5	50.4	100	100	100	100
STATE & LOCAL GOVT. (101)	14.6	16.5	16.5	16.4	17.1	16.4	100	99	104	99
FEDERAL GOVERNMENT (100,103)	38.2	37.8	37.8	37.8	37.9	37.8	100	100	100	100
TOTAL JOBS	157.4	185.5	186.0	185.1	193.2	184.9	100	100	104	99
CIVILIAN PERSONS EMPLOYED	113.8	140.6	141.0	140.2	147.4	140.0	100	99	105	99
CIVILIAN UNEMPLOYMENT RATE	4.4	5.3	5.2	5.2	5.8	5.8				
POPULATION	403.9	527.4	528.8	522.2	546.7	527.0	100	99	103	100
PER CAPITA INCOME	2806.2	3790.4	3798.0	3805.3	3885.4	3781.6	100	100	102	100
ENERGY USER SECTOR			**(TRILLIONS OF BTU'S)**							
NATURAL RESOURCES	6.9	5.8	5.8	5.8	5.9	5.8	100	100	102	100
CONSTRUCTION	5.6	6.9	6.9	7.0	13.4	6.0	101	100	193	86
MANUFACTURING	8.7	23.0	23.0	22.3	25.0	22.7	100	97	109	99
TRANSPORTATION INDUSTRY	2.9	6.6	6.7	6.6	7.2	6.6	101	99	108	99
PUBLIC UTILITIES	27.9	16.9	16.7	16.8	20.1	16.3	98	101	121	98
TRADE AND SERVICES	10.2	22.3	22.4	22.3	23.5	22.2	100	100	105	99
GOVERNMENT, EXC. TRANSPORTATION	1.5	2.1	2.1	2.1	2.2	2.2	100	99	103	99
CONSUMERS, EXC. TRANSPORTATION	13.1	23.6	23.7	23.5	24.7	23.6	100	100	104	99
USER-OPERATED TRANSPORTATION	19.0	33.5	33.6	33.4	35.2	33.4	100	100	105	99
TRANSPORTATION AIR POLLUTION			**(THOUSANDS OF TONS)**							
SULFUR OXIDES	1.2	1.7	1.7	1.7	1.9	1.7	100	99	106	99
PARTICULATE MATTER	0.9	1.3	1.3	1.3	1.4	1.3	100	99	105	99
CARBON MONOXIDE	159.9	254.1	255.0	253.4	266.4	253.4	100	100	104	99
HYDROCARBONS	28.5	44.3	44.5	44.1	46.4	44.2	100	99	104	99
NITROGEN OXIDES	17.0	24.5	24.6	24.5	25.8	24.5	101	99	105	99
OTHER AIR POLLUTION										
SULFUR OXIDES	48.0	29.0	28.5	28.7	34.1	27.9	98	101	120	98
PARTICULATE MATTER	63.9	111.3	108.6	103.4	117.9	107.5	98	95	108	99
CARBON MONOXIDE	48.8	34.6	35.0	35.7	34.8	35.3	101	102	99	101
HYDROCARBONS	13.1	13.0	14.3	14.2	17.2	13.9	110	99	120	97
NITROGEN OXIDES	14.2	9.3	9.2	9.3	10.5	9.0	99	101	115	99
WATER OXYGEN DEMAND	576.5	945.5	944.2	944.5	944.5	944.3	100	100	100	100
LAND SOLID WASTE	319.1	416.6	417.8	412.5	431.9	416.3	100	99	103	100

SUMMARY PROJECTIONS BY OBE ECONOMIC AREA UNDER FIVE ALTERNATIVE HIGHWAY SYSTEMS

129   AUSTIN, TEX.

	1970	1990 BASE YEAR	1990 COMPLETED INTERSTATE	1990 EXTENDED PRIMARY	1990 ECONOMIC DEVELOPMENT	1990 URBAN	PER CENT CI/BY	EP/CI	ED/CI	U/CI
JOBS BY INDUSTRY			(THOUSANDS)							
NATURAL RESOURCES (1-10)	19.0	16.2	16.1	16.1	16.2	16.1	99	100	101	100
CONSTRUCTION (11,12)	13.0	14.3	14.4	14.1	15.7	14.5	101	98	109	100
MANUFACTURING (13-74)	18.0	15.9	14.8	15.1	16.6	14.6	93	102	112	99
TRANSPORTATION INDUSTRY (75)	2.9	4.6	4.6	4.6	4.7	4.5	99	100	103	99
PUBLIC UTILITIES (76-80)	4.0	1.9	1.9	2.0	2.0	4.9	99	103	106	99
TRADE (81,86,89-99)	43.5	69.9	68.7	68.9	70.9	68.1	98	100	103	99
SERVICES (82-85,87,88,102)	48.5	127.6	127.6	127.4	127.7	127.5	100	100	100	100
STATE & LOCAL GOVT. (101)	36.7	50.0	49.6	49.6	50.2	49.5	99	100	101	100
FEDERAL GOVERNMENT (100,103)	13.7	15.1	15.0	15.0	15.2	15.0	99	100	101	100
TOTAL JOBS	199.2	315.5	312.6	312.8	319.3	311.8	99	100	102	100
CIVILIAN PERSONS EMPLOYED	175.9	282.7	280.1	280.4	286.2	279.4	99	100	102	100
CIVILIAN UNEMPLOYMENT RATE	3.0	2.4	2.1	2.2	2.1	2.2				
POPULATION	559.6	840.7	830.2	831.6	834.7	833.6	99	100	101	100
PER CAPITA INCOME	3037.8	4912.0	4889.3	4884.6	5012.1	4858.1	100	100	103	99
ENERGY USER SECTOR			(TRILLIONS OF BTU'S)							
NATURAL RESOURCES	8.6	7.4	6.9	6.8	7.2	6.8	93	100	105	99
CONSTRUCTION	11.2	24.5	23.1	24.4	29.5	20.8	94	106	128	90
MANUFACTURING	8.8	12.1	10.9	11.4	12.2	10.7	90	105	112	99
TRANSPORTATION INDUSTRY	2.5	7.1	6.7	6.8	7.3	6.6	95	100	108	98
PUBLIC UTILITIES	28.5	16.9	16.6	16.8	17.0	16.3	98	101	102	98
TRADE AND SERVICES	16.4	47.9	47.3	47.3	48.2	47.0	99	100	102	100
GOVERNMENT, EXC. TRANSPORTATION	4.9	7.3	7.2	7.2	7.3	7.2	99	100	101	100
CONSUMERS, EXC. TRANSPORTATION	20.4	45.3	44.7	44.7	45.8	44.6	99	100	102	100
USER-OPERATED TRANSPORTATION	35.0	78.9	78.0	78.0	79.6	77.8	99	100	102	100
TRANSPORTATION AIR POLLUTION			(THOUSANDS OF TONS)							
SULFUR OXIDES	1.3	2.5	2.4	2.4	2.5	2.4	97	100	104	99
PARTICULATE MATTER	1.2	2.3	2.3	2.3	2.3	2.2	98	100	103	100
CARBON MONOXIDE	272.3	567.7	560.9	561.3	573.1	559.7	99	100	102	100
HYDROCARBONS	48.1	98.7	97.5	97.6	99.6	97.3	99	100	102	100
NITROGEN OXIDES	26.2	50.3	49.6	49.8	50.9	49.5	99	100	103	100
OTHER AIR POLLUTION										
SULFUR OXIDES	67.4	92.7	91.7	91.1	92.8	90.9	99	100	101	99
PARTICULATE MATTER	67.9	61.9	61.7	61.5	62.4	61.8	100	100	101	100
CARBON MONOXIDE	50.0	29.0	29.2	29.1	29.2	29.0	101	100	100	99
HYDROCARBONS	17.3	30.3	18.0	23.4	26.1	16.9	59	130	145	94
NITROGEN OXIDES	23.9	55.6	55.1	54.6	55.7	54.9	99	100	101	99
WATER OXYGEN DEMAND	587.0	949.5	948.1	948.0	948.4	947.9	100	100	100	100
LAND SOLID WASTE	442.1	664.1	655.9	656.9	659.4	658.5	99	100	101	99

SUMMARY PROJECTIONS BY ORE ECONOMIC AREA UNDER FIVE ALTERNATIVE HIGHWAY SYSTEMS

130   TYLER, TEX.

	1970	1990 BASE YEAR	1990 COMPLETED INTERSTATE	1990 EXTENDED PRIMARY	1990 ECONOMIC DEVELOPMENT	1990 URBAN	CI/BY	EP/CI	ED/CI	U/CI
							PER CENT			
JOBS BY INDUSTRY		(THOUSANDS)								
NATURAL RESOURCES (1-10)	29.8	31.0	31.0	31.0	31.1	31.0	100	100	100	100
CONSTRUCTION (11,12)	10.1	4.9	4.5	4.5	6.8	3.8	97	101	152	84
MANUFACTURING (13-74)	49.4	76.5	74.2	76.0	78.3	73.7	97	102	106	99
TRANSPORTATION INDUSTRY (75)	4.5	1.6	1.5	1.6	1.8	1.5	96	105	118	98
PUBLIC UTILITIES (76-80)	4.5	1.6	1.6	1.6	2.2	1.5	96	104	142	97
TRADE (81,86,89-99)	38.8	39.9	38.7	40.1	42.7	38.1	97	104	110	98
SERVICES (82-85,87,88,102)	39.6	59.9	59.9	60.0	60.0	59.8	100	100	100	100
STATE & LOCAL GOVT. (101)	28.2	34.2	33.8	34.1	34.6	33.6	99	101	102	100
FEDERAL GOVERNMENT (100,103)	2.3	2.3	2.2	2.3	2.4	2.1	96	103	109	98
TOTAL JOBS	207.2	252.0	247.3	251.2	259.9	245.1	98	102	105	99
CIVILIAN PERSONS EMPLOYED	182.3	223.8	219.7	223.1	230.8	217.7	98	102	105	99
CIVILIAN UNEMPLOYMENT RATE	4.0	6.7	6.0	5.9	5.7	6.3				
POPULATION	553.4	745.5	731.7	740.8	750.0	728.3	98	101	102	100
PER CAPITA INCOME	2911.4	4217.8	4193.1	4230.0	4327.0	4174.5	99	101	103	100
ENERGY USER SECTOR		(TRILLIONS OF BTU'S)								
NATURAL RESOURCES	8.2	14.5	14.3	14.5	14.5	14.3	99	101	101	100
CONSTRUCTION	11.4	22.6	20.8	23.0	40.4	18.0	92	111	194	86
MANUFACTURING	42.6	93.0	91.4	93.1	94.4	90.9	98	102	103	99
TRANSPORTATION INDUSTRY	3.2	5.8	5.3	5.8	6.6	5.2	93	108	123	97
PUBLIC UTILITIES	47.2	30.0	29.4	29.6	36.2	28.8	98	101	123	98
TRADE AND SERVICES	14.9	28.3	27.7	28.4	29.2	27.4	98	102	108	99
GOVERNMENT, EXC. TRANSPORTATION	1.7	2.6	2.6	2.6	2.7	2.6	98	101	103	99
CONSUMERS, EXC. TRANSPORTATION	23.1	44.0	43.3	43.9	44.8	43.1	99	101	104	99
USER-OPERATED TRANSPORTATION	31.2	60.4	59.4	60.3	61.7	59.0	98	101	104	99
TRANSPORTATION AIR POLLUTION		(THOUSANDS OF TONS)								
SULFUR OXIDES	1.2	1.9	1.8	1.9	2.0	1.8	95	104	113	98
PARTICULATE MATTER	1.0	1.7	1.7	1.7	1.8	1.7	97	103	108	99
CARBON MONOXIDE	232.0	439.3	426.8	433.5	444.8	424.0	98	102	104	99
HYDROCARBONS	40.6	75.4	74.0	75.2	77.2	73.6	98	102	104	99
NITROGEN OXIDES	21.4	38.2	37.5	38.2	39.4	37.2	98	102	105	99
OTHER AIR POLLUTION										
SULFUR OXIDES	90.3	82.9	81.5	82.7	93.4	80.3	98	101	115	99
PARTICULATE MATTER	82.6	158.2	152.9	161.5	164.6	150.7	97	106	108	99
CARBON MONOXIDE	75.2	161.7	159.0	159.4	163.0	159.3	98	100	103	100
HYDROCARBONS	36.1	83.6	79.1	78.4	85.2	78.3	95	105	108	99
NITROGEN OXIDES	25.0	33.6	32.8	33.6	36.3	32.5	98	102	111	99
WATER OXYGEN DEMAND	953.5	1585.4	1582.1	1582.4	1585.8	1582.1	100	100	100	100
LAND SOLID WASTE	437.2	589.0	578.0	585.3	592.5	575.5	98	101	102	100

SUMMARY PROJECTIONS BY ORE ECONOMIC AREA UNDER FIVE ALTERNATIVE HIGHWAY SYSTEMS.

131   TEXARKANA, TEX.-ARK.

	1970	1990 BASE YEAR	1990 COMPLETED INTERSTATE	1990 EXTENDED PRIMARY	1990 ECONOMIC DEVELOPMENT	1990 ECONOMIC URBAN	PER CENT CI/BY	EP/CI	ED/CI	U/CI
JOBS BY INDUSTRY				(THOUSANDS)						
NATURAL RESOURCES (1-10)	20.3	20.8	20.8	21.4	21.2	20.8	100	103	102	100
CONSTRUCTION (11-12)	4.0	5.1	4.8	6.2	6.5	3.9	95	128	135	82
MANUFACTURING (13-74)	31.4	35.8	35.4	37.5	37.0	34.6	99	106	105	98
TRANSPORTATION INDUSTRY (75)	2.6	2.4	2.4	2.7	2.6	2.4	100	111	108	99
PUBLIC UTILITIES (76-80)	2.2	1.7	1.6	3.8	2.9	1.4	89	242	184	90
TRADE (81,86,89-99)	21.7	23.2	22.8	27.0	25.6	22.4	99	118	112	98
SERVICES (82-85,87,88,102)	19.1	31.2	31.1	31.3	31.2	31.1	100	100	100	100
STATE & LOCAL GOVT. (101)	16.5	19.1	19.0	19.8	19.5	18.9	99	104	103	99
FEDERAL GOVERNMENT (100,103)	8.1	8.7	8.7	8.9	8.8	8.7	100	102	101	100
TOTAL JOBS	125.9	148.0	146.7	158.4	155.3	144.3	99	108	106	98
CIVILIAN PERSONS EMPLOYED	104.5	124.4	123.3	132.8	130.4	121.3	99	108	106	98
CIVILIAN UNEMPLOYMENT RATE	7.2	1.2	1.0	0.7	0.8	1.0				
POPULATION	329.8	360.7	354.9	361.9	356.0	351.3	98	102	100	99
PER CAPITA INCOME	2634.8	4063.1	4069.2	4425.9	4364.3	4032.2	100	109	107	99
ENERGY USER SECTOR			(TRILLIONS OF BTU'S)							
NATURAL RESOURCES	6.3	8.3	8.3	8.9	8.6	8.2	100	107	104	99
CONSTRUCTION	5.6	8.1	8.2	9.6	13.1	4.4	100	117	160	54
MANUFACTURING	20.6	27.7	27.6	29.3	28.6	27.3	100	106	103	99
TRANSPORTATION INDUSTRY	1.9	3.0	2.9	4.0	3.6	2.8	97	136	123	96
PUBLIC UTILITIES	16.4	19.8	17.0	45.3	32.9	16.4	86	267	194	97
TRADE AND SERVICES	8.2	16.0	15.8	18.4	17.4	15.6	98	116	110	98
GOVERNMENT, EXC. TRANSPORTATION	1.1	1.5	1.5	1.5	1.5	1.4	99	106	104	99
CONSUMERS, EXC. TRANSPORTATION	10.8	18.4	18.3	19.6	19.2	19.0	99	107	105	99
USER-OPERATED TRANSPORTATION	16.7	29.6	29.3	31.4	30.7	28.9	99	107	105	99
TRANSPORTATION AIR POLLUTION			(THOUSANDS OF TONS)							
SULFUR OXIDES	.8	1.0	1.0	1.2	1.1	1.0	98	120	113	97
PARTICULATE MATTER	.7	.9	.9	1.0	1.0	.9	99	113	108	98
CARBON MONOXIDE	134.7	217.1	215.1	231.1	226.1	212.3	99	107	105	99
HYDROCARBONS	23.9	37.8	37.5	40.2	39.4	37.0	99	107	105	99
NITROGEN OXIDES	13.6	19.6	19.5	21.2	20.7	19.2	99	109	106	99
OTHER AIR POLLUTION										
SULFUR OXIDES	31.8	39.5	34.8	81.7	61.2	33.9	88	235	176	98
PARTICULATE MATTER	47.1	79.5	79.1	101.7	92.5	79.7	100	129	117	101
CARBON MONOXIDE	71.1	68.3	70.8	82.0	77.4	71.7	104	116	109	101
HYDROCARBONS	20.7	23.8	24.9	26.4	24.3	21.6	105	106	97	87
NITROGEN OXIDES	9.1	12.8	11.7	24.1	18.7	11.6	91	205	160	99
WATER OXYGEN DEMAND	747.5	1234.5	1234.7	1236.8	1236.2	1235.0	100	100	100	100
LAND SOLID WASTE	260.5	284.9	280.3	285.9	281.2	277.5	98	102	100	99

SUMMARY PROJECTIONS BY OBE ECONOMIC AREA UNDER FIVE ALTERNATIVE HIGHWAY SYSTEMS

132 SHREVEPORT, LA.

	1970	1990 BASE YEAR	1990 COMPLETED INTERSTATE	1990 EXTENDED PRIMARY	1990 ECONOMIC DEVELOPMENT	1990 URBAN	CI/BY	EP/CI	ED/CI	U/CI
								P E R C E N T		
JOBS BY INDUSTRY			(THOUSANDS)							
NATURAL RESOURCES (1-10)	13.5	6.8	6.8	6.8	7.1	6.6	99	101	105	97
CONSTRUCTION (11,12)	8.8	8.5	7.9	8.1	10.7	7.9	93	102	135	100
MANUFACTURING (13-74)	29.7	35.3	35.9	38.8	42.3	35.4	102	108	118	99
TRANSPORTATION INDUSTRY (75)	4.2	5.1	5.1	5.3	5.7	5.1	100	104	111	99
PUBLIC UTILITIES (76-80)	5.3	2.7	2.6	3.7	5.1	2.4	99	139	196	91
TRADE (81,86,89-99)	34.0	37.1	37.1	40.3	46.2	36.1	100	109	125	97
SERVICES (82-85,87,88,102)	26.1	52.4	52.4	52.5	52.8	52.4	100	100	101	100
STATE & LOCAL GOVT. (101)	22.0	25.8	25.8	26.5	27.7	25.7	100	103	107	100
FEDERAL GOVERNMENT (100,103)	10.3	10.1	10.1	10.3	10.5	10.1	100	102	104	100
TOTAL JOBS	153.8	183.7	183.7	192.3	208.1	181.5	100	105	113	99
CIVILIAN PERSONS EMPLOYED	134.7	162.7	162.6	170.5	185.0	160.6	100	105	114	99
CIVILIAN UNEMPLOYMENT RATE	6.4	6.3	6.5	7.0	6.5	6.9				
POPULATION	453.5	552.6	546.9	567.4	598.9	541.6	99	104	110	99
PER CAPITA INCOME	2557.0	4412.2	4451.3	4525.4	4719.2	4451.1	101	102	106	100
ENERGY USER SECTOR			(TRILLIONS OF BTU'S)							
NATURAL RESOURCES	4.6	9.3	9.2	9.5	10.5	8.9	99	104	115	97
CONSTRUCTION	7.6	10.4	10.4	11.1	22.9	10.1	100	106	220	98
MANUFACTURING	16.3	27.3	27.4	28.8	30.4	27.0	100	105	111	99
TRANSPORTATION INDUSTRY	4.7	8.7	8.7	9.6	11.1	8.4	100	110	128	97
PUBLIC UTILITIES	32.4	94.3	91.2	112.5	161.9	80.9	97	123	178	89
TRADE AND SERVICES	13.6	28.6	28.5	30.5	33.8	27.7	100	107	119	97
GOVERNMENT, EXC. TRANSPORTATION	11.0	14.6	14.6	14.7	14.8	14.6	100	101	101	100
CONSUMERS, EXC. TRANSPORTATION	20.7	40.7	40.6	41.8	44.0	40.4	100	103	108	99
USER-OPERATED TRANSPORTATION	47.4	80.3	80.2	82.0	85.4	79.9	100	102	106	100
TRANSPORTATION AIR POLLUTION			(THOUSANDS OF TONS)							
SULFUR OXIDES	1.3	2.6	2.6	2.7	3.1	2.5	100	106	119	98
PARTICULATE MATTER	1.0	2.0	2.0	2.1	2.3	1.9	100	105	114	99
CARBON MONOXIDE	193.0	397.5	397.2	411.0	437.7	394.3	100	103	110	99
HYDROCARBONS	33.8	69.7	69.6	72.0	76.6	69.1	100	103	110	99
NITROGEN OXIDES	18.8	38.7	38.7	40.3	43.2	38.4	100	104	112	99
OTHER AIR POLLUTION										
SULFUR OXIDES	61.9	193.4	188.0	222.9	304.6	170.9	97	119	162	91
PARTICULATE MATTER	36.3	93.0	91.0	102.5	128.2	85.1	98	113	141	94
CARBON MONOXIDE	58.1	116.3	114.1	119.3	131.8	110.4	98	105	116	97
HYDROCARBONS	22.7	51.4	52.2	56.8	59.1	51.4	99	109	113	99
NITROGEN OXIDES	19.9	65.1	63.7	72.5	93.5	59.3	98	114	147	93
WATER OXYGEN DEMAND	227.8	443.8	441.6	445.2	457.0	439.8	99	101	103	100
LAND SOLID WASTE	358.3	436.5	432.0	448.2	473.2	427.8	99	104	110	99

SUMMARY PROJECTIONS BY OBE ECONOMIC AREA UNDER FIVE ALTERNATIVE HIGHWAY SYSTEMS

133 MONROE, LA.

	1970	1990 BASE YEAR	1990 COMPLETED INTERSTATE	1990 EXTENDED PRIMARY	1990 ECONOMIC DEVELOPMENT	1990 URBAN	CI/BY	EP/CI	ED/CI	U/CI
								P E R	C E N T	
JOBS BY INDUSTRY			(THOUSANDS)							
NATURAL RESOURCES (1-10)	19.4	5.7	5.6	5.7	5.7	5.6	100	101	102	100
CONSTRUCTION (11,12)	27.8	8.8	8.8	9.6	18.9	8.7	100	109	216	100
MANUFACTURING (13-74)	23.1	35.9	35.5	36.5	38.3	34.9	99	103	108	98
TRANSPORTATION INDUSTRY (75)	4.2	4.2	4.2	4.3	4.4	4.2	100	102	105	99
PUBLIC UTILITIES (76-80)	3.3	3.8	3.7	3.8	1.0	3.6	97	107	132	87
TRADE (81,86,89-99)	30.3	37.7	37.3	38.3	40.8	36.7	99	103	109	98
SERVICES (82-85,87,88,102)	24.4	59.1	59.0	59.2	60.1	58.9	100	100	102	100
STATE & LOCAL GOVT. (101)	28.9	35.5	35.3	35.7	37.5	35.1	100	101	106	100
FEDERAL GOVERNMENT (100,103)	6.7	6.7	6.7	6.7	7.1	6.6	100	101	107	99
TOTAL JOBS	148.2	194.3	193.2	196.7	213.8	191.5	99	102	111	99
CIVILIAN PERSONS EMPLOYED	133.9	176.0	175.0	178.3	193.9	173.4	99	102	111	99
CIVILIAN UNEMPLOYMENT RATE	6.9	9.2	9.9	9.4	9.9	8.6				
POPULATION	532.8	764.9	765.8	769.4	829.4	753.9	100	100	108	98
PER CAPITA INCOME	2126.7	3263.1	3233.6	3299.6	3466.7	3236.0	99	102	107	100
ENERGY USER SECTOR			(TRILLIONS OF BTU'S)							
NATURAL RESOURCES	14.0	28.3	28.2	28.4	28.4	28.1	100	101	101	100
CONSTRUCTION	7.0	10.4	10.4	11.5	38.6	6.8	100	110	371	65
MANUFACTURING	18.7	45.0	44.7	45.5	45.9	44.2	99	102	103	99
TRANSPORTATION INDUSTRY	2.9	5.0	4.9	5.1	5.8	4.7	98	105	119	97
PUBLIC UTILITIES	15.7	9.3	9.2	9.3	12.7	9.0	98	101	139	98
TRADE AND SERVICES	12.6	26.0	25.7	26.2	27.6	25.4	99	102	107	99
GOVERNMENT, EXC. TRANSPORTATION	2.4	3.5	3.4	3.5	3.7	3.4	100	101	107	99
CONSUMERS, EXC. TRANSPORTATION	17.6	33.3	33.2	33.7	36.5	32.8	99	102	110	99
USER-OPERATED TRANSPORTATION	32.1	64.9	64.6	65.4	69.8	64.1	100	101	108	99
TRANSPORTATION AIR POLLUTION			(THOUSANDS OF TONS)							
SULFUR OXIDES	1.9	3.9	3.9	4.0	4.1	3.9	99	102	106	99
PARTICULATE MATTER	1.5	3.2	3.1	3.2	3.3	3.1	99	101	106	99
CARBON MONOXIDE	266.2	569.8	567.4	574.5	605.6	563.5	100	101	107	99
HYDROCARBONS	48.2	103.5	103.0	104.3	109.7	102.4	100	101	106	99
NITROGEN OXIDES	29.6	64.0	63.7	64.5	67.3	63.3	100	101	106	99
OTHER AIR POLLUTION										
SULFUR OXIDES	32.6	41.2	40.2	41.5	46.8	39.6	98	103	116	99
PARTICULATE MATTER	38.6	70.8	70.3	71.2	73.0	70.1	99	101	104	100
CARBON MONOXIDE	129.0	245.5	244.7	246.1	246.4	244.3	100	101	101	100
HYDROCARBONS	31.0	60.4	59.3	64.1	62.1	57.4	98	108	105	97
NITROGEN OXIDES	13.8	24.7	24.1	25.0	26.2	23.8	98	104	109	99
WATER OXYGEN DEMAND	287.2	554.7	549.6	558.0	556.3	547.9	99	102	101	100
LAND SOLID WASTE	420.9	604.2	605.0	607.8	655.2	595.6	100	100	108	98

134   GREENVILLE, MISS.

	1970	1990 BASE YEAR	1990 COMPLETED INTERSTATE	1990 EXTENDED PRIMARY	1990 ECONOMIC DEVELOPMENT	1990 URBAN	PERCENT CI/BY	PERCENT EP/CI	PERCENT ED/CI	PERCENT U/CI
JOBS BY INDUSTRY		(THOUSANDS)								
NATURAL RESOURCES (1-10)	23.2	14.8	14.8	15.6	15.3	14.6	99	106	104	99
CONSTRUCTION (11,12)	7.1	6.5	5.8	13.3	19.2	5.8	88	230	333	100
MANUFACTURING (13-74)	43.7	64.9	59.8	71.2	68.6	58.6	92	119	115	98
TRANSPORTATION INDUSTRY (75)	4.4	4.9	4.8	5.4	5.3	4.7	97	112	111	99
PUBLIC UTILITIES (76-80)	2.8	0.6	0.4	1.7	1.2	0.4	75	405	283	90
TRADE (81,86,89-99)	28.1	21.9	19.4	27.9	26.6	18.7	89	144	138	97
SERVICES (82-85,87,88,102)	32.2	60.5	60.3	60.9	61.3	60.3	100	101	102	100
STATE & LOCAL GOVT. (101)	21.4	25.7	24.7	27.6	27.5	24.5	96	112	112	99
FEDERAL GOVERNMENT (100-103)	2.5	2.0	1.8	2.4	2.4	1.7	89	137	136	98
TOTAL JOBS	165.5	201.8	191.6	225.9	227.6	189.3	95	118	119	99
CIVILIAN PERSONS EMPLOYED	144.9	176.9	168.2	192.9	199.5	166.1	95	118	119	99
CIVILIAN UNEMPLOYMENT RATE	6.4	6.4	6.0	6.0	5.1	5.6				
POPULATION	506.6	627.7	598.6	665.7	663.2	593.6	95	111	111	99
PER CAPITA INCOME	2306.1	3552.5	3422.5	3925.9	3938.7	3391.6	96	115	115	99
ENERGY USER SECTOR		(TRILLIONS OF BTU'S)								
NATURAL RESOURCES	23.3	12.5	12.3	13.3	13.0	12.1	99	108	106	99
CONSTRUCTION	10.6	18.5	14.7	29.2	47.6	12.9	80	198	323	87
MANUFACTURING	23.5	44.4	41.9	47.3	46.1	41.2	94	113	110	98
TRANSPORTATION INDUSTRY	4.4	7.9	7.1	9.6	9.2	6.9	90	134	129	97
PUBLIC UTILITIES	15.8	24.3	20.6	61.8	46.7	17.8	85	300	227	86
TRADE AND SERVICES	12.3	26.1	24.8	30.0	29.0	24.3	95	121	117	98
GOVERNMENT, EXC. TRANSPORTATION	3.5	4.9	4.8	5.1	5.1	4.7	98	107	107	100
CONSUMERS, EXC. TRANSPORTATION	16.2	29.4	27.9	32.6	32.6	27.5	95	117	117	99
USER-OPERATED TRANSPORTATION	29.8	53.7	51.3	58.7	58.7	50.8	96	114	114	99
TRANSPORTATION AIR POLLUTION		(THOUSANDS OF TONS)								
SULFUR OXIDES	2.9	2.7	2.5	3.0	3.0	2.5	94	120	118	98
PARTICULATE MATTER	2.0	2.0	1.9	2.2	2.2	1.9	95	117	115	99
CARBON MONOXIDE	280.5	383.7	366.1	420.9	420.2	362.4	95	115	115	99
HYDROCARBONS	52.4	68.0	64.9	74.4	74.3	64.3	96	115	114	99
NITROGEN OXIDES	37.1	39.5	37.8	43.3	43.1	37.4	96	115	114	99
OTHER AIR POLLUTION										
SULFUR OXIDES	34.5	59.1	53.2	121.1	96.5	48.4	90	228	181	91
PARTICULATE MATTER	68.3	65.8	64.1	90.6	82.1	62.1	98	141	128	97
CARBON MONOXIDE	223.6	177.9	178.0	196.6	191.6	175.7	100	110	108	99
HYDROCARBONS	68.8	70.7	66.2	74.4	72.9	65.4	94	112	110	99
NITROGEN OXIDES	14.3	25.4	24.1	41.8	35.5	22.8	95	173	147	95
WATER OXYGEN DEMAND	270.5	447.7	448.0	447.0	447.4	448.5	100	100	100	100
LAND SOLID WASTE	400.2	495.9	472.9	525.9	523.9	468.6	95	111	111	99

SUMMARY PROJECTIONS BY ORE ECONOMIC AREA UNDER FIVE ALTERNATIVE HIGHWAY SYSTEMS

135   JACKSON, MISS.

	1970	1990 BASE YEAR	1990 COMPLETED INTERSTATE	1990 EXTENDED PRIMARY	1990 ECONOMIC DEVELOPMENT	1990 URBAN	CI/BY	EP/CI	ED/CI	U/CI
								P E R C E N T		
JOBS BY INDUSTRY (THOUSANDS)										
NATURAL RESOURCES (1-10)	21.4	18.9	18.9	18.9	19.0	18.9	100	100	100	100
CONSTRUCTION (11,12)	12.1	15.9	16.1	15.7	18.0	16.1	101	97	112	100
MANUFACTURING (13-74)	34.9	61.2	60.3	57.8	64.9	57.3	98	96	108	95
TRANSPORTATION INDUSTRY (75)	2.9	.8	.8	.7	.8	.7	98	96	109	97
PUBLIC UTILITIES (76-80)	4.6	1.8	1.8	1.8	2.0	1.8	99	101	114	100
TRADE (81,86,89-99)	38.8	60.8	60.2	58.9	63.8	58.7	99	98	106	98
SERVICES (82-85,87,88,102)	51.6	111.8	111.8	111.6	111.9	111.7	100	100	100	100
STATE & LOCAL GOVT. (101)	31.2	45.1	44.9	44.3	46.0	44.4	100	99	102	99
FEDERAL GOVERNMENT (100,103)	7.2	9.3	9.2	9.1	9.5	9.1	99	99	103	99
TOTAL JOBS	204.7	325.6	323.9	318.8	335.9	318.8	99	98	104	98
CIVILIAN PERSONS EMPLOYED	186.3	296.3	294.8	290.2	305.8	290.1	99	98	104	98
CIVILIAN UNEMPLOYMENT RATE	4.1	5.1	5.8	5.3	5.0	5.4				
POPULATION	510.4	824.7	824.1	811.1	837.1	816.2	100	98	102	99
PER CAPITA INCOME	2823.8	4778.8	4740.3	4683.8	4927.7	4670.0	99	99	104	99
ENERGY USER SECTOR (TRILLIONS OF BTU'S)										
NATURAL RESOURCES	7.5	7.9	7.9	7.9	7.9	7.9	100	100	100	100
CONSTRUCTION	8.6	17.2	17.2	14.8	28.4	13.5	100	86	165	79
MANUFACTURING	14.3	35.8	35.1	33.5	38.0	33.5	98	95	108	95
TRANSPORTATION INDUSTRY	4.1	10.6	10.4	10.0	11.3	10.0	98	96	109	96
PUBLIC UTILITIES	22.6	15.0	14.7	14.9	24.1	14.5	98	101	163	98
TRADE AND SERVICES	16.1	43.9	43.6	43.6	45.6	42.9	99	99	105	98
GOVERNMENT, EXC. TRANSPORTATION	1.9	3.5	3.5	3.4	3.6	3.4	99	98	103	98
CONSUMERS, EXC. TRANSPORTATION	21.6	50.0	49.7	48.9	51.6	48.9	99	98	104	98
USER-OPERATED TRANSPORTATION	34.4	81.4	80.9	79.6	83.8	79.7	99	98	104	98
TRANSPORTATION AIR POLLUTION (THOUSANDS OF TONS)										
SULFUR OXIDES	1.5	3.0	3.0	2.9	3.2	2.9	98	97	106	97
PARTICULATE MATTER	1.2	2.5	2.5	2.4	2.6	2.4	99	98	105	98
CARBON MONOXIDE	253.6	576.3	572.9	562.9	594.2	563.6	99	98	104	98
HYDROCARBONS	44.5	100.0	99.4	97.7	103.1	97.8	99	98	104	98
NITROGEN OXIDES	24.4	52.0	51.8	50.9	53.9	50.8	99	98	104	98
OTHER AIR POLLUTION										
SULFUR OXIDES	52.7	69.8	68.9	67.8	84.1	68.2	99	98	122	99
PARTICULATE MATTER	55.5	112.4	108.1	96.1	115.2	106.2	96	89	107	98
CARBON MONOXIDE	42.9	66.5	67.1	68.4	67.3	68.3	101	102	100	102
HYDROCARBONS	14.7	35.3	34.1	32.2	40.8	32.2	97	94	120	95
NITROGEN OXIDES	17.0	31.2	30.8	29.9	34.7	30.6	99	97	113	99
WATER OXYGEN DEMAND	919.7	1524.7	1524.1	1524.6	1524.5	1524.7	100	100	100	100
LAND SOLID WASTE	403.2	651.5	651.0	640.8	661.3	644.8	100	98	102	99

SUMMARY PROJECTIONS BY ORE ECONOMIC AREA UNDER FIVE ALTERNATIVE HIGHWAY SYSTEMS

136   MERIDIAN, MISS.

	1970	1990 BASE YEAR	1990 COMPLETED INTERSTATE	1990 EXTENDED PRIMARY	1990 ECONOMIC DEVELOPMENT	1990 URBAN	CI/BY	EP/CI	ED/CI	U/CI
								P E R C E N T		
JOBS BY INDUSTRY			(THOUSANDS)							
NATURAL RESOURCES (1-10)	22.7	21.0	20.9	21.3	21.4	20.9	99	102	102	100
CONSTRUCTION (11,12)	5.5	7.3	6.8	9.0	13.3	6.9	94	131	194	101
MANUFACTURING (13-74)	32.2	31.0	30.7	34.8	35.0	30.3	99	113	114	98
TRANSPORTATION INDUSTRY (75)	6.4	13.3	13.2	13.5	13.6	13.1	99	102	103	99
PUBLIC UTILITIES (76-80)	2.6	1.1	1.0	1.6	1.7	1.0	95	158	158	99
TRADE (81,86,89-99)	25.3	32.0	31.5	36.1	37.4	31.0	98	114	119	98
SERVICES (82-85,87,88,102)	25.8	36.7	36.7	36.9	37.0	36.7	100	101	101	100
STATE & LOCAL GOVT. (101)	19.2	25.0	24.8	26.1	26.6	24.6	99	105	108	99
FEDERAL GOVERNMENT (100,103)	4.6	5.0	4.9	5.2	5.4	4.9	99	106	108	99
TOTAL JOBS	144.4	172.5	170.7	184.4	191.3	169.4	99	108	112	99
CIVILIAN PERSONS EMPLOYED	129.3	155.4	153.8	166.1	172.3	152.5	99	108	112	99
CIVILIAN UNEMPLOYMENT RATE	4.9	2.3	2.0	2.6	1.9	1.9				
POPULATION	393.9	460.3	451.2	492.4	504.5	448.8	98	109	112	99
PER CAPITA INCOME	2293.8	4225.9	4224.4	4389.2	4490.6	4193.0	100	104	106	99
ENERGY USER SECTOR			(TRILLIONS OF BTUS)							
NATURAL RESOURCES	5.1	5.2	5.0	5.3	5.6	4.9	96	107	112	98
CONSTRUCTION	4.2	7.4	7.2	13.4	31.6	7.1	98	185	437	99
MANUFACTURING	13.5	30.8	30.8	32.7	32.9	30.6	100	106	107	99
TRANSPORTATION INDUSTRY	3.7	7.6	7.5	8.5	8.8	7.4	98	113	118	99
PUBLIC UTILITIES	19.0	18.9	18.4	26.2	31.2	18.2	97	143	170	99
TRADE AND SERVICES	8.7	18.4	17.9	20.2	21.0	17.5	97	113	117	98
GOVERNMENT, EXC. TRANSPORTATION	1.8	2.7	2.7	2.8	2.9	2.7	99	105	108	99
CONSUMERS, EXC. TRANSPORTATION	12.6	24.7	24.4	26.5	27.4	24.2	99	109	112	99
USER-OPERATED TRANSPORTATION	20.1	40.2	39.7	43.1	44.4	39.4	99	108	112	99
TRANSPORTATION AIR POLLUTION			(THOUSANDS OF TONS)							
SULFUR OXIDES	1.0	1.9	1.8	2.0	2.1	1.8	98	111	116	99
PARTICULATE MATTER	.7	1.4	1.3	1.5	1.5	1.3	99	110	114	99
CARBON MONOXIDE	139.2	274.9	271.1	295.8	305.6	268.7	99	109	113	99
HYDROCARBONS	24.4	47.7	47.0	51.3	53.0	46.6	99	109	113	99
NITROGEN OXIDES	13.9	25.9	25.6	28.1	29.0	25.3	99	110	113	99
OTHER AIR POLLUTION										
SULFUR OXIDES	34.5	33.9	33.0	45.9	54.5	32.6	97	139	165	99
PARTICULATE MATTER	33.0	80.1	78.5	83.1	88.0	78.0	98	106	113	99
CARBON MONOXIDE	86.0	310.8	307.0	312.9	319.1	306.8	99	102	104	100
HYDROCARBONS	30.8	87.3	87.9	93.9	91.8	88.0	101	107	104	100
NITROGEN OXIDES	13.1	28.0	27.6	31.1	33.7	27.5	99	113	122	100
WATER OXYGEN DEMAND	503.2	933.0	931.4	932.7	934.1	932.1	100	100	100	100
LAND SOLID WASTE	310.5	363.7	356.4	389.0	398.5	354.6	98	109	112	99

SUMMARY PROJECTIONS BY OBE ECONOMIC AREA UNDER FIVE ALTERNATIVE HIGHWAY SYSTEMS

137   MOBILE, ALA.

	1970	1990 BASE YEAR	1990 COMPLETED INTERSTATE	1990 EXTENDED PRIMARY	1990 ECONOMIC DEVELOPMENT	1990 URBAN	PERCENT CI/BY	EP/CI	ED/CI	U/CI
JOBS BY INDUSTRY										
NATURAL RESOURCES (1-10)	11.2	9.2	9.7	8.9	10.1	9.4	105	92	104	98
CONSTRUCTION (11-12)	17.0	17.8	17.4	17.7	18.6	17.4	98	102	107	100
MANUFACTURING (13-74)	56.5	90.2	93.9	93.2	97.5	92.3	104	99	104	98
TRANSPORTATION INDUSTRY (75)	10.3	2.4	2.4	2.3	2.6	2.4	102	94	106	98
PUBLIC UTILITIES (76-80)	4.3	2.1	2.8	1.4	4.8	2.3	134	48	169	82
TRADE (81,86,89-99)	50.7	75.1	78.6	74.6	84.1	76.4	105	95	107	97
SERVICES (82-85,87,88,102)	53.4	79.0	79.2	79.1	79.3	79.1	100	100	100	100
STATE & LOCAL GOVT. (101)	31.3	39.6	40.5	39.9	41.8	40.1	102	98	103	99
FEDERAL GOVERNMENT (100,103)	25.5	26.2	26.4	26.3	26.7	26.3	101	99	101	100
TOTAL JOBS	260.2	341.7	351.0	343.2	365.5	345.7	103	98	104	98
CIVILIAN PERSONS EMPLOYED	233.2	310.9	319.6	312.3	333.4	314.6	103	98	104	98
CIVILIAN UNEMPLOYMENT RATE	5.2	7.7	6.5	6.9	6.6	6.7				
POPULATION	724.1	1075.7	1086.4	1069.3	1115.0	1075.0	101	98	103	99
PER CAPITA INCOME	2838.3	3874.4	3981.5	3927.6	4102.5	3941.2	103	99	103	99
ENERGY USER SECTOR (TRILLIONS OF BTU'S)										
NATURAL RESOURCES	4.7	4.6	5.0	4.2	5.5	4.8	110	83	110	96
CONSTRUCTION	15.5	22.8	23.5	22.5	36.4	23.1	103	96	155	98
MANUFACTURING	46.8	114.9	116.9	117.8	120.1	116.0	102	101	103	99
TRANSPORTATION INDUSTRY	9.4	18.3	19.3	18.2	20.6	18.8	105	94	107	97
PUBLIC UTILITIES	35.8	73.3	95.0	49.1	127.5	81.2	130	52	134	85
TRADE AND SERVICES	16.9	33.2	35.6	32.2	38.8	34.3	107	91	109	96
GOVERNMENT, EXC. TRANSPORTATION	33.0	44.0	44.1	44.0	44.2	44.0	100	100	100	100
CONSUMERS, EXC. TRANSPORTATION	29.1	56.0	57.3	56.3	59.4	56.5	102	98	104	99
USER-OPERATED TRANSPORTATION	18.9	189.8	191.9	190.2	195.2	190.7	101	99	102	99
TRANSPORTATION AIR POLLUTION (THOUSANDS OF TONS)										
SULFUR OXIDES	2.5	4.5	4.7	4.5	4.9	4.6	104	95	105	98
PARTICULATE MATTER	1.8	3.4	3.5	3.4	3.7	3.4	103	97	105	97
CARBON MONOXIDE	364.2	713.9	729.8	716.9	754.5	720.7	102	98	103	98
HYDROCARBONS	63.5	123.7	126.4	124.2	130.7	124.8	102	98	103	98
NITROGEN OXIDES	34.9	66.0	67.9	66.5	70.5	66.9	103	98	104	98
OTHER AIR POLLUTION										
SULFUR OXIDES	82.7	152.5	187.8	113.1	240.2	165.4	123	60	128	88
PARTICULATE MATTER	75.5	106.2	115.4	95.1	129.0	109.9	109	82	112	95
CARBON MONOXIDE	98.4	188.6	194.6	176.7	205.6	191.7	103	91	106	99
HYDROCARBONS	64.2	130.3	142.5	159.0	171.2	136.1	109	112	120	96
NITROGEN OXIDES	29.2	46.8	55.6	36.8	68.8	50.1	119	66	124	90
WATER OXYGEN DEMAND	246.2	468.5	471.2	470.3	473.6	471.3	101	100	101	100
LAND SOLID WASTE	572.1	849.8	858.3	844.8	880.9	849.2	101	98	103	99

SUMMARY PROJECTIONS BY OBE ECONOMIC AREA UNDER FIVE ALTERNATIVE HIGHWAY SYSTEMS

138   NEW ORLEANS, LA.

	1970	1990 BASE YEAR	1990 COMPLETED INTERSTATE	1990 EXTENDED PRIMARY	1990 ECONOMIC DEVELOPMENT	1990 URBAN	CI/BY	EP/CI	ED/CI	U/CI
							PERCENT			
JOBS BY INDUSTRY			(THOUSANDS)							
NATURAL RESOURCES (1-10)	61.1	57.8	58.5	57.6	58.0	58.3	101	98	99	100
CONSTRUCTION (11,12)	56.5	64.9	58.5	63.4	61.8	65.6	101	97	95	100
MANUFACTURING (13-74)	119.0	166.1	183.2	177.8	180.3	179.2	110	97	98	98
TRANSPORTATION INDUSTRY (75)	47.3	83.5	84.4	84.0	84.2	84.2	101	99	99	100
PUBLIC UTILITIES (76-80)	16.4	6.1	11.3	8.1	9.1	10.2	184	72	81	90
TRADE (81,86,89-99)	169.1	259.0	276.6	268.8	271.9	272.9	107	97	98	99
SERVICES (82-85,87,88,102)	155.9	281.1	282.6	282.2	282.3	282.5	101	100	100	100
STATE & LOCAL GOVT. (101)	109.1	143.4	148.1	146.1	146.8	147.2	103	99	99	99
FEDERAL GOVERNMENT (100,103)	19.6	23.1	24.2	23.7	23.9	24.0	105	98	99	99
TOTAL JOBS	754.0	1085.1	1134.3	1111.7	1118.3	1124.0	105	98	99	99
CIVILIAN PERSONS EMPLOYED	797.4	1127.9	1174.8	1153.4	1160.1	1166.9	104	98	99	99
CIVILIAN UNEMPLOYMENT RATE	4.7	5.1	5.5	5.4	5.5	5.4				
POPULATION	2148.6	3237.8	3337.3	3305.0	3318.1	3328.7	103	99	99	100
PER CAPITA INCOME	3114.4	5103.3	5201.4	5136.7	5148.8	5162.0	102	99	99	99
ENERGY USER SECTOR			(TRILLIONS OF BTU'S)							
NATURAL RESOURCES	33.9	94.9	100.1	97.7	98.8	99.4	106	98	99	99
CONSTRUCTION	54.7	99.6	110.4	104.6	103.4	109.0	111	94	93	98
MANUFACTURING	142.1	335.7	346.4	344.7	346.7	342.7	103	99	100	99
TRANSPORTATION INDUSTRY	66.4	155.3	160.5	158.5	159.4	159.4	103	99	99	99
PUBLIC UTILITIES	90.7	180.4	285.2	216.6	239.0	272.7	158	76	84	96
TRADE AND SERVICES	83.9	210.9	223.4	217.8	220.1	221.0	106	98	99	98
GOVERNMENT, EXC. TRANSPORTATION	24.7	34.6	35.1	34.9	35.0	35.0	101	99	100	100
CONSUMERS, EXC. TRANSPORTATION	69.7	155.8	162.9	159.7	160.6	161.4	105	98	98	99
USER-OPERATED TRANSPORTATION	162.0	327.8	338.9	333.9	335.3	336.5	103	99	99	99
TRANSPORTATION AIR POLLUTION			(THOUSANDS OF TONS)							
SULFUR OXIDES	13.2	30.0	30.9	30.3	30.5	30.6	103	98	99	99
PARTICULATE MATTER	7.3	16.4	17.0	16.8	16.8	16.9	104	99	99	99
CARBON MONOXIDE	937.7	2127.9	2213.4	2175.8	2186.8	2195.4	104	98	98	99
HYDROCARBONS	163.1	368.3	382.8	376.1	378.1	379.7	104	98	98	99
NITROGEN OXIDES	107.1	239.4	249.9	247.2	247.9	248.0	104	99	99	99
OTHER AIR POLLUTION										
SULFUR OXIDES	262.1	637.3	811.2	697.9	734.8	790.7	127	86	91	97
PARTICULATE MATTER	227.6	536.4	593.8	554.5	567.1	586.9	111	93	95	99
CARBON MONOXIDE	436.7	1636.1	1664.3	1663.9	1647.2	1659.2	102	99	99	100
HYDROCARBONS	389.8	1288.6	1326.1	1336.9	1350.1	1294.1	103	101	102	98
NITROGEN OXIDES	97.6	288.6	332.9	303.9	313.4	327.7	115	91	94	98
WATER OXYGEN DEMAND	802.7	1887.6	1907.0	1896.8	1900.3	1905.0	101	99	100	100
LAND SOLID WASTE	1697.4	2557.8	2636.5	2610.9	2621.3	2629.7	103	99	99	100

SUMMARY PROJECTIONS BY OBE ECONOMIC AREA UNDER FIVE ALTERNATIVE HIGHWAY SYSTEMS

139 LAKE CHARLES, LA.

	1970	1990 BASE YEAR	1990 COMPLETED INTERSTATE (THOUSANDS)	1990 EXTENDED PRIMARY	1990 ECONOMIC DEVELOPMENT	1990 URBAN	P E R C E N T CI/BY	EP/CI	ED/CI	U/CI
JOBS BY INDUSTRY										
NATURAL RESOURCES (1-10)	36.6	15.7	15.4	15.9	15.8	15.6	100	101	101	100
CONSTRUCTION (11,12)	17.1	16.1	15.4	13.4	21.2	12.7	95	87	138	83
MANUFACTURING (13-74)	22.8	26.7	25.6	26.7	28.1	25.3	96	105	110	99
TRANSPORTATION INDUSTRY (75)	7.5	8.9	8.7	9.1	9.3	8.6	98	104	106	99
PUBLIC UTILITIES (76-80)	5.0	.7	.7	1.0	1.0	.7	99	134	131	98
TRADE (81,86,89-99)	45.0	26.9	26.5	27.7	28.5	26.1	99	104	107	98
SERVICES (82-85,87,88,102)	33.4	84.5	84.6	84.5	84.7	84.5	100	100	100	100
STATE & LOCAL GOVT. (101)	34.5	38.7	38.3	38.5	39.5	37.9	99	100	103	99
FEDERAL GOVERNMENT (100,103)	28.6	27.3	27.2	27.3	27.5	27.1	100	100	101	100
TOTAL JOBS	230.6	245.4	242.7	244.0	255.5	238.7	99	101	105	98
CIVILIAN PERSONS EMPLOYED	195.4	210.0	207.5	208.7	219.6	203.7	99	101	106	98
CIVILIAN UNEMPLOYMENT RATE	6.8	11.7	11.0	11.3	11.2	11.0				
POPULATION	748.4	960.8	943.6	944.6	993.6	920.2	98	100	105	98
PER CAPITA INCOME	2234.9	3230.3	3228.3	3247.8	3290.6	3225.0	100	101	102	100
ENERGY USER SECTOR (TRILLIONS OF BTUS)										
NATURAL RESOURCES	25.1	41.3	41.2	43.2	42.3	41.1	100	105	103	100
CONSTRUCTION	19.7	23.6	23.8	24.1	39.8	14.5	101	101	167	61
MANUFACTURING	28.8	64.5	63.9	64.4	64.9	63.8	99	99	102	98
TRANSPORTATION INDUSTRY	9.0	10.9	10.3	10.8	11.0	10.1	99	104	107	98
PUBLIC UTILITIES	26.5	16.8	16.7	17.3	19.3	16.3	99	104	116	98
TRADE AND SERVICES	16.4	26.9	26.7	27.6	27.8	26.5	99	103	104	99
GOVERNMENT, EXC. TRANSPORTATION	17.5	23.2	23.1	23.1	23.3	23.1	100	100	101	100
CONSUMERS, EXC. TRANSPORTATION	24.4	42.9	42.4	42.6	44.3	41.7	99	100	104	98
USER-OPERATED TRANSPORTATION	81.5	134.0	133.2	133.6	136.2	132.2	99	100	102	99
TRANSPORTATION AIR POLLUTION (THOUSANDS OF TONS)										
SULFUR OXIDES	3.3	5.7	5.6	5.7	5.8	5.6	99	102	103	99
PARTICULATE MATTER	2.3	4.4	4.4	4.4	4.5	4.3	99	101	103	99
CARBON MONOXIDE	39.7	781.2	775.4	780.1	798.0	767.7	99	101	103	99
HYDROCARBONS	70.8	141.0	140.0	140.9	144.0	138.7	99	101	103	99
NITROGEN OXIDES	43.8	86.6	86.1	86.9	88.4	85.4	99	101	103	99
OTHER AIR POLLUTION										
SULFUR OXIDES	68.6	58.4	58.0	58.9	62.1	57.4	99	102	107	99
PARTICULATE MATTER	66.3	87.2	87.0	99.4	93.1	86.5	100	114	107	99
CARBON MONOXIDE	252.8	412.9	413.7	447.0	427.6	412.2	100	108	103	100
HYDROCARBONS	158.3	220.4	219.7	222.3	220.5	218.5	99	101	101	100
NITROGEN OXIDES	24.2	25.4	25.3	26.8	26.8	25.1	100	101	106	99
WATER OXYGEN DEMAND	248.7	497.1	496.4	512.1	503.2	494.8	100	103	101	100
LAND SOLID WASTE	591.3	759.1	745.4	746.2	785.0	727.0	98	100	105	98

SUMMARY PROJECTIONS BY ORE ECONOMIC AREA UNDER FIVE ALTERNATIVE HIGHWAY SYSTEMS

140   BEAU-P ART-ORANGE, TEX.

	1970	1990 BASE YEAR	1990 COMPLETED INTERSTATE	1990 EXTENDED PRIMARY	1990 ECONOMIC DEVELOPMENT	1990 URBAN	CI/BY	EP/CI	ED/CI	U/CI
								PERCENT		
JOBS BY INDUSTRY			(THOUSANDS)							
NATURAL RESOURCES (1-10)	7.1	7.5	6.9	6.7	6.7	6.8	92	97	97	98
CONSTRUCTION (11,12)	10.8	12.2	12.3	11.7	11.7	12.3	101	95	95	100
MANUFACTURING (13-74)	40.4	32.7	32.1	31.7	31.8	31.9	98	99	99	99
TRANSPORTATION INDUSTRY (75)	6.9	12.2	12.1	12.1	12.1	12.1	100	100	100	100
PUBLIC UTILITIES (76-80)	3.3	1.0	1.0	1.0	1.0	0.9	99	103	105	97
TRADE (81,86,89-99)	28.8	51.5	50.4	49.7	50.0	50.0	98	98	99	99
SERVICES (82-85,87,88,102)	27.2	39.7	39.7	39.6	39.6	39.7	100	100	100	100
STATE & LOCAL GOVT. (101)	15.0	19.1	18.8	18.6	18.6	18.8	99	99	99	100
FEDERAL GOVERNMENT (100,103)	1.7	1.9	1.8	1.8	1.8	1.8	97	97	98	100
TOTAL JOBS	141.2	177.7	175.1	173.0	173.3	174.3	98	99	99	100
CIVILIAN PERSONS EMPLOYED	137.8	173.2	170.6	168.6	169.0	169.9	99	99	99	100
CIVILIAN UNEMPLOYMENT RATE	6.5	6.7	6.5	6.5	6.5	5.8				
POPULATION	397.7	548.9	539.2	532.6	535.6	534.5	98	99	99	99
PER CAPITA INCOME	3330.7	4909.8	4910.1	4891.2	4874.5	4932.0	100	100	99	100
ENERGY USER SECTOR			(TRILLIONS OF BTU'S)							
NATURAL RESOURCES	5.5	11.6	10.3	9.2	9.4	10.0	89	89	91	97
CONSTRUCTION	12.1	24.2	20.6	19.3	20.8	19.5	85	94	101	95
MANUFACTURING	40.2	81.6	81.1	81.0	81.1	81.0	99	100	100	100
TRANSPORTATION INDUSTRY	10.4	24.4	24.0	23.8	23.9	23.9	98	99	100	100
PUBLIC UTILITIES	47.3	28.0	27.5	27.7	28.1	26.9	98	101	102	98
TRADE AND SERVICES	10.3	25.2	24.6	24.2	24.4	24.4	98	98	99	99
GOVERNMENT, EXC. TRANSPORTATION	33.2	44.1	44.0	44.0	44.0	44.0	100	100	100	100
CONSUMERS, EXC. TRANSPORTATION	16.9	33.5	33.1	32.7	32.8	33.0	99	99	99	100
USER-OPERATED TRANSPORTATION	97.8	144.3	143.7	143.1	143.2	143.5	100	100	100	100
TRANSPORTATION AIR POLLUTION			(THOUSANDS OF TONS)							
SULFUR OXIDES	2.2	4.7	4.7	4.6	4.6	4.6	98	99	99	99
PARTICULATE MATTER	1.3	2.6	2.6	2.6	2.6	2.6	99	99	99	99
CARBON MONOXIDE	184.5	358.7	354.1	350.0	350.7	352.8	99	99	99	99
HYDROCARBONS	32.2	62.1	61.2	60.5	60.6	61.0	99	99	99	99
NITROGEN OXIDES	20.4	39.5	39.2	38.9	38.9	39.0	99	99	99	99
OTHER AIR POLLUTION										
SULFUR OXIDES	103.9	118.4	117.1	116.4	117.2	115.9	99	99	100	99
PARTICULATE MATTER	40.5	62.1	57.0	49.4	50.7	55.4	92	87	89	97
CARBON MONOXIDE	162.8	468.7	457.8	437.7	440.9	453.7	98	96	96	99
HYDROCARBONS	157.9	462.0	457.8	456.3	456.6	457.4	99	100	100	100
NITROGEN OXIDES	27.3	32.9	31.9	30.4	30.8	31.4	97	95	96	98
WATER OXYGEN DEMAND	139.5	229.6	228.0	227.9	228.1	228.0	99	100	100	100
LAND SOLID WASTE	311.8	433.7	426.0	420.7	423.1	422.3	98	99	99	99

SUMMARY PROJECTIONS BY ORE ECONOMIC AREA UNDER FIVE ALTERNATIVE HIGHWAY SYSTEMS

141 HOUSTON, TEX.

	1970	1990 BASE YEAR	1990 COMPLETED INTERSTATE	1990 EXTENDED PRIMARY	1990 ECONOMIC DEVELOPMENT	1990 URBAN	P E R C E N T			
			(THOUSANDS)				CI/BY	EP/CI	ED/CI	U/CI
JOBS BY INDUSTRY										
NATURAL RESOURCES (1-10)	57.3	36.4	35.8	35.7	35.7	35.7	99	100	100	100
CONSTRUCTION (11-12)	95.8	97.4	98.5	95.4	92.8	98.6	101	97	94	100
MANUFACTURING (13-74)	177.8	271.5	252.7	243.8	243.4	243.8	93	96	96	96
TRANSPORTATION INDUSTRY (75)	50.5	78.4	77.8	77.4	77.4	77.4	99	99	99	99
PUBLIC UTILITIES (76-80)	25.9	13.4	11.8	10.9	11.1	11.1	88	92	95	94
TRADE (81,86,89-99)	239.7	397.4	385.9	377.6	377.4	379.3	97	98	98	98
SERVICES (82-85,87,88,102)	244.7	526.8	526.3	525.8	525.9	526.2	100	100	100	100
STATE & LOCAL GOVT. (101)	88.1	135.9	132.2	130.0	129.7	130.7	97	98	98	99
FEDERAL GOVERNMENT (100,103)	21.0	28.7	27.8	27.3	27.3	27.5	97	98	98	99
TOTAL JOBS	1001.1	1558.9	1548.9	1552.9	1520.7	1530.3	98	98	98	99
CIVILIAN PERSONS EMPLOYED	994.2	1559.6	1524.2	1500.4	1497.5	1506.3	98	98	98	99
CIVILIAN UNEMPLOYMENT RATE	3.6	5.0	5.6	5.1	5.8	5.7				
POPULATION	2362.8	3977.4	3927.5	3885.5	3892.2	3909.2	99	99	99	100
PER CAPITA INCOME	3833.5	5924.1	5828.9	5778.0	5750.9	5778.1	98	98	99	99
ENERGY USER SECTOR (TRILLIONS OF BTU'S)										
NATURAL RESOURCES	33.5	38.3	35.6	34.5	34.4	35.1	93	97	97	98
CONSTRUCTION	60.6	110.0	108.1	89.1	84.9	89.7	98	82	79	83
MANUFACTURING	251.2	589.8	573.3	568.0	567.5	562.6	98	99	99	98
TRANSPORTATION INDUSTRY	56.6	123.0	119.7	117.5	117.5	118.0	97	98	98	99
PUBLIC UTILITIES	104.4	96.7	78.2	71.8	72.7	71.7	81	92	93	92
TRADE AND SERVICES	123.2	277.5	272.0	268.4	268.3	268.9	98	99	99	99
GOVERNMENT, EXC. TRANSPORTATION	123.5	36.4	36.0	35.7	35.7	35.8	99	99	99	100
CONSUMERS, EXC. TRANSPORTATION	136.7	309.3	303.8	300.2	299.7	301.1	98	99	99	99
USER-OPERATED TRANSPORTATION	249.5	542.3	533.6	527.9	527.2	529.5	98	99	99	99
TRANSPORTATION AIR POLLUTION (THOUSANDS OF TONS)										
SULFUR OXIDES	13.8	28.1	27.3	26.7	26.8	26.9	97	98	98	98
PARTICULATE MATTER	9.3	19.3	18.9	18.7	18.7	18.7	98	99	99	99
CARBON MONOXIDE	1659.8	3695.9	3632.3	3590.3	3585.3	3601.6	98	98	99	98
HYDROCARBONS	290.0	640.3	629.1	621.7	620.9	623.8	98	99	99	98
NITROGEN OXIDES	167.4	354.1	348.6	345.3	344.4	345.4	98	99	99	99
OTHER AIR POLLUTION										
SULFUR OXIDES	365.4	666.3	636.2	625.4	626.8	625.5	95	98	98	98
PARTICULATE MATTER	385.5	598.9	586.7	572.6	572.1	583.0	98	98	98	98
CARBON MONOXIDE	687.4	1786.6	1774.5	1752.3	1750.8	1773.1	99	99	100	100
HYDROCARBONS	480.9	1680.2	1613.4	1588.2	1585.1	1501.4	96	98	98	93
NITROGEN OXIDES	133.3	285.6	277.3	273.2	273.5	274.6	97	99	99	99
WATER OXYGEN DEMAND	736.1	1396.2	1394.4	1396.0	1396.0	1396.0	100	100	100	100
LAND SOLID WASTE	1866.6	3139.8	3102.7	3066.5	3074.4	3008.2	99	99	99	100

142 SAN ANTONIO, TEX.

	1970	1990 BASE YEAR	1990 COMPLETED INTERSTATE	1990 EXTENDED PRIMARY	1990 ECONOMIC DEVELOPMENT	1990 URBAN	PERCENT CI/BY	EP/BY	ED/CI	U/CI
JOBS BY INDUSTRY			(THOUSANDS)							
NATURAL RESOURCES (1-10)	29.2	27.1	26.7	26.5	27.3	26.5	99	99	102	99
CONSTRUCTION (11,12)	24.0	23.1	22.9	23.7	28.0	22.9	99	104	122	100
MANUFACTURING (13-74)	50.0	60.3	59.6	61.2	63.8	58.4	99	103	107	98
TRANSPORTATION INDUSTRY (75)	9.9	4.2	4.1	4.2	4.4	4.1	99	101	106	98
PUBLIC UTILITIES (76-80)	7.6	3.1	2.8	2.9	3.3	2.7	90	103	118	95
TRADE (81,86,89-99)	103.8	113.9	113.0	114.2	117.7	111.4	99	101	104	99
SERVICES (82-85,87,88,102)	96.7	208.3	208.2	208.2	208.2	208.2	100	100	100	100
STATE & LOCAL GOVT. (101)	62.0	75.3	75.0	75.3	76.5	74.7	100	100	102	100
FEDERAL GOVERNMENT (100,103)	99.1	102.6	102.5	102.6	102.8	102.4	100	100	100	100
TOTAL JOBS	482.3	617.8	614.8	618.8	632.4	611.2	100	101	103	99
CIVILIAN PERSONS EMPLOYED	377.0	503.3	500.7	504.3	516.4	497.2	99	101	103	99
CIVILIAN UNEMPLOYMENT RATE	6.7	7.7	8.5	8.6	8.6	8.2				
POPULATION	1229.3	1845.6	1853.9	1847.7	1875.7	1827.4	100	100	101	99
PER CAPITA INCOME	2739.5	3419.6	3384.7	3432.5	3500.8	3393.6	99	101	103	100
ENERGY USER SECTOR			(TRILLIONS OF BTU'S)							
NATURAL RESOURCES	15.5	20.2	19.7	19.6	20.2	19.4	98	99	102	98
CONSTRUCTION	21.1	33.5	33.6	37.3	50.7	26.7	100	111	151	79
MANUFACTURING	30.0	33.7	33.3	34.7	37.5	32.5	99	104	113	98
TRANSPORTATION INDUSTRY	9.9	15.6	15.3	15.3	16.5	15.0	98	102	108	98
PUBLIC UTILITIES	37.8	25.6	25.0	25.2	36.9	24.5	98	101	147	98
TRADE AND SERVICES	37.2	68.9	68.5	68.9	70.4	67.8	99	101	103	99
GOVERNMENT, EXC. TRANSPORTATION	10.8	14.9	14.9	15.0	15.1	14.9	100	101	101	100
CONSUMERS, EXC. TRANSPORTATION	36.3	67.0	66.7	67.3	69.2	66.1	100	101	104	99
USER-OPERATED TRANSPORTATION	86.7	154.8	154.3	155.2	158.2	153.3	100	101	103	99
TRANSPORTATION AIR POLLUTION			(THOUSANDS OF TONS)							
SULFUR OXIDES	3.4	4.8	4.7	4.8	5.0	4.7	99	101	105	98
PARTICULATE MATTER	2.6	4.1	4.1	4.1	4.3	4.1	99	101	104	99
CARBON MONOXIDE	546.2	973.4	969.7	976.5	998.3	962.1	100	101	103	99
HYDROCARBONS	98.1	169.1	168.5	169.6	173.4	167.2	100	101	103	99
NITROGEN OXIDES	53.4	87.5	87.3	88.0	90.1	86.5	100	101	103	99
OTHER AIR POLLUTION										
SULFUR OXIDES	92.9	86.1	85.1	85.2	104.9	84.1	99	102	123	99
PARTICULATE MATTER	97.5	91.6	88.9	88.1	94.8	87.6	97	101	107	99
CARBON MONOXIDE	99.4	167.7	160.5	158.1	165.7	158.1	96	98	103	98
HYDROCARBONS	42.6	65.2	64.2	75.0	100.5	63.2	99	117	156	98
NITROGEN OXIDES	38.6	50.0	49.3	49.2	54.6	48.9	99	100	111	99
WATER OXYGEN DEMAND	1103.4	1833.3	1832.9	1833.0	1833.4	1833.6	100	100	100	100
LAND SOLID WASTE	971.1	1458.0	1464.6	1459.7	1481.8	1443.6	100	100	101	99

SUMMARY PROJECTIONS BY OBE ECONOMIC AREA UNDER FIVE ALTERNATIVE HIGHWAY SYSTEMS

143   CORPUS CHRISTI, TEX.

	1970	1990 BASE YEAR	1990 COMPLETED INTERSTATE	1990 EXTENDED PRIMARY	1990 ECONOMIC DEVELOPMENT	1990 URBAN	CI/BY	EP/CI	ED/CI	U/CI
JOBS BY INDUSTRY		(THOUSANDS)						P E R C E N T		
NATURAL RESOURCES (1-10)	16.6	16.9	16.9	16.9	16.9	16.9	100	100	100	100
CONSTRUCTION (11,12)	12.9	14.1	14.2	13.9	13.5	14.2	100	98	95	100
MANUFACTURING (13-74)	13.0	12.2	12.3	13.5	13.0	11.9	101	110	106	97
TRANSPORTATION INDUSTRY (75)	5.8	8.6	8.8	8.7	8.7	8.6	100	101	100	100
PUBLIC UTILITIES (76-80)	3.5	1.2	1.2	1.2	1.2	1.1	100	101	103	96
TRADE (81,86-89,99)	41.8	53.6	53.4	54.2	53.9	52.9	100	100	104	99
SERVICES (82-85,87,88,102)	33.5	62.6	62.6	62.6	62.5	62.5	100	100	101	100
STATE & LOCAL GOVT. (101)	22.8	29.0	29.0	29.1	29.0	28.9	100	100	101	100
FEDERAL GOVERNMENT (100,103)	19.5	20.3	20.3	20.4	20.3	20.3	100	100	100	100
TOTAL JOBS	169.3	218.5	218.4	220.4	219.1	217.3	100	101	100	99
CIVILIAN PERSONS EMPLOYED	152.9	200.1	200.0	201.9	200.7	199.0	100	101	100	99
CIVILIAN UNEMPLOYMENT RATE	6.8	8.4	7.8	8.5	8.2	8.1	100	101	101	100
POPULATION	516.3	701.2	699.9	704.2	705.9	697.6	100	101	101	100
PER CAPITA INCOME	2640.9	4002.6	4008.4	4028.9	3988.7	3997.5	100	100	100	100
		(TRILLIONS OF BTU'S)								
ENERGY USER SECTOR										
NATURAL RESOURCES	15.7	26.8	26.4	26.5	26.4	26.2	98	100	100	99
CONSTRUCTION	20.3	38.4	38.4	41.3	40.4	36.4	100	107	105	95
MANUFACTURING	15.3	35.8	35.9	36.3	36.2	35.7	100	101	101	99
TRANSPORTATION INDUSTRY	5.6	12.0	12.0	12.2	12.1	11.9	100	102	100	99
PUBLIC UTILITIES	48.5	29.7	29.2	29.4	29.7	28.5	98	101	101	98
TRADE AND SERVICES	12.8	27.5	27.4	27.7	27.6	27.2	100	101	101	99
GOVERNMENT, EXC. TRANSPORTATION	14.3	19.4	19.4	19.4	19.4	19.4	100	100	100	100
CONSUMERS, EXC. TRANSPORTATION	18.5	38.0	38.0	38.3	38.1	37.8	100	100	100	100
USER-OPERATED TRANSPORTATION	58.6	97.9	97.9	98.3	98.1	97.7	100	100	100	100
		(THOUSANDS OF TONS)								
TRANSPORTATION AIR POLLUTION										
SULFUR OXIDES	2.0	3.1	3.1	3.1	3.1	3.1	99	101	100	99
PARTICULATE MATTER	1.4	2.3	2.3	2.3	2.3	2.3	100	101	100	99
CARBON MONOXIDE	254.8	455.1	454.9	458.2	456.2	453.1	100	101	100	100
HYDROCARBONS	45.5	79.3	79.3	79.8	79.5	78.9	100	101	100	100
NITROGEN OXIDES	27.6	43.7	43.8	44.3	44.0	43.6	100	101	100	100
OTHER AIR POLLUTION										
SULFUR OXIDES	97.3	86.0	84.8	85.2	85.7	83.5	99	101	100	99
PARTICULATE MATTER	64.2	80.8	77.8	77.5	77.0	76.1	96	99	99	98
CARBON MONOXIDE	140.9	267.8	260.7	258.4	256.5	255.2	97	99	98	98
HYDROCARBONS	66.1	165.6	167.0	167.4	167.6	164.4	101	100	100	98
NITROGEN OXIDES	30.0	32.7	31.9	31.8	31.8	31.3	98	100	100	98
WATER OXYGEN DEMAND	353.2	591.3	590.8	589.3	589.6	589.5	100	100	100	100
LAND SOLID WASTE	407.9	553.9	552.9	556.3	557.7	551.1	100	100	101	100

SUMMARY PROJECTIONS BY ORE ECONOMIC AREA UNDER FIVE ALTERNATIVE HIGHWAY SYSTEMS

144 BROWN-HARL-S BENITO, TEX

	1970	1990 BASE YEAR	1990 COMPLETED INTERSTATE	1990 EXTENDED PRIMARY	1990 ECONOMIC DEVELOPMENT	1990 URBAN	CI/BY	EP/CI	ED/CI	U/CI
		(THOUSANDS)						P E R C E N T		
JOBS BY INDUSTRY										
NATURAL RESOURCES (1-10)	9.6	4.7	4.5	4.6	5.0	4.4	96	102	110	99
CONSTRUCTION (11,12)	4.6	4.4	4.2	5.0	11.7	4.2	95	120	283	101
MANUFACTURING (13-74)	8.1	12.9	11.3	12.4	13.3	11.2	87	110	118	99
TRANSPORTATION INDUSTRY (75)	2.1	.6	.4	.6	.4	.4	91	106	108	110
PUBLIC UTILITIES (76-80)	1.6	.6	.6	.6	.7	.5	96	105	120	96
TRADE (81,86,89-99)	29.5	25.3	24.5	25.1	26.5	24.2	97	102	108	99
SERVICES (82-85,87,88,102)	18.4	39.6	39.6	39.6	39.8	39.6	100	102	101	100
STATE & LOCAL GOVT. (101)	15.0	19.4	18.7	19.1	20.1	18.6	96	102	108	100
FEDERAL GOVERNMENT (100,103)	2.2	2.5	2.3	2.4	2.6	2.3	93	104	114	100
TOTAL JOBS	91.2	109.7	105.8	109.1	119.9	105.4	96	103	113	100
CIVILIAN PERSONS EMPLOYED	82.3	99.3	95.9	98.8	108.5	95.4	96	103	113	100
CIVILIAN UNEMPLOYMENT RATE	8.7	9.9	10.5	10.2	9.2	9.2				
POPULATION	355.2	527.3	512.4	520.4	551.1	507.6	97	102	108	99
PER CAPITA INCOME	1925.3	2814.3	2633.5	2752.6	2922.1	2645.7	94	105	111	100
ENERGY USER SECTOR		(TRILLIONS OF BTU'S)								
NATURAL RESOURCES	17.4	21.6	21.1	21.2	21.7	20.8	98	103	103	99
CONSTRUCTION	3.7	7.1	4.2	7.3	23.0	3.5	59	173	550	85
MANUFACTURING	8.1	8.1	6.1	7.7	8.0	5.9	76	125	130	96
TRANSPORTATION INDUSTRY	1.9	3.1	2.8	3.0	3.4	2.7	91	106	121	98
PUBLIC UTILITIES	16.7	10.0	9.7	9.8	12.0	9.5	97	101	123	98
TRADE AND SERVICES	7.9	16.0	15.6	15.8	16.5	15.4	97	102	106	99
GOVERNMENT, EXC. TRANSPORTATION	8.9	1.6	1.5	1.6	1.7	1.5	95	102	110	100
CONSUMERS, EXC. TRANSPORTATION	8.5	17.3	16.2	16.9	18.4	16.1	93	104	114	100
USER-OPERATED TRANSPORTATION	14.9	30.9	29.1	30.2	32.6	29.0	94	104	112	100
TRANSPORTATION AIR POLLUTION		(THOUSANDS OF TONS)								
SULFUR OXIDES	1.5	1.3	1.3	1.3	1.4	1.2	94	103	112	99
PARTICULATE MATTER	1.1	1.1	1.1	1.1	1.2	1.1	95	103	111	99
CARBON MONOXIDE	159.7	241.2	228.7	236.5	253.2	227.9	95	103	111	100
HYDROCARBONS	29.7	42.6	40.4	41.8	44.6	40.3	95	103	110	100
NITROGEN OXIDES	20.3	23.5	22.4	23.2	24.7	22.3	95	103	110	100
OTHER AIR POLLUTION										
SULFUR OXIDES	30.9	23.1	23.2	23.2	27.4	22.7	100	100	118	98
PARTICULATE MATTER	68.3	135.1	130.9	131.4	135.9	128.9	97	100	104	98
CARBON MONOXIDE	207.5	391.0	376.7	377.9	388.5	370.9	96	100	103	98
HYDROCARBONS	35.8	66.0	43.7	60.8	62.0	40.7	66	139	142	93
NITROGEN OXIDES	15.8	23.9	23.5	23.5	25.3	23.1	98	100	107	98
WATER OXYGEN DEMAND	141.1	242.0	238.7	238.0	238.6	238.5	99	100	100	100
LAND SOLID WASTE	280.6	416.6	404.8	411.1	435.3	401.0	97	102	108	95

145 EL PASO. TEX.

	1970	1990 BASE YEAR	1990 COMPLETED INTERSTATE	1990 EXTENDED PRIMARY	1990 ECONOMIC DEVELOPMENT	1990 URBAN	CI/BY	EP/CI	ED/CI	U/CI
JOBS BY INDUSTRY			(THOUSANDS)							
NATURAL RESOURCES (1-10)	17.7	13.3	12.7	13.9	14.4	12.5	95	101	113	98
CONSTRUCTION (11.12)	12.1	5.9	5.5	6.7	6.8	4.8	93	122	124	87
MANUFACTURING (13-74)	29.9	57.1	55.7	57.5	58.7	54.9	98	103	105	98
TRANSPORTATION INDUSTRY (75)	7.7	11.9	11.7	12.0	12.2	11.6	98	103	104	99
PUBLIC UTILITIES (76-80)	7.7	4.5	4.1	6.7	7.5	3.8	92	163	182	93
TRADE (81.86.89-99)	52.4	56.9	55.4	60.5	62.3	54.4	97	109	113	98
SERVICES (82-85.87.88.102)	44.5	80.4	80.2	80.3	80.4	80.2	100	100	100	100
STATE & LOCAL GOVT. (101)	31.7	37.0	36.4	37.6	38.0	36.2	99	103	104	99
FEDERAL GOVERNMENT (100.103)	49.4	49.9	49.8	50.1	50.2	49.8	100	101	101	100
TOTAL JOBS	252.8	317.0	311.5	325.3	330.5	308.0	98	104	106	99
CIVILIAN PERSONS EMPLOYED	205.5	267.0	261.9	274.8	279.6	258.7	98	105	107	99
CIVILIAN UNEMPLOYMENT RATE	5.4			.5						
POPULATION	681.5	737.2	724.1	761.7	773.7	720.8	98	105	107	100
PER CAPITA INCOME	2869.4	4718.5	4677.4	4752.9	4791.2	4626.3	99	102	102	99
ENERGY USER SECTOR			(TRILLIONS OF BTU'S)							
NATURAL RESOURCES	11.8	14.2	13.0	16.5	17.5	12.7	92	127	134	97
CONSTRUCTION	13.4	21.9	21.6	33.6	35.8	17.4	99	156	166	81
MANUFACTURING	8.9	13.8	13.4	14.6	15.1	13.0	97	109	113	97
TRANSPORTATION INDUSTRY	6.9	12.2	11.7	13.1	13.7	11.5	96	112	116	98
PUBLIC UTILITIES	37.8	124.7	102.2	137.2	162.4	93.4	82	134	159	91
TRADE AND SERVICES	20.5	40.5	39.7	43.0	44.0	39.2	98	108	111	99
GOVERNMENT. EXC. TRANSPORTATION	4.7	6.5	6.4	6.6	6.4	6.4	98	102	103	100
CONSUMERS. EXC. TRANSPORTATION	31.0	54.6	53.9	55.9	56.6	53.4	99	104	105	99
USER-OPERATED TRANSPORTATION	50.7	91.4	90.2	93.2	94.4	89.4	99	103	105	99
TRANSPORTATION AIR POLLUTION			(THOUSANDS OF TONS)							
SULFUR OXIDES	2.0	3.3	3.2	3.5	3.6	3.2	97	108	111	98
PARTICULATE MATTER	1.6	2.7	2.6	2.8	2.9	2.6	98	106	108	99
CARBON MONOXIDE	336.3	612.3	603.2	626.6	635.2	597.8	99	104	105	99
HYDROCARBONS	58.6	106.1	104.5	108.6	110.1	103.6	99	104	105	99
NITROGEN OXIDES	31.5	55.3	54.5	57.1	57.9	53.9	98	104	106	99
OTHER AIR POLLUTION										
SULFUR OXIDES	169.1	347.1	309.6	367.4	409.1	295.0	89	119	132	95
PARTICULATE MATTER	43.7	90.6	82.5	94.6	103.9	79.3	91	115	126	96
CARBON MONOXIDE	28.9	35.2	35.2	35.7	36.1	35.0	100	102	103	100
HYDROCARBONS	21.2	41.1	40.5	46.9	48.6	38.0	98	116	120	94
NITROGEN OXIDES	28.7	108.1	98.8	113.3	123.7	95.2	91	115	125	96
WATER OXYGEN DEMAND	225.7	366.6	365.3	366.5	366.8	365.2	100	100	100	100
LAND SOLID WASTE	538.4	582.4	572.0	601.8	611.2	569.5	98	105	107	100

146 ALBUQUERQUE, N. M.

	1970	1990 BASE YEAR	1990 COMPLETED INTERSTATE	1990 EXTENDED PRIMARY	1990 ECONOMIC DEVELOPMENT	1990 URBAN	CI/BY	EP/CI	ED/CI	U/CI
JOBS BY INDUSTRY			(THOUSANDS)					P E R C E N T		
NATURAL RESOURCES (1-10)	11.2	8.8	9.3	9.7	10.3	9.2	106	104	111	99
CONSTRUCTION (11,12)	11.8	6.0	6.2	6.5	6.8	5.8	103	105	110	94
MANUFACTURING (13-74)	12.7	19.6	21.8	22.3	25.4	21.0	111	103	117	97
TRANSPORTATION INDUSTRY (75)	6.3	10.1	10.4	10.5	10.8	10.3	103	101	104	99
PUBLIC UTILITIES (76-80)	4.2	1.8	3.3	3.7	5.8	2.7	182	114	177	84
TRADE (81,86,89-99)	42.6	46.5	49.5	50.4	54.8	48.3	106	102	111	98
SERVICES (82-85,87,88,102)	51.3	85.4	85.4	85.4	85.6	85.4	100	100	100	100
STATE & LOCAL GOVT. (101)	33.0	38.5	39.7	39.6	40.9	39.3	103	100	103	100
FEDERAL GOVERNMENT (100,103)	23.2	24.3	24.6	24.6	24.9	24.5	101	100	101	100
TOTAL JOBS	196.4	241.0	250.1	252.7	265.1	246.6	104	101	106	99
CIVILIAN PERSONS EMPLOYED	183.3	226.6	235.4	237.8	249.7	232.0	104	101	106	99
CIVILIAN UNEMPLOYMENT RAT⁻	7.1					0.7				
POPULATION	572.7	685.4	715.9	714.8	734.7	708.6	104	100	103	99
PER CAPITA INCOME	3172.3	4488.3	4581.0	4597.9	4810.2	4531.4	102	100	105	99
ENERGY USER SECTOR			(TRILLIONS OF BTU'S)							
NATURAL RESOURCES	7.6	15.6	16.1	16.9	18.4	16.0	103	105	114	99
CONSTRUCTION	11.9	16.9	17.7	26.1	26.5	17.4	105	148	150	98
MANUFACTURING	5.2	8.6	9.4	9.1	10.8	9.1	109	105	115	98
TRANSPORTATION INDUSTRY	6.3	11.0	11.8	12.0	13.2	11.5	108	102	112	97
PUBLIC UTILITIES	10.3	12.3	31.6	32.4	51.7	24.2	257	102	164	77
TRADE AND SERVICES	19.3	33.9	35.9	36.2	39.0	35.1	106	101	109	98
GOVERNMENT, EXC. TRANSPORTATION	6.4	8.4	8.6	8.5	8.7	8.5	102	100	101	100
CONSUMERS, EXC. TRANSPORTATION	23.0	38.4	40.1	40.2	42.3	39.5	104	100	105	99
USER-OPERATED TRANSPORTATION	52.3	90.6	93.2	93.3	96.6	92.3	103	100	104	99
TRANSPORTATION AIR POLLUTION			(THOUSANDS OF TONS)							
SULFUR OXIDES	1.7	3.0	3.1	3.2	3.4	3.1	106	101	109	98
PARTICULATE MATTER	1.4	2.4	2.6	2.7	2.7	2.5	105	101	106	98
CARBON MONOXIDE	310.6	563.8	583.5	584.6	608.8	576.6	103	100	104	99
HYDROCARBONS	53.9	97.6	101.0	101.2	105.4	99.8	103	100	104	99
NITROGEN OXIDES	28.1	50.4	52.5	52.8	55.2	51.8	104	101	105	99
OTHER AIR POLLUTION										
SULFUR OXIDES	29.9	49.0	80.6	81.8	113.6	68.5	165	102	141	85
PARTICULATE MATTER	33.4	37.7	43.5	44.4	51.2	41.1	115	102	118	95
CARBON MONOXIDE	14.8	39.1	38.3	41.9	40.8	38.7	98	109	107	101
HYDROCARBONS	16.2	16.2	17.6	22.6	23.2	17.3	109	128	132	98
NITROGEN OXIDES	14.8	29.1	36.9	37.5	45.4	33.9	127	102	123	92
WATER OXYGEN DEMAND	107.1	188.3	188.3	188.9	189.0	188.3	100	100	100	100
LAND SOLID WASTE	452.5	541.4	565.5	564.7	580.4	559.8	104	100	103	99

SUMMARY PROJECTIONS BY ORE ECONOMIC AREA UNDER FIVE ALTERNATIVE HIGHWAY SYSTEMS

147 PUEBLO, COL.

	1970	1990 BASE YEAR	1990 COMPLETED INTERSTATE	1990 EXTENDED PRIMARY	1990 ECONOMIC DEVELOPMENT	1990 URBAN	PER CENT CI/BY	EP/CI	ED/CI	U/CI
JOBS BY INDUSTRY				(THOUSANDS)						
NATURAL RESOURCES (1-10)	14.3	19.2	18.9	19.1	19.3	18.7	98	101	102	99
CONSTRUCTION (11,12)	7.7	7.5	7.6	8.2	8.0	7.6	101	109	106	100
MANUFACTURING (13-74)	19.2	37.8	37.3	37.9	38.8	36.7	99	102	104	98
TRANSPORTATION INDUSTRY (75)	5.0	5.7	5.7	5.7	5.8	5.6	99	101	102	99
PUBLIC UTILITIES (76-80)	3.8	8.4	7.8	7.8	8.7	7.3	93	100	112	94
TRADE (81,86,89-99)	36.1	38.1	36.9	37.4	38.6	36.0	97	101	105	98
SERVICES (82-85,87,88,102)	35.0	49.0	48.7	48.7	48.8	48.7	99	100	100	100
STATE & LOCAL GOVT. (101)	26.2	31.7	31.4	31.6	31.9	31.2	99	101	102	99
FEDERAL GOVERNMENT (100,103)	45.2	45.4	45.4	45.4	45.5	45.3	100	100	100	100
TOTAL JOBS	192.5	242.9	239.6	241.8	245.4	237.1	99	101	102	99
CIVILIAN PERSONS EMPLOYED	162.4	213.2	210.0	212.2	215.6	207.1	98	101	103	99
CIVILIAN UNEMPLOYMENT RATE	4.4									
POPULATION	509.4	518.7	509.6	514.9	522.9	506.8	98	101	103	99
PER CAPITA INCOME	3148.2	5945.9	5951.8	5968.6	5990.6	5907.5	100	100	101	99
ENERGY USER SECTOR				(TRILLIONS OF BTU'S)						
NATURAL RESOURCES	13.1	25.0	24.6	24.8	25.0	24.4	98	101	102	99
CONSTRUCTION	8.5	15.5	15.2	23.2	16.1	12.5	98	152	106	82
MANUFACTURING	18.3	42.0	41.6	41.7	42.4	41.3	99	100	102	99
TRANSPORTATION INDUSTRY	3.6	8.6	8.3	8.4	8.7	8.0	96	101	106	97
PUBLIC UTILITIES	14.9	102.0	93.2	90.6	103.2	88.2	91	97	111	95
TRADE AND SERVICES	13.4	32.1	31.0	31.1	32.0	30.4	97	100	103	98
GOVERNMENT, EXC. TRANSPORTATION	2.2	3.5	3.5	3.5	3.5	3.4	99	101	102	99
CONSUMERS, EXC. TRANSPORTATION	25.5	47.1	46.6	47.0	47.5	46.3	99	101	102	99
USER-OPERATED TRANSPORTATION	36.7	71.1	70.4	70.9	71.7	69.9	99	101	102	99
TRANSPORTATION AIR POLLUTION				(THOUSANDS OF TONS)						
SULFUR OXIDES	1.9	3.9	3.8	3.8	3.9	3.8	98	100	102	99
PARTICULATE MATTER	1.5	3.1	3.0	3.0	3.1	3.0	99	101	102	99
CARBON MONOXIDE	304.4	591.3	585.7	589.6	595.7	581.6	99	101	102	99
HYDROCARBONS	54.4	105.5	104.5	105.2	106.2	103.8	99	101	102	99
NITROGEN OXIDES	31.7	61.8	61.2	61.7	62.3	60.8	99	101	102	99
OTHER AIR POLLUTION										
SULFUR OXIDES	35.7	191.7	177.4	173.2	193.7	169.3	93	98	109	95
PARTICULATE MATTER	50.9	126.9	123.0	122.0	127.5	120.7	97	99	104	98
CARBON MONOXIDE	122.7	206.3	206.9	206.9	206.9	206.3	100	100	100	100
HYDROCARBONS	27.3	45.6	45.4	45.8	46.2	44.8	100	101	102	99
NITROGEN OXIDES	15.7	59.2	55.7	54.7	59.7	53.7	94	98	107	96
WATER OXYGEN DEMAND	917.2	1487.1	1485.7	1485.7	1487.0	1484.9	100	100	100	100
LAND SOLID WASTE	402.5	409.8	402.6	406.8	413.1	400.4	98	101	103	99

SUMMARY PROJECTIONS BY ORE ECONOMIC AREA UNDER FIVE ALTERNATIVE HIGHWAY SYSTEMS

148 DENVER, COL.

	1970	1990 BASE YEAR	1990 COMPLETED INTERSTATE	1990 EXTENDED PRIMARY	1990 ECONOMIC DEVELOPMENT	1990 URBAN	CI/BY	EP/CI	ED/CI	U/CI
								P E R C E N T		
JOBS BY INDUSTRY		(THOUSANDS)								
NATURAL RESOURCES (1-10)	33.2	41.2	41.0	39.8	40.0	40.7	99	97	98	99
CONSTRUCTION (11,12)	37.3	37.1	37.2	36.0	34.9	37.2	101	97	94	100
MANUFACTURING (13-74)	100.0	182.4	183.8	176.1	176.5	178.1	101	96	96	97
TRANSPORTATION INDUSTRY (75)	24.0	41.9	41.8	41.2	41.2	41.5	100	99	99	99
PUBLIC UTILITIES (76-80)	15.0	6.1	5.3	3.1	3.4	4.6	86	59	63	86
TRADE (81,86,89-99)	162.6	242.0	240.7	231.3	231.3	235.9	99	96	96	98
SERVICES (82-85,87,88,102)	153.9	258.2	258.4	257.6	257.6	257.7	100	100	100	100
STATE & LOCAL GOVT. (101)	87.1	118.1	118.1	115.7	115.7	116.8	100	98	98	99
FEDERAL GOVERNMENT (100-103)	42.4	46.8	46.8	46.3	46.3	46.5	100	99	99	99
TOTAL JOBS	654.8	974.0	973.0	947.1	946.9	958.9	100	97	97	99
CIVILIAN PERSONS EMPLOYED	608.4	912.7	911.7	887.3	887.1	898.4	100	97	97	99
CIVILIAN UNEMPLOYMENT RATE	3.8	3.1	3.1	3.4	3.6	3.5				
POPULATION	1523.4	2288.4	2285.6	2254.1	2225.5	2275.2	100	99	99	100
PER CAPITA INCOME	3950.6	6137.0	6139.1	6029.1	6030.6	6062.7	100	98	98	99
ENERGY USER SECTOR		(TRILLIONS OF BTU'S)								
NATURAL RESOURCES	41.7	80.2	80.5	78.1	78.6	79.5	100	97	98	99
CONSTRUCTION	37.3	71.5	71.3	69.4	64.7	65.7	100	97	91	92
MANUFACTURING	49.4	108.6	109.2	106.4	106.6	107.0	101	97	98	98
TRANSPORTATION INDUSTRY	37.2	82.3	81.9	79.3	79.4	80.6	100	97	97	98
PUBLIC UTILITIES	69.9	180.9	166.7	96.1	99.0	152.0	92	58	59	91
TRADE AND SERVICES	76.7	164.8	163.7	158.4	158.7	161.1	99	97	97	98
GOVERNMENT, EXC. TRANSPORTATION	8.5	14.3	14.3	14.0	14.0	14.1	100	98	98	99
CONSUMERS, EXC. TRANSPORTATION	60.1	129.7	129.6	125.8	125.7	127.5	100	97	97	98
USER-OPERATED TRANSPORTATION	104.8	227.7	227.5	221.6	221.5	224.3	100	97	97	99
TRANSPORTATION AIR POLLUTION		(THOUSANDS OF TONS)								
SULFUR OXIDES	9.2	20.2	20.1	19.5	19.5	19.8	99	97	97	99
PARTICULATE MATTER	5.7	12.5	12.5	12.2	12.2	12.3	100	98	98	99
CARBON MONOXIDE	839.3	1853.4	1851.5	1806.9	1806.3	1827.7	100	98	98	98
HYDROCARBONS	148.7	327.9	327.5	319.6	319.2	323.4	100	97	97	98
NITROGEN OXIDES	95.0	208.7	209.1	204.9	204.6	206.5	100	98	98	98
OTHER AIR POLLUTION										
SULFUR OXIDES	180.5	518.5	495.4	379.9	384.6	471.6	96	77	78	95
PARTICULATE MATTER	169.3	432.4	426.3	394.3	395.1	419.6	99	93	93	98
CARBON MONOXIDE	228.7	396.9	396.4	394.3	395.4	395.6	100	99	99	100
HYDROCARBONS	88.3	165.4	174.1	173.5	177.6	168.1	105	100	102	100
NITROGEN OXIDES	79.9	233.7	227.9	199.3	200.5	222.0	98	87	88	97
WATER OXYGEN DEMAND	3094.2	5054.1	5052.5	5050.2	5051.3	5049.9	100	100	100	100
LAND SOLID WASTE	1203.4	1807.8	1805.6	1780.7	1779.5	1797.4	100	99	99	100

SUMMARY PROJECTIONS BY ORE ECONOMIC AREA UNDER FIVE ALTERNATIVE HIGHWAY SYSTEMS

149   GRAND JUNCTION, COL.

	1970	1990 BASE YEAR	1990 COMPLETED INTERSTATE	1990 EXTENDED PRIMARY	1990 ECONOMIC DEVELOPMENT	1990 URBAN	CI/BY	EP/CI	ED/CI	U/CI
							P E R C E N T			
JOBS BY INDUSTRY (THOUSANDS)										
NATURAL RESOURCES (1-10)	19.1	21.8	22.9	25.2	24.8	22.4	105	110	108	98
CONSTRUCTION (11,12)	4.7	2.7	2.5	5.9	3.8	2.6	92	240	153	104
MANUFACTURING (13-74)	5.8	12.5	15.5	18.5	18.0	14.6	124	120	116	94
TRANSPORTATION INDUSTRY (75)	2.0	1.1	1.2	1.7	1.6	1.2	115	139	129	97
PUBLIC UTILITIES (76-80)	2.9	1.5	2.4	5.2	5.0	2.4	165	214	207	101
TRADE (81,86,89-99)	20.2	30.8	34.3	42.3	40.1	33.5	111	123	117	98
SERVICES (82-85,87,88,102)	18.9	32.3	32.4	33.0	32.7	32.4	100	102	101	100
STATE & LOCAL GOVT. (101)	13.8	18.5	19.6	21.9	21.1	19.2	106	112	108	98
FEDERAL GOVERNMENT (100,103)	3.6	4.2	4.5	5.0	4.8	4.4	106	111	108	98
TOTAL JOBS	91.0	125.3	135.2	158.6	151.9	132.7	108	117	112	98
CIVILIAN PERSONS EMPLOYED	83.2	115.3	124.2	145.4	139.3	121.9	108	117	112	98
CIVILIAN UNEMPLOYMENT RATE	5.4									
POPULATION	251.9	284.7	308.1	360.3	343.1	304.7	108	117	111	99
PER CAPITA INCOME	3063.2	6349.0	6450.1	6778.7	6751.3	6365.3	102	105	105	99
ENERGY USER SECTOR (TRILLIONS OF BTU'S)										
NATURAL RESOURCES	12.6	22.2	23.9	29.1	27.9	23.5	108	121	117	98
CONSTRUCTION	6.9	7.7	8.3	45.3	23.7	8.2	107	548	286	99
MANUFACTURING	3.1	9.9	10.8	12.1	12.0	10.4	110	112	111	96
TRANSPORTATION INDUSTRY	1.8	4.7	5.6	7.7	7.1	5.4	119	136	126	97
PUBLIC UTILITIES	25.4	20.2	24.7	63.8	55.8	24.1	122	258	226	97
TRADE AND SERVICES	7.5	18.1	20.0	24.6	23.4	19.7	111	123	117	98
GOVERNMENT, EXC. TRANSPORTATION	2.1	3.2	3.6	3.6	3.5	3.3	104	107	105	99
CONSUMERS, EXC. TRANSPORTATION	13.5	26.4	27.9	31.8	30.7	27.5	106	114	110	99
USER-OPERATED TRANSPORTATION	23.6	49.8	52.2	58.2	56.5	51.6	105	111	108	99
TRANSPORTATION AIR POLLUTION (THOUSANDS OF TONS)										
SULFUR OXIDES	1.0	2.1	2.3	2.7	2.6	2.2	108	118	113	98
PARTICULATE MATTER	0.9	1.8	2.1	2.1	2.1	1.8	106	114	110	99
CARBON MONOXIDE	180.1	377.7	395.3	439.5	427.3	390.7	105	111	108	99
HYDROCARBONS	32.0	66.7	69.8	77.4	75.3	69.0	105	111	108	99
NITROGEN OXIDES	18.2	36.9	38.8	43.3	42.0	38.3	105	112	108	99
OTHER AIR POLLUTION										
SULFUR OXIDES	51.4	69.7	77.0	141.9	128.4	76.0	111	184	167	99
PARTICULATE MATTER	24.4	47.3	48.7	63.6	59.9	48.6	103	131	123	100
CARBON MONOXIDE	69.6	192.8	191.1	191.6	190.9	191.6	99	100	100	100
HYDROCARBONS	33.1	103.8	106.2	111.0	111.1	104.7	102	105	105	99
NITROGEN OXIDES	17.6	36.6	38.5	54.7	51.3	38.3	105	142	133	99
WATER OXYGEN DEMAND	596.5	1001.5	1001.1	1000.5	1000.8	1001.4	100	100	100	100
LAND SOLID WASTE	199.0	224.9	243.4	284.6	271.1	240.7	108	117	111	99

SUMMARY PROJECTIONS BY ORE ECONOMIC AREA UNDER FIVE ALTERNATIVE HIGHWAY SYSTEMS

150 CHEYENNE, WYO.

	1970	1990 BASE YEAR	1990 COMPLETED INTERSTATE	1990 EXTENDED PRIMARY	1990 ECONOMIC DEVELOPMENT	1990 URBAN	PERCENT CI/BY	EP/CI	ED/CI	U/CI
JOBS BY INDUSTRY			(THOUSANDS)							
NATURAL RESOURCES (1-10)	13.3	14.9	15.5	16.1	16.4	15.3	104	105	105	98
CONSTRUCTION (11,12)	5.0	2.0	2.3	3.4	2.5	1.9	111	149	111	85
MANUFACTURING (13-74)	4.9	8.3	12.5	16.6	18.5	11.6	151	133	148	92
TRANSPORTATION INDUSTRY (75)	5.2	7.1	7.5	7.7	7.8	7.6	103	104	106	99
PUBLIC UTILITIES (76-80)	2.4	1.6	1.6	3.1	5.0	1.5	281	192	303	93
TRADE (81,86-89-99)	21.0	19.0	23.5	28.4	30.6	22.7	124	120	130	96
SERVICES (82-85,87,88,102)	18.5	21.3	21.4	21.6	21.6	21.4	101	101	101	100
STATE & LOCAL GOVT. (101)	16.3	18.4	19.6	20.6	21.0	19.3	106	105	107	99
FEDERAL GOVERNMENT (100,103)	7.5	7.4	7.7	7.9	8.0	7.6	103	103	104	99
TOTAL JOBS	94.1	99.1	111.5	125.3	131.5	108.6	113	112	118	97
CIVILIAN PERSONS EMPLOYED	85.8	90.9	102.6	115.5	121.3	99.9	113	113	118	97
CIVILIAN UNEMPLOYMENT RATE	5.0	7.1	6.5	5.5	5.0	7.5				
POPULATION	229.3	248.7	270.5	285.6	293.7	269.8	109	106	109	100
PER CAPITA INCOME	3153.8	5338.1	5665.5	6106.0	6188.2	5516.9	106	108	109	97
ENERGY USER SECTOR			(TRILLIONS OF BTU'S)							
NATURAL RESOURCES	10.7	23.2	25.8	28.1	28.8	24.9	111	109	111	97
CONSTRUCTION	6.7	6.9	9.5	22.0	10.4	7.4	137	232	110	78
MANUFACTURING	2.9	8.2	9.6	10.8	11.5	9.2	116	113	120	96
TRANSPORTATION INDUSTRY	3.3	7.5	8.8	10.1	10.7	8.6	117	114	121	97
PUBLIC UTILITIES	6.8	9.4	31.4	46.2	65.9	29.8	336	147	210	95
TRADE AND SERVICES	6.9	12.5	15.6	18.3	20.2	15.1	125	118	130	97
GOVERNMENT. EXC. TRANSPORTATION	3.2	4.3	4.5	4.6	4.6	4.4	103	102	106	99
CONSUMERS. EXC. TRANSPORTATION	11.1	20.1	21.8	23.6	24.2	21.4	109	108	111	98
USER-OPERATED TRANSPORTATION	30.4	55.9	58.6	61.4	62.4	58.1	105	105	106	99
TRANSPORTATION AIR POLLUTION			(THOUSANDS OF TONS)							
SULFUR OXIDES	1.0	2.2	2.5	2.7	2.8	2.4	112	110	115	98
PARTICULATE MATTER	0.9	1.7	1.9	2.0	2.1	1.9	109	108	111	98
CARBON MONOXIDE	188.9	372.9	393.9	415.3	423.3	389.5	106	105	107	99
HYDROCARBONS	33.0	65.0	68.7	72.4	73.7	67.9	106	105	107	99
NITROGEN OXIDES	17.6	35.0	37.4	39.7	40.7	36.9	107	106	109	99
OTHER AIR POLLUTION										
SULFUR OXIDES	17.1	27.4	63.6	87.8	120.0	60.8	232	138	189	96
PARTICULATE MATTER	12.0	18.3	25.7	32.7	40.4	24.8	140	127	157	97
CARBON MONOXIDE	48.8	124.8	124.9	127.6	127.4	124.1	100	102	102	99
HYDROCARBONS	32.6	99.0	103.1	107.2	106.5	100.7	104	104	103	98
NITROGEN OXIDES	7.0	9.8	18.7	24.8	32.5	17.9	191	133	174	96
WATER OXYGEN DEMAND	604.5	986.0	986.0	986.5	987.4	986.4	100	100	100	100
LAND SOLID WASTE	181.2	196.5	213.7	225.6	232.1	213.1	109	106	109	100

SUMMARY PROJECTIONS BY ORE ECONOMIC AREA UNDER FIVE ALTERNATIVE HIGHWAY SYSTEMS

151   SALT LAKE CITY, UTAH

	1970	1990 BASE YEAR	1990 COMPLETED INTERSTATE	1990 EXTENDED PRIMARY	1990 ECONOMIC DEVELOPMENT	1990 URBAN	CI/BY	PERCENT		
								EP/CI	ED/CI	U/CI
JOBS BY INDUSTRY			(THOUSANDS)							
NATURAL RESOURCES (1-10)	32.2	18.3	20.1	20.9	19.3	19.4	110	104	96	97
CONSTRUCTION (11,12)	16.7	16.4	16.6	16.9	15.6	16.6	101	102	94	100
MANUFACTURING (13-74)	51.3	64.9	71.3	73.1	69.4	68.6	110	103	97	96
TRANSPORTATION INDUSTRY (75)	16.0	26.4	27.0	27.2	26.8	26.8	102	101	99	99
PUBLIC UTILITIES (76-80)	8.7	9.2	14.7	14.3	11.8	13.7	160	98	80	94
TRADE (81,86,89-99)	90.8	106.5	115.9	117.7	111.8	113.1	109	102	96	98
SERVICES (82-85,87,88,102)	76.0	144.3	144.7	144.6	144.5	144.6	100	100	100	98
STATE & LOCAL GOVT. (101)	55.2	64.7	67.3	67.6	66.2	66.5	104	100	98	100
FEDERAL GOVERNMENT (100,103)	44.3	48.5	49.0	49.1	48.8	48.9	101	100	100	100
TOTAL JOBS	391.1	499.0	526.7	531.5	514.2	518.3	106	101	98	98
CIVILIAN PERSONS EMPLOYED	374.8	478.3	504.7	509.3	492.7	496.7	106	101	98	98
CIVILIAN UNEMPLOYMENT RATE	6.3	1.6	1.6	1.4	1.6	1.6	106	100	97	99
POPULATION	1061.7	1097.6	1160.6	1161.7	1127.6	1146.6	106	100	100	99
PER CAPITA INCOME	3179.8	5526.6	5630.0	5697.3	5606.1	5573.8	102	101	100	99
ENERGY USER SECTOR			(TRILLIONS OF BTU'S)							
NATURAL RESOURCES	20.7	33.8	38.6	40.3	37.3	37.4	114	104	97	97
CONSTRUCTION	18.8	25.9	32.5	45.7	29.6	28.0	125	141	91	86
MANUFACTURING	45.8	53.9	56.4	57.5	55.7	55.3	105	102	99	98
TRANSPORTATION INDUSTRY	15.1	30.2	33.1	33.5	31.9	32.3	110	101	96	98
PUBLIC UTILITIES	60.5	269.4	347.9	338.8	308.1	335.3	129	97	89	96
TRADE AND SERVICES	39.2	84.1	91.1	91.5	88.0	89.4	108	100	97	98
GOVERNMENT, EXC. TRANSPORTATION	8.2	11.3	11.5	11.6	11.4	11.4	103	100	99	99
CONSUMERS, EXC. TRANSPORTATION	43.5	77.8	81.8	82.5	80.0	80.5	105	101	98	98
USER-OPERATED TRANSPORTATION	76.6	134.9	141.0	142.1	138.2	139.1	105	101	98	99
TRANSPORTATION AIR POLLUTION			(THOUSANDS OF TONS)							
SULFUR OXIDES	3.9	7.1	7.7	7.7	7.4	7.5	108	101	97	98
PARTICULATE MATTER	2.7	4.9	5.2	5.3	5.1	5.1	107	101	97	98
CARBON MONOXIDE	505.1	909.2	956.9	965.2	935.3	942.5	105	101	98	98
HYDROCARBONS	88.4	158.1	166.3	167.7	162.6	163.9	105	101	98	99
NITROGEN OXIDES	50.5	89.1	94.5	95.6	92.4	93.0	106	101	98	98
OTHER AIR POLLUTION										
SULFUR OXIDES	248.2	840.4	969.4	954.3	904.1	948.9	115	98	93	98
PARTICULATE MATTER	119.7	193.5	218.3	215.9	205.6	214.2	113	99	94	98
CARBON MONOXIDE	147.7	259.3	257.3	258.7	255.9	252.3	99	101	99	100
HYDROCARBONS	64.6	160.6	168.2	175.5	166.7	164.6	105	104	99	98
NITROGEN OXIDES	42.5	139.5	171.5	167.9	155.2	166.4	123	98	90	97
WATER OXYGEN DEMAND	1208.1	2501.7	2510.3	2509.2	2504.0	2509.8	100	100	100	100
LAND SOLID WASTE	838.7	867.1	916.9	917.7	890.8	905.8	106	100	97	99

SUMMARY PROJECTIONS BY OBE ECONOMIC AREA UNDER FIVE ALTERNATIVE HIGHWAY SYSTEMS

152   IDAHO FALLS, IDAHO

	1970	1990 BASE YEAR	1990 COMPLETED INTERSTATE	1990 EXTENDED PRIMARY	1990 ECONOMIC DEVELOPMENT	1990 URBAN	CI/BY	EP/CI	ED/CI	U/CI
								P E R C E N T		
JOBS BY INDUSTRY			(THOUSANDS)							
NATURAL RESOURCES (1-10)	18.2	13.4	13.2	13.2	13.3	13.1	98	101	101	99
CONSTRUCTION (11-12)	4.9	6.6	6.6	6.7	6.2	6.7	101	101	94	100
MANUFACTURING (13-74)	17.0	24.1	24.1	24.8	24.4	23.6	100	103	101	98
TRANSPORTATION INDUSTRY (75)	4.4	6.1	6.0	6.0	6.0	6.0	98	101	101	99
PUBLIC UTILITIES (76-80)	2.1	1.8	1.8	2.0	2.1	1.7	84	114	117	93
TRADE (81,86,89-99)	30.2	38.1	37.3	38.2	38.1	36.7	98	102	102	98
SERVICES (82-85,87,88,102)	22.9	43.2	43.2	43.2	43.2	43.2	100	100	100	100
STATE & LOCAL GOVT. (101)	15.0	18.8	18.7	18.8	18.8	18.5	99	101	101	99
FEDERAL GOVERNMENT (100,103)	4.0	4.2	4.1	4.2	4.2	4.1	99	101	101	99
TOTAL JOBS										
CIVILIAN PERSONS EMPLOYED	118.5	156.6	155.0	157.1	156.3	153.4	99	101	101	99
CIVILIAN UNEMPLOYMENT RATE	115.5	152.1	150.6	152.6	151.9	149.0	99	101	101	99
POPULATION	3.7	1.4	1.3	1.2	1.4	1.3	99	101	101	99
PER CAPITA INCOME	300.2	335.3	330.7	333.9	333.9	328.5	99	101	101	100
	3157.2	6215.7	6227.6	6276.0	6229.4	6176.1	100	101	100	99
ENERGY USER SECTOR			(TRILLIONS OF BTU'S)							
NATURAL RESOURCES	22.1	13.6	13.3	13.5	13.5	13.3	98	101	101	100
CONSTRUCTION	4.9	7.7	7.5	10.7	7.6	6.2	98	143	102	83
MANUFACTURING	15.8	35.3	35.3	35.4	35.4	35.0	100	100	100	99
TRANSPORTATION INDUSTRY	2.8	5.1	4.9	5.1	5.1	4.8	97	103	103	98
PUBLIC UTILITIES	16.8	52.6	41.2	41.3	46.9	36.5	78	100	114	89
TRADE AND SERVICES	9.4	18.2	17.8	18.2	18.1	17.6	98	102	102	99
GOVERNMENT, EXC. TRANSPORTATION	1.4	1.8	1.8	1.8	1.8	1.8	99	102	101	99
CONSUMERS, EXC. TRANSPORTATION	12.8	26.0	25.8	26.1	26.0	25.5	99	101	101	99
USER-OPERATED TRANSPORTATION	24.7	51.7	51.4	51.8	51.7	50.9	99	101	101	99
TRANSPORTATION AIR POLLUTION			(THOUSANDS OF TONS)							
SULFUR OXIDES	2.4	2.3	2.2	2.3	2.3	2.2	98	101	101	99
PARTICULATE MATTER	1.8	1.9	1.9	1.9	1.9	1.9	99	101	101	99
CARBON MONOXIDE	273.7	415.2	412.6	416.3	414.9	409.6	99	101	101	99
HYDROCARBONS	50.9	73.3	72.9	73.5	73.3	72.3	99	101	101	99
NITROGEN OXIDES	34.8	40.5	40.2	40.6	40.5	39.9	99	101	101	99
OTHER AIR POLLUTION										
SULFUR OXIDES	32.8	102.4	83.4	83.4	92.7	75.6	81	100	111	91
PARTICULATE MATTER	47.3	71.7	66.5	66.2	69.2	64.4	93	99	104	97
CARBON MONOXIDE	154.1	78.2	78.0	78.3	78.2	78.5	100	100	100	101
HYDROCARBONS	43.3	46.0	47.2	47.7	48.0	45.6	102	101	102	97
NITROGEN OXIDES	13.1	32.3	27.6	27.5	29.9	25.7	85	100	108	93
WATER OXYGEN DEMAND	892.0	1478.8	1477.7	1477.8	1478.2	1478.0	100	100	100	100
LAND SOLID WASTE	237.1	264.9	261.3	263.7	263.8	259.5	99	101	101	99

SUMMARY PROJECTIONS BY OBE ECONOMIC AREA UNDER FIVE ALTERNATIVE HIGHWAY SYSTEMS

153 BUTTE, MONT.

	1970	1990 BASE YEAR	1990 COMPLETED INTERSTATE	1990 EXTENDED PRIMARY	1990 ECONOMIC DEVELOPMENT	1990 URBAN	PERCENT CI/BY	EP/CI	ED/CI	U/CI
JOBS BY INDUSTRY			(THOUSANDS)							
NATURAL RESOURCES (1-10)	10.5	6.8	6.8	6.8	7.1	6.8	99	101	105	101
CONSTRUCTION (11,12)	3.8	2.2	2.2	2.0	2.3	2.1	103	91	102	96
MANUFACTURING (13-74)	14.0	22.1	22.5	22.5	23.0	22.4	102	100	102	99
TRANSPORTATION INDUSTRY (75)	3.4	5.5	5.6	5.6	5.6	5.5	101	100	101	100
PUBLIC UTILITIES (76-80)	1.8	.4	.4	.5	.8	.5	118	102	155	98
TRADE (81,86,89-99)	18.6	23.0	23.5	23.3	24.6	23.3	102	99	105	99
SERVICES (82-85,87,88,102)	14.9	25.3	25.3	25.2	25.3	25.3	100	100	100	100
STATE & LOCAL GOVT. (101)	11.9	13.4	13.5	13.4	13.7	13.5	101	99	102	100
FEDERAL GOVERNMENT (100,103)	3.9	4.0	4.0	4.0	4.0	4.0	101	99	101	100
TOTAL JOBS	82.7	102.7	103.9	103.2	106.4	103.3	101	99	102	99
CIVILIAN PERSONS EMPLOYED	81.2	100.6	101.7	101.1	104.2	101.2	101	99	102	99
CIVILIAN UNEMPLOYMENT RATE	6.1	4.7	4.8	4.8	4.7	5.2				
POPULATION	234.9	305.2	309.5	306.6	312.9	310.3	101	99	101	100
PER CAPITA INCOME	3064.2	4506.9	4505.0	4459.5	4576.6	4470.7	100	99	102	99
ENERGY USER SECTOR			(TRILLIONS OF BTU'S)							
NATURAL RESOURCES	5.6	8.5	8.8	8.6	9.4	8.7	104	99	107	99
CONSTRUCTION	4.8	6.2	6.3	6.3	6.5	6.3	102	99	103	99
MANUFACTURING	9.5	24.7	25.1	25.0	25.5	25.0	102	100	102	99
TRANSPORTATION INDUSTRY	1.9	4.2	4.4	4.3	4.7	4.3	104	98	106	98
PUBLIC UTILITIES	16.6	10.1	11.3	11.4	15.4	11.0	112	101	136	98
TRADE AND SERVICES	6.0	14.4	14.7	14.5	15.3	14.6	102	99	104	99
GOVERNMENT, EXC. TRANSPORTATION	9.0	1.2	1.2	1.2	1.3	1.1	101	99	102	100
CONSUMERS, EXC. TRANSPORTATION	9.0	17.0	17.2	17.0	17.5	17.1	101	99	102	100
USER-OPERATED TRANSPORTATION	17.7	34.5	34.7	34.4	35.2	34.6	101	99	101	100
TRANSPORTATION AIR POLLUTION			(THOUSANDS OF TONS)							
SULFUR OXIDES	.8	1.6	1.7	1.6	1.7	1.7	102	98	103	99
PARTICULATE MATTER	.6	1.3	1.4	1.3	1.4	1.3	102	99	103	99
CARBON MONOXIDE	138.2	276.3	278.9	276.1	283.2	278.0	101	99	102	100
HYDROCARBONS	24.3	48.8	49.2	48.7	50.0	49.1	101	99	102	100
NITROGEN OXIDES	13.3	27.2	27.6	27.3	28.1	27.5	101	99	102	100
OTHER AIR POLLUTION										
SULFUR OXIDES	224.4	152.6	155.5	155.1	163.0	154.9	102	100	105	100
PARTICULATE MATTER	34.1	45.9	48.6	47.0	54.2	47.9	106	97	112	99
CARBON MONOXIDE	29.5	49.4	55.4	52.5	62.1	54.0	112	95	112	97
HYDROCARBONS	8.7	13.5	15.8	17.1	18.2	15.1	117	108	116	96
NITROGEN OXIDES	9.6	12.6	13.9	13.5	16.2	13.6	110	97	117	98
WATER OXYGEN DEMAND	327.2	638.7	646.0	641.5	650.2	644.4	101	99	101	100
LAND SOLID WASTE	185.6	241.1	244.5	242.2	247.2	245.2	101	99	101	100

154 SPOKANE, WASH.

	1970	1990 BASE YEAR	1990 COMPLETED INTERSTATE	1990 EXTENDED PRIMARY	1990 FCONOMIC DEVELOPMENT	1990 URBAN	CI/BY	PERCENT EP/CI	PERCENT ED/CI	PERCENT U/CI
JOBS BY INDUSTRY (THOUSANDS)										
NATURAL RESOURCES (1-10)	29.9	35.6	36.6	36.7	35.6	36.4	103	100	97	100
CONSTRUCTION (11,12)	9.8	13.3	13.6	14.4	12.6	13.0	101	107	94	97
MANUFACTURING (13-74)	34.0	43.7	52.0	56.6	48.1	49.4	119	109	93	95
TRANSPORTATION INDUSTRY (75)	8.8	5.9	6.3	6.6	6.0	6.2	107	105	95	99
PUBLIC UTILITIES (76-80)	4.2	1.6	2.6	3.5	1.7	2.4	167	136	65	93
TRADE (81,86,89-99)	58.5	73.3	82.7	87.2	77.3	80.9	113	106	93	98
SERVICE (82-85,87,88,102)	47.9	66.6	67.9	68.7	67.6	67.8	102	101	99	100
STATE & LOCAL GOVT. (101)	37.1	38.3	40.7	41.8	39.4	40.1	106	103	97	98
FEDERAL GOVERNMENT (100,103)	13.3	12.0	12.5	12.8	12.2	12.4	104	102	98	99
TOTAL JOBS	243.5	290.2	314.8	328.3	300.6	308.7	108	104	96	98
CIVILIAN PERSONS EMPLOYED	235.8	281.8	305.4	318.3	291.9	299.5	108	104	96	98
CIVILIAN UNEMPLOYMENT RATE	6.1	4.9	5.3	5.4	5.0	5.2				
POPULATION	687.2	764.2	830.7	861.1	786.4	813.5	109	104	95	98
PER CAPITA INCOME	3551.0	5419.0	5507.7	5587.2	5498.2	5489.7	102	101	100	100
ENERGY USER SECTOR (TRILLIONS OF BTU'S)										
NATURAL RESOURCES	39.1	65.7	67.7	68.5	65.9	67.3	103	101	97	100
CONSTRUCTION	13.7	15.7	20.4	37.1	16.5	17.2	130	182	81	85
MANUFACTURING	16.1	28.3	32.6	35.2	31.0	31.2	115	108	95	96
TRANSPORTATION INDUSTRY	7.0	12.6	15.0	16.1	13.7	14.6	119	107	91	97
PUBLIC UTILITIES	59.7	171.7	226.1	247.2	183.4	218.8	132	109	81	97
TRADE AND SERVICES	24.4	46.7	52.4	54.8	49.4	51.6	112	105	94	98
GOVERNMENT, EXC. TRANSPORTATION	2.8	3.6	3.9	4.0	3.7	3.8	107	103	96	98
CONSUMERS, EXC. TRANSPORTATION	26.5	47.7	51.1	53.1	49.2	50.2	107	104	96	98
USER-OPERATED TRANSPORTATION	40.7	68.1	73.9	76.9	70.6	72.4	108	104	96	98
TRANSPORTATION AIR POLLUTION (THOUSANDS OF TONS)										
SULFUR OXIDES	4.7	7.7	8.2	8.4	7.9	8.1	106	102	97	99
PARTICULATE MATTER	3.3	5.4	5.7	5.8	5.5	5.6	105	102	97	99
CARBON MONOXIDE	458.9	760.8	803.8	826.7	779.1	793.1	106	103	97	99
HYDROCARBONS	85.9	141.9	149.3	153.2	145.0	147.4	105	103	97	99
NITROGEN OXIDES	61.2	99.9	104.5	107.0	102.0	103.5	105	102	98	99
OTHER AIR POLLUTION										
SULFUR OXIDES	115.9	331.4	422.2	457.1	351.7	410.2	127	108	83	97
PARTICULATE MATTER	107.4	176.4	202.8	213.5	183.0	199.3	115	105	90	98
CARBON MONOXIDE	285.5	448.1	465.7	470.8	448.8	462.8	104	101	96	99
HYDROCARBONS	63.9	98.0	105.2	111.3	102.8	101.6	107	106	98	97
NITROGEN OXIDES	39.4	104.4	127.6	136.5	109.3	124.4	122	107	86	98
WATER OXYGEN DEMAND	737.2	1482.5	1493.2	1496.0	1486.7	1492.2	101	100	100	100
LAND SOLID WASTE	542.9	603.7	656.3	680.2	621	642.6	109	104	95	98

SUMMARY PROJECTIONS BY ORE ECONOMIC AREA UNDER FIVE ALTERNATIVE HIGHWAY SYSTEMS

155 SEATTLE-EVERETT, WASH.

	1970	1990 BASE YEAR	1990 COMPLETED INTERSTATE	1990 EXTENDED PRIMARY	1990 ECONOMIC DEVELOPMENT	1990 URBAN	CI/BY	EP/CI	ED/CI	U/CI
			(THOUSANDS)					PER CENT		
JOBS BY INDUSTRY										
NATURAL RESOURCES (1-10)	30.0	24.1	23.4	23.6	22.3	23.2	97	100	95	99
CONSTRUCTION (11,12)	44.6	52.6	52.8	51.6	49.9	52.6	100	98	94	100
MANUFACTURING (13-74)	192.3	273.6	269.3	270.2	258.0	262.7	98	100	96	98
TRANSPORTATION INDUSTRY (75)	35.6	63.8	63.6	63.6	62.8	63.3	100	100	99	99
PUBLIC UTILITIES (76-80)	19.0	17.8	15.6	15.0	10.0	13.7	87	96	65	88
TRADE (81,86,89-99)	201.2	316.7	311.4	311.2	298.6	306.1	98	100	96	98
SERVICES (82-85,87,88,102)	194.0	386.8	386.4	386.3	385.8	386.2	100	100	100	100
STATE & LOCAL GOVT. (101)	131.4	167.7	166.1	166.1	162.5	164.5	99	100	98	99
FEDERAL GOVERNMENT (100,103)	97.7	102.0	101.6	101.6	100.8	101.3	100	100	99	100
TOTAL JOBS	945.9	1405.0	1390.2	1389.2	1350.7	1373.5	99	100	97	99
CIVILIAN PERSONS EMPLOYED	977.7	1440.1	1425.7	1425.3	1388.9	1409.6	99	100	97	99
CIVILIAN UNEMPLOYMENT RATE	5.3	3.0	3.2	3.0	3.4	3.4				
POPULATION	2363.9	3633.0	3595.4	3584.8	3486.4	3570.6	99	100	97	99
PER CAPITA INCOME	4048.6	6354.3	6346.4	6358.3	6343.7	6308.5	100	100	100	100
ENERGY USER SECTOR			(TRILLIONS OF BTU'S)							
NATURAL RESOURCES	16.1	39.7	38.8	38.5	37.2	38.4	98	99	96	99
CONSTRUCTION	64.3	135.1	134.3	135.1	115.9	117.2	101	101	86	87
MANUFACTURING	78.8	167.9	165.7	166.5	160.6	162.4	99	100	97	98
TRANSPORTATION INDUSTRY	57.0	134.1	132.6	132.7	129.3	131.0	99	100	98	98
PUBLIC UTILITIES	132.1	309.2	270.6	262.4	183.3	251.0	88	97	68	93
TRADE AND SERVICES	105.8	263.8	260.0	260.0	251.8	256.4	99	100	97	99
GOVERNMENT, EXC. TRANSPORTATION	10.0	15.9	15.8	15.8	15.4	15.6	99	100	98	99
CONSUMERS, EXC. TRANSPORTATION	116.4	223.4	221.1	221.0	215.3	218.6	99	100	97	99
USER-OPERATED TRANSPORTATION	193.9	430.2	426.6	426.3	417.5	422.6	99	100	98	99
TRANSPORTATION AIR POLLUTION			(THOUSANDS OF TONS)							
SULFUR OXIDES	12.8	29.3	28.8	28.7	28.1	28.5	98	100	97	99
PARTICULATE MATTER	8.3	18.8	18.6	18.6	18.2	18.4	99	100	98	99
CARBON MONOXIDE	1451.6	3252.2	3226.0	3225.2	3158.7	3196.6	99	100	98	99
HYDROCARBONS	252.2	564.1	559.4	559.1	547.7	554.3	99	100	98	99
NITROGEN OXIDES	145.3	325.2	323.5	324.6	317.2	320.5	99	100	98	99
OTHER AIR POLLUTION										
SULFUR OXIDES	577.8	1204.8	1141.4	1128.2	997.6	1109.3	95	99	87	97
PARTICULATE MATTER	293.7	774.7	754.9	750.5	708.0	743.4	97	99	94	99
CARBON MONOXIDE	315.0	690.8	677.3	672.8	647.1	668.3	98	99	96	99
HYDROCARBONS	102.1	204.8	198.7	205.8	183.4	177.2	97	104	92	89
NITROGEN OXIDES	152.6	533.3	517.1	513.7	480.5	508.7	97	99	93	98
WATER OXYGEN DEMAND	1005.8	2033.9	2025.7	2025.4	2008.4	2021.0	100	100	99	100
LAND SOLID WASTE	1867.5	2870.0	2840.3	2832.0	2754.2	2820.7	99	100	97	99

SUMMARY PROJECTIONS BY ORE ECONOMIC AREA UNDER FIVE ALTERNATIVE HIGHWAY SYSTEMS

156 YAKIMA, WASH.

	1970	1990 BASE YEAR	1990 COMPLETED INTERSTATE	1990 EXTENDED PRIMARY	1990 ECONOMIC DEVELOPMENT	1990 URBAN	CI/BY	EP/CI	ED/CI	U/CI
								PERCENT		
JOBS BY INDUSTRY			(THOUSANDS)							
NATURAL RESOURCES (1-10)	18.9	22.8	24.5	23.8	24.2	24.4	107	97	99	100
CONSTRUCTION (11,12)	4.9	6.7	6.7	6.5	5.3	6.0	90	108	88	100
MANUFACTURING (13-74)	19.3	28.1	35.4	33.8	35.0	35.0	126	95	99	99
TRANSPORTATION INDUSTRY (75)	4.7	2.4	2.8	2.6	2.7	2.8	119	94	98	99
PUBLIC UTILITIES (76-80)	2.5	2.4	2.8	1.6	2.2	2.4	322	59	83	91
TRADE (81,86,89-99)	31.8	27.1	35.7	33.0	34.8	35.1	132	92	97	98
SERVICES (82-85,87,88,102)	30.3	62.3	63.3	63.4	63.5	63.3	102	100	100	100
STATE & LOCAL GOVT. (101)	20.3	22.0	24.2	23.6	23.9	24.1	110	100	100	100
FEDERAL GOVERNMENT (100,103)	5.9	5.7	6.2	6.0	6.1	6.1	109	98	99	99
TOTAL JOBS	138.6	177.9	200.8	194.4	197.8	199.2	113	97	98	99
CIVILIAN PERSONS EMPLOYED	131.4	168.9	190.5	184.4	187.6	188.9	113	97	98	99
CIVILIAN UNEMPLOYMENT RATE	7.7	10.8	9.8	10.4	10.6	9.4				
POPULATION	406.7	539.6	603.8	580.1	597.3	590.2	112	96	99	98
PER CAPITA INCOME	3275.6	4646.7	4773.2	4795.2	4746.2	4833.4	103	100	99	101
ENERGY USER SECTOR			(TRILLIONS OF BTU'S)							
NATURAL RESOURCES	27.5	43.9	45.7	45.2	45.4	45.7	104	99	99	100
CONSTRUCTION	8.6	7.4	9.6	8.9	9.4	9.5	130	92	97	98
MANUFACTURING	17.0	38.8	41.7	41.2	41.9	41.5	107	99	100	99
TRANSPORTATION INDUSTRY	3.6	7.4	10.0	9.2	9.8	9.8	135	93	98	98
PUBLIC UTILITIES	34.9	20.7	83.9	56.8	76.0	77.2	405	68	91	92
TRADE AND SERVICES	14.1	30.4	36.5	34.6	35.9	36.0	120	95	98	99
GOVERNMENT, EXC. TRANSPORTATION	1.6	2.1	2.3	2.3	2.3	2.3	112	97	98	99
CONSUMERS, EXC. TRANSPORTATION	12.7	23.0	26.2	25.4	25.8	26.0	114	97	98	99
USER-OPERATED TRANSPORTATION	26.9	50.6	55.6	54.3	55.0	55.2	110	98	99	99
TRANSPORTATION AIR POLLUTION			(THOUSANDS OF TONS)							
SULFUR OXIDES	3.1	5.3	5.8	5.6	5.7	5.8	109	97	99	99
PARTICULATE MATTER	2.2	3.8	4.1	4.0	4.1	4.1	107	98	99	99
CARBON MONOXIDE	317.3	563.2	601.3	591.2	596.8	598.2	107	98	99	99
HYDROCARBONS	59.6	104.8	111.3	109.6	110.5	110.8	106	98	99	100
NITROGEN OXIDES	42.3	72.3	76.5	75.5	76.1	76.2	106	99	99	100
OTHER AIR POLLUTION										
SULFUR OXIDES	66.2	52.3	162.6	117.2	149.1	151.4	311	72	92	93
PARTICULATE MATTER	67.7	76.0	109.8	97.0	105.0	107.3	144	88	96	98
CARBON MONOXIDE	223.7	311.5	342.8	331.8	336.7	341.8	110	97	98	100
HYDROCARBONS	63.1	95.4	104.5	106.5	109.5	103.2	110	102	105	99
NITROGEN OXIDES	24.9	25.5	56.7	44.8	53.0	53.9	223	79	94	95
WATER OXYGEN DEMAND	811.5	1607.4	1661.7	1653.1	1658.7	1660.6	103	99	100	100
LAND SOLID WASTE	321.3	426.3	477.0	458.3	471.8	466.3	112	96	99	98

SUMMARY PROJECTIONS BY ORE ECONOMIC AREA UNDER FIVE ALTERNATIVE HIGHWAY SYSTEMS

157   PORTLAND, ORE.-WASH.

	1970	1990 BASE YEAR	1990 COMPLETED INTERSTATE	1990 EXTENDED PRIMARY	1990 ECONOMIC DEVELOPMENT	1990 URBAN	CI/BY	EP/CI	ED/CI	U/CI
							PERCENT			
JOBS BY INDUSTRY			(THOUSANDS)							
NATURAL RESOURCES (1-10)	39.6	12.2	12.5	12.0	11.5	12.2	102	96	92	98
CONSTRUCTION (11,12)	28.7	27.7	27.8	27.0	26.1	27.8	100	97	94	100
MANUFACTURING (13-74)	139.6	194.6	206.2	206.5	202.1	201.1	106	100	98	98
TRANSPORTATION INDUSTRY (75)	26.9	44.4	44.8	44.7	44.5	44.5	101	100	99	99
PUBLIC UTILITIES (76-80)	14.0	9.5	11.3	9.3	7.3	10.0	118	82	65	88
TRADE (81,86,89-99)	150.7	169.0	168.5	166.0	161.3	164.6	105	99	96	98
SERVICES (82-85,87,88,102)	141.7	257.9	258.4	258.3	258.1	258.3	100	100	100	100
STATE & LOCAL GOVT. (101)	87.9	108.6	111.1	110.6	109.4	110.0	102	100	98	99
FEDERAL GOVERNMENT (100,103)	21.3	22.9	23.5	23.4	23.1	23.2	102	100	98	99
TOTAL JOBS	650.4	837.9	844.0	857.8	843.4	851.7	103	99	98	99
CIVILIAN PERSONS EMPLOYED	635.4	815.9	840.9	835.0	821.3	829.1	103	99	98	99
CIVILIAN UNEMPLOYMENT RATE	5.1	7.2	6.7	6.8	6.7	7.0				
POPULATION	1637.3	2292.6	2324.4	2304.2	2268.8	2311.5	101	99	98	99
PER CAPITA INCOME	3732.3	5817.1	5923.5	5931.5	5916.4	5867.2	102	100	100	99
ENERGY USER SECTOR			(TRILLIONS OF BTU'S)							
NATURAL RESOURCES	26.4	54.2	54.8	54.2	53.8	54.5	101	99	98	99
CONSTRUCTION	38.9	54.0	59.0	60.2	54.2	54.6	109	102	92	93
MANUFACTURING	79.9	122.8	132.2	133.9	131.6	127.4	108	101	100	96
TRANSPORTATION INDUSTRY	37.2	69.7	72.2	71.6	70.5	71.0	104	99	98	98
PUBLIC UTILITIES	93.1	219.9	245.5	218.7	197.5	229.6	112	89	80	94
TRADE AND SERVICES	85.9	166.9	172.1	170.4	167.9	169.4	103	99	98	98
GOVERNMENT, EXC. TRANSPORTATION	5.7	9.1	9.4	9.4	9.2	9.3	103	99	98	99
CONSUMERS, EXC. TRANSPORTATION	77.8	153.6	157.3	156.5	154.4	155.5	102	99	98	99
USER-OPERATED TRANSPORTATION	125.5	261.8	267.5	266.2	263.0	264.7	102	99	98	99
TRANSPORTATION AIR POLLUTION			(THOUSANDS OF TONS)							
SULFUR OXIDES	9.7	18.4	18.8	18.6	18.4	18.6	102	99	98	99
PARTICULATE MATTER	6.3	12.4	12.7	12.6	12.5	12.5	102	100	98	99
CARBON MONOXIDE	1029.5	2121.8	2165.3	2155.6	2131.2	2144.4	102	100	98	99
HYDROCARBONS	181.7	373.6	381.1	379.3	375.1	377.4	102	100	98	99
NITROGEN OXIDES	110.8	222.5	227.7	227.2	224.4	225.5	102	100	99	99
OTHER AIR POLLUTION										
SULFUR OXIDES	219.1	455.6	498.6	455.0	419.9	472.6	109	91	84	95
PARTICULATE MATTER	180.1	419.3	432.9	417.6	404.9	424.9	103	96	94	98
CARBON MONOXIDE	295.6	670.3	670.8	661.4	654.3	668.3	100	99	98	100
HYDROCARBONS	109.7	195.4	254.2	285.9	278.7	210.7	130	112	110	83
NITROGEN OXIDES	78.9	140.1	150.6	139.3	130.5	144.1	107	93	87	96
WATER OXYGEN DEMAND	936.6	1901.1	1906.4	1900.5	1896.7	1905.0	100	100	99	100
LAND SOLID WASTE	1293.4	1811.1	1836.3	1820.3	1792.3	1826.1	101	99	98	99

SUMMARY PROJECTIONS BY ORE ECONOMIC AREA UNDER FIVE ALTERNATIVE HIGHWAY SYSTEMS

158   EUGENE, ORE.

	1970	1990 BASE YEAR	1990 COMPLETED INTERSTATE	1990 EXTENDED PRIMARY	1990 ECONOMIC DEVELOPMENT	1990 URBAN	CI/BY	EP/CI	ED/CI	U/CI
JOBS BY INDUSTRY		(THOUSANDS)						P E R C E N T		
NATURAL RESOURCES (1-10)	14.4	4.9	4.8	5.3	5.0	4.7	98	110	104	99
CONSTRUCTION (11,12)	5.7	2.7	2.6	3.2	1.9	1.6	97	122	72	60
MANUFACTURING (13-74)	47.7	62.1	60.4	62.6	60.6	59.3	97	104	100	98
TRANSPORTATION INDUSTRY (75)	6.3	5.6	5.6	5.8	5.6	5.5	99	104	100	99
PUBLIC UTILITIES (76-80)	3.5	.8	.7	1.7	.8	.7	91	248	113	97
TRADE (81,86,89-99)	41.5	39.9	39.3	42.1	39.5	38.5	98	107	101	98
SERVICES (82-85,87,88,102)	32.5	83.3	82.5	82.6	82.2	81.8	99	100	100	99
STATE & LOCAL GOVT. (101)	27.5	32.5	32.1	32.8	32.1	31.8	99	100	100	99
FEDERAL GOVERNMENT (100,103)	6.8	5.4	5.3	5.5	5.3	5.2	98	103	100	98
TOTAL JOBS	186.0	237.2	233.3	241.6	233.0	229.2	98	104	100	98
CIVILIAN PERSONS EMPLOYED	193.5	245.0	241.3	249.3	241.1	237.3	98	103	100	98
CIVILIAN UNEMPLOYMENT RATE	5.6	8.1	9.0	9.1	8.4	9.2				
POPULATION	541.3	802.4	797.3	811.4	788.2	783.0	99	102	99	98
PER CAPITA INCOME	3100.9	4296.1	4238.1	4331.4	4275.3	4228.2	99	102	101	100
ENERGY USER SECTOR		(TRILLIONS OF BTU'S)								
NATURAL RESOURCES	7.6	7.5	6.9	9.1	8.0	6.7	92	132	116	96
CONSTRUCTION	9.9	15.6	15.8	23.2	9.7	6.7	101	147	61	43
MANUFACTURING	24.9	47.5	46.6	47.9	46.9	46.3	98	103	101	99
TRANSPORTATION INDUSTRY	6.1	10.3	10.1	11.0	10.2	9.8	98	109	101	98
PUBLIC UTILITIES	32.7	20.4	20.1	54.9	27.3	19.7	98	273	136	99
TRADE AND SERVICES	18.7	40.7	40.2	42.3	40.4	39.7	99	105	100	99
GOVERNMENT, EXC. TRANSPORTATION	2.1	3.5	3.4	3.5	3.4	3.4	99	102	100	99
CONSUMERS, EXC. TRANSPORTATION	21.5	40.5	40.1	41.1	40.1	39.7	99	102	100	99
USER-OPERATED TRANSPORTATION	42.9	85.7	84.8	86.6	84.8	83.9	99	102	100	99
TRANSPORTATION AIR POLLUTION		(THOUSANDS OF TONS)								
SULFUR OXIDES	2.0	3.2	3.2	3.3	3.2	3.1	98	106	101	98
PARTICULATE MATTER	1.6	2.8	2.7	2.9	2.8	2.7	99	104	101	99
CARBON MONOXIDE	339.0	653.9	647.1	662.7	647.7	640.2	99	102	102	99
HYDROCARBONS	59.5	113.7	112.5	115.2	112.6	111.3	99	102	100	99
NITROGEN OXIDES	32.8	58.9	58.3	60.2	58.5	57.6	99	103	100	99
OTHER AIR POLLUTION										
SULFUR OXIDES	64.0	44.8	44.3	101.6	56.2	43.5	99	230	127	98
PARTICULATE MATTER	48.5	45.1	41.8	66.9	50.9	40.0	93	160	122	96
CARBON MONOXIDE	85.5	94.2	85.3	127.2	105.2	80.1	91	149	123	94
HYDROCARBONS	18.0	25.3	20.4	30.2	23.7	18.4	80	148	116	90
NITROGEN OXIDES	21.6	15.5	15.1	30.6	18.7	14.7	97	203	124	97
WATER OXYGEN DEMAND	359.7	705.4	702.6	718.3	710.2	700.5	100	102	101	100
LAND SOLID WASTE	427.6	633.9	629.9	641.0	622.7	618.6	99	102	99	98

SUMMARY PROJECTIONS BY ORE ECONOMIC AREA UNDER FIVE ALTERNATIVE HIGHWAY SYSTEMS

159   BOISE CITY, IDAHO

	1970	1990 BASE YEAR	1990 COMPLETED INTERSTATE	1990 EXTENDED PRIMARY	1990 ECONOMIC DEVELOPMENT	1990 URBAN	PERCENT CI/BY	EP/CI	ED/CI	U/CI
JOBS BY INDUSTRY		(THOUSANDS)								
NATURAL RESOURCES (1-10)	12.2	9.0	9.0	9.0	9.4	9.0	100	100	104	100
CONSTRUCTION (11,12)	5.7	2.6	2.4	2.0	2.7	2.1	92	87	116	91
MANUFACTURING (13-74)	14.3	20.5	20.2	19.3	25.1	19.8	92	95	124	98
TRANSPORTATION INDUSTRY (75)	3.0	4.8	4.7	4.7	5.1	4.7	99	99	107	99
PUBLIC UTILITIES (76-80)	2.7	1.6	1.4	1.4	3.0	1.4	92	101	210	100
TRADE (81,86,89-99)	27.4	35.6	35.0	34.2	41.8	34.5	98	98	119	99
SERVICES (82-85,87,88,102)	22.2	41.3	41.4	41.1	41.8	41.3	100	100	101	100
STATE & LOCAL GOVT. (101)	14.7	19.0	18.8	18.5	20.4	18.7	99	98	108	99
FEDERAL GOVERNMENT (100,103)	8.5	8.9	8.9	8.8	9.2	8.9	100	99	104	100
TOTAL JOBS	110.6	143.2	141.8	139.1	158.5	140.5	99	98	112	99
CIVILIAN PERSONS EMPLOYED	96.1	126.0	124.7	122.4	139.8	123.5	99	98	112	99
CIVILIAN UNEMPLOYMENT RATE	4.9	3.5	3.3	3.2	2.6	3.2				
POPULATION	265.5	321.7	315.6	311.2	336.5	316.3	98	99	107	100
PER CAPITA INCOME	3130.4	5685.2	5711.9	5585.6	5279.9	5625.4	100	98	110	98
ENERGY USER SECTOR		(TRILLIONS OF BTU'S)								
NATURAL RESOURCES	11.4	8.1	8.0	8.0	8.3	8.0	99	100	104	100
CONSTRUCTION	5.0	9.0	8.9	7.7	12.9	7.9	98	87	145	89
MANUFACTURING	7.4	12.8	12.8	12.3	16.9	12.1	100	97	132	95
TRANSPORTATION INDUSTRY	3.7	6.8	6.6	6.4	8.1	6.5	98	97	122	98
PUBLIC UTILITIES	21.2	14.6	14.3	14.4	43.7	14.1	98	101	305	98
TRADE AND SERVICES	9.2	19.3	18.9	18.5	22.1	18.7	98	98	117	98
GOVERNMENT, EXC. TRANSPORTATION	.8	1.3	1.3	1.3	1.5	1.3	99	97	113	99
CONSUMERS, EXC. TRANSPORTATION	16.1	32.1	31.8	31.3	34.5	31.6	99	98	108	99
USER-OPERATED TRANSPORTATION	24.0	50.4	50.1	49.2	54.1	49.7	99	98	108	99
TRANSPORTATION AIR POLLUTION		(THOUSANDS OF TONS)								
SULFUR OXIDES	1.7	2.2	2.1	2.1	2.4	2.1	98	98	114	99
PARTICULATE MATTER	1.3	1.8	1.8	1.8	1.9	1.7	99	98	110	99
CARBON MONOXIDE	220.3	387.6	385.0	379.1	415.4	382.6	99	98	108	99
HYDROCARBONS	39.8	67.8	67.3	66.3	72.5	66.9	99	98	108	99
NITROGEN OXIDES	24.7	36.4	36.2	35.7	39.3	36.0	99	99	109	99
OTHER AIR POLLUTION										
SULFUR OXIDES	39.8	44.3	43.6	42.0	93.9	42.9	98	96	215	98
PARTICULATE MATTER	30.8	37.5	37.1	36.4	53.2	37.0	99	98	143	100
CARBON MONOXIDE	82.0	99.9	100.8	100.4	102.7	100.9	101	100	102	100
HYDROCARBONS	31.7	50.6	52.4	49.4	82.6	43.8	103	94	158	84
NITROGEN OXIDES	14.7	26.6	26.3	25.0	39.9	26.0	99	95	152	99
WATER OXYGEN DEMAND	704.6	1202.4	1198.5	1198.0	1197.9	1198.5	100	101	100	100
LAND SOLID WASTE	209.7	254.2	249.3	245.9	265.8	249.9	98	95	107	100

160   RENO, NEV.

	1970	1990 BASE YEAR	1990 COMPLETED INTERSTATE	1990 EXTENDED PRIMARY	1990 ECONOMIC DEVELOPMENT	1990 URBAN	PERCENT CI/BY	PERCENT EP/CI	PERCENT ED/CI	PERCENT U/CI
JOBS BY INDUSTRY			(THOUSANDS)							
NATURAL RESOURCES (1-10)	6.4	1.2	2.9	4.3	2.1	2.7	247	151	73	94
CONSTRUCTION (11,12)	4.3	1.8	1.7	2.8	1.5	1.5	97	162	85	90
MANUFACTURING (13-74)	4.0	5.0	5.8	8.3	5.8	5.4	117	144	100	94
TRANSPORTATION INDUSTRY (75)	3.3	1.6	1.7	2.1	1.7	1.7	109	124	97	98
PUBLIC UTILITIES (76-80)	3.0	1.3	1.5	3.0	1.6	1.4	113	203	105	96
TRADE (81,86,89-99)	18.5	19.2	21.3	26.4	20.8	20.9	111	124	98	98
SERVICES (82-85,87,88,102)	30.3	80.0	80.0	80.1	80.0	80.0	100	101	100	100
STATE & LOCAL GOVT. (101)	69.3	92.5	92.8	93.8	92.6	92.7	100	101	100	100
FEDERAL GOVERNMENT (100,103)	6.1	7.7	7.7	8.0	7.7	7.7	101	103	100	100
TOTAL JOBS	145.3	209.1	214.3	227.6	212.6	212.2	102	106	99	99
CIVILIAN PERSONS EMPLOYED	79.4	128.0	130.3	138.2	130.0	129.4	102	106	100	99
CIVILIAN UNEMPLOYMENT RATE	8.6	9.9	9.8	8.6	9.0	9.3				
POPULATION	206.7	302.0	310.3	321.4	305.1	304.0	103	104	98	98
PER CAPITA INCOME	5160.5	9419.2	9327.2	9608.6	9387.3	9442.3	99	103	101	101
ENERGY USER SECTOR			(TRILLIONS OF BTU'S)							
NATURAL RESOURCES	5.0	6.5	9.7	12.8	8.7	9.3	150	132	90	96
CONSTRUCTION	5.9	7.5	8.7	27.4	7.6	7.6	116	314	87	87
MANUFACTURING	3.1	5.2	5.6	6.9	5.5	5.4	108	124	99	97
TRANSPORTATION INDUSTRY	5.0	5.0	5.6	7.0	5.5	5.5	112	124	98	98
PUBLIC UTILITIES	26.0	16.1	21.9	66.5	24.1	21.4	136	303	110	98
TRADE AND SERVICES	11.1	20.4	21.4	23.9	21.2	21.2	105	112	99	99
GOVERNMENT, EXC. TRANSPORTATION	1.9	1.9	1.9	2.1	1.9	1.9	102	106	99	99
CONSUMERS, EXC. TRANSPORTATION	14.6	31.2	31.6	33.3	31.4	31.4	101	105	99	99
USER-OPERATED TRANSPORTATION	26.9	63.6	64.3	66.9	64.0	64.0	101	104	99	99
TRANSPORTATION AIR POLLUTION			(THOUSANDS OF TONS)							
SULFUR OXIDES	1.0	1.9	2.1	2.4	2.0	2.1	107	113	98	99
PARTICULATE MATTER	0.9	1.9	2.1	2.1	1.9	1.9	104	108	99	99
CARBON MONOXIDE	201.3	467.5	475.0	496.3	471.6	472.4	102	104	99	99
HYDROCARBONS	35.1	81.4	82.7	86.4	82.1	82.3	102	104	99	99
NITROGEN OXIDES	18.3	41.4	42.5	45.1	42.2	42.3	103	106	99	99
OTHER AIR POLLUTION										
SULFUR OXIDES	73.6	93.4	103.0	176.2	106.6	102.2	110	171	103	99
PARTICULATE MATTER	31.5	25.9	28.9	45.9	29.4	28.6	111	159	102	99
CARBON MONOXIDE	17.1	25.8	30.5	36.3	29.3	29.6	118	119	96	97
HYDROCARBONS	6.4	9.5	12.4	19.1	12.5	11.4	131	154	101	92
NITROGEN OXIDES	18.9	13.2	15.8	33.9	16.6	15.5	120	215	105	98
WATER OXYGEN DEMAND	383.8	753.5	772.9	785.7	767.5	771.8	103	102	99	100
LAND SOLID WASTE	163.3	238.6	245.1	253.9	241.0	240.2	103	104	98	98

SUMMARY PROJECTIONS BY OBE ECONOMIC AREA UNDER FIVE ALTERNATIVE HIGHWAY SYSTEMS

161   LAS VEGAS, NEV.

	1970	1990 BASE YEAR	1990 COMPLETED INTERSTATE	1990 EXTENDED PRIMARY	1990 ECONOMIC DEVELOPMENT	1990 URBAN	P E R C E N T CI/BY	EP/CI	ED/CI	U/CI
JOBS BY INDUSTRY		(THOUSANDS)								
NATURAL RESOURCES (1-10)	3.4	1.2	1.3	1.3	.9	1.0	94	116	83	90
CONSTRUCTION (11-12)	16.0	5.9	5.3	5.4	4.5	4.8	90	102	85	90
MANUFACTURING (13-74)	5.4	6.9	6.2	7.2	4.7	5.9	90	116	77	95
TRANSPORTATION INDUSTRY (75)	4.3	.9	.9	.9	.8	.9	96	105	92	98
PUBLIC UTILITIES (76-80)	3.4	1.7	1.2	1.6	.8	1.1	68	132	64	90
TRADE (81,86,89-99)	25.6	25.9	24.9	26.1	23.3	24.4	96	105	93	98
SERVICES (82-85,87,88,102)	54.7	70.7	70.3	70.3	70.3	70.3	99	100	100	100
STATE & LOCAL GOVT. (101)	27.3	32.7	32.4	32.5	32.0	32.3	99	100	99	100
FEDERAL GOVERNMENT (100,103)	12.8	12.6	12.6	12.6	12.5	12.5	99	100	99	100
TOTAL JOBS	152.7	158.6	154.9	157.9	149.7	153.1	98	102	97	99
CIVILIAN PERSONS EMPLOYED	112.7	121.7	118.8	121.3	114.9	117.3	98	102	97	99
CIVILIAN UNEMPLOYMENT RATE	6.1	7.8	7.6	8.0	7.2	7.9	97	102	96	98
POPULATION	317.3	373.4	363.5	369.6	349.1	357.4	97	102	96	98
PER CAPITA INCOME	3858.0	5522.0	5523.4	5525.8	5516.6	5559.4	100	100	100	101
ENERGY USER SECTOR		(TRILLIONS OF BTU'S)								
NATURAL RESOURCES	3.3	6.1	5.9	6.6	5.3	5.5	97	112	91	93
CONSTRUCTION	14.4	23.8	23.6	33.2	19.9	20.2	99	141	84	86
MANUFACTURING	6.4	12.2	11.7	12.5	10.3	11.5	96	107	88	98
TRANSPORTATION INDUSTRY	5.9	8.8	8.4	8.8	7.8	8.2	95	105	92	98
PUBLIC UTILITIES	16.0	57.7	40.5	43.2	20.4	34.9	70	107	50	86
TRADE AND SERVICES	20.7	34.1	33.0	33.3	31.6	32.7	97	101	96	99
GOVERNMENT, EXC. TRANSPORTATION	1.5	2.3	2.3	2.3	2.3	2.3	99	101	98	99
CONSUMERS, EXC. TRANSPORTATION	16.3	29.3	28.8	29.1	28.2	28.6	98	101	98	99
USER-OPERATED TRANSPORTATION	31.3	57.6	56.8	57.3	55.8	56.5	99	101	98	99
TRANSPORTATION AIR POLLUTION		(THOUSANDS OF TONS)								
SULFUR OXIDES	1.5	2.5	2.4	2.5	2.2	2.3	96	103	94	98
PARTICULATE MATTER	1.1	2.0	2.0	2.0	1.8	1.9	98	102	96	99
CARBON MONOXIDE	233.1	428.8	423.0	427.7	414.2	420.6	99	101	98	99
HYDROCARBONS	40.5	74.6	73.6	74.4	72.0	73.1	99	101	98	99
NITROGEN OXIDES	22.0	39.7	39.1	39.8	38.0	38.8	98	102	97	99
OTHER AIR POLLUTION										
SULFUR OXIDES	55.0	126.6	98.3	102.1	65.0	89.0	78	104	66	91
PARTICULATE MATTER	48.5	115.7	108.8	116.8	95.1	106.1	94	107	87	98
CARBON MONOXIDE	57.5	238.8	241.3	244.3	238.7	240.4	101	101	99	100
HYDROCARBONS	22.6	75.0	75.0	77.4	74.0	74.3	100	103	99	99
NITROGEN OXIDES	25.0	45.7	39.0	40.2	30.9	36.6	85	103	79	94
WATER OXYGEN DEMAND	179.7	448.0	446.8	453.4	439.4	446.5	100	101	98	100
LAND SOLID WASTE	250.7	295.0	287.1	292.0	275.8	282.3	97	102	96	98

SUMMARY PROJECTIONS BY ORE ECONOMIC AREA UNDER FIVE ALTERNATIVE HIGHWAY SYSTEMS

162 PHOENIX, ARIZ.

	1970	1990 BASE YEAR	1990 COMPLETED INTERSTATE	1990 EXTENDED PRIMARY	1990 ECONOMIC DEVELOPMENT	1990 URBAN	CI/BY	EP/CI	ED/CI	U/CI
JOBS BY INDUSTRY			(THOUSANDS)							
NATURAL RESOURCES (1-10)	30.8	24.9	25.0	24.9	25.4	24.9	101	99	101	99
CONSTRUCTION (11,12)	30.2	29.1	29.9	30.0	28.2	29.8	103	100	94	100
MANUFACTURING (13-74)	84.2	109.4	183.1	192.5	187.8	175.6	167	105	103	96
TRANSPORTATION INDUSTRY (75)	10.8	18.5	20.9	21.3	20.9	20.6	113	102	100	99
PUBLIC UTILITIES (76-80)	11.1	10.2	12.8	13.8	11.6	11.5	125	109	91	90
TRADE (81,86,89-99)	113.9	146.4	187.6	194.1	188.7	182.7	128	103	101	97
SERVICES (82-85,87,88,102)	114.0	281.3	285.8	285.8	285.7	285.5	102	100	100	100
STATE & LOCAL GOVT. (101)	64.9	89.9	104.0	105.6	104.3	102.4	116	102	100	99
FEDERAL GOVERNMENT (100,103)	31.6	35.2	38.3	38.7	38.4	38.0	109	101	100	99
TOTAL JOBS	491.4	744.8	887.2	906.7	891.0	871.0	119	102	100	98
CIVILIAN PERSONS EMPLOYED	449.2	687.7	820.1	838.5	824.0	804.8	119	102	100	98
CIVILIAN UNEMPLOYMENT RATE	5.2	.6	1.3	1.0	1.0	1.4				
POPULATION	1316.4	1684.3	2058.7	2080.7	2038.2	2039.6	122	101	99	99
PER CAPITA INCOME	3598.9	6538.2	6645.9	6739.1	6730.7	6570.1	102	101	101	99
ENERGY USER SECTOR			(TRILLIONS OF BTU'S)							
NATURAL RESOURCES	37.7	40.1	39.8	39.3	39.9	39.6	99	99	100	99
CONSTRUCTION	41.5	70.7	77.9	97.0	74.2	68.1	110	125	95	87
MANUFACTURING	34.6	56.7	77.0	79.5	77.9	75.2	136	103	101	98
TRANSPORTATION INDUSTRY	14.3	31.0	42.5	44.1	42.8	41.2	137	104	101	97
PUBLIC UTILITIES	94.7	337.4	385.6	393.4	373.1	365.6	114	102	97	95
TRADE AND SERVICES	54.4	129.2	149.8	152.7	149.8	147.0	116	102	100	98
GOVERNMENT, EXC. TRANSPORTATION	5.3	9.5	11.1	11.2	11.1	10.9	116	100	100	98
CONSUMERS, EXC. TRANSPORTATION	68.4	148.2	170.9	173.8	171.2	168.5	115	102	100	99
USER-OPERATED TRANSPORTATION	108.0	235.3	270.6	274.9	271.0	266.9	115	102	100	99
TRANSPORTATION AIR POLLUTION			(THOUSANDS OF TONS)							
SULFUR OXIDES	6.2	9.5	11.8	12.1	11.8	11.6	125	102	100	98
PARTICULATE MATTER	4.8	7.8	9.3	9.5	9.3	9.2	120	102	100	98
CARBON MONOXIDE	908.1	1748.2	2008.8	2041.4	2011.7	1981.3	115	102	100	99
HYDROCARBONS	162.1	304.6	349.5	355.1	350.0	344.8	115	102	100	99
NITROGEN OXIDES	95.5	161.2	187.4	191.1	187.9	184.6	116	102	100	99
OTHER AIR POLLUTION										
SULFUR OXIDES	541.9	1694.6	1773.7	1786.4	1753.3	1741.0	105	101	99	98
PARTICULATE MATTER	236.7	362.4	378.2	381.2	373.5	371.4	104	101	99	98
CARBON MONOXIDE	455.7	275.0	275.2	275.7	275.4	275.8	100	100	100	100
HYDROCARBONS	117.1	90.9	98.6	103.0	100.0	96.5	108	104	101	98
NITROGEN OXIDES	104.1	292.0	311.8	314.9	306.7	303.7	107	101	98	97
WATER OXYGEN DEMAND	1461.1	2224.4	2228.6	2228.7	2228.2	2227.8	100	100	100	100
LAND SOLID WASTE	1040.0	1330.6	1626.3	1643.8	1610.2	1611.3	122	101	99	99

SUMMARY PROJECTIONS BY OBE ECONOMIC AREA UNDER FIVE ALTERNATIVE HIGHWAY SYSTEMS

163   TUCSON, ARIZONA

	1970	1990 BASE YEAR	1990 COMPLETED INTERSTATE	1990 EXTENDED PRIMARY	1990 ECONOMIC DEVELOPMENT	1990 URBAN	P E R C E N T			
							CI/BY	EP/CI	ED/CI	U/CI
JOBS BY INDUSTRY										
NATURAL RESOURCES (1-10)	18.1	15.5	15.0	15.1	15.4	14.9	97	101	103	99
CONSTRUCTION (11,12)	11.6	11.5	11.7	11.8	11.0	11.6	101	101	94	100
MANUFACTURING (13-74)	10.0	8.9	7.8	9.0	7.4	7.0	88	115	95	90
TRANSPORTATION INDUSTRY (75)	3.5	5.6	5.6	5.6	5.5	5.5	98	101	99	99
PUBLIC UTILITIES (76-80)	3.2	.6	.5	.6	.5	.5	84	113	93	86
TRADE (81,86,89-99)	35.9	46.3	45.2	46.3	44.9	44.4	98	102	99	98
SERVICES (82-85,87,88,102)	35.3	68.5	68.4	68.5	68.3	68.4	100	100	100	100
STATE & LOCAL GOVT. (101)	24.6	29.3	28.8	29.2	28.7	28.6	98	102	100	99
FEDERAL GOVERNMENT (100,103)	24.8	25.0	24.9	25.0	24.9	24.8	100	100	100	100
TOTAL JOBS	167.0	211.3	207.8	211.0	206.6	205.6	98	102	99	99
CIVILIAN PERSONS EMPLOYED	137.1	178.5	175.3	178.3	174.3	173.3	98	102	99	99
CIVILIAN UNEMPLOYMENT RATE	6.3	6.5	7.1	6.3	6.2	7.1				
POPULATION	454.5	623.8	615.3	618.1	607.1	609.9	99	100	99	99
PER CAPITA INCOME	3311.1	4299.2	4209.3	4319.0	4229.2	4185.8	98	103	100	99
ENERGY USER SECTOR		(TRILLIONS OF BTU'S)								
NATURAL RESOURCES	12.4	22.2	21.0	21.0	20.8	20.7	95	100	99	99
CONSTRUCTION	11.4	22.9	22.9	29.2	20.4	17.4	100	128	89	76
MANUFACTURING	6.1	8.6	7.8	8.5	6.9	6.9	88	112	95	91
TRANSPORTATION INDUSTRY	3.0	5.8	5.5	5.8	5.4	5.3	94	105	98	96
PUBLIC UTILITIES	37.0	23.1	22.8	23.0	23.2	22.3	99	101	102	98
TRADE AND SERVICES	15.2	32.4	31.8	32.3	31.6	31.5	98	102	99	99
GOVERNMENT, EXC. TRANSPORTATION	1.6	2.5	2.5	2.5	2.5	2.4	98	102	100	99
CONSUMERS, EXC. TRANSPORTATION	17.8	33.1	32.4	32.9	32.3	32.1	98	102	100	99
USER-OPERATED TRANSPORTATION	33.4	62.2	61.0	62.1	60.7	60.5	98	102	100	99
TRANSPORTATION AIR POLLUTION		(THOUSANDS OF TONS)								
SULFUR OXIDES	1.2	2.0	1.9	1.9	1.9	1.8	96	103	99	98
PARTICULATE MATTER	1.1	1.8	1.8	1.8	1.7	1.7	97	102	99	99
CARBON MONOXIDE	249.5	446.7	438.2	445.9	436.0	434.4	98	102	100	99
HYDROCARBONS	43.7	77.5	76.1	77.4	75.7	75.4	98	102	100	99
NITROGEN OXIDES	23.1	39.4	38.6	39.4	38.4	38.2	98	102	100	99
OTHER AIR POLLUTION										
SULFUR OXIDES	222.9	290.9	289.9	290.4	290.2	289.0	100	100	100	100
PARTICULATE MATTER	56.2	73.7	72.9	74.2	72.3	72.3	99	102	99	99
CARBON MONOXIDE	34.5	61.1	61.3	64.1	60.5	60.9	100	105	99	99
HYDROCARBONS	17.8	45.0	34.3	45.0	30.8	27.5	76	131	90	80
NITROGEN OXIDES	31.7	62.4	61.9	62.3	61.7	61.5	99	101	100	99
WATER OXYGEN DEMAND	257.6	433.3	433.2	433.1	433.2	433.3	100	100	100	100
LAND SOLID WASTE	359.0	492.8	486.1	488.3	479.6	481.8	99	100	99	99

SUMMARY PROJECTIONS BY ORE ECONOMIC AREA UNDER FIVE ALTERNATIVE HIGHWAY SYSTEMS

164   SAN DIEGO. CALIF.

	1970	1990 BASE YEAR	1990 COMPLETED INTERSTATE	1990 EXTENDED PRIMARY	1990 ECONOMIC DEVELOPMENT	1990 URBAN	CI/BY	P E R C E N T EP/CI	ED/CI	U/CI
JOBS BY INDUSTRY			(THOUSANDS)							
NATURAL RESOURCES (1-10)	13.9	5.5	5.5	4.3	4.3	5.3	100	78	78	97
CONSTRUCTION (11,12)	23.0	9.2	8.6	6.6	6.5	7.0	93	77	75	81
MANUFACTURING (13-74)	74.6	127.2	136.3	124.9	126.8	131.9	107	92	93	98
TRANSPORTATION INDUSTRY (75)	9.1	15.8	16.1	15.3	15.4	15.8	102	95	95	98
PUBLIC UTILITIES (76-80)	11.1	19.1	19.3	11.7	12.5	17.3	101	60	65	90
TRADE (81,86,89-99)	103.2	153.5	159.1	145.4	147.3	153.6	104	91	93	97
SERVICES (82-85,87,88,102)	104.5	176.4	176.8	176.0	176.2	176.6	100	100	100	100
STATE & LOCAL GOVT. (101)	61.3	77.0	78.8	75.0	75.6	77.2	100	95	96	98
FEDERAL GOVERNMENT (100,103)	105.9	107.6	108.0	107.2	107.3	107.7	100	99	99	100
TOTAL JOBS	506.6	691.4	708.5	666.2	671.8	692.3	102	94	95	98
CIVILIAN PERSONS EMPLOYED	384.8	554.8	569.6	532.6	537.7	555.0	103	93	94	97
CIVILIAN UNEMPLOYMENT RATE	7.0	8.1	7.5	7.3	7.6	7.5				
POPULATION	1357.9	2081.2	2142.2	2018.4	2034.8	2103.5	103	94	95	98
PER CAPITA INCOME	3647.1	5173.7	5166.9	5132.4	5134.5	5128.4	100	99	99	99
ENERGY USER SECTOR			(TRILLIONS OF BTU'S)							
NATURAL RESOURCES	12.2	6.7	6.6	6.3	6.3	6.4	100	95	96	97
CONSTRUCTION	36.2	56.2	57.5	40.6	41.7	43.0	102	71	73	75
MANUFACTURING	22.1	49.2	52.2	46.9	47.8	49.1	106	90	92	94
TRANSPORTATION INDUSTRY	14.6	32.0	33.7	29.8	30.1	32.2	105	89	90	96
PUBLIC UTILITIES	20.3	68.9	76.8	26.1	30.1	60.7	112	34	39	79
TRADE AND SERVICES	43.8	102.2	104.7	95.3	96.5	101.6	102	91	92	97
GOVERNMENT. EXC. TRANSPORTATION	11.6	17.4	17.6	17.2	17.3	17.4	101	98	98	99
CONSUMERS. EXC. TRANSPORTATION	66.2	132.9	135.5	129.5	130.3	133.1	102	96	96	98
USER-OPERATED TRANSPORTATION	100.9	199.8	203.8	194.5	195.6	200.1	102	95	96	98
TRANSPORTATION AIR POLLUTION			(THOUSANDS OF TONS)							
SULFUR OXIDES	4.0	8.0	8.3	7.5	7.6	8.0	104	91	92	97
PARTICULATE MATTER	3.1	6.1	6.3	5.9	5.9	6.1	103	93	94	97
CARBON MONOXIDE	639.3	1305.9	1335.9	1266.0	1274.7	1308.3	102	95	95	98
HYDROCARBONS	111.4	226.3	231.4	219.3	220.8	226.6	102	95	95	98
NITROGEN OXIDES	60.5	120.2	123.6	116.6	117.4	120.8	103	94	95	98
OTHER AIR POLLUTION										
SULFUR OXIDES	80.1	156.2	169.4	86.6	92.6	143.5	108	51	55	85
PARTICULATE MATTER	116.8	99.5	102.1	81.6	83.2	96.1	103	80	82	94
CARBON MONOXIDE	215.4	124.2	122.6	121.0	121.5	121.4	99	99	99	99
HYDROCARBONS	55.1	72.5	77.0	55.7	60.5	49.7	106	72	79	64
NITROGEN OXIDES	54.2	72.7	75.9	54.8	56.4	69.3	104	72	74	91
WATER OXYGEN DEMAND	272.0	167.0	167.4	164.3	164.7	166.6	100	98	98	100
LAND SOLID WASTE	1072.7	1644.1	1692.3	1594.5	1607.5	1661.8	103	94	95	98

SUMMARY PROJECTIONS BY OBE ECONOMIC AREA UNDER FIVE ALTERNATIVE HIGHWAY SYSTEMS

165   L. A.--LONG BEACH, CALIF.

	1970	1990 BASE YEAR	1990 COMPLETED INTERSTATE	1990 EXTENDED PRIMARY	1990 ECONOMIC DEVELOPMENT	1990 URBAN	CI/BY	EP/CI	ED/CI	U/CI
								P E R C E N T		
JOBS BY INDUSTRY				(THOUSANDS)						
NATURAL RESOURCES (1-10)	79.4	46.0	45.5	44.3	44.4	45.8	99	97	98	101
CONSTRUCTION (11,12)	184.7	195.2	196.2	190.5	185.2	196.9	100	97	94	100
MANUFACTURING (13-74)	1068.1	1454.0	1405.3	1379.4	1385.5	1425.2	97	98	99	101
TRANSPORTATION INDUSTRY (75)	130.8	197.5	196.1	194.9	195.1	196.7	99	99	99	100
PUBLIC UTILITIES (76-80)	98.2	123.0	117.9	107.2	109.6	119.6	96	91	93	101
TRADE (81,86,89-99)	1003.5	1132.1	1104.8	1084.0	1086.5	1114.9	98	98	98	101
SERVICES (82-85,87,88,102)	1024.9	1711.2	1707.7	1706.6	1706.9	1708.5	100	100	100	100
STATE & LOCAL GOVT. (101)	496.6	627.4	618.4	611.2	611.7	622.1	99	99	99	101
FEDERAL GOVERNMENT (100,103)	172.1	183.2	181.2	179.6	179.7	182.0	99	99	99	101
TOTAL JOBS	4257.8	5669.7	5573.1	5497.7	5504.9	5611.7	98	99	99	99
CIVILIAN PERSONS EMPLOYED	4150.2	5528.1	5435.5	5363.9	5371.3	5472.2	98	99	99	99
CIVILIAN UNEMPLOYMENT RATE	5.6	7.0	7.3	7.2	7.0	7.2				
POPULATION	10436.1	15656.1	15516.2	15358.1	15314.1	15540.2	99	99	99	100
PER CAPITA INCOME	4392.4	6392.6	6345.3	6324.1	6347.9	6375.4	99	100	100	100
ENERGY USER SECTOR			(TRILLIONS OF BTU'S)							
NATURAL RESOURCES	91.0	74.9	73.2	68.4	68.4	75.3	98	94	93	103
CONSTRUCTION	273.9	414.4	410.8	382.6	375.1	429.0	99	93	91	104
MANUFACTURING	467.7	929.1	919.4	899.0	902.0	932.9	99	98	98	101
TRANSPORTATION INDUSTRY	227.4	388.8	381.1	375.5	376.4	383.8	98	99	99	101
PUBLIC UTILITIES	360.1	1286.5	1219.3	1109.4	1126.3	1237.0	95	91	92	101
TRADE AND SERVICES	546.6	970.2	954.6	942.1	943.8	959.6	98	99	99	100
GOVERNMENT, EXC. TRANSPORTATION	85.7	132.0	131.0	130.3	130.3	131.4	99	99	99	100
CONSUMERS, EXC. TRANSPORTATION	487.6	1024.7	1010.7	999.7	1000.3	1015.9	99	99	99	101
USER-OPERATED TRANSPORTATION	911.6	1842.0	1820.2	1802.7	1803.9	1828.3	99	99	99	100
TRANSPORTATION AIR POLLUTION			(THOUSANDS OF TONS)							
SULFUR OXIDES	53.7	90.8	88.2	87.3	87.6	89.3	98	98	99	101
PARTICULATE MATTER	35.6	64.2	63.2	62.6	62.6	63.6	99	99	99	101
CARBON MONOXIDE	6282.4	12669.0	12509.7	12383.7	12391.7	12569.3	99	99	99	100
HYDROCARBONS	1095.6	2194.9	2166.9	2144.6	2146.2	2177.2	99	99	99	100
NITROGEN OXIDES	633.3	1199.9	1186.9	1177.5	1176.9	1192.9	99	99	99	101
OTHER AIR POLLUTION										
SULFUR OXIDES	1192.6	2774.9	2664.1	2481.6	2509.4	2694.0	96	93	94	101
PARTICULATE MATTER	1237.9	1681.5	1658.7	1607.4	1613.4	1671.8	99	97	97	101
CARBON MONOXIDE	2017.9	1966.5	1981.0	1977.0	1976.1	1989.6	101	100	100	100
HYDROCARBONS	1119.9	1192.6	1214.3	1099.3	1130.9	1304.8	102	91	93	107
NITROGEN OXIDES	582.3	870.0	843.9	799.2	806.0	852.0	97	95	96	101
WATER OXYGEN DEMAND	3627.8	2532.0	2539.9	2541.8	2540.1	2538.8	100	100	100	100
LAND SOLID WASTE	8244.5	12368.2	12257.7	12132.8	12098.1	12276.7	99	99	99	100

166 FRESNO, CALIF.

	1970	1990 BASE YEAR	1990 COMPLETED INTERSTATE	1990 EXTENDED PRIMARY	1990 ECONOMIC DEVELOPMENT	1990 URBAN	PER CENT CI/BY	EP/CI	ED/CI	U/CI
JOBS BY INDUSTRY			(THOUSANDS)							
NATURAL RESOURCES (1-10)	55.2	32.5	32.3	32.7	31.5	32.0	99	101	98	99
CONSTRUCTION (11,12)	13.4	18.4	18.5	17.6	17.6	18.5	101	96	95	100
MANUFACTURING (13-74)	33.5	44.3	44.2	45.9	43.0	42.7	100	104	97	97
TRANSPORTATION INDUSTRY (75)	9.2	10.2	10.1	10.4	9.7	9.2	99	103	96	98
PUBLIC UTILITIES (76-80)	7.8	3.5	3.2	3.4	3.2	3.0	92	108	102	94
TRADE (81,86,89-99)	78.4	68.2	67.8	69.1	67.0	66.9	99	102	99	99
SERVICES (82-85,87,88,102)	58.9	107.9	106.9	106.9	106.7	106.9	99	100	100	99
STATE & LOCAL GOVT. (101)	53.8	58.8	58.6	58.9	58.1	58.2	100	100	99	100
FEDERAL GOVERNMENT (100,103)	21.2	20.3	20.3	20.4	20.2	20.2	100	100	99	100
TOTAL JOBS	331.3	364.2	361.8	365.6	357.0	358.2	99	101	99	99
CIVILIAN PERSONS EMPLOYED	318.5	349.9	347.6	351.2	343.1	344.2	99	101	99	99
CIVILIAN UNEMPLOYMENT RATE	7.6	12.6	12.6	12.1	12.4	10.7				
POPULATION	1036.7	1339.3	1334.0	1328.8	1316.2	1294.6	100	100	99	97
PER CAPITA INCOME	3276.6	4310.6	4297.6	4357.8	4284.1	4364.2	100	101	100	102
ENERGY USER SECTOR			(TRILLIONS OF BTU'S)							
NATURAL RESOURCES	85.1	47.3	47.2	47.7	47.1	47.0	100	101	100	100
CONSTRUCTION	19.5	23.8	23.7	24.2	19.6	19.7	100	102	83	83
MANUFACTURING	17.9	29.8	29.7	30.4	29.2	29.1	100	102	98	98
TRANSPORTATION INDUSTRY	9.9	10.8	10.6	11.0	10.3	10.3	99	104	97	97
PUBLIC UTILITIES	96.6	57.8	56.8	57.3	58.0	55.6	98	101	102	98
TRADE AND SERVICES	32.0	52.3	51.8	52.5	51.3	51.3	99	101	99	99
GOVERNMENT, EXC. TRANSPORTATION	11.7	16.9	16.8	16.9	16.8	16.8	100	100	100	100
CONSUMERS, EXC. TRANSPORTATION	39.3	68.2	67.8	68.3	67.0	67.1	100	101	99	99
USER-OPERATED TRANSPORTATION	84.1	142.6	142.1	142.9	140.9	141.0	100	101	99	99
TRANSPORTATION AIR POLLUTION			(THOUSANDS OF TONS)							
SULFUR OXIDES	9.0	6.1	6.1	6.1	6.0	6.0	99	101	99	99
PARTICULATE MATTER	6.3	5.1	5.0	5.1	5.0	5.0	100	101	99	99
CARBON MONOXIDE	858.8	1015.0	1011.2	1017.2	1002.6	1002.8	100	101	99	99
HYDROCARBONS	162.5	181.4	180.7	181.7	179.2	179.2	100	101	99	99
NITROGEN OXIDES	118.5	105.1	104.8	105.5	104.0	104.0	100	101	99	99
OTHER AIR POLLUTION										
SULFUR OXIDES	180.4	139.0	137.0	138.2	138.1	134.8	99	101	101	98
PARTICULATE MATTER	166.9	96.7	96.8	97.1	96.6	96.2	100	100	100	99
CARBON MONOXIDE	591.5	268.1	270.8	269.9	269.8	270.2	101	100	100	100
HYDROCARBONS	152.7	85.8	86.0	87.9	85.7	85.0	100	102	100	100
NITROGEN OXIDES	62.4	58.0	57.5	57.9	57.1	56.9	99	101	99	99
WATER OXYGEN DEMAND	1630.6	907.7	909.2	908.8	909.1	908.8	100	100	100	100
LAND SOLID WASTE	819.0	1058.0	1053.9	1049.8	1039.8	1022.7	100	100	99	97

167 STOCKTON, CALIF.

	1970	1990 BASE YEAR	1990 COMPLETED INTERSTATE	1990 EXTENDED PRIMARY	1990 ECONOMIC DEVELOPMENT	1990 URBAN	CI/BY	EP/CI	ED/CI	U/CI
JOBS BY INDUSTRY			(THOUSANDS)							
NATURAL RESOURCES (1-10)	34.6	14.6	14.6	14.6	14.6	14.6	100	100	100	100
CONSTRUCTION (11,12)	8.4	10.3	10.4	10.1	9.9	10.4	101	98	95	100
MANUFACTURING (13-74)	32.9	32.5	32.0	32.2	30.9	31.6	98	101	97	99
TRANSPORTATION INDUSTRY (75)	6.1	9.1	9.0	9.0	8.9	9.0	99	100	99	100
PUBLIC UTILITIES (76-80)	4.7	2.7	2.6	2.5	2.5	2.4	94	98	97	93
TRADE (81,86,89-99)	46.5	40.1	39.3	39.4	38.4	38.7	98	100	97	98
SERVICES (82-85,87,88,102)	36.2	67.3	66.8	66.7	66.6	66.8	99	100	100	99
STATE & LOCAL GOVT. (101)	37.1	38.0	37.8	37.8	37.5	37.7	99	100	99	100
FEDERAL GOVERNMENT (100,103)	16.5	15.7	15.7	15.6	15.6	15.6	100	100	100	100
TOTAL JOBS	223.2	230.3	227.9	228.0	224.8	226.7	99	100	99	99
CIVILIAN PERSONS EMPLOYED	233.8	244.3	242.0	242.1	239.2	240.8	99	100	99	99
CIVILIAN UNEMPLOYMENT RATE	8.0	8.5	8.6	8.3	8.1	8.5				
POPULATION	643.4	705.8	702.1	698.5	694.5	698.4	99	99	99	99
PER CAPITA INCOME	4003.9	5697.2	5674.8	5700.6	5652.4	5676.1	100	100	100	100
ENERGY USER SECTOR			(TRILLIONS OF BTU'S)							
NATURAL RESOURCES	33.2	15.9	16.0	16.0	16.0	16.0	101	100	100	100
CONSTRUCTION	12.6	18.0	17.9	17.9	16.2	16.3	99	100	90	91
MANUFACTURING	25.8	35.7	35.0	35.2	33.8	34.8	98	101	97	99
TRANSPORTATION INDUSTRY	8.7	13.5	13.2	13.2	12.9	13.1	98	100	98	99
PUBLIC UTILITIES	64.5	47.2	43.2	43.4	44.1	42.3	91	100	102	98
TRADE AND SERVICES	18.8	35.1	34.3	34.2	33.7	33.9	98	100	98	99
GOVERNMENT, EXC. TRANSPORTATION	4.0	5.6	5.6	5.6	5.5	5.6	100	100	99	99
CONSUMERS, EXC. TRANSPORTATION	18.8	26.4	26.1	26.1	25.8	26.0	99	100	99	99
USER-OPERATED TRANSPORTATION	44.5	71.5	71.0	70.9	70.2	70.7	99	100	99	99
TRANSPORTATION AIR POLLUTION			(THOUSANDS OF TONS)							
SULFUR OXIDES	4.5	4.2	4.1	4.1	4.1	4.1	98	100	98	98
PARTICULATE MATTER	3.1	3.0	3.0	3.0	3.0	3.0	99	100	99	99
CARBON MONOXIDE	452.8	558.0	554.2	554.2	548.6	552.0	99	100	99	99
HYDROCARBONS	83.7	98.7	98.0	98.0	97.1	97.6	99	100	99	99
NITROGEN OXIDES	57.6	57.8	57.5	57.6	57.0	57.3	99	100	99	99
OTHER AIR POLLUTION										
SULFUR OXIDES	119.2	123.3	116.0	116.5	115.9	114.4	94	100	100	99
PARTICULATE MATTER	123.6	203.1	199.2	199.8	187.0	197.0	98	100	94	99
CARBON MONOXIDE	251.6	279.5	288.2	284.9	290.3	287.9	103	99	101	100
HYDROCARBONS	64.4	83.7	87.1	86.8	88.2	86.4	104	99	101	99
NITROGEN OXIDES	40.8	66.4	64.9	64.9	64.3	64.4	98	100	99	98
WATER OXYGEN DEMAND	1268.8	805.8	809.0	807.3	810.4	808.4	100	100	100	100
LAND SOLID WASTE	508.3	557.6	554.7	551.8	548.6	551.7	99	99	99	99

168 SACRAMENTO, CALIF.

	1970	1990 BASE YEAR	1990 COMPLETED INTERSTATE	1990 EXTENDED PRIMARY	1990 ECONOMIC DEVELOPMENT	1990 URBAN	CI/BY	EP/CI	ED/CI	U/CI
JOBS BY INDUSTRY		*(THOUSANDS)*								
NATURAL RESOURCES (1-10)	27.5	12.1	12.0	12.1	11.8	12.0	99	100	98	100
CONSTRUCTION (11,12)	13.7	4.2	3.8	3.5	2.9	3.0	90	93	75	80
MANUFACTURING (13-74)	25.7	31.6	29.0	29.3	25.1	27.5	92	101	86	95
TRANSPORTATION INDUSTRY (75)	10.9	8.0	7.0	7.9	7.5	7.7	98	101	95	98
PUBLIC UTILITIES (76-80)	10.1	9.7	7.0	8.2	4.5	5.6	73	117	64	79
TRADE (81,86,89-99)	83.6	58.7	56.4	57.3	51.9	54.6	96	102	92	97
SERVICES (82-85,87,88,102)	73.9	105.6	105.3	105.3	104.9	105.2	100	100	100	100
STATE & LOCAL GOVT. (101)	93.5	98.3	97.2	97.4	95.8	96.5	99	100	99	99
FEDERAL GOVERNMENT (100,103)	54.7	54.0	53.8	53.8	53.5	53.6	100	100	99	100
TOTAL JOBS	393.5	382.2	372.3	374.9	357.9	365.8	97	101	96	98
CIVILIAN PERSONS EMPLOYED	366.9	357.5	348.0	350.5	334.3	341.8	97	101	96	98
CIVILIAN UNEMPLOYMENT RATE	8.2	10.8	12.4	12.4	12.5	11.9				
POPULATION	1089.4	1265.0	1252.0	1243.0	1214.2	1225.5	99	99	97	98
PER CAPITA INCOME	4132.7	4815.4	4731.5	4793.4	4658.0	4730.4	98	100	98	100
ENERGY USER SECTOR		*(TRILLIONS OF BTU'S)*								
NATURAL RESOURCES	38.4	22.4	22.0	22.2	20.7	21.7	98	101	94	99
CONSTRUCTION	23.1	32.3	31.7	32.3	23.3	23.8	98	102	73	75
MANUFACTURING	14.2	32.4	30.5	30.8	27.6	29.7	94	101	90	97
TRANSPORTATION INDUSTRY	10.1	14.9	13.9	14.3	12.3	13.3	94	103	88	95
PUBLIC UTILITIES	59.2	38.6	37.5	38.9	37.0	36.5	97	104	99	97
TRADE AND SERVICES	36.3	61.3	58.7	59.8	55.2	57.2	96	102	94	97
GOVERNMENT, EXC. TRANSPORTATION	5.6	7.0	6.8	6.9	6.7	6.8	98	100	98	99
CONSUMERS, EXC. TRANSPORTATION	69.0	108.8	107.4	107.8	105.2	106.3	99	100	98	99
USER-OPERATED TRANSPORTATION	95.7	150.9	148.7	149.2	145.2	147.0	99	100	98	99
TRANSPORTATION AIR POLLUTION		*(THOUSANDS OF TONS)*								
SULFUR OXIDES	6.0	5.8	5.6	5.7	5.3	5.5	97	101	94	98
PARTICULATE MATTER	4.7	5.0	4.9	5.0	4.7	4.8	98	101	96	98
CARBON MONOXIDE	843.8	1130.5	1113.9	1118.0	1087.8	1101.0	99	100	98	99
HYDROCARBONS	152.6	198.4	195.5	196.2	191.0	193.3	99	100	98	99
NITROGEN OXIDES	93.8	106.6	104.9	105.5	102.2	103.6	98	101	97	99
OTHER AIR POLLUTION										
SULFUR OXIDES	130.1	105.2	103.5	105.4	103.2	102.1	98	102	100	99
PARTICULATE MATTER	120.2	196.5	189.1	194.3	167.7	186.1	96	103	89	98
CARBON MONOXIDE	286.4	217.3	209.1	214.6	186.7	207.7	96	103	89	99
HYDROCARBONS	63.9	48.8	47.1	47.9	45.1	46.9	97	102	96	100
NITROGEN OXIDES	53.8	53.4	52.2	53.1	50.6	51.7	98	102	97	99
WATER OXYGEN DEMAND	575.6	362.4	358.3	359.2	357.2	359.6	99	100	100	100
LAND SOLID WASTE	860.6	999.3	989.1	982.0	959.2	968.2	99	99	97	98

PERCENT

SUMMARY PROJECTIONS BY ORE ECONOMIC AREA UNDER FIVE ALTERNATIVE HIGHWAY SYSTEMS

169 REDDING, CALIF.

	1970	1990 BASE YEAR	1990 COMPLETED INTERSTATE	1990 EXTENDED PRIMARY	1990 ECONOMIC DEVELOPMENT	1990 URBAN	CI/BY	EP/CI	ED/CI	U/CI
JOBS BY INDUSTRY			(THOUSANDS)					P E R C E N T		
NATURAL RESOURCES (1-10)	10.0	3.1	3.1	3.1	3.1	3.1	99	100	99	99
CONSTRUCTION (11-12)	1.4	.6	.5	.6	.2	.2	91	103	39	41
MANUFACTURING (13-74)	10.1	12.4	11.4	11.6	10.9	11.1	92	102	96	97
TRANSPORTATION INDUSTRY (75)	2.7	1.9	1.9	1.9	1.9	1.9	99	101	99	99
PUBLIC UTILITIES (76-80)	1.4	.7	.7	.7	.6	.6	101	101	103	95
TRADE (81,86,89-99)	10.8	11.3	10.9	11.1	10.6	10.6	97	101	97	97
SERVICES (82-85,87,88,102)	9.9	11.2	11.1	11.1	11.1	11.1	100	100	100	100
STATE & LOCAL GOVT. (101)	11.3	12.4	12.2	12.2	11.9	12.0	98	100	98	98
FEDERAL GOVERNMENT (100,103)	4.1	4.1	4.1	4.1	4.0	4.0	99	100	99	99
TOTAL JOBS	61.7	57.7	56.0	56.3	54.4	54.7	97	101	97	98
CIVILIAN PERSONS EMPLOYED	60.4	56.5	54.9	55.2	53.4	53.6	97	101	97	98
CIVILIAN UNEMPLOYMENT RATE	8.0	14.0	13.9	12.9	13.8	13.3				
POPULATION	176.9	224.2	218.3	213.7	211.0	208.8	97	98	97	96
PER CAPITA INCOME	3647.5	4763.8	4738.4	4846.2	4666.3	4768.0	99	102	98	101
ENERGY USER SECTOR			(TRILLIONS OF BTU'S)							
NATURAL RESOURCES	4.6	2.7	2.5	2.5	2.4	2.4	93	99	94	94
CONSTRUCTION	5.0	7.7	7.8	8.0	3.2	3.1	101	103	40	40
MANUFACTURING	5.0	13.4	12.6	12.6	12.4	12.6	93	101	99	100
TRANSPORTATION INDUSTRY	2.2	3.6	3.5	3.5	3.4	3.4	97	101	97	97
PUBLIC UTILITIES	20.2	12.1	11.8	11.9	12.1	11.6	98	101	102	98
TRADE AND SERVICES	5.5	9.4	9.1	9.2	9.0	9.0	98	100	98	98
GOVERNMENT, EXC. TRANSPORTATION	8.9	1.3	1.3	1.3	1.3	1.3	98	100	98	98
CONSUMERS, EXC. TRANSPORTATION	9.9	18.4	18.1	18.1	17.7	17.7	98	100	98	98
USER-OPERATED TRANSPORTATION	19.1	35.3	34.9	34.9	34.3	34.3	99	100	98	98
TRANSPORTATION AIR POLLUTION			(THOUSANDS OF TONS)							
SULFUR OXIDES	.9	1.2	1.2	1.2	1.2	1.2	97	100	98	98
PARTICULATE MATTER	.7	1.1	1.1	1.1	1.0	1.0	98	100	98	98
CARBON MONOXIDE	151.2	259.2	256.0	256.3	251.7	252.2	99	101	99	99
HYDROCARBONS	26.8	45.1	44.5	44.6	43.8	43.9	99	100	99	99
NITROGEN OXIDES	15.1	23.3	23.0	23.1	22.7	22.7	99	100	99	99
OTHER AIR POLLUTION										
SULFUR OXIDES	36.7	22.7	22.3	22.4	22.7	21.9	98	101	102	98
PARTICULATE MATTER	19.8	16.9	16.8	16.8	16.5	16.6	99	100	98	98
CARBON MONOXIDE	33.8	26.6	25.5	25.2	24.6	24.8	96	99	97	98
HYDROCARBONS	7.6	15.2	7.3	7.4	6.6	6.3	48	101	90	86
NITROGEN OXIDES	11.5	7.6	7.4	7.4	7.4	7.2	98	100	100	98
WATER OXYGEN DEMAND	317.9	177.5	177.5	177.5	177.5	177.5	100	100	100	100
LAND SOLID WASTE	139.7	177.2	172.5	168.8	167.0	164.9	97	98	97	96

	1970	1990 BASE YEAR	1990 COMPLETED INTERSTATE	1990 EXTENDED PRIMARY	1990 ECONOMIC DEVELOPMENT	1990 URBAN	PER CENT CI/BY	EP/CI	ED/CI	U/CI
JOBS BY INDUSTRY			(THOUSANDS)							
NATURAL RESOURCES (1-10)	4.0	1.3	1.3	1.3	1.3	1.3	100	101	101	100
CONSTRUCTION (11,12)	1.7	.3	.1	.6	.1	.1	18	2714	97	96
MANUFACTURING (13-74)	11.2	6.3	6.6	6.7	6.6	6.0	105	101	99	91
TRANSPORTATION INDUSTRY (75)	.9	.1	.2	.2	.1	.1	104	108	97	95
PUBLIC UTILITIES (76-80)	1.1	1.3	1.7	1.8	1.5	1.7	126	107	91	103
TRADE (81,86,89-99)	7.9	6.6	6.8	7.4	7.4	6.5	103	108	98	96
SERVICES (82-85,87,88,102)	6.0	5.6	5.3	5.4	5.3	5.3	95	101	100	100
STATE & LOCAL GOVT. (101)	7.3	7.6	7.4	7.9	7.4	7.3	97	106	99	98
FEDERAL GOVERNMENT (100,103)	1.1	.9	.8	.9	.8	.8	95	112	99	97
TOTAL JOBS	40.4	30.1	30.2	33.0	29.7	29.2	100	110	99	97
CIVILIAN PERSONS EMPLOYED	38.6	28.8	28.8	31.6	28.4	27.9	100	110	99	97
CIVILIAN UNEMPLOYMENT RATE	11.8	20.7	22.3	21.7	21.8	22.5				
POPULATION	121.9	140.7	143.6	151.6	140.1	134.6	102	106	98	94
PER CAPITA INCOME	4001.0	5610.0	5328.1	5588.7	5381.2	5534.0	95	105	101	104
ENERGY USER SECTOR			(TRILLIONS OF BTU'S)							
NATURAL RESOURCES	3.2	1.8	1.7	1.7	1.7	1.7	94	100	100	99
CONSTRUCTION	2.5	4.1	1.6	10.8	1.1	1.1	40	654	67	66
MANUFACTURING	5.4	10.3	10.1	10.2	10.1	9.8	98	101	100	97
TRANSPORTATION INDUSTRY	1.3	1.8	1.8	2.0	1.8	1.7	103	108	98	95
PUBLIC UTILITIES	16.7	20.0	29.2	30.3	24.7	32.0	146	104	85	110
TRADE AND SERVICES	3.6	6.4	6.4	6.7	6.2	6.2	100	105	98	98
GOVERNMENT, EXC. TRANSPORTATION	3.5	.7	.7	.8	.7	.7	97	107	99	98
CONSUMERS, EXC. TRANSPORTATION	4.3	7.2	7.0	7.5	7.0	6.9	98	107	99	98
USER-OPERATED TRANSPORTATION	9.2	15.5	15.2	16.3	15.1	14.9	98	107	99	98
TRANSPORTATION AIR POLLUTION			(THOUSANDS OF TONS)							
SULFUR OXIDES	.4	.5	.5	.6	.5	.5	100	107	98	96
PARTICULATE MATTER	.3	.5	.5	.5	.5	.5	99	107	99	97
CARBON MONOXIDE	68.1	112.3	110.3	117.7	109.2	108.2	98	107	99	98
HYDROCARBONS	11.9	19.5	19.1	20.4	18.9	18.8	98	107	99	98
NITROGEN OXIDES	6.4	10.0	9.9	10.6	9.8	9.7	99	107	99	98
OTHER AIR POLLUTION										
SULFUR OXIDES	29.9	35.5	50.5	52.4	43.2	55.1	142	104	85	109
PARTICULATE MATTER	29.4	22.5	25.8	25.6	24.5	26.7	115	99	95	103
CARBON MONOXIDE	57.5	33.9	35.9	32.9	36.0	36.0	106	92	100	100
HYDROCARBONS	6.2	9.8	6.4	8.8	6.2	6.2	66	138	97	96
NITROGEN OXIDES	10.6	11.0	14.8	15.1	13.0	15.9	134	102	88	108
WATER OXYGEN DEMAND	94.6	56.5	58.4	56.6	58.4	58.5	103	97	100	100
LAND SOLID WASTE	96.3	111.2	113.5	119.7	110.7	106.3	102	106	98	94

SUMMARY PROJECTIONS BY ORE ECONOMIC AREA UNDER FIVE ALTERNATIVE HIGHWAY SYSTEMS

171 S FRAN-OAKLAND, CALIF.

	1970	1990 BASE YEAR	1990 COMPLETED INTERSTATE	1990 EXTENDED PRIMARY	1990 ECONOMIC DEVELOPMENT	1990 URBAN	CI/BY	EP/CI	ED/CI	U/CI
								PERCENT		
JOBS BY INDUSTRY		(THOUSANDS)								
NATURAL RESOURCES (1-10)	49.0	19.3	18.7	18.6	18.0	18.7	97	100	96	100
CONSTRUCTION (11,12)	99.2	100.1	100.9	97.7	94.8	101.2	101	97	94	100
MANUFACTURING (13-74)	378.7	355.0	324.8	315.0	305.2	326.3	91	97	94	100
TRANSPORTATION INDUSTRY (75)	101.0	165.3	164.2	163.9	163.5	164.3	99	100	100	100
PUBLIC UTILITIES (76-80)	58.1	85.3	81.7	80.8	76.5	81.4	96	99	94	100
TRADE (81,86,89-99)	459.2	553.8	530.9	526.9	517.5	533.0	96	99	97	100
SERVICES (82-85,87,88,102)	508.0	839.0	838.0	837.6	837.2	838.3	100	100	100	100
STATE & LOCAL GOVT. (101)	277.0	335.7	328.7	327.1	324.1	328.9	98	99	99	100
FEDERAL GOVERNMENT (100,103)	200.4	208.4	206.5	206.5	205.9	206.9	99	100	100	100
TOTAL JOBS	2130.7	2662.0	2594.8	2574.1	2542.6	2598.9	97	99	98	100
CIVILIAN PERSONS EMPLOYED	1944.0	2453.1	2389.4	2369.9	2340.1	2393.1	97	99	98	100
CIVILIAN UNEMPLOYMENT RATE	6.5	7.8	8.2	8.1	9.0	7.8				
POPULATION	5090.9	6874.1	6929.7	6790.5	6802.3	6840.9	101	98	98	99
PER CAPITA INCOME	4688.8	7083.2	6861.2	6944.9	6861.9	6950.2	97	101	100	101
ENERGY USER SECTOR		(TRILLIONS OF BTU'S)								
NATURAL RESOURCES	41.7	21.7	19.9	19.5	18.8	20.1	92	98	94	101
CONSTRUCTION	149.2	232.5	230.0	211.8	192.0	235.2	99	92	84	102
MANUFACTURING	209.8	457.8	441.8	434.9	424.6	441.0	97	98	96	100
TRANSPORTATION INDUSTRY	184.3	346.0	339.2	338.5	336.0	339.6	98	100	99	100
PUBLIC UTILITIES	435.2	258.6	254.2	256.1	259.4	250.2	98	101	102	98
TRADE AND SERVICES	288.0	514.3	500.6	498.1	491.5	502.1	97	99	98	98
GOVERNMENT, EXC. TRANSPORTATION	58.4	84.7	83.9	83.8	83.4	84.0	99	100	99	100
CONSUMERS, EXC. TRANSPORTATION	199.2	391.7	381.9	378.7	374.5	382.0	98	99	98	100
USER-OPERATED TRANSPORTATION	429.3	794.2	778.9	773.8	767.3	778.9	98	99	99	100
TRANSPORTATION AIR POLLUTION		(THOUSANDS OF TONS)								
SULFUR OXIDES	38.2	68.0	66.3	65.8	65.4	66.4	98	99	99	100
PARTICULATE MATTER	21.5	38.2	37.5	37.4	37.1	37.5	98	100	99	100
CARBON MONOXIDE	2841.7	5316.4	5203.7	5169.3	5120.4	5204.7	98	99	98	100
HYDROCARBONS	496.7	920.0	900.1	893.7	885.5	900.7	98	99	98	100
NITROGEN OXIDES	325.5	579.8	570.7	570.4	564.0	570.9	98	100	99	100
OTHER AIR POLLUTION										
SULFUR OXIDES	1086.3	1003.1	995.1	997.7	1002.0	989.1	99	100	101	100
PARTICULATE MATTER	768.1	1079.3	1069.3	1065.1	1054.2	1074.2	99	100	99	100
CARBON MONOXIDE	1374.2	1287.9	1281.2	1279.0	1278.0	1283.8	99	100	100	100
HYDROCARBONS	698.4	1204.1	1159.3	1097.4	1018.4	1129.3	96	95	88	97
NITROGEN OXIDES	467.4	449.6	446.2	446.4	446.7	445.3	99	100	100	100
WATER OXYGEN DEMAND	1512.1	981.3	978.8	978.5	970.9	983.0	100	100	101	100
LAND SOLID WASTE	4021.8	5430.5	5474.5	5364.5	5373.8	5409.3	101	98	99	99

SUMMARY PROJECTIONS BY ORE ECONOMIC AREA UNDER FIVE ALTERNATIVE HIGHWAY SYSTEMS

172   ANCHORAGE, ALASKA

	1970	1990 BASE YEAR	1990 COMPLETED INTERSTATE	1990 EXTENDED PRIMARY	1990 ECONOMIC DEVELOPMENT	1990 URBAN	CI/BY	EP/CI	ED/CI	U/CI
								PERCENT		
JOBS BY INDUSTRY										
NATURAL RESOURCES (1-10)	4.2	2.4	2.4	2.4	2.4	2.4	100	99	99	99
CONSTRUCTION (11,12)	4.7	5.1	5.0	4.8	4.7	5.0	98	96	93	99
MANUFACTURING (13-74)	6.7	15.6	14.7	13.1	13.5	14.4	94	89	92	98
TRANSPORTATION INDUSTRY (75)	7.1	12.3	12.3	12.2	12.2	12.3	100	99	92	100
PUBLIC UTILITIES (76-80)	1.6	1.4	1.7	1.0	.7	1.5	119	56	42	88
TRADE (81,86,89-99)	17.0	27.4	27.0	25.3	25.2	26.6	98	94	93	98
SERVICES (82-85,87,88,102)	17.3	25.9	25.8	25.7	25.8	25.8	100	100	100	100
STATE & LOCAL GOVT. (101)	17.7	22.1	22.0	21.4	21.4	21.9	100	97	97	100
FEDERAL GOVERNMENT (100-103)	45.7	46.7	46.7	46.6	46.6	46.7	100	100	100	100
TOTAL JOBS	122.1	159.0	157.6	152.4	152.3	156.5	99	97	97	99
CIVILIAN PERSONS EMPLOYED	86.7	122.6	121.3	116.4	116.4	120.3	99	96	96	99
CIVILIAN UNEMPLOYMENT RATE	11.0	1.1	1.1	1.1	1.1	1.1				
POPULATION	300.4	318.6	317.9	301.3	300.8	313.5	99	96	96	100
PER CAPITA INCOME	4698.9	7730.7	7775.7	7768.7	7759.0	7749.2	101	100	100	100
ENERGY USER SECTOR		(TRILLIONS OF BTU'S)								
NATURAL RESOURCES	4.6	7.8	7.8	7.6	7.5	7.7	100	97	97	99
CONSTRUCTION	12.7	22.9	17.2	15.3	15.3	15.6	75	89	89	91
MANUFACTURING	7.3	27.4	26.9	26.3	26.4	26.8	98	98	98	100
TRANSPORTATION INDUSTRY	15.2	32.1	31.9	31.5	31.5	31.8	100	99	99	100
PUBLIC UTILITIES	20.4	17.9	21.5	18.3	14.8	20.2	120	85	69	94
TRADE AND SERVICES	9.7	23.1	22.9	21.7	21.5	22.6	99	95	94	99
GOVERNMENT, EXC. TRANSPORTATION	2.3	3.3	3.3	3.3	3.3	3.3	100	98	98	100
CONSUMERS, EXC. TRANSPORTATION	10.7	13.0	12.9	12.1	12.1	12.8	99	94	93	99
USER-OPERATED TRANSPORTATION	8.0	9.3	9.1	7.9	8.0	8.8	98	87	88	97
TRANSPORTATION AIR POLLUTION		(THOUSANDS OF TONS)								
SULFUR OXIDES	2.6	5.4	5.3	5.2	5.2	5.3	99	98	98	98
PARTICULATE MATTER	1.2	2.3	2.2	2.2	2.2	2.2	100	98	98	99
CARBON MONOXIDE	70.8	93.8	92.6	84.0	84.3	90.6	99	91	91	98
HYDROCARBONS	12.1	16.0	15.7	14.2	14.3	15.4	98	90	91	98
NITROGEN OXIDES	12.0	20.7	20.8	20.2	20.0	20.6	101	97	96	99
OTHER AIR POLLUTION										
SULFUR OXIDES	44.9	39.4	45.2	40.4	34.8	43.2	115	89	77	96
PARTICULATE MATTER	32.5	75.8	77.4	73.8	71.7	76.4	102	95	93	99
CARBON MONOXIDE	49.4	156.5	155.7	152.1	150.8	154.7	100	98	97	99
HYDROCARBONS	8.8	30.2	25.5	25.0	24.9	25.4	84	98	97	99
NITROGEN OXIDES	18.0	19.4	20.8	19.5	18.1	20.2	107	94	87	98
WATER OXYGEN DEMAND	19.5	62.3	61.9	61.6	61.5	61.8	99	100	99	100
LAND SOLID WASTE	237.3	251.7	248.8	238.0	237.6	247.7	99	96	96	100

SUMMARY PROJECTIONS BY ORE ECONOMIC AREA UNDER FIVE ALTERNATIVE HIGHWAY SYSTEMS

173 HONOLULU, HAWAII

	1970	1990 BASE YEAR	1990 COMPLETED INTERSTATE	1990 EXTENDED PRIMARY	1990 ECONOMIC DEVELOPMENT	1990 URBAN	CI/BY	EP/CI	ED/CI	U/CI
								P E R C E N T		
JOBS BY INDUSTRY		(THOUSANDS)								
NATURAL RESOURCES (1-10)	8.5	3.2	4.4	3.1	3.1	4.6	139	70	70	104
CONSTRUCTION (11-12)	26.6	37.5	40.0	38.5	37.6	40.1	101	96	94	100
MANUFACTURING (13-74)	28.0	51.6	62.7	52.1	52.3	61.8	122	83	83	99
TRANSPORTATION INDUSTRY (75)	14.3	25.8	26.6	25.7	25.7	26.6	103	97	97	100
PUBLIC UTILITIES (76-80)	7.3	8.9	15.5	8.6	8.5	16.0	174	56	55	103
TRADE (81,86,89-99)	73.6	108.0	121.2	108.7	108.9	120.7	112	90	90	100
SERVICES (82-85,87,88,102)	76.9	140.3	141.0	140.3	140.3	141.1	101	99	100	100
STATE & LOCAL GOVT. (101)	42.9	64.4	69.2	64.9	65.0	69.2	107	94	94	100
FEDERAL GOVERNMENT (100-103)	62.5	67.2	68.3	67.3	67.4	68.3	102	99	99	100
TOTAL JOBS	340.6	509.0	549.0	509.3	508.8	548.3	108	93	93	100
CIVILIAN PERSONS EMPLOYED	272.6	426.8	462.2	427.0	426.7	461.4	108	92	92	100
CIVILIAN UNEMPLOYMENT RATE	3.2	7.7	7.9	7.7	7.8	7.8	110	91	92	99
POPULATION	768.6	1319.2	1452.4	1324.0	1332.3	1439.3	110	91	92	99
PER CAPITA INCOME	4555.9	5968.6	6010.4	5961.0	5919.6	6048.1	101	99	98	101
ENERGY USER SECTOR		(TRILLIONS OF BTU'S)								
NATURAL RESOURCES	4.3	5.8	7.0	6.3	6.3	7.4	121	89	90	105
CONSTRUCTION	59.5	114.2	119.1	96.3	97.4	112.4	104	81	82	94
MANUFACTURING	16.3	37.7	44.7	39.1	39.1	44.6	118	88	87	100
TRANSPORTATION INDUSTRY	25.3	59.8	64.0	60.2	60.3	63.9	107	94	94	100
PUBLIC UTILITIES	35.5	127.1	238.6	134.1	131.2	252.6	188	56	55	106
TRADE AND SERVICES	31.7	86.6	97.1	87.6	87.7	97.2	112	90	90	100
GOVERNMENT, EXC. TRANSPORTATION	4.1	6.9	7.5	7.0	7.0	7.5	107	94	94	100
CONSUMERS, EXC. TRANSPORTATION	24.2	53.6	60.8	53.7	53.7	60.6	113	88	88	100
USER-OPERATED TRANSPORTATION	49.2	103.7	115.0	104.1	104.0	114.7	111	90	90	100
TRANSPORTATION AIR POLLUTION		(THOUSANDS OF TONS)								
SULFUR OXIDES	5.0	11.6	12.5	11.6	11.6	12.4	107	93	93	100
PARTICULATE MATTER	2.8	6.3	6.8	6.3	6.3	6.8	109	93	93	100
CARBON MONOXIDE	361.4	787.5	873.2	791.0	790.3	871.1	111	91	91	100
HYDROCARBONS	62.8	136.7	151.4	137.1	137.0	151.1	111	90	90	100
NITROGEN OXIDES	41.0	90.8	100.2	92.3	92.0	100.0	110	92	92	100
OTHER AIR POLLUTION										
SULFUR OXIDES	128.7	447.6	634.8	461.4	456.7	658.2	142	73	72	104
PARTICULATE MATTER	90.6	250.0	311.5	261.6	261.4	320.8	125	84	84	103
CARBON MONOXIDE	51.4	73.7	90.2	80.1	81.7	97.0	122	89	91	108
HYDROCARBONS	17.4	38.8	42.8	38.6	38.7	42.4	110	90	90	99
NITROGEN OXIDES	67.5	229.2	276.8	233.6	232.5	282.9	121	84	84	102
WATER OXYGEN DEMAND	37.0	79.7	118.2	97.9	97.6	121.0	148	83	83	102
LAND SOLID WASTE	607.2	1042.1	1197.4	1046.0	1052.5	1137.0	110	91	92	99

SUMMARY PROJECTIONS BY ORE ECONOMIC AREA UNDER FIVE ALTERNATIVE HIGHWAY SYSTEMS

UNITED STATES

	1970	1990 BASE YEAR	1990 COMPLETED INTERSTATE	1990 EXTENDED PRIMARY	1990 ECONOMIC DEVELOPMENT	1990 URBAN	CI/BY	EP/CI	ED/CI	U/CI
JOBS BY INDUSTRY			(THOUSANDS)							
NATURAL RESOURCES (1-10)	4245.3	2323.2	2323.2	2323.2	2323.2	2323.2	100	100	100	100
CONSTRUCTION (11,12)	3794.1	3904.7	3904.7	3904.7	3904.7	3904.7	100	100	100	100
MANUFACTURING (13-74)	20101.2	26829.4	26829.4	26829.4	26829.4	26829.4	100	100	100	100
TRANSPORTATION INDUSTRY (75)	2858.0	3819.6	3819.6	3819.6	3819.6	3819.6	100	100	100	100
PUBLIC UTILITIES (76-80)	1753.4	1467.6	1467.6	1467.6	1467.6	1467.6	100	100	100	100
TRADE (81,86,89-99)	17976.2	24438.5	24438.5	24438.5	24438.5	24438.5	100	100	100	100
SERVICES (82-85,87,88,102)	17770.7	31058.8	31058.8	31058.8	31058.8	31058.8	100	100	100	100
STATE & LOCAL GOVT. (101)	9922.0	12525.1	12525.1	12525.1	12525.1	12525.1	100	100	100	100
FEDERAL GOVERNMENT (100,103)	4512.5	4785.7	4785.7	4785.7	4785.7	4785.7	100	100	100	100
TOTAL JOBS	82933.4	111152.7	111152.7	111152.7	111152.7	111152.7	100	100	100	100
CIVILIAN PERSONS EMPLOYED	77956.9	104925.3	104925.3	104925.3	104925.3	104925.3	100	100	100	100
CIVILIAN UNEMPLOYMENT RATE	4.6	3.9	3.9	3.9	3.9	3.9	100	100	100	100
POPULATION	203165.5	269656.6	269656.6	269656.5	269656.6	269656.6	100	100	100	100
PER CAPITA INCOME	3755.2	6151.4	6152.3	6152.2	6152.6	6151.8	100	100	100	100
ENERGY USER SECTOR			(TRILLIONS OF BTU'S)							
NATURAL RESOURCES	3002.7	5346.5	5346.5	5346.5	5346.5	5346.5	100	100	100	100
CONSTRUCTION	4582.1	8003.1	8003.1	8003.1	8003.1	8003.1	100	100	100	100
MANUFACTURING	11109.1	23501.1	23501.1	23501.1	23501.1	23501.1	100	100	100	100
TRANSPORTATION INDUSTRY	3774.6	7977.9	7978.5	7979.0	7977.7	7978.5	100	100	100	100
PUBLIC UTILITIES	12137.4	26707.9	26707.8	26707.2	26707.2	26707.2	100	100	100	100
TRADE AND SERVICES	9071.2	19790.8	19790.8	19790.8	19790.8	19790.8	100	100	100	100
GOVERNMENT, EXC. TRANSPORTATION	1355.9	2016.1	2016.1	2016.1	2016.1	2016.1	100	100	100	100
CONSUMERS, EXC. TRANSPORTATION	8847.5	17397.3	17397.3	17397.3	17397.3	17397.3	100	100	100	100
USER-OPERATED TRANSPORTATION	14930.5	30262.9	30262.9	30262.9	30262.9	30262.9	100	100	100	100
TRANSPORTATION AIR POLLUTION			(THOUSANDS OF TONS)							
SULFUR OXIDES	984.0	1998.3	1990.4	1982.5	1986.4	1990.4	100	100	100	100
PARTICULATE MATTER	655.0	1327.7	1328.8	1329.9	1329.3	1328.8	100	100	100	100
CARBON MONOXIDE	110900.0	228161.0	228202.2	228243.3	228222.8	228202.2	100	100	100	100
HYDROCARBONS	19530.0	40029.0	40024.7	40020.5	40022.6	40024.9	100	100	100	100
NITROGEN OXIDES	11688.0	23652.6	23721.9	23791.2	23756.6	23721.9	100	100	100	100
OTHER AIR POLLUTION										
SULFUR OXIDES	32634.0	71788.6	71788.6	71788.6	71788.6	71788.6	100	100	100	100
PARTICULATE MATTER	24915.0	49883.9	49883.9	49883.9	49883.9	49883.9	100	100	100	100
CARBON MONOXIDE	36010.0	67810.7	67810.7	67810.7	67810.7	67810.7	100	100	100	100
HYDROCARBONS	15160.0	30559.0	30559.0	30559.0	30559.0	30559.0	100	100	100	100
NITROGEN OXIDES	11001.0	24248.9	24248.9	24248.9	24248.9	24248.9	100	100	100	100
WATER OXYGEN DEMAND	156674.1	281351.9	281351.8	281351.8	281351.8	281351.8	100	100	100	100
LAND SOLID WASTE	160500.0	213027.7	213027.7	213027.7	213027.7	213027.7	100	100	100	100

Index

About the Author

Curtis C. Harris, Jr. is Professor of Economics at the Bureau of Business and Economic Research and at the Department of Economics of the University of Maryland. He has been with the U.S. Department of Commerce and the University of California, Davis. Professor Harris received the B.S. in economics from the University of Florida in 1956, and the M.A. and Ph.D. from Harvard.

Professor Harris has published numerous articles in professional journals. He is co-author of a 1972 book on Locational Analysis, and author of a 1973 book on The Urban Economies, 1985. He has served as a consultant to the Federal Government and private industry. Professor Harris specializes in regional and urban economics at the University of Maryland.